GUINNESS
MOVIE
FACTS & FEATS

PATRICK ROBERTSON

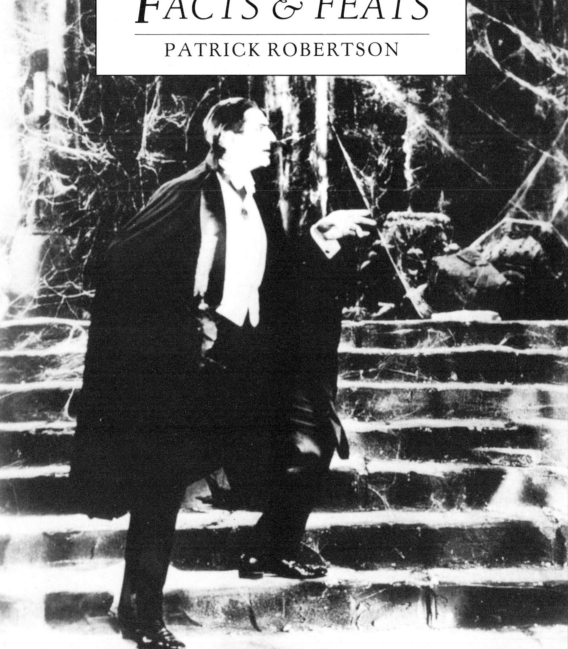

GUINNESS PUBLISHING

Project Editor: Honor Head
Editor: Beatrice Frei
Design: Christie Archer
Picture Editing and Research: P. Alexander
Goldberg and James M. Clift

Frontispiece: Dracula (US 31)

THE AUTHOR

Patrick Robertson has had a passion
for movies which began at the age of
three when he was taken to see *For
Me and My Gal* on a wet afternoon
in Lyme Regis in 1943. In his spare
time he runs a props hire business,
supplying vintage magazines, comics
and newspapers for set dressing in
film and television productions. He
is also Chairman of the Ephemera
Society and author of *The Shell Book
of Firsts* and *Movie Clips*.

COUNTRY ABBREVIATIONS

Afg	Afghanistan	Fr	France	Kor	Korea	Swz	Switzerland
Alg	Algeria	Ger	Germany	Lby	Libya	Syr	Syria
Arg	Argentina	GDR	Germany, East	Mex	Mexico	Sen	Senegal
Aus	Australia	FRG	Germany, West	Mor	Morocco	S. Kor	South Korea
Aut	Austria	Gha	Ghana	Moz	Mozambique	Tai	Taiwan
Ban	Bangladesh	Gre	Greece	Mau	Mauritania	Tha	Thailand
Bel	Belgium	Gab	Gabon	Neth	Netherlands	Tun	Tunisia
Bra	Brazil	HK	Hong Kong	NZ	New Zealand	Tur	Turkey
Bul	Bulgaria	Hun	Hungary	Nor	Norway	US	United States
Can	Canada	Ind	India	Phi	Philippines	Uru	Uruguay
Chn	China	Ice	Iceland	Pol	Poland	Ven	Venezuela
Col	Colombia	Ire	Ireland	Por	Portugal	Yug	Yugoslavia
Cz	Czechoslovakia	Isr	Israel	Rom	Romania		
CayI	Cayman Islands	It	Italy	Rus	Russia		
Cur	Curacao	IvC	Ivory Coast	Sin	Singapore		
Den	Denmark	Jam	Jamaica	SA	South Africa	The abbreviation i.p. after a	
Egy	Egypt	Jap	Japan	Sp	Spain	film title instead of a date	
Fin	Finland	Ken	Kenya	Swe	Sweden	signifies 'in production'.	

CONTENTS

PREFACE

Most books on films are concerned about quality—the cinema as art. This book is unashamedly about *quantity*—together with 'firsts', records, oddities, remarkable achievements, historic landmarks and the wilder extravagances of the motion picture business during the 100 years of its colourful history. It is not the place to seek potted biographies of favourite stars or great directors, but it does offer a gamut of film facts, ranging from the significant to the absurd, many of which have never appeared in any film book before. For the historically minded there are old orthodoxies explored and often rejected—Who really 'invented' the close-up? What was the first western? Where did full-length feature films begin? Hollywood receives due attention, of course, as the centre of world film production, but many other countries—no less than 80 in all—have been approached for information. There is something about each of them, including a chart which records the number of features made each year by every film producing nation since the earliest days (pp. 14–15).

To the First Lady of the Silver Screen—
Miss Lillian Gish.

Devotees of Dracula will find a complete filmography; Shakespeare buffs a listing of all 73 versions of Hamlet, including the four in which the Prince was played by a woman; film fans may read about other film fans, including Queen Victoria, Stalin, Hitler and the last Emperor of China (who wore Harold Lloyd spectacles as a tribute to his favourite star). Records range from the largest and smallest cinema theatres, the longest career in movies, the biggest cast (300,000) and the most remakes to the heaviest actress, the last silent picture and the longest and shortest film titles.

This is the fourth edition of the *Guinness Book of Movie Facts & Feats*. It contains not only updated and revised material, but many new features. The position of women in movies is considered from a number of perspectives, with detailed analysis of the ages of leading ladies (p. 109)—the age profile has shown a marked shift towards the mature woman—and of the proportion of films in which actresses are top billed (p. 174). In silent days, more female stars than male stars got the main credit; now, in the era of equal opportunities, there are four male stars billed first for every one woman. A survey of the occupations of the leading characters in movies (p. 65) also reveals some significant facts about Hollywood and its resistance to social change. Generally, male stars play roles in which they give the orders, female leads still take them. And hardly any lead characters in Hollywood movies have blue collar jobs, unless the collar is on a police uniform—there are more films about cops than ever before.

Other new features include one on reality in the movies (cinema literate audiences today tend to take it for granted that everything is achieved by artifice—it is not always so) and another, in the 'Locations' section, is about where famous films were shot. There is also an analysis of reviews published in five population centres of the US and UK which shows where the sternest critics operate. And if you want to know the only one of the five where there are more favourable notices than unfavourable, you will find the answer on p. 221.

There are very few stars whose performances never got a bad notice, but one of them is an actress whose screen career has spanned an astonishing 75 years. For us she remains 'The First Lady of the Silver Screen' and this book is repsectfully dedicated to her in her 99th year—Miss Lillian Gish.

Special thanks are due to Marion Brett for her valuable help in preparing the manuscript.

ONE

FADE IN

The first motion picture films were taken with a camera patented in Britain by French-born Louis Aimé Augustin Le Prince (1842–90?) in November 1888. Two fragments survive: one taken at a speed of 10–12 frames per second early in October 1888 in the garden of his father-in-law, Mr Joseph Whitley, at Roundhay, Leeds; the other taken at 20 frames per second later in the month and showing traffic crossing Leeds Bridge. According to Le Prince's mechanic, James Longley, the latter film was shown on a projector incorporating a Maltese cross for intermittent picture shift. He claimed that the image obtained was sufficiently clear for smoke to be visible rising from the pipe of a lounger on the bridge. Both films were made on sensitized paper rolls 2⅛ in wide and it was not until a year later that Le Prince was able to obtain Eastman celluloid roll film, which had just been introduced into Britain. This provided a far more suitable support material and it seems likely that the inventor was able to start the commercial development of his motion picture process by the beginning of 1890. A new projector was built so that a demonstration could

The LePrince camera of 1888.

be given before M. Mobisson, the Secretary of the Paris Opera. On 16 September 1890 Le Prince boarded a train at Dijon bound for Paris, en route to New York where he intended to present his invention in public for the first time. He never arrived in the French capital. No trace of his body was ever found and after exhaustive enquiries the police were unable to offer any rational explanation of his disappearance. The mystery has never been solved.

The fullest account of Le Prince's life and his mysterious disappearance is Christopher Rawlence's *The Missing Reel* (Collins 1990), described by *Variety* as 'an important rewriting of film history'.

The first commercially developed motion picture process was instigated by Thomas Alva Edison (1847–1931), American electrical engineer. His initial attempt to produce an illusion of movement, by means of an apparatus called the 'optical phonograph', resulted in failure, and in January 1889 Edison assigned William Kennedy Laurie Dickson (1860–1935), an assistant at his laboratories in West Orange, NJ, to work on the development of what was to become the Kinetoscope, a film-viewing machine designed for use in amusement arcades. Dickson, the French-born son of English parents, had early training as a photographer and was better suited to this kind of research than his mentor who knew little of optics. Abandoning the use of rectangular sheets of celluloid for camera work, he substituted 50 ft lengths of celluloid film produced by the firm of Merwin Hulbert. These long rolls were first purchased on 18 March 1891, which is the earliest date at which it seems likely that Dickson could have made successful films for viewing in the peep-show Kinetoscope apparatus.

The first public demonstration of motion pictures took place at the Edison Laboratories at West Orange, NJ, on 22 May 1891, when 147 representatives of the National Federation of Women's Clubs, having lunched with Mrs Edison at Glenmont, were taken over her husband's workshops and allowed to view the new Kinetoscope. The New York *Sun* reported: 'The surprised and pleased clubwomen saw a small pine box standing on the floor. There were some wheels and belts near the box, and a workman who had them in charge. In the top of the box was a hole perhaps an inch in diameter. As they looked through the hole they saw the picture of a man. It was a most marvellous picture. It bowed and smiled and waved its hands and took off

The earliest known motion-picture film—*Traffic Crossing Leeds Bridge* (GB 88).

its hat with the most perfect naturalness and grace. Every motion was perfect . . . .' The film used for this demonstration appears to have been taken with a horizontal-feed camera without sprockets. This would have been an imperfect apparatus at best, and not until October 1892 is there evidence that William Dickson had built an effective vertical-feed camera using perforated film. In that month the *Phonogram* published an illustration showing sequences from four films evidently taken with such a device. These included pictures of Dickson himself, together with his helper, William Heise, and also shots of wrestling and fencing. By this date, then, it can be positively asserted that Dickson had overcome all the obstacles that had stood in the way of making films suitable for commercial exhibition. He was to receive little thanks for his work. After Dickson left West Orange in 1895, following a dispute with his employer, Edison steadfastly refused to concede that anyone but himself was responsible for bringing the invention to fruition. Most historians were content to accept Edison's own version of events until the appearance in 1961 of a painstaking work of scholarship titled *The Edison Motion Picture Myth*. The author, Gordon Hendricks, demonstrates by reference to hitherto unpublished papers in the Edison archives that all the experimental work on the Kinetoscope was conducted by Dickson, or under his direction, and that Edison himself can be credited with little more than instigating the research programme and providing facilities for carrying it out.

The practical development of motion pictures in Britain can be dated from a camera built in 1895 by Birt Acres (1854–1918) and R. W. Paul (1869–1943) at the latter's optical instrument works in Saffron Hill. Paul's interest in films had been aroused the previous October when he was approached by a Greek showman, George Trajedis, with a request to manufacture some Edison Kinetoscopes. This Paul agreed to do on learning that Edison had omitted to patent the machine in Britain. Since Edison's agents understandably refused to sell films for the pirated machines, Paul approached Acres with the suggestion that they should construct a camera together (later each claimed to have been the only begetter of the apparatus) so that they could make their own Kinetoscope subjects. Acres was to be cameraman. Using film obtained from the American Celluloid Co. of Newark, NJ, Acres tried out the camera for the first time with a scene of a cricketer (his assistant Henry Short) coming out of Acres' home Clovelly Cottage, in Barnet. This was followed by what Paul described as 'our first saleable film', *The Oxford and Cambridge University Boat Race*, which was premièred in a Kinetoscope at the India Exhibition, Earls Court on 27 May 1896. This film, together with *The Derby* and *The Opening of the Kiel Canal* (see News

Film, p. 193), formed the first programme presented on screen in Britain since Le Prince's experiments, when Acres gave a private show with his Kineopticon projector in a coach-house at Wrotham Cottage, Barnet in August 1895. Acres was also the first to give a public screening (see below), while Paul became the first manufacturer of projectors (q.v.) and Britain's pioneer film producer.

The first commercial presentation of motion pictures took place at Holland Bros' Kinetoscope Parlor, 1155 Broadway, New York, which opened for business on 14 April 1894. The Kinetoscopes were arranged in two rows of five, and for 25c viewers were allowed to watch five films—to see the whole programme they had to pay double entrance money. The first day's take of $120 suggests that this first 'cinema audience' totalled nearly 500. The films, made in the Edison 'Black Maria' (see Film

Studio, p. 139) at West Orange, were titled: *Sandow, Bertholdi (mouth support), Horse Shoeing, Bertholdi (table contortion), Barber Shop, Blacksmiths, Cock Fight, Highland Dance, Wrestling, Trapeze.*

The first commercial presentation of films in Britain took place at the Kinetoscope parlour opened by the Continental Commerce Co. of New York at 70 Oxford Street, London, on 18 October 1894. The twelve machines offered such titillating delights as *Carmencita* (a buxom vaudeville artiste) and *Annabelle Serpentine Dance*, as well as more prosaic fare like *Blacksmith Shop, Wrestling Match* and *The Bar Room.*

The first film presented publicly on screen was *La Sortie des Ouvriers de l'Usine Lumière* (Fr 94) which was shown before members of the Société d'Encouragement pour l'Industrie Nationale by

---

HOW THE CINEMA SPREAD ROUND THE WORLD

Few inventions have spread more rapidly than cinematography. By the end of 1896, a mere twelve months after the real start of commercial cinema in France, nearly all the major countries of the western world had witnessed their first demonstration of the new art. It is clear from the following chronology that the Lumière brothers of Lyon were the most positive force in introducing motion pictures to the world. (The designation 'Lumière' below signifies that the programme was made up of Lumière films.) The presentations listed were public shows before a paying audience unless otherwise indicated.

1895
March 22 FRANCE *La Sortie des Ouvriers des l'Usine Lumière* (Fr 94), presented by Louis and Auguste Lumière before the Société d'Encouragement pour l'Industrie Nationale at 44 rue de Rennes, Paris (see p. 3-4).
May 20 UNITED STATES *Young Griffo* v. *Battling Charles Barnett* (US 95) presented before paying audience at 153 Broadway, New York (see p. 5).
November 1 GERMANY Eight short films (for subjects, see Production: firsts by countries, p. 5) presented by Max and Emil Skladanowski at Berlin Wintergarten.
November 10 BELGIUM Lumière programme before invited audience of scientists etc., in Brussels. First before paying audience at 7 de la Galerie du Roi, Brussels, 1 Mar 1896.

1896
January 14 UNITED KINGDOM Programme (subjects see p. 5) presented by Birt Acres before Royal Photographic Society, London. First before paying audience: Lumière programme by F. Trewey at Regent Street Polytechnic, London, 20 Feb 1896.
February ?? ITALY Lumière presented by Vittorio Calcina at the Ospedale di Carita, Turin.
March 19 AUSTRIA Lumière presented by E. J. Dupont at the Graphic Arts Teaching & Research Centre, Vienna.
April 6 NORWAY Skladanowski programme presented at Circus Variété, Oslo.
April 20 IRELAND Unidentified programme presented at Star of Erin Variety Theatre, Dublin.
May 4 RUSSIA Lumière presented by Francis Doublier at Aquarium Theatre, St Petersburg.

May 6 SOUTH AFRICA R. W. Paul's Theatrograph programme—*Highland Dancers* (GB 96), *Street Scenes in London* (GB 96), *Trilby Dance* (GB 96), *A Military Parade* (GB 96), *The Soldier's Courtship* (GB 96) —presented at Empire Theatre of Varieties, Johannesburg.
May 10 HUNGARY Lumière presented at Royal Hotel, Budapest. Included street scenes taken in front of Opera House and Chain Bridge, Budapest, and Hungarian Millenary Procession.
May 15 SPAIN Lumière presented by M. Promio at 34 Carrera de San Jeronimo, Madrid.
May 27 ROMANIA Lumière presented at Salon l'Independenta Romana, Bucharest.
June 7 YUGOSLAVIA (SERBIA) Lumière presented at Kod Zlatnog Krsta Café, Belgrade.
June 7 DENMARK Lumière presented by Vilhelm Pacht in Raadhuspladsen, Copenhagen.
June 9 NETHERLANDS Lumière presented at the Kurhaus, Scheveningen.
June 18 PORTUGAL Lumière (?) presented by Erwin Rousby at Real Coliseu, Rua da Palma, Lisbon.
June 28 SWEDEN Lumière presented by C. V. Roikjer at the Industrial Exhibition, Malmö.
June 28 FINLAND Lumière presented at the Societetshuset, Helsinki.
July 7 INDIA Lumière presented at Watson's Hotel, Bombay.
July 8 BRAZIL 'Omniographo' presented at 57 Rua do Ouvidor, Rio de Janiero.
July 15 CZECHOSLOVAKIA Lumière presented at the Lázenský dům, Karoly Vary.
July 21 CANADA Edison Vitascope programme presented at West End Park, Ottawa.
July 28 ARGENTINA Lumière presented by Francisco Pastos and Eustaquio Pellier at Colón Theatre, Buenos Aires.
August 11 CHINA French programme (negative evidence suggests *not* Lumière) presented as act of variety show at Hsu Gardens, Shanghai.
August 15 MEXICO Lumière presented by engineering student Salvador Toscano Barragan at 17 Calle de Jesus, Mexico City.
August 22 AUSTRALIA R. W. Paul programme presented by conjurer Carl Hertz at Melbourne Opera House.
September 26 GUATEMALA Lumière presented by Arnold Tobler at 11 Passage Aycinena, Guatemala City.
October 13 NEW ZEALAND R. W. Paul (?)

programme of English films presented by Profs Hausmann and Gow at Auckland Opera House.
October ?? POLAND Edison programme presented at Lvov.
Date unknown EGYPT unidentified programme at Zavani Café, Alexandria.

1897
January 24 CUBA Lumière presented by Gabriel Veyre at Teatro Tacón, Havana.
January 28 VENEZUELA Edison presented by Manuel Trujillo at Teatro Baralt, Maracaibo.
February/March ?? BULGARIA Lumière presented in port town of Russe.
March 2 PERU Edison Vitascope presented on the Plaza de Armas, Lima.
June 10 THAILAND Lumière presented by S. G. Marchovsky in Bangkok.
June ?? JAPAN Lumière presented by Katsutaro Inahata at Osaka.
December 25 URUGUAY Lumière at Montevideo.
Date unknown TUNISIA Lumière at store show established by Albert Samama on rue Es-Sadika, Tunis.

1898
Spring GREECE Lumière at Place Kolokotronis, Athens.

1899
Date unknown TURKEY unidentified programme presented privately before Sultan by Spaniard Don Ramirez and then publicly at his Electric Circus, Constantinople.

1900
November 30 (?) INDONESIA Nederlandsche Bioscope Maatschappij presented at Batavia.
Date unknown KOREA free film show sponsored by Anglo-American Tobacco Co. of Shanghai. Admission in exchange for cigarette coupons.
Date unknown SENEGAL Lumière presented at Dakar.
Date unknown IRAN unidentified programme presented before Shah by Mirza Ebrahim Khan at Royal Palace, Teheran. First public show opened in Avenue Cheraq Gaz, Teheran, by Sahâf Bâshi in 1905.

Probably the earliest pictorial poster advertising a cinema show in Britain, believed to date from the latter half of 1897. The claim to have been the 'first' was advertising puffery. In fact the Egyptian Hall was the third place of entertainment to show films in London. (*Museum of London*)

Auguste and Louis Lumière at 44 rue de Rennes, Paris, on 22 March 1895. Believed to have been taken in August or September 1894, the film showed workers leaving the Lumière photographic factory at Lyons for their dinner-hour.

The first public screening in Britain was given by Birt Acres at the London headquarters of the Royal Photographic Society, 14 Hanover Square on 14 January 1896. The programme, comprised of films

taken by Acres himself, consisted of *The Opening of the Kiel Canal, The Derby, Boxers, Three Skirt Dancers* and *Rough Seas at Dover.*

The first film to be screened before a paying audience was a four-minute boxing subject, *Young Griffo v. Battling Charles Barnett,* presented by Major Woodville Latham of the Lamda Co. at 153 Broadway, New York on 20 May 1895. The projector was a primitive and imperfect machine called the Eidoloscope, designed for the Lamda Co. (the first film company established as such) by former Edison employee Eugene Lauste. Although some authorities have cast doubt on the Eidoloscope's ability to create an illusion of movement on a screen, it must have achieved a sufficient level of technical acceptability, however jerky and inadequate the picture, for Latham to have attracted paying customers. Another commercial show was given by C. Francis Jenkins and Thomas Armat, using a projector they had designed themselves, at a purpose-built temporary cinema at the Cotton States Exposition at Atlanta, Ga., in September 1895. After making various improvements to the machine, Armat came to an arrangement with Thomas Edison, who had failed to produce a workable projector himself, by which the celebrated inventor would be allowed to exploit it as his own. As the Edison Vitascope, the improved machine was debuted at Koster and Bial's Music Hall on Broadway on 23 April 1896, an occasion which has often and erroneously been heralded as the first time that motion pictures were presented on a screen to a paying audience.

The first screening before a paying audience in Europe was given by Max and Emil Skladanowski with a projector of their own invention at the Berlin Wintergarten on 1 November 1895. The films were made up of endless loops and the action lasted only a few seconds before it was repeated. Taken at the rate of eight pictures a second, the films were flickering and jerky, but the fact that there was movement on the screen at all was sufficient for the Nazis to claim, some 40 years later, that Germany was the cradle of the cinema industry. In fact neither the work of Lauste and Latham in America, nor that of the Skladanowskis in Germany was destined to have any lasting effect on the development of the cinema. It is generally agreed that the première of the Lumière brothers' show, before a paying audience at the Grand Café, 14 Boulevard des Capucines, Paris, on 28 December 1895, marks the debut of the motion picture as a regular entertainment medium. Their projector was the first to advance beyond the experimental stage and the first to be offered for sale.

The first screening before a paying audience in Britain took place at the Regent Street Polytechnic on 20 February 1896, when the French magician Felicien Trewey exhibited the Lumière Cinématographe with accompanying commentary by M. Francis Pochet. Admission was 1s and the engagement lasted three weeks, hours 2–4 p.m. The opening programme included the Lumière films *Arrival of a Train at a Station, The Baby and the Goldfish, The Family Tea Table* and *M. Trewey: Prestigidateur.* The first commercial show outside London was by Birt Acres at Cardiff Town Hall on 5 May 1896.

TWO

THE INDUSTRY

FEATURE FILMS

The world's first full-length feature film was *The Story of the Kelly Gang* (Aus 06), made in Australia in 1906. No other country established regular production of features until 1911. (*Backnumbers*)

The first feature film, according with the Cinematheque Française definition of a feature being a commercially made film over one hour duration, was Charles Tait's *The Story of the Kelly Gang* (Aus 06), which was 4000 ft long and had a running time of 60–70 min. A biopic of Victoria's notorious bushranger Ned Kelly (1855–80), the film was produced by the theatrical company J. & N. Tait of Melbourne, Victoria, and shot on location over a period of about six months at Whitehorse Road, Mitcham (Glenrowan Hotel scenes, including the last stand of the Kelly Gang); at Rosanna (railway scenes); and on Charles Tait's property at Heidelberg, Vic. (all other scenes). The actual armour which had belonged to Ned Kelly—a bullet-proof helmet and jerkin fashioned from ploughshares— was borrowed from the Victorian Museum and worn by the actor playing the role, an unidentified Canadian from the Bland Holt touring company who disappeared before the film was finished. It had to be completed with an extra standing in as Ned, all these scenes being taken in long shot. Elizabeth Veitch played Kate Kelly, and others in the cast included Ollie Wilson, Frank Mills, Bella Cole and Vera Linden.

Made on a budget of £450, *The Story of the Kelly Gang* was premièred at the Athenaeum Hall, Melbourne, on 24 December 1906 and recovered its cost within a week, eventually grossing some £25,000, including receipts from the English release. No complete print survives but stills from the film were issued as picture postcards and give the impression of a vigorous, all-action drama made with imaginative use of outdoor locations—a significant advance on the studio-bound one-reelers being turned out in Europe and America at this period. It was long believed that the film had been totally lost, but recently a 210 ft long fragment was discovered in Melbourne. Other versions of the Ned Kelly story survive. There were remakes in 1910, 1917, 1920, 1923, 1934, 1951 and 1970, all of them Australian productions except the last, a British film with Mick Jagger in the title role.

Australia was the only country in the world to have established regular production of feature-length films prior to 1911. For figures on early output, see Production: World Output (pp. 14).

The first feature-length film made in Europe was Michel Carré's 90-minute long production *L'Enfant prodigue* (Fr 07), premièred at the Théâtre des Variétés in the Boulevard Montmartre, Paris, on 20 June 1907. This was a screen representation of a stage play, with little or no adaptation.

THE FIRST 12 FEATURE FILMS PRODUCED IN THE USA

May 1912 *Oliver Twist* (5 reels) H. A. Spanuth
Oct 1912 *From the Manger to the Cross* (6 reels) Kalem Co.
Oct 1912 *Richard III* (4 reels) Sterling Camera & Film Co.
Nov 1912 *Cleopatra* (6 reels) Helen Gardner Picture Plays
Nov 1912 *The Adventures of Lieutenant Petrosino* Feature Photoplay Co.
Feb 1913 *One Hundred Years of Mormonism* (6 reels) Utah Moving Picture Co.; Ellay Co.
Feb 1913 *A Prisoner of Zenda* (4 reels) Famous Players Film Co.
March (?) 1913 *Hiawatha* (4 reels) Frank E. Moore
June 1913 *The Battle of Gettysburg* (5 reels) NY Motion Picture Co.
July 1913 *The Seed of the Fathers* (6 reels) Monopol Film Co.
Aug (?) 1913 *Victory* (5 reels) Victory Co.
Sept 1913 *Tess of the D'Urbervilles* (5 reels) Famous Players Film Co.
It is worthy of note that neither Cecil B. DeMille's *The Squaw Man* (US 14) nor D. W. Griffith's *Judith of Bethulia* (US 14), each of which has been cited as the first feature produced in the US, appears above.

THE FIRST 12 FEATURE FILMS PRODUCED IN THE UK

Aug 1912 *Oliver Twist* (4 reels) Hepworth
Dec 1912 *Lorna Doone* (5 reels) Clarendon
May 1913 *East Lynne* (6 reels) Barker
July 1913 *The Battle of Waterloo* (5 reels) British & Colonial
July 1913 *Ivanhoe* (6 reels) Zenith Films
July 1913 *A Message from Mars* (4 reels) United Kingdom Films
Aug 1913 *David Copperfield* (8 reels) Hepworth
Sept 1913 *King Charles* (4 reels) Clarendon
Sept 1913 *A Cigarette-Maker's Romance* (4 reels) Hepworth
Sept 1913 *The House of Temperley* (5 reels) London Films
Oct 1913 *The Grip* (4 reels) Britannic Films
Oct 1913 *Hamlet* (6 reels) Hepworth

COUNTRIES PRODUCING FEATURE FILMS BY 1914

By the outbreak of World War I, the following countries had commenced feature-film production:

1906 Australia
1909 France
1911 Denmark, Germany, Italy, Poland, Russia, Spain, Yugoslavia (Serbia)
1912 Austria, Greece, Hungary, Japan, Norway, Romania, United Kingdom, United States
1913 Brazil, Finland, India, Netherlands, Sweden, Venezuela, Canada
1914 Argentina

FILM PRODUCING NATIONS

The following list chronicles, wherever known, the first motion picture production, the first dramatized (i.e. acted) production, the first feature film (over one hour duration) and the first talkie feature of each of the film-producing countries of the world, signified by the abbreviations Film, Drama, Feature, Talkie. The first feature film in natural colour is included for major film-producing nations. The first motion picture production means a film made by a native or permanent resident of the country, as opposed to a visiting cameraman or non-resident producer. Where a category has been omitted no information is available. Drama/Feature and Feature/Talkie signify respectively that the first feature-length film was also the first dramatic production of any length and that the first talkie was also the first feature-length production. Other abbreviations: doc.=documentary; f.=filmed; d.=directed; pr.=première; prod.=produced.

ALGERIA
Film: *La Prière du muezzin* (1906), d. Felix Mesguich.
Drama: *Ali Bouf a l'huile* (1907), d. Felix Mesguich.
Feature/Talkie: *Peuple en marche* (1963), d. Ahmed Rachedi and René Vautier.

ANGOLA
Film: *Monangambé* (1968), d. Sarah Maldoror.
Feature/Talkie: *Des fusils pour Banta* (1970), d. Sarah Maldoror.

ARGENTINA
Film: *La Bandera Argentina* (1897), d. Eugenio Py.
Drama: *El Fusilamiento de Dorrego* (1908), d. Mario Gallo and Salvador Rosich.
Feature: *Amalia* (1914), d. Enrique Garcia Velloso.
Talkie: *Muñequitas porteñas* (1931), with Maria Turguenova—Vitaphone system.

AUSTRALIA
Film: *The Melbourne Cup* (3 Nov 1896), d. Marius Sestier.
Drama: untitled 75 ft drama by Joseph Perry of the Salvation Army about man sent to gaol for stealing bread and helped by Army's 'prison-gate brigade' on release, c. 1897.
Feature: *The Story of the Kelly Gang* (pr. 26 Dec 1906), d. Charles Tait. (NB: **First feature film** (q.v.) **in world.**)
Talkie: *Fellers* (press shown 23 May 1930), d. Arthur Higgins and Austin Fay, prod. Artaus Films, starring Arthur Tauchert.

AUSTRIA
Drama: *Ein Walzertraum* (scene from opera) f. 2 Mar 1907.
Feature: *Zweierlei Blut* (1912), starring Luise Kohn and Jakob Fleck.
Talkie: *G'schichten aus der Steiermark* (pr. 23 Aug 1929), d. Hans Otto Löwenstein, prod. Eagle Film and Ottoton film, starring Hilde Maria and Anny Burg.

BANGLADESH
Feature/Talkie: *Mukh O Mukhosh* (1956), d. Jabbar Khan.

BELGIUM
Film: *Le Marché aux poissons de Bruxelles* (1897) and other actualities, d. M. Alexandre.
Drama: *'chand d'habits* (1897), d. M. Alexandre
Feature: *Belgique meurtrie* (1920), d. Paul Flon.
Talkie: *La Famille Klepkens* (1930), d. Gaston Schoukens and Paul Flon.

BOLIVIA
Film: actualities by Luis Castillo, 1913.
Feature: *La Profecia del Lago* (1923), d. José Maria Velasco Maidana (film banned).
Talkie: *La Guerra del Chaco* (1936), d. José Luis Bazoberry.

BRAZIL
Film: *View of Guanabara Bay* (f. 19 July 1898), d. Alfonso Segreto.
Drama: *Os Estranguladores* (1906)—crime film based on true story in police files, d. Isaac Sandenberg.
Feature: *O Crime dos Banhados* (1913), d. Francisco Santos, prod. Guarany Film.
Talkie: *Acabaram-se os Otarios* (1930), country comedy d. Luis de Barros, starring Genésio Arruda and Tom Bill.

BULGARIA
Film: actuality about Bulgarian army, 1910.
Drama: *Such is the War* (1914).
Feature: *The Bulgar is a Gentleman* (1915), satire about Sofia snobbery, d. Vassil Guendov, starring ditto and Mara Lipina.
Talkie: *A Song of the Balkan Mountains* (1934), d. Peter Stoychev.

BURKINA FASO
Film: *A Minuit . . . l'Independence* (1960).
Feature/Talkie: *Le Sang des parias* (1973), d. Mamadou Djim Kolas.

BURMA
Film: *The Funeral of U Tun Shein* (1920) actuality made by U Ohn Maung.
Feature: *Dana Pratap* (1925), prod. London Art Photo Co. of Rangoon.
Talkie: *Shwe ein the* (1932), prod. British Burma Film Co.

CAMEROON
Film: *L'Aventure en France* (1962), d. Jean-Paul N'Gassa.
Feature/Talkie (doc.): *Une Nation est née* (1972).
Feature/Talkie (drama): *Pousse-pousse* (1975), d. Daniel Karawa.

CANADA
Film: actualities of life on the prairies made by James Freer of Brandon, Manitoba, 1897.
Drama: *The Great Unknown* (1913), d. Oscar Lund, starring Barbara Tennent and Fred Truesdell.
Feature: *Evangeline* (1913), d. E. P. Sullivan and W. H. Cavanaugh, prod. Canadian Bioscope Co., starring Laura Lyman and John F. Carleton.
Talkie (English): *North of '49* (1929), d. Neal Hart, prod. British Canadian Pictures.
Talkie (French): *Notre-dame de la Mouise* (1941).
Colour: *Talbot of Canada* (1938), Kodachrome.

CAPE VERDE ISLANDS
Feature/Talkie: *Os Flagelados do Vento Leste* (1988), d. António Faria, starring Carlos Alhinho and Arciolinda Almeida.

CHILE
Film: *Un Ejercicio General de Bomberos*, pr. 26 May 1902.
Feature: *La Baraja de la muerte* (1916), d. Salvador Giambastiane.
Talkie: *Norte y Sur* (1934), d. Jorge Délano.

CHINA
Film/Drama: *Tingchun Mountain* (1908), d. Lin Tenlun of the Feng Tai Photo Shop, Peking, starring Tan Hsin-pei.
Feature: *Yen Rei-sun* (1921), about embezzler who murders prostitute, d. Ren Pun-yen, prod. China Film Research Society, starring Chun Tso-Tze and Wang Tsai-yun.
Talkie: *Singsong Girl Red Peony* (1930), d. Chang Shih-chuan, prod. Star Film Co., starring Butterfly Wu.

COLOMBIA
Film/Drama: *The Life of General Rafael Uribe* (1914), d. brothers Di Domenico.
Feature: *La Maria* (1922), d. Alfredo Del Diestro.
Talkie: *Flowers of the Valley* (1939), d. Pedro Moreno Garzón.

CONGO
Film: *Kayako* (c. 1967), d. Sébastien Kamba.
Feature/Talkie: *La Rançon d'une alliance* (1973), d. Sébastien Kamba.

COSTA RICA
Drama: *El Retorno* (1926), d. Romulo Bertoni.
Feature: *La Segua* (1984), d. Antonio Yglesias.

CUBA
El Brujo desapareciendo (1898), d. José E. Casasús.
Drama: *El Cabildo de ña Romualda* (1908), d. Enrique Diaz Quesada, prod. Metropolitan Films.
Feature: *El Rey de los campos de Cuba* (1913), d. Enrique Diaz Quesada, starring Gerardo Artecona and Evangelina Adams.
Talkie: *El Caballero de Max* (1930), d. Jaime San-Andrews, starring Nancy Norton and Wilfredo Genier—Vitaphone. (The Cuban government had made a sound-on-film documentary by the Phonofilm process in 1926.)

CURAÇAO
Feature/Talkie: *Ava & Gabriel. Un Historia di Amor* (1990), d. Felix de Rooy, starring Nashaira Desbarida and Cliff San-A-Jong.

CYPRUS
Feature/Talkie: *Avrianos Polemistis/Tomorrow's Warrior* (1981), d. Michael Papas, prod. Cyprian (MP) Films, starring Christos Zannidea.

CZECHOSLOVAKIA
Film/Drama: *Výstavní Párkař a Lepič Plakátů* (1898), *Dostavencícko Ve Mlýniči* (1898), *Pláč a Smích* (1898), etc., actualities and short comedies featuring Bohemian cabaret artiste Josef Šváb-Malostranský, d. Prague student Jan Kříženecký.
Feature: *Pražští Adamité* (1917), d. Antonín Fencl, prod. Lucernafilm, starring Josef Vošalik.
Talkie (Czech): *Tonka of the Gallows* (1930), d. Karel Anton. Talkie (Slovak): *The Singing Land* (1932), d. Karel Plicka.
Colour: *Jan Roháč of Duba* (1947), d. Vladamír Borský.

DAHOMEY (BENIN)
Film: *Ganvié, mon village* (1966), d. Pascal Abikanlou.
Feature/Talkie: *Sous le signe du Vaudoun* (1974), d. Pascal Abikanlou.

DENMARK
Film: *Kørsel med grønlandske Hunde* (1896), d. Peter Elfelt.
Drama: *Henrettelsen* (1903), d. Peter Elfelt, starring Francesca Nathansen and Victor Betzonich.
Feature: *Den sorte Drøm* (pr. 4 Sept 1911), circus drama, d. Urban Gad, starring Valdemar Psilander and Asta Nielsen.
Talkie: *Eskimo* (pr. 9 Oct 1930), d. G. Schneevogt, starring Mona Martenson and Paul Richter.
Colour: *Tricks* (pr. 7 May 1956), d. Erik Balling.

DOMINICAN REPUBLIC
Drama: *Las Emboscados de Cupido* (1924), d. Francisco Palau.
Feature/Talkie: *La Serpiente de la Luna de los Piratas* (1972), d. Jean-Louis Jorge.

ECUADOR
Feature/Talkie: *Se Conocieron en Guayaquil* (1949), d. Alberto Sanatana, prod. Ecuador Sono Films.

EGYPT
Film: *Dans les rues d'Alexandrie* (1912), d. M. de Lagarne.
Drama: *Sharaf el Badawi* (1918), prod. Italo-Egyptian Cinematographic Co.
Feature: *Koubla Fil Sahara'a* (1927), d. Ibrahim Lama, prod. Condor Film. (NB: Shooting on *Laila* (1927), generally credited as first Egyptian feature, started earlier, but the film was released later.)
Talkie: *Onchoudet el Fouad* (pr. 14 Apr 1932), d. Mario Volpi.

FAROE ISLANDS
Feature/Talkie: *Atlantic Rhapsody* (1989), d. Katrin Ottardottir, starring Erling Eysturoy and Katrin Ottarsdottir, prod. Kaledidoskop.

FINLAND
Film: *Pupils of Nikolai Street School during Break* (1904).
Drama: *Salaviinanpolttajat* (1907), d. Louis Sparre, starring Teuvo Puro and Jussi Snellman.
Feature: *Kun Onni Pettää* (pr. 23 Nov 1913), d. Konrad Tallroth, starring Axel Precht and Sigrid Precht.
Talkie: *The Log-Driver's Bride* (1931), d. Erkki Karu.

FRANCE
Film: *La Sortie des Usines* (1894), d. Louis Lumière.
Drama: *L'Arroseur arrosé* (1895), d. Louis Lumière, starring Lumière's gardener M. Clerc and apprentice boy Duval.
Feature: *L'Enfant prodigue* (pr. 20 June 1907), d. Michel Carré.
Talkie: *Les Trois masques* (1929), d. André Hugon, prod. Pathé-Natan, starring Renée Heribel and Marcel Vibert.
Colour: *L'Eternal amour* (1921), d. Gaston Colombani in Héraute Colour.

GABON
Film: *M'Bolo Gabon* (1967).
Feature/Talkie: *Où vas-tu Koumba* (1971), d. Alain Ferrari and Simon Auré.

GERMANY
Films: *Italian Dance, Kangaroo Boxer, Juggler, Acrobats, Russian Dance, Serpentine Dance, Lutte, Apothéose* (all pr. 1 Nov 1895), d. Max and Emil Skladanowski.
Feature: *In dem grossen Augenblick* (pr. 11 Aug 1911), d. Urban Gad, prod. Deutsche Bioscop GmbH, starring Asta Nielsen and Hugo Hink.

Talkie: *Melodie der Welt* (pr. 12 Mar 1929), d. Walter Ruttman, starring J. Kowal Samborsky and Renée Stobrawa.

GHANA
Drama: *Amenu's Child* (1949), d. Sean Graham.
Feature/Talkie: *Boy Kumasenu* (1951), d. Sean Graham.

GIBRALTAR
Feature/Talkie: *Instant Justice* (1985), d. Denis Amar, prod. Mulloway Ltd, starring Michael Paré and Tawny Kitaen.

GREECE
Film: Olympic Games actuality (1906).
Drama: *Quo Vadis Spiridion* (1911), comedy, d. Spiros Dimitracopoulos, prod. Athina Films.
Feature: *Golfo* (1912), d. Costas Bahatoris from Spiros Peressiadis' folk-story play.
Talkie: *Les Apaches d'Athenes* (1930), musical, d. D. Gaziadis, prod. Dag Films, starring Mary Sayannou and Petros Epitropakis.

GUATEMALA
Drama: *Agent No 13* (1912), d. Alberto de la Riva.
Feature/Talkie: *El Sombreron* (1950).

GUINEA
Film: *Mouramani Mamadou Touré* (1953).
Feature/Talkie: *Sergeant Bakary Woolén* (1966), d. Lamine Akin.

GUINEA-BISSAU
Feature/Talkie: *Ntturudu* (1986), d. Umban U'Kset, prod. Republic of Guinea-Bissau, starring Mario Acqlino.

GUYANA
Feature/Talkie: *Aggro Seizeman* (1975), d. James Mannas and Brian Stuart-Young, starring Gordon Case and Martha Gonsalves.

HONG KONG
Dramas: *The Widowed Empress, The Unfilial Son, Revealed by the Pot, Stealing the Cooked Ducks* (all 1909), d. Benjamin Polaski, prod. Asia Film Co.

HUNGARY
Film: *The Emperor Franz Josef Opening the Millenial Exhibition* (1896), d. Arnold Sziklay.
Drama: *Siófoki kaland* (pr. 29 Apr 1898) — shown as sequence in stage production *Mozgáfényképek/Moving Pictures*.
Feature: *Ma és holnap* (1912), d. Mihály Kertész (Michael Curtiz).
Talkie: *A Kék Bálvány* (pr. 25 Sept 1931), d. Lajos Lázár, starring Pál Jávor.
Colour: *Ludas Matyi* (1949), d. K. Nádasdy.

ICELAND
Film: various short subjects shot 1904.
Drama: *Aevintýri Jóns og Gvendar/The Adventures of Jön and Gvendur* (1923), d. Loftur Gudmundsson.
Feature/Talkie: *Milli fjalls og fjöru/Between Mountain and Shore* (1948), d. Loftur Gudmundsson.

INDIA
Film: *Cocoanut Fair* (1897), maker unknown, probably English. First by Indian: *The Wrestlers* (f. Nov 1899), d. Harishchandra S. Bhatvadekar of Bombay.
Drama: *Pundalik* (pr. 18 May 1912), d. R. G. Torney.
Feature: *Raja Harischandra* (pr. 17 May 1913), d. D. G. Phalke of Bombay.
Talkie (Hindi): *Alam Ara* (pr. 14 Mar 1931), d. A. M. Irani, prod. Imperial Film Co., starring Master Vithal and Zubeida.

Talkie (Bengali): *Jamai Sasthi* (1931), prod. Madan Theatres.

Colour: *Kisan Kanya* (1937), d. Moti B. Gidwani, prod. Imperial Film Co.—Cinecolor.

INDONESIA
Feature: *Loetoeng Kasaroeng* (1927), d. G. Kruger at Bandung.

Talkie: *Njai Dasima* (1931), d. Lie Tek Soi and Bakhtiar Effendi, prod. Tan's Film.

IRAN
Film: scenes of religious procession and of Shah's private zoo, d. Mirza Ebrahim Khan (Court Photographer to Shah Mozaffareddin) 1900.

Drama/Feature: *Abi and Rabi* (1932), comedy, d. Oranes Ohanian.

Talkie: *Dokhta Lor* (1934), d. Abdol Hoseyn Sepenta.

IRAQ
Drama/Feature/Talkie: *Leila in Iraq* (1949).

IRELAND
Film: Visit of King Edward VII to Lismore Castle 2 May 1904, f. by Thos Horgan of Youghal.

Drama: *Fun at Finglas Fair* (1915), d. F. J. McCormick. Never released, as all prints destroyed in Easter Rising.

Feature: *A Girl of Glenbeigh* (1917), starring Kathleen O'Connor, prod. Film Co. of Ireland.

Talkie (English): *The Voice of Ireland* (1932), d. Col Victor Haddick. Talkie (Irish): see Languages: Irish Gaelic (p. 157).

ISRAEL
Film: documentary about Jewish settlement in Palestine (1912), d. Akiva Arie Weiss.

Drama: *Yerahmiel the Shlemiel* and other short comedies (1926), d. Nathan Axelrod.

Feature: *Oded Hanoded* (1933), d. Nathan Axelrod.

Talkie: *Me'al Hekhoravot* (1936), d. Nathan Axelrod.

ITALY
Film: *Arrivo del treno stazione di Milano* (1896), d. Italo Pacchioni.

Drama: *La Presa di Roma* (1905), d. Filoteo Albernini, starring Carlo Rosaspina.

Feature: *La Portatrice di pane* (1911), d. S. De Montépin, prod. Vesuvio Films, Naples.

Colour Feature: *Cyrano de Bergerac* (1925), d. Augusto Genina, prod. Unione Cinematographica Italia, starring Pierre Magnier.

Talkie: *La Canzone dell' amore* (1930), d. Genarro Righelli.

IVORY COAST
Film: *Sur la dune de la solitude* (1964), d. Timité Bassori.

Feature/Talkie: *Korogo* (1964), d. Georges Keita.

JAMAICA
Feature/Talkie: *The Harder They Come* (1972), d. Perry Henzell, starring Jimmy Cliff and Janet Bartley.

JAPAN
Film: street scenes in Tokyo's Ginza and shots of geisha from Shimbasi and Gion districts, d. Tsunekichi Shibata of the Mitsukoshi Department Store's photo dept., 1897.

Drama: *Momiji-gari* (1897), Noh drama, d. Tsunekichi Shibata, starring Kikugoro V and Danjuro IX.

Feature: *The Life Story of Tasuke Shiobara* (1912).

Talkie: *Taii no Musume* (1929), prod. Nikkatsu Co.

Colour: *Karumen Kokyo ni Kaeru* (1951).

JORDAN
Feature/Talkie: *Watani Habibi* (1964).

KOREA
Drama: *The Righteous Revenge* (1919), d. Kim Do-san.

Feature: *A Pledge in the Moonlight* (1923), morality tale about importance of keeping money in banks, d. Yun Paek-nam.

Talkie: *Chun Hyang-jon* (1935), d. Yi Pil-u and Yi Myong-u.

KUWAIT
Feature/Talkie: *Bas Ya Bahar* (1972), d. Khaled el Seddik, starring Mohamad Monsour and Amal Baker.

LAOS
Feature/Talkie: *Gun Shots in the Valley of the Jugs* (1983).

LEBANON
Drama/Feature: *The Adventures of Elias Mabrouk* (1929), comedy about Lebanese emigrant returning from USA, d. Jordano Pidutti.

Talkie: *In the Ruins of Ba'albak* (1936), d. George Costi, prod. Lumnar Film Co.

LIBYA
Feature/Talkie: *Lorsque le destin s'acharne* (1972), d. A. Zarrouk.

LUXEMBOURG
Feature/Talkie: *Wât huet e gesôt?* (1980), d. Paul Scheuer, prod. AFO-Film.

MADAGASCAR
Film: Centenary celebrations of martyrdom of Malagasy hero Rasalama, d. M. Raberono 1937.

Feature/Talkie: *Le Retour* (1973), d. Randrasana Ignace Solo.

MALAYSIA (MALAYA)
Talkie: *Chandu* (1939), prod. Malayan Films Inc.

MALI
Drama: *Bambo* (1968).

Feature/Talkie: *Les Wandyalankas* (1973), d. Alkaly Kaba.

MALTA
Feature/Talkie: *Katarin* (1977), d. Cecil Satariano, starring Anna Stafrace.

MAURITANIA
Feature/Talkie: *Soleil O* (1971), d. Med Hondo.

MEXICO
Drama: *Don Juan Tenorio* (1898), d. Salvador Toxano Barragan.

Feature: *Fatal Orgullo* (1916), prod. México Lux.

Talkie: *Más fuerte que el deber* (1930), d. Raphael J. Sevilla.

Colour: *Novillero* (1936), d. Boris Maicon—Cinecolor.

MOROCCO
Feature/Talkie: *Itto* (1934), d. Jean Benoit-Levy.

NEPAL
Feature/Talkie: *Harischandra* (1951).

NETHERLANDS
Drama: *Muis Hamel bij den Criffeur* (1904), d. Albert and Willy Mullens.

Feature: *De Levende Ladder* (1913), d. Maurits H. Binger, prod. Hollandia.

Talkie: *Vader des Vaderlands* (1933), d. G. J. Teunissen.

NEW ZEALAND
Film: *Opening of the Auckland Exhibition* (f. 1 Dec 1898), d. A. E. Whitehouse.

Drama: *A Message from Mars* (1903), d. W. F. Brown.

Feature: *The Test* (1916), d. and starring Rawdon Blandford.

Talkie: *Down on the Farm* (1935), d. Lee Hill and Stuart Pitt, prod. Sound Film Productions Ltd.

NICARAGUA
Feature/Talkie: *Alsino y el Condor* (1982), d. Miguel Littin.

NIGER
Film: *Aouré* (1962), d. Mustapha Allasane.

Feature/Talkie: *FVVA* (1971), d. Mustapha Allasane.

NIGERIA
Drama: *My Father's Burden* (1961), d. Segun Olusola.

Feature/Talkie: *Two Men and a Goat* (1966), d. Edward Jones Horatio.

NORWAY
Film: reception of the newly-elected King Haakon VII in Oslo, 1905.

Drama: *The Dangerous Life of a Fisherman* (1907), prod. Norsk Kinematograf A/S, starring Alma Lund.

Feature: *Anny—Story of a Prostitute* (1912), d. Adam Eriksen, starring Julie Jansen.

Talkie: *The Great Christening* (pr. 26 Dec 1931), d. Einar Sissener and Tancred Ibsen, starring Einar Sissener.

OUTER MONGOLIA
Feature/Talkie: *At the Frontier* (1937).

PAKISTAN
Feature/Talkie: *Teri Yaad* (1948), prod. Dewan Pictures, d. Dawood Chand, starring Asha Posley and Nasir Khan. Urdu.

PARAGUAY
Feature/Talkie: *Cerro Cora* (1978), starring Rosa Ros and Roberto de Felice, d. Ladislao Gonzalez.

PERU
Film: *Peruvian Centaurs* (1908), actuality of cavalry manoeuvres.

Drama: *Negocio al Agua* (1913), d. Frederico Blume.

Feature: *Luis Pardo* (1927), biopic of brigand of that name, d. and starred Enrique Cornejo Villanueva.

Talkie: *Resaca* (1934), d. Alberto Santana.

PHILIPPINES
Film: *El Fusilamiento de Rizal* (1908).

Feature: *Dalagang Bukid* (1919), d. José Nepomuceno.

Talkie: *Ang Aswang/The Vampire* (1932).

POLAND
Film: actualities made by Kazimierz Proszynski with a camera of his own invention—the 'pleograph'—1894.

Drama: *His First Visit to Warsaw* (1908), comedy starring Antoni Fertner.

Feature: *Dzieje Grzechu* (pr. 26 Aug 1911), d. Antoni Bednarczyk, starring Maria Mirska and Teodor Roland.

Talkie: *The Morals of Madame Dulska* (1930), d. B. Newolyn.

PORTUGAL
Film: *Leaving the Factory* (1896), d. Aurelio Da Paz Dos Reis.

Drama: *Rapto duma Actriz* (1907), d. Lino Ferreira, starring Carlos Leal and Luz Velozo.

Feature: *A Rosa do Adro* (1919).

Talkie: *A Severa* (pr. 17 June 1931), d. Jose Leitao de Barros, prod. Super-Filmes, starring Dina Teresa and Conde Marialava.

ROMANIA
Film: actualities of Bucharest race-course, a fair

FILM PRODUCING NATIONS (continued)

and the Capsa coffee house (1897), d. Paul Menu.
Drama: *Amor fatal* (pr. 26 Sept 1911), d. Grigore Brezeanu, starring Lucia Sturdza and Tony Bulandra.
Feature: *Razboiul Independentei* (pr. 1 Sept 1912), d. Grigore Brezeanu, starring C. Nottra and Ar. Demetriade.
Talkie: *Ciuleandra* (pr. 30 Oct 1930), d. Martin Berger, starring Jeana Popovici-Voinea.

SAUDI ARABIA
Feature/Talkie: *Sinbad, the Little Sailor* (1990).

SENEGAL
Film: *C'était il y a 4 ans* (1955), d. Paulin Vieyra.
Feature/Talkie: *La Noire de . . .* (1967), d. Ousmane Sembene.

SINGAPORE
Feature/Talkie: *White Golden Dragon* (1936).

SOMALIA
Film/Drama: *The Love that Knows no Barrier* (1961), d. Hossein Manrok.
Feature/Talkie: *Town and Village* (1968), d. El Hadji Mohamed Giumale.

SOUTH AFRICA
Film: scene taken from front of tram travelling down Commissioner Street, Johannesburg, d. Edgar Hyman, 1896.
Drama: *The Star of the South* (1911), about theft of diamond found on banks of Vaal by a Hottentot, prod. Springbok Film Co.
Feature: *De Voortrekkers* (pr. 16 Dec 1916), d. Harold Shaw, prod. African Film Productions Ltd, starring Dick Cruickshanks and Zulu actor Goba as Dingaan. Claimed (in S. Africa) that *The Covered Wagon* (US 23) was inspired by this film.
Talkie (Afrikaans): *Mocdertjie* (1931), d. Joseph Albrecht, starring Carl Ricjter and Joan du Toit.
Talkie (English): *They Built a Nation* (1938), d. Joseph Albrecht, prod. African Film Productions Ltd.

SPAIN
Film: *Salida de misa de doce en la Iglesia del Pilar en Zaragoza* (1896), d. Eduardo Jimeno.
Drama: *Riña en un Café* (1897), d. Fructuoso Gelabert.
Feature: *Lucha por la herencia* (1911), d. Otto Mulhauser, prod. Alhambra Films.
Talkie: *Yo quiero que me lleven a Hollywood* (pr. 20 June 1932), d. Edgar Neville.
Colour: *En un rincon de España* (1949), d. Jerónimo Mihura.

SRI LANKA
Feature/Talkie: *Banda Nagarayata Pemineema* (1953).

SUDAN
Feature/Talkie: *Hopes and Dreams* (1969), d. Al Rachid Mehdi.

SURINAM
Feature/Talkie: *Wan Pipel* (1976), d. Pim de la Parra, starring Borger Breeveld and Diana Gangaram.

SWEDEN
Film/Drama: *Slagsmål i Gamla Stockholm* (pr. 3 July 1897), two 17th-century cavaliers fighting over a girl, d. Ernest Florman, prod. Numa Handels & Fabriks AB.
Feature: *Blodets Röst* (pr. 20 Oct 1913), d. Victor Sjöström, prod. Svenska Biografteatern, starring Victor Sjöström and Ragna Wettergreen.
Talkie: *Konstgjorda Svensson* (pr. 14 Oct 1929), d. Gustaf Edgren, prod. Film AB Minerva, starring Fridolf Rhudin and Brita Apelgren.
Colour: *The Bells in Old Town* (1947), d. Ragnar Hylton-Cavallier, prod. Europa Film—Cinecolor, starring Edvard Person.

SWITZERLAND
Films: *Zürcher Sechseläuten-Umzug* (c. 1901) and *Montreux Fête des Narcisses* (c. 1901), d. Georges Hipleh-Walt.
Drama: *Une Adventure de Redzipet* (1908), d. Albert Roth-de-Markus, starring Paul Marville.
Feature: *Le Spectre de minuit/Lo Spettro di mezzanotte* (1915), d. Giovanni Zannini, prod. Talia-Film, starring Giovanni Zannini and Lina Pellegrini.
Talkie: *Bünzli's Grosstadtabenteuer* (1930), d. Robert Wohlmut, starring Freddy Scheim.

SYRIA
Drama/Feature: *Al Moutaham al Bari* (1928), gangster movie, d. and starring Ayoub Badri, prod. Hermon Film.
Talkie: *Leila Al-Amira* (1947), d. Niazi Mustafa.

TAIWAN
Drama: *The Orphan who Saved his Grandfather* (1922).

TANZANIA
Feature/Talkie: *Gumu* (1935).

THAILAND
Drama/Feature: *Miss Suwan* (1922), d. and prod. Henry McRay and the Wasuvati family. Performers were 'noble families and high-ranking government officials'.

TRINIDAD
Drama: *Callaloo* (1937), starring Ursula Johnson.
Feature/Talkie: *The Right and Wrong* (1970), d. Harbance Kumar, prod. De Luxe Films, starring Ralph Maharaj and Jesse Macdonald.

TUNISIA
Drama: *Ain el Ghezal* (1924), d. Haydée Samama-Chikly, starring Si Haj Hadi Djeheli.
Feature: *The Secret of Fatouma* (1928), d. Dedoncloit, starring Véra de Yourgaince.
Talkie: *Tergui* (1935), d. Abdelaziz Hassine.

TURKEY
Film: *Collapse of the Russian Monument in Ayestafanos* (1914), d. Fuat Uzkinay.
Drama: *The Wedding of Himmet Aga* (1916).
Feature: *Pençe* (1917), d. Sedat Simavi.
Talkie: *Istanbul Sokaklarinda* (1931), d. Muhsin Ertugrul, prod. Ipek Film.

UK
Film: *Traffic Crossing Leeds Bridge* (1888), d. Louis Aimé Augustin Le Prince.
Drama: *The Soldier's Courtship* (f. Apr 1896), d. Robert Paul, starring Fred Storey.
Feature: *Oliver Twist* (1912), d. Thomas Bentley, prod. Hepworth, starring Ivy Millais and Alma Taylor.
Colour Feature: *The World, the Flesh and the Devil* (1914), d. F. Martin Thornton, prod. Union Jack Photoplays and Natural Colour Kinematograph Co., starring Frank Esmond.
Talkie: *Blackmail* (pr. 21 June 1929), d. Alfred Hitchcock, prod. British International Pictures, starring Anny Ondra and John Longden.

URUGUAY
Film: *Una Carrera de Ciclismo en el Velodrome de Arroyo Seco* (1898), d. Felix Oliver.
Drama: *Oliver, Juncal 108* (1900), d. and starring Felix Oliver.

Feature: *Del Pingo al Volante* (1928), d. Roberto Kouri, prod. Bonne Garde.
Talkie: *Dos Destinos* (1936), d. Juan Etchebchere, prod. Estudios Ciclolux, starring Pepe Corbi.

USA
Film: actualities of fencers and wrestlers, etc., d. W. K. L. Dickson, prod. Edison Co., 1892.
Drama: *The Execution of Mary Queen of Scots* (f. 28 Aug 1895), d. Alfred Clark, prod. Raff & Gammon and Edison Co., starring Mr R. L. Thomas (as Mary!)
Feature: *Oliver Twist* (pr. 20 May 1912), prod. H. A. Spanuth, starring Nat C. Goodwin and Winnie Burns.
Colour Feature: *The Gulf Between* (pr. 21 Sept 1917), prod. Technicolor Motion Picture Corp., starring Grace Darmond and Niles Welch.
Talkie: *The Jazz Singer* (pr. 6 Oct 1927), d. Alan Crosland, prod. Warner Bros, starring Al Jolson.

USSR
Film: *Cossack Trick Riders* (f. 29 Sept 1896), d. amateur cinematographer A. P. Fedetsky at Kharkov.
Drama: *Boris Gudonov* (1907), d. A. O. Drankov, starring F. G. Martini and Z. Lopanskaya.
Feature: *The Defence of Sebastopol* (pr. 15 October 1911), d. Vasili Goncharov and Aleksandr Khanzhonkov, starring Andrei Gromov.
Soviet Feature: *Signal* (1918), d. Alexander Arkatov, prod. Moscow Cinema Committee, starring Grabevetskaya.
Talkie: *The Earth Thirsts* (1930), d. Yuli Raizman.
Colour: *Nightingale, Little Nightingale* (1936), d. Nikolai Ekk.

VENEZUELA
Film: *Muchachas bañádose en el Lago* (1897) and *Un gran especialista sacando muelas en el Hotel Europa* (1897), d. Manuel Trujillo Durán at Maracaibo.
Drama: *Carnival in Caracas* (1909), d. Augusto Gonzalez Vidal and M. A. Gonham.
Feature: *The Lady of Cayenas* (1913), parody of *Camille*, d. E. Zimmerman.
Talkie: *El Rompimiento* (1938), d. Antonio Delgado Gomez, starring Rafael Guinard.

VIETNAM
Drama: *Vie du Detham* (1910), biopic of guerilla leader, d. Rene Batisson.
Talkie: *The Flower from the Cemetry* (1939), prod. Société Indochine Films et Cinéma.

YUGOSLAVIA
Film: *Odhod od mase v Ljutomeru* (1905), made in 17.5 mm by Ljutomer lawyer Karl Grossman.
Drama/Feature: *Zivot i Dela Besmrtnog Vožda Karadjordje* (pr. 17 Nov 1911), biopic of 'Immortal Leader Karadjordje', d. I. Stojadinović, starring M. Petrović.
Talkie: *Nevinost Bez Zastite* (1939), d. D. Aleksić.

ZAIRE
Feature/Talkie: *La Nièce captive* (1969), d. Luc Michez.

The first European feature film scripted for the screen was a four-reel version of *Les Misérables* (Fr 09), produced by Pathé from the novel by Victor Hugo.

The first feature film exhibited in the United Kingdom was Charles Tait's *The Story of the Kelly Gang* (Aus 06), which had its British première at the Assembly Rooms, Bath, in January 1908. The film was released by the Colonial Picture Combine.

The first feature film produced in the United Kingdom was Thomas Bentley's *Oliver Twist* (GB 12), a Hepworth production in four reels starring ex-beauty queen Ivy Millais as Oliver Twist, Alma Taylor as Nancy and John McMahon as Fagin. It was released in August 1912, two months after Vitagraph's version in America (see below).

The first feature film produced in the United States was Vitagraph's four-reel production of *Les Misérables* (US 09), released in separate one-reel parts between 18 September and 27 November 1909. Charles Kent's Vitagraph production of *The Life of Moses* (US 09), in five reels, was also released in separate parts (4 December 1909–19 February 1910) because the producers did not consider that the American public were prepared to sit through a film that lasted over an hour. The first feature film to be released in its entirety in the USA was *Dante's Inferno* (It 11) in August 1911. *Queen Elizabeth* (Fr 12), which is nearly always cited as the first feature film shown in America, was in fact the third, because in the meantime the first domestic feature-length production to be shown whole had been released. This was *Oliver Twist* (US 12), produced by H. A. Spanuth and starring Nat C. Goodwin and Winnie Burns, which was premièred on 20 May 1912, seven weeks before *Queen Elizabeth* (12 July 1912). However, the prejudice against long films was so insistent in America (at least amongst producers and distributors) that even in 1913 the major European success of that year, August Blom's feature *Atlantis* (Den 13), had to be compressed into a half-length version for US release. Domestic production was a modest two in 1912 and twelve in 1913, the real watershed being in 1914, when no less than 212 features were produced. The delay in going over to feature-film making suggests that the impact of *Queen Elizabeth*'s successful exploitation by Adolph Zukor in 1912 may not have been so influential as historians of the cinema have generally believed. Competition from the major European film-producing nations, most of whom had a two-year lead on America in feature production (see p. 7), may in fact have been the deciding factor.

*P*RODUCTION OUTPUT

Total world output of feature films is nearly 4000 annually. Asian countries (including Australasia) account for approx. 50 per cent of output, European countries (including USSR) for approx. 33 per cent, the Middle East and Africa for approx. 5.5 per cent, North America for approx. 6 per cent, and Latin America for approx. 5.5 per cent.

The country with the largest production output in the world is India, with a total of 948 full-length feature releases in 1990 and an annual output that has exceeded 700 each year since 1979.

India has also produced more feature films than any other country, a total of 24,293 from 1913 to 1990 inclusive.

The twelve major film-producing countries of the past decade in terms of output are the following (average annual output in brackets): India (810); Japan (309); USA (257); Taiwan (186); Philippines (160); USSR (155); France (152); Turkey (c. 150); Hong Kong (136); Thailand (c. 130); China (c. 115); Italy (91).

FEATURE-FILM PRODUCTION

The following countries have held the production record since the inception of feature films:

1906–11 Australia	1922–32 Japan	1940 Japan
1912 Hungary	1933–35 USA	1941–53 USA
1913 Germany	1936–38 Japan	1954–70 Japan
1914–22 USA	1939 USA	1971– India

The smallest country with an established film industry is Iceland, whose population of 251,000 are among the most frequent filmgoers in the world with an average of five visits a year (about twice the Scandinavian average). Feature production began in 1948 with Loftur Gudmundsson's *Between Mountain and Shore* and continued sporadically through the next three decades with a dozen features made up to 1977. The breakthrough for the establishment of a permanent film industry came in 1978 with the setting up of the Icelandic Film Fund by Act of Parliament. The first grants from the fund were made the following year and three full-length features went into production immediately. The number of features released annually since then has fluctuated between two and five, and it is estimated that the more successful productions are seen by as many as a quarter of the population of the nation.

Iceland's first full-scale film studio able to accommodate the making of feature films was built in 1988 by Jon Thor Hannesson and Snorri Thorisson. The following year Icelandic cinema, once regarded as a curiosity, achieved international recognition when Gudny Halldorsdottir's *Under the Glacier* (Ice 89) won the Lübecker Lens, top prize at Lübeck's annual Nordic Film Days Festival.

The best year for UK film production was 1936, with 192 features released. The most productive year of the silent era was 1920, with 155 features.

The worst year for UK film production (since 1914) was 1988 when only 27 features were released. The worst years of silent pictures were

1925 and 1926 with 33 releases. On two occasions in the past 65 years, production in Britain has come to a total halt. No films were made during November 1924 and for a three-week period in 1975.

The best year for US film production was 1921 with 854 feature releases.

The worst year for US film production (since 1913) was 1963 with 121 feature releases.

The highest output of any Hollywood studio was 101 features from Paramount in 1921; highest of the sound era was 68 by Paramount in 1936 and the same number from Warner's in 1937. The two most prolific studios of 1990 were 20th Century Fox and Warner Bros with 20 starts each, down on Universal's 23 starts in 1989.

The largest number of foreign films released in the USA in any one year was 361 in 1964. The number of domestic releases was 141. The lowest number of foreign films was 30 in 1943, against 397 Hollywood productions. In 1990 there were 113 foreign releases, 45 of them English language.

Worldwide Production of Feature Films 1906-90

The figures given in the chart on pp. 14-15 refer to feature films of an hour or more in length, including co-productions and feature-length documentaries. Television movies (TVMs) are excluded unless they have had a theatrical release. Production is attributed to the country in which the production company is registered. It should be noted that figures are for the number of new pictures released, which in most cases is not far short of the number produced. In the case of the USA, however, the gap has been widening considerably in recent years. In 1983, for example, there were 336 feature movies produced, of which 85 failed to secure a release; by 1988 no less than 297 features remained on the shelf out of a total of 573.

ACCIDENTS

The largest number of fatalities incurred in the production of a film took place in 1989 when fire engulfed the set of Indian TVM *The Sword of Tipu Sultan*, killing over 40 people.

Reports of prodigious death rolls on Hollywood movies tend to be exaggerated. Neither version of *Ben Hur* (US 25 and US 59) resulted in any deaths, except of horses. **Hollywood's worst accident** took place during production of *Such Men Are Dangerous* (US 30), when two planes collided on the way to shoot a scene. Ten members of the film crew were killed.

Deaths in the course of production have a macabre tendency to come in threes. A helicopter crash during the making of *Twilight Zone* (US 82) resulted in three dead, two of them child actors; three stuntmen were killed shooting the Cooper River rapids for *The Trail of '98* (US 28); three extras were drowned in the *Noah's Ark* (US 28) flood scenes; three aerial stuntmen were killed on *Hell's Angels* (US 30), though only one of them while actually filming; three horsemen died in the cavalry charge in *They Died with Their Boots On* (US 41). One of the latter was Bill Mead, whose horse tripped as he rode by the side of Errol Flynn. He had the presence of mind to fling his sword forward to avoid falling with it, but by incredible mischance the hilt stuck in the ground and Mead fell on the tip of the blade, impaling himself.

Greater safety precautions on Hollywood sets since the *Twilight Zone* disaster noted above have resulted in a sharp decline in accidents. In 1982 there were 214 accidents involving members of the Screen Actors Guild; in 1986 the figure was down to 65, though this included two deaths—stuntmen Dar Robinson and Vic Magnotta.

It is rare for scenes of actual deaths during filming to be retained in the completed picture, but one known example is the anti-British propaganda drama *Mein Leben für Irland* (Ger 41). In the final battle scene several extras were killed when one stepped on a live land-mine, and the footage was included in the release prints.

> In a uniquely tragic episode almost the entire cast of a film were struck down—two years after its completion. They were the non-professional performers from the town in northwestern Iran used in Abbas Kiarostami's award-winning and much acclaimed production *Where Is My Friend's House?* (Iran 88). In the June 1990 Iranian earthquake the town was destroyed, its population wiped out. The only person appearing in the film who survived was a boy who was out of town when the disaster occurred.

ARCHIVES

The first film archive was the Danish Statens Arkiv for historiske Film og Stemmer, which had its origins in the spring of 1910 when Anker Kirkeby of the Copenhagen newspaper *Politiken* approached Ole Olsen of Nordisk Films with the idea of preserving a selection of films likely to be of historic interest in the future. During the ensuing three years a collection of films was assembled, including a number, specially taken for the archive, which showed Danish writers, scientists, politicians, etc., and shots of parts of old Copenhagen due for redevelopment. The archive was formally established at the Royal Library in Copenhagen on 9 April 1913.

By the outbreak of war in 1914, film collections had been formed at the Louvre in Paris, the National Records Office in Madrid, the New York Public Library, and in Brussels, Rome, Berlin, and the Indian state of Baroda. These pioneer efforts, and those that followed in the 1920s, were generally concerned with the preservation of films as a record of national or civic history.

The first National Film Archive formed as a record of the film industry, rather than as a retrospective of public events, was the Reichsfilmarchiv established in Germany at the instigation of Arnold Raether on 4 February 1935. The Svenska Filminstituter Archive claims an earlier date of foundation, but it originated with the Filmhistorika Samlingarna, a private collection formed in 1933 by Einar Lauritzen.

Two other major archives were founded in 1935. The British Film Institute (founded 1933) set up the National Film Archive under Ernest Lindgren in May, and in New York Iris Barry and John Abbott established the Museum of Modern Art Film Library. The following year, Henri Langlois formed the Cinémathèque Française from his own private film collection and this rapidly grew into a national institution, though the government support enjoyed since the end of World War II was withdrawn in 1969 when the French government established its own archive. The USSR's giant Gosfilmofond, which occupies a 150-acre site at Bielye Stolbi near Moscow and employs a staff of 600, was not founded until 1948.

The world's largest service film archive is Britain's National Film Archive, with 135,000 films. The Centre Nationale de la Cinématographie in Paris holds 95,000 films, while the Soviet Union's Gosfilmofond has about 45,000.

The smallest national archive is the Icelandic Film Archive, which contains some 225 films about or made in Iceland.

The country with the most complete visual record of its cinema heritage is Czechoslovakia, whose Prague Film Archive holds an estimated 95 per cent of all the Czech fiction films made since production began. Britain's National Film Archive holds 79 per cent of all British feature films made since the advent of talkies in 1929. Elsewhere the picture is bleaker. Worldwide it is estimated that half of all the feature films made before 1951 have been irretrievably lost; three out of every four feature films made before 1930; and four out of every five features made before 1920.

The biggest single loss of archive film occurred in March 1982 when 6506 films were destroyed by fire and explosions at the Cineteca Nacional in Mexico City. A commentator described the disaster as 'the most terrible cultural loss in modern Mexican history—the filmic memory of our country is erased'.

The largest collection of film stills in the world is the National Film Archive Stills Collection in London, which consists of 6.5 million black-and-white stills and over 1 million colour transparencies from over 80,000 films.

This was the only known copy of an historic New Zealand film, *The Birth of New Zealand* (NZ 22). Archives all over the world are racing against time to transfer old nitrate prints to acetate film before they decompose like this one. (*New Zealand Film Archive*)

According to the organizers of Nitrate Project 2000, there is 189,786,700 ft of pre-1953 nitrate film in the UK, totalling some 35,000 hours of running time. This is equivalent in length to about 20,000 full-length feature films. Cost of transferring all of the footage to acetate is estimated at £14.5 million. Nitrate Project 2000's aim is to save the best of it by the end of the century.

CO-PRODUCTIONS

The first co-production was *Das Geheimnis der Lüfte* (Aut/Fr 13), a full-length feature thriller starring Julius Brandt. The Austrian production company was Wiener Autorenfilm; the French company is believed to have been Pathé.

The first Anglo-American co-production was *Charley's Aunt* (US/GB 25), starring Syd Chaplin, a Christie comedy co-produced with Ideal Films Ltd of London, which opened at the Colony Theater, New York, on 8 February 1925.

The first Anglo-Soviet co-production was *Anna Pavlova* (USSR/GB 85), made by Mosfilm (Moscow) and Poseidon films (London) and starring Galina Belayeva as Pavlova, Martin Scorcese and James Fox.

The first US–Soviet co-production was *The Blue Bird* (US/USSR 76), based on Maurice Maeterlinck's fantasy about a dream trip in search of the elusive bluebird of happiness. The cast was predominately American (Elizabeth Taylor, Jane Fonda, Ava Gardner and Cicely Tyson as a cat) and British (Robert Morley, Harry Andrews, George Cole and a very young Patsy Kensit). The Russians, including ballerina Nadejda Pavlova as the Blue

WORLDWIDE FEATURE FILM PRODUCTION 1906-1990

Year	Algeria	Argentina	Australia	Austria	Bangladesh	Belgium	Brazil	Bulgaria	Canada[1]	China[4]	Cuba	Cz	Denmark	Egypt	Eire	Finland	France	Ger. W	Ger. E	Greece	Hong Kong[3]	Hungary	India	Indonesia[2]	Iraq
1906	0	0	1	0		0	0	0	0	0	0	0	0	0	0	0	—	0		0	—	0	0	0	0
1907	0	0	2	0		0	0	0	0	0	0	0	0	0	0	0	—	1		0	—	0	0	0	0
1908	0	0	0	0		0	0	0	0	0	0	0	0	0	0	0	—	0		0	—	0	0	0	0
1909	0	0	0	0		0	0	0	0	0	0	0	0	0	0	0	—	1		0	—	0	0	0	0
1910	0	0	3	0		0	0	0	0	0	0	0	0	0	0	0	—	0		0	—	0	0	0	0
1911	0	0	16	0		0	0	0	0	0	0	1	0	0	0	0	—	1		0	—	0	0	0	0
1912	0	0	8	1		0	0	0	0	0	0	0	2	0	0	0	—	3		0	—	14	0	0	0
1913	0	0	4	6		3	2	0	1	0	1	0	13	0	0	1	—	49		0	—	11	3	0	0
1914	0	0	3	9		0	—	0	0	0	0	0	16	0	0	0	—	29		0	—	19	1	0	0
1915	0	4	8	10		0	3	1	1	0	1	0	24	0	0	0	—	60		0	—	27	0	0	0
1916	0	12	15	7		0	6	0	2	0	1	0	34	0	0	1	—	107		1	—	52	0	0	0
1917	0	16	6	9		0	4	2	2	0	3	1	40	0	1	0	—	117		0	—	77	3	0	0
1918	0	2	13	40		0	2	0	1	0	1	13	21	0	0	0	—	211		1	—	107	7	0	0
1919	0	15	16	56		1	6	0	2	0	2	23	20	0	0	0	—	345		0	—	48	8	0	0
1920	0	5	10	48		1	6	0	2	0	5	17	8	0	3	1	—	485		0	—	54	27	0	0
1921	0	11	15	47		7	2	3	0	—	8	25	10	0	0	2	—	646		0	—	25	44	0	0
1922	0	10	7	64		8	4	3	8	—	5	30	8	0	3	3	—	474		0	—	6	64	0	0
1923	0	15	7	45		3	6	1	2	—	0	18	15	0	0	3	—	347		2	—	13	52	0	0
1924	0	13	10	30		4	4	0	0	—	0	8	9	0	0	4	68	271		1	—	9	54	0	0
1925	0	15	9	24		10	12	1	0	—	0	17	8	0	2	2	73	228		2	—	3	86	0	0
1926	0	7	16	17		2	12	0	0	80	3	31	7	0	0	2	55	195		2	—	3	94	1	0
1927	0	6	4	18		2	10	2	2	75	2	24	6	1	0	6	74	241		2	—	8	90	1	0
1928	0	6	13	19		1	10	2	3	50	1	16	4	4	0	3	94	226		2	—	2	109	2	0
1929	0	4	3	22		4	13	7	0	40	3	35	3	2	0	7	52	194		4	—	5	140	5	0
1930	0	5	3	17		3	14	3	1	—	2	23	5	4	0	2	98	180		13	—	3	194	7	0
1931	0	4	6	9		3	4	2	0	—	0	23	4	2	0	7	157	199		6	—	3	228	5	0
1932	0	2	4	11		5	8	0	0	60	0	24	6	6	1	3	156	150		6	—	8	148	5	0
1933	0	6	7	18		1	6	2	1	—	0	44	10	6	0	5	152	129		2	—	9	144	1	0
1934	0	6	9	17		6	2	2	2	69	0	34	8	7	0	4	119	142		1	—	12	171	3	0
1935	0	13	3	32		5	2	0	3	80	0	34	11	12	1	5	128	111		0	—	18	233	3	0
1936	0	15	6	25		3	3	1	5	—	0	31	6	13	1	9	145	128		0	—	28	217	2	0
1937	0	28	5	18		7	0	1	6	75	1	49	13	17	0	12	124	108		1	150	36	179	3	0
1938	0	41	7	11		5	3	1	0	86	2	41	10	10	2	20	122	113		3	55	35	172	4	0
1939	0	50	4	11		3	2	1	1	58	8	41	9	15	0	21	94	118		1	100	27	165	4	0
1940	0	49	3	10		2	7	2	0	—	1	31	12	12	0	22	40	89		0	—	39	170	13	0
1941	0	47	3	5		3	1	4	0	—	1	21	16	12	0	15	41	71		1	—	41	167	31	0
1942	0	56	1	6		5	1	1	0	—	1	11	18	22	0	18	74	64		0	—	48	173	1	0
1943	0	36	0	10		1	1	3	0	—	3	10	18	15	0	22	81	83		3	—	53	161	0	0
1944	0	24	1	8		1	7	1	1	—	1	9	18	23	0	16	27	75		2	—	22	127	6	0
1945	0	23	1	1		9	5	2	0	—	2	3	10	42	0	20	50	72		5	—	3	99	0	0
1946	0	32	3	4		8	11	4	3	—	1	11	13	52	0	20	81	1	3	4	—	2	200	0	0
1947	0	38	1	13	0	3	9	3	2	—	2	19	13	55	0	15	88	6	4	6	—	4	281	0	2
1948	0	41	1	25	0	3	14	0	2	—	2	17	10	49	0	16	84	21	7	6	—	5	263	3	0
1949	0	47	4	25	0	1	18	0	5	10	4	20	8	44	0	16	97	56	12	8	256	7	291	8	3
1950	0	56	1	17	0	2	30	1	3	26	10	20	14	48	0	14	104	61	10	6	202	4	241	23	0
1951	0	53	3	28	0	1	22	2	3	17	5	8	18	52	0	19	109	69	8	12	192	9	221	40	0
1952	0	35	1	19	0	2	31	2	1	8	5	16	12	59	0	28	100	73	6	17	259	5	233	42	0
1953	0	37	1	28	0	4	31	1	2	10	4	18	12	62	0	15	111	103	7	19	188	6	260	50	0
1954	0	45	2	22	0	5	25	4	2	24	11	14	13	65	0	28	98	109	9	19	167	8	278	59	0
1955	0	43	2	28	0	5	24	2	0	23	7	16	13	51	0	30	110	128	13	16	235	10	289	64	1
1956	0	36	2	37	1	8	21	9	2	40	5	21	13	39	0	18	129	122	19	26	311	20	295	36	1
1957	0	15	3	26	0	3	36	5	3	41	3	25	16	40	1	21	142	107	22	28	223	15	294	21	3
1958	0	32	1	23	0	12	41	9	3	101	6	29	16	55	3	17	126	115	17	38	237	13	294	19	5
1959	0	22	2	19	3	6	30	3	4	79	5	33	14	58	2	15	133	106	28	59	239	18	304	16	1
1960	0	31	2	20	2	9	29	10	2	59	2	30	19	59	0	18	158	94	24	68	293	14	318	38	2
1961	0	25	1	23	5	9	36	9	5	26	2	39	22	52	1	18	167	80	27	56	303	19	298	37	0
1962	0	32	1	20	5	11	28	8	4	33	2	35	23	49	0	21	125	61	24	78	261	17	315	12	7
1963	1	27	0	15	4	4	21	9	5	39	4	36	21	48	0	14	141	66	20	66	260	21	302	19	6
1964	0	37	0	19	17	2	23	10	14	28	6	38	19	45	0	6	148	77	16	94	235	18	310	19	3
1965	3	30	3	16	12	5	26	8	15	43	4	40	16	43	0	9	142	69	14	96	204	20	322	15	1
1966	1	34	3	18	24	3	30	12	10	12	2	31	18	39	0	7	130	60	16	106	171	20	311	13	1
1967	2	27	2	12	22	31	41	15	11	0	3	40	20	33	0	3	120	96	20	76	169	22	329	13	4
1968	4	32	1	7	34	10	47	6	13	0	4	36	19	40	1	12	117	107	6	95	156	21	349	8	5
1969	2	29	6	3	30	15	46	14	25	0	1	25	23	44	0	9	154	121	13	88	158	20	379	9	2
1970	8	28	14	7	41	12	70	25	46	2	0	38	28	48	0	13	138	113	—	86	138	20	398	21	2
1971	1	38	10	5	6	16	69	18	32	2	4	37	33	46	0	9	127	99	12	83	127	20	432	52	0
1972	9	32	7	9	28	20	81	22	32	5	2	35	17	41	1	6	169	85	17	63	133	21	411	50	1
1973	6	39	12	6	31	27	58	18	43	4	3	36	12	43	0	8	200	98	16	63	201	18	448	58	0
1974	10	38	11	8	30	16	82	19	41	17	2	38	14	44	0	3	234	80	15	38	147	19	432	84	0
1975	3	33	24	6	34	21	90	25	39	25	2	39	17	49	0	5	222	81	16	47	109	19	470	39	1
1976	4	21	16	5	44	11	78	20	30	37	5	46	20	47	0	9	214	61	17	38	112	17	507	58	0
1977	1	21	17	8	31	30	73	21	39	19	3	42	20	50	1	7	142	60	15	21	116	19	555	124	3
1978	5	22	10	3	42	20	101	21	39	45	3	46	16	51	2	10	227	64	17	18	135	23	612	81	2
1979	2	33	18	9	52	10	93	22	55	62	6	46	11	39	0	9	234	66	17	—	145	25	714	51	3
1980	0	34	14	8	44	21	102	21	54	83	4	45	12	34	—	11	189	49	15	26	132	21	742	68	—
1981	0	24	9	11	39	9	80	—	33	105	0	44	12	43	—	16	231	76	16	25	127	24	737	71	—
1982	5	17	21	13	42	5	86	17	27	114	3	44	7	41	1	19	164	70	16	46	126	27	763	52	—
1983	3	17	19	11	45	11	84	22	34	127	8	41	12	46	2	17	131	77	16	48	114	26	741	74	—
1984	3	31	15	14	50	8	90	20	27	143	6	34	13	63	3	20	161	77	—	37	125	23	800*	78	—
1985	5	24	16	18	63	7	83	17	58	127	7	44	8	75	2	15	151	77	19	23	105	27	912	62	—
1986	3	37	23	12	70	6	79	23	63	125	12	56	10	91	2	29	134	73	16	26	109	26	840	64	—
1987	4	33	23	14	65	12	60	26	61	142	10	39	11	70	2	15	133	74	—	22	113	24	806	54	—
1988	—	32	34	—	—	15	—	15	—	158	10	42	15	58	1	9	—	57	—	—	151	19	773	83	—
1989	—	32	32	16	—	—	25	20	—	195	6	41	17	—	2	10	137	68	—	—	199	18	781	104	—
1990	—	9	16	14	—	—	—	19	—	—	10	54	13	—	3	13	144	48	—	—	272	8	948	—	—

— No data available   [1] Completions per year   [2] Starts per year   [3] Financial year April-March   [4] 1949-66: 614   * estimated

Japan	Korea, S	Malaysia	Mexico	Neths	NZ	Norway	Pakistan	Philippines	Poland	Portugal	Romania	Singapore	S Africa	Spain	Sri Lanka	Sweden[3]	Swz	Thailand	Tunisia	Turkey	UK	Uruguay	USA	USSR	Ven	Yug
0	0	0	0	0	0	0		0	0	0	0	0	0	0	0	0	0	0	0	0	0	0	0	0	0	0
0	0	0	0	0	0	0		0	0	0	0	0	0	0	0	0	0	0	0	0	0	0	0	0	0	0
0	0	0	0	0	0	0		0	0	0	0	0	0	0	0	0	0	0	0	0	0	0	0	0	0	0
0	0	0	0	0	0	0		0	0	0	0	0	0	0	0	0	0	0	0	0	0	0	0	0	0	0
0	0	0	0	0	0	0		0	0	3	0	0	0	—	0	0	0	0	0	0	0	0	0	1	0	1
2	0	0	0	0	0	1		0	0	2	1	0	0	—	0	0	0	0	0	0	2	0	2	9	0	0
0	0	0	0	1	0	0		0	5	0	10	0	0	—	0	4	0	0	0	0	18	0	12	31	1	—
5	0	0	0	5	0	0		0	5	0	0	0	0	—	0	5	0	0	0	0	15	0	212	17	0	—
3	0	0	0	7	0	0		0	3	0	0	0	0	—	0	2	1	0	0	0	73	0	419	44	1	—
—	0	0	1	9	1	2		0	5	0	0	0	14	—	0	4	0	0	0	0	107	0	677	74	0	—
—	0	0	11	5	0	3		—	7	0	0	0	7	—	0	7	1	0	0	2	66	0	687	57	0	—
—	0	0	6	10	0	3		—	6	0	0	0	5	—	0	6	1	0	0	0	76	0	841	27	0	6
—	0	0	13	5	0	2		—	7	4	0	0	6	17	0	11	2	0	0	3	122	0	646	12	0	—
—	0	0	7	10	0	2		—	8	2	2	0	4	12	0	20	0	0	0	0	155	1	797	8	0	—
—	0	0	8	10	0	3		—	17	3	1	0	2	8	0	7	3	0	1	3	137	0	854	5	0	—
—	2	0	4	11	2	3		—	15	2	0	0	3	4	0	11	4	1	2	2	110	0	748	9	0	—
875	2	0	0	6	1	1		—	11	7	1	0	1	8	0	23	5	1	0	3	68	1	576	12	0	—
—	6	0	7	2	1	2		—	5	0	0	0	1	38	0	18	5	2	0	0	33	0	579	76	0	—
—	6	0	4	4	0	5	3	8	1	4	0	0	0	39	0	18	1	3	0	0	33	0	740	77	1	—
648	—	0	2	1	2	5	4		12	1	3	0	0	25	0	11	2	3	2	0	48	1	678	106	0	—
798	—	0	2	1	1	3	—		12	1	4	0	0	12	0	6	2	8	2	1	80	1	641	125	3	0
850	—	0	2	1	0	2	—		16	1	5	0	0	21	0	6	2	—	1	1	81	1	562	103	1	—
—	—	0	1	1	0	2		16	12	5	3	0	0	8	0	13	2	—	1	0	75	0	509	123	0	—
—	—	0	1	0	0	1		16	10	2	3	0	2	2	0	24	4	—	0	1	93	0	501	88	1	—
498	—	0	6	1	0	5		20	14	0	1	0	0	9	0	22	4	—	0	1	110	0	489	67	1	4
450	—	0	21	0	0	3	—	11	0	0	0	0	0	17	0	22	3	—	0	7	115	0	507	35	3	2
413	—	0	23	8	0	2	—	14	3	2	0	0	0	23	0	19	7	—	0	3	145	0	480	59	0	0
470	—	0	22	9	1	1	—	14	1	0	0	0	0	44	0	20	7	—	2	0	165	0	525	34	0	0
558	—	0	25	11	3	1		15	24	1	0	1	1	19	0	28	9	—	0	0	192	1	522	49	0	0
583	5	0	38	5	0	2		32	28	3	1	—	0	10	0	22	1	—	1	1	176	0	538	45	1	0
554	—	0	57	3	0	5		55	21	4	0	—	1	4	0	27	5	10	1	1	134	3	455	41	0	0
437	—	0	37	4	0	4	—	18	1	3	—	1		20	0	30	7	12	0	4	84	0	483	52	2	1
497	—	6	29	2	1	4	—	0	3	0	0	0	3	40	0	36	11	—	0	4	50	0	477	50	1	0
232	—	0	37	—	1	4	—	0	2	0	0	0	0	33	0	34	14	—	0	1	46	0	492	50	1	0
87	—	1	47	—	0	5	—	0	4	1	0	0	0	49	0	34	12	—	0	4	39	0	488	26	2	0
61	—	0	70	—	0	4	—	0	4	2	0	0	0	53	0	43	5	—	0	2	47	0	397	27	0	0
46	—	0	73	—	0	3	—	0	3	0	0	0	1	34	0	43	2	—	0	2	35	0	401	21	0	0
38	—	0	82	2	0	4	—	0	4	1	0	0	0	33	0	44	2	—	0	3	39	0	350	20	4	0
57	4	0	72	1	0	6	10	1	6	4	—	4		41	0	36	1	—	0	6	41	1	378	19	1	0
97	13	2	58	0	0	1	0	24	2	7	0	—	2	48	0	43	2	—	0	12	58	1	369	22	0	2
123	22	3	81	2	0	4	0	—	2	4	0	—	1	44	0	40	2	—	1	16	74	1	366	22	3	4
156	20	3	108	2	0	3	4	—	3	7	1	—	4	37	0	34	4	10	0	18	101	2	356	13	4	3
215	5	8	124	0	0	2	15	—	4	2	0	—	2	49	0	25	3	—	0	21	81	2	383	14	4	4
212	5	11	101	1	0	7	10	—	2	2	2	15	5	41	0	31	1	—	1	32	75	1	391	10	1	6
258	—	18	99	1	1	7	7	—	4	8	1	14	1	41	0	25	3	—	0	52	101	2	324	20	3	5
302	—	16	83	2	0	6	10	—	3	4	2	21	5	43	6	31	3	—	0	50	102	0	344	42	1	9
370	18	11	105	0	0	9	7	—	10	3	3	13	5	69	5	30	2	—	1	53	110	0	253	35	1	7
423	15	9	84	2	0	9	19	—	8	0	4	20	4	56	7	30	3	—	0	64	95	0	254	84	2	14
514	42	9	87	0	0	8	31	—	6	4	3	12	2	75	7	34	3	—	0	52	91	0	272	98	3	10
443	44	16	106	3	0	9	27	—	16	1	8	13	2	72	8	32	5	—	1	60	115	1	300	144	2	15
516	80	23	92	4	0	9	33	97	16	4	4	19	5	75	9	29	7	—	1	80	111	2	241	130	1	15
500	109	28	84	1	0	6	34	92	16	5	4	17	6	68	9	24	6	50	1	71	99	1	187	145	1	14
555	85	13	64	6	0	6	38	112	21	2	9	12	8	73	9	23	4	43	0	68	110	0	154	139	1	14
537	91	19	49	1	0	6	34	108	23	2	10	19	19	91	8	18	7	35	1	116	109	0	131	137	0	32
378	115	18	—	5	0	6	34	152	23	5	8	27	13	89	6	17	6	96	0	127	126	0	147	97	3	22
363	146	15	—	2	0	6	46	142	26	8	10	21	7	113	11	18	4	48	0	125	107	0	121	96	4	18
346	148	13	—	3	1	6	67	161	25	8	11	19	8	123	15	24	1	44	0	178	75	0	141	108	9	17
487	189	12	52	1	0	8	54	161	20	6	14	11	6	133	15	19	2	44	1	214	80	0	153	127	3	20
442	124	9	—	6	1	7	72	201	26	5	15	12	10	152	20	25	1	54	2	238	69	0	156	131	3	21
410	155	10	48	7	0	6	66	180	21	7	14	10	9	138	21	27	4	51	7	206	89	0	178	136	2	31
494	219	11	90	4	0	5	99	175	18	4	7	5	12	117	20	34	7	52	3	177	73	0	180	121	5	36
494	229	11	93	6	0	5	91	169	22	4	12	5	12	123	20	24	—	64	5	229	85	0	177	141	1	29
423	209	9	—	3	0	11	85	194	25	4	8	4	17	105	17	20	7	73	4	225	103	0	231	130	4	23
421	202	2	—	4	1	6	79	253	25	7	13	3	17	107	14	19	—	74	2	266	97	0	223	133	4	23
400	122	2	81	6	0	8	99	181	20	8	16	3	24	104	20	14	—	70	4	298	90	0	224	127	1	21
405	125	3	48	11	1	12	93	146	25	6	16	4	22	112	18	18	18	81	2	208	80	0	201	150	5	16
333	141	6	44	9	0	12	107	120	31	11	18	1	34	115	41	24	15	83	2	188	81	0	179	140	3	11
333	94	4	40	14	1	14	111	143	36	10	23	4	30	102	31	20	15	90	3	124	80	0	161	148	5	19
356	134	4	43	8	0	12	109	174	28	18	22	2	25	90	30	16	10	130	1	164	64	0	188	149	13	18
337	102	3	59	8	4	10	74	141	32	19	20	2	24	97	75	22	—	98	2	225	43	0	157	143	29	15
326	117	4	63	9	2	6	87	135	27	5	23	0	19	79	35	17	10	148	3	123	49	0	162	141	12	16
335	96	5	85	14	3	13	80	170	32	6	28	0	22	73	29	18	—	150	2	195	38	1	167	151	9	24
320	91	9	108	7	2	10	58	173	37	13	32	0	20	110	75	26	—	142	4	—	41	1	200	151	5	26
332	87	14	87	11	5	10	84	179	41	8	31	0	20	92	56	25	16	138	3	—	32	1	181	145	4	24
322	97	13	74	13	5	10	66	149	33	7	30	0	15	146	65	18	13	117	3	—	37	—	187	158	7	32
363	91	15	80	15	4	7	85	143	32	4	32	0	35	99	33	23	17	109	3	—	33	—	231	148	9	28
379	81	13	77	12	8	7	82	138	32	8	26	0	80	75	34	23	17	141	3	—	42	—	262	150	15	34
329	80	8	73	16	12	10	92	158	—	2	—	0	85	77	26	20	21	134	—	—	47	—	264	142	15	30
311	73	10	88	13	5	10	106	177	33	4	—	0	56	60	18	27	28	102	—	—	30	—	311	142	16	28
286	90	13	82	17	6	8	76	167	—	5	—	0	78	69	18	25	36	130	—	—	30	—	332	151	14	26
265	—	—	112	10	8	9	88	—	42	9	—	0	52	63	—	20	—	—	—	—	27	—	325	171	7	—
255	—	—	99	13	9	11	101	162	35	7	—	0	19	47	—	17	—	—	—	—	38	—	276	138	—	—
239	—	—	100	13	9	9	84	—	27	4	—	0	12	36	11	21	24	—	—	—	29	—	304	300	—	—

Bird, were consigned to the bottom half of the bill.

Soviet production facilities came as something of a rude shock to the visiting Hollywood film-makers. When director George Cukor arrived in Leningrad with Elizabeth Taylor and Ava Gardner he remarked to the Soviet studio head what an honour it was to be filming in the very studio where Eisenstein had shot his classic *The Battleship Potemkin* in 1925. 'Yes', beamed their proud host, 'and with the very same equipment'.

The first US-Chinese co-production was *A Great Wall* (US/China 85), made by W & S Productions of New York and the Nanhai Film Co. of Beijing. It starred Chinese-American actor Peter Wang, who also directed, as a San Francisco computer executive experiencing culture shock on a visit to relatives in the old country.

The most cosmopolitan co-productions are the seven-nation films *Soldaty svobody* (USSR/Bul/Hun/GDR/Pol/Rom/Cz 77) and *West Indies Story* (Tun/Mali/IvC/Mau/Alg/Sen/Fr 79). *Soldaty svobody* involved the most production companies, namely Mosfilm (USSR), Za Ugrakbu Film (Bul), Mafilm (Hun), Defa (GDR), PRF EF (Pol), Bukuresti (Rom), Barrandov (Cz) and Koliba (Cz). Sembene Ousmane's *Almamy Samori Toure*, currently in production (1991), is a co-production between France, Japan, Italy and nine African countries.

Hollywood in 1911, the year the moviemakers arrived. (*Kobal Collection*)

HOLLYWOOD

The first European inhabitant of the area now known as Hollywood, then called Nopalera, was Mexican-born Don Tomas Urquidez, who built an adobe dwelling in 1853 at what is now the northwest corner of Franklin and Sycamore Avenues.

The name 'Hollywood' was conferred on her Cahuenga Valley ranch by Mrs Harvey Henderson Wilcox, wife of one of the district's earliest real-estate developers, in 1886. The name had nothing to do with holly-bushes imported from England, as some accounts have it. Mrs Wilcox had been travelling by train to her old home in the east when she met a lady with a summer home near Chicago called 'Hollywood'. She was so charmed by the name that she decided to borrow it for her own property. In 1903 the village of Hollywood and its environs were incorporated as a municipality, but in 1910 the citizens voted to become a district of Los Angeles in order to secure water supplies. At that date the population was 5000; by 1919 it was 35,000 and by 1925 it had grown to 130,000.

The largest private house in the Hollywood area is producer Aaron Spelling's 123-room 'The Manor' in Holmby Hills. Built on the site of Bing Crosby's former home, which Spelling bought for $10 million and demolished, the house is in the style of a French château and contains a theatre, gymnasium, four bars, three kitchens, an Olympic-size swimming pool, a doll museum, eight two-car garages, 12 fountains, a bowling alley and a bomb-

proof anti-terrorist room. It was completed in 1990 at an estimated cost of $45 million.

Beverly Hills

The exodus of Hollywood's upper crust to Beverly Hills began when Douglas Fairbanks rented sports goods manufacturer Syl Spaulding's 36-room house on Summit Drive in 1919. At that time Beverly Hills was mainly agricultural land given over to the cultivation of beans and there was only one house between Fairbanks' rented property and the sea seven miles away. Early in 1920 he bought a hunting lodge adjacent to the Spaulding mansion and rebuilt it in a style befitting his new bride, Mary Pickford. Named 'Pickfair' after the first syllables of their names, Doug's wedding gift to Mary was, and remained, Beverly Hills' most regal establishment, a magnet that drew the elite of the film colony to what was soon to become America's richest suburb. In 1980, following the death of Mary Pickford, the 45-room mansion was put up for sale, but it was not until 1988 that international financier Meshulam Riklis paid the equivalent of £12 million for it as a home for his diminutive actress wife Pia Zadora. Riklis announced that he would spend another £3.5 million to 'spruce it up'.

. . . and Malibu

The first film star to settle in Malibu Beach was Anna Q. Nilsson, who built a house on a sandy strip of deserted beach just north of Malibu Creek in 1928. Clara Bow, Gloria Swanson, Ronald Colman and Frank Capra soon followed her and within two years the area had been dubbed the Malibu Motion Picture Colony.

> What is the biggest business in Los Angeles? Certainly not movies, per *Los Angeles Business Journal*. Some 547,000 Angelenos are employed in banking and related services, 328,000 in the tourist business, 289,000 in the aerospace industry and only 80,000 in movie and TV production.

The first dramatic film made in the Los Angeles area was Francis Boggs' *The Count of Monte Cristo* (US 08), a Selig production made partly in Colorado and partly in the Laguna and Venice districts of what is now Greater Los Angeles. The first made wholly in LA was Francis Boggs' *The Power of the Sultan* (US 09), starring Hobart Bosworth, a Broadway actor who had lost his voice through TB and was seeking recuperative sunshine. The movie was shot in three days, 8–10 May 1909, on a rented lot next to a Chinese laundry on Olive and Seventh Streets, Los Angeles. Boggs, who might have become prominent as California's pioneer director, was unfortunately cut down in his prime, murdered by a crazed Japanese studio gardener in 1911.

The first studio in the Los Angeles area was established by the Selig Co. at 1845 Allesandro Street, Edendale. Construction began in August 1909 and enlargements were made in 1910 and again in 1911, so that within two years of opening it was occupying a 230×220 ft building.

The first film made in Hollywood was D. W. Griffith's *In Old California* (US 10), a Biograph melodrama about the liaison between a Spanish maiden (Marion Leonard) and a dashing hero, destined to become Governor of California (Frank Grandin), who have an illegitimate wastrel son (Arthur Johnson). It was shot in two days, 2–3 February 1910, and released on 10 March.

> At the 1984 American Film Institute Life Achievement Award presentation to 90-year-old Lillian Gish, John Houseman recalled that many years ago Miss Gish and her sister Dorothy were offered the chance of buying the Sunset Strip in Hollywood for $300. The Gish sisters talked the matter over, weighing the pros and cons. They then went down to fashionable Bullock's and bought a dress each instead.

The first studio in Hollywood was established there as the result of a toss of a coin. Al Christie, chief director of the Centaur Co., wanted to make westerns in California, since he was tired of having to simulate sagebrush country in New Jersey. Centaur's owner, David Horsley, thought that Florida would be better, but agreed to abide by a heads-or-tails decision. Christie tossed and won. After viewing various possible sites in Southern California, he found a derelict roadhouse on Sunset Boulevard which looked suitable and cost only $40 a month to rent. This building was converted into a studio in October 1911. It was called the Nestor Studio, after the name of the western branch of the company. Today the site is occupied by the West Coast headquarters of CBS. By the end of the following year there were 15 film companies operating in Hollywood. Uninterrupted sunshine and a comforting distance from the agents of the Patents Co. were not the only attractions of Southern California as a film-making base. The astonishing range and variety of its scenery enabled locations to be found that could reasonably represent any terrain from Cornwall to the Urals; westerns could be located in the real west rather than New Jersey, South Sea island pictures could be shot on Catalina and neighbouring islands, an oil field in Los Angeles itself served for Texan oilman dramas, Spanish missions set the scene for old Mexico, and there were even sufficient baronial mansions to cater for the needs of

The Nestor Studios on Sunset Boulevard 1911. Formerly a derelict roadhouse, it was Hollywood's first studio.

pictures playing in Hollywood's England. Only a jungle was missing, but studios like Selig and Universal established their own zoos and built their African locales on the back-lot.

The first talking picture made in Hollywood was a Fox Movietone short *They're Coming to Get Me* (US 26), with comedian Chic Sale, released in May 1926.

The Celebrated Hollywood Sign

The sign was erected on Hollywood Hills in 1923 at a cost of $21,000. Originally it spelt out the word HOLLYWOODLAND, in letters 30 ft wide and 50 ft tall and built up from 3×9 ft sheet metal panels attached to a scaffolding frame. Each letter was studded with 20-watt light bulbs at eight-inch intervals. A man called Albert Kothe, who lived on the job—in a hut behind one of the 'L's'—was employed full time to change the bulbs when they burned out. The sign has often been featured in movies as a means of establishing locale, for example as shown in *The Day of the Locust* (US 75) and *1941* (US 79). It has been put to more macabre use for frequent suicide attempts. First to take a death dive from the top of the sign was failed starlet Peg Entwhistle in 1932.

Declared an historic landmark in 1973, the original and much dilapidated sign was replaced five years later after a fund for this purpose had been established by Gene Autry, Alice Cooper and Playboy chief Hugh Hefner. The new sign cost $27,000 for each letter. The remains of the old one were sold to a Mr Hank Berger, who cut the scrap metal into one-inch squares and retailed them to the more obsessive nostalgia buffs at $29.95 a time.

A group calling themselves 'The Environmental Pranksters' have made newspaper headlines several times recently by their depredations on the famous sign. Using black plastic sheeting to cover up whole letters, or parts of letters, they converted HOLLY-WOOD to HOLYWOOD to celebrate the Pope's visit in 1987, to HOLLYWEED after laws on marijuana possession had been relaxed, and to OLLYWOOD in tribute to Col. 'Olly' North's performance at the Senate's Irangate hearings.

The first footprints outside Grauman's Chinese Theater in Hollywood were Norma Talmadge's on 18 May 1927. Legend has it that she stepped on the wet cement by accident, thereby giving Sid Grauman the idea for his celebrated and still continuing publicity stunt.

Selection for the Hollywood Walk of Fame is a high honour for those who have achieved distinction in the motion picture and entertainment business. It is also expensive for the recipient of the honour. The Hollywood Historic Trust, which adminsters the Walk of Fame, has upped the price to $3500. Most celebrities are prepared to pay, though a few have refused to dip into their own pockets for the price of sidewalk immortality. By December 1990 there were 1925 stars embedded in the concrete, with 578 remaining slots.

Biting the Hand . . .

☆ 'A town that has to be seen to be disbelieved'—Walter Winchell

☆ 'It's a great place to live—if you're an orange'—Fred Allen

☆ 'Hollywood is a sewer—with service from the Ritz Carlton'—Wilson Mizner

☆ 'There is one word which aptly describes Hollywood—*nervous!*'—Frank Capra

☆ 'They've great respect for the dead in Hollywood, but none for the living'—Errol Flynn

☆ 'Hollywood is the only community in the world where the entire population is suffering from rumourtism'—Bert Lahr

☆ 'Hollywood is pretty painful even in small quantities'—Constance Bennett. (It grew a little less painful when her salary leaped from $8000 a week to $30,000 a week—the highest in Hollywood—shortly after saying this.)

☆ 'It's somehow symbolic of Hollywood that Tara was just a facade, with no rooms inside'—David O Selznick

☆ 'Hollywood stinks'—Frank Sinatra

☆ 'I saw Hollywood born and I've seen it die . . .'—Mary Pickford in old age

☆ 'Hollywood is a place where they'll pay you $50,000 for a kiss and 50c for your soul'—Marilyn Monroe

☆ 'Hollywood is where, if you don't have happiness,

you send out for it'—Rex Reed

☆ 'This town's motivated by fear—the fear of failure'—Amanda Donohoe

☆ 'Here, it is boring, incredibly boring, so boring I can't believe it is true'— Greta Garbo in 1926

☆ 'Hollywood's a place where they shoot too many pictures and not enough actors'—Walter Winchell again

*L*ONGEST FILMS

The longest film ever made was the 85-hour *The Cure for Insomnia* (US 87), directed by John Henry Timmis IV and premièred in its entirety at the School of Art Institute of Chicago from 31 Jan to 3 Feb 1987. Much of the film consists of L. D. Groban reading his own 4080 page poem, also titled *The Cure for Insomnia*, interspersed with scenes of rock band J.T.4 and Cosmic Lightning and what the makers describe as some 'X-rated footage'. A short

'clean' version lasting a mere 80 hours is available without the erotic scenes.

The longest commercially-made film was *The Burning of the Red Lotus Temple* (Chn 28–31), adapted by the Star Film Co. from a newspaper serial *Strange Tales of the Adventurer in the Wild Country* by Shang K'ai-jan. It was released in 18 feature-length parts over a period of three years. Although never shown publicly in its 27-hour entirety, some cinemas would put on all-day performances of half-a-dozen parts in sequence.

The longest commercially-made American movie to be released uncut was Erich von Stroheim's *Foolish Wives* (US 22), which was distributed to Latin American countries in its original 6 hr 24 min version. In the United States, however, it was seen only in a severely cut form, a 12-reel version for the road show and a 10-reel version for general release.

The 42-reel version of von Stroheim's masterpiece

FILMS RUNNING FOUR HOURS

The following are films shown in public in a version lasting four hours or longer. The list includes films issued in parts, but not serials. The duration of the silent films listed is calculated on the assumption that they were projected at 16 f.p.s.

Hours	Film	Hours	Film	Hours	Film
4 hr	*Chusingura* (Jap 55)		*La Hora de los Hornos* (Arg 68)	6 hr 30 min	*Sleep* (US 63)
	Gosta Berlings Saga (Swe 24)	4 hr 34 min	*Atvaltozas/Point of Departure* (Hun 84)	6 hr 40 min	*Hitler: a Film from Germany* (FRG 77)
	Heaven's Gate (US 81) [1]	4 hr 38 min	*The Memory of Justice* (FRG 76)	7 hr	*Der Hund von Baskerville* (Ger 14–20)
	Ludwig (It/Fr/FRG 73) [2]	4 hr 40 min	*Amerikanske Billeder* (Den 81)		
	Manon des Sources (Fr 54)		*The Prodigal Son* (GB 23)	7 hr 45 min	*Français si vous savez* (Fr 73)
4 hr 3 min	*Cleopatra* (US 63)	4 hr 45 min	*Rameau's Nephew by Diderot* (Can 74)	7 hr 58 min	*Iskry Plamja* (Rus 25)
4 hr 5 min	*The Keys of Happiness* (Rus 13)			8 hr	*Empire* (US 64)
	Siberiade (USSR 79)	4 hr 57 min	*Darkness* (Fr 88)	8 hr 27 min	*War and Peace* (USSR 63–67) [6]
4 hr 12 min	*L'Amour Fou* (Fr 68)	4 hr 58 min	*Percal* (Mex 50)	8 hr 32 min	*La Roue* (Fr 21) [7]
4 hr 15 min	*Parsifal* (FRG/Fr 82)	5 hr 2 min	*Winifred Wagner und die Geschichte des Hauses Wahnfried* (FRG 75)	9 hr	*Wagner* (GB/Hun/Aut 83) [8]
	Paths of Life (GDR 81)				*Napoleon* (Fr 27) [9]
	Molière (Fr 78)	5 hr 5 min	*Les Misérables* (Fr 27)	9 hr 21 min	*Shoah* (Fr/Swz 85)
	Out 1: Spectre (Fr 72)	5 hr 6 min	*Petersburgskije truscoby* (Rus 15)	9 hr 29 min	*The Human Condition* (Jap 58–60)
	Mera Naam Joker (Ind 70)	5 hr 14 min	*Potop/The Deluge* (Pol 74)	12 hr 40 min	*Out 1: Noli me Tangerey* (Fr 71) [10]
4 hr 16 min	*The Age of Cosimo de Medici* (It 72)	5 hr 16 min	*1900* (It 78)	12 hr 43 min	*Comment Yukong deplace les montagnes* (Fr 76)
	Gustaf Wasa (Swe 28)	5 hr 20 min	*Vindicta* (Fr 23)		
4 hr 17 min	*Les Plouffe* (Can 81)	5 hr 32 min	*Les Misérables* (Fr 33)	13 hr	*The Old Testament* (It 22)
4 hr 20 min	*Amor der Perdicao* (Por 80)	5 hr 37 min	*La Révolution Française* (Fr/GDR/It/Can 89)	14 hr 33 min	*The Journey* (Can 87)
	Boris I (Bul 85)			15 hr 21 min	*Berlin Alexanderplatz* (FRG/It 80) [11]
	The Greatest Story Ever Told (US 62) [3]	5 hr 50 min	*Fanny and Alexander* (Swe 83) [4]	15 hr 40 min	*Heimat* (FRG 84)
	Rubens (Neth 78)	5 hr 54 min	*Soldati Svobodi* (USSR/Bul/Hun/Cz/GDR/Rom/Pol 77)	24 hr	* * * * (US 67) [12]
4 hr 25 min	*The Idiot* (Jap 51)	5 hr 57 min	*Little Dorrit* (GB 87)	27 hr	*The Burning of the Red Lotus Temple* (Chn 28–31)
	The Tokyo Trial (Jap 85)	6 hr	*Charles XII* (Swe 27)	42 hr	*Cinématon Part 1* (Fr 86)
4 hr 27 min	*Hotel Terminus: The Life and Times of Klaus Barbie* (Fr 88)		*Idade de Terra* (Bra 79)	48 hr	*The Longest Most Meaningless Movie in the World* (GB 70) [13]
			Khan Asparouch (Bul 82)		
4 hr 30 min	*Measure for Measure* (Bul 81)		*Monte Cristo* (Fr 28)	50 hr	*Mondo Teeth* (US 70)
	Imagen de Caracas (Ven 68)	6 hr 10 min	*Die Nibelungen* (Ger 24)	85 hr	*The Cure for Insomnia* (US 87)
	The Great Citizen (USSR 38)	6 hr 24 min	*Foolish Wives* (US 22) [5]		
	Time of Violence (Bul 87)				
	Le Chagrin et la Pitié (Fr 70)				

[1] Long version shown Venice Film Festival 1982 and elsewhere.

[2] General release print 3 hr; 4-hr version shown Rome 1980, Paris 1983.

[3] At première only. Release prints were 3 hr 58 min.

[4] Long version shown at Venice Film Festival 1983.

[5] Released at this length in South America only. US general release: 10 reels.

[6] Russian language version. English language version 6 hr 13 min.

[7] Released in 4-hr version, but VGIK in Moscow has print of 8½ hr original.

[8] Premièred in 9-hr entirety at Dominion, Tottenham Court Road, May 1983. Release version 5 hr.

[9] Abel Gance's 42-reel version *définitive*; trade and press shown at the Apollo, Paris in 1927 and believed to have been shown commercially in Nice and other provincial centres. The version shown at the Paris première was 3 hr 40 min. The 7½-hr version reconstructed by Kevin Brownlow was first

shown at Don Bosch, Netherlands on 24 November 1984.

[10] Shown only once at this length, then re-edited as 4½-hr *Out 1: Spectre*.

[11] Long version: see **Longest film shown commercially** entry above.

[12] Shown only once, then re-edited as two features of conventional length.

[13] Premièred at this length, then cut to 1½ hr.

Greed (US 24)—**Hollywood's longest-ever film in its original form**—was shown only once at a 9-hour screening at MGM on 12 January 1924. Idwal Jones, drama critic of the *San Francisco Daily News*, who was present, commented that it had 'every comma of the book put in'. It was subsequently cut to 24 reels by an aggrieved von Stroheim, who had already spent four unpaid months editing the original footage down to 48 reels; then to 18 reels by Rex Ingram, and finally 10 reels by Joe Farnham. The 32 reels of cut negative were melted down by MGM to retrieve the minute quantity of silver nitrate they contained.

The longest commercially-made American movie released in America was the ill-fated $43 million epic *Cleopatra* (US 63) at a seemingly endless 4 hr 3 min. The only other Hollywood productions longer than *Gone with the Wind* (US 39), which ran for 3 hr 40 min, were *The Greatest Story Ever Told* (US 65) at 3 hr 45 min and Bob Dylan's 3 hr 55 min *Renaldo and Clara* (US 77). Otto Preminger's *Exodus* (US 60) was exactly the same length as *Gone with the Wind*. Prior to *Gone with the Wind* the record for the longest Hollywood talkie was held by MGM's *The Great Ziegfeld* (US 36), which ran for 2 hr 59 min.

The longest commercially-made British film was Christine Edzard's monumental screen adaptation of Charles Dickens's *Little Dorrit* (GB 87), starring Sir Alec Guinness, Derek Jacobi and talented newcomer Sarah Pickering in the title role. With a total running time of 5 hr 57 min, the film was released in two parts, playing on alternate days, the first part of 2 hr 56 min duration, the second 3 hr 1 min.

The longest film to be shown commercially in its entirety was Rainer Werner Fassbinder's 15 hr 21 min opus *Berlin Alexanderplatz* (FRG 83) at the Vista cinema in Hollywood on 6–7 August 1983. Tickets cost $20 and there was a two-hour break for dinner. The slightly longer *Heimat* (FRG 84), at 15 hr 40 min, was shown in several German cities and at the London Film Festival during 1984, but these were weekend shows with a night in between the first half and the second.

CINEMA MUSEUMS

The following museums are either wholly devoted to cinema or have substantial cinema collections. Film archives are only included if they also administer a museum.

ARGENTINA
  Museo Municipal de Arte Moderno, Mendoza.

AUSTRALIA
  Australian Film Institute Museum, Canberra.
  Movie Museum, Buderim.

AUSTRIA
  Österreichisches Filmmuseum, Vienna.

BELGIUM
  Foto en Kinematografie Museum Sterckshof, Antwerp.
  Musée de la Photographie et du Cinéma, Brussels.
  Provinciaal Museum voor Kunstambachten het Sterckshof, Deurne.

BRAZIL
  Embrafilme Cinema Museum, Rio de Janeiro.
  The Cinema Museum, São Paulo.

CZECHOSLOVAKIA
  Museum of Animated and Puppet Films, Kratochvile Castle, Bohemia.

DENMARK
  Det Danske Filmmuseum, Copenhagen.

FRANCE
  Henri Langlois Film Museum, Palais de Chaillot, Paris.
  Musée du Cinéma, Rue de Courcelles, Paris.
  Musée du Cinéma, Lyons (Lumière collection).
  Pirates Galleon Museum, Cannes. Housed in the galleon built at a cost of £7m for Roman Polanski's *Pirates* (US/Tun 86).

GERMANY
  Kreismuseum, Bitterfeld.
  Munich City Museum (Film and Photography Department).
  Deutsches Film Museum, Frankfurt-am-Main.

GREAT BRITAIN
  Barnes Museum of Cinematography, St Ives, Cornwall.
  The National Museum of Photography, Film and Television, Bradford.
  Kay Kendall Memorial Museum, Withernsea Lighthouse, Yorks.
  Laurel & Hardy Museum, Ulverston, Cumbria (birthplace of Stan Laurel).
  Buckingham Movie Museum (home movies).
  The Museum of the Moving Image, South Bank, London.
  The Cinema Museum, Effra Road, Brixton.

HUNGARY
  The Ciné-Museum, Kaposvár.

ITALY
  Museo Nazionale del Cinema, Turin.

JAPAN
  Masei University *Gone With the Wind* display—2000 items on the book and the film.

MEXICO
  Cinematica Luis Bunuel, Puebla.
  Cinematica Mexicana, Mexico City.
  Anda Museum, Mexico City. Established 1987 by actors' union Anda to preserve momentos of Mexican stars.

NETHERLANDS
  Stichting Nederlands Filmmuseum, Amsterdam.

NORWAY
  Norsk Filminstitutt, Oslo.

SOUTH KOREA
  Cheju Island Movie Town Museum (opening 1992).

SWEDEN
  Asta Nielsen Filmmuseum, Lund.

SWITZERLAND
  Museum des Films, Basel.

USA
  James Dean Museum, Fairmount, Indiana (birthplace).
  Tom Mix Museum, Dewey, Oklahoma.
  Laurel and Hardy Museum, Harlem, Ga (birthplace of Oliver Hardy).
  Will Rogers Memorial, Claremore, Oklahoma.
  International Museum of Photography, George Eastman House, Rochester, NY.
  Museum of Modern Art, New York.
  Hollywood Stuntmen's Hall of Fame, Mojave, California.
  The Hollywood Museum, 7051 Hollywood Boulevard.
  Hollywood Studio Museum, opened 1987 in what was formerly known as the De Mille Barn, site of the original Lasky Studio where Cecil B. De Mille filmed *The Squaw Man* in 1913.
  American Museum of the Moving Image, Kaufman Astoria Studios, Queens, New York. Billed as first museum in the US devoted to 'the art, history and technology of motion pictures and television'.

USSR
  Ukrainian State Museum of Theatrical, Musical and Cinema Art, Kiev.
  Cinema History Museum, Odessa (history of cinema in Georgia).
  The Eisenstein Museum, Moscow (housed in Eisenstein's widow's small apartment).

YUGOSLAVIA
  Muzej Jugoslavenske Kinoteke, Belgrade.

*C*INEMA MUSEUMS

The first cinema museum was the Česco-slovenskyé Filmové Museum, founded by Jindrrich Brichta at Prague in 1923.

The first cinema museum in America was the Crocker Museum which Charles Chaplin's assistant Harry Crocker, who had a mania for collecting movie memorabilia, established on Sunset Boulevard, Hollywood in 1928. The exhibits consisted of props and costumes from silent movies, including Chaplin's original tramp costume, Harold Lloyd's glasses, William S. Hart's first leather chaps, Keaton's pancake boater, Gloria Swanson's 'Sadie Thompson' costume, the cabin that tottered on the brink from *The Gold Rush* (US 24), and the winning chariot from *Ben Hur* (US 26).

*P*UBLICITY

The largest publicity budget was the $48.1 million allocated by the Walt Disney Co. for promoting *Dick Tracy* (US 90) worldwide. The negative cost of the film was slightly less than this at $46.5 million.

Average marketing cost for a movie given a general release by one of the Hollywood majors is about $7 million. Movie advertising billings in the US in 1989 totalled $536 million, of which $387 million was spent on TV and $149 on press.

Slogans

Slogans extolling movies have tended towards hyperbole ever since impresario George Belmont announced his presentation of the 'Theatrograph' at Sadler's Wells in 1896 with the words: 'A mighty mirror of Promethean Photographs and a superb, brilliant, and electrifying entertainment specially adapted to cheer the toiling millions'.

A travelling bioscope showman encountered by a correspondent of *The Pelican* in a Kentish village in 1908 stretched credulity with a sign proclaiming: 'The most extraordinary invention of modern times, as presented before the Emperor Napoleon!'

Innocence of a different type during the early years of the movies is represented by a local billsheet for a Mary Pickford film showing in Haddington, Scotland. It proffered 'What Happened to Mary Twice Nightly'.

Impressive figures have often engaged the attention of publicists. India's first feature film *Raja Harischandra* (Ind 12) was advertised as 'a performance with 57,000 photographs . . . a picture two miles in length . . . all for only three annas!' *After Rain, Clear Sky* (Chn 31), one of China's earliest all-talkies, was promoted with the information that 'on the 977 occasions for dialogue, 6935 sentences are spoken'. The quantitative attractions of Twentieth Century-Fox's

The Egyptian (US 54) stimulated a slogan writer to even greater flights of figurative fancy with the claim that it had '10,965 pyramids, 5337 dancing girls, one million swaying bulrushes, 802 sacred bulls'.

Promoting a film to the wrong audience may be deliberate, in the case of a weak attraction, or perpetrated through sheer ignorance. In 1918 a Chicago theatre urged: 'Tomorrow—Ibsen's *Doll's House*—Bring the Kiddies!' Equally inappropriate was a Toronto cinema's slogan for David Lean's gentle evocation of middle-aged suburban romance *Brief Encounter* (GB 45): 'Girls who live dangerously'. A cinema on New York's 42nd Street, an area noted for vice, booked a nature film titled *The Love Life of a Gorilla* (US 37) and brought the crowds flocking in with a poster asking the searing question 'Do native women live with apes?' Anyone paying good money to see the film was rewarded with the answer—no, they don't.

Carl Laemmle knew that what audiences really want is escapist nonsense and signalled the fact loud and clear by billing his *Fighting American* (US 24) as the picture 'guaranteed not to make you think'.

The slogan used to boost the Joan Crawford starrer *Mildred Pierce* (US 45) entreated moviegoers 'Don't tell what Mildred Pierce did!'. The line was parodied all over. A diner in downtown Los Angeles put up a sign reading: 'For 65c we'll not only serve you a swell blue plate—we'll tell you what Mildred Pierce did.'

Attempts to summarize the story in a phrase could involve criminal assault on the English language. *Bridal Suite* (US 39) was encapsulated: 'Howl Bent for Laugh Heaven, Four Zanies Tangle with Cock-Eyed Love'. Real extravagance of prose style, though, was reserved for the epics. Cecil B. De Mille's *King of Kings* (US 27) was advertised in New York as abounding in 'Dramatic Magnificence, Spectacular Splendor, Riotous Joy, Tigerish Rage, Undying Love, Terrifying Tempests, Appalling Earthquakes'. (Audiences might be forgiven for not recognizing this as the story of the Gospels.)

In contrast, publicity could hardly be more downbeat than the announcement on the marquee of a drive-in in Cleveland County, NC in 1960: 'Two Features'. The manager explained that he never advertised the titles of the films because 'the people who patronize this drive-in don't care what's playing'.

Devastating honesty was seldom an attribute of movie publicists, but individual cinema managers would occasionally give a frank opinion of their offerings. Ray S. Hanson broke the house record for his Fox Theater in Fertile, Minnesota in November 1940 when he advertised *Windjammer* (US 40) with the slogan 'See a lousy show and win $70'. In 1947 an exhibitor in Hastings, Neb. announced: 'Double Feature—One Good Show and One Stinker'.

Slogans could be used to take a side-swipe at another star. Fox's advertising to promote George

O'Brien in *The Iron Horse* (US 24), which declared 'He's not a Sheik or a Caveman or a Lounge Lizard—He is a Man's Man and An Idol of Women', was clearly meant to draw a denigratory comparison with Latin lover Rudolph Valentino.

If the star was not the main attraction, someone else might be. When Oscar, the well-known Negro bootblack on the Paramount lot, played a bit part in *Gambling Ship* (US 33), a black cinema on Los Angeles' Central Avenue billed the film with the legend: 'Sensational star in *Gambling Ship*, Oscar supported by Cary Grant'. The pictures outside were entirely of Oscar.

There is nothing like a good scandal to hype an indifferent picture. Released at the time of the Profumo affair, *The Man who Couldn't Walk* (US/Can 64) was billed as 'the story behind the scandal that shocked London . . . baring untold secrets of vice, intrigue and international party girls'. What was actually delivered on screen amounted to no more than a routine meller about safecrackers. There was no character remotely resembling the Defence Minister and none that bore any connection with Miss Keeler.

Another attempt at topicality was made by the British distributors of a florid Indian romance titled *Red Rose* (Ind 82). The original slogan ran 'Petals from a beautiful film flower named Red Rose', to which some enterprising publicist had added 'Adapted from "The Yorkshire Ripper"'.

Howard Hughes made immediate impact with the posters promoting his controversial picture *The Outlaw* (US 43) when it was briefly released in 1943 before being withdrawn again. The slogan—'Mean, Moody and Magnificent'—was spread below a picture of a rampant-breasted Jane Russell standing bare-legged bestride a haystack with a pistol in each fist. When released in 1946 a far more decorous though equally striking copy-line had taken its place, a quote from Judge Twain Michelsen, who had tried the film for indecency: 'We have seen Jane Russell. She is an attractive specimen of American womanhood. God made her what she is.'

Briefer, but equally apt, was the slogan promoting Tony Richardson's *The Loved One* (US 65): 'The Picture with Something to Offend Everyone'. Briefer still and perhaps even more effective was the slogan accompanying *Baby Doll* (US 56): 'Condemned by Cardinal Spellman'.

The first colour stills were taken in the Uvachrome process by Max Hofstetter of the Powers Photo Engraving Co. of New York on the set of the Rudolph Valentino movie *Monsieur Beaucaire* (US 24) at the Paramount Astoria Studio on Long Island, NY. Hofstetter had great difficulty taking the pictures, partly because nobody could understand his broken English, but more particularly on account of the yellow make-up used by the cast to counteract the effect of the blue light radiated from the Cooper-Hewitt mercury vapour lamps with which the set was illuminated. Despite the producers' objections that it would cost $10,000 an hour to make up the cast again, and the need to scout the town for incandescent floodlights to supplement the mercury vapour lamps, Hofstetter succeeded in getting his shots. Later, one of them became the first colour photograph transmitted by wire when it was sent from Chicago to New York by Dr Hubert E. Ives of the Bell Telephone Laboratories.

The most valuable movie poster sold at auction was Boris Blinsky's two-sheet for Fritz Lang's *Metropolis* (Ger 26), which fetched $21,100 at the Druout auction rooms in Paris on 8 December 1989.

These are the earliest known 'lobby cards' for display in the lobbies of cinemas. They date from 1913 and are now in the collection of Michael Hawks of Los Angeles.

THE BATTLE OF SAN JUAN HILL

THE GUERILLA MENACE

WOMAN AND WAR

Modern movie publicity depends on the mystique of the market researcher. Touchstone Pictures made sure that all the ads for *Splash* (US 84), in which Daryl Hannah played an on-shore mermaid, revealed the blonde beauty's seemingly endless legs. Research had shown, in the words of one of the marketing executives on the picture, that 'the target audience of young men just didn't believe you could screw a fish'.

The first trailers were clips of film which Georges Méliès projected on a screen above the entrance of this Théâtre Robert Houdin, Paris in 1898 to give passers-by an idea of the delights awaiting them within. The modern trailer—as an *advance* announcement of films to come—was originated by National Screen Services of New York in 1920.

Nowadays, there are 20 major specialist production houses providing the Hollywood studios with trailers for their films and cost per is in the region of $100,000, exclusive of prints—these can run to as many as 6000. Standard length was 90 seconds until 1990, when by agreement with the Motion Picture Producers Association it was increased to 120 seconds. Some movies have more than one trailer and in the case of the recent kidpic *Teenage Mutant Ninja Turtles* (US 90) there were no less than five. One was targeted at young males, a 'sweet one' at young females, another was for family viewing, an alternative consisted of funny one-liners, and the fifth was for Hispanics. The specialist trailer houses aim for a creative angle the studios might miss. In the words of one New York based creative director: 'The trailer should always be better than the movie.'

US distributor of foreign pictures, Miramax, faced a considerable marketing problem when Pedro Almodovar's *Tie Me Up! Tie Me Down!* (Sp 90) was X-rated by the censorship board—usually the kiss of death at the box office. The off-beat tale of a man's infatuation for an unattainable girl whom he kidnaps and keeps roped to a bed, it was promoted by Miramax with a neat allusion to the ratings' brouhaha: 'A love story . . . with strings attached.' Similarly, when Peter Greenaway's *The Cook, The Thief, His Wife and Her Lover* (GB 89) fell foul of the censors in the US, Miramax responded by plastering the ads with a quote from *Time* magazine's film critic: 'X as in excellent, exciting, exemplary and extraordinary.'

The most licences for merchandising in respect of a single picture were issued by Warner Bros for *Batman* (US 89), with over 160 at the time of the film's première. It was also the most successful merchandising operation in terms of licence fees, which added an estimated $50 million to the movie's box office gross of $250 million.

Publicity Stunts

These began decorously enough in the early days of cinema and became progressively more outrageous during the days of Hollywood's greatest extravagances, the 1920s. Initially a little ingenuity was made to go a long way. One of the earliest stunts, reported by *Kinematograph Weekly* in 1907, was dreamed up by the proprietor of a Chicago nickelodeon who had letters printed in simulated handwriting purporting to be from a girl called Lizzie, on a visit to the city, writing to her friend Mary about an exciting excursion to the cinema. They were scattered in the streets and the advertiser relied on the baser human impulse to read other people's letters. Other gimmicks employed in the USA prior to World War I included making arrangements with grocers to give 13 eggs for every dozen ordered, the extra egg being paid for by the cinema and stamped with details of the next attraction; distributing oversized neckties of a garish hue and offering free seats to any man willing to wear one throughout the performance; and giving free admission to anyone slender enough to pass through a narrow wicket set up in the lobby or alternatively short enough to pass under a low bar.

The Vaudette Theater of West Point, Ga. announced that they would be giving away a free 'one-piece coat and garment hanger' to every patron on an advertised date in 1914. Those who attended were handed a very small envelope which contained a two-inch nail. The distributors of *Neptune's Daughter* (US 14), in which Annette Kellerman was clad in rather less than that customary for the period, sent out 36-inch tape measures which bore, at appropriate intervals, Miss Kellerman's vital statistics.

When Kalem reissued *The Colleen Bawn* (US 11), they had several tons of earth shipped from Killarney to New York and made up into four foot square sods for distribution to cinemas exhibiting the film. For the price of a theatre ticket, Irish immigrants could savour the pleasure of once again standing on Irish soil.

One of the most sure-fire stunts, repeated in small towns all over the USA from about 1912, was known as 'Giving Away a Baby'. The exhibitor announced that a baby would be given away on the stage on a certain day. He then arranged for someone to write to the local newspaper deploring this act of inhumanity, to which the cinema manager would reply in a hurt tone saying that the baby had made no objection and the mother was indifferent to its fate. This would provoke a shoal of letters, a lively public debate in the community, and threats of police prosecution. On the appointed night a packed house, usually includ-

In the twenties and thirties every big picture was ballyhooed with publicity stunts organized by local exhibitors. This not very hostile looking tank was helping to boost *The Big Parade* (US 25) into the biggest grossing silent picture of them all.

ing a contingent of police, would see the manager give away a baby pig.

As a promotion for the serial *Bride 13* (US 20), the manager of the Lyric Theater at Easley, S. Carolina persuaded an engaged couple to be married in front of the screen immediately following the first episode. A capacity audience watched the event, which included an unscheduled moment of drama when the bride's mother, who was present but had no idea that her daughter was involved in the stunt, shouted 'Stop!' from the stalls. She was persuaded, in the interests of her daughter's happiness and the manager's profits, to let the show go on.

Hollywood's tsars were not above a little stunt work themselves. Carl Laemmle turned the expensive luxury of employing Erich von Stroheim as a director to good account by erecting a mammoth electric sign on Broadway flashing out the prodigious budget allo-

cated for *Foolish Wives* (US 22), then in the course of its year-long shooting schedule. As von Stroheim's extravagances pushed the budget ever higher, Laemmle arranged for the New York Fire Brigade to tear down Broadway every Wednesday to change the light bulbs to the latest spiralling figure. The 'S' in Stroheim was replaced on the billboard by a $ sign.

It was about this period that publicity stunts involving stars reached their apogee. During a dip in Valentino's popularity, Harry Reichenbach, archexponent of ballyhoo, persuaded the great lover to grow a beard, and then proceeded to orchestrate a chorus of protest from outraged legions of female fans and the proprietors of barber shops. A few months later he arranged a ceremonial debearding by experts nominated by the Master Barbers of America.

To promote Raoul Walsh's *The Honor System* (US 25), the producers arranged for a practical demonstration of the 'honor' system in action, with a prisoner being released for a single day on his honour to return. Alas, he was not seen again.

Another stunt that backfired was the misguided one perpetrated by Universal when *The Phantom of the Opera* (US 25) was brought to England. By some means the studio publicity department persuaded Lt. Col. W. H. Barrell, Commanding Officer of the 153rd Heavy Brigade of the Royal Artillery, to give the English release prints a military escort from Southampton docks to the station and from Waterloo to Wardour Street. For the ceremonial march through London, the prints were preceded not only by troops but also an armoured car and a full regimental band. Press and public were equally scandalized by the vulgarity of the operation and the 'outrage on British troops', as one newspaper put it. There was a full-scale War Office enquiry and questions were asked in the House. To make matters worse, Universal's English representative, James Bryson, confessed that the military had been escorting empty boxes, since the prints of *The Phantom of the Opera* had been left safely in his trunks on the *Berengaria*, the liner which had brought them from New York. The uproar was so great that the film was never released in Britain and when, some years later, there was a second and more discreet attempt to bring it over, permission was flatly refused.

When *The Man I Killed* (US 32) went on release, an American exhibitor engaged a man to be buried alive for 24 hours. Unfortunately, a storm during the night obliterated the grave marker and long after the 24 hours were up, a team of 30 rescuers were desperately digging to release the entombed man. His first demand on being brought to the surface was for overtime pay.

Publicist Pete Smith was inspired with the idea of getting Sam Goldwyn to say that there were only 13 real actors in Hollywood and to name them. Goldwyn liked the stunt, but for the fact that he felt that as a result he would only be on speaking terms with 13 actors. He found the solution himself, naming twelve of the actors and leaving Hollywood to guess the name of the 13th.

Mom and Dad aka *A Family Story* (US 47), an exploitation movie with a live childbirth scene, was shown to sexually segregated audiences. According to publicity, this was 'so as not to offend the delicate'. To improve the effect, promotional manager Joe Solomon arranged to have a nauseous chemical put into the ventilation system and then called the local press to take pictures of the women reeling and retching out of the cinema. This ensured a full house of men in the evening.

As producer-director of *Psycho* (US 60) master showman Alfred Hitchcock had it written into every booking contract that no one was to be admitted into the cinema after the film began. The master showman created a publicity gimmick that was actually enforceable in law. When one cinema manager called the studio to complain about angry patrons forced to wait in the rain until the next show, Hitchcock intercepted the call and told him 'Buy them umbrellas'.

The distributors of *Snuff* (Arg/US 74), a tasteless exploitation movie based on the unfounded rumours

Those who did were rewarded with mild electric shocks whenever the Tingler was on the prowl. It was quite a thrill in small town America 1959. (*Ronald Grant Archive*)

then circulating that young girls were being killed for real on camera in Latin America sex pix, hired rentamob teams to picket cinemas showing the film in order to attract adverse but none the less beneficial publicity.

Rather more tasteful in both senses was the tie-in with Gabriel Axel's *Babette's Feast* (Den 88) when it opened in New York at the Lincoln Plaza Cinema. Patrons were able to carry on to the Petrossian restaurant afterwards to partake of the magnificent gourmet dinner they had just witnessed on screen.

When *Too Scared to Scream* (US 85) premièred at Hollywood's Paramount Theater a contest was held on the sidewalk outside to find the girl who could scream loudest and scariest. One hundred contestants were judged for howl quality by the picture's producer and star Mike Connors.

While the real 24-carat hype seems to have gone out of movie promotion, some publicists succeed in preserving their cherished tradition of plumbing the depths of bad taste and insensitivity. French video distributors GCR excelled with their giveaway promo for *Mississippi Burning* (US 86) —free Ku Klux Klan masks.

*R*EMAKES

The story which has been remade the most times is *Cinderella*, of which there have been 94 productions, including cartoon, modern, ballet, operatic, pornographic and parody versions, from *Cinderella and the Fairy Godmother* (GB 98), starring Laura Bayley, to Yoram Gross Studios' *The Magic Riddle* (Aus 91), an animated feature in which Cinderella encounters Snow White, Pinocchio, Little Red Riding Hood and the Three Little Pigs.

In addition to *Cinderella*, the following works have been the subject of 12 or more movie remakes: Shakespeare's *Hamlet* - 55 + 6 modern + 12 parodies; *Carmen* (Merimée's story and Bizet's opera - 56+2 parodies; *Faust* (Marlowe, Goethe and Gounod's opera) - 51; R. L. Stevenson's *Dr Jekyll and Mr Hyde* - 51 (including parodies and variants); Shakespeare's *Romeo and Juliet* - 32+6 modern+11 parodies; Defoe's *Robinson Crusoe* - 44 (inc. 2 porno); Dumas fils' *La Dame aux camélias* - 36; Cervantes's *Don Quixote* - 36; Shakespeare's *Macbeth* - 27+4 modern+1 parody; Hugo's *Les Misérables* - 31; Dumas père's *The Three Musketeers* - 33+10 variants featuring the character d'Artagnan; the Hindu epic *Harischandra* - 25 in 9 languages; Tolstoy's *Resurrection* - 23; Dumas père's *The Count of Monte Cristo* - 22+13 variants featuring the character Edmund Dantes; Dickens's *Oliver Twist* - 22; Shakespeare's *A Midsummer Night's Dream* - 21; Dickens's *A Christmas Carol* - 20; Shakespeare's *Julius Caesar* - 18+1 modern; Tolstoy's *Anna Karenina* - 19; Lewis Carroll's *Alice in Wonderland* - 17; Dostoevsky's *Crime and Punishment* - 16; *Othello* (Shakespeare and Verdi's opera) - 16; *William Tell* (Schiller and legend) - 16; Shakespeare's *King Lear* - 15 including Godard's 'free' version (the director admitted he had not read the play); Brandon Thomas's *Charley's Aunt* - 15; R. L. Stevenson's *Treasure Island* - 15; Harriet Beecher Stowe's *Uncle Tom's Cabin* - 14; Tolstoy's *The Living Corpse* - 13; Dumas père's *The Corsican Brothers* - 13; Mrs Henry Wood's *East Lynne* - 13; Sir Arthur Conan Doyle's *The Hound of the Baskervilles* - 13.

'If I had my life to live over I would do everything the exact same way—with the possible exception of seeing the movie remake of *Lost Horizon*.'—Woody Allen

---

The first director to make a remake of his own original was Cecil B. De Mille with the second, 1918 version of *The Squaw Man*, which he had first filmed in 1913. He had a third go at it in 1931.

The longest interval between the original version of a film and the remake was 72 years in the case of *Camila* (Arg 12), starring Bianca Podestá in the title role, and *Camila* (Arg/Sp 84) with Susú Pecoraro. The real-life story of aristocratic young beauty Camila O'Gorman, both films related how she fell in love with a Jesuit priest, their elopement and their tragic end before a firing squad. Although the events had taken place in the 1840s, passions about the affair still ran so high a century later that all attempts to bring it to the screen again between 1912 and 1984 were blocked either by open censorship or by political manoeuvring.

The longest interval between the original version of a film and the remake with the same actor playing the same role was 34 years in the case of Tito Lusiardo's performances in *El Dia que me Quitas/The Day You Leave Me* (US 35 and Arg 69). The longest interval for an actress was 28 years between Sophia Loren's performances as the mother in *Two Women* (It 61 and It 89).

The distinguished German actress Lil Dagover appeared in the remake of *The Spiders* (FRG 79), 60 years after performing (in a different role) in the 1919 original. Jean Simmons played Miss Havisham's ward Estella in David Lean's *Great Expectations* (GB 46) and Miss Havisham in the 1989 remake. Jane Greer played the heroine in *Out of the Past* (US 47) and the heroine's mother in the remake *Against All Odds* (US 85). Magda Schneider starred in *Liebelei* (Aut 32); her daughter Romy Schneider in the remake *Christine* (Fr 59). Barry Norton played a leading role in *What Price Glory?* (US 26) and a bit part in the 1952 remake; Jack Pennick played a bit in the silent original and a leading role in the talkie.

The most versions of a film to be shown collectively were 11 *Les Misérables* (out of a total of 31) during a season of Victor Hugo adaptations at the Cinémathèque Française in 1985. They included the French versions of 1912, 1925, 1933, 1957, 1971 and 1982, the Hollywood versions of 1918, 1935 and 1952, the Italian version of 1947 and the 1937 Soviet version titled *Garoche*.

Usually the producers of remakes have an optimistic though often mistaken belief that they can improve on the script of the original. No such ambitions prompted Edmund Goulding's remake of *The Dawn Patrol* (US 38) with Errol Flynn and Basil Rathbone. Exactly the same script was used as for Howard Hawks' original version of 1930 with Richard Barthelmess and Douglas Fairbanks Jr as the intrepid WWI fliers.

SEQUELS

The longest interval between a sequel and its original was 46 years in the case of Walt Disney Productions' *Return to Oz* (US 85), starring Fairuza Balk as Dorothy, which resumed the story six months after the previous Dorothy (Judy Garland) had returned to Kansas in MGM's *The Wizard of Oz* (US 39). The sequel was based on the second and third of Frank Baum's 14 Oz books, *The Land of Oz* and *Ozma of Oz*.

The longest interval between a sequel and its original with the same stars was 20 years and one day in the case of Claude Lelouche's *A Man and a Woman* (Fr 66), which premièred at the Cannes

Lee Patrick looks as if she had a higher regard for the cigarette-smoking Humphrey Bogart in *The Maltese Falcon* (US 41) (*below*) than she had for cigar-chomping George Segal in the sequel, *The Black Bird* (US 75).

Film Festival on 10 May 1966, and *A Man and a Woman: 20 Years Later* (Fr 86), which also bowed at Cannes, on 11 May 1986. The co-stars of both pictures were Jean-Louis Trintignant and Anouk Aimée. Lelouche has promised *A Man and a Woman: 40 Years Later* for May 2006.

The Hollywood record is held by Peter Bogdanovich's *The Last Picture Show* (US 71) and *Texasville* (US 90). Jeff Bridges and Cybill Shepherd co-starred, playing small-town teens in the first and middle-aged lovers in the second. Although only 19 years separate the two pictures, the action of *The Last Picture Show* was set in 1951, while *Texasville* takes place 33 years later in 1984. In the former, Bridges and Shepherd had to play younger than their real ages (22 and 21); in the latter, they were playing characters about ten years older than themselves.

In at least two instances individual stars have reprised their roles in sequels made a quarter of a century later. Paul Newman played pool player 'Fast' Eddie Felson in *The Hustler* (US 61) and *The Color of Money* (US 86), while Hayley Mills appeared in her dual roles as Sharon Ferris and Susan Corey in Disney's *Parent Trap II* (US 86 TVM) 25 years after the original story of the identical twins from East and West Coasts who secretly swap families. Lee Patrick exceeded this time span as a featured player when she made a welcome return as Effie, Sam Spade's secretary in *The Maltese Falcon* (US 41), in the sequel *The Black Bird* (US 75). Thirty-four years on Spade's son (George Segal) had inherited her along with his father's detective agency.

'Prequels'

These are sequels that relate the story that *preceded* the original film. *Another Part of the Forest* (US 47) recounted the earlier lives of the Hubbard family por-

Paul Newman reprised his role of Fast Eddie Nelson in *The Color of Money* (US 86) 25 years after he had played the character—looking about 40 years younger—in *The Hustler* (US 61).

trayed in *The Little Foxes* (US 41); Steve McQueen's title role in *Nevada Smith* (US 66) centred on the earlier life of the character played by Alan Ladd in *The Carpetbaggers* (US 64); Michael Winner's *The Night Comers* (GB 71) told the story of how the ghosts in *The Innocents* (GB 61)—the manservant Quint and the 'former governess'—lost their lives; *Rhapsody* (US 54), from Henry Handel Richardson's novel *Maurice Guest*, was followed 25 years later by the film of the preceding volume of the story, *The Getting of Wisdom* (Aus 79); Richard Lester's *Butch and Sundance—The Early Days* (US 79) recounts the story of how the outlaw pair (Tom Berenger and William Katt) met and teamed up together, while the earlier George Roy Hill picture *Butch Cassidy and the Sundance Kid* (US 69) related the events leading up to the death of Butch and Sundance (Paul Newman and Robert Redford) in a shoot-out with the Bolivian army. Zoltán Fábri brought Jósef Baláz's novel *Hungarians* (Hun 79) to the screen before embarking on the preceding story of the hero's father in his youth, told in *Bálint Fábián's Encounter with God* (Hun 80). Both Bálint Fábián and his son András were played by the same actor, Gábor Koncz. *Indiana Jones and the Temple of Doom* (US 84) was set in 1935, preceding by three years the action of the earlier Indiana Jones caper *Raiders of the Lost Ark* (US 81). *Missing in Action 2—The Beginning* (US 85) related what happened to Col. Braddock (Chuck Norris) in Vietnam before his escape to the

Glenda Jackson played Gudrun in Ken Russell's film of D. H. Lawrence's *Women in Love* (GB 70). In the prequel, *The Rainbow* (GB 89), she was Gudrun's mother.

the sexual awakening of Ursula, Sammi Davis takes the role of the turn-of-the-century country girl being initiated into lesbian love, while the mature Ursula of *Women in Love* was played by Jennie Linden. The role of Gudrun, for which Glenda Jackson won an Oscar in *Women in Love*, is portrayed by Glenda McKay in *The Rainbow*, but Glenda Jackson reappears as the mother of the girl she had played in the earlier film.

The only prequel-sequel movie was Francis Ford Coppola's *The Godfather Part II* (US 74), which ranged back and forth in time to reveal events which had taken place before those in *The Godfather* (US 71) as well as events which followed on. A rare instance of a sequel-prequel-sequel arose with Claude Berri's *Jean de Florette* (Fr 86), from the Marcel Pagnol story of the destruction of a hunchback townsman (Gerard Depardieu) who seeks to settle on the land in Provence in the 1920s, which was the prequel to Pagnol's own film *Manon des Sources* (Fr 53), in which the hunchback's daughter (Jacqueline Pagnol) wreaks vengeance on the village. A remake of *Manon des Sources* (Fr 87), also by Claude Berri and with Emanuelle Béart in the title role, provided a new sequel to the prequel.

US and return to Vietnam to locate missing comrades, as depicted in *Missing in Action* (US 84).

Ken Russell waited nearly 20 years after his interpretation of D. H. Lawrence's *Women in Love* (GB 70) before bringing the earlier story of Ursula Brangwen and her sister Gudrun to the screen in *The Rainbow* (GB 89). In the prequel, which recounts

THREE

BOX OFFICE AND BUDGETS

BOX OFFICE

The film with the highest earnings is *E.T. The Extra-Terrestrial* (US 82), which has grossed $700 million worldwide ($400 million in the home market). Distributor MCA estimates that some 240 million cinemagoers have seen the picture.

Previous box office champions were *Snow White and the Seven Dwarfs* (US 37), which was the first talkie to overtake the record for silent pictures set by *The Big Parade* (US 25) (see below); *Gone with the Wind* (US 39), which held the record from 1940 until overtaken by *The Sound of Music* (US 65) in August 1966 and again in 1971–2 as the result of a

reissue; *The Godfather* (US 72), which set a new record the year of its release; and *Jaws* (US 75), also a record-breaker in its first year and box office champion until surpassed by *Star Wars* in 1977. The crown passed to *E.T. The Extra-Terrestrial* (US 82) in January 1983, 31 weeks after its release.

The top grossing silent film was King Vidor's *The Big Parade* (US 25), with worldwide rentals of $22 million. No exact figure is available for D. W. Griffith's *The Birth of a Nation* (US 15), which was long thought of as the top grossing silent, with estimates of up to $50 million receipts in the domestic

---

ANNUAL TOP MONEYMAKER USA

Prior to 1947 there are no consistent records. Since that date *Variety* has identified the following pictures as top moneymaker of the year in the domestic market (US and Canada). Where the top moneymaker is a non-American production, the top American grosser is listed second:

1947 *The Best Years of Our Lives*
1948 *The Road to Rio*
1949 *Jolson Sings Again*
1950 *Samson and Delilah*
1951 *David and Bathsheba*
1952 *The Greatest Show on Earth*
1953 *The Robe*
1954 *White Christmas*
1955 *Cinerama Holiday*
1956 *Guys and Dolls*
1957 *The Ten Commandments*
1958 *The Bridge on the River Kwai* (GB)
  Peyton Place (US)
1959 *Auntie Mame*
1960 *Ben Hur*
1961 *The Guns of Navarone* (GB)
  The Absent-Minded Professor (US)

1962 *Spartacus*
1963 *Cleopatra*
1964 *The Carpetbaggers*
1965 *Mary Poppins*
1966 *Thunderball* (GB)
  Doctor Zhivago (US)
1967 *The Dirty Dozen*
1968 *The Graduate*
1969 *The Love Bug*
1970 *Airport*
1971 *Love Story*
1972 *The Godfather*
1973 *The Poseidon Adventure*
1974 *The Sting*
1975 *Jaws*
1976 *One Flew Over the Cuckoo's Nest*
1977 *Star Wars*
1978 *Grease*
1979 *Superman* (GB)
  Every Which Way But Loose (US)
1980 *The Empire Strikes Back*
1981 *Raiders of the Lost Ark*
1982 *E. T. The Extra-Terrestrial*
1983 *Return of the Jedi*

1984 *Ghostbusters*
1985 *Back to the Future*
1986 *Top Gun*
1987 *Beverly Hills Cop II*
1988 *Who Framed Roger Rabbit*
1989 *Batman*
1990 *Ghost*

Of the 48 top grossers listed above, 9 were contemporary dramas, 9 were comedies, 8 were historical epics, 6 were musicals, 6 were science-fiction/fantasy, 4 were war films, 2 were adventure films, one was a Bond movie and one a Cinerama travelogue. Only one was a straight crime drama (*The Godfather*).

Usually the top grosser in the US is also the top grosser worldwide. A notable exception occurred in 1986, when *Top Gun* wasn't; it was outgunned by Australia's all-time sleeper *Crocodile Dundee*. And in 1990, despite *Ghost*'s spirited performance at home, it was unable to match the charms of *Pretty Woman* worldwide.

ANNUAL TOP MONEYMAKER GB

The following have been the annual top moneymaking British films in the domestic market since 1936:

1936 *The Ghost Goes West*
1937 *Good Morning Boys*
1938 *A Yank at Oxford*
1939 *Pygmalion*
1940 *Convoy*
1941 *49th Parallel*
1942 *The First of the Few*
1943 *In Which We Serve*
1944 *This Happy Breed*
1945 *The Seventh Veil*
1946 *The Wicked Lady*
1947 *The Courtneys of Curzon Street*
1948 *Spring in Park Lane*
1949 *The Third Man*
1950 *The Blue Lamp*
1951 *Laughter in Paradise*
1952 *Where No Vultures Fly*
1953 *The Cruel Sea*
1954 *Doctor in the House*

1955 *The Dam Busters*
1956 *Reach for the Sky*
1957 *Doctor at Large*
1958 *The Bridge on the River Kwai*
1959 *Carry on Nurse*
1960 *Doctor in Love*
1961 *The Swiss Family Robinson*
1962 *The Young Ones*
1963 *From Russia with Love*
1964 *Goldfinger*
1965 *Help!*
1966 *Thunderball*
1967 *You Only Live Twice*
1968 *Up the Junction*
1969 *Oliver!*
1970 *Battle of Britain*
1971 *On the Buses*
1972 *Diamonds are Forever*
1973 *Live and Let Die*
1974 *Confessions of a Window Cleaner*
1975 *The Man with the Golden Gun*
1976 *The Return of the Pink Panther*

1977 *The Spy Who Loved Me*
1978 *The Revenge of the Pink Panther*
1979 *Moonraker*
1980 *Monty Python's Life of Brian*
1981 *Superman II*
1982 *Chariots of Fire*
1983 *Octopussy*
1984 *Never Say Never Again*
1985 *A View to a Kill*
1986 *Santa Claus—The Movie*
1987 *The Living Daylights*
1988 *A Fish Called Wanda*
1989 *Scandal*
1990 *Memphis Belle*

Of the 55 films listed, 18 were comedies, 10 were war films, 13 were Bond movies, 8 were contemporary dramas, 3 were historical, 2 were musicals, and one was science-fiction. Significantly only one straight crime drama (*The Blue Lamp*) is included.

market alone. This is now considered to be a wildly exaggerated figure, and *Variety* quotes $5 million as a reasonable 'guestimate'. Griffith himself stated in 1929 that the film had earned $10 million world-wide.

THE TWENTY-FIVE TOP GROSSING FILMS

The list below was published by the American trade paper *Variety* in 1991 and represents the North American (US and Canada) rentals for the 25 top grossing films of all time. As a very approximate guide, until recently films which were successful in the North American market could usually expect to earn about the same in overseas rentals as they did in domestic rentals. Since c.1986 the ratio has generally been closer to about 60/40 in favour of the home market.

1	*E.T. The Extra-Terrestrial* (US 82)	$228,618,939
2	*Star Wars* (US 77)	$193,500,000
3	*Return of the Jedi* (US 83)	$168,002,414
4	*Batman* (US 89)	$150,500,000
5	*The Empire Strikes Back* (US 80)	$141,600,000
6	*Ghostbusters* (US 84)	$132,720,000
7	*Jaws* (US 75)	$129,549,325
8	*Raiders of the Lost Ark* (US 81)	$115,598,000
9	*Indiana Jones and the Last Crusade* (US 89)	$115,500,000
10	*Indiana Jones and the Temple of Doom* (US 84)	$109,000,000
11	*Beverly Hills Cop* (US 84)	$108,000,000
12	*Back to the Future* (US 85)	$105,493,534
13	*Grease* (US 78)	$96,300,000
14	*Tootsie* (US 82)	$94,910,000
15	*Ghost* (US 90)	$94,000,000
16	*The Exorcist* (US 73)	$89,000,000
17	*Rain Man* (US 88)	$86,813,000
18	*The Godfather* (US 72)	$86,275,000
19	*Superman* (GB 78)	$82,800,000
20	*Close Encounters of the Third Kind* (US 77)	$82,750,000
21	*Pretty Woman* (US 90)	$81,903,000
22	*Three Men and a Baby* (US 87)	$81,356,000
23	*Who Framed Roger Rabbit* (US 88)	$81,244,000
24	*Beverly Hills Cop II* (US 87)	$80,857,776
25	*Home Alone* (US 90)	$80,000,000

NB: By April 1991 *Home Alone* had overtaken *Jaws* in the rank order.

The highest grossing film from outside the USA was the phenomenal Australian success *Crocodile Dundee* (Aus 86), starring Paul Hogan as the irrepressible crocodile hunter from the Northern Territory who takes on New York and wins hands down. It took $70 million in rentals in North America, some $80 million in the rest of the world, and earned a worldwide gross estimated at $375 million. It was also the highest grossing film of all time in Britain, taking over £20 million at the box office.

The most successful foreign-language film released in the US is *I Am Curious (Yellow)* (Swe 67), which grossed $19 million during its 1969 release. Runners up are Fellini's *La Dolce Vita* (It 59) at $18 million and *La Cage aux Folles* (It/Fr 80) at $17 million. Most successful of the last decade is *Cinema Paradiso* (It 88), which grossed $11.3 million.

The most successful video release is MCA Home Video's *E.T. The Extra-Terrestrial* (US 82), which sold over 15 million copies in the year it was first issued, 1989. The most successful in Britain is Buena Vista's *Lady and the Tramp* (US 55), which

was released on video for Christmas 1990 and sold 1.7 million copies in three months.

> Few American films do better overseas than on home territory. Of the exceptions, the one with proportionately the widest gap between foreign rentals and domestic rentals is Steven Spielberg's *Empire of the Sun* (US 87), which took a modest $10 million in North America, $30 million elsewhere. Normally a successful Hollywood picture's revenue is divided about 60–40 in favour of the home market, though many earn an even higher proportion at home. Failure of Spielberg's compelling film in the United States has been put down to its alien setting (China under Japanese occupation) and the fact that only one of the leading characters was American.

The country with the highest box office gross is the USA, whose record year was 1989 with 1130 million paid admissions worth $5030 million.

The highest single day gross for any film was achieved by Warner Bros' *Batman* (US 89), which took $14.54 million at 2880 screens on Saturday 24 June 1989. It also scored the **highest opening day gross** on 23 June at $13.12 million and the **weekend record** (23–25 June) at $40.49 million. *Batman* passed the $100 mark in 11 days, eight days earlier than previous record holder *Indiana Jones and the Last Crusade* (US 89).

> Do Bergman-reared Scandinavians really prefer their movies slow-paced and gloomy? Possibly, per audience statistics which reveal that 17 per cent of all box office returns in the Nordic countries are for art films. The US box office for 'message movies' is less than 1 per cent.

The lowest reported box office gross for any film in the last decade was $1500 for *Contaminacion* (Col 82).

The highest loss on any film was incurred by United Artists on the ill-fated *Heaven's Gate* (US 80), which earned $1,500,000 in North American rentals against an estimated negative cost of $44 million and a total cost, including distribution and studio overheads, of $57 million. It brought in a better return (or lesser loss) per dollar, however, than the $15 million *Orphans* (US 87), which earned only $100,000 in North American rentals and in terms of budget/box office ratio is Hollywood's biggest box office flop of all time.

Steven Spielberg's *Empire of the Sun* (US 87) reversed the usual trend by doing three times as much business overseas as it did in the US. Christian Bale starred as the boy who spent the war years in a Japanese internment camp. Here he salutes the heroism of the kamikaze pilots who made their last flights from an adjacent airfield.

Box Office Disasters

Megabuck pix ($20 million and over) which have returned less than a tenth of their budget in North American rentals:

The Fall of the Roman Empire (US 64)
  Cost $20 million Earned $1.9 million
Heaven's Gate (US 80)
  Cost $44 million Earned $1.5 million
Honky Tonk Freeway (US 81)
  Cost $24 million Earned $0.5 million
Inchon (Kor 82)
  Cost $46 million Earned $1.9 million
King Kong Lives (US 86)
  Cost $21 million Earned $1.7 million
Omar Mukhtar—Lion of the Desert
(GB/Lby/US 81)
  Cost $30 million Earned $1.5 million
Once Upon a Time in America (US 84)
  Cost $30 million Earned $2.5 million
One from the Heart (US 82)
  Cost $26 million Earned under $1 million
Pirates (US/Tun 86)
  Cost $31 million Earned $0.7 million
Revolution (GB 85)
  Cost $28 million Earned $0.2 million
Tai-Pan (US 86)
  Cost $25 million Earned $2 million
Waterloo (It/USSR 70)
  Cost $25 million Earned $1.4 million

BUDGETS

The most expensive film was the Caroleo production *Terminator 2: Judgement Day* (US 91), which had a negative cost reported to be $104 million. A further $20 million was spent on prints and publicity. The picture starred Arnold Schwarzenegger at a fee of $15 million. *Terminator 2*'s budget far exceeded the spend on any previous film. Cost of *The Godfather Part III* (US 90) was estimated at between $55 million and $60 million, *Die Hard II* (US 90) at $62 million, *Rambo III* (US 88) at $63 million, *Total Recall* (US 90) at between $60 million and $70 million (per *Variety*—other estimates were as high as $75 million), and *Who Framed Roger Rabbit* (US 88) at $70 million. As costs have spiralled over the last few years, budgeting of major motion pictures has become an increasingly inexact science. The studios seldom reveal budgets and estimates made by the trade press vary so widely that they have to be treated with reserve. The figures suggested here are not, therefore, claimed as definitive.

In terms of real cost (inflation adjusted) *Cleopatra* (US 63) remains the most expensive movie ever made. Its $44 million budget is equivalent to $186 million in 1990 dollars.

The most expensive silent film was Fred Niblo's *Ben Hur* (US 25) at $3.9 million.

The record for the most expensive production has been held successively by the films listed below. Figures quoted are those reported at the time the films were produced and in most cases are impossible to verify.

$30,000 *Napoleon* (US 08)	$3,950,000 *Hell's Angels* (US 30)
$34,000 *For the Term of his Natural Life* (Aus 08)	$4,250,000 *Gone with the Wind* (US 39)
$47,500 *Queen Elizabeth* (Fr 12)	$5,200,000 *Wilson* (US 44)
$50,000 *The Prisoner of Zenda* (US 13)	$6,000,000 *Duel in the Sun* (US 46)
$210,000 *Cabiria* (It 14)	$8,700,000 *Joan of Arc* (US 48)
$575,000 *Intolerance* (US 16)	$13,500,000 *The Ten Commandments* (US 56)
$1,000,000 *A Daughter of the Gods* (US 16)	$15,000,000 *Ben Hur* (US 59)
$1,100,000 *Foolish Wives* (US 22)	$19,000,000 *Mutiny on the Bounty* (US 62)
$1,500,000 *When Knighthood was in Flower* (US 22)	$44,000,000 *Cleopatra* (US 63)
$1,800,000 *The Ten Commandments* (US 23)	$55,000,000 *Superman* (GB 78)
$2,000,000 *The Thief of Baghdad* (US 24)	$63,000,000 *Rambo III* (US 88)
$3,900,000 *Ben Hur* (US 25)	$70,000,000 *Who Framed Roger Rabbit* (US 88)
	$104,000,000 *Terminator 2: Judgement Day* (US 91)

The least expensive full-length feature film on record is Victorian Film Productions' part-colour *The Shattered Illusion* (Aus 27), which took twelve months to complete and included spectacular scenes of a ship being overwhelmed by a storm. Total cost of production was £300 ($1460).

The least expensive all-colour talkie was Pat Rocco's 80-minute psychological drama *Someone* (US 65), with Joe Adair and four other paid performers, which was made on an eight-day schedule for $1200 (£500).

Other low budget movies which have achieved box office and/or critical success include Marco Bellocchio's *I Pugni in Tasca* (It 66), which cost $78,000; Truffaut's *The Four Hundred Blows* (Fr 59), $65,000; *Never on Sunday* (Gre 59), $100,000; Nasser Gholam-Rezai's highly acclaimed *How Starry was My Night* (Iran 77), $28,000; Philippe Garrel's *La Concentration* (Fr 68), $14,000; Celestino Coronado's *Hamlet* (GB 77), $5000; Jon Jost's colour feature *Angel City* (US 76), $6000; Ingmar Bergman's *The Seventh Seal* (Swe 57), $40,000; Ermano Olmi's *Il Posto* (It 61), $15,000; Akira Kurosawa's *Rashomon* (Jap 50), $40,000; Claude Lelouch's *Smic, Smac, Smoc* (Fr 71), $30,000; Wim Verstappen's award-winning *Joszef Katus* (Neth 67), $2400; Jon Jost's *Last Chants for a Slow Dance* (US 77), $3000; Josef Rodel's *Albert—Why* (FRG 78), winner of the 1979 German Critics' Film Prize, $5000. *The Night of the Living Dead* (US 68) was made for $114,000 and brought in $12 million in worldwide rentals; John Waters' *Pink Flamingos* (US 72), billed as 'An Exercise in Poor Taste' and described in one review as 'the sickest movie ever made', cost $12,000 to produce and grossed $1,250,000 in two years; while the notorious *Deep*

Throat (US 71), made for $25,000, grossed $4.6 million over the same length of time. Wayne Wang's thriller *Chan is Missing* (US 81), set in San Francisco's China Town, came in at $20,000.

Rick Schmidt, author of *Feature Film-making at Used Car Prices*, practised what he preached when he brought in his *Morgan's Cake* (US 89) for $15,000. Gregg Araki is more accustomed to making films at wrecked car prices. Hailed by *Variety* as 'Los Angeles' lowest budget film-maker', he lived up to this accolade by producing his 87-minute black and white feature *The Long Weekend* (US 89) for $5,000.

Sam Raimi's *Evil Dead* (US 82) cult classic was made for $90,000 culled from a group of Mid-Western dentists and doctors, all of whom were rewarded for their faith in the fledgling director by a 350 per cent return on their investment.

In a rather higher bracket at $262,000, but still comparable with the cost of many 30-second TV commercials, was the Canadian sleeper *I've Heard the Mermaids Singing* (Can 87), which sold to 32 countries after winning the Prix de Jeunesse at the 1987 Cannes Film Festival. Writer, director, editor and co-producer Patricia Rozema recounted how her two main sources of funds, Telefilm Canada and the Ontario Film Development Company, had tried to persuade her to accept more money, but she had refused as she 'didn't want to be obligated to have a huge audience'. Among the highpoints in the picture is a scene in which the heroine Polly takes off into the air and flies effortlessly over Toronto. Per Ms Rozema: 'The special-effect flying was a $60 effect. A fan, some scaffolding, a little bit of smoke and there you go.'

The lowest budgeted British film to win an international release was Bill Forsyth's *That Sinking Feeling* (GB 79), made for £6000. Cost of dubbing new voices for the North American release in 1983—the original Glaswegian accents were impenetrable to US audiences—exceeded the budget of the picture.

The record budget/box office ratio was 1:285 in the case of the $350,000 Australian production *Mad Max* (Aus 80), which grossed $100 million in its first two years of international distribution.

Average Budgets

The earliest feature films made in Britain prior to World War I cost in the region of £4000–£5000, a figure which by the early twenties had risen to £6000–£7000. By the end of the twenties the average budget had virtually doubled, one estimate in 1927 being £17,000. There could be wide disparity though—supporting features were probably still within the £8000–£10,000 range, while Michael Balcon has quoted £30,000–£35,000 as a reasonable average for good-class pictures at the end of the silent era. The 1930s saw a vast outpouring of 'Quota

Quickies' with budgets determined solely by length, the fixed rate being £1 per foot of screened film. The average length being 6000 ft, the average budget was £6000, allowing for a 12-day shooting schedule.

Average budgets of Hollywood features from the earliest days to the present are listed below. As in Britain, a lot of budgets were way below the general level. The 'B' pictures of the thirties and forties ground out at $15,000-$20,000, the budget set to realize an anticipated profit margin of $2000-$3000. Failure to reap the forecast return could put a small Poverty Row studio into serious financial difficulties. Quality was hardly a consideration. Sam Newfield, who could manufacture a 'B' western in three or four days with quite a bit of stock footage as padding, was once urged by a studio executive to hurry things up on a particular picture: 'You don't really mean', he drawled in reply, 'that there's someone out there waiting to see this junk'. Amongst the lowest budget features ever made in the USA were the so-called 'Ghetto movies'—all-black films for all-black audiences. Budgets could be trimmed to as little as $5000 by the simple expedient of failing to pay the actors.

AVERAGE HOLLYWOOD BUDGETS FOR FEATURE FILMS ($)

1913 13,000 (5 reels)	**1955** 900,000	**1980** 7,500,000
1915 21,800 (5 reels)	**1960** 1,000,000	**1981** 9,750,000
1919 60,000 (5 reels)	**1965** 1,500,000	**1982** 10,900,000
1924 300,000	**1970** 1,750,000	**1983** 9,700,000
1932 153,000	**1972** 1,890,000	**1984** 11,300,000
1935 209,000	**1974** 2,500,000	**1986** 11,900,000
1940 314,000	**1976** 4,000,000	**1988** 12,400,000
1941 400,000	**1978** 5,300,000	**1990** 18,100,000
1948 1,000,000	**1979** 6,700,000	

Figures prior to 1972 are quoted from *Motion Picture Almanac*. The decrease in the average budget between 1924 and the early 1930s may be accounted for by the increase in the number of cheap 'B' pictures, economies forced on studios by the Depression, and a decline in the general index of prices. Early talkies also tended to have smaller casts and less elaborate sets than the silent features of the 1920s. The apparent stability between 1948 and 1960 is harder to explain, particularly as this period saw a vogue for expensive historical epics, a substantial increase in the use of colour, and the demise of the 'B' picture. The figures quoted for this decade should therefore be regarded with caution.

Raising Coin

Finding finance for films is never easy in India, but director John Abraham literally drummed up the money for his award-winning *Amma Ariyan* (Ind 87). He spent six years touring round remote villages soliciting funds by banging a drum as he went. Master film-maker Shyam Benegal also believes in involving the common people. When he made a film called *Manthan* (Ind 76) which was set in a milk co-operative, the money came from the co-op's own members. His acclaimed *Susman* (Ind 87), about the handloom weavers of Andra Pradesh, was financed by the weavers themselves.

The budget for *The Diary of a Madman* (Fr 87), from Gogol's short story, was mustered by producers Fanny Cotençon and Roger Coggio, who also star in

It is an old axiom of the movie business that you should never use your own money to produce a picture. Claude Berri dug into his own pocket for the $25 million to make *The Bear* (Fr 89) and proved the wiseacres wrong when the virtually no dialogue story of nature in the raw became an international hit. (*Kobal*)

the film, by the simple device of selling tickets in advance. Six months before release they had managed to sell 300,000 tickets at 23 francs (about £2.35) apiece. Debut black helmer Robert Townsend raised the seed coin for his comedy *Hollywood Shuffle* (US 87), about Hollywood's perceptions of blacks, by using 10 different unsolicited credit cards to charge up $40,000 of expenses. The film stock came free when he succeeded in begging the short-ends from two films he was acting in, *Ratboy* and *Odd Jobs*. Using his salary from these performances, plus the money he earned as a stand-up comic, he was able to finance the film entirely from his own resources—a total of some $100,000—but the 17 days of shooting had to be spread over two years to enable him to take to the road again whenever funds ran low. His efforts paid off when the picture grossed $5 million.

Miguel Pereira hustled the money for his powerful film *The Debt* (Arg 88), winner of the Silver Bear at the Berlin Film Festival and the grand jury prize at the Chicago Film Festival, by getting up early every morning and begging donations from local merchants in the remote Andes township where they were filming. 'No one denied me anything', he recalled, 'but by the end of filming people were crossing the street to avoid me . . .'

Journalist Michael Moore's idiosyncratic *Roger and Me* (US 90) turned out to be the third most successful feature-length documentary of all time, grossing over $6.7 million at the US box office. It told of his quest to interview Roger Smith, the General Motors chairman who had closed down the auto factories in the company's birthplace of Flint, Michigan, leaving 30,000 unemployed. Moore, also unemployed and himself born in Flint, set about raising a $250,000 budget from scratch by running Saturday night bingo games in the town. When the money from the bingo games ran out, he started scouring the streets for empty soda pop bottles on which he could claim the deposit.

Not all newcomers have to exercise such ingenuity. According to Paul Hogan, when he decided it was 'time to have a go at this film-making business', Aussie investors were so eager to put up coin for *Crocodile Dundee* (Aus 86) that 'we had to send $3,500,000 back'.

Not all major Hollywood movies are financed in America. The $12 million budget for *Wired* (US 88), based on Bob Woodward's best selling biography of John Belushi, was put up by New Zealand's Lion Breweries.

It is virtually unknown for major motion pictures to be financed from the pockets of an individual, but a notable exception was the remarkable no-dialogue French film *The Bear* (Fr 89). The whole budget of $25 million, highest ever for a French film, was put up by its producer Claude Berri. His faith in the unusual picture, about two bears and two hunters and four years in the making, was well rewarded. It grossed over $100 million worldwide. Berri himself, son of a Romanian mother and a Polish father, reached his pre-eminence in the French film industry—he directed the huge international successes *Jean de Florette* (Fr 86) and *Manon des Sources* (Fr 87)—by virtue of not succeeding in his original intentions. Critic Oscar Moore wrote of him: 'He dreamed of becoming an actor, but when no director gave him a part, he wrote his own screenplays. When no one would make his screenplays, he became a director, and when no one would finance him as a director, he became a producer. Finally, when he couldn't sell his films, he distributed them himself.'

FOUR

STORY AND SCRIPT

AUTHORS

Producers began turning to literature for their plots soon after the turn of the century. In 1902 Ferdinand Zecca of Pathé succeeded in compressing Zola's *L'Assommoir* into five minutes of screen time as *Les Victimes d l'Alcolisme* (Fr 02), while Edwin S. Porter of the Edison Co. presented *Uncle Tom's Cabin* (US 02) in 14 'tableaux' lasting some 17 minutes. Probably the first novel to be adapted at sufficient length for an adequate presentation of the story was *Robbery Under Arms*, by Rolf Boldrewood, which was brought to the screen by the Australian producer C. McMahon in a five-reel version premièred at the Athenaeum Theatre, Melbourne, on 2 November 1907. The first in Europe was Viggo Larsen's three-reel version of Guy Boothby's *Dr. Nicola* (Den 09), starring August Blom. In America the same year Vitagraph produced a four-reel version of Dickens' *Oliver Twist* (US 09) and soon found they had set a trend, eight versions of the story appearing in various countries during the following three years. Among them was Britain's first essay at a 'full-length' screen adaptation, Thomas Bentley's *Oliver Twist* (GB 12), with Ivy Millais in the title role.

The payment of film rights was first put on an organized basis in France, where the Société Cinématographique des Auteurs et Gens de Lettres was established in 1908 to act as a performing rights society interceding between companies like Film d'Art—who based all their films on works of literature—and the members of the two leading literary associations, the Société des Auteurs and the Société des Gens de Lettres.

It was only the previous year that the matter of film rights to an author's work had arisen for the first time, when the Kalem Co. produced a one-reel version of *Ben Hur* (US 07). The publishers of Lew Wallace's novel, Harper's, and the producers of the very successful play based on the book, promptly sued. Kalem defended themselves on the grounds that neither publisher nor author had suffered damage and that the film was a good advertisement for the book and the play. The case lasted four years, Kalem finally conceding defeat and settling for $25,000.

The first copyright fee paid in the US for film rights had been negotiated in the meantime between Biograph and Little, Brown & Co., publishers of Helen Hunt Jackson's *Ramona*, a bestselling romance about an Indian maiden, originally published in 1884. The film of *Ramona* (US 10)

Some books have been turned into movies for the unlikeliest of reasons. Orson Welles decided to make a movie of Sherwood King's novel *If I Die Before I Wake* without having read so much as a synopsis. In a desperate financial situation over a stage play he was producing in Boston, Welles called Harry Cohn of Columbia to ask him for a $50,000 loan. When Cohn sounded reluctant, Welles offered to direct a film for him and added that he had an excellent thriller in mind which could be produced very inexpensively. The director was momentarily nonplussed when Cohn asked the title, but glancing over his shoulder he noticed that the wardrobe mistress was reading a paperback and signalled to her to hold it up so that he could see the cover. He told Cohn the title was *If I Die Before I Wake* and was promised a loan in exchange for making the film. It was released as *The Lady from Shanghai* (US 48) with Welles himself playing opposite Rita Hayworth.

was directed by D. W. Griffith with Mary Pickford in the title role. The fee was $100 and the authoress received the rare distinction of a credit following the main title.

Film rights were not to remain on this modest level for long. In Italy Gabriele D'Annunzio (1863–1938) signed an historic contract with Ambrosio-Films in May 1911 disposing of rights to six of his works at 40,000 lire each, equivalent to $7845 at the then rate of exchange. Ambrosio later bought eight more, but far from delighting in this good fortune D'Annunzio displayed only contempt for the medium which had so wholeheartedly embraced his work. He saw only one of the films, *La Leda senza cigno* (It 12), which he dismissed as 'childish and grotesque'. So far as the 40,000 lire fees were concerned, he declared that they were just a means of buying meat for his dogs.

The record fees noted below do not take account of *The Birth of a Nation* (US 15), for which the copyright fee was paid on a royalty basis. The film was based on a disagreeably racist novel called *The Clansman*, for which author Thomas Dixon had demanded an unprecedented (for the US) rights fee of $25,000. Producer–director D. W. Griffith was unable to raise such a sum and offered him a $2000 advance against a 25 per cent royalty instead. Dixon ultimately received some $750,000, **the** highest sum made by the author of any silent film property.

The highest sum paid for rights during the silent era was $600,000 (£170,000) by the Classical Cinematograph Corporation in 1921 for *Ben Hur*, the Lew Wallace novel made into a 1925 movie.

The first million dollar property was Garson Kanin's Broadway show *Born Yesterday*. Kanin had instructed his agent to refuse any offers from Columbia owing to a long-standing feud with production chief Harry Cohn. The unprecedented size of the offer undermined Kanin's resolve and Columbia made the picture (US 50) with Judy Holliday and Broderick Crawford.

The highest ratio of rights to budget was 78 per cent in the case of Pathé's *Les Misérables* (Fr 11). The film had a budget of 230,000f, of which 180,000f was paid to the Victor Hugo estate for the rights.

The highest sum made by any novelist in film history has almost certainly accrued to William Peter Blatty, author of *The Exorcist*. The amount of money involved is indeterminate, since Mr Blatty, as producer of the film, was on 40 per cent of the gross. *The Exorcist* (US 73) has grossed over $89 million in North American rentals alone.

The highest reported fee for the rights to a novel is the $5 million paid by Warner Bros to Tom Wolfe for his *Bonfire of the Vanities*, made into a 1990 movie by Brian De Palma with Tom Hanks, Bruce Willis and Melanie Griffith in the leads.

The highest price ever paid for film rights is the $9,500,000 (£4,950,000) by Columbia in 1978 for Charles Strouse's Broadway musical *Annie*. When the $35 million picture was eventually released in 1982, *Variety* remarked in a thumbs-down review that the price of the rights was 'about what the whole film should have cost'.

Potentially the most lucrative rights deal is in respect of Andrew Lloyd Webber and his Really Useful Group's 1990 contract with Warner Bros for the film version of the composer's global stage success *Phantom of the Opera*. This gives Lloyd Webber and the Really Useful Group 3 per cent each of the gross if profits exceed $100 million. Should the income from the movie pass this trigger point, the rights will probably be worth $60 million or more. But if the film fails to achieve the specified profit level, Lloyd Webber and his company will get nothing.

Starring . . . The Author

Novelists and playwrights have occasionally appeared in the screen versions of their own works, the earliest known example being Jean Richepin's starring role as the Count de la Roque in *Gypsy Passion* (Fr 22), from his story *Miarka, the Child of the*

Mickey Spillane as his own creation Mike Hammer in *The Girl Hunters* (US 63). Britain's Shirley Eaton is the girlfriend. (*SI*)

Bear. Elinor Glyn, the one who preferred to sin on a tiger skin, played herself in her own *It* (US 27), overshadowed only by the 'It Girl' herself, Clara Bow. With the coming of sound Peter Frauchen, author of bestseller *Der Eskimo*, featured as the villain in MGM's *Eskimo* (US 33), but no other examples are noted until after the war, when Sir Compton Mackenzie played Captain Buncher in *Whisky Galore!* (GB 49), from his popular novel of the same name—for US release the picture was retitled *Tight Little Island*—and author Birgit Tengroth took a leading role in Ingmar Bergman's sombre rendering of *Törst/Thirst* (Swe 49). The first American writer to literally get into the act was black novelist Richard Wright, who took the lead in an Argentinian film, *Native Son* (Arg 50), from his story about a black youth afflicted by racism in the Chicago ghetto. Eynon Evans was cast as Amos in *The Happiness of Three Women* (GB 54), based on his play *The Wishing Well* and a few years later Erich Maria Remarque, author of *All Quiet on the Western Front*, put in a distinguished performance as the schoolmaster Pohlmann in the film of his novel *A Time to Love and a Time to Die* (US 58). The role of private eye Mike Hammer was played by his creator Mickey Spillane in *The Girl Hunters* (US 63) and paperback queen Jacqueline Susann did a bit part as an interviewer in her own *Valley of the Dolls* (US 67). Another cameo role by the author was Peter Benchley as the reporter in his mighty *Jaws* (US 75). He also appeared in *The Deep* (US 77), from his novel of that name, as the first mate who had served aboard the *Goliath*. Gore Vidal appeared as a senator in the film of his play *The*

First of Stephen King's bestsellers to be adapted for the screen by the author himself was the horror thriller *Pet Sematory* (US 89). And it was also the first in which the author makes a personal appearance—in the cameo role of a minister at a funeral.

Best Man (US 64). Anne-Cath Vestly starred in *Mormor og de Atte Ungene I Byen* (Nor 76), based on her own short stories, while another Norwegian film, *Anette* (Nor 80), not only featured the author of the novel, Astri Nustad, but was directed by her son. Amos Kolek, son of the Mayor of Jerusalem, had the satisfaction of playing a character based on himself in the film of his autobiographical novel *Don't Ask Me Why I Love* (Isr 79). Another autobiographical novel brought to the screen was Vergilio Ferreira's *Manha Submersa* (Por 80), in which the author played the rector of a seminary to which a boy is sent against his will to train for the priesthood. The boy's experiences were based on Ferreira's own. Similarly Gavino Ledda, the shepherd lad whose deprived childhood was so movingly portrayed in *Padre Padrone* (It 77), starred in as well as wrote and directed the autobiographical *Ybris/Habris* (It 84), which recounted the story of the scholar shepherd grown to manhood.

Recent examples of authors performing in the films of their own works have come from Switzerland, where Ingrid Puganigg played the title role in *Martha Dubronski* (Swz 85), and Canada, where Gordon Pinsent directed and starred in the film of his novel *John and the Missus* (Can 87), a mining drama set in the economically depressed Newfoundland of the early sixties. *Last Exit to Brooklyn* author Hubert Rechy played a hit-and-run driver in the 1987 West German film of his novel and Tama Janowitz had a small speaking part in the 1989 Merchant–Ivory adaptation of her anecdotal stories *Slaves of New York*. In *Pet Sematory* (US 89), based on Stephen King's bestseller of the same title, the much-filmed novelist had a cameo role as a minister presiding over a funeral. Over 40 years after the publication of his classic 1949 novel *The Sheltering Sky*, 80-year-old Paul Bowles appeared in Bernardo Bertolucci's 1990 film version observing the protagonists (John Malkovich and Debra Winger) from a sidewalk café in Tangiers.

The youngest author to have had a novel filmed was F. J. Thwaites (1908–79) of Sydney, Australia, whose first book, *Broken Melody*, written when he was 17, was brought to the screen by Ken Hall in a 1938 Cinesound production.

In 1990 Academy Entertainment and Artec announced that they would co-produce and Martha Coolidge would direct a film of Tamela Larimer's *Buck*. The novel had been published by Avon two years earlier when Miss Larimer was 17.

The most filmed author is William Shakespeare (1564–1616), whose plays have been presented in 299 straight or relatively straight film versions, 39 'modern versions' (where the story line has been loosely based on Shakespeare, e.g. *West Side Story*) and innumerable parodies. Not surprisingly *Hamlet* has appealed most to film-makers, with 73 movie versions (see filmography and also Remakes, p. 25), followed by *Romeo and Juliet*, which has been filmed 49 times, and *Macbeth*, filmed 32 times.

It will be noted from the checklist below that on four occasions Hamlet has been played by a woman: Sarah Bernhardt in a French synchronized sound short of 1900 (see also Sound Film, First, p. 149); the great Danish star Asta Nielsen in a German version of 1920 where Hamlet is revealed at the

Authors may be accustomed to storylines being changed when translated to the screen, but few have suffered quite such distortion of their work as British writer Pat Barker. Her novel *Union Street* is the story of seven women struggling against poverty in a grim town in the North of England. One of them is Iris, an overweight 50-year-old cleaner who subsists on chip butties. In the screen version, adapted as *Stanley and Iris* (US 90), six of the women have disappeared from the narrative altogether and Iris has become a svelte, independent thirtysomething living on the coast of California and enjoying the radiant good health associated with Jane Fonda, who plays her. Boyfriend Stanley (Robert De Niro), whose relationship with Iris the film is about, does not figure in the novel at all.

very end to have been a girl raised as a boy; Caroline Johnson, who interchanged with male thespian Rick McKenna in the 1971 film version of Toronto's Theatre of God production; and Fatma Girik in the explicitly titled *Female Hamlet* (Tur 77).

Among the more bizarre film versions of Shakespeare's greatest play is one in which the Prince of Denmark has undergone a metamorphosis into a gunslinger in the Wild West—*Quella sporca storia del West* (It 68). Hamlet has yet to meet Frankenstein's Monster, but one fears this is only a matter of time. Even the most well-intentioned treatment of Shakespeare's work can be subject to the grossest liberties. One of the most inexplicable is the translation of the sub-titles on the US/GB release prints

of Grigori Kozintsev's *Hamlet* (USSR 64), intended as a word-for-word film version of the play. The title-writer has given a modern English rendering of Boris Pasternak's scrupulous Russian translation of Shakespeare's original text. Other debasements of the bard's work have been more deliberate. We may be thankful that there has been no follow-up to the soft-porn British film *The Secret Sex Life of Romeo and Juliet* (GB 70) and even more so that among the many projected Shakespeare films that have failed to go into production was Joseph Goebbels' viciously anti-semitic version of *The Merchant of Venice.*

The most filmed novelist is Edgar Wallace (1875–1932), whose books and short stories have been made into at least 179 British, American and German films. In addition there have been other films based on Edgar Wallace plays, scripts and unidentified sources, making him the most filmed 20th-century writer. The first movie derived from one of Wallace's works of fiction was *The Man who Bought London* (GB 16), from his novel of the same name. Despite the royalties from his prodigious literary output, his film rights (over 50 of the films were made in his lifetime), and fees for scriptwriting, directing, and chairing the board of British Lion, Edgar Wallace died owing $315,000.

The most filmed American writer is Edgar Allan Poe (1809–49), with 111 films of his works. Apart from Edgar Wallace, the only writers who have been filmed more often than Poe are Alexander Dumas (père) (1802–70), author of *The Count of Monte Cristo* and *The Three Musketeers*, whose works have been brought to the screen in 121 films, and Charles Dickens (1812– 70), with 114 films to his credit. (NB: It has not been possible to deter-

---

HAMLET FILMOGRAPHY

Fr 00 with Sarah Bernhardt
Fr 07 with Georges Méliès
Fr 08 with Haques Gretillat
It 08 (Cornerio)
It 08 (Milano)
It 08 (Cines)
Fr 09 with Mounet-Sulley
It 10 with Dante Capelli
It 10 with Amleto Palermi
Fr 10 with Jacques Grétillat
Den 10 with Alwin Neuss
Nor 11
GB 12 with Charles Raymond
Fr 13 with Paul Mounet-Sully
GB 13 with Sir Johnston Forbes-Robertson
US 13 with Maurice Costello
It 14 with Hamilton A. Revelle
US 14 with James Young
GB 14 with Eric Williams
US 14 with Alla Nazimova (there is some doubt whether this film was ever made, nor is it known whether Nazimova played Hamlet or Ophelia if it was)
It 17 with Ruggero Ruggeri
Ger 20 with Asta Nielsen
Blood for Blood (Ind 27)
Khun-E-Nahak (Ind 28)

US 33 with John Barrymore (test reel of Act I Scene 5 and Act II Scene 2)
Ind 35 with Sohrab Modi
Strange Illusion (US 45)
GB 48 with Sir Laurence Olivier
I, Hamlet (It 52) with Erminio Macario
Ind 54 with Kishore Sahu
US 58 (Baylor Theater production)
US 59 (Encyclopaedia Britannica 16 mm production)
Ger 60 with Maximilian Schell
Pol 60 (short directed by Jerzy Skolimowski)
The Bad Sleep Well (Jap 60)
US 64 with Richard Burton
USSR 64 with Innokenti Smoktunowski
Hamile aka *The Tongo Hamlet* Gha 65 with Kofi Middleton-Mends
Hun 65 (animated)
GB 69 with Nicol Williamson
US 70 with Richard Chamberlain (TVM)
Heranca aka *Hamlet* Bra 70 with David Cardaso
US 71 with David Suchet (16 mm)
Can 71 (musical) with Rick McKenna and Caroline Johnson
GB 72 with Ian McKellen (TVM)
Un Amleto di meno It 73 with Carmelo Bene
A Gay Hamlet (GB 76)
Dogg's Troupe Hamlet GB 77

Female Hamlet Tur 77 with Fatma Girik
GB 78 with Anthony and David Meyer
Dome to Elsinore USSR 78—made by workers of the Paris Commune Shoe Factory, Moscow.
GB 80 with Derek Jacobi
Den 85 with Stine Bierlick*
Rosencrantz and Guildenstern Are Dead (GB 90) from Tom Stoppard's play. Hamlet (Iain Glen) is a background character
US 90 with Mel Gibson
US 90 with Kevin Kline (TVM)
MODERN VERSIONS
Der Rest ist Schweigen Ger 59 with Hardy Kruger
Ophelia Fr 61 with André Jocelyn
Ithele na yini vasilas/He Wanted to be King Gre 67 with Angelos Theodoropoulos
Quella sporca storia del West It 68 with Enio Girolami
Johnny Hamlet (It 72) with Chip Corman
Hamlet Goes Business (Fin 87) with Pirkka-Pekka Petelius.
PARODIES

GB 15	GB 19	US 19	US 37
US 16	GB 19	Den 22	It 73
US 16	GB 19	Den 32	
It 16			

* At 18 the youngest screen Hamlet

mine how many of over 200 films featuring the character of Sherlock Holmes—see p. 45—were based on actual stories by Sir Arthur Conan Doyle.)

The most filmed living writer is the Swedish children's novelist Astrid Lindgren (1907–), whose works have been adapted for 37 movies. Most recent is *Lotta on Rascal Street* (Swe 91), shot in the 'Astrid Lindgren Village' theme park at the author's birthplace Vimmerly, which is based on the houses in her books.

CLASHES

The simultaneous release of Gregory Ratoff's *Oscar Wilde* (GB 60), with Robert Morley, and Ken Hughes's *The Trials of Oscar Wilde* (GB 60), with Peter Finch, drew attention to a phenomenon which has been commoner in the history of movies than is generally realized. As early as 1912 the first feature film made in Britain and the first feature film made in America were rival versions of *Oliver Twist* and that same year no less than three different productions of *The Last Days of Pompeii* were made in Italy. Here are some of the more notable examples of movie 'clashes':

☆ Two Russian adaptations of *War and Peace* were actually released on the same day, 13 February 1915, and the same thing happened the next year in America when both the Francis X. Bushman–Beverly Bayne and Harry Hilliard–Theda Bara versions of *Romeo and Juliet* were premièred on 22 Oct 1916.

☆ As many as eight biopics of the rascally monk Rasputin were made in 1917, four in Russia, three in the USA and one in Germany.

☆ Two versions of Max Marcin and Charles Guernon's play *Eyes of Youth* were made in 1919, one with an all white cast headed by Clara Kimball Young, the other with an all black cast headed by Abbie Mitchell.

☆ In 1934 Marlene Dietrich's bravura performance in and as *The Scarlet Empress* (US 34) eclipsed Elizabeth Bergner's less vibrant interpretation of *Catherine the Great* (GB 34).

☆ The following year there was another clash of costume dramas with Josef von Sternberg's American version of *Crime and Punishment*, starring Peter Lorre, and Pierre Chanal's French production with Pierre Blanchar.

☆ America and France clashed again in 1936 when audiences could choose between the Hollywood biopic *Louis Pasteur* with Paul Muni or the more authentic portrayal of the great scientist by Sacha Guitry in the version titled simply *Pasteur*.

☆ Two feature-length cartoon versions of *Cinderella* appeared in 1950, one from Walt Disney in America, the other from Estela Film in Spain.

☆ Disney had competition again the following year when his cartoon version of *Alice in Wonderland* was on release at the same time as Lou Bunin's puppet and live-action version with Carol Marsh as Alice.

☆ Twin films about the July plot to kill Hitler, *The 20th July*, and *It Happened on 20th July*, were released in Germany on successive days in 1955.

☆ Mario Lanza was not the only actor to play *The Great Caruso* (US) in 1951. Ermanno Randi starred in a rival biopic, *Enrico Caruso, Legend of a Voice* (It).

☆ When the Italian director Franco Zeffirelli made a British production of *Romeo and Juliet* in 1968 with Leonard Whiting and Olivia Hussey, an Italian production of the great love story was made by Ricardo Freda with Gerald Meynier and Rosemarie Dexter. This version was brought to London for dubbing, but hoping to penetrate the lucrative American market, Signor Freda chose to have it done in that most unromantic of accents, Brooklynese!

☆ Another clash of classics—this time with some real competition at the box office—came in 1975 with the simultaneous release of Patrick Garland's *A Doll's House*, with Claire Bloom as Nora, and Joseph Losey's *A Doll's House* with Jane Fonda. Both these were British productions, but there was also a German version the same year, directed by Rainer Werner Fassbinder and starring Margit Carstensen.

☆ Two biopics titled *Harlow* (US 65), one with Carroll Baker as the thirties star, the other with Carol Lynley, were joined by a third from the Andy Warhol stable titled *Harlot* (US 65). In this rather unconventional version, the Blonde Venus was portrayed by Mario Montez in drag.

☆ The well-loved children's classic *The Little Mermaid* appeared in three different versions in 1976—a Czech production, a Finnish production, and a USSR–Bulgarian co-production. There were another two in 1990, both of them cartoon features: Disney's *The Little Mermaid* (US 90) and Saban's *Adventures of The Little Mermaid* (Swz 90).

☆ *The Elephant Man* (GB 80), with John Hurt, was one of the box office successes of 1980, but not many people were aware of the Canadian version produced the same year.

☆ Released within twelve months of each other, if not the same year, were the three treatments of the Entebbe Raid story, *Victory at Entebbe* (US 76), *Raid on Entebbe* (US 76), and the most accurate version of the events, *Operation Thunderbolt* (Isr 77).

☆ Opera buffs were confronted with no less than seven versions of *Carmen* in 1984, albeit three of them from the same director. Peter Brook filmed his French stage production with three different casts, the title role being taken by Helene Delavault, Zehava Gal and Eva Saurova. Julia Migenes-Johnson took the part in Francesco Rossi's Italian-French co-production, Anne-Marie Mühle in Roland Sterner's Swedish production, Stefania Toczyska in Mate Rabinovski's French production and Laura del Sol in

Carlos Saura's Spanish production. An eighth version of Carmen, based on Merimée's story, was *Carmen Nue* with Pamela Prati in the title role.

☆ *Wills and Burke* (Aus 85) was released a week before *Burke and Wills* (Aus 85). The latter is a straight presentation of the story of Australia's most celebrated explorers, the former a parody. Uniquely in a clash situation there were two actors, Peter Collingwood and Chris Haywood, who appeared in both versions. (Any listing of either actor's credits is going to read like a mistake.)

☆ Raymond Radiguet's novel *Le Diable au corps*, about a love affair between a 17-year-old boy and a married woman, was filmed by Scott Murray with a World War II Australian setting as *Devil in the Flesh* (Aus 86) and by Marco Bellocchio with a 1985 Rome setting as *Il Diavolo in Corpo* (It 86). The Australian version did not contain the fellatio scene which caused Bellocchio censorship problems in the Italian version.

☆ In 1987 both mainland China and Taiwan produced rival biopics of the leader of the 1911 revolution and 'Father of modern China' Dr Sun Yat-Sen. As the two films had the same booking dates, audiences were confused as to which version was which. There were also two biopics of China's last Emperor, Pu Yi, Bertolucci's *The Last Emperor* (It/GB/Chn 87) and the Chinese production *The Last Empress* (Chn 87). The latter concentrates mainly on Pu Yi's relationship with his official wife Wanrong and his two concubines Wenxlu and Tan Yuling.

☆ Stephen Frears' *Dangerous Liaisons* (US 88) and Milos Forman's *Valmont* (Fr/GB 89), each based on Choderlos de Laclos' 18th-century French novel of high class sexual shenanigans. were both on general release in 1989. The Valmont role was played by John Malkovich in the Frears version, by Colin Firth in Forman's version; the Marquise de Merteuil by Glenn Close and Annette Bening respectively; Madame de Tourvel by Michelle Pfeiffer and Meg Tilly; and 15-year-old Cécile by Uma Thurman and Fairuza Balk. Frears, a British director, had his 18th-century French aristocrats speaking in uncompromising American; Forman, a Czech, in the Queen's English.

☆ Morgan Creek's $50 million *Robin Hood* starring Kevin Costner and 20th Century Fox's more modestly budgeted $15 million *Robin Hood Prince of Thieves* with Patrick Bergin were both shot in England at the same time, both claim to be the first historically accurate rendering and both were released in the summer of 1991.

SCRIPT

The first scriptwriter was New York journalist Roy McCardell, who was hired in 1900 by Henry Marvin of the American Mutoscope & Biograph Co. to write ten scenarios a week at $15 each. Since most of the films made by Biograph at that time were 50–100 ft in length (about 1½ minutes), McCardell found he was able to complete his first week's assignment in a single afternoon.

The first contract writer (i.e. full-time employee of a studio) was Louis Feuillade, who joined the Gaumont Studios in Paris in 1905.

Britain's first regular scriptwriter was Harold Brett, engaged by H. O. Martinek of the British & Colonial Kinematograph Co., whose earliest known scenario was for a spy picture called *A Soldier's Honour* (GB 11). Previously it had been the custom of British film producers to shoot without a script or write their own screenplays.

The first writer of literary distinction to be engaged to produce a scenario was the French playwright Henri Lavedan, whose *L'Assassination du Duc de Guise* (Fr 08) was made by Film d'Art.

In the USA the first eminent writer under contract was Emmett Campbell Hall, who was engaged by D. W. Griffith to script the Biograph pictures *His Trust* (US 11) and *His Trust Fulfilled* (US 11), a two-part story of the American Civil War.

> Spencer Tracy was asked what qualities he sought in a film script. The laconic reply: 'Days off.'

The first scriptwriter to 'have his name in lights'—in other words, to be credited on a cinema marquee—was H. H. Van Loon, author and adaptor of *The Virgin of Stamboul* (US 20), who was afforded this tribute by the Strand Theater, San Francisco, in November 1920.

The first scriptwriters to write dialogue for a sound feature film were Joseph Jackson and Edward T. Lowe Jr, who composed the four talking sequences of Warner Bros' crime melodrama *Tenderloin* (US 28). The dialogue was so ludicrous that two of the sequences were cut after the first week of the film's run. (The dialogue sequences in *The Jazz Singer* (US 27) had been ad libbed by Al Jolson in the title role.)

The shortest dialogue script since the introduction of talkies was written for Mel Brooks' *Silent Movie* (US 76), which had only one spoken word throughout. The dialogue sequence in the otherwise silent movie occurs when mime artist Marcel Marceau, having been invited by telephone (silently) to appear in a silent movie, replies (audibly) 'Non!'. The person making the call is asked (according to the inter-title) 'What did he say?' Response, also by inter-title: 'I don't know. I don't understand French.'

The only other film with but a single word of dialogue, Paul Fejos's *Marie, A Hungarian Legend* (Hun 32), used a longer word—the name 'Marie'.

The most co-writers credited for any film was 21 in the case of *Forever and a Day* (US 43). They included C. S. Forester, John van Druten, Christopher Isherwood, R. C. Sherriff, James Hilton and Frederick Lonsdale.

A Yank at Oxford (GB 38) credited only eight scriptwriters, but at least 31 are known to have been employed by MGM on the screenplay. Among those uncredited were Herman J. Mankiewicz, John Paddy Carstairs, Hugh Walpole and F. Scott Fitzgerald.

The highest fee ever paid for a commissioned script was $2 million by Carolco Pictures to Oscar-winning *Rain Man* scriptwriter Ronald Bass for an adaptation of T. R. Wright's supernatural thriller *Manhattan Ghost Story*. The deal was announced in October 1990.

The highest fee ever paid for a speculative script (i.e. a script offered to the highest bidder rather than commissioned) was the $3 million by Carolco Pictures to Joe Eszterhas for 1990 opus *Basic Instinct*. A cop thriller, the script was described by *Variety* as 'devoid of any noticeably redeeming social merit'. Esterhas was subsequently taken off the picture due to creative differences with director Paul Verhoeven, but received payment in full.

The lowest fee paid for the script of a major Hollywood feature was the $10 earned by Preston Sturges for *The Great McGinty* (US 40). Sturges was a scriptwriter who wanted to direct. The deal with Paramount was that he should be given the opportunity in return for doing the script for a nominal fee.

Alan Dwan made his full-length feature *Night Life in New York* (US 25) so quickly that writer Edgar Selwyn had not started on his script when the film was completed five days after shooting began. The director had made the film according to the storyline that Selwyn had told him over lunch a month earlier. Returning from a quick trip to Europe, Selwyn was dismayed to find the picture finished, but Dwan gave him the writer's credit on screen.

The longest delay between the completion of a movie script and the making of the movie was 39 years in the case of Freddie Francis's *The Doctor and the Devils* (GB 86), starring Timothy Dalton. The script, about the Edinburgh grave robbers Burke and Hare, was written by the Welsh poet Dylan Thomas in 1947. It was originally to have been filmed by the Rank Organization. When this came to naught, further attempts were made by Nicholas Roeg in the 1960s and by Mel Brooks in 1983 before it was finally brought to the screen by Brooksfilm in an adaptation by Ronald Harwood.

Profanities, Obscenities and Expletives

It is Hollywood myth that Clark Gable's celebrated closing line in *Gone with the Wind* (US 39) — 'Frankly, my dear, I don't give a damn'—was the first occasion on which the word 'damn' had been spoken on the screen. It was said by both Leslie Howard and Marie Lohr in *Pygmalion* (GB 38) and had featured in several earlier Hollywood pictures. Fred Stone said 'Damn you!' to the heroine's boss (who had wronged her) in *Alice Adams* (US 35) and three years before that Emma Dunn had exclaimed 'Well, I'll be damned' in *Blessed Event* (US 32). Even at the beginning of the talkie era there were three 'damns' in *Glorifying the American Girl* (US 29) and 'It's me, goddamit' could be heard in *Hell's Angels* (US 30), as well as 'What the hell', 'For Chrissake', 'Jesus!' and 'That son-of-a-bitch!'. Nothing stronger, however, was allowed until the sixties, the obscenities voiced by Mickey Shaughnessy in *Don't Go Near the Water* (US 56) being bleeped out. A similar device had been used a generation earlier in the Astaire-Rogers musical *Swing Time* (US 36). Victor Moore's angry response to a street cop was deliberately rendered inaudible by the honking of a motor horn. Little skill in lip-reading is needed to discern that the words spoken were 'Motherfucking son-of-a-bitch!'.

British censors had less reserve about the use of realistic language where it was appropriate. 'Bloody' was heard for the first time in *Pygmalion* (GB 38), 'fanny' in *Convoy* (GB 40), 'arse' in *The Guinea Pig* (GB 49) and 'bastard' in *The Blue Lamp* (GB 49). The British also pioneered the on-screen use of 'bugger' in *Poor Cow* (GB 67) and the most over-used four-letter word in *I'll Never Forget Whatshisname* (GB 68), in which Marianne Faithfull made a little piece of film history by breaking the ultimate 'word barrier'. (Critic Kenneth Tynan had, however, said it earlier on television.) The Americans were first, however, with 'shit', which was heard in *In Cold Blood* (US 67) a year earlier than its first appearance on a British soundtrack in *Boom!* (GB 68), while the permissive Danes led with the first on-screen use of a four-letter word in reference to female genitalia in *Quiet Days in Clichy* (Den 69). This was the era of the permissive society and the breakdown of old taboos, aptly summed up by Bob Hope in 1968: 'Last year Hollywood made the first pictures with dirty words. This year we made the pictures to go with them.'

The film with the doubtful distinction of over-using the most over-used four letter word the most times was *Scarface* (US 84), in which it is spoken 206 times—an average of once every 29 seconds.

The televison watchdogs tend to be more sensitive about indecorous language than the film censors, particularly where young children are likely to be viewing. In the case of *E.T. The Extra-Terrestrial* (US 82), it was Steven Spielberg himself who doctored the movie for the living-room audience. There are three occasions when a four letter word beginning with 's' is used in the cinema version. For television the word became a five letter one beginning with 's'—'shoot!'.

Most of the above words had been used at one time or other by actors in silent films. When Edmund Lowe and Victor McLaglen indulged in a fine exchange of Billingsgate in *What Price Glory* (US 26), the studio received hundreds of letters of protest from outraged lip-readers. Likewise in *Sadie Thompson* (US 28), lip-readers would be the only ones to appreciate the full rich flavour of Gloria Swanson's language as Sadie—which made no concessions to the censors. The title cards only reproduced what she was *not* saying.

Who was going to escape from Casablanca with whom? Bogart was the only one who knew.

> Most movie buffs know the oft-repeated tale of how Michael Curtiz directed *Casablanca* (US 42) without a completed script and no denouement to the story. The truth of the matter is no less intriguing. There was indeed a detailed shooting script which had been completed by Julius and Irving Epstein, with the classic ending in which Humphrey Bogart as Rick sacrifices his love to allow Ingrid Bergman as Ilsa and her husband Laszlo (Paul Henreid) to escape from Nazi retribution. (Although Howard Koch did a rewrite, the ending remained the same.) But Curtiz pretended that he did not know the ending in order that his cast should be as uncertain of what fate had in store for them as the characters they were playing. In the love scene in Rick's apartment Ilsa, torn with doubt, says: 'I don't know the finish yet'. This was true for the actress as well as the character, and she went in anguish to scriptwriter Howard Koch to demand 'How can I play a love scene when I don't know which man I'm going to end up with?'. Bogart, however, did know what was going to happen on the tarmac of a mist-shrouded Casablanca airport—as a major star his contract gave him the right to script approval.

The most hackneyed line in movie scripts is 'Let's get outta here'. A survey of 350 American features of the period 1938–85 showed that it was used at least once in 81 per cent of Hollywood productions and more than once in 17 per cent. Film critic David McGillivray disputes this finding with the assertion that no single phrase has been so over-worked in movie scripts as 'Try to get some sleep now'.

Also nominated for the golden cliché award is 'I've never been so serious about anything in my life' in answer to the kind of question that John McEnroe puts to tennis umpires.

The fastest time for writing the script of a full-length feature film was two days for *Weird Science* (US 85) by John Hughes, who also directed.

This was an improvement on previous efforts—it had taken him three days to script *The Breakfast Club* (US 84), a full four days for *National Lampoon's Vacation* (US 83), and no less than a week for *Mr Mom* (US 83).

The most improbable scenario ever to reach the screen must be a matter of opinion, but the author would like to nominate George Dewhurst's plot for the Hepworth production *Mist in the Valley* (GB 23), in which Alma Taylor played an ex-nun who marries an amnesia victim and is framed for allegedly murdering a usurping uncle who was posing as her father.

The longest monologue in a dramatic film is a 20-minute speech by Edwige Feuillère in *L'Aigle à deux têtes/The Eagle has Two Heads* (Fr 48).

The longest monologue in a Hollywood movie is by Lionel Barrymore in *A Free Soul* (US 31). Six cameras were used to film the 14-minute speech in one take, since sound editing had yet to be perfected.

> John Wayne had only one line in his role of the centurion at the Crucifixion in *The Greatest Story Ever Told* (US 65), but on the first take it lacked dramatic impact. Director George Stevens asked the Duke if he could add an awe to his words. An obliging actor who could take direction, Wayne did as he though he had been bidden. On the next take he declaimed 'Aw, truly this man was the Son Of God'.

Statesmen as Scriptwriters

A number of statesmen have turned their hands to scriptwriting, including Sir Winston Churchill, who was under contract to London Films from 1934 until the war and worked on such films as *The Twenty Five Year Reign of King George V* (uncompleted) and *Conquest of the Air* (GB 38). He is also said to have contributed a speech to the script of *Lady Hamilton/ US That Hamilton Woman* (GB 42). On the other side of the Atlantic, President Roosevelt wrote the original scenario for *The President's Mystery* (US 36), about a lawyer (Henry Wilcoxson) who fakes his own death so that he can right the wrongs he did in the name of big business. Carmine Gallone's vast and sprawling epic *Scipio Africanus* (It 37), a story of Roman victories in Africa intended to parallel Mussolini's contemporary victories in Abyssinia, was alleged to have been written by Il Duce himself. Some years earlier Mussolini's melodrama *The Cardinal's Mistress* had been made into a successful silent movie. Another dictator with a screenplay to his credit was General Franco who wrote the scenario for *The Spirit of Race* (Sp 41), an adaptation of his own novel, under the pen-name Jaime de Andrade. He also scripted and shot his own animated cartoons. In more recent times former Thailand Prime Minister Kukrit Pramoj wrote *Fai Dang/The Red Bamboo* (Phi 79). Field Marshal Idi Amin Dada, before he was deposed as President-for-Life of Uganda, scripted an adulatory biopic of himself, but happily this was never made. India's former premier Moraji Desai is probably the only world leader to have scripted a film while in office. Having committed himself to producer J. G. Mohla before being gaoled under Mrs Gandhi's State of Emergency, and finding himself Prime Minister shortly after his release, he nevertheless felt under an obligation to fulfil his undertaking. Working in the early mornings he completed his English-language script of *Yogeshwar Krishna*, the story of Lord Krishna, a few months later. Originally written as a play, Pope John Paul II's *The Jeweller's Shop*, first performed in Poland in 1960, was filmed in Montreal in 1987 with Burt Lancaster, Ben Cross and Olivia Hussey in the leading roles.

Royalty has also turned a hand to scriptwriting, HRH Prince Charles assisting John Cleese with the dialogue of environmental comedy *Grimes Goes Green* (GB 90), in which he and the hero of *A Fish Called Wanda* co-star. The following year he co-scripted the 25-minute cartoon telefilm *The Old Man of Lochnagar* (GB 91), based on his bestselling book of the same title. Made for STV and S4C, the picture was produced in three versions, English, Gaelic and Welsh.

FIVE

CHARACTER AND THEMES

SCREEN CHARACTERS

The character most often portrayed on screen since the inception of the story film has been Sherlock Holmes, the master detective created by Sir Arthur Conan Doyle (1859–1930), who has been played by 72 actors, including one black (Sam Robinson), in 204 films produced between 1900 and 1991 (see filmography). The only actor to have played both Sherlock Holmes and Dr Watson was Reginald Owen, who was Watson in *Sherlock Holmes* (US 32) and Holmes in *A Study in Scarlet* (US 33).

When the Allies reached Berlin in 1945, the contents of Hitler's bunker revealed a number of interesting sidelights to his character and tastes. The two movies they found were both Sherlock Holmes adventures—*The Hound of the Baskervilles* (Ger 37) and *The Man Who Was Sherlock Holmes* (Ger 37).

Is this the real Sherlock Holmes—suave, sophisticated, a mental giant? Fear not—Mr Caine is masquerading as an actor who is masquerading as the Great Detective in the aptly titled *Without a Clue* (US 88). *(British Film Institute)*

SHERLOCK HOLMES FILMOGRAPHY

The filmography below includes feature-length TVMs, but excludes filmed television series. Where known the actor playing Sherlock Holmes is included.

Sherlock Holmes Baffled (US 00)
Maurice Costello *The Adventures of Sherlock Holmes* (US 03)
Sherlock Holmes Returns (US? 06?)
Bauman Károly *Sherlock Holmes* (Hun 08)
Viggo Larsen *Sherlock Holmes I Livsfare* (Den 08); *Sherlock Holmes II* (Den 08); *Sherlock Holmes III* (Den 08)
Sherlock Holmes in the Great Murder Mystery (US 09)
Viggo Larsen *Sangerindens Diamanter* (Den 09)
August Blom *Droske No 519* (Den 09)
Viggo Larsen *Den Graa Dame* (Den 09)
The Latest Triumph of Sherlock Holmes (Fr 09)
Sherlock Holmes (It 09?)
Viggo Larsen *Der Alte Sekretar* (Ger 10); *Der Blaue Diamant* (Ger 10); *Die Falschen Rembrandts* (Ger 10); *Die Flucht* (Ger 10)
Otto Lagoni *Sherlock Holmes I Bondefangerklør* (Den 10)
Forrect Holger-Madsen (?) *Forklaedte Barnepige* (Den 11)
Holger Rasmussen *Medlem af den Sorte Hand* (Den 11)

Alwin Neuss *Millionobligation* (Den 11)
Hotel Mysterierne (Den 11)
Viggo Larsen *Arsène Lupins Ende* (Ger 11); *Sherlock Holmes contra Professor Moryarty* (Ger 11)
Henri Gouget *Les Aventures de Sherlock Holmes* (Fr 11)
Schlau, Schlauer, am Schlauesten (Fr 12) French title unknown
Georges Treville *The Speckled Band* (GB 12); *The Reigate Squires* (GB 12); *The Beryl Coronet* (GB 12); *The Adventure of the Copper Beeches* (GB 12); *A Mystery of Boscombe Vale* (GB 12); *The Stolen Papers* (GB 12); *Silver Blaze* (GB 12); *The Musgrave Ritual* (GB 13)
Verrater Zigarette (Ger 13)
Schwarze Kappe (Ger 13)
Gli artigli di griffard (It 13)
Forte di Sherlock Holmes (It 13)
Harry Benham *Sherlock Holmes Solves the Sign of Four* (US 13)
Ferdinand Bonn *Sherlock Holmes contra Dr Mors* (Ger 14)
En Raedsom Nat (Den 14)
Em Gregers (?) *Hvem er Hun?* (Den 14)
James Bragington *A Study in Scarlet* (GB 14)
Francis Ford *A Study in Scarlet* (US 14)
Alwin Neuss *Der Hund von Baskerville* (Ger

14); *Der Hund von Baskerville II* (Ger 14); *Der Hund von Baskerville III* (Ger 15); *Der Hund von Baskerville IV* (Ger 15)
Eugen Burg *Der Hund von Baskerville V* (Ger 15)
Alwin Neuss *Ein Schrei in der Nacht* (Ger 15)
Bloomer Tricks Sherlock Holmes (It 15)
Alwin Neuss *William Voss* (Ger 15)
William Gillette *Sherlock Holmes* (US 16)
H. A. Saintsbury *The Valley of Fear* (GB 16)
Alwin Neuss *Sherlock Holmes auf Urlaub* (Ger 16); *Sherlock Holmes Nächtliche Begegnung* (Ger 16)
Hugo Flink *Der Erstrommotor* (Ger 17); *Die Kasette* (Ger 17); *Der Schlangenring* (Ger 17); *Die Indische Spinne* (Ger 17)
Viggo Larsen *Rotterdam-Amsterdam* (Ger 18)
Ferdinand Bonn *Was er im Spiegel sar* (Ger 18); *Die Giftplombe* (Ger 18); *Das Schicksal der Renate Yongk* (Ger 18); *Die Dose des Kardinals* (Ger 18)
Sam Robinson *Black Sherlock Holmes* (US 18) only time Holmes has been played by a black
Viggo Larsen *Drei Tage Tot* (Ger 19)
Kurt Brenkendorff *Der Mord im Splendid Hotel* (Ger 19)
Erich Kaiser-Titz (?) *Dr Macdonald's Sanatorium* (Ger 20)

Adolf D'Arnaz (?) *Harry Hill contra Sherlock Holmes* (Ger 20)

Lu Jurgens (?) *Das Haus ohne Fenster* (Ger 20)

Eille Norwood *The Dying Detective* (GB 21); *The Devil's Foot* (GB 21); *A Case of Identity* (GB 21); *The Yellow Face* (GB 21); *The Red-Headed League* (GB 21); *The Resident Patient* (GB 21); *A Scandal in Bohemia* (GB 21); *The Man with the Twisted Lip* (GB 21); *The Beryl Coronet* (GB 21); *The Noble Bachelor* (GB 21); *The Copper Beeches* (GB 21); *The Empty House* (GB 21); *The Tiger of San Pedro* (GB 21); *The Priory School* (GB 21); *The Solitary Cyclist* (GB 21); *The Hound of the Baskervilles* (GB 21); *Charles Augustus Milverton* (GB 22); *The Abbey Grange* (GB 22); *The Norwood Builder* (GB 22); *The Reigate Squires* (GB 22); *The Naval Treaty* (GB 22); *The Second Stain* (GB 22); *The Red Circle* (GB 22); *The Six Napoleons* (GB 22); *Black Peter* (GB 22); *The Bruce-Partington Plans* (GB 22); *The Stockbroker's Clerk* (GB 22); *The Boscombe Valley Mystery* (GB 22); *The Musgrave Ritual* (GB 22); *The Golden Pinz-Nez* (GB 22); *The Greek Interpreter* (GB 22)

John Barrymore *Sherlock Holmes* (US 22)

Eman Fiala *The Abduction of Banker Fusee* (Cz 23)

Eille Norwood *Silver Blaze* (GB 23); *The Speckled Band* (GB 23); *The Gloria Scott* (GB 23); *The Blue Carbuncle* (GB 23); *The Engineer's Thumb* (GB 23); *His Last Bow* (GB 23); *The Cardboard Box* (GB 23); *Lady Frances Carfax* (GB 23); *The Three Students* (GB 23); *The Missing Three-Quarter* (GB 23); *Thor Bridge* (GB 23); *The Stone of Mazarin* (GB 23); *The Dancing Men* (GB 23); *The Crooked Man* (GB 23); *The Final Problem* (GB 23); *The Sign of Four* (GB 23)

Philip Beck *Kobenhavns Sherlock Holmes* (Den 25)

Carlyle Blackwell *Der Hund von Baskerville* (Ger 29)

Clive Brook *The Return of Sherlock Holmes* (US 29); *Paramount on Parade* (US 30)

Arthur Wontner *The Sleeping Cardinal* (GB 31)

Raymond Massey *The Speckled Band* (GB 31)

Robert Rendel *The Hound of the Baskervilles* (GB 32)

Clive Brook *Sherlock Holmes* (US 32)

Arthur Wontner *The Sign of Four* (GB 32); *The Missing Rembrandt* (GB 32)

Martin Fric *Lelicek ve Sluzbach Sherlocka Holmese* (Cz 32)

Richard Gordon *The Radio Murder Mystery* (US 33)

Reginald Owen *A Study in Scarlet* (US 33)

Arthur Wontner *The Triumph of Sherlock Holmes* (GB 35); *Silver Blaze* (GB 37)

Bruno Güttner *Der Hund von Baskerville* (Ger 37)

Hermann Speelmans *Die Graue Dame* (Ger 37)

Hans Albers *Der Mann, der Sherlock Holmes War* (Ger 37)

Basil Rathbone *The Hound of the Baskervilles* (US 39); *The Adventures of Sherlock Holmes* (US 39); *Sherlock Holmes and the Voice of Terror* (US 42); *Sherlock Holmes and the Secret Weapon* (US 42); (cameo role) *Crazy House* (US 43); *Sherlock Holmes in Washington* (US 43); *Sherlock Holmes Faces Death* (US 43); *Sherlock Holmes and the Spider Woman* (US 44); *The Scarlet Claw* (US 44); *The Pearl of Death* (US 44); *The House of Fear* (US 45); *The Woman in Green* (US 45); *Pursuit to Algiers* (US 45); *Terror by Night* (US 45); *Dressed to Kill* (US 45)

John Longden *The Man with the Twisted Lip* (GB 51)

Peter Cushing *The Hound of the Baskervilles* (GB 59)

Christopher Lee *Sherlock Holmes und das Halsband des Todes* (FRG 62)

The other fictitious or legendary characters most frequently represented on screen have been Count Dracula—158 films (see p. 56); Frankenstein's monster—112; Tarzan—98; Zorro—70; Hopalong Cassidy—66 (see p. 105); the Durango Kid—64; Robin Hood—58; Charlie Chan—49.

1920: Gene Pollar was the second of the Tarzans, after Elmo Lincoln.

Jerome Raphel *The Double-Barrelled Detective Story* (US 65)

John Neville *A Study in Terror* (GB 65)

Nando Gazzolo *La Valle della paura* (It 68, TVM); *L'Ultimo dei Baskerville* (It 68)

Uncredited *The Best House in London* (GB 69)

Robert Stephens *The Private Life of Sherlock Holmes* (GB 70)

Radovan Lukavsky *Touha Sherlocka Holmese* (Cz 71)

George C. Scott *They Might Be Giants* (US 72) (as character who thinks he is SH)

The Case of the Metal-Sheathed Elements (GB 72) cartoon

Stewart Granger *The Hound of the Baskervilles* (US 72, TVM)

Keith McConnell *Murder in Northumberland* (GB 74)

Rolf Becker *Monsieur Sherlok Holmes* (Fr 74, TVM)

Harry Reems *Sherlock Holmes* (US 75) porno

Douglas Wilmer *The Adventure of Sherlock Holmes' Smarter Brother* (GB 75)

Roger Moore *Sherlock Holmes in New York* (US 76, TVM) released theatrically in Europe

Keith McConnell *Murder by Death* (US 76) SH role cut in some release prints

Sherlock Holmes (Swz 76)

A Case of Royal Murder (GB 77)

The Case of the Exhumed Client (GB 77)

Nicol Williamson *The Seven-Per-Cent Solution* (GB 77)

Trevor Ainsley *The Case of the Mounting Fortune* (GB 78)

Peter Cook *The Hound of the Baskervilles* (GB 78)

Vasilij Livanov *Sherlock Holmes and Doctor Watson* (USSR 79); *The Adventures of Sherlock Holmes and Doctor Watson* (USSR 80); *The Hound of the Baskervilles* (USSR 81); *The Treasure of Agra* (USSR 83); *The Sign of Four* (USSR 83); *Trouble in Bohemia* (USSR 83); *The Twentieth Century is Starting* (USSR 86) —all TVMs

Christopher Plummer *Murder by Decree* (GB/Can 79)

Jeremy Young *The Case of the Fantastical Passbook* (GB 79)

Aljgis Masjulis *The Blue Carbuncle* (USSR 80, TVM)

Peter O'Toole (voice) *Sherlock Holmes and the Baskerville Curse* (Aus 81); *The Sign of Four* (Aus 81); *A Study in Scarlet* (Aus 81); *A Valley of Fear* (Aus 81) —all animated

Ian Richardson *The Hound of the Baskervilles* (GB 83); *The Sign of Four* (GB 83)

Guy Rolfe *The Case of Marcel Duchamp* (Fr 83)

Peter Cushing *The Masks of Death* (GB 84, TVM)

Nicholas Rowe *Young Sherlock Holmes* (GB 86)

Vassily Livanov (voice) *Sherlock Holmes and I* (USSR 86) —animated

Basil Rathbone (voice—posthumously) *The Great Mouse Detective* (US 86) —animated

Jeremy Brett *The Sign of Four* (GB 87)

Michael Caine *Without a Clue* (US 88) (NB Caine character is imposter)

Jeremy Brett *The Hound of the Baskervilles* (GB 88, TVM)

Rodney Litchfield *Testimony* (GB 88)

Edward Woodward *Hands of a Murderer* (GB/US 90, TVM)

Charlton Heston *The Crucifer of Blood* (US 91)

Christopher Lee *Sherlock Holmes and The Leading Lady* (US/Lux 91, TVM)

Christopher Lee *Sherlock Holmes: Incident at Victoria Falls* (US/Lux 91, TVM)

COMIC STRIP CHARACTERS

A host of comic strip characters have been portrayed on screen in live action feature-length movies. This list is confined to English language films. The name following the abbreviation 'Orig' is that of the originator of the comic strip.

☆ Ginger Meggs, cartoon larrikin in Australian newspapers, was played by Ray Griffin in *Those Terrible Twins* (Aus 25). Orig: James Bancks.

☆ *Ella Cinders* (US 26) with Colleen Moore. Orig: William Counselman and Charles Plumb.

☆ Fatty Finn, an urchin of the backstreets of Sydney, was played by 'Pop' Ordell in *The Kid Stakes* (Aus 26). Orig: Syd Nicholls.

☆ *Tillie the Toiler* (US 27) with Marion Davies as the office girl heroine. Orig: Russ Westover in the *New York American*.

☆ *Harold Teen* (US 28) with Arthur Lake. Orig: Carl Ed.

☆ J. Farrell MacDonald played Jiggs and Polly Moran played Maggie in *Bringing Up Father* (US 28). Orig: George McManus.

☆ *Skippy* (US 30) with Jackie Cooper. Orig: Percy Crosby.

☆ *Sooky* (US 31) with Robert Coogan in the name part and Jackie Cooper as Skippy. Orig: Percy Crosby.

☆ *Little Orphan Annie* (US 32) with Mitzi Green. Orig: Harold Gray and Al Lowenthal.

☆ *Harold Teen* (US 34) with Hal LeRoy. Orig: Carl Ed.

☆ *Tailspin Tommy* (US 34) with Maurice Murphy as the young flying ace. First serial based on comic strip. Orig: Hal Forrest.

☆ *Palooka* (US 34) with Stuart Erwin. Orig: Ham Fisher.

☆ *Tailspin Tommy and the Great Air Mystery* (US 35) with Clark Williams. Orig: Hal Forrest.

☆ *Flash Gordon* (US 36) with Buster Crabbe. Serial. Orig: Alex Raymond.

☆ *Jungle Jim* (US 37) with Grant Withers. Serial. Orig: Alex Raymond.

☆ *Tim Tyler's Luck* (US 37) with Frankie Thomas. Serial. Orig: Lyman Young.

☆ *Dick Tracy* (US 37) with Ralph Byrd. Serial. Orig: Chester Gould.

☆ *Radio Patrol* (US 37) with Grant Withers. Serial. Orig: Eddie Sullivan and Charles Schmidt.

☆ *Blondie* (US 38) with Penny Singleton in the title role and Arthur Lake as Dagwood. First of a

RALPH BYRD

DICK TRACY RETURNS

with LYNN ROBERTS

Based on *cartoon strip* by CHESTER GOULD

Directed by WILLIAM WITNEY · JOHN ENGUSH

Associate Producer · ROBERT BECHE

A *Republic* SERIAL in 15 SMASHING CHAPTERS

Dick Tracy returned long before Warren Beatty. The year was 1938 and war had broken out—on the streets of comic strip Hollywood. (*Kobal*)

series of 28 supporting features made by Columbia 1938–50. Orig: Chic Young.

☆ *Little Orphan Annie* (US 38) with Ann Gillis. Orig: Harold Gray and Al Lowenthal.

☆ *Flash Gordon's Trip to Mars* (US 38) with Buster Crabbe. Serial. Orig: Alex Raymond.

☆ *Dick Tracy Returns* (US 38) with Ralph Byrd. Serial. *Tracy's G-Men* (US 39). Orig: Chester Gould.

☆ John Trent as Tailspin Tommy in *Sky Patrol* (US 39). Serial. Orig: Hal Forrest.

☆ *Planet Outlaws* (US 39) with Buster Crabbe as Buck Rogers. Orig: Dick Calkins and Phil Nolan.

☆ *Buck Rogers* (US 39) with Buster Crabbe. Serial. Orig: Dick Calkins and Phil Nolan.

☆ *Mandrake the Magician* (US 39) with Warren Hull. Serial. Orig: Lee Falk and Phil Davis.

☆ *Li'l Abner* (US 40) with Granville Owen. Orig: Al Capp.

☆ *Flash Gordon Conquers the Universe* (US 40) with Buster Crabbe. Serial. Orig: Alex Raymond.

☆ *Adventures of Captain Marvel* (US 41) with Tom Tyler. Orig: C. C. Beck.

☆ *Tillie the Toiler* (US 41) with Kay Harris. Orig: Russ Westover.

☆ *Private Snuffy Smith* (US 42) with Bud Duncan. Orig: Billy de Beck.

☆ Bud Duncan as Snuffy Smith in *Hillbilly Blitzkrieg* (US 42). Orig: Billy de Beck.

☆ *Winslow of the Navy* (US 42) with Don Terry. Serial. Orig: Lt Com Frank Martinek.

☆ *Batman* (US 43) with Lewis Wilson as Batman, Douglas Croft as Robin. Serial. Orig: Bob Kane.

☆ *Don Winslow of the Coastguard* (US 43) with Don Terry. Serial. Orig: Lt Com Frank Martinek.

☆ *The Phantom* (US 43) with Tom Tyler. Serial. Orig: Lee Falk.

☆ *Dixie Dugan* (US 43) with Lois Andrews. Orig: Joseph McEvoy. In this case McEvoy's strip had itself been based on a film—*Show Girl* (US 28).

☆ *Captain America* (US 44) with Dick Purcell. Orig: Jack Kirby and Joe Simon.

☆ *Dick Tracy* (US 45) with Morgan Conway. Orig: Chester Gould.

☆ *Joe Palooka, Champ* (US 46) with Joe Kirkwood, who also starred in eight other Palooka movies 1947–51. Orig: Ham Fisher.

☆ Joe Yule as Jiggs and Renie Riano as Maggie in *Bringing Up Father* (US 46); also in *Jiggs and Maggie in Society* (US 48) and *Jiggs and Maggie Out West* (US 50). Orig: George McManus.

☆ *Dick Tracy vs Cueball* (US 46) with Morgan Conway. Orig: Chester Gould.

☆ *Dick Tracy's Dilemma* (US 47) and *Dick Tracy Meets Gruesome* (US 47) with Ralph Byrd. Orig: Chester Gould.

☆ *Superman* (US 48) with Kirk Alyn. Serial. Orig: Jerry Siegel and Joe Schuster.

☆ *Jungle Jim* (US 48) with Johnny Weissmuller in this and seven other Columbia low budgeters. Orig: Alex Raymond.

☆ *Bomba the Jungle Boy* (US 49) with Johnny Sheffield; first of series of 12 which continued to 1955. Orig: Roy Rockwell.

☆ *Batman and Robin* (US 49) with Robert Lowery as Batman, John Duncan as Robin. Serial. Orig: Bob Kane.

☆ *The Adventures of Jane* (GB 49) with Christabel Leighton-Porter. Orig: Norman Pett.

☆ *Atom Man vs Superman* (US 50) with Kirk Alyn as Superman. Serial. Orig: Jerry Siegel and Joe Schuster.

☆ Scotty Beckett as Corky and Jimmy Lydon as Skeezix in *Gasoline Alley* and *Corky of Gasoline Alley* (both US 51). Orig: Frank O. King.

☆ *Superman and the Mole Men* (US 51) with George Reeves. Orig: Jerry Siegel and Joe Schuster.

☆ *Blackhawk* (US 52) with Kirk Alyn. Orig: Reed Crandall and Charles Guidera.

☆ *Prince Valiant* (US 54) with Robert Wagner. Produced in colour and Cinemascope.

☆ *The Sad Sack* (US 57) with Jerry Lewis. Orig: George Baker.

☆ *Li'l Abner* (US 59) with Peter Palmer. Orig: Al Capp.

☆ *Dondi* (US 61) with David Kory. Orig: Gus Edson and Irwin Hasen.

☆ *Modesty Blaise* (GB 66) with Monica Vitti in title role and Terence Stamp as Willie Garvin. Orig: Peter O'Donnell and Jim Holdaway.

☆ *Batman* (US 66) with Adam West in title role and Burt Ward as Robin. Orig: Bob Kane.

☆ *Barbarella* (Fr/It 67) with Jane Fonda. Orig: Jean-Claude Forest.

☆ *The Adventures of Barry McKenzie* (Aus 72) with Barry Crocker; sequel *Barry McKenzie Holds His Own* (Aus 74). Orig: Barry Humphries—the only comic strip artist to have appeared in the films based on his strip.

☆ *Tiffany Jones* (GB 73) with Anouska Hempel. Orig: Pat Tourret and Jenny Butterworth.

☆ *Wonder Woman* (US 74, TVM) with tennis star Cathy Lee Crosby and *The New, Original Wonder Woman* (US 75, TVM) with Lynda Carter. Orig: Charles Moulton.

☆ *Friday Foster* (US 75) with Pam Grier, based on first comic strip with black heroine. Orig: Jorge Langaron.

☆ *Brenda Starr* (US 75, TVM) with Jill St John. Orig: Dale Messick.

☆ *The Incredible Hulk* (US 77, TVM) with Lou Ferrigno. Orig: Stan Lee.

☆ *Spider-Man* (US 77, TVM), *Spider-Man Strikes Back* (US 78) and *The Dragon's Challenge* (US 80) with Nicholas Hammond. Orig: Stan Lee.

☆ *Dr Strange* (US 78, TVM), with Peter Hooten. Orig: Stan Lee.

☆ *Superman* (GB 78) with Christopher Reeve; followed by *Superman II* (GB 81), *Superman III* (GB 84) and *Superman IV* (US 87). The first in the series was claimed to have been the most expensive film ever made. Orig: Jerry Siegel and Joe Schuster.

☆ *Captain America* (US 79, TVM) and *Captain America II* (US 79, TVM) with Reb Brown. Orig: Jack Kirby and Joe Simon.

☆ *Mandrake* (US 79, TVM) with Anthony Herrerra. Orig: Lee Falk and Phil Davis.

☆ *Buck Rogers* (US 79) with Gil Gerard. Orig: Dick Calkins.

☆ *Fatty Finn* (Aus 80) with Ben Oxenbould. Orig: Syd Nicholls.

☆ *Flash Gordon* (GB 80) with Sam J. Jones. Orig: Alex Raymond.

☆ *Popeye* (US 80) with Robin Williams and Shelley Duvall as Olive Oyl. Orig: Elzie Crisler Segar.

☆ *Swamp Thing* (US 82) with Dick Durock as the Thing. Orig: DC Comics.

☆ *Conan the Barbarian* (82) with Arnold Schwarzenegger. Orig: Robert E. Howard.

☆ *Annie* (US 82) with Aileen Quinn as Little Orphan Annie. Orig: Harold Gray and Al Lowenthal.

☆ *Ginger Meggs* (Aus 82) with Paul Daniel. Orig: James Bancks.

☆ *Supergirl* (GB 84) with Helen Slater. Orig: Otto Binder.

☆ *Conan the Destroyer* (US 84) with Arnold Schwarzenegger. Orig: Robert E. Howard.

☆ *Sheena Queen of the Jungle* (US 84) with Tanya Roberts. Orig: Sam Iger and Will Eisner.

☆ *Howard the Duck* (US 86) with Ed Gale, Chip Zien, Tim Rose, Steve Sleap, Peter Baird, Mary Wells, Lisa Sturz and Jordan Prentice taking it in turns to play the eponymous hero. Orig: Steve Gerber.

☆ *Jane and the Lost City* (GB 87) with Kirsten Hughes. Orig: Norman Pett.

☆ *The Spirit* (US 87, TVM) with Sam Jones. Orig: Will Eisner.

☆ *The Incredible Hulk Returns* (US 88, TVM), *The Trial of the Incredible Hulk* (US 89, TVM), *The Death of the Incredible Hulk* (US 90, TVM) with Lou Ferrigno as Hulk, Bill Bixby as alter ego David Banner. Orig: Stan Lee.

☆ *Batman* (US 89) with Michael Keaton. Orig: Bob Kane.

☆ *The Return of Swamp Thing* (US 89) with Dick Durock. Orig: DC Comics.

☆ *Spider-Man* (US 89) with Don Michael Paul. Orig: Stan Lee.

☆ *The Punisher* (Aus 90) with Dolph Lundgren as Frank Castle. Orig: Marvel Comics.

☆ *Archie: To Riverdale and Back Again* (US 90, TVM) with Christopher Rich. Orig: John L. Goldwater.

☆ *The Flash* (US 90, TVM) with John Wesley Shipp. Orig: Harry Lampert.

☆ *Dick Tracy* (US 90) with Warren Beatty. Orig: Chester Gould.

☆ *Brenda Starr* (US 91) with Brooke Shields. Orig: Dale Messick.

☆ *Teenage Mutant Ninja Turtles* (US 90) with Josh Pais as Raphael, Michelan Sisti as Michelangelo, Leif Tilden as Donatello, David Forman as Leonardo. *Teenage Mutant Ninja Turtles II: The Secret of Ooze* (US 91) with Ken Troum and Mark Caso. Orig: Kevin Eastman and Peter Laird.

☆ *The Rocketeer* (US 91) with Bill Campbell. Orig: Dave Stevens.

*B*IOPICS

The historical character who has been represented most often on screen is Napoléon Bonaparte (1769–1821), Emperor of the French. The role has been played in at least 194 films to date.

Other historical characters most often represented on screen include Jesus Christ, of whom there are 147 recorded film portrayals; Vladimir Ilich Lenin (1870–1924) —86; Adolf Hitler (1889–1945) —74; Cleopatra (69–30 BC) —40; Queen Victoria (1819–1901) —38; Josef Stalin (1879–1953) —38; Henry VIII (1491–1547) —34; Queen Elizabeth I (1553–1603) —32; Pancho Villa (1877–1923) —30; Grigori Rasputin (1871?– 1916) —29; St Joan of Arc (c. 1412–31) —29; Sir Winston Churchill (1874–1965) —21. The US President most often portrayed on screen has been Abraham Lincoln in 136 films. See pp. 50. Queen Elizabeth II (1926–) was portrayed for the first time by Jeanette Charles in *Marcia* (GB 77) and subsequently by Dana Winter in *The Royal Romance of Charles and Diana* (US 82, TVM), Jeanette Charles again in *The Naked Gun* (US 89) and by Mary Reynolds in *Bullseye!* (US 90). The first screen portrayal of Mrs Thatcher (1925–) was by Janet Brown in the James Bond movie *For Your Eyes Only* (GB 81), with John Wells as Denis, fol-

lowed by Kathleen Smith in *Bullseye!* (US 90).
David Lloyd Austin brought President Gorbachev
to the screen for the first time in *The Naked Gun*
(US 89). See also Western heroes (p. 71–72).
**The first portrayal of a reigning British mon-
arch** was by Thomas R. Mills, who played King
George V (1865–1936) in a fictionalized version of
Sir Roger Casement's life *Whom the Gods Destroy*
(US 16).

A courtly Leslie Nielson bows to the waist in this
close encounter with HM Queen Elizabeth II
(Jeannette Charles) in *The Naked Gun* (US 89).
(British Film Institute)

US PRESIDENTS

The President of the United States **most often
portrayed on film,** as well as **America's most
oft portrayed historical character,** is
Abraham Lincoln (1809–65). The role has been
played in the 136 films listed, as well as a
quantity of educational subjects. This
filmography of representations of US Presidents
cites the actor playing the presidential role
where known, though in some films the actor
has been uncredited. The date preceding the
presidents' names is the year of inauguration.

1789 GEORGE WASHINGTON (1732–99)
Washington at Valley Forge (US 08)
Barbara Freitchie (US 08)
Benedict Arnold and Major Andre (US 09)
Phillips Smalley *A Heroine of '76* (US 11)
Peter Leon *Washington at Valley Forge* (US 14)
William Worthington *The Spy* (US 14)
Charles Ogle *Molly, the Drummer Boy* (US 14)
Joseph Kilgour *The Battle Cry of Peace* (US 15)
Joseph Kilgour *The Dawn of Freedom* (US 16)
George MacQuarrie *Betsy Ross* (US 17)
Noah Beery *The Spirit of '76* (US 17)
A Daughter of War (US 17)
George MacQuarrie *The Beautiful Mrs Reynolds*
(US 18)
Harold Judson *Deliverence* (US 19)
Schoolmaster Matsumoto (Jap 19)
Arthur Dewey *America* (US 24)
Joseph Kilgour *Janice Meredith* (US 24)
Francis X. Bushman *The Flag* (US 27)

Edward Hern *The Winners of the Wilderness* (US
27)
Alan Mowbray *Alexander Hamilton* (US 31);
The Phantom President (US 32)
Aaron Edwards *Are We Civilized?* (US 34)
George Houston *The Howards of Virginia* (US
40)
Montague Love *Remarkable Andrew* (US 42)
Alan Mowbray *Where Do We Go From Here?*
(US 45)
Douglass Dumbrille *Monsieur Beaucaire* (US
46)
Robert Barrat *The Time of their Lives* (US 46)
Richard Gaines *Unconquered* (US 47)
James Seay *When the Redskins Rode* (US 51)
John Crawford *John Paul Jones* (US 59)
Howard St John *Lafayette* (Fr 62)
Washington at Valley Forge (US 71)
Lorne Green *Washington—The Man* (US c. 75)
Patrick O'Neal *Independence* (US 76)
Barry Bostwick *George Washington* (US 84,
TVM); *George Washington II: The Forging of a
Nation* (US 86 TVM)
Frank Windsor *Revolution* (GB 86)

1797 JOHN ADAMS (1735–1826)
Jack Drumier *The Beautiful Mrs Reynolds* (US
18)
John Paul Jones (US 59)
William Daniels *1776* (US 72)
Pat Hingle *Independence* (US 76)
Hal Holbrook *George Washington* (US 84,
TVM)

Paul Collins *George Washington II: The Forging
of a Nation* (US 86, TVM)

1801 THOMAS JEFFERSON (1743–1826)
A Continental Girl (US 15)
Charles Jackson *The Heart of a Hero* (US 16)
Albert Hart *The Beautiful Mrs Reynolds* (US
18)
P. R. Scammon *My Own United States* (US 18)
Lionel Adams *Janice Meredith* (US 24)
Frank Walsh *America* (US 24)
Albert Hart *The Man Without a Country* (US
25)
Old Ironsides (US 26)
Montague Love *Alexander Hamilton* (US 31)
The Phantom President (US 32)
George Irving *Hearts Divided* (US 36)
Guy Bates Post *Maytime* (US 37)
The Howards of Virginia (US 40)
Gilbert Emery *The Remarkable Andrew* (US
42); *The Loves of Edgar Allan Poe* (US 42)
Grandon Rhodes *The Magnificent Doll* (US 46)
Holmes Herbert *Barbary Pirate* (US 49)
Herbert Heyes *The Far Horizons* (US 55)
John Paul Jones (US 59)
Ken Howard *1776* (US 72); *Independence* (US
76)
Jeffrey Jones *George Washington II: The Forging
of a Nation* (US 86, TVM)

1809 JAMES MADISON (1751–1836)
Burgess Meredith *The Magnificent Doll* (US 46)
Guy Paul *George Washington II: The Forging of a
Nation* (US 86, TVM)

US PRESIDENTS (continued)

1817 JAMES MONROE (1758–1831)
Charles Brandt *The Beautiful Mrs Reynolds* (US 18)
The Spirit of Lafayette (US 19)
Emmett King *The Man Without a Country* (US 25)
Morgan Wallace *Alexander Hamilton* (US 31)
Robert Kelly *George Washington II: The Forging of a Nation* (US 86, TVM)

1825 JOHN QUINCY ADAMS (1767–1848)
No portrayals on screen

1829 ANDREW JACKSON (1767–1845)
F. C. Earle *My Own United States* (US 18)
George Irving *The Eagle of the Sea* (US 26)
Russell Simpson *The Frontiersman* (US 27)
Lionel Barrymore *The Gorgeous Hussy* (US 36)
Hugh Sothern *The Buccaneer* (US 38)
Edward Ellis *Man of Conquest* (US 39)
Brian Donlevy *The Remarkable Andrew* (US 42)
Der unendliche Weg (Ger 43)
Lionel Barrymore *Lone Star* (US 52)
Charlton Heston *The President's Lady* (US 53)
Basil Ruysdael *Davy Crockett, King of the Wild Frontier* (US 55)
Carl Brenton Reid *The First Texan* (US 56)
Charlton Heston *The Buccaneer* (US 58)
John Anderson *Bridger* (US 76, TVM)
G. D. Spradlin *Houston: The Legend of Texas* (US 86, TVM)
Matt Salinger (young Jackson) and David Hemmings (older Jackson) *Davy Crockett: Rainbow in the Thunder* (US 88, TVM)

1837 MARTIN VAN BUREN (1782–1862)
Charles Trowbridge *The Gorgeous Hussy* (US 36)

1841 WILLIAM HENRY HARRISON (1773–1841)
Douglass Dumbrille *Ten Gentlemen from West Point* (US 42)
George Eldredge *Brave Warrior* (US 52)

1841 JOHN TYLER (1790–1862)
No portrayals on screen

1845 JAMES KNOX POLK (1795–1849)
Addison Richards *The Oregon Trail* (US 59)
Noble Willingham *Dream West* (US 86, TVM)

1849 ZACHARY TAYLOR (1784–1850)
The Fall of Black Hawk (US 12)
Harry Holden *The Yankee Clipper* (US 27)
Robert Barrat *Distant Drums* (US 51)
Fay Roope *Seminole* (US 53)

1850 MILLARD FILLMORE (1800–74)
No portrayals on screen

1853 FRANKLIN PIERCE (1804–69)
Porter Hall *The Great Moment* (US 44)

1857 JAMES BUCHANAN (1791–1868)
No portrayals on screen

1861 ABRAHAM LINCOLN (1809–65)
Uncle Tom's Cabin (US 03)
The Blue and the Grey (US 08)
The Reprieve (US 08)
The Life of Abraham Lincoln (US 08)
The Assassination of Abraham Lincoln (US 09)
Stirring Days in Old Virginia (US 09)
George Stelle *The Sleeping Sentinel* (US 10)
Abraham Lincoln's Clemency (US 11)
The Old Man and Jim (US 11)
The Fortunes of War (US 11)
James Dayton *Lieutenant Grey* (US 11)
Ralph Ince *Under One Flag* (US 11)
A Romance of the '60's (US 11)
Ralph Ince *The Battle Hymn of the Republic* (US 11)
Grant and Lincoln (US 11)
Ralph Ince *The Seventh Son* (US 12)

H. G. Lonsdale *The Fall of Black Hawk* (US 12)
Ralph Ince *Lincoln's Gettysburg Address* (US 12)
Francis Ford *On Secret Service* (US 12); *When Lincoln Paid* (US 12)
When Lincoln was President (US 13)
Hugh Ford *With Lee in Virginia* (US 13)
From Rail Splitter to President (US 13)
William Clifford *The Toll of War* (US 13)
Lincoln for the Defense (US 13)
Ralph Ince *Songbird of the North* (US 13)
Willard Mack *The Battle of Gettysburg* (US 13)
Ralph Ince *Lincoln the Lover* (US 14); *The Man Who Knew Lincoln* (US 14)
Benjamin Chapin *Lincoln's Thanksgiving Story* (US 14) not released
The Sleeping Sentinel (US 14)
Benjamin Chapin *Old Abe* (US 15)
The Magistrate's Story (US 15)
Joseph Henabery *The Birth of a Nation* (US 15)
Francis Ford *The Heart of Lincoln* (US 15)
William Ferguson *The Battle Cry of Peace* (US 15)
Frank McGlynn *The Life of Abraham Lincoln* (US 15)
The Heart of Maryland (US 15)
Samuel Drane *The Crisis* (US 16)
Benjamin Chapin 10 one-reelers collectively known as *The Lincoln Cycle* (US 17)
Ralph Ince *Battle Hymn of the Republic* (US 17)
Clarence Barr *Madame Who* (US 18)
Gerald Day *My Own United States* (US 18)
Benjamin Chapin *Down the River* (US 18)
Rolf Leslie *Victory and Peace* (GB 18)
Benjamin Chapin *Lincoln's Thanksgiving Story* (US 18); *Children of Democracy* (US 18); *Son of Democracy* (US 18)
Meyer F. Stroell *The Copperhead* (US 19)
The Land of Opportunity (US 20)
Ralph Ince *The Highest Law* (US 21)
Ellery Paine *Lincoln's Gettysburg Address* (US 22) talkie
Wild Bill Hickock (US 23)
The Heart of Abraham Lincoln (US 24)
Ellery Paine (?) *An Episode in the Life of Abraham Lincoln* (US 24) talkie
George A. Billings *Barbara Freitchie* (US 24); *The Dramatic Life of Abraham Lincoln* (US 24)
Charles E. Bull *The Iron Horse* (US 24)
George A. Billings *The Man Without a Country* (US 25); *Hands Up* (US 26)
Charles E. Bull *The Heart of Maryland* (US 27)
Rev. Lincoln Caswell *Lincoln's Gettysburg Address* (US 27) talkie
Uncle Tom's Cabin (US 27)
The Heart of Lincoln (US 27)
Frank Austin *Court Martial* (US 28)
Walter Houston *Two Americans* (US 29)
George A. Billings *Lincoln's Gettysburg Address* (US 30)
Only the Brave (US 30)
Walter Houston *Abraham Lincoln* (US 30)
The Phantom President (US 32)
Frank McGlynn *Abraham Lincoln, the Pioneer* (US 33); *Abraham Lincoln, the Statesman* (US 33); *Are We Civilized?* (US 34); *The Littlest Rebel* (US 35); *Roaring West* (US 35)
Chic Sale *The Perfect Tribute* (US 35)
Frank McGlynn *The Prisoner of Shark Island* (US 36); *Hearts in Bondage* (US 36)
Segraren vid Hampton Roads (Swe c. 36)
Bud Buster *Cavalry* (US 36)
Frank McGlynn *Western Gold* (US 37); *Wells Fargo* (US 37); *The Man Without a Country* (US 37); *The Plainsman* (US 37)
Albert Russell *Courage of the West* (US 37)
Triumph (GB? 37)
Percy Parsons *Victoria the Great* (GB 37)

Frank McGlynn *The Lone Ranger* (US 37); *The Mad Empress* (Mex 39)
A Failure at Fifty (US 39)
Frank McGlynn *Lincoln in the White House* (US 39)
Frank McGlynn and Walter Huston *Land of Liberty* (US 39) compilation film
John Carradine *Of Human Hearts* (US 39)
Henry Fonda *Young Mr Lincoln* (US 39)
Raymond Massey *Abe Lincoln in Illinois* (US 39)
Gene Reynolds *The Blue Bird* (US 40)
Victor Killain *Virginia City* (US 40)
Charles Middleton *Sante Fe Trail* (US 40)
A Dispatch from Reuters (US 40)
Dreams (US 40)
Not Long Remember (US 41)
Charles Middleton *They Died With Their Boots On* (US 41)
Ed O'Neill *Tennessee Johnson* (US 42)
Joel Day *The Days of Buffalo Bill* (US 46)
Charles Middleton *The Decision of Christopher Blake* (US 48)
Jeff Corey *Rock Island Trail* (US 50); *Transcontinent Express* (US 50)
G. William Horsley *Lincoln in Illinois* (US 50)
Hans Conreid *New Mexico* (US 51)
Leslie Kimmell *The Tall Target* (US 51)
Thomas Mitchell (?) *The Lincoln-Holmes Incident, a Folktale* (US 52)
Richard Hale *San Antone* (US 53)
Suddenly (US 54)
James Griffith *Apache Ambush* (US 55)
Stanley Hall *The Prince of Players* (US 55)
The Palmetto Conspiracy (US 55)
Tom Tryon *Springfield Incident* (US 55)
The Abductors (US 57) corpse only
Austin Green *The Story of Mankind* (US 57)
Royal Dano *Lincoln: The Young Years* (US c. 59, TVM)
Lincoln at Gettysburg (US 60)
The Boyhood of Abraham Lincoln (US 62)
Raymond Massey *How the West was Won* (US 63)
Uncle Tom's Cabin (FRG 65)
Jeff Corey *Der Schatz der Azteken* (FRG/Fr/It/Yug 65)
Dennis Weaver *The Great Man's Whiskers* (US 71)
Charlton Heston *Lincoln's Gettysburg Address* (US 73)
Arthur Hill *The Rivalry* (US 75)
William Deprato *The Faking of the President* (US 76)
John Anderson *The Lincoln Conspiracy* (US 77)
Ford Rainey *Guardian of the Wilderness* (US 77)
Gregory Peck *The Blue and the Gray* (US 82, TVM)
Hal Holbrook *North and South* (US 85, TVM); *North and South Book II* (US 86, TVM)
F. Murray Abraham *Dream West* (US 86, TVM)
Sam Waterston *Gore Vidal's Lincoln* (US 88, TVM)
Robert V. Barron *Bill and Ted's Excellent Adventure* (US 89)
The Rose and the Jackal (US 90, TVM)
Jason Robards *The Perfect Tribute* (US 91, TVM)

1865 ANDREW JOHNSON (1808–75)
Van Heflin *Tennessee Johnson* (US 42)
Bill Hindman *The Ordeal of Dr Mudd* (US 80, TVM)

1869 ULYSSES SIMPSON GRANT (1822–85)
Barbara Freitchie (US 08)
Stirring Days in Old Virginia (US 08)
The Blue and the Gray (US 08)
The Old Soldier's Story (US 09)

The Bugle Call (US 09)
From Wallace to Grant (US 11)
Alvin Wyckoff *Lieutenant Grey of the Confederacy* (US 11)
Grant and Lincoln (US 11)
With Lee in Virginia (US 13)
John Smiley *The Battle of Shiloh* (US 13)
The Littlest Rebel (US 14)
Paul Scardon *The Battle Cry of Peace* (US 15)
Donald Crisp *The Birth of a Nation* (US 15)
Frank Murray *My Own United States* (US 18)
Wilbur J. Fox *The Warrens of Virginia* (US 24)
Walter Rogers *Abraham Lincoln* (US 24)
Dixie (US 24)
Walter Rogers *Flaming Frontier* (US 26); *The Heart of Maryland* (US 27); *The Little Shepherd of Kingdom Come* (US 28)
Court-Martial (US 28)
Fred Warren *Abraham Lincoln* (US 30)
Guy Oliver *Only the Brave* (US 30)
Fred Warren *Secret Service* (US 31)
Walter Rogers *Silver Dollar* (US 32)
Fred Warren *Operator 13* (US 34)
Gold is Where You Find It (US 38)
Joseph Crehan *Union Pacific* (US 39); *Geronimo* (US 39)
Harrison Greene *The Son of Davy Crockett* (US 41); *Tennessee Johnson* (US 42)
Joseph Crehan *They Died With Their Boots On* (US 42); *The Adventures of Mark Twain* (US 44)
Reginald Sheffield *Centennial Summer* (US 46)
John Hamilton *The Fabulous Texan* (US 47)
Joseph Crehan *Silver River* (US 48)
Sunset at Appotomax (US 53)
John Hamilton *Sitting Bull* (US 54)
Hayden Rorke *Drum Beat* (US 54)
Morris Ankrum *From the Earth to the Moon* (US 58)
Stan Jones *The Horse Soldiers* (US 59)
Henry Morgan *How the West was Won* (US 63)
Buffalo Bill, l'eroe del Far West (It/Fr/FRG 65)
Antonio Albaisin (?) *Ringo e Gringo contro tutti* (It 66)
John McLiam *Freedom Road* (US 79, TVM)
Jason Robards *The Legend of the Lone Ranger* (US 81)
Rip Torn *The Blue and the Gray* (US 82, TVM)
Mark Moses *North and South* (US 85, TVM)
Anthony Zerbe *North and South, Book II* (US 86, TVM)
Alan North *Liberty* (US 86, TVM)
James Gamman *Gore Vidal's Lincoln* (US 88, TVM)
Stanley Anderson *Son of the Morning Star* (US 91, TVM)

1877 RUTHERFORD BIRCHARD HAYES (1822–93)
John Dilson *Buffalo Bill* (US 44)

1881 JAMES ABRAM GARFIELD (1831–81)
Night Raiders (US 39)
Lawrence Wolf *No More Excuses* (US 68)
Van Johnson *Il prezzo del potere* (It/Sp 69)

1881 CHESTER ALAN ARTHUR (1831–86)
Emmett Corrigan *Silver Dollar* (US 32)
Larry Gates *Cattle King* (US 63)

1885 and **1893** STEPHEN GROVER CLEVELAND (1837–1908)
Topack *Lively Political Debate* (US 94)
William B. Davison *Lillian Russell* (US 40)
Pat McCormick *Buffalo Bill and the Indians* (US 76)
Wilford A. Brimley *The Wild Wild West Revisited* (US 79, TVM)
Haji Washington (Iran 83)

1889 BENJAMIN HARRISON (1833–1901)
Steele *Lively Political Debate* (US 94)
Roy Gordon *Stars and Stripes Forever* (US 52)

1897 WILLIAM MCKINLEY (1843–1901)
A Message to Garcia (US 16)
Del Henderson *A Message to Garcia* (US 36)
Frank Conroy *This is My Affair* (US 37)

1901 THEODORE ROOSEVELT (1858–1919)
Terrible Teddy, The Grizzly King (US 01)
The 'Teddy' Bears (US 07)
Big Game Hunting in Africa (US 09) reconstruction newsfilm with actor portraying T.R.
Up San Juan Hill (US 09)
T.R. as himself in unidentified one-reel comedy starring Matty Roubert (US 14)
T.R. himself in *Womanhood, the Glory of a Nation* (US 17)
W.E. Whittle *Why America Will Win* (US 18)
W. E. Whittle *General Pershing* (US 19)
Francis J. Noonan (boy), Herbert Bradshaw (young man), E. J. Ratcliffe *The Fighting Roosevelts* (US 19)
Jack Ridgeway *The Copperhead* (US 19)
E. J. Radcliffe *Sundown* (US 24)
Buck Black *Lights of Old Broadway* (US 25)
Frank Hopper *The Rough Riders* (US 27)
The Man Who Dared (US 33)
I Loved a Woman (US 33)
Erle C. Kent *The End of the Trail* (US 36)
Sidney Blackmer *This Is My Affair* (US 37)
Wallis Clark *Jack London* (US 43)
Sidney Blackmer *In Old Oklahoma* (US 43); *Buffalo Bill* (US 44)
John Merton *I Wonder Who's Kissing Her Now?* (US 47)
Sidney Blackmer *My Girl Tisa* (US 48)
Take Me Out to the Ballgame (US 49)
John Alexander *Fancy Pants* (US 50)
Edward Cassidy *The First Travelling Saleslady* (US 56)
Karl Swenson *Brighty of the Grand Canyon* (US 66)
Brian Keith *The Wind and the Lion* (US 75)
William Phipps *Eleanor and Franklin* (US 76, TVM)
David Healy *Eleanor and Franklin: The White House Years* (US 77, TVM)
James Whitmore *Bully* (US 78)
Robert Boyd *Ragtime* (US 81)
Walter Massey *Cook and Peary: The Race to the Pole* (US 83, TVM)
Bob Boyd *The Indominatable Teddy Roosevelt* (US 85)

1909 WILLIAM HOWARD TAFT (1857–1930)
The Sculptor's Nightmare (US 08)
Ross Durfee *The Winds of Kitty Hawk* (US 78, TVM)

1913 THOMAS WOODROW WILSON (1856–1924)
himself in introduction to *The Battle Cry of Peace* (US 15)
himself *The Adventures of a Boy Scout* (US 15)
himself *Womanhood, the Glory of a Nation* (US 17)
Ralph C. Faulkner *Why America Will Win* (US 18)
Ralph C. Faulkner *On the Dump* (US 18)
Ralph C. Faulkner *The Prussian Cur* (US 18)
Orlo Eastman *The Kaiser, The Beast of Berlin* (US 18)
Fred C. Truesdell *The Great Victory* (US 19)
Ralph C. Faulkner *General Pershing* (US 19)
Turn Back the Clock (US 33)
Alexander Knox *Wilson* (US 44)
Earl Lee *The Story of Will Rogers* (US 52)
L. Kovsakov *The Unforgettable Year 1919* (USSR 52)
Frank Forsyth *Oh! What a Lovely War* (GB 69)
Jerzy Kaliszewski *Polonia Restituta* (Pol/USSR/Hun/Cz/GDR 81)
Robert Webber *Shooting Star* (US 83, TVM)

1921 WARREN GAMALIEL HARDING (1865–1923)
No portrayals on screen

1923 JOHN CALVIN COOLIDGE (1872–1933)
Ian Wolfe *The Court Martial of Billy Mitchell* (US 55)

1929 HERBERT CLARK HOOVER (1874–1964)
Tom Jensen *Fires of Youth* (US 31)
Franklin Cover *The Day the Bubble Burst* (US 82, TVM)

1933 FRANKLIN DELANO ROOSEVELT (1882–1945)
himself (Assistant Secretary to the Navy) *The Battle Cry of Peace* (US 15)
Capt. Jack Young *Yankee Doodle Dandy* (US 42); *This is the Army* (US 43)
Herr Roosevelt Plaudert (Ger 43)
Jack Young *Mission to Moscow* (US 43)
Godfrey Tearle *The Beginning or the End?* (US 47)
Nikolai Cherkasov *The First Front* (USSR 49)
Secret Mission (USSR 50)
Beau James (US 57)
Ralph Bellamy *Sunrise at Campobello* (US 60)
Richard Nelson *The Pigeon that Took Rome* (US 62)
McHale's Navy Joins the Air Force (US 68)
Stephen Roberts *First to Fight* (US 67)
Stanislav Jaskevik *Liberation* (USSR 70–71)
Edward Herrmann *Eleanor and Franklin* (US 76, TVM)
Dan O'Herlihy *MacArthur—The Rebel General* (US 77)
Stephen Roberts *Ring of Passion* (US 77, TVM)
Edward Herrmann *Eleanor and Franklin: The White House Years* (US 77, TVM)
Howard Da Silva *The Private Files of J. Edgar Hoover* (US 78)
Stephen Roberts *Ike* (US 79, TVM)
Jason Robards *F.D.R.: The Last Year* (US 80, TVM)
Stephen Roberts *Enola Gay* (US 80, TVM)
Teheran '43 (USSR/Fr/Swz 81)
Edward Herrmann *Annie* (US 82)
Ralph Bellamy *The Winds of War* (US 83, TVM)
Robert Vaughan *Murrow* (US/GB 86, TVM)
Jack Denton *Crossings* (US 86, TVM)
David Ogden Stiers *J. Edgar Hoover* (US 87, TVM)
Margaret Bourke-White (US 89, TVM)

1945 HARRY S. TRUMAN (1884–1972)
Art Baker *The Beginning or the End?* (US 47)
Secret Mission (USSR 50)
Call Me Madam (US 53)
uncredited child *Alias Jesse James* (US 59)
James Whitmore *Give 'Em Hell, Harry!* (US 75)
E. G. Marshall *Collision Course* (US 76)
Ed Flanders *MacArthur—The Rebel General* (US 77)
Robert Symonds *Tail Gunner Joe* (US 77, TVM)
Enola Gay (US 80, TVM)
Richard McKenzie *Eleanor, First Lady of the World* (US 82)
Algimantas Masiulis *Victory* (USSR 86)
Ed Nelson *Brenda Starr* (US 1991)

1953 DWIGHT DAVID EISENHOWER (1890–1969)
Willis Bouchey *Red Planet Mars* (US 52)
The Outsider (US 61)
Harry Carey Jr *The Long Grey Line* (US 55)
Henry Grace *The Longest Day* (US 72)
James Flavin *Francis Gary Powers* (US 76, TVM)
Andrew Duggan *Tail Gunner Joe* (US 77, TVM)
Robert Duvall *Ike* (US 79, TVM)
Robert Beer *The Right Stuff* (US 83)
Richard Dysart *The Last Days of Patton* (US 86, TVM)

1961 JOHN FITZGERALD KENNEDY (1917–63)
Kennedy in his True Colours (Chn 62)

 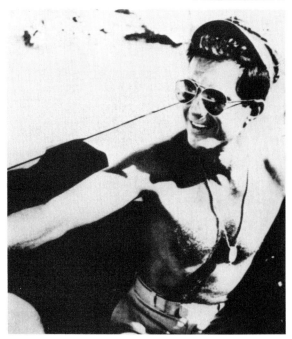

Left: John Fitzgerald Kennedy as a young PT boat commander during World War II. *Right*: Cliff Robertson as the future President in *PT 109* (US 63).

Cliff Robertson *PT 109* (US 63)
Gas-s-s-s (US 70)
Martin Sheen *The Missiles of October* (US 74, TVM)
William Jordan *The Private Files of J. Edgar Hoover* (US 77)
Sam Chew *Young Joe, the Forgotten Kennedy* (US 77, TVM)
Paul Rudd *Johnny We Hardly Knew Ye* (US 77, TVM)
William Jordan *King* (US 78, TVM)
James Franciscus *Jacqueline Bouvier Kennedy* (US 82, TVM)
Sam Groom *Blood Feud* (US 83, TVM)
Martin Sheen *Kennedy* (GB 83, TVM)
Robert Hogan *Prince Jack* (US 84, TVM)
Cliff DeYoung *Robert Kennedy and His Times* (US 85, TVM)
Charles Frank *LBJ The Early Years* (US 87, TVM)

1963 LYNDON BAINES JOHNSON (1908–73)
Ivan Treisault *How to Succeed in Business without Really Trying* (US 67)
Colpo di Stato (It 68)
The Wrecking Crew (US 69)
Andrew Duggan *The Private Files of J. Edgar Hoover* (US 77)
Warren Kemmerling *King* (US 78, TVM)
Nesbitt Blaisdell *Kennedy* (GB 83, TVM)
Forrest Tucker *Blood Feud* (US 83, TVM)
Donald Moffat *The Right Stuff* (US 83)
Kenneth Mars *Prince Jack* (US 84, TVM)
GD Spradlin *Robert Kennedy and His Times* (US 87, TVM)
Rip Torn *J. Edgar Hoover* (US 87, TVM)
Randy Quaid *LBJ The Early Years* (US 87, TVM)

1969 RICHARD MILHOUS NIXON (1913–)
Jean-Pierre Biesse *Made in USA* (Fr 67)
The Statue (GB 70)
Cold Turkey (US 71)
Million Dollar Duck (US 71)
Jim Dixon *Is There Sex After Death?* (US 71)
Dan Resin as young Nixon and Richard Dixon as older Nixon in *Richard* (US 72)
Richard Dixon *The Faking of the President 1974* (US 76) ; *The Private Files of J. Edgar Hoover* (US 77) ; *Tail Gunner Joe* (US 77, TVM)

Anderson Humphreys *The Cayman Triangle* (CayI 77)
Harry Spillman *Born Again* (US 78)
Richard M. Dixon *Hopscotch* (US 80) ; *Where the Buffalo Roam* (US 80)
Philip Baker Hall *Secret Honor: The Last Testament of Richard M. Nixon* (US 84, TVM)
Anthony Palmer *J. Edgar Hoover* (US 87, TVM)

1974 GERALD RUDOLPH FORD (1913–)
Dick Crockett *The Pink Panther Strikes Again* (GB 76)

1977 JAMES EARL CARTER (1924–)
Ed Beheler *The Cayman Triangle* (CayI 77)
Black Sunday (US 77)
Walt Hanna *Sadat* (US 83, TVM)
himself *Special Counsel* (US 88)
Ken Jenkins *The Final Days* (US 90, TVM)

1981 RONALD REAGAN (1911–)
himself in *It's a Great Feeling* (US 49)
Bryan Clark *Without Warning: The James Brady Story* (US 91, TVM)

1989 GEORGE BUSH (1924–)
Fred Travelena *Comedy in the Oval Office* (US 89, TVM)

*B*LACK FILMS

The first black film was *The Railroad Porter* (US 12), a chase comedy with an all-black cast directed by pioneer black film-maker Bill Foster.

The first black production company was the Lincoln Motion Picture Co., founded in Los Angeles in 1915 by black actors Clarence Brooks and Noble Johnson, a prosperous black druggist called James T. Smith and white cameraman Harry Grant. The company's first release was *The Realisation of a*

Negro's Ambition (US 16), with Noble Johnson starring as an oil engineer who makes good.

The first black feature film was the Frederick

Romance between white and black was treated for the first time in an English-language film in *Pool of London* (GB 50), with Susan Shaw and Earl Cameron (*top left*). In America the subject remained too hot to handle until *Island in the Sun* (US 59) offered twin romances between John Justin and Dorothy Dandridge (*above*) and Harry Belafonte and Joan Fontaine (*left*).

Douglass Film Co.'s six-reel *The Coloured American Winning his Suit* (US 16), which was premièred at Jersey City on 14 July 1916. The all-black cast was largely amateur, made up of 'young men and women of the race from . . . the best families in New Jersey'.

The first black talkie was Christie Comedies' two-reel *Melancholy Dame* (US 28), featuring Roberta Hyson and Spencer Williams. The picture was about black 'high society' in Birmingham, Ala.

The first feature-length black talkie was MGM's *Hallelujah!* (US 29), directed by King Vidor and starring Daniel Haynes. **The first made by a black production company** was the Oscar Micheaux Corporation's *The Exile* (US 31), directed by Oscar Micheaux and starring Stanley Murrell.

The first feature-length film produced by blacks in Britain was Horace Ové's *Reggae* (GB 70), a 60-minute documentary about the distinctive Jamaican music form. **The first dramatic feature** was Horace Ové's *Pressure*, made on location in the Ladbroke Grove area of London in 1974, but not released until February 1978. Originally commissioned by the BBC, but rejected as 'too heavy', the film told the story of a British-born younger son (Herbert Norville) of an immigrant family from Trinidad who finds himself adrift between two cultures. **The first dramatic feature released** in Britain was *Black Joy* (GB 77), a delightful comedy about an innocent and unsophisticated Guyanan immigrant (Trevor Thomas) exposed to the hustlin' way of life of the Brixton ghetto.

Black Films Made by the Major Studios

During the silent period the 'majors' showed little or no interest in black movies and even when black characters were required they were generally played by white actors in black-face. D. W. Griffith's *The*

Birth of a Nation (US 15) had a large cast of black roles, since the controversial plot revolved round the black 'takeover' of the South following the Civil War, yet only one genuine black—the curiously named Madame Sul-Te-Wan—was employed on the film.

The coming of sound altered the picture, since the trend towards greater realism demanded that blacks be played by blacks, though their roles were generally confined to the menial or the comic (usually both combined). At the same time the major studios began to turn out the occasional all-black picture,

> Miscegenation ceased to be controversial in the 70s, though it can still arouse passions, albeit different ones. In 1990 the *New York Times* refused to accept an advertisement for *How to Make Love to a Negro without Getting Tired* (Fr 89), based on a comic novel of the same title by black Haitian writer Dary Laferrière. According to the distributors, no black people had objected, only white liberals. The *New York Times* admitted they had turned down the ad because they found the title 'racially offensive'.

most of them dependent upon the vocal talents of the black American and aimed principally at white audiences. Those made prior to the sudden explosion of 'superspade' black exploitation pictures in the late sixties were as follows: *Hallelujah!* (MGM 29) with Daniel Haynes; *Hearts in Dixie* (Fox 29) with Clarence Muse; *Green Pastures* (Warner 36) with Rex Ingram; *Stormy Weather* (TCF 43) with Bill Robinson, Lena Horne; *Cabin in the Sky* (MGM 43) with Eddie Anderson, Lena Horne; *Bright Road* (MGM 51) with Dorothy Dandridge; *Carmen Jones* (TCF 54) with Harry Belafonte, Dorothy Dandridge; *Anna Lucasta* (United Artists 58) with Sammy Davis Jr., *Porgy and Bess* (Goldwyn 59) with Sidney Poitier, Dorothy Dandridge.

No Hollywood films took the subject of contemporary race relations as a main theme until 1949 when three such films came to the screen almost simultaneously, led by *Home of the Brave*, the story of a black veteran undergoing psychiatric treatment following traumatic war experiences. The other two films, *Pinky* and *Lost Boundaries*, dealt with light-skinned blacks passing for white.

The Hays Code ban on miscegenation as a theme was breached by *Island in the Sun* (US 59), which offered twin romances between John Justin and Dorothy Dandridge (who marry in the end) and Harry Belafonte and Joan Fontaine (who part). In Britain the subject had been tackled much earlier in *Pool of London* (GB 50), which depicted the relationship between a Jamaican ship's steward (Earl Cameron) and a white cinema cashier (Susan Shaw).

Production output: A total of 49 all-black silent features are recorded in the US for the period 1917–30; exactly 150 all-black talkies were made in the US 1931–50.

The first black film with an all-African cast was the Stoll Co.'s *Nionga* (GB 25), about a young betrothed couple in Central Africa and the tragic ending to their romance, the man being accidentally killed and the bride burned alive in her hut according to local custom. Such films were rare, the only

> One of the mysteries of Hollywood is why it is so difficult to get financing for black films. Although blacks make up only 10 per cent of the population of the US, they represent no less than 23 per cent of the total cinema audience.

other pre-war examples on record being *Zeliv* (It 28), a story of tribal life enacted entirely by Zulus, *Samba* (Ger 28) and *Stampede* (GB 30). All these films were aimed at white audiences, a fact made abundantly clear in the sub-titles to *Nionga*, which referred to its protagonists as 'the savages'.

The first African film drama made by a black African was Ousmane Sembene's *La Noire de . . .* (Sen 67), premièred at the Théâtre Sorano in Dakar on 4 February 1967.

JEWISH FILMS

The first Jewish film with an all-Jewish cast was Stanislaw Sebel's screen version of Gordin's *Satan* (Pol 12), produced by Madame Yelizariantz's Sila Co. with a cast drawn from Warsaw's Fishon Theatre. Within a year there were four Polish companies specializing in Jewish films, Sila having been joined by Variag (also run by a woman, Madame Stern), Mintus and Kosmofilm.

The first British example was *The Jewish King Lear* (GB 12), filmed at the Pavilion Theatre and premièred at New King's Hall in the Commercial Road. **America's first Jewish picture** was *A Passover Miracle* (US 14), released by Kalem in two versions, one with English sub-titles, the other with Yiddish.

The first talkie in Yiddish was Sidney M. Goldin's *Style and Class* (US 29), a Judea Films production with Goldie Eisenman and Marty Baratz.

Production Output

According to Rob Edelman's filmography of feature films in Yiddish (*Films in Review* June/July 1978), there were 53 produced in America 1924–61, 17 in Poland pre-1940, 4 in Russia 1925–33 and solitary examples from West Germany in 1948 and Italy in 1949. Mr Edelman believes there may also have been Romanian and Hungarian Yiddish features.

After *Three Daughters* (US 61), production ceased entirely for nearly 20 years. Then in 1980 came Samy Szlingerbaum's *Brussels-Transit* (Bel 80), a story of Polish-born survivors of the holocaust settling in Brussels after World War II. The film, which had a Yiddish commentary and part-Yiddish dialogue, was followed by *The Dybbuk* (Pol 82), a Jewish State Theatre of Poland production from the play by Syymon Szurmiez, and an Israeli offering called *If They Give, Take* (Isr 82). A short directed by David Greenwald, *The Well* (US 84), renewed production of Yiddish films in America.

The revival of interest in Yiddish films was stimulated by the founding of the National Centre for Jewish Film at Brandeis University, Waltham, Mass., established in 1976 with 30 mainly incomplete films from the estate of producer Joseph Seiden. It now houses over 2000 films on Jewish subjects as well as an extensive photo and rare book collection. Despite the lack of any recent product, a Yiddish Film Festival was held in New York in 1978 and the following year a season of Yiddish films ran at Cineplex in Toronto. In Europe, retrospectives of Yiddish cinema were held in Frankfurt by Walter Schobert in 1980, 1982 and 1984. Two feature-length documentaries, *Das Jiddische Kino* (FRG 83) and *Almonds and Raisins* (GB 84), have also been made on the history of Yiddish films. The former introduced a season of Yiddish features on West Germany's ZDF television station in April 1983. As part of London's 1987 Jewish East End celebration, the National Film Theatre presented a retrospective of Yiddish films dating back to the Molly Picon comedy *East and West* (Aut 23).

Yiddish films, after their tentative revival on the festival circuit, have recently become available to the living room audience since the National Centre for Jewish Film began releasing pre-World War II classics on video cassette in late 1989. Inaugural titles included *Green Fields* (US 37), *Jolly Paupers* (Pol 37), *Tevye* (US 39) and a poignant documentary *Jewish Life in Vilna* (Lithuania 39), depicting a community about to be destroyed for ever.

Anti-Semitic Films

These have been rare. In 1935, when Joseph Goebbels ordered a search to be made for foreign anti-Semitic films that could be released in Germany, the only example that could be obtained was a primitive Swedish talkie called *Pettersson and Bendel* (Swe 33). Curiously the Nazi-controlled film industry of the Third Reich made no overtly anti-Semitic pictures until just before the war, when Hans Heinz Zerlett directed *Robert und Bertram* (Ger 39), a comedy about two German tramps who get the better of a rascally Jew and save the innkeeper's lovely Aryan daughter from the fate of marrying him. The following year cinematic Jew-baiting began in earnest with *Jud Süss* (Ger 40), *Die Rothschilds* (Ger 40) and *Der ewige Jude* (Ger 40), three films whose virulent hatred was a presage of the vengeance to be wreaked on the race they vilified. Of these *Jud Süss* is undoubtedly the most notorious; it is also the only one to have been released since the war. Dubbed in Arabic, it was distributed in the Arab states in 1955 by the USSR agency Sovexport.

Molly Picon, seen here in Joseph Green's *Mamele/ Little Mother* (Pol *c.* 37), was the Yiddish cinema's foremost star.

After the collapse of the Third Reich, anti-Semitic films were mercifully sparse, but in 1952 the semi-official Cifesca company of Spain produced Luis Marquina's *Amaya* (Sp 52). This film blamed the Muslim conquest of Spain on treacherous Jews who were portrayed as funding the invasion in order to make more profit as part of the Islamic empire. One of the characters states that to the Jews, a Christian is no different from a Muslim, simply someone to be exploited for profit. The Jews in the film are depicted as rascally, cunning and devious; the Spanish characters are not unlike the Nordic heroes and heroines in similar types of Nazi film.

> Leon Liebgold and Lili Liliana, foremost stars of pre-war Yiddish cinema in Poland—they co-starred as husband and wife (which they were in real life) in the classic and uncharacteristically lavish production *The Dybbuk* (Pol 38)— owed their survival to the exigencies of movie making. The couple were in New York with their theatre troupe in 1939 when Liebgold was approached by the great Yiddish actor/director Maurice Schwartz to appear in his film *Tevye* (US 39). Liebgold agreed, provided shooting of his scenes could be completed in ten days, as he had tickets for his and Lili's return to Poland. Despite Schwartz's best efforts to keep to schedule, shooting was constantly interrupted by the buzzing of aeroplanes over their Long Island location. The day of the sailing came and went with Liebgold's scenes uncompleted and he booked for the next sailing instead. But he and Lili never boarded. Two days later Germany invaded Poland. The two stars, who would otherwise have been part of the grim harvest of the holocaust, remained in New York, where they live to this day.

HORROR

The character most frequently portrayed in horror films is Count Dracula, the creation of the Irish writer Bram Stoker (1847–1912), whose novel *Dracula* was published in 1897. Representations of the Count or his immediate descendants on screen outnumber those of his closest rival, Frankenstein's monster, by 160 to 112 (see filmography).

The peak year for production of horror films was 1972, with a total of 189. Of these, 83 emanated from the USA. The horror boom rapidly abated, with only 58 screamers going into production worldwide in 1975. Nevertheless, this was the year in which horror pictures garnered the largest share of the North American box office, with 22 per cent of all motion picture rentals. The upsurge was largely due to the overwhelming success of *Jaws* (US 75) and a strong performance by Mel Brooks' horror-spoof *Young Frankenstein* (US 74).

The list below records **the most successful horror film** each year since 1970. The top rankings are based on North American rentals, though in practice this almost invariably reflects worldwide box office performance. All films listed are US productions.

1970 *House of Dark Shadows*
1971 *Willard*
1972 *Frenzy*
1973 *Legend of Hell House*
1974 *The Exorcist*
1975 *Jaws*
1976 *The Omen*
1977 *King Kong*
1978 *Jaws II*
1979 *Alien/Amityville Horror*
1980 *The Shining*
1981 *An American Werewolf in London*
1982 *Poltergeist*
1983 *Jaws 3-D*
1984 *Gremlins*
1985 *Teen Wolf*
1986 *Aliens*
1987 *Witches of Eastwick/Predator*
1988 *A Nightmare on Elm Street 4*
1989 *Pet Sematory*
1990 *Arachnophobia*

DRACULA FILMOGRAPHY

The filmography excludes the frequent appearances that Dracula has made in cartoon films. The name of the artiste portraying the vampire is given before the title where this is known. (* amateur productions)

Drakula (Hun 21)
Max Schreck *Nosferatu, eine Symphonie des Grauens* (Ger 22)
Bela Lugosi *Dracula* (US 31)
Carlos Villarias *Dracula* (US 31) Spanish language
Gloria Holden *Dracula's Daughter* (US 36) Dracula himself seen as corpse only
Lon Chaney Jnr *Son of Dracula* (US 43) despite title, Chaney plays Dracula himself, there is no son in the picture

John Carradine *House of Frankenstein* (US 44); *House of Dracula* (US 45)
Bela Lugosi *Abbott and Costello Meet Frankenstein* (US 48)
Atif Kaptan *Drakula Istanbula* (Tur 53)
El Fantasma de la operatta (Arg 55)
German Robles *El Castillo de los monstruos* (Mex 57)
Victor Fabian *Frankenstein Meets Dracula* (US 57); *Return of the Wolfman* (US 57); *Revenge of Dracula* (US 57)
Francis Lederer *The Return of Dracula* (US 58)
*Black Inferno** (US 58)
Christopher Lee *Dracula* (GB 58)
*Castle of Dracula** (GB 58)
*Dracula** (US 59)

Gene Gronemeyer *The Teenage Frankenstein** (US 59); *Slave of the Vampire** (US 59)
Donald Glut (as Dracula's son) *I Was a Teenage Vampire** (US 59)
Richard Christy *Pawns of Satan** (US 59)
Chimi Kim *The Bad Flower* (S. Kor 61)
Frankenstein, el vampiro y cia (Mex 61)
Donald Glut (as Dracula's son) *Monster Rumble** (US 61)
Yechoon Lee *Ahkea Khots* (S. Kor 61)
Jeffrey Smithers *House on Bare Mountain* (US 62)
Donald Glut (as Dracula's son) *Dragstrip Dracula** (US 62)
Escala en Hi-Fi (Sp 63)
Kiss Me Quick! (US 64)
Sexy Proibitissimo (It 64)

Jack Smith *Batman Dracula* (US 64)

John Carradine *Billy the Kid versus Dracula* (US 65)

Mga Manugang ni Drakula (Phi 65)

Christopher Lee *Dracula—Prince of Darkness* (GB 65)

Pluto Felix *The Worst Crime of All!* (US 66)

Glenn Sherrard *Horror of Dracula** (US 66)

Mitch Evans *Dr Terror's Gallery of Horrors* (US 66)

Cesar Del Campo (?) *El Imperio de Dracula* (Mex 66)

Chappaqua (US 66)

Cesar Silva *La Sombra del murcielago* (Mex 66)

Dracula's Wedding Day (US 67)

Harrison Marks *Vampire* (GB 67)

Dante Rivero *Batman Fights Dracula* (Phi 67)

Harrison Marks *The Naked World of Harrison Marks* (GB 67)

Bill Rogers (as descendant of Dracula) *A Taste of Blood* (US 67)

John Carradine *Las Vampiras* (Mex 67)

Christopher Lee *Dracula Has Risen from the Grave* (GB 68)

Santo en el tesoro de Dracula (Mex 68)

Dracula Meets the Outer Space Chicks (US 68)

Mondo Keyhole (US(?) 68)

Isabell, A Dream (It 68)

Aldo Monti *El Vampiro y el Sexo* (Mex 68)

Vince Kelly (as descendant of Dracula) *Dracula, the Dirty Old Man* (US 69)

Men of Action Meet Women of Dracula (Phi 69)

Christopher Lee *One More Time* (GB 69)

Alex d'Arcy *The Blood of Dracula's Castle* (US 69)

Tales of Blood and Terror (US/GB 69)

Does Dracula Really Suck (US 69) homosexual Dracula

Gabby Paul (?) *Il Risveglio di Dracula* (It 69)

Christopher Lee *El Conde Dracula* (FRG/Sp/It 69)

Marty Feldman *Every Home Should Have One* (GB 70)

Des Roberts *Guess What Happened to Count Dracula?* (US 70)

Dennis Price *Vampyros Lesbos/Die Erbin des Dracula* (Sp/FRG 70)

Tunnel Under the World (It 70)

Christopher Lee *Taste the Blood of Dracula* (GB 70); *The Scars of Dracula* (GB 70)

Eva Renzi (as descendant of Dracula) *Beiss mich Liebling* (FRG 70)

Des Roberts *Dracula's lusterne vampire/Dracula's Vampire Lust* (Swz 70)

Paul Albert Krumm *Jonathan, Vampire sterben nicht* (FRG 70)

Denholm Elliott *Dracula* (GB 71, TVM)

Britt Nichols (as Dracula's Daughter) *La Fille de Dracula* (Fr/FRG 71)

Mori Kishida *Chi o Su Me/Lake of Dracula* (Jap 71)

Paul Naschy *Hombre que vino de ummo* (Sp/FRG 71)

Zandor Vorkov *Dracula versus Frankenstein aka Blood of Frankenstein* (US 71)

Howard Vernon *Dracula contra el Dr Frankenstein* (Sp/Fr 71)

Jim Parker *The Mad Lust of a Hot Vampire* (US 71)

The Lust of Dracula (US 71)

Once Upon a Prime Time (Can 71)

Ferdy Mayne *Happening der Vampire* (FRG 71)

Charles McCauley *Blacula* (US 72)

Dennis Price *Go For a Take* (GB 72)

Dracula, A Family Romance (US 72)

Paul Naschy *La Messe nere della Contessa Dracula* (It 72)

Narcisso Ibañez Menta *La Saga de los Draculas* (Sp 72)

Des Roberts *Dracula Vampire Sexuel* (Swz 72)

Howard Vernon *La Hija de Dracula* (Sp 72)

Christopher Lee *Dracula AD 1972* (GB 72)

David Azivu (?) *Santo y Blue Demon contra Dracula y el Hombre Lobo* (Mex 72)

Cesar Silva *La Invasion de los Muertos* (Mex 72)

Chabelo y Pepito contra los monstruos (Mex 73)

Paul Naschy *El Gran amor del Conde Dracula* (Sp 73)

Udo Kier *Blood for Dracula* (It/Fr 73)

Christopher Lee *The Satanic Rites of Dracula* (GB 73)

Harry Nillson (as Dracula's son) *Son of Dracula* (GB 73)

The House of Dracula's Daughter (US 73)

Christopher Lee *Tendre Dracula* (Fr 73)

Shadow of Dracula (Can 73)

Jack Palance *Dracula* (GB 74, TVM)

John Forbes-Robertson *Legend of the 7 Golden Vampires* (GB/HK 74)

David Niven *Vampira* (GB 74)

Dracula's Blood (US 74)

Hope Stansbury (as Dracula's daughter) *Blood* (US 74)

Dracula Goes to RP (Phi 74)

Tiempos duros para Drácula (Arg/Sp 75)

Peter Wechsburg (as illegitimate son of Dracula) *Deafula* (US 74)

Dracula is not Dead (GB 75)

Evil of Dracula (Jap 75)

Jay Robinson *Train Ride to Hollywood* (US 75)

El Jovencito Dracula (Sp 76)

Joe Rigoli (?) *El Pobrecito Dracula* (Mex 76)

Rossano Brazzi (?) *Il cav. constante nicosia demoniaco ovvero Dracula in Brianza* (It 76)

Christopher Lee *Dracula Père et Fils* (Fr 77)

Evelyne Kraft *Lady Dracula* (FRG 77)

Louis Jourdan *Count Dracula* (GB 77, TVM)

Geoffrey Land *Doctor Dracula* (US 77)

Suzanne Krazna as Countess Dracula in *Halloween with the Addams Family* (US 77, TVM)

Michael Pataki (as Dracula's grandson) *Dracula's Dog* (US 78)

John Carradine *Nocturna* (US 78) 'the first soft-porn-vampire-disco-rock movie'

Christopher Lee *Count Dracula and His Vampire Bride* (GB 78)

Fabian Forte *La Dinastia Dracula* (Mex 78)

Enrique Alvarez Felix *Dracula* (Mex 78)

Stefan Sileanu (as the historical Dracula, Vlad the Impaler) *Vlad Tepes/US: The True Life of Dracula* (Rom 79)

George Hamilton *Love at First Bite* (US 79)

Klaus Kinski *Nosferatu: Phantom der Nacht* (FRG 79)

Judd Hirsch *Halloween That Almost Wasn't* (US 79, TVM)

Frank Langella *Dracula* (US 79)

Gianni Garko *Dracula in Oberbayern* (FRG 79)

The Diabolic Loves of Nosferatu (Sp 79)

Peter Lowey *Dracula Bites the Big Apple* (US 79)

Johnny Harden *Star Virgin* (US 79)

Masumi Okada *Kyuketsuki Dorakyura Kobe Ni Arawaru: Akuma wa Onna wo Utsukushiku Suru* (Jap 79)

Jamie Gillis *Dracula Sucks* (US 80)

Gerald Fielding *Dracula's Last Rites* (US 80)

Andreas Voutsinas *Les Charlots Chez Dracula Junior* (Fr 80)

Louise Fletcher *Mama Dracula* (Fr/Bel 80)

Andres Garcia *El Macho Bionico* (Mex 81)

Jamie Gillis *Dracula Exotica* (US 81)

Les Jeux de la Comtesse Dolingen de Gratz (Fr 81)

Charlie Callas *Hysterical* (US 82)

Buenas Noches, Senor Monstruo (Sp 82)

Kung Fu from Beyond the Grave (HK 82?)

Dracula, Sovereign of the Damned (US? 83)

Kostas Soumas *Dracula Tan Exarchia* (Gre 83)

Gayracula (US 83)

Edmund Purdom *Fracchia contro Dracula* (It 86)

Trond Kirkraag (as descendent) *Something Entirely Different* (Nor 86)

Carlitos Espejel *Chiquidrácula* (Mex 86)

Duncan Regehr *Monster Squad* (US 87)

Ferdy Mayne *Freckles and Ghosts* (Cz 88)

Brenden Hughes *To Die For* (US 89)

Klaus Kinski *Nosferatu in Venice* (FRG 89)

Miles O'Keeffe *Waxwork* (US 89)

Michael Praed *Son of Darkness: To Die For II* (US 91)

Dracula with designer stubble: Miles O'Keeffe in *Waxwork* (US 89). (*British Film Institute*)

MUSICALS

The first musical with an original score was MGM's *The Broadway Melody* (US 29), with Bessie Love, Anita Page and Charles King, which was premièred at Grauman's Chinese Theatre in Hollywood on 1 February 1929. The songs were: *Give My Regards to Broadway* (George M. Cohan); *The Wedding Day of the Painted Doll, Love Boat, Broadway Melody, Boy Friend, You Were Meant For Me* (Arthur Freed and Nacio Herb Brown); and *Truthful Deacon Brown* (Willard Robison).

The first British musical was BIP's *Raise the Roof* (GB 30), directed by Walter Summers with Betty Balfour as an actress bribed by a rich man to ruin his son's touring review.

The first musical wholly in colour was Warner Bros' *On With the Show*, directed by Alan Crosland in two-colour Technicolor with Betty Compson and Joe E. Brown and premièred in New York on 28 May 1929. **The first British** was BIP's *Harmony Heaven* (GB 30) with Polly Ward and Stuart Hall.

The musical with the most song numbers was Madan Theatres' *Indra Sabha* (Ind 32), a Hindi movie with 71 songs.

The Hollywood musical with the most songs was RKO's *The Story of Vernon and Irene Castle* (US 39). In the course of its 93 minutes running time the film proffered, in the words of *Variety*, 'one original song and 40 old pop songs by divers tunesmiths'.

SERIES

The longest series of films was the 85 Hong Kong-made features about the 19th-century martial arts hero Huang Fei-Hong, starting with *The True Story of Huang Fei-Hong* (HK 49) and continuing to *Magnificent Butcher* (HK 80). Of the total, 77 starred Kwan Tak-Hing and no less than 25 of the films premièred in a single year, 1956. All but five were in Cantonese, the others, all made in the 1970s, being in Mandarin.

The longest series still continuing is Shochiku Studios' *Tora-San* comedy series, of which the first was premièred in August 1969 and the 44th in December 1991. The hero of the series, played by Kiyoshi Atsumi, is a Chaplinesque 'little man' who owns nothing, does little or no work and gets into scrapes. All the films have almost identical plots—ne'er do well pedlar Tora-San returns from his wanderings to home and family, who try to persuade him to marry and settle down. He falls in love with his 'madonna'—a different girl each time—whom he always loses before setting off again on his travels. Tora-San was originally devised as an antidote to those national characteristics of ruthless effi-

Japan's Tora-San movies are the longest series of films still running. The feckless hero, played by Kiyoshi Atsumi, has been falling in love with a different sweet-natured girl from the first in the series *Tora-San, Our Lovable Tramp* (Jap 69) (top) to the 43rd, *Tora-San Takes a Vacation* (Jap 90) (bottom). The secret of Tora-san's success is simply this: in a world of corporate conformity he stands for the individual kicking against the system. (*Shockika Co.*)

ciency and success-at-any-price. The formula was spectacularly successful; whilst the first *Tora-San* movie was seen by 282,000 people, the audience nowadays for each new film averages three million with a box office take of some $20 million.

The most successful series at the box office has been United Artists' and Eon Productions' British-made James Bond movies, which topped $2000 million in worldwide aggregate rentals with the release of their 15th 007 adventure *The Living Daylights* (GB 87).

SEX

Sex on screen followed rapidly on the emergence of cinema as a public entertainment. The pioneer producer of sex films was Eugène Pirou, beginning with a three-minute long production titled *Le Coucher de la mariée* (Fr 96), starring blonde and chubby Louise Willy. Based on an act performed by Mlle Willy at the Olympia music-hall in Paris the previous year, the film showed a newly-wed couple preparing for bed. The girl's husband removes her satin slipper and presses it ecstatically to his lips, then she disrobes and puts on her night attire while her husband watches with evident desire. Finally Mlle Willy does a provocative little dance before the couple retire to bed. The film caused a sensation when it was premièred in the basement of the Café de Paris in November 1896 and was soon showing at two other *salles* as well, one in the boulevard Bonne-Nouvelle and the other at 86 rue de Clichy. Pirou followed this success with other sex subjects, such as *Bain de la Parisienne* (Fr 97), *Lever de la Parisienne* (Fr 97) and *La Puce* (Fr 97), most of them based on striptease acts playing in the Paris music halls. *La Puce*, for example, showed a maiden afflicted with a flea who removes her garments one by one to locate the offending insect.

Pirou's chief rival in the blue-movie field was Georges Méliès, whose *Les Indiscrets/The Peeping Toms* (Fr 96) came out at the end of 1896. Méliès was the man who brought nudity to the screen in *Après le bal* (Fr 97) and won a wide following with such sensational subjects as *En Cabinet particulier/A*

Private Dinner (Fr 97), *L'Indiscret aux Bains de mer/ Peeping Tom at the Seaside* (Fr 97) and *La Modèle irascible/An Irritable Model* (Fr 97). In England these films were distributed by the Warwick Trading Co., who described them as 'welcome at any smoking concert or stag party'.

The earliest known American film on a sexual theme is American Mutoscope & Biograph's *The Downward Path* (US 02), a five-scene melodrama about a share-cropper's daughter who follows a downward path to prostitution—in one of the scenes she is encountered soliciting in the streets.

While most of the above films were very much of the 'What the Butler Saw' genre, the longer sex drama designed for general release emerged with Foto-rama's *The White Slave Traffic* (Den 10), a two-reel shocker of such drawing power at the box office that within a few months Nordisk had produced a rival version with the same name. It was no less sensational. A publicity still shows a scene of a kidnapped girl being savagely beaten. Ole Olsen of Nordisk recalled that at the trade show in Berlin, the German

> Former British Board of Film Censors Secretary John Trevelyan recalled an occasion when Customs officers seized an imported film titled *Games in Bed*. On screening the film they found it was about ways of entertaining a sick child.

cinema managers all clambered on to their seats for a better view. It was the success of these Danish sexploitation films—other titles included *The Last Victim of the White Slave Traffic* (Den 11) and *Dealer in Girls* (Den 12)—that inspired George Loane Tucker to make the first American feature-length sex picture, *Traffic in Souls* (US 13), starring Jane Gail and Matt Moore. Made clandestinely—not because of the subject, but because Universal did not believe that the American public were ready for feature films—Tucker's $5700 movie garnered record earnings of $450,000.

Nudity on Screen

The First leading lady to appear nude on screen was Audrey Munson in George Foster Platt's *Inspiration* (US 15), a Thanhouser production released by the Mutual Film Corporation on 18 November 1915. It related the story of an inexperienced country girl who becomes a 'life model' for a sculptor with whom she falls in love. The nude scenes aroused opposition from some, others considered them 'artistic' and 'educational'. Audrey Munson was a well-known artist's model in real life. She performed in two other films: *Purity* (US 16), in which she was also seen naked, and *The Girl O' Dreams* (US 16).

The sensation caused in the 1930s by Hedy Lamarr's nude bathing scenes in *Extase* (Cz 33) has

Probably the earliest surviving still from a pornographic film. Title and date unknown but probably French, c. 1900. *(Kobal)*

As early as 1915 Audrey Munson braved the wrath of America's moral guardians to become the first star to appear on screen in the nude.

given wide currency to the mistaken idea that Miss Lamarr was the first nude actress on screen. She was not even the first nude in Czech movies, a distinction earned by Ira Rina in Gustav Muchaty's *Eroticon* (Cz 29).

Other nude scenes of the pre-*Extase* period were legion. Celio Film's *Idolo Infranto* (It 13) contained a scene set in an artist's studio with a nude model. 'The Naked Truth' was represented by a nude girl in woman director Lois Weber's *The Hypocrites* (US 15). This Paramount release was banned in Ohio and the Mayor of Boston demanded that clothes be painted on to the image of 'Naked Truth', frame by frame. The nude was uncredited, but has been variously claimed as a Miss Margaret Edwards and Lois Weber herself.

D. W. Griffith hired a number of prostitutes to appear naked in the Belshazar's Feast sequence of *Intolerance* (US 16). Joseph Hanabery, Griffith's assistant, had been ordered to shoot nude scenes, but decided it was more than he could get away with and had his actresses lightly draped for the orgy. Meanwhile Griffith, who was back in New York, did some close shots of nude prostitutes and these were intercut with Hanabery's more discreet scenes. When the film was reissued, in 1942, the New York Censor Board insisted that Griffith's nude inserts be cut.

The same year saw no less than three films in which the leading lady appeared in the nude. Apart from Audrey Munson's second nude role in *Purity* (US 16)—see above—the nymph-like Australian swimming star turned actress Annette Kellerman was seen as nature intended in Fox's *Daughter of the Gods* (US 16) and winsome 16-year-old blue-eyed newcomer June Caprice was filmed running naked through the woods in *The Ragged Princess* (US 16). Miss Kellerman, the Esther Williams of silent movies, had been the centre of controversy five years earlier when she had worn the first one-piece bathing suit, though strangely when she wore nothing at all it aroused far less indignation. Esther Williams played Miss Kellerman in *Million Dollar Mermaid* (US 52), but by that date the austere provisions of the Hays Code precluded any presentation of the naked human form.

A nude girl on a crucifix was portrayed in *The Penitentes* (US 16) and a 'Miss Ray' appeared nude

> Romain Gary shot two versions of *Kill* (US 71), one clothed and the other unclothed. The undraped version, he explained, was for Protestant countries and the other for Catholic countries.

in *Le Film du Diable* (Bra 17). In *The Tree of Knowledge* (US 20), Yvonne Gardelle appeared naked as Lillith, the temptress who seeks to seduce Adam in the Garden of Eden before the creation of Eve. There were nude bathing scenes in *The Branding Iron* (US 20), *Isle of Love* (US 22)—in the night club scene naked girls threw themselves into a swimming pool as midnight struck—and in Henry Hathaway's *To the Last Man* (US 33), with Esther Ralston as one of the participants. Clara Bow took to nude bathing in *Hula* (US 27).

Lili Damita was seen in the buff in *Red Heels* (US 26) and Hope Hampton in *Lovers' Island* (US 26), while in *In Line of Duty* (US 32), a picture set in Arctic regions, Sue Carol bravely stripped off twice. Sally Rand performed an alfresco dance wearing nothing but a pair of shoes in *Paris at Midnight* (US 26) and a rather more circumspect Elissa Landi played a naked Christian girl bound to the stake in a Roman arena in *The Sign of the Cross* (US 32). Jean Vigo's *A Propos de Nice* (Fr 30) contains a scene of a nude sitting at a cafe table. The 35 mm prints of the film imported into Britain had the scene cut, but the sub-standard gauge prints retained it, since 16 mm film is not subject to censorship in Britain. A full-length nude is observed in the prison scene in *The Yellow Ticket* (US 31), about prostitution in Czarist Russia. The first nude scene in a Russian film, of a widow hysterically mourning in *Earth* (USSR 30), was cut by order of the authorities.

Nude scenes also appeared in *A Man's World* (US 18), *The Tree of Knowledge* (US 20), *Man, Woman and Marriage* (US 21), *Heedless Moths* (US 21) — the earliest known instance of a nude stand-in being used for the star, Jane Thomas—*Quo Vadis* (Ger/It 24), *Dante's Inferno* (US 24), *Wege zur Kraft und Schonheit* (Ger 25), *Metropolis* (Ger 26), *Beatrice Cenci* (It 26), *Casanova* (Fr/It 26), *Faust* (Ger 26), *Mandrin* (Fr 28?) and *Secrets of the Orient* (Ger/Fr 28). In most of these films the nakedness was tastefully discrete. Stefan and Franciszka Themerson's *Europa* (Pol 30) had what has been claimed as 'the first full-frontal nude'. The censor demanded that the scene should be cut, but Stefan neglected to do so and the film was released intact.

Following the introduction of the 1934 Hays Code, nudity disappeared from the Hollywood screen for 30 years. The first picture to bypass the ban was Sidney Lumet's *The Pawnbroker* (US 64), in which a woman was shown naked to the waist. The film was passed uncut by the Production Code Administration on the grounds that the scene was an essential element in the narrative. This decision opened the way for artistically valid scenes of nudity and sexual explicitness; it also hastened the end of the Administration itself, since a more liberal attitude towards sex on screen was difficult to accommodate within a code of prohibitions, and a ratings system was adopted instead.

The first film containing nude scenes to be passed by the British Board of Film Censors was *One Summer of Happiness* (Swe 51), in which a young couple were seen embracing in a pool of bulrushes. The decision was based on the fact that, in the words of former

> The first real 'nudie pic' was a UFA documentary on naturism titled *The Way to Strength and Beauty* (Ger 27). *Variety* referred to the 'dumb-looking German women' as 'very sturdy heifers'.

BBFC Secretary John Trevelyan, 'it was generally accepted in this country that in Scandinavia people bathed in the nude'. The prohibition of nudity, which had remained absolute since the founding of the Board in 1913 until this breach in 1952, was abandoned for good the following year after a naturist movie called *The Garden of Eden* (US 53) was banned by the BBFC but certified for exhibition by over 180 local authorities including the LCC. Some even gave it a U Certificate. The Board wisely

decided that its original decision had been out of keeping with changing social attitudes and modified its policy on nudity. Another 14 years were to pass, however, before the Board felt the public was ready to accept a full frontal nude, and again it was a Swedish film which stimulated the change. *Hugs and Kisses* (Swe 66) was passed by the BBFC in 1967 complete with a scene in which a girl undressed in front of a full-length mirror. This was also the first time that pubic hair was displayed so forthrightly, though there had been some revealing 'flashes' during the scene in *Blow Up* (GB 67) in which David Hemmings wrestles on the floor with Jane Birkin and Gillian Hills.

The cinema of the Eastern world took longer to come to terms with nudity. The same year that *The Pawnbroker* (US 64) was restoring bare bosoms to the American screen, the first Indian films were released in which girls were permitted to be seen in bathing costumes—*April Fool* (Ind 64) and *Sangam* (Ind 64). India still bans nudity and has only recently allowed kissing (q.v.). In Japan, however, nudity had arrived on screen in the fifties, with a scene in *The Princess Yang* (Jap 55) where the heroine enters the bath. Since the heroine was the distinguished dramatic actress Machiko Kyo, it was unthinkable that she should be seen *in person* in the nude, so a stripper was hired from the Ginza to double for her. Foreign films continued to be subject to strict censorship, though not always simply by cutting. In the Japanese release prints of *A Clockwork Orange* (GB 71) the nude scenes went out of focus, while *Woodstock* (US 69) had the emulsion scraped off the footage contain-

In *Les Années Folles* (Fr 32) Alicia Bertoni became one of the first actresses to bare her bosom straight to camera. (Kobal)

ing nudes. Nevertheless, Japan has come a long way since a scene of Cary Grant embracing Sylvia Sidney in *Madame Butterfly* (US 32) was cut by the Japanese censor because Miss Sidney's elbow was exposed. Among the last of the Far Eastern countries to succumb was Red China, where nudity reached the screen in 1985 with a picture called *The Rickshaw Boy* (Chn 85). In this a girl was seen totally naked— but from the rear only.

Full frontal nudity came to Soviet cinema in 1990 with the Odessa Filmstudio's *The Weakness Syndrome* (USSR 90). A seemingly impregnable bastion was breached the same year when Ferid Boughedir's *Halfouine—Child of the Terraces* (Tunisia 90) became the first film from a Muslim country to strip away the veils and reveal the naked female form.

The first full-frontal male nudity to be seen on screen appeared fleetingly in *Dante's Inferno* (It 12). The first explicit scene revealing male genitalia in a commercial feature was the nude wrestling match between Alan Bates and Oliver Reed in Ken Russell's *Women in Love* (GB 69).

The naked form in serious films is usually justified on 'artistic' grounds. Derek Jarman, director of the all-male *Sebastiane* (GB 75), vouchsafed a refreshingly practical explanation for the abundant nudity in this study of religious sexuality in Romano-Britain: 'the budget wouldn't run to authentic costumes'.

The first film made for theatrical release in which the sex act was depicted was *Extase* (Cz 33). The young heroine (Hedwig Kiesler, later known as Hedy Lamarr), who has flown from an impotent husband, runs naked through the woods, bathes, and then has sex with a young engineer in a hut. Curiously *Extase* is celebrated as the first motion picture containing a nude scene, which it was not, rather than the first to show sexual intercourse, which it was.

Sex was depicted on screen in a Soviet film for the first time in Vassili Pitchul's portrait of post-glasnost alienated youth *Little Vera* (USSR 88).

The first theatrical release to contain a scene of unsimulated sexual intercourse was Jan Lindqvist and Stefan Jarl's *Dom Kallar Oss Mods/They Call Us Misfits* (Swe 67), starring Kenta Gustafsson and Stoffe Svensson.

The earliest known pornographic film which can definitely be dated is *A l'Ecu d'Or ou la bonne auberge* (Fr 08).

There is no doubt that pornographic film-making was well established even by this early date, though for obvious reasons records are sparse. It was in the same year as *A l'Ecu d'Or* was released, 1908, that Russia enacted a law against obscene movies, known there as 'the Paris Genre'. In Moscow the Mephistopholes Kino decided to test its enforcement by presenting a full programme of such films and was promptly closed down.

The oldest surviving pornographic films are contained in America's Kinsey Collection. *Am Abend* (Ger c.10) is a ten-minute film which begins with a woman masturbating alone in her bedroom and progresses to scenes of her with a man performing straight sex, fellatio and anal penetration. An Argentinian film believed to date from 1907–12, *El Satario*, opens with a group of women bathing in a river in savannah country—probably filmed at Tigre, near Buenos Aires. One of their number is abducted by a satyr, who performs a wide variety of unmentionable acts with her, which she apparently enjoys. Eventually they are disturbed by the other women and the satyr flees back into the forest.

> Pornography received 'professional recognition' in the USA in 1974, when the Screen Actors Guild relaxed the rule against its members appearing in hardcore movies. Formerly any SAG members performing in porno pics did so anonymously.

The first full-length erotic cartoon film was Osamu Tezuka's *A Thousand and One Nights* (Jap 69) —claimed (inaccurately) as 'the first animated film for adults'. David Grant's *Sinderella* (GB 72) was declared obscene by both Bow Street Magistrates' Court and the High Court of Appeal, but later passed by the British Board of Film Censors with cuts amounting to only 26 seconds.

'Soft porn' for theatrical release first started in Japan in 1950 with a wave of teenage sexploitation films with titles like *Teenager's Sex-Manual, Virgin's Clinic, A Virgin's Sex Manual, Bitch* and *Bad Girl*. The title role in the latter was played by the aristocratic Yoshiko Kuga, daughter of a Japanese peer, which gave it an added piquancy for some. The films reflected—and exploited—the revolution in social values of post-war Japan, where a confused generation of teenagers was apt to identify freedom with license. Remarkably the production of these movies began only three years after the first Japanese screen kiss.

The genesis of the American 'skinflick' is generally attributed to ex-Signal Corps cameraman Russ Meyer, who made his soft-porn debut with *The Immoral Mr Teas* (US 59), a comedy about a man with the unusual ability to undress girls mentally. This modest pioneer effort, shot on a budget of $24,000 in four days, inspired no less than 150 imitations within a year of its release.

The first hardcore pornographic feature film to be shown in public cinemas in the US was *Deep Throat* (US 72), which opened at the New Mature World Theater in New York in the summer of 1972. The owner of the cinema was twice arrested for promoting obscenity, but by the time the New Mature World Theater was ordered closed in March 1973, the picture had been seen by more than a quarter of a million people and grossed over one million dollars (it cost $24,000 to make). The peculiar fascination of the movie, apart from the notoriety conferred on it by the courts, was the engaging conceit that the protagonist (Linda Lovelace) had her clitoris not in the usual place but nine inches down the eponymous throat, whence it could be reached only by those sufficiently well endowed.

Although sexploitation movies are generally profitable in relation to their modest budgets, the first to achieve an outstanding box office success, even by comparison with major studio productions, was *Emmanuelle* (Fr 74). Of the 607 new films released in Paris in 1974 *Emmanuelle* scored the highest number of admissions (1,342,921), ahead of such notable box-office draws as *The Sting* (US 73) — 1,154,952 admissions and *The Exorcist* (US 73) — 655,092 admissions.

The most prolific producer of pornographic films was the Nikkatsu Company of Tokyo, Japan, which made over 1100 softcore films between 1971 and 1988. The studio went 'straight' under a new name, Ropponica, after deciding that video had killed off the market for theatrical porno movies.

The first film about overt homosexuality was Richard Oswald's *Anders als die Andern* (Ger 19), starring Conrad Veidt, which dared to confront the cinema-going public with a subject still proscribed in literature. Following the resumption of censorship, male homosexuality received no further attention until Gustaf Gründgens' *Zwei Welten* (Ger 40). The story by Felix Lutzkendorff was an innocuous romance about two boys and two girls working together on a farm in the summer holidays. Under the direction of Gründgens it became transformed into an idyll between the two boys.

Elsewhere the theme attracted less sympathetic treatment. During the Japanese occupation of Shanghai, the Japanese made a film in China for native consumption called *Chu Hai-tang* (Jap/Chn 43), which attempted to propagate the idea of the Chinese as a decadent race with the story of a Chinese General embroiled with a female impersonator from the Peking Opera.

In Britain the subject remained unbroached on screen until Terence Young's *Serious Charge* (GB 59), about a priest (Anthony Quayle) falsely accused by a youth (Andrew Ray) of making homosexual advances. This made relatively little

> The earliest gay gag in a movie features in Mutual's Charlie Chaplin comedy *Behind the Screen* (US 16). Eric Campbell as the heavy, thinking the heroine Edna Purviance, dressed in male clothing, is a boy, goes all coy and twee, protruding his bottom provocatively.

impact, and it was left to Basil Deardon to make a film sufficiently explicit to actually use the word 'homosexual' in the dialogue. The picture was *Victim* (GB 61), in which Dirk Bogarde portrayed a respected barrister who becomes the victim of blackmail as a result of his relationship with a young vagrant (Peter McEnery). In the meantime American director Joseph Mankiewicz had directed Gore Vidal's screen adaptation of *Suddenly, Last Summer* (GB 59), the story of a homosexual poet whose beautiful cousin (Elizabeth Taylor) lures Italian beach boys for his delectation. Other British films on homosexual themes followed *Victim* in fairly quick succession, including *A Taste of Honey* (GB 61), *The Leather Boys* (GB 63) and *The Servant* (GB 63), but there was little further development of the theme by American film-makers between *Suddenly, Last Summer* and John Huston's *Reflections in a Golden Eye* (US 67), again with Elizabeth

The first film to deal explicitly with homosexuality was *Anders als die Andern* (Ger 19). The two lovers at a gay ball were played by Conrad Veidt and Reinhold Schünzel. (*Stiftung Deutsche Kinemathek*)

> The earliest known scene of men coupling on screen occurs in a pornographic French film titled *Le Télégraphiste* dating from the early 1920s. A telegraph boy delivers a telegram at a house where he becomes sexually involved first with the maid, then with the mistress of the house, finally with her husband. To what extent the scene of male congress is a reference to the known proclivity of telegraph boys is uncertain. In Britain at the time of Oscar Wilde, it was customary practice amongst certain gay men of leisure to send themselves sixpenny telegrams for the pleasure afforded on delivery.

Taylor, this time as the wife of an army officer (Marlon Brando) infatuated with a young recruit.

Lesbian love was treated with delicacy and discretion in Leontine Sagan's *Mädchen in Uniform* (Ger 31), a tender study of a girl's infatuation for a teacher in a repressive Prussian boarding school. The film's two principals, Dorothea Wieck and Hertha Thiele, were reunited two years later in a homo-erotic melodrama *Anna and Elizabeth* (Ger 33), in which the older, wealthy Elizabeth becomes possessively dependent on the sensual Anna when cured of her lameness by the younger woman's seemingly miraculous powers.

It was another 30 years before Hollywood broached the subject. In *Walk on the Wild Side* (US 62) Barbara Stanwyck played the madame of a brothel who looks to inmate Capucine for the 'affection' she cannot receive from her maimed husband. Rather more explicit in treatment—*Wild Side* took a fairly oblique look at the relationship—was *The Children's Hour* (US 62), the second film version of Lillian Hellman's play of the same name. Both pictures were directed by William Wyler, but in the earlier version, titled *These Three* (US 36), the original story of two schoolmistresses having an affair was changed to a heterosexual triangle involving two female teachers and a man. Wyler's remake had Shirley Maclaine and Audrey Hepburn in a sensitively-handled adaptation true to the spirit and the purpose of the play.

Kissing

The first screen kiss was performed in close up by May Irwin and John Rice in a filmed scene from the stage play *The Widow Jones* (US 96) and was described by a contemporary journal, *The Chap Book*, as 'absolutely disgusting'.

The first French kiss in a Hollywood movie was between Natalie Wood and Warren Beatty in *Splendor in the Grass* (US 61).

The first erotic kiss between two members of the same sex occurs during the orgy scene in Cecil B. DeMille's *Manslaughter* (US 22). The first leading lady to kiss another woman on screen was Marlene Dietrich, provocatively dressed in a white tuxedo, in Josef von Sternberg's *Morocco* (US 30).

The first far eastern country to permit kissing in films was China, the first oriental screen kiss being bestowed on Miss Mamie Lee in *Two Women in the House* (Chn 26). In Japan, where kissing was considered 'unclean, immodest, indecorous, ungraceful and likely to spread disease'—at least by Tokyo's Prefect of Police—some 800,000 ft of kissing scenes were cut from American movies that same year. Indians reacted much the same way, though with less rigour about cuts. According to *The Report of the Indian Cinematograph Committee*

(1928), during western films 'when a kissing scene is shown, the ladies turn their heads away'.

Japan's first screen kiss was seen in *Hatachi no Seishun/Twenty-Year-Old Youth* (Jap 46), directed by Yasushi Sasaki. The honour of directing the inaugural kiss should have gone to Yasuki Chiba, who was planning to introduce the daring innovation in his aptly titled *Aru Yo no Seppun/A Certain Night's Kiss* (Jap 46), but he lost his nerve at the last moment and the big clinch between the two lovers was discreetly obscured by an open umbrella. Only four years later the sex act itself was brought to the Japanese screen in *Yuki Fujin Ezu/Picture of Madame Yuki* (Jap 50).

The first screen kiss in a movie from a Muslim country took place in *The Blazing Sun* (Egypt 53), in which Omar Sharif made his second screen appearance.

The last major film producing countries still banning kissing in films are Iran and Turkey.

Kissing in Indian Films

Kissing was voluntarily renounced by the film producers themselves in the mid-thirties on the grounds that Indians did not kiss in public, and to see them doing so on the screen was pandering to an alien custom. After Independence, when the producers decided that there were sound commercial reasons for a little occidental decadence, they found themselves up against the stern morality of the censors. Some latitude was permitted, however, if at least one of the partners in the act was a foreigner, or in the case of 'international' versions of films for overseas release only. In one instance two Indians were allowed to be seen kissing each other because the girl was playing the part of a Portuguese. The breakthrough came only in 1977, when for the first time in over 40 years two Indians playing Indians were able to kiss in a major film shown in their own country. The historic embrace took place between Zeenat Aman, a former Miss Asia, and the sub-continent's most romantic leading man, Shashi Kapoor, in Raj Kapoor's *Satyam Shivam Sundaram* (Ind 77), a musical melodrama about a man who falls in love with the compelling voice of an adivasi girl and only learns on their wedding night that half of her face is hideously disfigured by a burn.

The longest screen kiss in a commercial feature movie occupied 3 min 5 sec of Regis Toomey's and Jane Wyman's time in *You're in the Army Now* (US

Singapore has special rules about 'suggestive prolonged kissing': it is not allowed in Malay language films, but is acceptable in others. In Pennsylvania in the 1930s, horizontal screen kisses were banned, vertical allowed.

40). Naomi Levine spent the full duration of Andy Warhol's non-commercial 50-minute *Kiss* (US 63) kissing Rufus Collins, Gerald Malanga and Ed Saunders.

The most kisses in a single film were the 127 bestowed by John Barrymore on Mary Astor and Estelle Taylor in *Don Juan* (US 26).

Only two Hollywood leading ladies never kissed their leading men on screen. One was Mae West, who exuded such powerful sexuality that actual physical contact would have seemed like overkill. The other was the Chinese-American star Anna May Wong (1907–61). She nearly achieved it in *The Road to Dishonour* (GB 29); Indeed her kissing scene with John Longden was shot, but cut by the censor on the grounds that inter-racial love would be offensive to some patrons. One other heroine of the American screen also faced a kissing ban: Margeurite Clark (1881–1940), at one time Mary Pickford's chief rival as 'America's Sweetheart'. In this case the ban was imposed by her husband Harry Palmerson-Williams, whom she married in 1918. Although she made another dozen films, her career was severely damaged by the marital edict and she retired in 1921.

Cinema and the Call of Nature

It was sometimes remarked, in the days before stark realism invaded the screen, that nobody in films ever seemed to feel the call of nature. As early as 1912, though, a Hungarian company called Hunnia had made a film titled *Bitter Love or Hunyadi János* (Hun 12) which was entirely about going to the lavatory— the plot centring round an aperient water called Hunyadi János which had an extraordinarily stimulating effect on the bowels. Not surprisingly, Hollywood was a good deal more reticent on the subject and it was not until 1928 that King Vidor's *The Crowd* (US 28), better remembered as the first feature film to make extensive use of outdoor New York locations, pioneered in another direction with a bathroom set which actually showed a lavatory bowl. Luis Bunuel advanced scatological film-making when he showed a woman actually sitting on the lavatory in his controversial *L'Age d'or* (Fr 30). It was the down-to-earth Russians, though, who were the first to depict people actually performing the natural functions. This was in Alexander Dovzhenko's *Earth* (US 30). Like most Soviet films of the period it was about tractors, and during the scene in question one of them runs out of water and peasants urinate in the radiator. Many years were to pass before the bowel action was depicted on screen and it was Orson Welles, always a pioneer and always of regal bearing, who led the way when he was found on the throne in *Catch-22* (US 70). Maria Schneider could have been performing either function as she squatted on the lavatory in *Last Tango in Paris* (Fr 72), but there was no room for doubt when a girl was seen performing the golden shower on her lesbian lover in Pedro Almodóvor's outrageous first feature *Pepi, Luci, Bom and the Other Girls* (Sp 80).

Meanwhile in *La Grande Bouffe* (Fr 72) Michel Piccoli had perished in his own excrement as a result of overeating. This was also the first film in which a character audibly breaks wind, a theme pursued by Dustin Hoffman in the close confines of a telephone box also containing Tom Cruise in *Rain Man* (US 89). Although this film was garlanded with awards, it was the rather less celebrated *Silent But Deadly* (US 89) which won *Variety's Gone With the Wind* New Genre Citation at the 1989 MIFED sales convention. The genre was flatulence.

The quirky Canadian film *Urinal* (Can 88) was about 'cottaging' rather than urinating, but contained informative asides on the history of the toilet seat and the first public lavatories. The 1990s offered a number of new perspectives, literally so in the case of *I Bought a Vampire Motorcycle* (GB 90) with a shot taken from inside a lavatory bowl on which someone is going about their business. This film also introduced the novelty of a talking turd. Jaime Humberto Hermosillo's *Bathroom Intimacies* (Mex 90) took place entirely in a bathroom while the fixed camera, standing in for the bathroom mirror, records the movements—in more than one sense of the word—of a family of four and their maid.

Probably the most cherished scene for scatology buffs is the one in *The War of the Roses* (US 90) in which a vengeful Michael Douglas urinates into an elaborate fish dish estranged wife Kathleen Turner is about to serve to important business associates.

TOP JOBS

Ever since silent days the occupations of leading characters in Hollywood feature movies have tended to be confined to a surprisingly narrow spectrum. Only half a dozen forms of employment are represented by no less than 46 per cent of the 2305 lead roles 1920–90 analysed in a special survey exclusive to *The Guinness Book of Movie Facts and Feats*: law enforcement, show business, medicine, journalism, the law and the armed forces. Manual workers scarcely feature in leading roles except occasionally in comedies, while working class occupations in general are rare other than certain stereotypes— golden-hearted prostitutes, spunky chorus girls, rookie soldiers from the Middle West and their grizzled sergeants, monosyllabic but incorruptible cops. Apart from these, blue collar jobs represent less than 2 per cent. Certain other occupations, numerically prominent within the world-at-large, have been almost wholly neglected by Hollywood. The count of 2305 leads includes only four barbers, three accountants, two garage mechanics, one elevator operator—and not even a single civil servant.

The survey demonstrates that the changing position of women in society has yet to be fully reflected on the large screen. Employment for the ladies in the movies of 1990 was generally on stage or on their backs—*Pretty Woman's* lovely Julia Roberts was only one of eight happy hookers and *The Baker Boys'* gorgeous Michelle Pfeiffer but one of 17 who were hoofing, warbling or thesping their way in show biz. Dedicated lady doctors and battling policewomen were also to the fore, but most of the hot-shot lady lawyers were practising their advocacy on the smaller screen.

MALE	1920	1930	1940	1950	1960	1970	1980	1990	Total*	%
Policeman/Sheriff Federal Agent	16	12	35	71	10	7	10	40	201 (12)	12.7
Doctor/Psychiatrist	28	2	21	20	4	2	5	9	91 (13)	5.7
Armed Services: Officer	11	20	10	13	11	8	4	6	83 (1)	5.3
Lawyer	22	15	12	10	6	3	–	10	78 (9)	5.0
Armed Services: Non-Com	4	25	5	8	7	4	1	7	61 (2)	3.9
Journalist	10	9	21	9	1	1	4	6	61 (28)	3.9
Businessman	21	12	4	3	1	7	3	7	58 (2)	3.6
Sportsman	8	8	6	18	1	3	5	5	54 (–)	3.4
Musician/Songwriter/ Composer	6	14	9	3	4	3	6	4	49 (12)	3.1
Farmer/Rancher	17	7	11	5	2	–	1	1	44 (18)	2.8
Private Detective	10	2	13	1	1	2	5	9	43 (3)	2.7
Writer	12	4	5	5	4	4	3	6	43 (10)	2.7
Singer/Dancer	2	11	8	12	1	1	6	1	42 (154)	2.7
Student (college)	2	10	3	1	4	6	3	7	36 (24)	2.3
Clergy/Missionary/ Evangelist	10	3	1	6	4	3	1	4	32 (7)	2.0
Artist/Sculptor	15	2	4	1	1	1	1	6	31 (7)	2.0
Banker/Broker/ Financier	15	4	3	–	1	1	–	6	30 (4)	1.9
Scientist/Inventor	3	–	5	1	5	2	3	11	30 (11)	1.9
Engineer	14	2	3	6	3	–	–	2	20 (–)	1.9
Teacher (school/ college)	1	1	6	3	4	7	4	4	30 (22)	1.9
Actor	2	6	3	3	–	5	2	6	27 (72)	1.7
Secret Agent	9	1	2	6	2	2	2	2	26 (22)	1.6
Farm-hand/Ranch-hand	9	3	7	3	1	1	–	–	24 (2)	1.5
Manufacturer/Mine Owner	15	1	–	1	1	–	2	3	23 (5)	1.5
Merchant Marine	4	7	5	3	–	–	3	–	22 (1)	1.4
Hotelier/Restaurateur/ Bar Owner	3	4	1	3	3	–	3	3	20 (20)	1.3
Pilot	2	1	8	4	1	1	2	1	20 (4)	1.3
Broadcaster/TV	–	1	6	2	–	1	3	4	17 (7)	1.1
Office Worker	4	4	4	–	–	1	1	1	15 (5)	1.0
Truck Driver	2	1	3	1	–	–	5	1	13 (–)	0.8
Film-maker	–	1	2	–	1	4	2	2	12 (–)	0.8
Gold-miner	8	2	1	–	1	–	–	–	12 (–)	0.8
Hotel, Restaurant Bar Worker	2	2	2	–	–	1	–	5	12 (24)	0.8
Advertising Exec	1	–	2	1	–	2	1	4	11 (–)	0.7
Oil-driller	4	–	3	–	1	1	2	–	11 (–)	0.7
Circus Performer	2	5	–	3	–	–	–	–	10 (7)	0.6
Shop Owner	–	–	3	–	–	–	–	1	10 (4)	0.6
Cab-driver	1	–	2	1	–	2	1	2	9 (–)	0.6
Theatre Producer	–	1	3	3	1	–	1	–	9 (1)	0.6
Travelling Salesman	1	2	1	2	1	1	–	1	9 (3)	0.6
Factory Worker	1	1	–	1	1	1	2	1	8 (4)	0.5
Chauffeur	3	2	–	–	–	–	–	2	7 (–)	0.5
Fisherman	1	2	–	3	–	–	1	–	7 (–)	0.5
Architect	3	–	–	–	2	–	1	1	6 (–)	0.4
Forestry Worker	–	2	2	2	1	–	–	–	7 (–)	0.5
Astronaut	–	1	–	2	2	–	1	–	6 (–)	0.4
Insurance Investigator	–	–	3	2	1	–	–	–	6 (1)	0.4
Fireman	–	3	1	1	–	–	–	–	5 (1)	0.3
Insurance Agent	–	2	2	–	–	1	–	–	5 (–)	0.3
Plumber	–	3	2	–	–	–	–	–	5 (–)	0.3
Servant	1	3	–	–	–	–	–	1	5 (–)	0.3
								Others	78	
								Total	1586	

* The figure in brackets is for the equivalent female occupation.

The men of the movies in 1990 were doctors, law-yers, Wall Street wizards or artistic types—if they were not cops or private eyes, which is what over 25 per cent of all gainfully employed male leads were in a year where the movies seemed to be either about the rich and successful or about those who protect society on their behalf.

The charts below enumerate the main occupations of the leading male and female characters in all the American feature productions of the years tabulated. The sample consists of approximately 10 per cent of total Hollywood production (excluding porno movies) since the inception of the feature-length film.

FEMALE	1920	1930	1940	1950	1960	1970	1980	1990	Total*	%
Singer/Dancer	36	41	31	26	2	4	8	6	154 (42)	21.5
Actress	16	16	8	11	3	3	4	11	72 (27)	10.0
Office Worker/Secretary	14	12	6	9	2	4	6	4	57 (15)	8.0
Nurse	3	2	10	9	1	3	1	4	33 (-)	4.6
Journalist	5	–	13	2	–	–	5	3	28 (61)	3.9
Prostitute/Madam	3	1	1	–	4	6	3	8	26 (1)	3.6
Hotel, Restaurant, Bar Worker	5	8	5	1	–	1	2	2	24 (12)	3.3
Student (college)	2	4	1	1	4	–	3	4	24 (36)	3.3
Secret Agent	4	4	2	4	–	2	2	4	22 (26)	3.1
Teacher (school/college)	8	1	4	4	2	1	1	1	22 (30)	3.1
Hotelier, Restaurateur, Bar owner	1	3	4	7	1	–	2	2	20 (20)	2.8
Model	2	3	4	5	–	2	1	2	19 (-)	2.6
Farmer/Rancher	3	3	6	4	1	–	–	1	18 (43)	2.5
Servant	6	4	–	–	1	1	1	1	14 (5)	2.0
Doctor/Psychiatrist	–	–	–	2	–	2	2	7	13 (91)	1.8
Shop Assistant	4	4	3	–	–	–	–	2	13 (4)	1.8
Musician/Songwriter	4	2	3	2	–	–	1	–	12 (49)	1
Policewoman	–	–	1	4	–	–	1	6	12 (201)	1
Scientist	–	–	1	–	1	1	4	4	11 (30)	1.5
Writer	2	1	5	–	–	–	–	2	10 (43)	1.4
Lawyer	–	1	1	1	–	–	3	3	9 (78)	1.3
Artist/Sculptor	4	–	–	–	–	1	1	1	7 (30)	1.0
Broadcaster/TV	–	–	1	–	–	–	3	3	7 (17)	1.0
Circus Performer	4	1	1	1	–	–	–	–	7 (10)	1.0
Missionary/Evangelist/Nun	2	1	–	–	1	1	2	–	7 (32)	1.0
Social Worker	2	–	–	2	–	1	1	1	7 (1)	1.0
Air Stewardess	–	–	2	–	1	2	1	–	6 (-)	0.8
Garment Worker	5	–	–	–	–	–	–	–	5 (2)	0.7
Manufacturer	1	1	1	–	1	–	1	–	5 (23)	0.7
								Others	57	
								Total	719	

* The figure in brackets is for the equivalent female occupation.
See also pp. 68–69

Combining the male and female figures gives the following overall ranking (occupations representing 1% or more of the total): Police—9.2% (213); Singer/Dancer—8.5% (196); Doctor/Psychiatrist—4.5% (104); Actor/Actress—4.3% (99); Journalist—3.8% (89); Lawyer—3.8% (87); Armed Services, Officer—3.7% (84); Office Worker—3.1% (71); Armed Services, Non-Com—2.7% (63); Farmer/Rancher—2.7% (62); Musician/Songwriter/Composer—2.7% (61); Student—2.6% (60); Businessman—2.6% (60); Sportsman—2.3% (54); Writer—2.3% (53); Teacher—2.3% (52); Secret Agent—2.1% (48); Private Detective—2.0% (46); Scientist—1.8% (41); Hotelier, Restaurateur, Bar Owner—1.7% (40); Clergy, Missionary, Evangelist—1.7% (39); Artist/Sculptor—1.6% (38); Hotel/Restaurant/Bar Worker—1.6% (36); Banker/Broker/Financier—1.5% (34); Nurse—1.4% (33); Engineer—1.3% (30); Manufacturer—1.2% (27); Prostitute—1.2% (27); Farm-hand/Ranch-hand—1.1% (26) %; Broadcaster/TV— 1% (24); Pilot—1% (24).

The roster of the most prominent screen professions in each decade is not only repetitive but, seen in a wider social context, an indictment.

	Male	Female
1920	Doctor	Singer/Dancer
1930	Soldier/Sailor	Singer/Dancer
1940	Police	Singer/Dancer
1950	Police	Singer/Dancer
1960	Army/Navy Officer	Prostitute and Student (=)
1970	Army/Navy Officer	Prostitute
1980	Police	Secretary
1990	Police	Actress

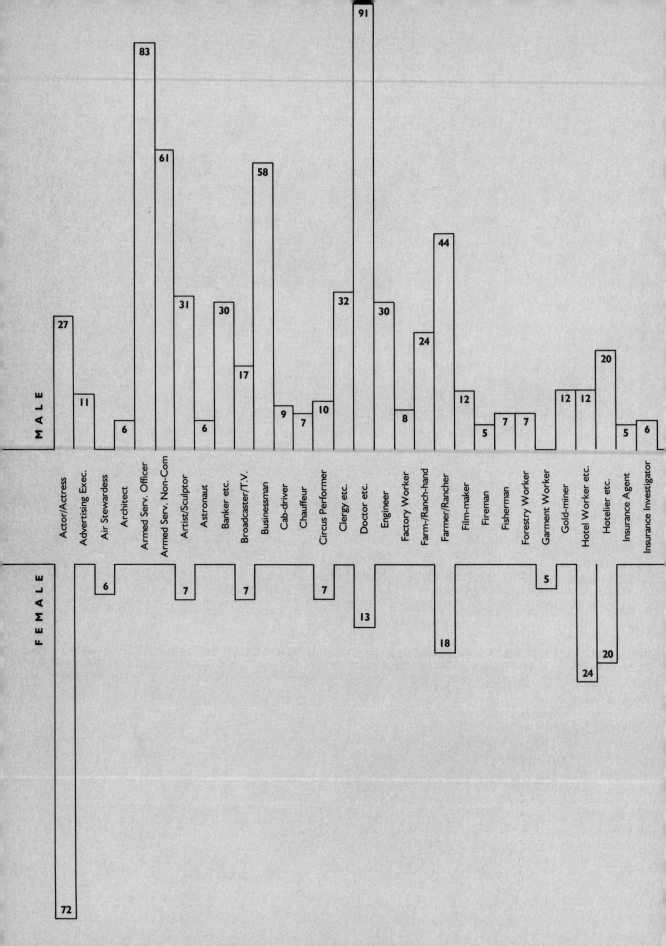

MALE

Occupation	Value
Actor/Actress	27
Advertising Exec.	11
Air Stewardess	6
Architect	83
Armed Serv. Officer	61
Armed Serv. Non-Com	31
Artist/Sculptor	30
Astronaut	6
Banker etc.	17
Broadcaster/T.V.	58
Businessman	9
Cab-driver	7
Chauffeur	10
Circus Performer	32
Clergy etc.	91
Doctor etc.	30
Engineer	8
Factory Worker	24
Farm-/Ranch-hand	44
Farmer/Rancher	12
Film-maker	5
Fireman	7
Fisherman	7
Forestry Worker	12
Garment Worker	12
Gold-miner	20
Hotel Worker etc.	5
Hotelier etc.	6

FEMALE

Occupation	Value
Air Stewardess	6
Artist/Sculptor	7
Banker etc.	7
Circus Performer	7
Clergy etc.	13
Farm-/Ranch-hand	18
Garment Worker	5
Hotel Worker etc.	24
Hotelier etc.	20
Actor/Actress	72

For full details of film role occupations see Tables on pp. 66–67.

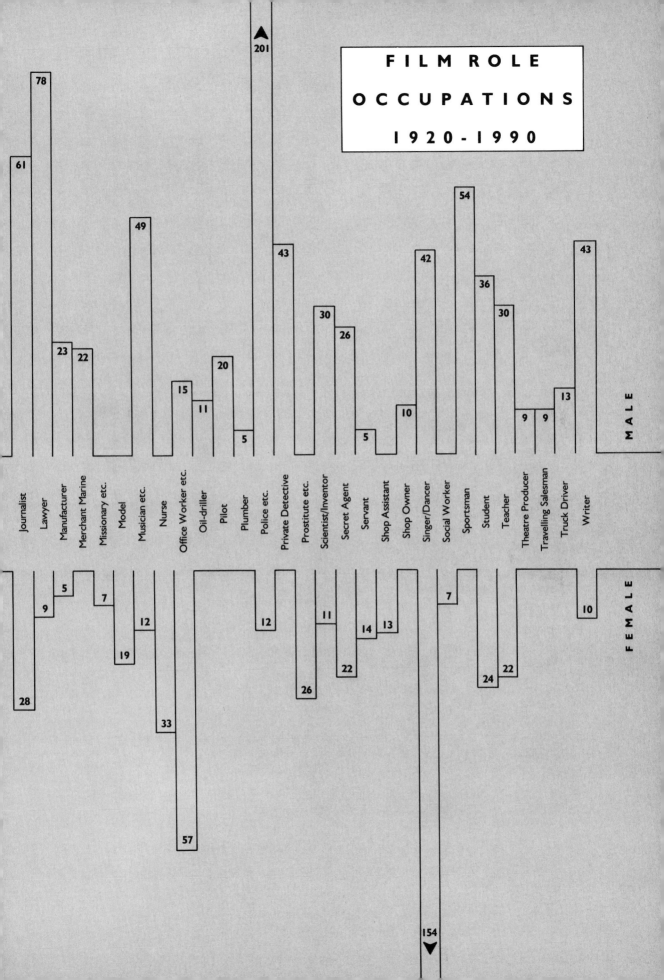

FILM ROLE OCCUPATIONS 1920-1990

MALE

Occupation	Male	Female
Journalist	61	28
Lawyer	78	9
Manufacturer	23	5
Merchant Marine	22	
Missionary etc.		7
Model		19
Musician etc.	49	12
Nurse		33
Office Worker etc.	15	57
Oil-driller	11	
Pilot	20	
Plumber	5	
Police etc.	201	
Private Detective	43	12
Prostitute etc.		26
Scientist/Inventor	30	11
Secret Agent	26	22
Servant	5	14
Shop Assistant		13
Shop Owner	10	
Singer/Dancer	42	154
Social Worker		7
Sportsman	54	
Student	36	24
Teacher	30	22
Theatre Producer	9	
Travelling Salesman	9	
Truck Driver	13	
Writer	43	10

FEMALE

HOLLYWOOD AND SPORT—THE LEAGUE TABLE

Hollywood has made a total of 799 feature films with a sports background up to the end of 1990. The most popular sport as a subject for screen drama is boxing, with just under 25 per cent of the total, followed by horse racing with 17.3 per cent, American football with 13.5 per cent and motor racing with 10.7 per cent. The number of films devoted to each sport in each decade is listed below, with the various sports in rank order according to their individual totals. Only films about competitive sport have been included, so few of the films of Esther Williams, for example, have been counted under swimming.

	1910–19	1920–29	1930–39	1940–49	1950–59	1960–69	1970–79	1980–89	1990	Total
Boxing	7	61	39	29	28	4	11	14	1	194
Horse Racing	20	32	44	21	11	5	3	2	–	138
American Football	2	23	38	14	10	5	8	8	–	108
Motor Racing	2	23	20	3	10	16	8	2	1	85
Baseball	8	9	7	7	13	1	7	14	1	67
Athletics	–	8	2	–	3	3	8	5	1	30
Basketball	–	2	2	–	3	2	12	3	–	24
Wrestling	–	–	2	1	–	–	7	9	–	19
Golf	1	1	4	–	3	4	1	4	–	18
Motor Cycle Racing	–	2	1	–	1	3	6	2	–	15
Polo	–	6	4	–	–	–	–	–	–	10
Rowing	1	5	4	–	–	–	–	–	–	10
Skiing	–	–	1	1	–	2	2	4	–	10
Speedboat Racing	–	1	6	–	–	–	2	–	–	9
Cycle Racing	–	–	1	–	–	–	1	6	–	8
Ice Hockey	–	–	3	1	1	–	1	1	–	7
Swimming	–	2	–	–	1	–	1	2	1	7
Tennis	–	1	1	–	1	–	3	1	–	7
Roller Skating	–	–	–	–	1	–	4	–	–	5
Pool	–	–	–	–	–	1	1	2	–	4
Skateboarding	–	–	–	–	–	–	2	2	–	4
Soccer	–	–	–	–	–	–	1	2	–	3
Gymnastics	–	–	–	–	–	–	–	2	–	2
Ice Skating	–	–	1	–	–	–	1	–	–	2
Showjumping	–	–	–	–	–	1	–	1	–	2
Volleyball	–	–	–	–	–	–	–	1	1	2
Yacht Racing	–	–	1	–	–	1	–	–	–	2
Angling	–	–	–	–	–	1	–	–	–	1
Bowling	–	–	–	–	–	–	1	–	–	1
Cockfighting	–	–	–	–	–	–	1	–	–	1
Dog Racing	–	–	1	–	–	–	–	–	–	1
Fencing	–	1	–	–	–	–	–	–	–	1
Ice Yachting	–	1	–	–	–	–	–	–	–	1
Kickboxing	–	–	–	–	–	–	–	1	–	1
Weightlifting	–	–	–	–	–	–	1	–	–	1

WESTERNS

The earliest subjects of western interest were *Sioux Indian Ghost Dance, Indian War Council* and *Buffalo Dance*, made by the Edison Co. at West Orange, NJ on 24 September 1894. *Bucking Broncho* followed on 16 October and is notable for the first appearance of a cowboy in a film—Lee Martin of Colorado, who is seen riding *Sunfish* in a corral, while his 'pardner' Frank Hammit stands on the rails and discharges the first of many tens of thousands of pistol shots that were to be seen (and later heard) in almost every western that followed. Annie Oakley, immortalized in *Annie Get Your Gun* (US 50), made her film debut a fortnight later on 1 November 1894.

The first westerns were copyrighted by the American Mutoscope & Biograph Co. on 21 September 1903. One was titled *Kit Carson* (US 03) and related the story of its hero's capture by Indians and subsequent escape through the agency of a beautiful Indian maiden. There were 11 scenes and the film had a running time of 21 minutes, making it the longest dramatic picture (other than Passion Plays) produced in America at that time. The other film, titled *The Pioneers* (US 03), showed the burning of a settler's homestead by Indians, who kill the homesteader and his wife and carry off his daughter. The picture ends with the dramatic rescue of the child by frontiersmen who have found the bodies of her parents. Running time was approximately 15 minutes. Both pictures were directed by Wallace McCutcheon and filmed on location in the Adirondack Mountains of New York State. *Kit Carson* was made on 8 September 1903 and *The Pioneers* two days later.

The more celebrated *The Great Train Robbery* (US 03), generally and erroneously described as the first western and often as the first film to tell a story, was copyrighted by the Edison Co. some six weeks later, on 1 December 1903.

Until 1906 all westerns were shot in the Eastern states, generally in New Jersey. **The first western made in the West** was Biograph's *A California Hold Up* (US 06), shot by O. M. Grove.

The first feature-length western was Lawrence

B. McGill's *Arizona* (US 13), an All Star Feature Corporation production with Cyril Scott and Gertrude Shipman. It was released in August 1913, six months before Cecil B. DeMille's *The Squaw Man* (US 14), usually credited as the first feature.

The first western in colour was a British production by a Dutch director, Theo Bouwmeester's *Fate* (GB 11), made in Kinemacolor by the Natural Colour Kinematograph Co. Set in Texas, it was about an Englishman who becomes leader of a tribe of renegade Indians.

The first feature-length colour western was the Famous Players–Lasky production *Wanderer of the Wasteland* (US 24), a Zane Grey horse opera from the novel of the same name. Photographed in two-colour Technicolor by Arthur Ball, it was directed by Irvin Willar, starred Jack Holt, Noah Beery and Billie Dove, and was premièred in Los Angeles on 21 June 1924.

The first western talkie was Fox–Movietone's *In Old Arizona* (US 28), directed by Raoul Walsh and Irving Cummings and starring Edmund Lowe,

> There has been at least one western in which not a single gunshot is heard. *They Passed This Way* aka *Four Faces West* (US 48) starred Joel McCrea as a bank robber on the run from Charles Bickford's Pat Garrett. Strong characterization and suspense proved no substitute for the traditional showdown in Main Street as far as the fans were concerned and the film bombed at the box office.

Warner Baxter and Dorothy Burgess. It was premièred at the Criterion Theater, Los Angeles, on 25 December 1928.

The first feature-length film with an all-Indian cast was Edward S. Curtis's *The Land of the Head Hunters* (US 14), a story of the son of a tribal chief and his quest for manhood. It was filmed on location on the North-West coast of America.

The first western with Indian dialogue was Universal's talkie serial *The Indians Are Coming* (US 31), in which Chief Thunderbird spoke in his native Sioux. In 1970 Dame Judith Anderson, an Australian, successfully coped with all-Sioux dialogue in her role as Buffalo Cow Head in *A Man Called Horse* (US 70).

The highest earning western was Kevin Costner's *Dances with Wolves* (US 90), which had earned $175 million in North American rentals by June 1991. The previous record was held for 21 years by *Butch Cassidy and the Sundance Kid* (US 69) with $29.2 million. The extraordinary success of Costner's film, after Hollywood had dismissed the western genre as box office poison, was all the more remarkable for the fact that much of the dia-

logue was in the Sioux language Lakota. It was also the first western to win the Oscar for Best Film since *Cimarron* in 1931.

The first western star was G. M. 'Broncho Billy' Anderson (1881–1971), who was to have been cast as one of the villains for his western debut in *The Great Train Robbery* (US 03), but proved so inept on a horse that he had to be relegated to extra work. Notwithstanding this inauspicious start to a career dedicated to the relationship of man and horse, Anderson starred in *Life of an American Cowboy* (US 06) and then went west with a Selig location crew to make one of the earliest westerns shot in the real west—*The Girl from Montana* (US 07). The following year he established a West Coast studio for Essany at Niles, California, and decided to embark on a series of one-reelers based on a central character, reasoning that the weakness of the Edison, Selig and Essany westerns he had played in was that they lacked clearly-defined heroes. His original intention had been to find an actor expert in horsemanship whom he could direct, but actors of any kind being in short supply in California, he eventually decided to cast himself in the role. *Broncho Billy and the Baby* (US 10), a sentimental story of a man-gone-wrong who is reformed by the love of a good woman, was the first in a series of nearly 400 Broncho Billy pictures which established Anderson as a major star. A curious feature of the films was their total lack of continuity. If Broncho Billy married in one picture, he would be a bachelor again in the next; he would be reformed inexhaustibly by a succession of good women; and death would only interrupt his career in the saddle until the opening scenes of the next one-reeler. Anderson turned to features in 1918, but competition from his successors, Tom Mix and W. S. Hart, was too strong. After a period of producing Stan Laurel comedies for Metro, he retired in 1923. Nearly half a century after his last silent western role in *The Son of a Gun* (US 18), he made a single excursion into talkies with a guest appearance in *The Bounty Killer* (US 67).

The most popular western star was determined annually with a poll of exhibitors conducted by *Motion Picture Herald* between 1936 and 1954 (when the 'B' western ended). Buck Jones won in 1936, Gene Autry each year from 1937–42, and Roy Rogers from 1943–54 inclusive.

The western hero most often portrayed on screen has been William Frederick Cody (1846–1917), otherwise known as 'Buffalo Bill', a character who has appeared in 53 dramatic films to date. William Bonney (1860–81), alias Billy the Kid, has been portrayed in 49 films; Jesse James (1847–82) in 38 films; Wild Bill Hickock (1837–76) in 37 films; General George Armstrong Custer (1839–76) in 32 films; and Wyatt Earp (1848–1929) in 23 films.

Emilio Estevez (right) as the 48th screen incarnation of Billy the Kid in *Young Guns II* (US 90).

The days of the 'real West' overlapped with the movies' version to the extent that there were still authentic western heroes alive—such as 'Buffalo Bill' Cody (d. 1917) and Marshal Wyatt Earp (d. 1929)—when Hollywood was busy creating mythology. One early western, the Selig Co.'s *Custer's Last Stand* (US 08), included among its cast three aged Sioux Indians who had actually participated in the Battle of the Little Big Horn (1876) as young warriors. The producer's hope that he could depend on them as historical advisers came, however, to naught. 'The most we could get out of them,' he declared, 'was that the fight was over so quickly that they could remember little about it.'

The most prolific western directors were Lesley Selander (1900–79), with at least 107 known feature-length westerns made between 1935 and 1967, and Lambert Hillyer (1893–), with 106 recorded titles between 1917 and 1949.

The only western directed by a woman was Ruth Ann Baldwin's curiously titled Universal production '49-'17 (US 17).

Western Output

It is estimated that there have been over 3500 multi-reel westerns made since the first two-reeler, the Oklahoma Natural Mutoscene Co.'s *The Bank Robbery* (US 08).

'You need Indians . . . You can get them right from the reservoir.'—Samuel Goldwyn.

PERFORMERS

The first motion picture film to employ the use of actors was a brief costume drama, *The Execution of Mary Queen of Scots* (US 95), which was shot by Alfred Clark of Raff & Gammon, Kinetoscope proprietors, at West Orange, NJ on 28 August 1895. The part of Mary was played by Mr R. L. Thomas, Secretary and Treasurer of the Kinetoscope Co. After approaching the block and laying his head on it, Thomas removed himself, the camera was stopped, and a dummy substituted. The camera was then started again for the decapitation scene. This was **the first use of trick photography or special effect work** in a film.

The first person employed to play a comedy role in a film was M. Clerc, a gardener employed by Mme Lumière at Lyons, France. He was aptly cast in the part of the gardener in the Lumière production *L'Arroseur arrosé* (Fr 95), a film premièred at the Grand Café in Paris on 28 December 1895. Clerc is seen watering flowerbeds with a hose. A mischievous boy, played by a 14-year-old Lumière apprentice called Duval, creeps up behind the gardener and places his foot on the hose to stop the flow of water. As the perplexed gardener holds the nozzle up to his eye to see if there is a blockage, young Duval removes his foot and capers with joy as a burst of water gushes into M. Clerc's face. Clerc and Duval were the first performers to be seen on the screen, as *The Execution of Mary Queen of Scots* had been made for viewing in Edison's 'peep-show' Kinetoscope.

The first professional actors to perform in movies made their screen debuts almost simultaneously on either side of the Atlantic. In America John Rice and May Irwin performed the first screen kiss in *The Widow Jones* aka *May Irwin Kiss* (US 96), which was a scene from the Broadway comedy *The Widow Jones* filmed by Raff and Gammon in April 1896. At about the same time in Britain, Fred Storey played the title role in R. W. Paul's *The Soldier's Courtship* (GB 96), a short comedy made on the roof of the Alhambra Theatre, Leicester Square, and premièred underneath. Storey also got to kiss the heroine, Julie Seale of the Alhambra Ballet. Performers of established reputation rarely appeared in films prior to about 1908 in France and Britain and later elsewhere. There were, however, a few notable exceptions during the primitive period, including Auguste van Biene's role as the cellist in Esme Collings' *The Broken Melody* (GB 96), from the play of the same name; Joseph Jefferson's performance in American Mutoscope & Biograph's *Rip*

Van Winkle (US 96); Beerbohm Tree and Julia Neilson in *King John* (GB 99); Sarah Bernhardt in *Hamlet* (Fr 00); Coquelin in *Cyrano de Bergerac* (Fr 00); Marie Tempest and Hayden Coffin in *San Toy* (GB 00); and Marie Tempest, Ben Webster and H. B. Warner in *English Nell* (GB 00). The only one of these to make a career as a screen actor was H. B. Warner (1876–1958), whose most notable performances were in *King of Kings* (US 27) as Jesus Christ, *Mr Deeds Goes to Town* (US 36), *Lost Horizon* (US 37) and *Victoria the Great* (GB 37).

The Star System

This emerged in the United States and Europe simultaneously. Previous to 1910 it was the deliberate policy of film-makers not to give their lead players any star billing, lest they should overvalue their services. First to break with this was the American production company Kalem, which in January 1910 began issuing star portraits and posters with the artistes names credited. A few weeks later Carl Laemmle, who had succeeded in luring the still anonymous Florence Lawrence away from Biograph to work for IMP, pulled the kind of outrageous publicity stunt that has enlivened and bedevilled the industry ever since, and in the process created the first real movie star. He began by arranging for a story to break in the St Louis papers that the actress had been killed in a street-car accident. Public interest in the supposed tragedy having been fully aroused, Laemmle placed the following advertisement in the same papers on 10 March 1910: 'The blackest and at the same time the silliest lie yet circulated by the enemies of IMP was the story foisted on the public of St Louis last week to the effect that Miss Lawrence, "The Imp Girl", formerly known as "The Biograph Girl", had been killed by a street car. It was a black lie so cowardly. We now announce our next film *The Broken Path*.' This was followed up with personal appearances by Miss Lawrence and a long interview in the *St Louis Post-Dispatch*; within a year her name was appearing on film posters in larger type than the title.

In Europe the practice of publicizing star names began the same year with the outstanding success of two films, one from Denmark, the other from Germany. Asta Nielsen's bravura performance in *The Abyss* (Den 10), one of the first long films to demonstrate a true sense of dramatic construction, brought a hitherto little-known actress almost immediate international recognition and the first of the really prodigious star salaries (c.f. Artistes' earnings, pp.

75–76). Germany's box office success of the year was *Das Liebesglück der Blinden/The Love of the Blind Girl* (Ger 10), starring 'The Messter Girl', a designation that cloaked the identity of Oskar Messter's leading player Henny Porten, who had also scripted the picture. It was received with such acclaim by filmgoers that Messter was persuaded to reveal her name. Once her name was on the credits, Henny proceeded to justify the producers' worst fears by demanding an increase in salary—from the equivalent of $50 a month to $56. Messter refused and she walked straight out of the studio. Having failed to call what he thought was a bluff, the producer sent his assistant, Kurt Stark, to fetch the girl back with a promise that she could have the raise. Henny returned to the studio, married Stark, and went on to become Germany's idol of the silent screen.

Not Charlie Chaplin

No actor has been portrayed on screen by *other* actors as often as Charlie Chaplin. It started with Leslie Henson playing Chaplin in a satire by James Barrie called *The Real Thing At Last* (GB 16), which was about an American film producer modernizing *Macbeth*. In the same year Fred Evans did a Chaplin role in *Pimple—Himself and Others* (GB 16) and meanwhile Australia's Ern Vockler was doing Chaplin impersonations on stage and appeared as the little tramp in a film titled *Charlie at the Sydney Show* (Aus 16). Essany followed with *Chase Me Charlie* (US 17), in which Graham Douglas impersonated Chaplin (who had left Essany for Mutual) in a compilation of genuine Chaplin extracts made into a story with linking footage. The Ming Hsing Film Co. of Shanghai made two 'Chaplin films' in the early twenties—*The King of Comedy Visits China* (Chn 22) and *Disturbance at a Peculiar Theatre* (Chn 22)—with British amateur actor Richard Bell taking the part of Charlie. Japan also had a home-grown Chaplin in the person of Katsuo Mikoshiba, who looked almost indistinguishable from the real thing in his baggy pants, bowler and toothbrush moustache, and Germany had her own Charlie Kaplin. The Chaplin impersonation industry seems to have come to a halt with a full-scale biopic, an unauthorized *Life Story of Charles Chaplin* (GB 26) starring Chick Wango in the title role, which was suppressed and never shown. Recently, however, there has been a Chaplin 'comeback'. Chinese comedian Dean Saki played the title role in *Chinese Chaplin and the Kung Fu Kid in Laughing Times* (HK 81), in which the little tramp befriends a poor but beautiful orphan girl obviously inspired by Paulette Goddard's barefoot waif in *Modern Times* (US 36).

Katsuo Mikoshiba, the Nipponese Chaplin.

Artistes' Earnings

Earnings which have now reached as much as $20 million plus for a single film began at a level commensurate with the penny gaff milieu of early filmmaking. The earliest known wage rate was the gold Louis ($4.30 or 17s) per day paid in the late 1890s by Star Films of Paris, but not all production companies were so generous. Gene Gauntier was offered $3 to play the lead in Biograph's *The Paymaster* (US 06), the story of a mill-girl in love with the manly young paymaster of the mill. Miss Gauntier was required to be thrown into the millstream by the villain, which she allowed him to do, not liking to mention that she was unable to swim. The producer was so pleased with her pluck that the $3 fee was raised to $5. Alma Lund, who played the female lead in the first film drama made in Norway—*Dangerous Life of a Fisherman* (Nor 07)—was paid the equivalent of $1.50 for her part; the boy who played her son got 75c. R. W. Paul paid Britain's first professional film actor, Johnny Butt, a daily wage of 5s ($1.25) in 1899, which was rather better than the 4s ($1) a day accorded to Chrissie White when she joined the Hepworth Co. at Walton-on-Thames in 1908. 'When I really got on,' she recalled, 'I received 8s a day, and when I was a star they paid me 50—shillings, not pounds.' Dave Aylott, who joined Cricks & Martin of Mitcham in 1909, remembered that their terms were 7s 6d a day for principal parts, 5s for minor parts, plus 1s 6d travelling expenses to Mitcham and a bread and cheese lunch with beer. In America at this time the $5 a day received by Mary Pickford when she joined Biograph in 1909 seems to have become standard throughout the industry, nothing extra being paid for 'star' roles.

The escalation in salaries, when it came, was rapid and had to do with two factors: the use of major names from the stage, who had to be paid highly to demean themselves in this way; and the introduction of the 'star' system (cf Star system, pp. 73–74) from

1910 onwards. The change began with Film d'Art in Paris, a company established in 1908 to produce prestige films with prestige players. Their leading artistes were paid the equivalent of $40 for each rehearsal and $200 for the actual shoot. Featured players, however, received as little as $2 to $3 a day for services in a major film like *Germinal* (Fr 13), for which the star, Henry Krauss, was paid $700. In England Will Barker paid Sir Herbert Beerbohm Tree a record £1000 to play Wolsey in *Henry VIII* (GB 11), a two-reeler which was shot in a single day. How far this was from the norm is indicated by the fact that the following year Barker was able to secure the lead player of his *Hamlet* (GB 12), Charles Raymond, for just 10s—which included his services as director of the film!

The first superstar salary was earned not by any of the rising American players, but by Denmark's Asta Nielsen. For her debut in *The Abyss* (Den 10) she was paid a modest 200kr ($53.60), but the film rocketed her to stardom and by the end of 1912 she was under contract to Berlin producer Paul Davidson with guaranteed annual earnings of $80,000. Compared to Asta Nielsen's salary of over $1500 a week, the highest paid stars in America were Gene Gauntier at $200 a week and Florence Lawrence at $250 a week. At this time Mary Pickford, who was soon to eclipse them all, was trailing at $175 a week at Biograph. The following year, however, Adolph Zukor lured her to Famous Players at $500 a week and this was doubled in 1914 and doubled again in 1915. Already the highest paid woman in the world,

Samuel Goldwyn on doing business with Mary Pickford: 'It took longer to make one of Mary's contracts than it did to make one of Mary's pictures.'

on 24 June 1916 she signed a new contract that put her on a par with the highest paid man in the world—Charles Chaplin, who had contracted with Mutual earlier in the year at a salary of $670,000. Miss Pickford's earnings were now half the profits of all her pictures, with a $10,000 p.w. minimum, plus a $300,000 single payment bonus, plus $150,000 p.a. to her mother for 'goodwill', plus $40,000 for examining scenarios prior to signing.

In the meantime Francesca Bertini, Italian 'diva', had become Europe's highest paid star in 1915 at $175,000 p.a., only slightly behind the $200,000 p.a. that Mary Pickford was then earning. European earnings, however, were never to rise above this before World War II, apart from the $450,000 that Alexander Korda paid Marlene Dietrich to star in *Knight Without Armour* (GB 37). American earnings continued to spiral upward, but with the three highest paid stars—Mary Pickford, Charlie Chaplin and Douglas Fairbanks—combined together as producers under the distribution banner of United Artists from 1919 onwards, it is hard to assess their new

earning power. In that same year Roscoe 'Fatty' Arbuckle had become the first star with a guaranteed minimum of $1 million a year, but his contract with Paramount only lasted until scandal destroyed his career in 1922 and he became the first star to be formally banned.

No other star of the silent era matched Arbuckle's salary, but Nazimova was reported to be the highest salaried woman star in 1920 at $13,000 p.w., Tom Mix, the most popular cowboy star of the silents, was earning $17,500 p.w. in 1925 and Harold Lloyd's weekly wage was reported to be $40,000 p.w. in 1926. Salaries in Britain were a sad contrast. Alma Taylor, the most popular female star of the early twenties, was paid £60 p.w. by the Hepworth Co., but they were less generous with their leading male

Edna Purviance, Chaplin's 'star soubrette' of the 1915-23 period, made no films after 1926, yet remained under contract to Chaplin on full salary until her death 32 years later.

actor, Stewart Rome, who earned only £10 p.w. Ivor Novello, a matinee idol with a strong stage reputation, could command £3000-£4000 per film at his height in the late twenties, while the highest sum for a silent film was the £10,000 paid to music hall artiste Sir Harry Lauder for his role as a retired grocer in George Pearson's *Huntingtower* (GB 27).

The coming of sound and the Depression, almost simultaneously, forced most star salaries downward. In 1927 over 40 stars were reputedly earning $5000 or more a week. By 1931 only 23 stars had salaries of $3500 or more. Top earners in that year were Constance Bennett and John Barrymore at $30,000 p.w., a sum soon to be matched by Greta Garbo, who earned $250,000 for *The Painted Veil* (US 34) and the same for *Anna Karenina* (US 35). Highest earnings of 1935 were the $480,833 reported by Mae West to the tax authorities, well in excess of the highest earnings of 1938—Shirley Temple's $307,014, or 1939—James Cagney's $368,333, or even 1946 when Bing Crosby topped both at the box office (rated No. 1 in the Quigley Poll) and at the bank with $325,000. During the forties and fifties top star salaries per film were generally in the $250,000-$400,000 region, with a new peak of $500,000 for a British film—Elizabeth Taylor in *Suddenly Last Summer* (GB 59)—and $750,000 for an American production, earned by both John Wayne and William Holden (plus 20 per cent of the net) on *The Horse Soldiers* (US 59). The 1960s saw the era of the $1 million star salary for single pictures and in the 1970s the multi-million dollar contract. In the mid 1970s Charles Bronson was reported to be earning $20,000-$30,000, plus $2500 living allowance, per day. However, this was far exceeded by Marlon Brando's reputed $3.5 million for 12 days shooting on *Superman* (GB 78), which works out at $290,000 per day. According to a special *Newsweek* report on Hollywood in 1978, the world's highest paid stars were Paul Newman, Robert Redford and Steve McQueen, commanding some $3 million per picture. Each of the three had turned down a $4 million offer to take the starring role in *Superman* (GB 78). Dustin Hoffman accepted precisely that amount for his transvestite role in *Tootsie* (US 82), but an even higher figure of $5 million plus percentage had already been paid to Burt Reynolds for *The Cannonball Run* (US 81). Sean Connery became the highest paid British star when he was lured back into Bond movies with a $5 million bait for *Never Say Never Again* (GB 83).

Barbra Streisand became the first woman to reach the $5 million plateau with the less than sensational *Nuts* (US 88), then headed upwards again with $6 million for *Prince of Tides* (US 91). Probably the only other actresses in this kind of price bracket are Meryl Streep; Sigourney Weaver, who earned $5 million for *Aliens III* (US 91), and Madonna—with neophyte Julia Roberts treading hard on their heels. Goldie Hawn signed a contract with Disney in 1989 worth an estimated $30 million for seven films. Meanwhile the gap between the highest male earnings and the highest female earnings has become a yawning chasm. Al Pacino was paid $8 million for reprising his Michael Corleone role in *The Godfather III* (US 90), plus $50,000 per diem for six days of extra shooting. Tom Cruise earned $9 million plus a substantial percentage for *Days of Thunder* (US 90). Michael Douglas also weighs in at $9 million a picture, while Sean Connery has maintained his position as highest paid British star with fees of $10 million per for *The Hunt for Red October* (US 90) and *The Russia House* (US 91). Eddie Murphy is also in the $10 million league and Bruce Willis, reputedly paid $10 million

> 'I'm a sensitive writer, actor and director. Talking business disgusts me. If you want to do business, call my disgusting personal manager.'—Sylvester Stallone, whose sensitivity commands over $20 million a picture.

for doing the baby voice-over in *Look Who's Talking Too* (US 90), was signed for *The Last Boy Scout* (US i.p.) at $14 million.

He-man Arnold Schwarzenegger, who arrived in the US from his native Austria with nothing but a duffelbag of clothes, realised the American dream when he banked $25 million as his percentage of the box office hit *Twins* (US 89). His emolument for *Total Recall* (US 90), at a fee variously quoted at $10 million to $13 million plus 15 per cent of the net profits, will probably exceed that. He also received a private jet as a bonus. His total earnings for 1989–90 of $55 million, including royalties from earlier films, put

him second in the league table of highest paid movie stars. Top is the redoubtable Sylvester Stallone with $63 million. Having been the first to crash the $10 million barrier, he now commands more than double that sum per film. His earnings for acting and scripting chores on *Rocky V* (US 90) were reported to be $27.5 million plus 35 per cent of the gross.

Besides Schwarzenegger and Stallone, three other stars enjoy the same kind of earning capacity. Dustin Hoffman made $20 million for his percentage deal on

> During the suit brought by Art Buchwald contending (successfully) that he was the originator of *Coming to America* (US 88), it was revealed that Paramount had paid Eddie Murphy $8 million for his performance, plus $1.7 million signing fee, plus $1 million living allowance. Murphy's itemized expenses included $200 for a breakfast (with entourage) at McDonald's.

Rain Man (US 88). Warren Beatty was originally expected to earn twice this from his contract as director and star of *Dick Tracy* (US 90), but the picture failed to break box office records and the final accounting may yield something below $40 million. The only actor reputed to have earned more is Jack Nicholson for his bravura performance as the Joker in *Batman* (US 89). His profit-related deal has been variously estimated to be worth $50 million and $60 million; either way it vies with Stallone's deal on *Rocky V* for the largest amount earned by any actor for a single film.

The lowest salaries of the last 30 years or so have seldom fallen below the £1500 that Olivia Hussey claimed she was paid for 11 months work while she was playing the female lead in Zeffirelli's *Romeo and Juliet* (GB 68) —at least in the west. In eastern countries and even Eastern Europe, different standards prevail. Teresa Izewska, star of the award-winning *Kanal* (Pol 57), revealed at the Cannes Film Festival that she earned the equivalent of $12 a month and that the Polish authorities had bought her one dress and one pair of shoes in order to represent them at the Festival. In 1973 *Variety* reported that China's biggest box office star, Shih Chung-chin, drew a salary of $20 a month. She slept in a communal dormitory with other actresses. By 1980 a top Chinese star could earn a maximum of 250 yuan ($168) a month, though not all were so generously recompensed. Joan Chen, star of the first Anglo-Chinese co-production *The Last Emperor* (It/GB/Chn 88) and latterly of TV's *Twin Peaks*, was earning less than $8 a month in 1980 when she won the 100 Blossoms award as most popular actress. Her salary then went up to $24 a month. Top salary per film for Soviet stars is 6000 roubles

And well might Joker Jack Nicholson toss around a few greenbacks in *Batman* (US 89)—his earnings from the role are reputed to be a record $50–$60 million.

And well might poor Miss Streisand look like she was on the breadline in *Nuts* (US 88)—but she was the first actress to take home $5 million for a movie.

(approx. £6000 at the official rate) for a 50-day schedule, and this modest emolument is subject to a ten per cent withholding tax.

The lowest paid players in American pictures were found in black movies. White director Edgar G. Ulmer recalls paying the 50 chorus girls in *Moon Over Harlem* (US 39) 25c a day each. The shooting schedule was four days and the girls had to pay their car fares from Harlem to the studio in Jersey out of the $1 they earned for a week's work. A record zero budget for an entire cast was achieved by Action Pictures Co. for their all-black feature *Sugar Hill Baby* (US 38). The casting director announced with disarming frankness that there was no money available for salaries, the only inducement offered being the somewhat doubtful 'chance to continue to work in future in productions at good salaries'.

Leading players in Hollywood films expect rather more immediate rewards, but even for major motion pictures salaries may, on occasions, be modest. For what many fans reckon to be the most memorable role in movie history, that of Scarlett O'Hara in *Gone With the Wind* (US 39), Vivien Leigh (by no means a newcomer to the screen) was paid a not very princely $15,000. This was less than ice-skating champion turned film star Sonja Henie was then being paid for a week's work. Frank Sinatra earned only $8000 for his Oscar-winning performance in *From Here to Eternity* (US 53). Nodules on his throat had brought his singing career to a temporary halt and he was desperate to get back into movies at any price. A few years later his co-star in *The Man with the Golden Arm* (US 56), Kim Novak, was hired at her regular salary from Colum

bia of $100 a week, though producer Otto Preminger had to pay the studio $100,000 for her services. In the mid-1950s Paul Newman was getting a relatively meagre $17,500 for each of his Warner Bros' pictures; by the mid-1960s he was on $750,000 a film plus percentage. In the same kind of price bracket was James Dean, paid $18,000 for his standout performance in *East of Eden* (US 55). It was his fifth film but his first starring role and it rocketed him to instant stardom.

Perhaps the last of the great western stars, Clint Eastwood had already been in movies for ten not very productive years when he was offered $15,000 to appear in a spaghetti western called *A Fistful of Dollars* (It 64). By 1972 he was the No. 1 star at the box office and between the mid-seventies and mid-eighties his pictures grossed a record $1400 million. Another star who found fame and fortune in the sixties was Dustin Hoffman. His worth was rated at $17,000 for the smash hit *The Graduate* (US 67) and $425,000 a couple of years later for the floppo *John and Mary* (US 69).

All of these stars were generously remunerated in comparison with Steve McQueen, whose total reward for playing the lead in tacky horror movie *The Blob* (US 58) was $3000. He was not invited to appear in the sequel, *Son of Blob* (US 71). By that time his fee would have been several times the whole budget of the movie. According to Sylvester Stallone, the world's highest paid film star, the only recompense he received for playing a leading role in *The Lords of Flatbush* (US 74) was 25 free T-shirts. Today as ever a performer may be bargain basement one moment and in the megabuck league the next.

Age before beauty. Bogarde's pay for *Death in Venice* (It 71) was one hundred times as much as co-star Bjorn Andresen's. (*Kobal*)

The difference between the earnings of co-stars can be wide. Bjorn Andresen, the luminous youth who was the object of Dirk Bogarde's unspoken passion in *Death in Venice* (It 71), was paid $5000 for the role. Bogarde later revealed to Bjorn that he had been paid exactly one hundred times as much.

One Stephen J. Lewicki cast an unknown rock singer for the lead in *A Certain Feeling* (US 84) and has since been able to congratulate himself all the way to the bank that he secured the services of Madonna for $100 all in.

The first screen artiste to work on percentage was Nellie Stewart, who was paid £1000 plus a per cent of the gross for her role in *Sweet Nell of Old Drury* (Aus 11).

The first American artiste to receive a percentage deal was James O'Neill (father of Eugene), who played the wronged Edmond Dantes in Famous Players' maiden production *The Count of Monte Cristo* (US 13). O'Neill had played the part on stage no less than 4000 times over a period of 30 years and was both too old (65) and too ham for the screen version, but Daniel Frohman knew that his was the name which would draw theatregoers to the cinema and he offered the star 20 per cent of the net profits as an inducement. Returns were undermined by a rival Selig version of *The Count of Monte Cristo*, but the Famous Players version eventually grossed $45,539.32, of which O'Neill received $3813.32.

Percentage deals were anathema to the Hollywood moguls throughout the great days of the studio system. There may been the occasional exception. RKO producer Pandro S. Berman has attested that Fred Astaire received a percentage of the profits on several of his RKO musicals of the 1930s, though this was kept a closely guarded secret at the time. The breakthrough came with the deal negotiated with Universal by James Stewart's agent Lew Wasserman for *Winchester 73* (US 50). Stewart was able to command up to $250,000 as a fixed fee for a picture, but this was beyond the resources of Universal after a series of flops. It was agreed that Stewart should receive a 50 per cent share of the picture's net profits. These were to be defined as anything over twice the negative cost of the film. If *Winchester 73* had earned less than this figure, Stewart would not have earned anything. As it turned out his share of the profits was $600,000, rather more than 'The King of Hollywood', Clark Gable, was paid by MGM for a year's work. For subsequent films Stewart received his standard $250,000 up front plus 10 per cent of the gross.

The most highly-paid stars have sometimes been victims of ingenious attempts by the unscrupulous to benefit from their box office drawing power without the formality of payment. In 1917 a film processor in Chicago created his own Chaplin feature film—at a time when Chaplin was the highest paid star in the world—by matching together shots from his old comedies and then interpolating material from Fox's sensational *The Daughter of the Gods* (US 16), in which Australian star Annette Kellerman appeared in the nude. By clever optical work, he succeeded in creating scenes in which Chaplin and the naked Antipodean beauty appeared to be performing together. The film was released to the underground trade as *Charlie, Son of the Gods*.

Even more audacious was Soviet director Sergei Komarov's deception that secured him the gratuitous services of not one but two superstars, Mary Pickford and Douglas Fairbanks. During the visit of the couple to Moscow in July 1926, Komarov posed as a newsreel cameraman and followed them round with a camera, shooting enough footage to piece together a full-length comedy feature after their departure. Titled *The Kiss of Mary Pickford* (USSR 26), it was an engaging tale of a film extra who is determined to kiss the 'world's sweetheart'—and succeeds! Most remarkable of all was the climactic sequence of the close embrace between Soviet hero and Hollywood heroine. Although the film has now been shown publicly in the west, no one has been able to offer a convincing explanation of how Komarov managed to contrive this scene.

BIOPICS OF SCREEN STARS

Increasingly common as television movies, these often concentrate on an aspect of the performer's life other than their screen career. The biopics of Diana Barrymore and Lillian Roth were concerned with their subjects' alcoholism, those of Eddie Cantor and Al Jolson dwelt mainly on their singing careers, and Annette Kellerman's on her swimming exploits, while *The George Raft Story* recounted the star's pre-Hollywood days in the gangster milieu of 20s New York. The following performers have had their life stories, in whole or in part, portrayed in feature movies:

BUD ABBOTT (1895–1974) and LOU COSTELLO (1906–59) *Bud and Lou* (US 78, TVM). Harvey Korman and Buddy Hackett in a behind-the-scenes story of the comedy duo's stormy personal relationship.

DIANA BARRYMORE (1921–60) *Too Much Too Soon* (US 58) with Dorothy Malone in the story, based on Miss Barrymore's memoirs, of how she went to Hollywood to look after her alcoholic father John Barrymore (Errol Flynn) and herself succumbed to drink.

JOHN BELUSHI (1949–82) *Wired* (US 89). Based on Bob Woodward's biography, with Michael Chiklis as the overweight comic genius who died of a drug overdose.

HUMPHREY BOGART (1899–1957) *Bogie* (US 80, TVM) with Kevin O'Connor, based on Joe Hyams' biography of the same title.

EDDIE CANTOR (1892–1964) *The Eddie Cantor Story* (US 53) with Keefe Brasselle in the name role. Cantor himself played a bit part and also sang the songs off-screen. On seeing the finished picture, he remarked: 'If that was my life, I didn't live.'

LON CHANEY (1883–1930) *The Man of a Thousand Faces* (US 57) with James Cagney as the character actor and contortionist extraordinary of the silent screen.

CHARLES CHAPLIN (1889–1977) *The Life Story of Charles Chaplin* (GB 26) with Chick Wango in a British attempt to cash in on the popularity of the cockney lad who had made it in Hollywood. The first biopic of a screen star, but never released due to a threat of legal action from its subject.

JOAN CRAWFORD (1906–77) *Mommie Dearest* (US 81) was based on Christina Crawford's controversial expose of her adoptive mother, here portrayed by Faye Dunaway as an insecure but savagely egotistical woman given to beating her children with coathangers.

MARION DAVIES (1879–1961) *The Hearst and Davies Affair* (US 85, TVM). Virginia Madsen as the chorus girl who became the lifetime lover of press baron William Randolph Hearst (Robert Mitchum)—he bought her stardom by financing her films and ballyhooing them in his newspapers. Lorne Kennedy as Charlie Chaplin.

JAMES DEAN (1931–55) *James Dean* (US 76, TVM) was scripted by the moody rebel's friend Bill Bast and recounted the story of their lives together as aspiring young actors when they were room-mates in the early fifties. Dean was portrayed by Stephen McHattie, Bast by Michael Brandon.

LEILA DINIZ (194?–6?) *Leila Diniz* (Bra 87) with Louise Cardoso as the unconventional and rebellious Brazilian star of the sixties who became a symbol of the period before perishing in a plane crash at the age of 27.

PATTY DUKE (1946–) *Call Me Anna* (US 90, TVM). Rare example of an autobiopic, with Patty Duke playing herself as an adult (Ari Meyers plays her as a child, Jenny Robertson as a teenager). Tele-film, based on Duke's autobiography of the same title, depicts her horrific childhood as the molested victim of monstrous foster parents, the actress's drug and alcohol abuse as an adult, and her desperate attempts to find love.

FRANCES FARMER (1914–70) *Committed* (US 84) was an earnest black-and-white docu-drama with Sheila McLaughlin in an intense performance as the overwrought, alcoholic, leftist and eventually lobotomized Hollywood beauty whose neuroses led to commitment to an asylum. The title is a play on words signifying Farmer's other commitment, to various 'progressive' causes.

Jessica Lange underwent the straitjacketing and lobotomy in a standout performance in Graeme Clifford's *Frances* (US 82), a version with less emphasis on politics and more on the relationship with monstrous mother Lillian Farmer, played for hisses by Kim Stanley.

W. C. FIELDS (1879–1946) *W. C. Fields and Me* (US 76) with Rod Steiger in another study of a star disintegrating from drink. The 'Me' of the title was Fields' mistress Carlotta Monti (Valerie Perrine), who nursed the tyrant comic through his alcoholism to the detriment of her own career.

ERROL FLYNN (1909–59) *My Wicked, Wicked Ways—The Legend of Errol Flynn* (US 85, TVM) with Canadian Duncan Regehr as the swashbuckling Australian. Barbara Hershey played his fiery Spanish actress wife Lili Damita, Barrie Ingham his fellow drunk John Barrymore and Lee Parcell the too perfect Olivia de Havilland.

Flynn (Aus 90 and 91). Guy Pearce, known to thousands of pre-teens as the rather wimpish teacher Mike in Aussie soap *Neighbours*, was the surprise choice to play the title role in this rampage through Flynn's early life as policeman, gold prospector, slave trader, spy and murder suspect following his deapture from his native New Guinea from his native Australia. The reason two dates are given above is that there were two versions. The one premièred at the 1990 Cannes Film Festival had Australian actors Paul Steven and Jeff Truman in major supporting roles. The other had British actor/playwright Steven Berkoff and American actor John Savage in the same roles, apparently to give the picture a better chance in overseas markets. Reportedly some 40 per cent of the film was reshot for the second version. The new footage was shot in Fiji, allegedly to prevent action by Australian Equity, who declared the replacements 'an absolute bloody disgrace'.

CLARK GABLE (1901–60) *Gable and Lombard* (US 76) with James Brolin struggling bravely in a generally misconceived attempt to portray 'the man rather than the star'. See also LOMBARD.

GRETA GARBO (1905–90) *Moviola: The Silent Lovers* (US 80, TVM). Swedish actress Kristina Wayborn played the divine one very competently—and looked sensationally beautiful—in this tele-pic of Garbo's early years in Hollywood and her celebrated on-off romance with the doomed John Gilbert. Harold Gould portrayed mogul Louis B. Mayer as a monster.

BIOPICS OF SCREEN STARS *(continued)*

JUDY GARLAND (1922–69) *Rainbow* (US 78, TVM) Judy's early life from her days starting out in vaudeville aged 10 to her triumph in *The Wizard of Oz* (US 39) when she was 17. Andrea McArdle played Judy, Moosie Drier the teenage Mickey Rooney and Johnny Doran played Jackie Cooper, who directed *Rainbow*. Probably the only occasion the director of a movie has been portrayed in it.

RUTH GORDON (1896–1985) *The Actress* (US 53). The young Jean Simmons, then 24, played the even younger Ruth Gordon as a stagestruck teenager, in a warm and humorous evocation of growing up in New England in the early years of the century. (Gordon was to make her screen debut in *Camille* in 1915.) The screenplay was by the actress herself, from her own autobiographical play *Years Ago*.

CORINNE GRIFFITH (1898–1979) *Papa's Delicate Condition* (US 63), based on silent screen heroine Corinne Griffith's own book, is possibly the only biopic about the infancy of a star. Linda Bruhl played the six-year-old Corrie, Jackie Gleason her inebriate father.

JEAN HARLOW (1911–37) *Harlow* (US 65) with Carroll Baker in a travesty of the star's life of which the producer, director and screen-writer should be thoroughly ashamed.

Harlow (US 65) with Carol Lynley in a rather better attempt at the subject, released in an Electronovision version.

RITA HAYWORTH (1918–87) *The Love Goddess* (US 83, TVM) Lynda Carter chronicles the flame-haired beauty's rise from café dancer to screen legend and her eventual meeting with husband-to-be Prince Aly Khan, played by Israeli actor Aharon Ipale. Edward Edwards essayed Orson Welles, while Terri Lynn looked suitably vacuous as Kim Novak.

ROCK HUDSON (1925–85) *Rock Hudson* (US 90, TVM) with Thomas Ian Griffith as the homosexual star. Recounts his arranged marriage to his agent's secretary Phyllis Gates (Daphne Ashbrook) and relationship with lover Marc Christian (William Moses), to whom he never confided that he was suffering from AIDS.

SAMMO HUNG (–) *Painted Faces* (HK 88). Ching-ying as the martial arts superstar of Hong Kong action-comedy films, playing opposite Sammo Hung himself as his teacher. Tells the story of Hung's early life as a pupil undergoing the gruelling training in a monastic type martial arts/Chinese opera school where he was incarcerated from the age of seven to seventeen with virtually no contact with the world outside.

AL JOLSON (1886–1950) *The Jolson Story* (US 46) and *Jolson Sings Again* (US 49) with Larry Parks in both highly successful films. Jolson himself did the voice-over for the songs and is also seen in long shot during the 'Swanee' sequence of the first picture.

BUSTER KEATON (1895–1966) *The Buster Keaton Story* (US 57) with Donald O'Connor in what Leslie Halliwell has described as 'a dismal tribute'. Once again the theme is one of drink being the curse of the starring classes.

ANNETTE KELLERMAN (1888–1978) *Million Dollar Mermaid* (US 53) with Esther Williams playing the Australian girl who invented the one-piece bathing suit and became one of the first star actresses to appear on the screen in the nude (not depicted in the biopic).

GRACE KELLY (1928–82) *Grace Kelly* (US 83, TVM). Made with Princess Grace's consent and participation, shortly before her death in September 1982. Cheryl Ladd succeeded,

where so many have failed in star biopics, in looking like the original. Ian McShane played Prince Rainier and there was a galaxy of star portrayals: Rita Gam (Marta DuBois); Mady Christians (Salome Jens); Raymond Massey (Paul Lambert); Clark Gable (Boyd Holister); Alec Guinness (Arthur Berggren); William Holden (Van Corwith). Lomax Stucly had the difficult task of impersonating Alfred Hitchcock.

BRUCE LEE (1940–73) *A Dragon Story*/GB: *The Bruce Lee Story* (US 74) with Hsiao Lung as the Chinese-American actor who achieved international stardom in Hong Kong martial arts movies.

A succession of wholly or semi-fictitious martial arts films followed which purported to portray Bruce Lee: *The Story of the Dragon* (HK 76) with Ho Tsung-tao (Bruce Li); *Bruce Lee—True Story* (HK 76) with Bruce Li; *Bruce Lee and I* (HK 76) with Li Msiu Hsien; *The Dragon Lives* (HK 78) with Bruce Li; *Bruce Lee: the Man, the Myth* (HK 78) with Bruce Li; *Bruce Lee, The Tiger of Manchuria* (HK 78) with Hang Yong Chul; *Young Bruce Lee* (HK 79) with Chuck Norris; *Sexy Isla Meets Bruce Lee in the Devil's Triangle* (Can 7?); *Bruce Lee versus the Gay Power* (Bra 7?). *The Death of Bruce Lee* (HK 76) merely invoked the name, not the character.

VIVIEN LEIGH (1913–67) and LAURENCE OLIVIER (1907–90) *Darlings of the Gods* (Aus/GB 90, TVM). Anthony Higgins as a somewhat wooden Sir Larry and Mel Martin as an effectively lookalike Vivien Leigh in the story of their triumphant but turbulent tour of Australia in 1948 with the Old Vic Company. As the marriage starts to collapse under the pressures of Vivien's erratic behaviour and insatiable sexual appetite, she seeks solace in the arms of young Australian actor Peter Finch (Jerome Ehlers).

LEKHA (–) *Lekha's Death, a Flashback* (Ind 84). The life and death of a teenage superstar of the thriving Malayalam cinema, with Nalini as Lekha. Director K. G. George speculates on the reasons for her suicide in a partly fictional account of her escape from prostitution into the false glamour of the 'filmi' world.

CAROLE LOMBARD (1908–42) *Gable and Lombard* (US 76) with Jill Clayburgh as the love of Gable's life, killed tragically in an aeroplane accident at the age of 34. The film failed to illuminate either the romantic myth of the legendary affair or the earthy reality (Lombard commented to a friend 'He's not what you'd call a helluva great lay'). Though even Hollywood could not bring itself to nominate the film for an Oscar, it did succeed in picking up Harvard Lampoon's 1976 Victor Mature Memorial Award for the most embarrassing line of dialogue. The citation read: '*Gable and Lombard*, for the screen's greatest insouciant comment following the incendiary demise of his beloved in a plane crash, as he gazes fondly over the twisted wreckage: "She should have taken the train".'

SOPHIA LOREN (1934–) *Sophia Loren: Her Own Story* (US 80, TVM). Sophia Loren as herself and as her mother in a poor girl makes good story aptly summed up by her own remark 'Everything you see, I owe to spaghetti'. John Gavin made his last screen appearance, playing Cary Grant, before his appointment by former colleague Ronald Reagan as Ambassador to Mexico.

JAYNE MANSFIELD (1932–67) *The Jayne Mansfield Story* (US 80, TVM). Fictionalised biopic of the 50s plantinum-blonde sex siren, played by

Sophia Loren is one of the few stars to have played themselves in a film of their life story. In this scene from *Sophia Loren: Her Own Story* (US 80, TVM) she re-enacts the birth of her first child, Carlo Ponti Jr. The baby was played by 11-day-old Anita Cookson of Clapham, whose 20-year-old mother Sharon was present at the shoot to watch her daughter's 'rebirth' as a boy. *(Hulton-Deutsch Collection)*

Loni Anderson. Arnold Schwarzenegger, in his first starring role on television, played her muscle-bound second husband Mickey Hargitay.

MARILYN MONROE (1926–62) *Goodbye, Norma Jean* (US/Aus 75) with Misty Rowe, a reasonable look-alike but nothing more, in an exploitation movie that concentrates on Norma Jean Baker's seedy and often degrading existence before her metamorphosis into Marilyn Monroe superstar.

Catherine Hicks essayed the difficult role of legendary sex goddess in *Marilyn the Untold Story* (US 80), a TVM theatrically released in Europe. Based on Norman Mailer's biography, it in fact told little that had not been told before, but then neither did the book. One unusual feature was the portrayal of living and active stars by other actors—Tony Curtis by Bruce Neckels, Jack Lemmon by Brad Blaisdell and Laurence Olivier by Anthony Gordon.

Constance Forslund starred as MM in the other tele-biopic of 1980 *Moviola: This Year's Blonde* aka *The Secret Love of Marilyn Monroe* (US 80, TVM). This one was about her relationship with the agent who launched her in the face of jibes that she was no more than 'this year's blonde'.

Goodnight, Sweet Marilyn (US/Aus 89) was both a follow-up to and a reworking of *Goodbye, Norma Jean* by the same producer/director, Larry Buchanan. It focuses on the last day of MM's life, with extensive flashbacks taken from the Misty Rowe movie. The older Marilyn is played by Paula Lane.

PATRICIA NEAL (1926-) *The Patricia Neal Story* (US 81, TVM). Glenda Jackson as Patricia Neal, the actress who won an Oscar for *Hud* (US 63) but was struck down by a series of major strokes at the peak of her career. Her husband, the best-selling writer Roald Dahl, was portrayed by Dirk Bogarde and Rock Hudson played himself.

LAURENCE OLIVIER see VIVIEN LEIGH.

ELVIS PRESLEY (1935-77) *Elvis* (US 79, TVM) with Kurt Russell playing the Pelvis, Ronnie McDowell dubbing the songs. Theatrically released in Europe.

GEORGE RAFT (1895-1986) *The George Raft Story* (US 61) with Ray Danton as the professional athlete, gambler, nightclub dancer and intimate of gangsters who turned it all to good account in Hollywood.

BILL 'BOJANGLES' ROBINSON (1878-1949) *Stormy Weather* (US 43) with 'Bojangles' himself in an all-black fictionalized version of his own life story. Also subject of 1979 Broadway musical *Bojangles*.

WILL ROGERS (1879-1935) *The Story of Will Rogers* (US 50) with Will Rogers Jnr playing his father in a bland homage to the celebrated crackerbarrel philosopher and latecomer movie star.

LILLIAN ROTH (1910-80) *I'll Cry Tomorrow* (US 55) with Susan Hayward as the Broadway/Hollywood star of the early thirties whose career became another write-off to alcoholism.

THERESA SALDANA (1964-) *Victims for Victims: The Theresa Saldana Story* (US 84, TVM). TS starred as herself in this recounting of the horrific attack on her by a crazed fan in 1982, shortly after she had appeared opposite Robert De Niro as Jake LaMotta's sister-in-law in *Raging Bull* (US 80), and its aftermath when she became spokeswoman for the Victims for Victims support organisation.

MARGARET SULLAVAN (1911-60) *Haywire* (US 80, TVM). Based on Brooke Hayward's best-selling biography of her parents, film and stage star Margaret Sullavan, played by Lee Remick in the film, and the theatrical agent/producer Leland Hayward (Jason Robards). Produced by their son William Hayward.

KINUYO TANAKA (1910-77) *Actress* (Jap 87). Sayuri Yoshinaga as one of the greatest Japanese screen actresses, star of the first successful talkie made in Japan *A Madame and a Wife* (Jap 31). Almost a potted history of the Japanese film industry, the picture includes recreated scenes of Kenji Mizoguchi (played by Bunta Sugawara) directing Tanaka in his masterpiece *The Life of Oharu* (Jap 52).

RUDOLPH VALENTINO (1895-1926) *Valentino* (US 51) with Anthony Dexter in a flat biopic made at a time when Hollywood's attempts to portray the twenties invariably mixed period cliché with blundering anachronisms.

The Legend of Valentino (US 75) with Franco Nero in a version billed as 'romantic fiction'—a precaution against litigation from any of the surviving personalities in Valentino's tempestuous life.

Valentino (GB 77) with Rudolf Nureyev charismatic in Ken Russell's lush and stimulating evocation of man, myth, place and period.

HANSA WADKAR (1920-71) *Bhumika* (Ind 78) with Smita Patil as the popular Hindi star of the thirties and forties. One of the few foreign-language star biopics.

MAE WEST (1892-1980) *Mae West* (US 82, TVM). Ann Jillian in a sanitized version of the raunchy star's life from age seven until her triumphant Broadway return in *Diamond Lil* in 1948. Chuck McCann played W. C. Fields.

PEARL WHITE (1889-1938) *The Perils of Pauline* (US 47) with Betty Hutton recreating the career of the silent serial queen in uncompromisingly forties style.

Extras

The first film with a 'cast of thousands' in a literal sense was Luigi Maggi's Napoleonic epic *Il Granatiere Rolland* (It 10), for which 2000 extras were employed. A similar number participated in Britain's first extravaganza, Charles Weston's feature-length *The Battle of Waterloo* (GB 13).

The largest number of extras employed on a film appeared in the funeral scene of Sir Richard Attenborough's *Gandhi* (GB 82) and comprised a crowd believed to have been in excess of 300,000. Announcements by loudspeaker van, in newspapers and on television and radio summoned over 200,000 volunteer extras to Delhi's ceremonial mall, the Raj-path, where they were supplemented by another 94,560 contracted performers, the majority of whom were paid a fee equivalent to 40p each. The sequence had to be shot in a single morning, that of Saturday 31 January 1981, the 33rd anniversary of Gandhi's funeral. Eleven camera crews shot 20,000 ft of film, more than the total footage of the 188-minute release print of the movie. The edited funeral sequence with its 300,000 performers ran for only 125 seconds of screen time.

The largest number of soldiers used as extras was 187,000 in the last Nazi-made motion picture epic *Kolberg* (Ger 45). For this story about Napoleon's siege of Kolberg, whole army divisions were diverted from the front to play Napoleonic soldiers at a time when Germany was facing the prospect of her defeat. The film was started in 1943 and completed at the end of the following year, with drafts of fresh extras continuously replacing those who had to return to more earnest military duties. Released in January 1945, at a time when few Berlin cinemas were still functioning, *Kolberg* was seen by a considerably smaller total audience than the number which had appeared in it.

Other considerable casts include: 157,000 for monster movie *Wang Ma Gwi/Monster Wang-magwi* (S.Kor 67); 120,000 for *War and Peace* (USSR 67); 106,000 for *Ilya Muromets* (USSR 56); over 100,000 on *Tonko* (Jap 88), claimed as 'the most expensive film ever made in Japan'; 80,000 for *The War of Independence* (Rom 12); 68,894 for *Around the World in 80 Days* (US 56); 60,000 for *Intolerance* (US 16)—publicity for the picture claimed 125,000; 60,000 for *Dny Zrady* (Cz 72); 50,000 for *Ben Hur* (US 59), *Exodus* (US 60), *Inchon* (Kor/US 81) and *Khan Asparouch* (Bul 82); 36,000 in *Metropolis* (Ger 26), including 1100 bald men in the Tower of Babel sequence; and 30,000 in *Michael the Brave* (Rom 70).

The year that the largest number of extras were employed in Hollywood was 1927, when a total

> In Samuel Fuller's war picture *Big Red One* (US 80), all the Nazi concentration camp guards were played by Jews. The location was a military base in Israel and the jackbooted jailers were Israeli soldiers lent for the production.

The cast of *Metropolis* (Ger 26) included 1100 bald extras in the Tower of Babel sequence. (*Kobal*)

When Mario Mattoli was filming his comedy *Imputato, alzateri!/Defendant Stand Up!* (It 39) at Cinecitta Studios in Rome, he was dismayed to hear that on the last day of shooting he had to play host to 200 Japanese tourists. Knowing that it would be all but impossible to control such a herd of non-Italian speaking oriental shutterbugs, he made the best of a bad job. Hastily rewriting the script, Mattoli devised an end scene involving a mob of Japanese tourists and filmed his 200 unpaid extras to hilarious effect.

of 330,397 days were worked (227,415 by men, 102,892 by women), an average daily call of 1056. Since there were 14,000 extras registered with Central Casting that year, average employment rate was approximately one day in 14.

Extras who Became Stars

Comparatively few major stars began their film careers as extras, the majority having had stage or, latterly, television experience before entering movies. Those who did do extra work include Theda Bara, Gary Cooper, Marlene Dietrich, Clark Gable, Janet Gaynor, John Gilbert, Paulette Goddard, Stewart Granger, Jean Harlow, Harold Lloyd, Sophia Loren, Marilyn Monroe, David Niven, Ramon Novarro, Merle Oberon, Norma Shearer, Erich von Stroheim, Constance Talmadge, Rudolph Valentino, Michael Wilding and Loretta Young.

Despite the fact that he was registered at Central Casting as 'Anglo-Saxon type 2008', David Niven's first role was as a Mexican in a blanket in a Hopalong Cassidy oater. He was subsequently an extra in 26 other westerns.

Sadly the reverse process could also apply. Leading players who ended their careers as extras were King Baggot, Mae Busch, Ethel Clayton, Grace Cunard, western star Franklyn Farnum, Flora Finch, Francis Ford (brother of John Ford and a leading man in the late teens), John Ince (brother of early mogul Thomas Ince), Douglas Fairbanks' leading lady Julanne Johnston, Alice Lake, original 'Biograph Girl' Florence Lawrence, western star Kermit Maynard, Marshall Neilan, who had once commanded $125,000 per picture, Florence Turner, who was the first star to be put under contract, and 'country boy' hero Charles Ray. May McAvoy, romantic lead of the twenties who played opposite Al Jolson in *The*

School, college and regimental reunions are commonplace, but a reunion of film extras? Veteran Australian producer-director Ken Hall organized, at the age of 89, what is believed to have been the first such event when he brought together the surviving walk-ons from his 1931 classic *On Our Selection* (Aus 31) nearly 60 years later. All those who had appeared in the Picnic Race scenes were invited to attend the reunion at Agnes Bank, NSW, which was held on 10 June 1990 together with the outback town's annual Picnic Race.

Jazz Singer (US 27), retired when talkies took over but later tried to make a comeback as a character actress. She never succeeded in securing a speaking part and ended her career as an extra with MGM in the 1940s.

The dream of stardom via Central Casting occasionally comes true even today. Sixteen-year-old French schoolgirl Sandrine Bonnaire applied for a role as an extra in Maurice Pialat's *A Nos Amours* (Fr 83). She was given the lead instead, winning plaudits from the critics for her performance and sharing in the accolade of a César award, the French Oscar, for 'Best Film' of the year.

Black Extras

Demand for black extras in the USA began with the flood of Civil War movies that followed the 50th anniversary in 1911. Tarzan and other jungle movies, together with epics of the ancient world, maintained a steady flow of work and the number of blacks registered with Central Casting peaked at 6816 in 1926. The following year was the best for employment, with some 10,000 black roles cast—the total for the previous three years had been 17,000. There was a decline with the coming of talkies and generally the films of the thirties were more confined in their settings than those of the silent era, requiring smaller crowd scenes. World War II brought an almost complete stop to black casting; despite the million black Americans under arms, Hollywood's doughboy was resolutely white. After the war there was little improvement—in 1948 only 130 black roles were cast in pictures.

Contracts, Legal and Binding . . .

In the days when studios 'owned' stars, the price of security and gigantic salaries was often freedom of behaviour. All big stars had morality clauses in their contracts (first to sign had been Maryon Aye in 1922), but Joan Crawford's with MGM in 1930 even specified the hour by which she had to be in bed. Mary Miles Minter's contract with the Realart Co. in 1919 was dependent upon her remaining unmarried for 3½ years. Others enjoined to remain single were Clara Bow, at Paramount's insistence, and Alice White, whose contract with First National further obliged her to learn two languages during the course of 1930, preferably French and Spanish. Walter Pidgeon, much in demand for musicals before he became a father figure, was forbidden to sing tenor lest he impair his rich baritone voice. Buster Keaton's famous unsmiling face was a contractual obligation. His contract with MGM in the twenties precluded him from smiling on screen, while Charles Butterworth's with Warner Bros prevented him from smiling in public. Similarly, Roscoe Ates' stutter was legally binding in his contract with RKO. First National demanded of Douglas Fairbanks Jr that he never travel in 'planes. Joe E. Brown was forbidden to grow a moustache. A clause in teetotaller Frank McHugh's contract with First National required that he play drunkards whenever required, while Maurice Chevalier's with Paramount, signed as talkies were coming in, insisted that he remain in character—it was rendered invalid if he ever lost his French accent. In 1931 boxing fan Vivienne Segal was directed by her contract with Warner's not to yell at prize fights in case she strained her voice.

Possibly the most difficult contractual obligation to enforce was the one enjoined on Lois Moran not to grow sophisticated for a year after the release of *Stella Dallas* (US 26). Clara Bow was offered a $500,000 bonus by Paramount in 1926 provided she kept herself free of scandal during its tenure. She failed to collect. All the cast of Cecil B. DeMille's reverential life

of Christ, *King of Kings* (US 27), were bound by contract not to accept any roles without DeMille's consent for ten years after the film's release. Dorothy Cummings, who played the Madonna, was further denied the right to divorce, which she promptly did 3 months after the première.

Occasionally the stars were able to impose unusual conditions on their masters, the studios. At the Warner studios in the early thirties, George Arliss's contract provided that he did not have to remain on set after 4.30 p.m., while John Barrymore's gave him the privilege of not being on set before 10.30 a.m. Moran and Mack, the Two Black Crows, were the only Paramount stars allowed to drive their car within the studio gates. Garbo's desire to be alone was protected by a clause preventing MGM from demands that she make any public appearances. When stage player Margaret Sullavan was persuaded by director John Stahl to accept the lead in *Only Yesterday* (US 33), she was so reluctant to enter films that she had a clause inserted in her contract to the effect that she could quit after ten days if she disliked Hollywood as much as she anticipated. Although she loathed Tinsel Town, she completed the picture and many others. Joe E. Brown's contract with Warner's demanded that the studio co-operate with him in running a baseball team. Virginal Evelyn Venable's contract with Paramount in 1933 had a clause inserted by her father preventing her from being kissed on screen. The rather less virginal Clara Bow wrote into her contract with Paramount that none of the workmen or technicians were to use profane language to her or in her presence.

Even today, producers are known to make grudging concessions if the name of the star is big enough. Roger Moore will not sign any contract unless he is guaranteed an unlimited supply of hand-rolled Monte Cristo cigars from Cuba. On one of the Bond movies, the bill of 007's cigars came to £3176.50. Audrey Hepburn also knows how to wipe the thin-lipped smile from producers' faces. Before agreeing to star in *Sidney Sheldon's Bloodline* (US/FRG 83), she imposed a condition that all her costumes were to be designed by Paris couturier Givenchy; and furthermore that, when filming was completed, she would be given the $100,000 wardrobe.

Cricket fanatic Trevor Howard had a clause in his contracts relieving him of having to be on set during Test Matches, while Peter Sellers stipulated that he was to have accommodation which allowed his bed to be positioned east–west—any other way and he could not sleep. Personal vanity also has its part to play in deal making. Warren Beatty will not sign any contract that requires him to be filmed without his shirt. Sylvester Stallone will only be shot in profile from his good side, otherwise the deal's off.

Woody Allen's conditions for starring in Disney's *Scenes from a Mall* (US 91) included a clause entitling the whole of his surrogate family, including Mia

Farrow and her many children, to be flown out to Disneyland and personally conducted round its attractions by studio head Jeffrey Katzenberg. At the bottom line, though, superstar contracts are about money—lots of it. Michael Ovitz, reputedly Hollywood's most powerful agent, secured a unique concession for Sean Connery when he negotiated terms for the Scottish star's appearance in *The Hunt for Red October* (US 90). He demanded extra money to compensate for the dollar's decline against the pound. 'I don't think the studio had heard the argument before', Connery confided, 'but funnily enough they came round to my way of thinking.'

FILM STARS WHO HAVE PLAYED THEMSELVES IN MOVIES

Rex Allen *Trail of Robin Hood* (US 51)
June Allyson *Words and Music* (US 48)
Eddie 'Rochester' Anderson *Star Spangled Rhythm* (US 42)
Arletty *L'Amour Madame* (Fr 52)
Fred Astaire *Dancing Lady* (US 33)
Steve Astin *Without You I'm Nothing* (US 90)
Mary Astor *Hollywood* (US 23)
Lew Ayres *The Cohens and the Kellys in Hollywood* (US 32)
Lauren Bacall *Two Guys from Milwaukee* (US 46)
Carroll Baker *Jack of Diamonds* (US/FRG 67)
Anne Bancroft *Silent Movie* (US 76)
Tallulah Bankhead *Stage Door Canteen* (US 43); *Main Street to Broadway* (US 53)
Brigitte Bardot *Dear Brigitte* (US 65)
Wendy Barrie *It Should Happen to You* (US 54)
Ethel Barrymore *Main Street to Broadway* (US 53)
John Barrymore *Nearly a King* (US 14); *The Nightingale* (US 14)
Lionel Barrymore *Free and Easy* (US 30); *Main Street to Broadway* (US 53)
Freddie Bartholomew *Sepia Cinderella* (US 47)
Noah Beery *Hollywood* (US 23)
Dorothy Bellew *The Kinema Girl* (GB 14)
William Bendix *Duffy's Tavern* (US 45); *Variety Girl* (US 47)
Constance Bennett *It Should Happen to You* (US 54)
Edgar Bergen *Stage Door Canteen* (US 43); *Song of the Open Road* (US 44)
Milton Berle *Let's Make Love* (US 60); *Broadway Danny Rose* (US 84)
Humphrey Bogart *Thank Your Lucky Stars* (US 43); *Two Guys from Milwaukee* (US 46); *Always Together* (US 47); *The Love Lottery* (US 54)
John Boles *Stand Up and Cheer* (US 34)
Ray Bolger *The Great Ziegfeld* (US 36)
Clara Bow *Fascinating Youth* (US 26)
Joe E. Brown *Hollywood Canteen* (US 44)
Johnny Mack Brown *The Marshal's Daughter* (US 53)
Coral Browne (as herself in 1958) *An Englishman Abroad* (GB 84)
James Caan *Silent Movie* (US 76)
Eddie Cantor *Thank Your Lucky Stars* (US 43); *Hollywood Canteen* (US 44); *The Story of Will Rogers* (US 52)
Jack Carson *It's a Great Feeling* (US 49)
Charles Chaplin *Show People* (US 29)
Cyd Charisse *Words and Music* (US 48)
Chevy Chase *L.A. Story* (US 91)
Cher *Good Times* (US 67)
Maurice Chevalier *L'Homme du Jour* (Fr 37) (also plays hero); *Pepe* (US 60)
Julie Christie *Nashville* (US 75)
Betty Compson *Hollywood* (US 23); *Hollywood Boulevard* (US 36)
Chester Conklin *Fascinating Youth* (US 26); *The Perils of Pauline* (US 47)
Sean Connery *Memories of Me* (US 88)
Eddie Constantine *Les Septs péchés capitaux* (Fr/It 62); *Warnung vor einer Heiligen Nutte* (FRG/It 71); *Flight to Berlin* (GB 84)
Jackie Coogan *Free and Easy* (US 30)

Gary Cooper *Variety Girl* (US 47); *It's a Great Feeling* (US 49); *Starlift* (US 51)
Ricardo Cortez *Hollywood* (US 23)
Dolores and Helene Costello *How Cissy Made Good* (US 14)
Broderick Crawford *A Little Romance* (US 79)
Joan Crawford *Hollywood Canteen* (US 44); *It's a Great Feeling* (US 49)
Bing Crosby *Star Spangled Rhythm* (US 42); *Duffy's Tavern* (US 45); *Variety Girl* (US 47); *Angels in the Outfield* (US 52); *The Greatest Show on Earth* (US 52); *Let's Make Love* (US 60); *Pepe* (US 60)
Finlay Currie *6.5. Special* (GB 58)
Karl Dane *Free and Easy* (US 30)
Bette Davis *Thank Your Lucky Stars* (US 43); *Hollywood Canteen* (US 44)
Sammy Davis Jr *Pepe* (US 60); *Moon Over Parador* (US 88)
Doris Day *Starlift* (US 51)
Olivia de Havilland *Thank Your Luck Stars* (US 43)
Dolores Del Rio *Torero!* (Mex 56)
Catherine Deneuve *L'Enfant de l'Art* (Fr 88)
Marlene Dietrich *Follow the Boys* (US 44); *Jigsaw* (US 49)

Richard Dix *Fascinating Youth* (US 26)
Diana Dors *Allez France* (Fr 64)
Sidney Drew *Pay Day* (US 18)
Jimmy Durante *Pepe* (US 60)
Douglas Fairbanks *Hollywood* (US 23); *The Kiss of Mary Pickford* (USSR 26); *Show People* (US 29)
Marianne Faithfull *Made in USA* (Fr 67)
Peter Falk *Der Himmel über Berlin* (FRG/Fr 87)
William Farnum *The Perils of Pauline* (US 47); *Trail of Robin Hood* (US 51)
Alice Faye *Four Jills in a Jeep* (US 44)
Stepin Fetchit *Stand Up and Cheer* (US 34)
Gracie Fields *Stage Door Canteen* (US 43)
W. C. Fields *Sensations of 1945* (US 44); *Song of the Open Road* (US 44); *Follow the Boys* (US 44)
Flora Finch *How Cissy Made Good* (US 14)
Barry Fitzgerald *Variety Girl* (US 47)
Rhonda Fleming *The Patsy* (US 64)
Cyril Fletcher *Yellow Canary* (GB 43)
Errol Flynn *Always Together* (US 47); *Cuban Rebel Girls* (US 60)
Henry Fonda *Jigsaw* (US 49); *Main Street to Broadway* (US 53); *Fedora* (FRG 78)
Jane Fonda *Leonard Part 6* (US 87)

Jane Wyman as Jane Wyman, John Garfield as John Garfield and Bette Davis as Bette Davis in Warner Bros' *Hollywood Canteen* (US 44). (*Kobal*)

Kay Francis *Four Jills in a Jeep* (US 44)
Zsa Zsa Gabor *Pepe* (US 60) ; *Jack of Diamonds* (US/FRG 67) ; *California Girls* (US 85, TVM) ; *Smart Alex* (US 86)
Greta Garbo *A Man's Man* (US 29)
Ava Gardner *The Band Wagon* (US 53)
John Garfield *Thank Your Lucky Stars* (US 43) ; *Hollywood Canteen* (US 44) ; *Jigsaw* (US 49)
Judy Garland *Words and Music* (US 48)
Greer Garson *The Youngest Profession* (US 43) ; *Pepe* (US 60)
John Gilbert *Married Flirts* (US 24) ; *A Man's Man* (US 29)
Paulette Goddard *Star Spangled Rhythm* (US 42) ; *Variety Girl* (US 47)
Elliott Gould *Nashville* (US 75) ; *The Muppets Take Manhattan* (US 84)
Betty Grable *Four Jills in a Jeep* (US 44)
Cary Grant *Without Reservations* (US 46)
Greta Gynt *I'm a Stranger* (GB 52)
Larry Hagman *I am Blushing* (Swe 81)
Creighton Hale *Mary of the Movies* (US 23)
Monte Hale *Trail of Robin Hood* (US 51)
Rex Harrison *Main Street to Broadway* (US 53)
W. S. Hart *Hollywood* (US 23) ; *Show People* (US 29)
Laurence Harvey *The Magic Christian* (GB 70) as self playing Hamlet
Sessue Hayakawa *Night Life in Hollywood* (US 22)
Sterling Hayden *Variety Girl* (US 47)
Susan Hayward *Star Spangled Rhythm* (US 42)
Sonja Henie *Hello London* (GB 58)
Katherine Hepburn *Stage Door Canteen* (US 43)
William Holden *Variety Girl* (US 47)
Jack Holt *Hollywood Speaks* (US 32)
Bob Hope *Duffy's Tavern* (US 45) ; *Variety Girl* (US 47) ; *The Greatest Show on Earth* (US 52) ; *The Oscar* (US 66)
John Houseman *Scrooged* (US 88)
Rock Hudson *The Patricia Neal Story* (US 81, TVM)
John Hurt *Spaceballs* (US 87)
Betty Hutton *Star Spangled Rhythm* (US 42) ; *Duffy's Tavern* (US 45)
Sidney James *The Beauty Contest* (GB 64)
Al Jolson *Hollywood Cavalcade* (US 39) ; *Rhapsody in Blue* (US 44) ; *Jolson Sings Again* (US 49) —scene of Jolson meeting Larry Parks and congratulating him on his portrayal of Jolson in *The Jolson Story*
Boris Karloff *The Cohens and the Kellys in Hollywood* (US 32) ; *Bikini Beach* (US 64)
Danny Kaye *It's a Great Feeling* (US 49)
Buster Keaton *Hollywood Cavalcade* (US 39) ; *Sunset Boulevard* (US 50)
Gene Kelly *Words and Music* (US 48) ; *Love is Better than Ever* (US 52) ; *Let's Make Love* (US 60)
George Kennedy *The Legend of Lylah Clare* (US 68) ; *Modern Romance* (US 81)
Alan Ladd *Star Spangled Rhythm* (US 42) ; *Duffy's Tavern* (US 45) ; *Variety Girl* (US 47)
Veronica Lake *Star Spangled Rhythm* (US 42) ; *Variety Girl* (US 47)
Dorothy Lamour *Star Spangled Rhythm* (US 42) ; *Duffy's Tavern* (US 45) ; *Variety Girl* (US 47) ; *Here Comes the Groom* (US 51)
Carole Landis *Four Jills in a Jeep* (US 44)
Harry Langdon *Ella Cinders* (US 26)
Laurel and Hardy *Pick a Star* (US 37)
Peter Lawford *Pepe* (US 60)
Janet Leigh *Pepe* (US 60)
Jack Lemmon *Pepe* (US 60)
Peter Lorre *Hollywood Canteen* (US 44)
Bessie Love *Night Life in Hollywood* (US 22) ; *Mary of the Movies* (US 23)
Linda Lovelace *Linda Lovelace for President* (US 75)
Ida Lupino *Thank Your Lucky Stars* (US 43)
Jeanette MacDonald *Follow the Boys* (US 44)

Virginia McKenna *An Elephant called Slowly* (GB 69) ; *The Lion at World's End* (GB 71)
Fred MacMurray *Star Spangled Rhythm* (US 42)
Gordon MacRae *Starlift* (US 51)
Lee Majors *Scrooged* (US 88)
George Marshall *Variety Girl* (US 47)
Harpo Marx *Stage Door Canteen* (US 43)
Marcello Mastroianni *L'Ingorgo/Bottleneck* (It/Fr/Sp/FRG 79)
Victor Mature *Head* (US 68)
Kermit Maynard *Trail of Robin Hood* (US 51)
Virginia Mayo *Starlift* (US 51)
Adolphe Menjou *Fascinating Youth* (US 26)
Burgess Meredith *Jigsaw* (US 49)
Ray Milland *Star Spangled Rhythm* (US 42) ; *Variety Girl* (US 47)
Liza Minnelli *Silent Movie* (US 76) ; *The Muppets Take Manhattan* (US 84)
Tom Mix *The Cohens and the Kellys in Hollywood* (US 32)
Bull Montana *Hollywood* (US 23)
Yves Montand *Trois places pour le 26* (Fr 88)
Owen Moore *Hollywood* (US 23)
Dennis Morgan *It's a Great Feeling* (US 49)
Paul Muni *Stage Door Canteen* (US 43)
Mae Murray *Married Flirts* (US 24) ; *Show People* (US 29)
Ornella Muti *Grandi Magazzini* (It 86)
Nita Naldi *Hollywood* (US 23)
Patricia Neal *It's a Great Feeling* (US 49)
Pola Negri *Hollywood* (US 23)
Paul Newman *Silent Movie* (US 76)
Anna Q. Nillson *Sunset Boulevard* (US 50)

Kim Novak *Pepe* (US 60)
Merle Oberon *Stage Door Canteen* (US 43) ; *The Oscar* (US 66)
Donald O'Connor *Follow the Boys* (US 44)
Lili Palmer *Main Street to Broadway* (US 53) ; *Le Rendezvous de Minuit* (Fr 66) (also played two fictitious characters) ; *Jack of Diamonds* (US/FRG 67)
Larry Parks *Jolson Sings Again* (US 49) —also played Jolson
Mary Pickford *Hollywood* (US 23) ; *The Kiss of Mary Pickford* (USSR 26) made by Sergei Komorov without Miss Pickford being aware of her own participation
Walter Pidgeon *The Youngest Profession* (US 43)
ZaSu Pitts *Mary of the Movies* (US 23) ; *Make Me a Star* (US 32)
Eddie Polo *Dangerous Hour* (US 23)
Dick Powell *Star Spangled Rhythm* (US 42)
Jane Powell *Song of the Open Road* (US 44)
William Powell *The Youngest Profession* (US 43)
Robert Preston *Variety Girl* (US 47)
Dennis Price *Go for a Take* (GB 72)
George Raft *Broadway* (US 42) ; *Stage Door Canteen* (US 43) ; *The Patsy* (US 64) ; *Casino Royale* (GB 67) ; *Sextette* (US 78)
Tony Randall *The King of Comedy* (US 83)
Ronald Reagan *It's a Great Feeling* (US 49)
Wallace Reid *Night Life in Hollywood* (US 22)
Michael Rennie *The Body Said No!* (GB 50)
Burt Reynolds *Silent Movie* (US 76)
Debbie Reynolds *Pepe* (US 60)
Ralph Richardson *The Volunteer* (GB 43)
Tex Ritter *Nashville Rebel* (US 66) ; *What Am I Bid?* (US 67)

Gloria Swanson as herself in *Airport 75* (US 74). More than half a century earlier she had also played herself in *Hollywood* (US 23).

Joan Rivers as President of the USA Joan Rivers in *Les Patterson Saves the World* (Aus 87)

Edward G. Robinson *It's a Great Feeling* (US 49)

May Robson *How Molly Malone Made Good* (US 15)

Patricia Roc *Holiday Camp* (GB 47)

Roy Rogers *Hollywood Canteen* (US 44)

Will Rogers *Hollywood* (US 23)

Sabrina *Just My Luck* (GB 57)

Randolph Scott *Starlift* (US 51)

Larry Semon *Go Straight* (US 25)

Norma Shearer *Married Flirts* (US 24)

Martin Sheen *In the King of Prussia* (US 82)

Brooke Shields *The Muppets Take Manhattan* (US 84)

Sylvia Sidney *Make Me a Star* (US 32)

Phil Silvers *Take It or Leave It* (US 44)

Frank Sinatra *Pepe* (US 60); *The Oscar* (US 66); *Cannonball Run II* (US 83)

Barbara Stanwyck *Hollywood Canteen* (US 44); *Variety Girl* (US 47)

Tommy Steele *Kill Me Tomorrow* (GB 55); *The Tommy Steele Story* (GB 57)

Anita Stewart *Mary of the Movies* (US 23); *Hollywood* (US 23); *Go Straight* (US 25)

Edith Storey *How Cissy Made Good* (US 14)

Gloria Swanson *Hollywood* (US 23); *Airport 75* (US 74)

Blanche Sweet *Souls for Sale* (US 23)

Constance Talmadge *In Hollywood with Potash and Perlmutter* (US 24)

Norma Talmadge *In Hollywood with Potash and Perlmutter* (US 24); *Show People* (US 29)

Estelle Taylor *Mary of the Movies* (US 23); *Hollywood* (US 23)

Robert Taylor *The Youngest Profession* (US 43)

Bill Travers *An Elephant called Slowly* (GB 69); *The Lion at World's End* (GB 71)

Lana Turner *The Youngest Profession* (US 43)

Ben Turpin *Hollywood* (US 23); *Make Me a Star* (US 32)

Liv Ullman *Players* (US 79)

Peter Ustinov *Players* (US 79)

Conrad Veidt *Die Grosse Sehnsucht* (Ger 30)

Vera-Ellen *Words and Music* (US 48)

H. B. Warner *Sunset Boulevard* (US 50)

Paul Wegener *The Golem and the Dancer* (Ger 14)

Johnny Weissmuller *Stage Door Canteen* (US 43)

Orson Welles *Follow the Boys* (US 44); *Someone to Love* (US 87)

Cornel Wilde *Main Street to Broadway* (US 53)

Michael Wilding *Hello London* (GB 58)

Natalie Wood *The Candidate* (US 72); *Willie and Phil* (US 81)

Monty Woolley *Night and Day* (US 46)

Jane Wyman *Hollywood Canteen* (US 44); *It's a Great Feeling* (US 49); *Starlift* (US 51)

Ed Wynn *The Patsy* (US 64)

Michael York *Fedora* (FRG 78)

Susannah York *Scruggs* (GB 66) —also played heroine; *Long Shot* (GB 78)

Pia Zadora *Troop Beverly Hills* (US 90)

> Garbo's last screen appearance? No, not *Two-Faced Woman* (US 41). It was in tacky sex movie *Adam and Yves* (US 74). She was depicted as herself walking down a street in New York—needless to say her participation was without her consent and unpaid.

NON-ACTORS WHO HAVE PLAYED THEMSELVES IN FILMS

The list excludes the many bandleaders and vocalists appearing in sound movies. All roles were acted—documentary material and newsreel footage is excluded. (* Autobiopics)

Bella Abzug, US Congresswoman *Manhattan* (US 79)

Princess Aicha Abidir *Pierrot-le-Feu* (Fr/It 65)

Frankie Albert, All-American quarterback *The Spirit of Stanford** (US 42)

Buzz Aldrin, astronaut *The Boy in the Plastic Bubble* (US 76, TVM)

Dragljub Aleksić, acrobat *Nevinost bez Zastite** (Yug 68)

Queen Alexandra *The Great Love* (US 18); *Women Who Win* (GB 19)

Muhammed Ali, heavyweight boxing champion *The Greatest** (US 77); *Body and Soul* (US 81)

Alfredo Alvarado, exhibition dancer *El Rey del Jorapo** (Ven 80)

Vijay Amritraj, Indian tennis champion *Octopussy* (GB 83)

Mario Andretti, motor-racing driver *Speed Fever* (It 78)

Duke and Duchess of Argyll *Bullseye!* (US 90)

Lady Astor, first woman MP to sit in House of Commons *Royal Cavalcade* (GB 35)

Lt-Commander Auten VC, RNR re-enacted exploit which won him VC in *Q Ships* (GB 28)

Lord Baden-Powell, defender of Mafeking and founder of the Scout movement *Boys of the Otter Patrol* (GB 18); *The Man Who Changed His Mind* (GB 28); *The Woodpigeon Patrol* (GB 30)

Admiral Badger *Victory* (US 13)

Max Baer, boxer *The Prizefighter and the Lady* (US 33)

Bruce Bairnsfather, creator of cartoon character 'Old Bill' *Old Bill Through the Ages* (GB 24)

Joan Bakewell, TV personality *The Touchables* (GB 67)

Sonny Barger, Hell's Angels leader *Hell's Angels on Wheels* (US 67); *Hell's Angels '69* (US 69)

Adolf Beck, convicted of false murder charge *The Martydom of Adolf Beck** (GB 09)

The Duchess of Bedford *The Beauty Contest* (GB 64)

The Duke of Bedford *The Iron Maiden* (GB 62)

Alec Bedser, cricketer *The Final Test* (GB 53)

Saul Bellow, novelist *Zelig* (US 83)

Yogi Berra, baseball star *That Touch of Mink* (US 62)

Daniel and Phillip Berrigan, radical Jesuits *In the King of Prussia* (US 82)

Roy Best, Warden of Canon City Penitentiary *Canon City* (US 48)

Ronald Biggs, train robber *The Great Rock 'n' Roll Swindle* (GB 80); *Honeymoon* (FRG 80)

Danny Blanchflower, soccer star *Those Glory Glory Days* (GB 83)

Jasmine Bligh, TV announcer *Band Wagon* (GB 40)

Ada Bodart, assisted Nurse Edith Cavell in establishing her World War I escape organization *Dawn* (GB 28)

Evangeline Booth, Commandant of US Salvation Army *Fires of Faith* (US 19)

Lord Boothby, politician *Rockets Galore* (GB 58)

Muhammed Ali as himself in the autobiopic *The Greatest* (US 77). (*Kobal*)

Bjorn Borg, tennis champion *Racquet* (US 79)

Horatio Bottomley, politician and financier, three times charged with fraud (convicted 1922) *Was It He?* (GB 14)

The Bowen Family, of Guyra, NSW, victims of psychic phenomena *The Guyra Ghost Mystery* (Aus 21)

Jack Brabham, motor-racing driver *The Green Helmet* (GB 61)

Melvyn Bragg, adenoidal broadcaster *The Tall Guy* (GB 89)

Sir David Brand, premier of Western Australia *Nickel Queen* (Aus 71)

RSM Ronald Brittain, Regimental Sergeant Major of ferocious demeanour *You Lucky People* (GB 55)

Dr Joyce Brothers, sexologist *Stand Up and Be Counted* (US 71); *Embryo* (US 76); *The Lonely Guy* (US 84); *Last of the Great Survivors* (US 84, TVM); *Troop Beverly Hills* (US 90)

Joe Brown, New York speakeasy proprietor *Dressed to Kill* (US 28)

Judge Willis Brown of Salt Lake Juvenile Court *A Boy and the Law* (US 14)

Maurice Buckmaster, spy-master *Odette* (GB 50)

Sir Matt Busby, football manager *Cup Fever* (GB 65)

Jeanne Marie Calment of Arles, aged 114, last person alive who knew Van Gogh *Vincent and Me* (Can 90)

José Capablanca, chess Grand Master *Chess Fever* (USSR 25)

Vernon and Irene Castle, exhibition dancers (played by Fred Astaire and Ginger Rogers in *The Story of Vernon and Irene Castle* (US 39)) in *The Whirl of Life* (US 15)*

Andrew Carnegie, multi-millionaire industrialist *Our Mutual Girl* (US 14)

James Earl Carter, US President *Special Counsel* (US/Is 88)

George Washington Carver, distinguished black scientist *George Washington Carver** (US 40)

Dick Cavett, TV chat show presenter *Health* (US 80)

César, sculptor who created the César (French Oscar) *T'es folle ou quoi?* (Fr 82)

HRH Prince Charles *Grimes Goes Green* (GB 90)

Arthur Christiansen, ex-editor of the *Daily Express The Day the Earth Caught Fire* (GB 61)

Cicciolina (Ilona Staller), Italian politician and former prostitute *Sexploitation* (Hun 90)

M. E. Clifton-James, ex-actor who impersonated Montgomery to deceive Nazi Intelligence *I Was Monty's Double** (GB 58)

Ty Cobb, baseball player *Somewhere in Georgia* (US 17); *Angels in the Outfield* (US 51)

Sir Alan Cobham, aviator *The Flight Commander* (GB 27)

William Cody, Buffalo Bill *The Life of Buffalo Bill** (US 09); *Buffalo Bill's Far West and Pawnee Bill's Far East* (US 10); *The Indian Wars* (US 13); *Sitting Bull—The Hostile Indian Chief* (US 14); *Patsy of the Circus* (US 15)

Dennis Compton, cricketer *The Final Test* (GB 53)

Douglas 'Wrong Way' Corrigan, aviator *The Flying Irishman** (US 39)

Edwina Currie MP, former junior health minister and victim of egg jokes *News Hounds* (GB 90, TVM)

Michael Curtiz, film director *It's a Great Feeling* (US 49)

Emmett Dalton, youngest of the Dalton brothers, notorious desperadoes *Beyond the Law* (US 18)

Josephus Daniels, US Secretary of the Navy *Victory* (US 13)

Clarence Darrow, criminal lawyer *From Dusk to Dawn* (US 13)

Jimmie Davis, Governor of Louisiana *Louisiana** (US 47)

Moshe Dayan, Israeli Minister of Defence *Operation Thunderbolt* (Isr 77)

Count de Bauford in unidentified Carl Laemmle film (US 10) about his romance with an American heiress

Cecil B. DeMille, film producer and director *Hollywood* (US 23); *Free and Easy* (US 30); *Star Spangled Rhythm* (US 42); *Variety Girl* (US 47); *Sunset Boulevard* (US 50)

Jack Dempsey, heavyweight boxing champion *Sweet Surrender* (US 53); *Big City* (US 37); *Off Limits* (US 53); *Requiem for a Heavyweight* (US 62)

Joe Di Maggio, baseball player *Angels in the Outfield* (US 51)

Richard Dimbleby, BBC commentator *The Twenty Questions Murder* (GB 50); *John and Julie* (GB 55); *Rockets Galore* (GB 58); *Libel* (GB 59)

Georgi Dimitrov, communist revolutionary tried and acquitted in the 1933 Reichstag Fire trial, Prime Minister of Bulgaria 1946–49 *Kämpfer* (USSR 36)

Walt Disney, creator of Mickey Mouse, etc *Once Upon a Time* (US 44)

Sir Arthur Conan Doyle, novelist and creator of Sherlock Holmes *The $5,000,000 Counterfeiting Plot* (US 14)

Joni Eareckson, paraplegic *Joni** (US 80)

Sgt Arthur Guy Empsey, war hero *Over the Top** (US 18)

Godfrey Evans, cricketer *The Final Test* (GB 53)

Robert Fabian, police detective *Passport to Shame* (GB 59)

Emerson Fittipaldi, motor-racing driver *Speed Fever* (It 78)

Margot Fonteyn, prima ballerina *The Little Ballerina* (GB 51)

Michael Foot, socialist politician *Rockets Galore* (GB 58)

John Ford, director *Big Time* (US 29)

Joe Frazier, boxer *Rocky* (US 77)

Tito Fuentes, baseball player *Solomon King* (US 74)

Samuel Fuller, director *Pierrot-le-Feu* (Fr 65); *Scotch Myths—The Movie* (GB 83)

Paul Gallico, novelist *Madison Square Garden* (US 32)

Dorothy Gibson, Titanic survivor *Saved from the Titanic* (GB 12)

André Gide, writer *La Vie commence demain* (Fr 52)

Frank Gifford, American footballer *Paper Lion* (US 68); *Viva Knievel!* (US 77)

Alan Ginsberg, poet *Ciao! Manhattan* (US 72)

Raymond Glendenning, sports commentator *The Galloping Major* (GB 51); *Make Mine a Million* (GB 59); *The Iron Maiden* (GB 62)

Elinor Glyn, pioneer of the sex novel and creator of 'It' *It* (US 27); *Show People* (US 29)

Barbara Goalen, model *Wonderful Things!* (GB 58)

Pancho Gonzalez, tennis coach *Players* (US 79)

John Gorton, Prime Minister of Australia *Don's Party* (Aus 76)

Steffi Graf, tennis champion *Otto-Der Ausserfriesische* (FRG 89)

Billy Graham, American evangelist *Souls in Conflict* (GB 55); *Two a Penny* (GB 67)

Sheila Graham, journalist and mistress of F. Scott Fitzgerald (played by Deborah Kerr in biopic *Beloved Infidel* (US 59)) *College Confidential* (US 60)

Angèle Grammont, who escaped from old people's home near Lausanne *Angèle** (Swz 68)

Zane Grey, Western novelist *White Death* (Aus 36)

Grock, clown *Grock** (Ger 31)

Earl Haig, World War I Commander-in-Chief *Remembrance* (GB 27)

Ernest Haigh, ex-Chief Inspector of Police *Leaves from My Life** (GB 21)

Giscele Halimi, defence counsel in notable 1972 abortion trial *L'Une chante l'autre pas* (Fr/Bel/Cur 76)

David Hamilton, photographer *Tiffany Jones* (GB 73)

General Sir Ian Hamilton, leader of the Gallipoli Expedition *Tell England* (GB 31)

Oscar Hammerstein, composer *Main Street to Broadway* (US 53)

Judge James Hannon, judge who tried Arlo Guthrie for throwing litter *Alice's Restaurant* (US 69)

Gilbert Harding, crusty TV personality, famous for rudeness *Simon and Laura* (GB 55); *As Long as They're Happy* (GB 55); *An Alligator Named Daisy* (GB 55); *My Wife's Family* (GB 56); *Left, Right and Centre* (GB 59); *Expresso Bongo* (GB 59)

Mickey Hargitay, ex-Mr Universe, ex-husband of Jayne Mansfield *Mr Universe* (Hun 88)

Tom Harmon, All-American quarterback *Harmon of Michigan** (US 41)

Norman Hartnell, couturier *The Beauty Contest* (GB 64)

Len Harvey, boxer *The Bermondsey Kid* (GB 33)

Edith Head, Hollywood costume designer *The Oscar* (US 66)

Hugh Hefner, founder of Playboy empire (played by Cliff Robertson in *Star 80* (US 83)) *How Did a Nice Girl Like You Ever Get Into This Business* (FRG 70)

Graham Hill, motor-racing driver *The Fast Lady* (GB 62)

Dennis Hills, captive of Idi Amin *The Rise and Fall of Idi Amin* (Ken 81)

David Hockney, artist *A Bigger Splash** (GB 74)

John Hodge MP, Minister of Pensions *Broken in the Wars* (GB 19)

Ben Hogan, golfer *The Caddy* (US 53)

Hedda Hopper, movie gossip columnist *Sunset Boulevard* (US 50); *Pepe* (US 60); *The Patsy* (US 64)

William Morris Hughes, Prime Minister of Australia *Smithy* (Aus 46)

Hubert Humphrey, US Senator *The Candidate* (US 72)

James Hunt, motor-racing driver *Speed Fever* (It 78)

Len Hutton, cricketer *The Final Test* (GB 53)

Father Iliodor, rascally monk, first protégé then opponent of Rasputin *The Fall of the Romanoffs* (US 18)

David Jacobs, broadcaster *Otley* (GB 68)

James J. Jeffries, boxing champion *Pennington's Choice* (US 15)

Admiral Lord Jellicoe *Q Ships* (GB 28)

Al Jennings, convicted bank and train robber *The Bank Robbery* (US 08); *Beating Back** (US 15); *The Lady of the Dugout* (US 18)

Amy Johnson, aviatrix *Dual Control* (GB 32)

Jack Johnson, boxer *Jack Johnson's Adventures in Paris* (Fr 13); *As the World Rolls On* (US 21)

José José, alcohol and drug addicted popular singer *Gavilán o Paloma** (Mex 85)

Anatoly Karpov, chess Grandmaster *Fool's Mate* (FRG 89)

Helen Keller, deaf-blind scholar *Deliverance** (US 19)

Murray King, Long Island insurance salesman *Murray, King** (US 69)

Evel Knievel, motorcycle stuntman *Viva Knievel!* (US 77)

Not the first Prince of Wales to act in a movie. His great uncle Edward VIII appeared in three silent pictures, but Charles was the first member of the British Royal Family to speak on screen in a fiction movie—*Grimes Goes Green* (GB 90). Here the manic John Cleese as Grimes realises that the person behind the newspaper whom he has been abusing is not who he thought it was. (*Mail Newspapers*)

HRH Prince Charles made his screen acting debut opposite John Cleese in Video Arts' environmental film *Grimes Goes Green* (GB 90). He plays himself on a royal visit to a factory whose managing director Grimes considers green issues are only for the beards and sandals brigade. Cleese as Grimes fails to recognise the Prince, who is buried behind the *Daily Telegraph* in reception, and harangues him with 'Oh, another one from the Palace, eh? Well, I suppose you'll be wanting to see the drains then. Let me guess—you're the Royal Sanitary Inspector, eh?'. The Prince lowers his paper to reveal himself and Grimes instantly becomes cringingly obsequious as he listens to the Prince's formula for going green. Equally sycophantic was the reaction of most newspapers, praising the 'Clown Prince' as a 'Video King'. A striking exception was *Today*, which panned his performance with the criticism that his nerves had got the better of him, resulting in some unnatural body movement, and that his lines had been delivered so unimaginatively that even the most attentive of audiences would find their minds wandering. 'We all love him', the paper summed up, 'but the truth is he can't act.'

Edward J Koch, Mayor of New York in *The Muppets Take Manhattan* (US 84); Woody Allen's *Oedipus Wrecks* segment of *New York Stories* (US 89)

Somchai Koonperm, village chief *Kamnan Poh** (Tha 80)

Jim Laker, cricketer *The Final Test* (GB 53)

Fritz Lang, film director (played by Marcel Hillaire in *Take the Money and Run* (US 69)); *Contempt* (Fr 64)

Nikki Lauda, motor-racing driver *Speed Fever* (It 78)

Henry Lawson, Australian poet *While the Billy Boils* (Aus 21)

Dr Timothy Leary, guru of LSD *Cheech and Chong's Nice Dreams* (US 81); *Fatal Skies* (US 90)

Stan Lee, cartoonist, creator of Spider-Man and the Incredible Hulk *The Ambulance* (US 91)

Suzanne Lenglen, Wimbledon tennis champion *Things Are Looking Up* (GB 35)

Oscar Levant, composer *Rhapsody in Blue* (US 45)

Bernard Levin, journalist *Nothing But the Best* (GB 63)

Prinz Eduard von und zu Liechtenstein, of the Royal House of Liechtenstein *Johann Strauss an der schönen blauen Donau* (Aut 13)

Sir Thomas Lipton, millionaire grocer and yachtsman *The Lipton Cup* (US 13)

Vincent Lombardi, American footballer *Paper Lion* (US 68)

Chief Lomoiro, Masai tribal leader *Visit to a Chief's Son* (US 74)

Captain James Lovell, astronaut *The Man Who Fell to Earth* (GB 76)

Joan Lowell, yachtswoman *Adventure Girl** (US 34)

Paul and Linda McCartney, ex-Beatle and photographer wife *Give My Regards to Broad Street* (GB 84); Paul only in *Eat the Rich* (GB 87)

Windsor McCay, cartoonist (*Little Nemo*, etc) and pioneer film animator *The Great White Way* (US 24)

Jem Mace, boxer *There's Life in the Old Dog Yet* (GB 08)

John McEnroe, tennis champion *Players* (US 79)

George McGovern, US Senator *The Candidate* (US 72)

Marshall McLuhan, Canadian academic, expert on media and communications *Annie Hall* (US 77)

George McManus, cartoonist (*Bringing Up Father*, etc) *The Great White Way* (US 24)

Leonard Maltin, film critic *Gremlins 2: The New Batch* (US 90)

Alice Marble, tennis champion *Pat and Mike* (US 52)

Queen Mary *Women Who Win* (GB 19)

Dan Maskell, tennis player *Players* (US 79)

Bob Mathias, twice winner of Olympic decathlon *The Bob Mathias Story** (US 54)

Yehudi Menuhin, violinist *Stage Door Canteen* (US 43)

Cliff Michelmore, TV personality *A Jolly Bad Fellow* (GB 63)

Lewis Milestone, film director *Fascinating Youth* (US 26)

Freddie Mills, boxer *6.5 Special* (GB 58)

Leslie Mitchell, Britain's first TV announcer (1936) and Movietone commentator *Geneviève* (GB 53)

Jim Mollison, aviator who made first east–west crossing of N. Atlantic *Dual Control* (GB 32)

Gussie Moran, tennis champion *Pat and Mike* (US 52)

Stirling Moss, motor-racing driver *The Beauty Contest* (GB 64)

James Mossman, broadcaster *Masquerade* (GB 64)

Malcolm Muggeridge, journalist and pundit *I'm All Right Jack* (GB 59) ; *Heavens Above* (GB 63) ; *Herostratus* (GB 67) ; *The Naked Bunyip* (Aus 70)

Audie Murphy, most decorated US Soldier of World War II and subsequently professional actor *To Hell and Back** (US 55)

Pete Murray, disc jockey *6.5 Special* (GB 58)

A disclaimer before the end credits of *Players* (US 79) insisted that all the characters in the film were wholly fictitious; it was immediately followed by a cast list that included no less than 14 famous tennis personalities, including John McEnroe, playing themselves.

Albert Namatjira, Aboriginal artist *The Phantom Stockman* (Aus 53)

Ilie Nastase, Romanian tennis champion *Players* (US 79)

Bess Nielsen, Parisian girl given to amorous adventures *On n'est pas sérieux quand on a 17 ans** (Fr 74)

Officer Obie, policeman who arrested Arlo Guthrie for casting litter *Alice's Restaurant* (US 69)

Dan O'Brien, San Francisco Chief of Police *Poison* (US 24)

Barney Oldfield, motor-racing driver *Barney Oldfield's Race for Life* (US 16)

Ignace Paderewski, pianist, Prime Minister and later President of Poland *Moonlight Sonata* (GB 37)

Arnold Palmer, golfer *Call Me Bwana* (GB 63)

Emmeline Pankhurst, sufragette leader *Eighty Million Women Want—?* (US 13)

Huang Pao-Mei, girl spinner in China's Cotton Mill No 17 *Huang Pao-mei** (Chn 58)

Michael Parkinson, TV personality *Madhouse* (GB 74)

Louella Parsons, movie gossip columnist *Hollywood Hotel* (US 37) ; *Stagedoor Canteen* (US 43)

Nicholas Parsons, TV personality *Mr Jolly Lives Next Door* (GB 87)

Princess Patricia *Women Who Win* (GB 19)

Floyd Patterson, boxing champion *Terrible Joe Moran* (US 84, TVM)

Lieutenant Harold R. Peat *Private Peat** (US 18)

Betty Ting Pei, Bruce Lee's lover *Bruce Lee and I** (HK 76)

Pele, Brazilian soccer player *Young Giants* (US 83)

Shimon Peres, Prime Minister of Israel *Special Counsel* (US/Isr 88)

Marshal Pétain, French Commander-in-Chief World War I, Head of Vichy Government World War II *Verdun, Visions d'Histoire* (Fr 28)

Pablo Picasso, artist *La Vie commence demain* (Fr 52) ; *Le Testament d'Orphée* (Fr 60)

Wiley Post, first aviator to circumnavigate world solo *Air Hawks* (US 35)

Andre Previn, conductor *Pepe* (US 60)

Luis Procuna, matador *Torero!** (Mex 56)

Yizhak Rabin, Prime Minister of Israel *Operation Thunderbolt* (Isr 77) ; *Special Counsel* (US/Isr 88)

Dame Marie Rambert, founder of the Ballet Rambert *The Red Shoes* (GB 48)

Paul Raymond, eroticist *Erotica* (GB 81)

Jean Renoir, film director *The Christian Licorice Store* (US 71)

Carlos Reutemann, motor-racing driver *Speed Fever* (It 78)

Robert Ripley, originator of *Believe It or Not The Great White Way* (US 24)

Charlie Rivel, circus clown *Scö-ö-ön** (Ger 43)

Jackie Robinson, first black to play major league baseball *The Jackie Robinson Story** (US 50)

Robert Robinson, broadcaster *French Dressing* (GB 64)

Sugar Ray Robinson, boxer *Paper Lion* (US 68)

Richard Rodgers, composer *Main Street to Broadway* (US 53)

Franklin Delano Roosevelt, Assistant Secretary to the Navy, later President *The Battle Cry of Peace* (US 15)

Theodore Roosevelt, ex-President of the USA *Womanhood, The Glory of a Nation* (US 17)

Jonathan Ross, TV presenter *The Tall Guy* (GB 89)

Lady 'Bubbles' Rothermere, society hostess *The Stud* (GB 78)

Damon Runyon, writer *The Great White Way* (US 24) ; *O, Baby* (US 26) ; *Madison Square Garden* (US 32)

'Babe' Ruth, baseball player *Speedy* (US 28) , *Pride of the Yankees* (US 42)

Gunther Sachs, millionaire industrialist and playboy *Cadillac* (FRG 69)

Col. Harlan T. Sanders of Kentucky Fried Chicken fame *The Big Mouth* (US 67)

Margaret Sanger, birth control pioneer *Birth Control* (US 17)

Jean-Paul Satre, philosopher *La Vie commence demain* (Fr 52)

Ichijo Sayuri, stripper *Ichijo Sayuri: Wet Desire** (Jap 74)

Joe Schmidt, American footballer *Paper Lion* (US 68)

Charles E. Sebastian, ex-Mayor of Los Angeles *The Downfall of a Mayor** (US 17)

Mlle Segree, lover of Landru, murderer of 11 women *Landru* (Fr 24)

Caporal Sellier, bugler who sounded the World War I armistice, re-enacted scene in *The Soul of France* (Fr 28)

Mack Sennet, founder of the Keystone Kops *Hollywood Cavalcade* (US 39)

Ma Sha, reformed pimp and killer *The First Error Step** (Sin 79)

Barry Sheene, world motorcycling champion, and his girlfriend Stephanie McLean *Space Riders* (GB 83)

William Shirer, historian *The Magic Face* (US 51)

Harry Siegenberg, bookmaker *The Stolen Favourite* (SA 19)

O. J. Simpson, football player *The Klansman* (US 74)

George R. Sims, crusading journalist gaoled in celebrated 1885 Maiden Tribute of Modern Babylon case *The Martyrdom of Adolf Beck* (GB 09)

Alfred E. Smith, Governor of New York (and first politician to appear on TV, 1928) *The Volcano* (US 19)

Sir Charles Kingsford Smith, Australian aviator *Splendid Fellows* (Aus 34)

Kate Smith, singer *Hello Everybody* (US 33) (fictionalized biopic)

Susan Sontag, writer *Zelig* (US 83)

Mickey Spillane, thriller writer *Ring of Fear* (US 54)

Ringo Starr, ex-Beatle *Give My Regards to Broad Street* (GB 84)

Isobel Lillian Steele, American victim of Gestapo *Captive of Nazi Germany** (US 36)

Charles Stragusa, narcotics agent who led 10-year quest to nail mobster Lucky Luciano *Re: Lucky Luciano* (It/Fr 73)

Preston Sturges, film director *Star Spangled Rhythm* (US 42)

Anne Sullivan, who taught blind deaf-mute Helen Keller to speak and read *Deliverance* (US 19)

Ed Sullivan, TV personality *The Patsy* (US 64)

William Sulzer, impeached Governor of New York *The Shame of the Empire State** (US 13)

Hannen Swaffer, journalist *Spellbound* (GB 41)

Crown Princess of Sweden *Women Who Win* (GB 19)

Fuji Takeshi, world junior welterweight boxing champion *Fuji Takeshi Monogatari** (Jap 68)

Yukio Tani, martial arts exponent *Ju-Jitsu to the Rescue* (GB 13)

Alderman C. E. Tatham, Mayor of Blackpool *Sing As We Go* (GB 34)

A. J. P. Taylor, historian *Rockets Galore* (GB 58)

Evelyn Nesbitt Thaw, beauty whose husband murdered her lover, architect Stanford White (played by Joan Collins in *The Girl in the Red Velvet Swing* (US 55) and by Elizabeth McGovern in *Ragtime* (US 81)) *The Great Thaw Trial* (US 07) ; *Redemption* (US 17)

Wynford Vaughan Thomas, broadcaster *John and Julie* (GB 55)

William 'Big Bill' Thompson, Mayor of Chicago *Is Your Daughter Safe?* (US 27)

William Tilghman, Marshal of Cache, Oklahoma (played by Rod Steiger in *Cattle Annie and Little Britches* (US 80)) *The Bank Robbery* (US 08) ; *Passing of the Oklahoma Outlaw* (US 15)

Sir Frederick Treves, surgeon (played by Anthony Hopkins in *The Elephant Man* (GB 80)) *The Great Love* (US 18)

Donald Trump, tycoon *Another You* (US 91)

Mark Twain, humorous writer *A Curious Dream* (US 07)

Senator Jo Valentine of Western Australia *The Pursuit of Happiness* (Aus 88)

John van Druten, playwright *Main Street to Broadway* (US 53)

Princess Victoria *Women Who Win* (GB 19)

King Vidor, film director *It's a Great Feeling* (US 49)

Guillermo Vilas, tennis player *Players* (US 79)

The Prince of Wales, later King Edward VIII *The Warrior Strain* (GB 19) ; *The Power of Right* (GB 19) ; *Remembrance* (GB 27)

Lech Walesa, founder of Solidarity, President of Poland *Man of Iron* (Pol 81)

Jimmy Walker, Mayor of New York *Glorifying the American Girl* (US 29)

Raoul Walsh, film director *It's a Great Feeling* (US 49)

Cyril Washbrook, cricketer *The Final Test* (GB 53)

Alan Whicker, TV commentator *The Angry Silence* (GB 60)

Gough Whitlam, Prime Minister of Australia *Barry McKenzie Holds His Own* (Aus 74)

District Attorney Whitman *Our Mutual Girl* (US 14) ; *Smashing the Vice Trust* (US 14)

Frank Wills, Watergate security guard who discovered break-in *All the President's Men* (US 76)

Peter Wilson, Chairman of Sotheby's *Laughter in the Dark* (GB 69)

Woodrow Wilson, President of the USA *The Adventures of a Boy Scout* (US 15)

FILM STARS WHO HAVE PLAYED THEMSELVES IN MOVIES *(continued)*

The only British monarch to have acted in films was King Edward VIII when he was Prince of Wales. In March 1919 he performed in two patriotic war dramas—like Indian stars of today he economized on time by playing his scenes for both films at the same time. This was made easier by the fact that he was portraying himself in each and that they had remarkably similar plots. *The Power of Right* (GB 19), directed by F. Martin Thornton for Harma Photoplays, was about a colonel's son who joins the cadets and succeeds in killing

an escaped German internee, while *The Warrior Strain* (GB 19) was also about a cadet, this time an Earl's son, who foils a dastardly plot by a German baron to signal the enemy from Brighton. In the latter film the Prince played a scene with Sydney Wood (as the boy's father), and another in which he presents each of the members of the cadet section with a gold watch as a reward for thwarting the wicked baron. Some years later he again played himself in BIP's *Remembrance* (GB 27), a story about disabled war veterans.

Walter Winchell, influential American columnist (played by Lew Ayres in *Okay America!* (US 32)); *Wake Up and Live* (US 37); *Love and Hisses* (US 37); *The Helen Morgan Story* (US 57); *College Confidential* (US 60); *Wild in the Streets* (US 68)

Godfrey Winn, journalist *Very Important Person* (GB 61); *Billy Liar!* (GB 63)

Maharishi Narish Yogi, guru *Candy* (It/Fr 68)

Sam Yorty, Mayor of Los Angeles *The Candidate* (US 72)

Jimmy Young, broadcaster *Otley* (GB 68)

Krzysztof Zanussi, film director *Amator/Camera Buff* (Pol 79)

Florenz Ziegfeld, impresario *Glorifying the American Girl* (US 29)

Adolf Zukor, film producer *Glorifying the American Girl* (US 29)

NON-ACTORS IN FILMS

Personalities who have played roles other than themselves (see also Personalities playing themselves, pp. 86–90) include:

Horacio Accavallo, world flyweight boxing champion, lead in *Destino para dos* (Arg 67)

Muhammed Ali, world heavyweight boxing champion, as young fighter in *Requiem for a Heavyweight* (US 62); as Gideon Jackson, first black US Senator, in *Freedom Road* (US 79, TVM)

Viscount Althorp, brother of Princess of Wales, as public schoolboy in *Another Country* (GB 84)

Sydney Biddle Barrows, NY socialite who ran high class call-girl ring, as Peggy Eaton in biopic of Barrows (Candice Bergen) *Mayflower Madam* (US 87, TVM)

Max Baer, boxer, in *The Prizefighter and the Lady* (US 33)

Mrs Morgan Belmont, society leader and member of New York's '400', played the upper crust Diana Tremont in *Way Down East* (US 20)

Peter Benchley, author of *Jaws*, played a reporter in *Jaws* (US 75)

Godfrey Binaisa, President of Uganda, bit parts in *King Solomon's Mines* (US 50) and *The African Queen* (GB 51)

Ex-Detective Sergeant Bishop as Detective Sergeant in *Blackmail* (GB 29)

Bricktop, black nightclub proprietor famous in cafe society, as mother figure in *Honeybaby, Honeybaby* (US 74)

RSM Ronald Brittain, Regimental Sergeant Major at Sandhurst Military Academy during 1950s, appeared (usually as a Sergeant Major) in *Carrington VC* (GB 54), *The Missing Note* (GB 61), *The Amorous Prawn* (GB 62), *Joey Boy* (GB 65) and *The Spy with a Cold Nose* (GB 66)

Dr Joyce Brothers, sexologist, in *Burnin' Love* (US 87); as baseball announcer in *The Naked Gun* (US 89)

Joe Bugner, heavyweight boxing champion, as forest ranger in *Sher Mountains Killing Mystery* (Aus 90)

William Burroughs, sex writer, as a mafia don in *It Don't Pay to be an Honest Citizen* (US 85); as defrocked junkie priest in *Drugstore Cowboy* (US 89)

Maria Callas, opera diva, in non-singing title role of *Medea* (It/Fr/FRG 70)

Truman Capote, author, leading role in detective fiction parody *Murder by Death* (US 76)

Primo Carnera, boxer, as boxer in *The Prizefighter and the Lady* (US 33); as Pyrhon Macklin in *A Kid for Two Farthings* (GB 55); as Corfa in *Casanova's Big Night* (US 54)

Georges Carpentier, boxer, as hero in *Toboggan* (Fr 34)

Viscount Castlerosse, bon viveur, as the man in the bath chair in *Kipps* (GB 41)

Fidel Castro, dictator, bit player in *Holiday in Mexico* (US 46)

Juan Chacon, trade union leader, as Mexican strike leader in *Salt of the Earth* (US 54)

G. K. Chesterton, author, in *Rosy Rapture—The Pride of the Beauty Chorus* (GB 14)

Michael Chow, restaurateur, as underworld boss Fong Wei Tan in *Hammett* (US 82)

Daniel Cohn-Bendit, revolutionary, in Godard's *Vent d'est* (FRG/It 70); as friend of heroine who bemoans his resemblance to Daniel Cohn-Bendit in *Un Amour à Paris* (Fr 87)

Jackie Collins, best-selling novelist, sister of Joan, as teenager June in *All at Sea* (GB 57)

Henry Cooper, boxer, as prizefighter John Gully in *Royal Flash* (GB 75)

Carmine Coppola, composer, as man in the lift in Francis Coppola's *One from the Heart* (US 82); as street musician in *New York Stories* (US 89)

James John Corbett, heavyweight boxing champion of the world, as 'Gentleman Jim' (lead) in *The Man from the Golden West* (US 13); as Raffles (lead) in *The Burglar and the Lady* (US 14); as pugilist Kid Garvey in *The Other Girl* (US 16); also in *The Midnight Man* (US 19)

Gregory Corso, American beat poet, as 'unruly stockholder' in *The Godfather III* (US 90)

Quentin Crisp, free spirit (played by John Hurt in *The Naked Civil Servant* (GB 75, TVM))

as Polonius in *Hamlet* (GB 76); as Dr Zaklus in *The Bride* (GB 85); as partygoer in *Fatal Attraction* (US 87)

Fred Demara, imposter (played by Tony Curtis in *The Great Imposter* (US 60)) as imposter impersonating actor impersonating doctor in *The Hypnotic Eye* (US 59)

Jack Dempsey, world heavyweight boxing champion, as boxer in *The Prizefighter and the Lady* (US 33)

Lt Col Hugh Dickens, CO 9th/12th Royal Lancers, as Nazi officer in *Indiana Jones and the Last Crusade* (US 89)

Dionne Quins, world's first surviving quintuplets, in *The Country Doctor* (US 36), *Reunion* (US 36) and *Five of a Kind* (US 38)

Steve Donaghue, champion jockey, as Steve Baxter, hero of *Riding for a King* (GB 26), *Beating the Book* (GB 26), *The Golden Spurs* (GB 26) and *The Stolen Favourite* (GB 26)

Terry Downes, boxer, as Chunky in Sherlock Holmes movie *A Study in Terror* (GB 65)

Bob Dylan, rock musician, as Alias in *Pat Garrett and Billy the Kid* (US 73), as avant garde artist who uses buzz-saw as brush in *Catchfire* (US 89)

Gertrude Ederle, first woman to swim the English Channel, in *Swim, Girl, Swim* (US 28)

Princess Elizabeth of Toro, as the Sharma in *Sheena—Queen of the Jungle* (US 84)

David Frost, television commentator, as reporter in *The VIPs* (GB 63)

Princess Ira von Furstenberg as femme lead Arabella in *Matchless* (It 67)

Paul Getty III, grandson of oil tycoon, as film scriptwriter Dennis in *The State of Things* (US/Por 82)

Althea Gibson, black tennis star, as maid in John Ford's *The Horse Soldiers* (US 59)

Allen Ginsberg, poet, as a lawyer in *It Don't Pay to be an Honest Citizen* (US 85)

Jerry Goldsmith, film composer (*Rambo, Gremlins*) as patron in ice cream parlor in *Gremlins 2: The New Batch* (US 90)

Robert Graves, poet and novelist, as partygoer in *Deadfall* (GB 68)

Graham Greene, author, as the insurance representative in *Day for Night* (Fr 73)

Germaine Greer, women's liberationist, as Clara Bowden in *Universal Soldier* (GB 71)

Jerry Hall, statuesque model and Mrs Mick Jagger, in *Running Out of Luck* (US 85) and *Topo Galileo* (It 88)

Lorenz Hart, of Rodgers and Hart, played the bank teller in *Hallelujah, I'm a Bum* (US 33)

Len Harvey, British boxing champion, played a glass collector turned boxer in *Excuse My Glove* (GB 36)

Patty Hearst, kidnap victim (played by Natasha Richardson in *Patty Hearst* (US/GB 88)) as upper-crust mother in *Cry Baby* (US 90)

Hugh Hefner, founder of Playboy empire (played by Cliff Robertson in *Star 80* (US 83)) as pipe smoking ancient Roman in *History of the World—Part I* (US 81)

Ernest Hemingway, author, uncredited bit part in *The Old Man and the Sea* (US 58)

Xaviera Hollander, prostitute and writer, lead in *My Pleasure is My Business* (Can 74)

Christopher Isherwood, novelist, as partygoer in *Rich and Famous* (US 81)

Bianca Jagger, jet-setter, leads in *Flesh Colour* (US 79) and *The Great American Success Company* (US 79)

Clive James, Australian pundit, as most drunken of Bazza's mates in *Barry McKenzie Holds His Own* (Aus 77)

James Jones, novelist, as a poker player in *The Marseilles Contract* (GB/Fr 74)

Thomas Keneally, Australian novelist, as Father Marshall in *The Devil's Playground* (Aus 76)

Jomo Kenyatta, President of Kenya 1963–78, played an African chief in *Sanders of the River* (GB 35)

Stephen King, novelist, as minister at funeral in *Pet Sematary* (US 89)

Jerzy Kosinksy, controversial Polish-American novelist, as Bolshevik revolutionary Zinoviev in *Reds* (US 81)

Jake LaMotta, prizefighter (played by Robert De Niro in *Raging Bull* (US 80)) as rebel Julio in *Rebellion in Cuba* (US 61); as army deserter Joe Shenken in *House in Naples* (US 70)

Dr Emmanuel Lasker, world chess champion, played Napoleon's chess partner in Lupu Pick's *Napoléon a Sainte-Hélène* (Fr 29)

Dr Timothy Leary, proponent of hallucinogenic drugs, as TV evangelist in *Shocker* (US 89); as diner at 'The Nouveau Woodstock' in *Rude Awakening* (US 90)

John Lindsay, Mayor of New York, played Senator Donnovan in *Rosebud* (US 75)

Joe Louis, boxer, played lead as young fighter in all-black *Spirit of Youth* (US 38)

Victor Lowndes, chairman of Playboy UK, as Reeve Passmore in *Fledglings* (GB 65)

John McAllister, Sinn Fein activist, as Sinn Fein activist in *Hidden Agenda* (GB 90)

Compton MacKenzie, author, as Capt Buncher in film of his own novel *Whisky Galore!* (GB 49); as Sir Robert Dysart in *Chance of a Lifetime* (GB 50)

Norman Mailer, writer, as 'The Prince' in *Wild 90* (US 68); as Lt Francis Xavier Pope of NY Police in *Beyond the Law* (US 68); as film director and presidential candidate 'Kingsley' in *Maidstone* (US 70); as New York architect Stanford White (murdered in celebrated turn-of-century crime of passion) in *Ragtime* (US 81); as Lear (in opening scenes—Burgess Meredith then takes over) in *King Lear* (US/Swz 87)

Yehudi Menuhin, violinist, in *The Magic Bow* (GB 46)

Freddie Mills, British champion boxer, in *Emergency Call* (GB 52), *Kill Me Tomorrow*

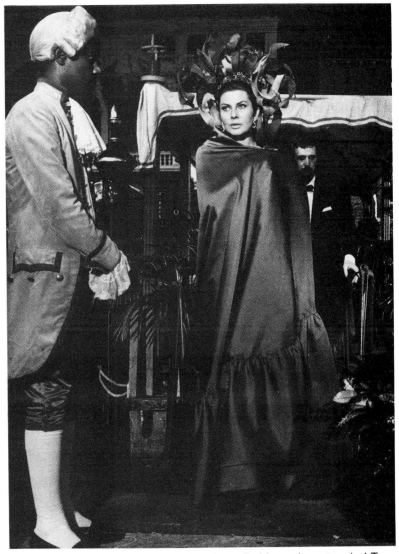

Ex-Empress Soraya played herself and two fictitious characters in *I Tre Volti* (It 65). (*Kobal*)

(GB 55), *Fun at St Fanny's* (GB 56), *Breakaway* (GB 56), *Chain of Events* (GB 58), *Carry on Constable* (GB 60), *Carry on Regardless* (GB 61), *The Comedy Man* (GB 63), *Saturday Night Out* (GB 64)

Ján Miró, Spanish painter, played the museum curator in *El Umbracle* (Sp 73)

Stirling Moss, motor-racing driver in *Casino Royale* (GB 67)

Benito Mussolini, Italian dictator, extra in *The Eternal City* (US 14)

Beverly Nichols, author, as the Hon. Richard Wells in *Glamour* (GB 31)

Mrs Richard Nixon, wife of ex-President Nixon, walk-on parts in *Becky Sharp* (US 36) and *Small Town Girl* (US 37)

HRH Nana Agyefi Kwame II de Nsein, as the mad King Bossa Ahadee in *Cobra Verde* (FRG 88)

John O'Hara, novelist, as a reporter on a train in *The General Died at Dawn* (US 36)

Charley Paddock, US Olympic athlete (played by Dennis Christopher in *Chariots of Fire* (GB

81)) as hero in *The Olympic Hero* (US 28)

Princess Pearl, daughter of White Rajah of Sarawak, as Princess Paula in Ruritanian romance *Everything is Rhythm* (GB 36)

Pelé, Brazilian football star, as soccer hero in *Hotshot* (US 87); *Solidão* (Br 89) Paloma Picasso, daughter of Pablo, as Countess Bathory, she who bathed in the blood of virgins, in *Immoral Tales* (US 74)

Harold Pinter, playwright, as 'society man' in *The Servant* (GB 63); as lawyer Saul Abrahams in *Rogue Male* (GB 76); as bookshop customer in *Turtle Diary* (GB 85)

Nosher Powell, minder, in lead role as Home Secretary in *Eat the Rich* (GB 87)

Kukrit Pramoj, Prime Minister of Thailand (1974), as Prime Minister of the fictitious state of 'Sarkhan' in *The Ugly American* (US 62)

Erich Maria Remarque, author of *All Quiet on the Western Front*, as the schoolmaster Pohlmann in the film of his novel *A Time to Love and a Time to Die* (US 58)

David Robinson, film critic of *The Times*, in *If* (GB 60), *Fragments of Life* (Hun 70), *Britannia Hospital* (GB 81), and as 1930s drama critic of *The Times* in *Mephisto* (Hun 81)

Sugar Ray Robinson, boxer, as Zero in *Candy* (It/Fr 68)

Babe Ruth, baseball player (played by William Bendix in *The Babe Ruth Story* (US 48) and John Goodman in *The Babe* (US i.p.)), as hero in *Headin' Home* (US 20); as ball player Babe Dugan in *The Babe Comes Home* (US 27)

Pierre Salinger, John F. Kennedy's Press Secretary, as poker player in *The Marseilles Connection* (GB/Fr 73)

Max Schmeling, boxer, as hero Max Breuer, playing opposite wife Anny Ondra, in *Knockout* (Ger 36)

Martin Scorsese, film director, as the Director of the Metropolitan Opera House in *Pavlova—A Woman for All Time* (GB/USSR 83)

George Bernard Shaw, playright, in *Rosy Rapture—The Pride of the Beauty Chorus* (GB 14)

Jean Shrimpton, model, leading lady in *Privilege* (GB 67)

Ex-Empress Soraya in triple role as herself, Linda and Mrs Melville in *I Tre Volti* (It 65)

Steven Spielberg, producer/director, as Cook County Clerk in *The Blues Brothers* (US 80)

Mickey Spillane, detective novelist, as straw-chewing sleuth in *Ring of Fear* (US 54); as his own creation Mike Hammer in *The Girl Hunters* (US 63)

Jacqueline Susann, novelist, as reporter in film of her own book *Valley of the Dolls* (US 67)

Leslie 'Squizzy' Taylor, Melbourne gangster gunned down in 1927, in race-track drama *Bound to Win* (Aus 19)

Jim Thorpe, Oklahoma Indian who was stripped of his Olympic Gold Medals (played by Burt Lancaster in *Jim Thorpe—All American* (US 51)), as Captain of the Guard in *She* (US 35); as prisoner in *White Heat* (US 49)

Bill Tilden, tennis champion, as Joles in *The Music Master* (US 27)

Franz von Trauberg, first post-war Mayor of Berlin, as kidnapped ambassador in *Guernica* (It 72)

Leon Trotsky, revolutionary and founder of the Red Army, played a bit part as a nihilist in Vitagraph's spy drama *My Official Wife* (US 14) and also appeared in *The Battle Cry of Peace* (US 15)

Margaret Trudeau, estranged wife of Premier of Canada, Pierre Trudeau, starred in *The Guardian Angel* (Can 78) and *Kings and Desperate Men* (Can 79)

Donald Trump, tycoon, as 'Mr Speculator' in *Ghosts Can't Do It* (US 89)

Ivana Trump, socialite, wife of above, as heroine in *Pantau* (Cz 70)

Gene Tunney, heavyweight boxing champion as Marine in *The Fighting Marine* (US 26)

Roger Vadim, film director, as partygoer in *Rich and Famous* (US 81)

Gore Vidal, polemicist, as bearded preacher in *Gore Vidal's Billy the Kid* (US 89)

Hugh Walpole, author, as the vicar in *David Copperfield* (US 35)

Senator John Warner, ex 'Mr Elizabeth Taylor', as a fisherman in *The Mirror Crack'd* (GB 81)

Judge Joseph N. Welch, presiding judge at the McCarthy hearings, played a judge in *Anatomy of a Murder* (US 59)

Bombardier Billy Wells, British boxing champion, starred as the pilot in *The Silver Lining* (GB 19) and played the hangman in *The Beggar's Opera* (GB 53)

White Man-Runs Him, last survivor of the Battle of the Little Big Horn (at which Gen. Custer's force was massacred in 1876), played in a Ken Maynard western *The Red Raiders* (US 27)

Gough Whitlam, Prime Minister of Australia, as 'man in night club' in *The Broken Melody* (Aus 38); see also under Non-actors who have played themselves

Godfrey Winn, journalist, played an announcer in *The Bargee* (GB 64) and Truelove in *The Great St Trinian's Train Robbery* (GB 65)

Jersey Joe Walcott, boxer, as 'George' in *The Harder They Fall* (US 56)

Alexander Woolcott, writer and critic, as literary sophisticate Vanderveer Veyden in *The Scoundrel* (US 35)

Brig. Gen. Chuck Yeager, first pilot to break sound barrier and US astronaut, as Fred the barman in *The Right Stuff* (US 83). Yeager portrayed in same film by Sam Shepard—one of the rare instances of a name appearing on both sides of the cast list

Yevgeny Yevtushenko, poet, played leading role as Russian space pioneer Konstantin Tsiolkovsky in *Take-Off* (USSR 79); also in *The Kindergarten* (USSR 85)

Black Actors

The first black actor to play a leading role in a feature film was Sam Lucas, cast in the title role of *Uncle Tom's Cabin* (US 14).

The first black actor to make a career in films was Noble Johnson, who made his debut in a Lubin western in 1914 playing an Indian chief. After arriving in Hollywood in 1915, he graduated from stunt work and bit parts with the formation of the Lincoln Motion Picture Co., an all-black production company specializing in ghetto films, of which he was president as well as leading player. Johnson starred in three Lincoln productions—*The Realisation of a Negro's Ambition* (US 16), *The Trooper of Company K* (US 17) and *The Law of Nature* (US 18) — before leaving the company to concentrate on the Universal serials he had been making between Lincoln pictures. In 1932 he had the unusual distinction of becoming the only black actor to have played a white man in a straight role (others have in comedy roles) when he appeared as a Russian 'heavy' in Radio Pictures' *The Most Dangerous Game* (US 32).

The first black performer to be awarded a studio contract was six-year-old 'Sunshine Sammy' Morrison by Hal Roach in 1919. The original two-year contract was later renewed and over a five-year period Sunshine Sammy appeared in 114 Hal Roach Studios comedy shorts, including 28 of the *Our Gang* series in 1922-24. As an adult Morrison worked in vaudeville before leaving show business for the aerospace industry.

According to a Screen Actors Guild survey, black actors were cast in 1,583 speaking roles in 1989 or about 10 per cent of all male roles cast by the major studios. Black actresses scored the same percentage with 873 speaking roles. This was up from 9 per cent in 1987 and 1988 for black actors and up from 8 per cent in these years for black actresses.

While things appear to be getting a little better for performers in featured roles, the prospects for blacks in leading roles show no signs of improvement. The peak was reached in 1973, when 45 US features, 21 of them from major studios, starred black leading players. In 1990 there were less than half a dozen.

Britain's first black screen actor was Bermuda-born Ernest Trimmingham, who made his debut in the British & Colonial production *Her Bachelor Guardian* (GB 12). **The first black actor to play**

a leading role in a British film was Paul Robeson as Bosambo in Alexander Korda's *Sanders of the River* (GB 35). He also starred in *Song of Freedom* (GB 37), *Big Fella* (GB 37), *King Solomon's Mines* (GB 37) and *Jericho* (GB 37).

The performer who played in the most movies made for general release was Tom London (1883–1963), who was born in Louisville, Ky., and made the first of his over 2000 appearances on screen in *The Great Train Robbery* (US 03). He was given the role of the locomotive driver, which was also his job in real life. By 1919 he was playing starring roles at universal under his real name, Leonard Clapham, which he changed to Tom London in 1924. When he became too old for lead roles he receded comfortably into character parts, specializing in sheriffs in 'B' westerns. His last picture was Willard Parker's *The Lone Texan* (US 59).

John C. Holmes (1944–88) claimed in 1985 to have appeared in 2274 mainly hardcore sex pictures. Of these, probably not more than 200 were features, the remainder being shorts, most of them made in the 1960s, known in the trade as 'porno loops'. Holmes admitted to being arrested 13 times during his career, usually for indecency. In 1981 he was tried and acquitted of a charge of bludgeoning to death four people in Laurel Canyon, but gaoled for contempt of court.

The performer who has played the most leading roles in feature films is the Indian comedienne Manorama, who made her screen debut in 1958 and completed her 1000th film in 1985. Of the total, 999 were in Tamil and one in Hindi (a language she does not speak). Manorama works on as many as 30 films at the same time.

The Hollywood star who played the most leading roles in feature films was John Wayne (1907–79), who appeared in 153 movies from *The Drop Kick* (US 27) to *The Shootist* (US 76). In all except 11 of these films he played leading roles. The Duke summed up his simple yet enduring qualities thus: 'I've never had a goddam artistic problem in my life, never, and I've worked with the best of them. John Ford isn't exactly a bum, is he? Yet he never gave me any manure about art.' And: 'I play John Wayne in every part regardless of the character, and I've been doing okay, haven't I?'

The international star with the most screen credits who is still performing in movies is Christopher Lee (born London 1922), star of English, French, Spanish, German, Dutch, Italian, Swedish, Norwegian, Russian, American, Canadian and Australian films. The 201 feature films and TVMs and two shorts he has played in from *Corridor of Mirrors* (GB 47) to *Gremlins 2: The New Batch* (US 90) include 14 in which he recreated his most celebrated role, that of Count Dracula, and one in which he played HRH Prince Philip.

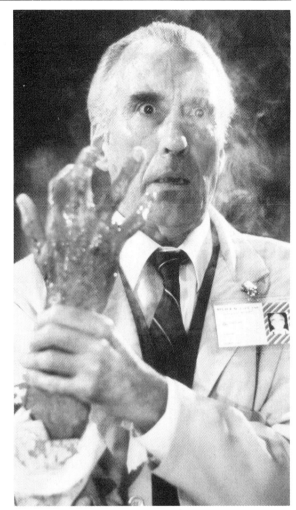

Christopher Lee played his 203rd film role in *Gremlins II: The New Batch* (US 90).

The Most Popular Actors and Actresses

The earliest recorded popularity poll was conducted by a Russian fan magazine in 1911 and was headed by dapper French comedian Max Linder, followed by Denmark's tragic actress Asta Nielsen, with another Danish star, Valdemar Psilander, in third place. America's first poll was staged by *Motion Picture Story Magazine* in March 1912 and resulted in Maurice Costello being voted most popular male star and the now forgotten Dolores Cassinelli most popular actress. By 1914 Mary Pickford, 12th in the 1912 poll, had displaced her and for the next ten years 'the girl with the golden curls', otherwise known as 'America's sweetheart', topped virtually every popularity poll held throughout the world, including those conducted in Soviet Russia (where her husband Douglas Fairbanks was voted most popular male star in 1925). The most durable star of talkies would appear to be John Wayne, who featured in the annual

'Ten Top Box Office Stars' Quigley Poll 25 times 1949–74 and headed it in 1950, 1951, 1954 and 1971. For the most popular Hollywood stars of the 1970s, see Quigley Poll results.

The first popularity poll confined to British-born stars was conducted by *Pictures and the Picturegoer* in 1915 with the following results: 1 Alma Taylor; 2 Elizabeth Risdon; 3 Charles Chaplin; 4 Stewart Rome; 5 Chrissie White; 6 Fred Evans.

Ten years later the *Daily News* poll showed Alma Taylor and Chrissie White, both of whom had joined

> Gene Hackman recalls that he and Dustin Hoffman were voted by fellow students at the Playhouse Acting School in California as the members of their class 'least likely to succeed'.

the Hepworth Co. as child actresses in 1908, still firmly in the public favour: 1 Betty Balfour; 2 Alma Taylor; 3 Gladys Cooper; 4 Violet Hopson; 5 Matheson Lang; 6 Fay Compton; 7 Chrissie White; 8 Stewart Rome; 9 Owen Nares; 10 Ivor Novello.

During the 1930s America's box office was dominated by children, elderly ladies and gentlemen, and a mouse. Marie Dressler topped the Quigley Poll at age 63 in 1932 and again in 1933; Will Rogers came first aged 55 in 1934; then Shirley Temple rose to the top, aged 7, and remained there for the following three years, until 1939, when Mickey Rooney, 18 years old and playing a high school kid in the *Andy Hardy* series, took the lead and held first place for three years. Mickey Mouse was not eligible for the Quigley Poll, but he beat Emil Jannings by 400,000 votes as No. 1 star in a popularity contest held in

Australia in 1931, and knocked Wallace Beery into second place in Japan in 1936.

Bridging this period and the John Wayne era were the Bing Crosby–Betty Grable years of the 1940s. Cumulative Quigley Poll results for the 1960s give the following hierarchy of the biggest box-office draws of the decade: 1 John Wayne; 2 Doris Day; 3 Cary Grant, Rock Hudson and Elizabeth Taylor; 6 Jack Lemmon; 7 Julie Andrews; 8 Paul Newman; 9 Sean Connery; 10 Elvis Presley. (Of course no such list is definitive. Sophia Loren, who never appeared in the annual Top Ten, was nevertheless voted the most popular star in the world by the US Foreign Press Corps in 1969.) The order for the 1970s: 1 Clint Eastwood; 2 Burt Reynolds; 3 Barbra Streisand; 4 Paul Newman; 5 Robert Redford; 6 Steve McQueen; 7 John Wayne; 8 Woody Allen; 9 Dustin Hoffman; 10 Sylvester Stallone. The order for the 1980s: 1 Clint Eastwood; 2 Eddie Murphy; 3 Burt Reynolds; 4 Tom Cruise; 5 Sylvester Stallone; 6 Harrison Ford; 7 Michael J. Fox, Paul Hogan; 9 Arnold Schwarzenegger; 10 Michael Douglas. Top woman star of the decade, despite rare appearances on screen and few successes, was Jane Fonda in 11th place.

A new method of measuring popularity was introduced by Marketing Evaluations of New York in 1990. Dubbed the Q Score, it is based on a poll in which a panel of representative Americans are asked to rate personalities on a scale of 1 to 5. Although it covers all fields of endeavour, six luminaries of the big screen appear in the initial top ten listing, led by Dustin Hoffman and Bugs Bunny, who each have a Q Score of 45, and followed by Robin Williams (44), Tom Hanks (43), Mickey Mouse (42) and Clint Eastwood (42).

QUIGLEY PUBLICATIONS POLL

The annual Quigley Poll is a poll of exhibitors to determine the top box-office draws. Listed below are the top male and the top female star for each year—the rating of whichever was not No. 1 is given in brackets after the name. For example the (12) after Meryl Streep's name for 1983 signifies that, although she was rated most popular actress, 11 male stars scored higher popularity ratings in that year. Significantly no woman has headed the poll since Julie Andrews in 1967.

1915	William S. Hart Mary Pickford (2)	1923	Thomas Meighan Norma Talmadge (2)	1937	Shirley Temple Clark Gable (2)	1951	John Wayne Betty Grable (3)
1916	William S. Hart Mary Pickford (2)	1924	Norma Talmadge Rudolph Valentino (3)	1938	Shirley Temple Clark Gable (2)	1952	Dean Martin and Jerry Lewis Doris Day (7)
1917	Douglas Fairbanks Anita Stewart (3)	1925	Rudolph Valentino Norma Talmadge (2)	1939	Mickey Rooney Shirley Temple (5)	1953	Gary Cooper Marilyn Monroe (6)
1918	Douglas Fairbanks Mary Pickford (2)	1926	Colleen Moore Tom Mix (2)	1940	Mickey Rooney Bette Davis (9)	1954	John Wayne Marilyn Monroe (5)
1919	Wallace Reid Mary Pickford (3)	1927	Tom Mix Colleen Moore (2)	1941	Mickey Rooney Bette Davis (8)	1955	James Stewart Grace Kelly (2)
1920	Wallace Reid Marguerite Clark (2)	1928	Clara Bow Lon Chaney (2)	1942	Abbott & Costello Betty Grable (8)	1956	William Holden Marilyn Monroe (8)
1921	Mary Pickford Douglas Fairbanks (2)	1929	Clara Bow Lon Chaney (2)	1943	Betty Grable Bob Hope (2)	1957	Rock Hudson Kim Novak (11)
1922	Mary Pickford Douglas Fairbanks (2)	1930	Joan Crawford William Haines (2)	1944	Bing Crosby Betty Grable (4)	1958	Glenn Ford Elizabeth Taylor (2)
		1931	Janet Gaynor Charles Farrell (2)	1945	Bing Crosby Greer Garson (3)	1959	Rock Hudson Doris Day (4)
		1932	Marie Dressler Charles Farrell (4)	1946	Bing Crosby Ingrid Bergman (2)	1960	Doris Day Rock Hudson (2)
		1933	Marie Dressler Will Rogers (2)	1947	Bing Crosby Betty Grable (2)	1961	Elizabeth Taylor Rock Hudson (2)
		1934	Will Rogers Janet Gaynor (3)	1948	Bing Crosby Betty Grable (2)	1962	Doris Day Rock Hudson (2)
		1935	Shirley Temple Will Rogers (2)	1949	Bob Hope Betty Grable (7)	1963	Doris Day John Wayne (2)
		1936	Shirley Temple Clark Cable (2)	1950	John Wayne Betty Grable (4)	1964	Doris Day Jack Lemmon (2)

1965	Sean Connery Doris Day (3)	1978	Burt Reynolds Diane Keaton (7)
1966	Julie Andrews Sean Connery (2)	1979	Burt Reynolds Jane Fonda (3)
1967	Julie Andrews Lee Marvin (2)	1980	Burt Reynolds Jane Fonda (4)
1968	Sidney Poitier Julie Andrews (3)	1981	Burt Reynolds Dolly Parton (4)
1969	Paul Newman Katharine Hepburn (9)	1982	Burt Reynolds Dolly Parton (6)
1970	Paul Newman Barbra Streisand (9)	1983	Clint Eastwood Meryl Streep (12)
1971	John Wayne Ali MacGraw (8)	1984	Clint Eastwood Sally Field (5)
1972	Clint Eastwood Barbra Streisand (5)	1985	Sylvester Stallone Meryl Streep (10)
1973	Clint Eastwood Barbra Streisand (6)	1986	Tom Cruise Bette Midler (5)
1974	Robert Redford Barbra Streisand (4)	1987	Eddie Murphy Glenn Close (7)
1975	Robert Redford Barbra Streisand (2)	1988	Tom Cruise Bette Midler (7)
1976	Robert Redford Tatum O'Neal (8)	1989	Jack Nicholson Kathleen Turner (10)
1977	Sylvester Stallone Barbra Streisand (2)	1990	Arnold Schwarzenegger Julia Roberts (2)

Valentino. At 30 he was voted the biggest box office draw in the world. At 31 he was dead.

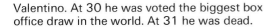

The largest number of members of one family to have appeared in films is 31 in the case of the Luevas of Los Angeles. Matriarch Augustina Lueva (b. La Refugio, Mexico 1852), 18 of her 21 children and 12 of her grandchildren were reported to be actively employed as film actors in 1928. Six of the children and four of the grandchildren appeared together in an unidentified film of that year.

Other films in which families have appeared together are: *Hearts of the World* (US 18), in which Bobby Harron played the lead, his mother played a French woman, her two daughters Jessie and Mary played her screen daughters, and Bobby's brother Johnny played 'a boy with a barrel'; *Mr Smith Goes to Washington* (US 39) with brothers and sisters Coy, Vivian, Gloria, Louise, Harry, Billy, Delmar, Garry and Bobs Watson playing the Governor's children; and *Ein Tag ist Schoener als der Andere* (FRG 70), featuring the seven von Eichborn children, Clarissa, Justina, Evelyn, Jacqueline, Wolfram, Holger and Isabella. More recently Blake Edwards's *That's Life* (US 86) starred his wife Julie Andrews opposite Jack Lemmon, and featured his own daughter Jennifer Edwards and Jack's son Chris Lemmon, as well as Julie's daughter Emma Walton and Jack's wife Felicia Farr. When Mia Farrow starred as Hannah in *Hannah and Her Sisters* (US 86), there were no sisters around, but her mother Maureen O'Sullivan, her three children by André Prévin and four of her adopted children were all in the picture. Three generations were also represented in *Kung Fu Master* (Fr 88), with Jane Birkin's parents (mother is actress Judy Campbell) playing her parents in the film, and her children

Charlotte Gainsbourg and Lou Doillon playing her on-screen daughters. Maurice, Philippe and Louis Garrel replicated their real life relationship as grandfather, son and grandson in *Les Baisers de secours* (Fr 89) and Robert, Christopher and Bentley C. Mitchum did the same in *Promises to Keep* (US 85, TVM).

Soviet director Vladimir Basov solved the problem of the 25-year-time span in his film of J. B. Priestley's *Time and the Conways* (USSR 84) by casting four fathers and sons and three mothers and daughters to play the characters in their older and younger personas respectively.

Some film families deliberately avoided working with each other. All six McLaglen brothers were film actors, Victor in America, the others mainly in Britain. When the youngest, Leopold, tried to break into Hollywood pictures in the mid-1930s, eldest brother Victor took out an injunction restraining him. 'There's only room for one McLaglen in Hollywood,' asserted Victor.

The most generations of screen actors in a family is four in the case of the Redgraves. Roy Redgrave (1872–1922), father of Sir Michael, made his screen debut in *The Christian* (Aus 11) and continued to appear in Australian movies until 1920. Sir Michael Redgrave (1908–85) married actress Rachel Kempson (1910–), and their two daughters Vanessa (1937–) and Lynn (1943–) and son Corin (1939–) all went into movies. Vanessa's daughters Natasha and Joely made their debut in *The Charge of the Light Brigade* (GB 68) and subsequently appeared in *Dead Cert* (GB 74) and *Joseph Andrews* (GB 77), while Corin's daughter Jemima appeared for the first time in *Joseph Andrews*. All three actress members of the fourth generation have successfully transferred to adult leading roles, Joely in *Wetherby* (GB 85), *Drowning by Numbers* (GB 88) and *Shining Through* (GB 91), Natasha in *Gothic* (GB 86), *A Month in the Country* (GB 87), *Patty Hearst* (US/GB 88), *The Handmaid's Tale* (US/FRG 90) and *The Comfort of Strangers* (GB 91), and Jemma (her adult name) in *The Dream Demon* (GB 88).

Mums and Dads

A number of artistes have portrayed their own parents in films. Marie Lloyd Jr played 'Queen of the Halls' Marie Lloyd Sr in *Variety Jubilee* (GB 43), while on the other side of the Channel playwright Sacha Guitry took the role of his father, actor Lucien Guitry, in *The Private Life of an Actor* (Fr 48) —he also played himself. Will Rogers Jr portrayed Will Rogers Sr in three films—*Look for the Silver Lining* (US 49), *The Story of Will Rogers* (US 52) and *The Eddie Cantor Story* (US 53). Dick Powell Jr was seen in a cameo role as lookalike father Dick Powell Sr in *The Day of the Locust* (US 74) and Marcel Cerdan Jr had a leading role as his father in *Edith and Marcel* (Fr 84), the story of Edith Piaf's love affair with middleweight boxing champion Marcel Cerdan Sr. In *Adolf Hitler—My Part in His Downfall* (GB 72), Jim Dale plays Spike Milligan, while Milligan appears as his own father.

Chynna Phillips portrayed her own mother Michelle Phillips, formerly of the sixties pop group The Mamas and the Papas and ex live-in-lover of both Jack Nicholson and Warren Beatty, in *California Dreamin'* (US 88). The only recorded example of a character being played by his own brother is in Raj Kapoor's two autobiographical movies *Awara* (Ind 51) and *Shree 420* (Ind 55), with Shashi Kapoor in the roles based on Raj Kapoor.

Albert Wimscheider took the part of his own uncle in *Autumn Milk* (FRG 89), based on his wife's autobiographical story of how she ran their farm while he was away at the war. Another story of war and its aftermath, the 1989 Berlin Film Festival Silver Bear winner *The Summer of Aviya* (Isr 89), starred Gila Almagor as her own mother, a mentally disturbed Holocaust survivor.

Marie Osmond played her mother Olive Osmond while her daughter Amy Osmond appeared as Marie in *Side by Side: The True Story of the Osmond Family* (US 82, TVM). Patty Duke's brother Ray Duke portrayed their father in his sister's autobiopic *Call Me Anna* (US 90, TVM).

Only one actor has played his own grandfather and only one his own great grandfather. Stalin's grandson Eugene Djugasvili played the tyrant in *War Is War For Everyone* (USSR 90). In *American Friends* (GB 91) Michael Palin stars as a middle-aged Oxford classics don based on his great grandfather, the Rev. Edward Palin, who had to resign his post after deciding to marry a teenage American girl he met on a walking tour of Switzerland. The story was based on a few cryptic entries Palin discovered in his great grandfather's diary.

The largest cast of credited performers in a film was 260 in *Dny Zrady/Days of Treason* (Cz 72), the story of the betrayal of Czechoslovakia in 1938, including Gunnar Möllar as Hitler, Jaroslav Radimecky as Chamberlain, Alexander Fred as Goebbels, Rudolf Jurda as Goering and Vladamir Stach as Mussolini.

Sacha Guitry's *Napoleon* (Fr 54) had 101 credited roles, but was claimed to have 300 speaking parts. MGM claimed 365 speaking parts (73 credited) for *Ben Hur* (US 59), but this seems impossible for a 217-minute film unless it includes groups of people all speaking at once. As many as 430 speaking parts were claimed for the 188 minute *Gandhi* (GB 83), with 138 credited. The British film with the largest cast of credited performers is *Little Dorrit* (GB 87) with 211.

Other films with large casts (credited) include: *Mission to Moscow* (US 43) with 195; *Rottenknechte* (GDR 70) with 194; *A Cry in the Dark* (Aus 88) with 168; *Baron Muenchhausen* (Ger 45) with 150; *Sweden for the Swedes* (Swe 80) with 142; *Around the World in 80 Days* (US 56) with 138; *A Bridge Too Far* (GB 77) with 137; *Oh! What a Lovely War* (GB 69) with 125; and Karl Ritter's *Pour la Merité* (Ger 38) with 102.

For **the largest cast including extras**, see p. 81.

The largest all-female cast consisted of the 135 speaking roles in MGM's *The Women* (US 39), starring Joan Crawford, Norma Shearer, Rosalind Russell, Paulette Goddard and Joan Fontaine.

The smallest cast in a live-action dramatic feature, excluding movies with an all-animal cast, is none. Kostas Sfikas' *Model* (Gre 74) had no performers, only robots seen in a single set representing a factory yard. The 1 hr 45 min film was intended as a critique of the 'implacable process that transforms mankind into negotiable goods and mere accessories of an industrial machine'.

There have been a number of movies with a cast of one. Olaf Fønns, leading Danish romantic hero of the World War I period, played alone in Fritz Magnussen's *Remorse* (Den 19), made for Dansk Astra Film. The story is of a wealthy man who is ruined and loses his mistress (represented only by a pair of arms), then returns to her in a starving condition, is rejected and kills her. He restores his fortune but, relentlessly pursued by his own accusing shadow, eventually gives himself up. In addition to its solo performance, the film was distinguished by having no inter-titles.

Sunil Dutt's *Yaadein/Recollections* (Ind 64), in which he starred as well as directed and produced, was a single set, solo movie about a husband deserted by his wife. At the end of the film the woman's shadow seen against a wall indicates that she has returned to him. Robert Carlisle's *Sofi* (US 68), an adaptation of Gogol's *Diary of a Madman*, had Tom Troupe as its only performer. Thierry Zeno's *Vase de noces* (Bel 73) starred Dominique Garny, who does not speak throughout the film. It tells the story of a simple man living alone amongst his poultry and pigs who eventually hangs himself. Danilo-Bata Stojković played alone as a man fleeing from imaginary pursuers in Milos Radivojević's *Testament* (Yug 75), which was also without speech. Jean-Pierre Lefebvre's *L'Amour blessé* (*Confidences de la nuit*) (Can 75) starred Louise Cuerrier as a lonely woman spending a dull evening in her room listening to a talk show, while Britain's first single artiste film had Monica Buferd in the rather more compelling role of *St Joan* (GB 77). James Whitmore gave a standout performance as Harry S Truman in his solo biopic of the President's life and times *Give 'Em Hell, Harry!* (US 75).

Other examples of solo performances are by Anne Flannery in *A State of Siege* (NZ 78), Willeke van Ammelrooy in Frans Zwartje's *It's Me* (Neth 79), and by Alain Cavalier in *Ce repondent ne prend pas de message* (Fr 79).

Julie Harris played Charlotte Brontë in Delbert Mann's evocation of the author's life and times *Brontë* (US/Ire 83). Interaction with the other members of the Brontë family was conveyed by having Charlotte handle both sides of the conversation. Another powerful portrayal of a real-life character was by Philip Baker Hall as Richard Nixon in Robert Altman's *Secret Honor* (US 84), delivering an 80-min monologue described as 'a fictional meditation'. In Luc Besson's wordless *The Last Battle* (Fr 83) Pierre Jolivet is the last survivor on earth after the apocalypse.

Another last survivor was the ape-man played by Peter Elliott in *The Missing Link* (US 88), all the other members of his genus having been killed off when the mentally superior but violent *homo sapiens* discovered the axe. In *A Fine Film of Ashes* (GB 88) Steve Shill, who also directed, plays an estate agent who has returned from his father's funeral to ruminate over the ashes in the old man's living room, the only set. *Private Code* (It 88) also had a single set, the ornate flat belonging to a girl (Ornella Muti) whose rich and famous lover has flown off to a conference, perhaps with no intention of returning. Interaction with other, unseen characters is via telephone and computer. In a rare Irish production, Ronan O'Leary's *Fragment of Isabella* (Ire 89), Gabrielle Reidy solo stars as Auschwitz survivor Isabella Leitner.

Stanislaw Rojewicz's *The Body Snatchers* (Pol/Cz 89), declared by *Sight and Sound* to be the oddest film screened at the 1989 Gdansk Festival, achieved the remarkable feat of translating R. L. Stevenson's novel of the same name to the screen with only one body in evidence—that of a lively, lovely nude actress. As remarkable, and perhaps even odder, was the Belgian verison of *Romeo and Juliet* in which the eponymous lovers and all the other Shakespearian characters are played by cats. The only human being in *Romeo-Juliet* (Belg 90) is an old Venetian bag-lady—played in drag by John Hurt.

Unusual Casts

☆ There have been only four full-length feature films with casts composed entirely of American Indians, and none since the advent of talkies. The tally: *Hiawatha* (US 13), with a cast of 150 headed by Soon-goot as Minnehaha; *Before the White Man Came* (US 20), with a cast drawn from the Crow and Cheyenne tribes; *The Daughter of Dawn* (US 20), with a cast from the Comanche and Kiowa tribes; and *The Silent Enemy* (US/Can 30), starring Chief Yellow Robe of the Obizibway Indians of Canada, one of only four members of the cast who had ever seen a motion picture.

☆ The only feature film with a cast composed entirely of Lapps was *The Pathfinder* (Nor 87).

☆ There have been two fiction films with all-Eskimo casts, *Kivalina of the Ice Lands* (US 25) and *Igloo* (US 32), and three Hollywood movies with all-Balinese casts—*Virgins of Bali* (US 32); *Goona-Goona* (US 32) and *Legond, Dance of the Virgins* (US 32). One American film has been made with an all-Chinese cast, Universal's *The War of the Tongs* (US 17), starring Lee Gow and Lin Neong; one with an all-Siamese cast, *Chang* (US 27); and one with an all-Sudanese cast, *Stampede* (US 30).

☆ In *Sitting Bull* (US 54), the Indians and the US Cavalry were all played by Mexicans. In Samuel Fuller's war picture *Big Red One* (US 80), all the Nazi concentration camp guards were played by Jews.

☆ *The Writing on the Wall* (Fr/Bel 82) was a story of the Northern Ireland troubles in which all the Protestants were played by Catholics and the Catholics by Protestants.

☆ There have been many films about nuns, but only two in which they were actually played by nuns. *Francesca* (FRG 87) is about a fictitious star of yester-year who was raised by nuns in Bavaria. The Mother Superior is played by real-life Mother Superior Roswitha Schneider and the nuns by the Sisters of St Mary's Convent in Niederviebach, Bavaria. One hundred cloistered nuns of the Clarissa order perform in *Invisible Things* (It 90, TVM), directed by Capuchin monk Fr Serafino Rafaiani.

☆ Nearly all the performers in *Amy* (US 81) were deaf—they were recruited from the California School for the Deaf at Riverside. Mentally-handicapped actor Richard Mulligan was cast as the most brilliant and intellectual teacher on campus in the off-beat high-school social comedy, *Teachers* (US 84). The title role in *Annie's Coming Out* (Aus 84), based on a true story about a brain damaged teenager, was played by real-life spastic Tina Arhondis.

☆ Members of the International Brigade played in André Malraux's *Man's Hope* (Sp 45), filmed from his own novel during the bombardment of Barcelona in 1938. For three allied fliers who were shot down over Switzerland in World War II, not only was it the end of their war but the opportunity to star in a film. John Hoy and E. G. Morrison of the RAF and Ray Reagan, USAAF sergeant, were given the leading roles in the Swiss film *Last Chance* (Swz 45), playing escaped prisoners leading a party of refugees over the Alps to neutral Switzerland. The refugees, all of different nationalities, were played by real refugees.

☆ All the leading players in *Dionysus* (Fr 84), about a US university professor who comes to Paris to defend a thesis on Dionysus and ends up running an assembly line at Citroën, were played by real life university professors.

☆ Beauty queens have often been given a chance to break into movies, but never so many all at once as in *Yankee Pasha* (US 54). A costumer about a New England girl sold into a Moroccan harem, the cast included the Misses USA, Japan, Panama, Norway, Uruguay, South Africa, Australia and Miss Universe, Christiane Martel.

☆ RKO tried an unusual experiment in 1944 with a film called *Days of Glory* (US 44), in which all 19 featured players were making their screen debut. One of the 19 went on to stardom—Gregory Peck.

☆ Von Stroheim used real hookers to play the prostitutes in *The Wedding March* (US 27) and similarly the inmates of the bordello in John Huston's *Under the Volcano* (US 85) were real-life members of their calling. Not so in *Maya* (Fr 49). A set representing a red light district was built in false perspective to give an illusion of depth. The prostitutes seen at the far end of the street were played by little girls of 6 to 8 years old outfitted in the gaudy raiment of harlotry.

☆ When lesbian producer/star Nazimova starred in her own production of *Salome* (US 23), she employed only gay actors as a 'homage' to Oscar Wilde.

☆ The masochists receiving the punishing attentions of Bulle Ogier in *Maitresse* (Fr 79) were not actors. They were deviants who were invited to bring along their own chains and whips.

☆ The extras engaged to play convicts in *Hell's Highway* (US 32) were all ex-cons themselves.

☆ There have been many prison dramas and war films with all male casts, but very few films with all-female casts. Best known is probably *The Women* (US 39), whose 135 speaking roles included those played by Joan Crawford, Norma Shearer, Rosalind Russell, Paulette Goddard and Joan Fontaine. Others have been: *Maedchen in Uniform* (Ger 31)

witn Dorothea Wieck; *The Mad Parade* (US 31) with Evelyn Brent; *The Blossoms Have Fallen* (Jap 38), about the constraints of life in a geisha house; *Cry Havoc* (US 43), starring Margaret Sullavan, Ann Sothern and Joan Blondell; *The Bitter Tears of Petra von Kant* (FRG 72) with Margit Carstensen; *Cries and Whispers* (Swe 72) with Harriet Andersson, Ingrid Thulin and Liv Ulmann; and *Friendships, Secrets and Lies* (US 79) with Sondra Locke, Tina Louise and Paula Prentiss. All-women films of the 1980s include *Black Mirror* (Can 81), a French-Canadian movie set in a women's prison, *Les Chicks* (Fr 85) and *Les Nanas* (Fr 85) with Marie-France Pisier. Cynthia Scott's *The Company of Strangers* (Can 90), seventh in a series of National Film Board of Canada features in which non-professionals play themselves in a fictitious setting, has a cast of seven elderly ladies (oldest 88) and one young one in a story of how they are marooned in an abandoned country house when their bus breaks down.

☆ Equally rare are films with all-child casts. Since the inception of talkies there have been five features in which the children are playing children, of which the earliest was *Torn Shoes* (USSR 34)—all the performers were under 13. Peter Brook's *The Lord of the Flies* (GB 63) was from William Golding's novel about schoolboy castaways on an uninhabited island who revert to barbarism, while *Leave Us Alone* (Den 75) had a similar theme of children adapting to life on a desert island. Mexico's *Poison for Fairies* (Mex 86), winner of five Ariels (Mexico's equivalent to the Oscar), is set in a girls' school and confronts the dangerous world of childhood fantasies. The only adult characters are represented by an arm or a leg seen at the side of the screen. *Maramao* (Fr/It 87) had a cast composed entirely of 5 to 13 year olds, headed by Italian moppet Vanessa Grevina. In addition there have been three films in which children play adults. *General Spanky* (US 37), starring Spanky McFarland of Our Gang fame, was a burlesque melodrama of the Civil War, while *Bugsy Malone* (GB 76) parodied the gangster movies of the thirties with a then unknown Jodie Foster as a 13-year-old femme fatale. The cast of *The Annunciation* (Hun 84), in which Adam, the first man, is guided through the darker passages of man's tormented history, were all between 8 and 12, with the part of Satan played by a 9-year-old girl.

☆ All the leading roles in Shusuki Kanedo's *Summer Vacation 1999* (Jap 89), a story of teenage homosexual love at a boys' boarding school in Japan, were played by children. But the remarkable feature of this film was that all the boys were played by 14-year-old girls. Their voices were dubbed by young males.

☆ There have been isolated examples of children playing adults in straight dramas. Blanche Sweet played a married woman at the age of 13 in *A Man with Three Lives* (US 09) and 12-year-old Gladys

Seventy-five years separate Lillian Gish's performances in *An Unseen Enemy* (US 12)—kneeling on the right—and *The Whales of August* (US 87).

Leslie took the role of a debutante in *The Beloved Imposter* (US 19). Mickey Rooney played an adult midget in *Orchids and Ermine* (US 27) at the age of seven and this led to a persistent rumour that the child star was in reality a midget posing as a child. The reverse principle, of adults playing children, was not uncommon in silent days, when actresses like Mary Pickford and Lillian Gish specialized in such roles. More unusual examples are the 33-year-old Richard Barthelmess playing a six-year-old boy in the opening scenes of *The Little Shepherd of Kingdom Come* (US 28) and Bette Davis's portrayal of a 13-year-old in *Payment on Demand* (US 51) when she was 43.

☆ Veteran producer Mario Cecchi Gori assembled a mammoth cast for his 125th picture *The Department Store* (It 86) which included every available performer who had appeared in his previous 124 films.

The longest screen career is that of Berlin comedian and character actor Curt Bois (b. 1900), who made his film debut in 1909 at the age of nine in *Mutterliebe* (Ger 09). Bois left Germany in 1933 on the accession of the Nazis and made his way to the US via Prague, Vienna, London and Paris. He went to New York to star in a stage play which closed after only one night and thence to Hollywood in 1938. He appeared in such notable films as *Casablanca* (US 42) and Max Ophuls' *Caught* (US 49) before returning to Berlin in the early fifties. He was to be seen recently as an old man who regards himself as the last storyteller of his tribe in Wim Wenders' enigmatic story of angels come to Earth *Wings of Desire* (FRG 88).

The actress with the longest screen career is Helen Hayes (b. 1900), who made her debut in *Jean and the Calico Doll* (US 10) and performed in the religious docudrama *Divine Mercy, No Escape* (US 88) at the age of 88. Since her other screen work in the last ten years has been confined to television movies, the record for the most enduring actress of the large screen goes to Lillian Gish (b. 1893), first seen as a 19-year old in *An Unseen Enemy* (US 12) and more recently playing leading roles in *Hambone and Hillie* (US 84), *Sweet Liberty* (US 85) and *The Whales of August* (US 87).

The British-based performers with the longest screen careers are the Irish actor Cyril Cusack (b. 1910), who made his debut in *Knocknagow* (Ire 18), and Sir John Gielgud (b. 1904), whose film debut was in *Who Is the Man?* (GB 24).

'Acting is all about honesty. If you can fake that you've got it made.'—veteran star George Burns

---

The largest number of roles played by one actor in a single film is not, as generally believed, the eight members of the d'Ascoyne family portrayed by Alec Guinness in *Kind Hearts and Coronets* (GB 49), but the 27 parts taken by Rolf Leslie in Will Barker's life story of Queen Victoria *Sixty Years a Queen* (GB 13). Others who have equalled or exceeded Sir Alec's eight roles are Lupino Lane, who played all 24 parts in *Only Me* (US 29), Joseph Henabery, cast as Abraham Lincoln and 13 other characters in *The Birth of a Nation* (US 15), Robert Hirsch, seen in 12 roles in *No Questions on Saturday* (US 64), Michael Ripper, with nine in *What a Crazy World* (GB 63), Flavio Migliaccio, who had eight parts in *Como Vai, Vai Bem* (Bra 69) and Rolv Wesenlund, portraying eight characters in the comedy *Norske Byggeklosser* (Nor 71). Perhaps the most economically cast film of recent years was *The Great McGonagall* (GB 74) which had five actors playing 34 parts between them.

What might be described as a double Dutch movie, *Ongedaan gedaan* (Neths 89), did the opposite. The four principal roles were played by eight performers, each character by two actors or actresses.

Actresses Who Have Played Men

There have been many examples of films in which female characters disguised themselves in male attire and in the silent days it was not infrequent for young women to play boys, but few actresses have played adult males. Those who have:

☆ Francesca Bertini in the title role of *Histoire d'un Pierrot* (It 13).
☆ Mathilde Comont as the Persian prince in *The Thief of Bagdad* (US 24).
☆ Elspeth Dudgeon (billed as 'John Dudgeon') as the aged man in the upstairs bedroom in *The Old Dark House* (US 32).
☆ Virginia Engels as old man who falls down the stairs during saloon brawl in *San Antonio* (US 45).
☆ Jean Arless as Warren (also as his wife Emily) in *Homicidal* (US 61).
☆ Sena Jurinac as Octavian in *Der Rosenkavalier* (GB 62).
☆ Ivy Ling Po as the hero Chang in *The Mermaid* (HK 66).
☆ Caroline Johnson as the Prince of Denmark in *Hamlet* (Can 71).
☆ Anne Heywood as Roy, a transsexual man, in *I Want What I Want* (GB 72).
☆ Victoria Abril as an effeminate young man who undergoes a sex change in *I Want To Be a Woman* (Sp 77).
☆ Li Ching-hsia as effeminate young man, Pao Yu, with voracious sexual (hetero) appetite in *Dream of the Red Chamber* (HK 77).
☆ Ethel Merman as a shell-shocked soldier suffering from the delusion he is Ethel Merman in *Airplane* (US 80).
☆ Linda Hunt, 4 ft 9 in American actress, as the male Eurasian cameraman Billy Kwan in *The Year of Living Dangerously* (Aus 82).
☆ Eva Mattes as a male film director based on Rainer Werner Fassbinder in *A Man Like Eva* (FRG 83).
☆ Ina-Miriam Rosenbaum as Jesus Christ in *Johannes' Hemmelighed* (Den 85).
☆ Vanessa Redgrave as Richard Radley, who underwent a sex change and became tennis champion Renee Richards, in *Second Score* (US 86, TVM).
☆ Gillian Jones as Sebastian (also Viola) in *Twelfth Night* (Aus 86).
☆ Debra Winger as redheaded male archangel Emmett, who is in charge of Heaven, in *Made in Heaven* (US 87). (Ms Winger played the role on condition she was neither credited nor identified.)
☆ Theresa Russell as King Zog of Albania in husband Ken Russell's segment of portmanteau film *Aria* (GB 87).
☆ Lanah Pellay as black waiter-turned-revolutionary Alex in *Eat the Rich* (GB 87).
☆ Barbara Leary as Moustachioed Russian heavy Dimitri in *9½ Ninjas* (US 91).

Names

The most usual reasons for actors and actresses changing their names are that those they were born with are too long, too difficult to pronounce, or simply unglamorous. It is not hard to understand why Herbert Charles Angelo Kuchacewich ze Schluderpacheru decided to drop it in favour of Herbert Lom, or why Derek Julius Gaspard Ulrich Niven van den Bogaerde thought he would go further with a name like Dirk Bogarde. Equally Larushka Mischa Skikne had good reason to change his to Laurence Harvey and nobody complained when Walter Matuschanskayasky chose to call himself Matthau instead (though he was billed as Walter Matuschanskayasky when he played a recurring cameo role as a drunk in *Earthquake* (US 74)).

Briefer names may be just as unacceptable. Sarah Jane Fulks was distasteful to Jane Wyman, as was Alexandra Zuck to Sandra Dee and Diana Fluck to Diana Dors. Olga Kronk preferred Claire Windsor,

Myrna Williams from Raidersberg, Montana found that her almond eyes and high cheek bones made her a natural for oriental parts. Just to make sure casting directors took the point, she changed her name to Myrna Loy.

and not surprisingly Doris Day was as relieved to be free of Doris Kappelhoff as was Cyd Charisse not to have to answer to Tula Finklea. Burl Ivanhoe substituted Ives, while Fabian Forte Bonaparte was satisfied to get along with just his first name. Robert Taylor had rather more appeal for a romantic hero than Spangler Arlington Brugh and Septimus Ryott was undoubtedly correct in thinking that his female fans would prefer him as Stewart Rome. Austrian actor Jake Kratz doubted he would be able to play hot-blooded Latin lovers with a name like that and changed it to Ricardo Cortez. Many performers born with Latin names preferred something Anglo-Saxon: Dino Crocetti opted for Dean Martin, Margarita Carmen Cansino for Rita Hayworth, Luis Antonio Damaso de Alonso for Gilbert Roland and Anna Maria Luisa Italiano for Anne Bancroft. A few

Glenda McKay, who plays Gudrun in Ken Russell's *The Rainbow* (GB 88), was named by her mother after Glenda Jackson. Her mother in the film was played by . . . Glenda Jackson.

reversed the process, and changed Anglo-Saxon names into something more exotic: Bonar Sullivan became Bonar Colleano, Peggy Middleton assumed the more romantic Yvonne de Carlo and Muriel Har-

ding decided that Olga Petrova held a greater air of mystery for a *femme fatale*.

Some actors chose names that others had discarded. Bernard Schwarz chose Tony Curtis, while the real Tony Curtis had become Italy's best loved comedian Toto. American actor Bud Flanagan changed his name to Dennis O'Keefe, while British actor Robert Winthrop altered his to Bud Flanagan. It was fortunate for James Stewart that his British namesake had already decided to change James Stewart into Stewart Granger before the other James Stewart went into movies.

Alternatively an artiste could sometimes get away with adopting a name which already had cachet. Cambodia's leading female star before the communist takeover, Kim Nova, selected her screen name in unabashed imitation of Kim Novak. In 1974 a Cambodian starlet called herself Kim Novy in imitation of the imitation. Charles Chaplin sued a Mexican comedian called Charles Amador who had changed his name to Charles Aplin, but was unable to do anything about a German comedian who appeared on screen as Charlie Kaplin. Hong Kong's Bruce Li found fame and fortune treading in the footsteps of the late Bruce Lee.

It was also perfectly possible to have several actors with a legitimate claim to the same name. There were three Robert Lee's working in Hollywood during the 1920s and four Charles Mack's, two of them styled themselves Charles E. Mack, and additionally a Mrs Charles Mack, who performed under that name. When Pernilla Wahlgren and Pernilla Wallgren were both cast in Bo Wideberg's *The Serpent's Way Across Helle Mountain* (Swe 86), the latter decided to change her screen name to Ostergren—her married name—to avoid confusion.

Some were satisfied simply to change their Christian name: Leslie/Bob Hope; James/David Niven; William/Pat O'Brien; Clarence/Robert Cummings; Hubert/Rudy Vallee; John/Arthur Kennedy; Julius/Groucho Marx; Virginia/Bebe Daniels; Sari/Zsa Zsa Gabor; Marilyn/Kim Novak; Adolf/Anton Walbrook; Julia/Lana Turner; Ruth/Bette Davis.

Joseph Keaton assumed the first name of 'Buster' at the age of six months when he fell downstairs and Harry Houdini, a family friend, remarked to his father: 'That's some buster your baby took!' Harry Crosby acquired 'Bing' from avid reading of a comic strip called *The Bingville Bugle* when he was at school.

Even simpler was to change a single letter of the name: Conrad Veidt (Weidt); Beulah Bondi (Bondy); George Raft (Ranft); May Robson (Robison); Ronald Squire (Squirl); Gerard Philipe (Philippe); Dorothy Malone (Maloney); Warren Beatty (Beaty); Yul Brynner (Bryner). James Baumgarner was content to drop the 'Baum', Anna Maria Pierangeli split her surname down the middle and eschewed her first names, while Banky Vilma just switched to Vilma Banky.

Choice of a new name is dictated by varied circumstances. Judy Garland (Frances Gumm) took her stage surname from the theatre pages of a Chicago newspaper, whose reviews were written by Robert Garland. It was chosen by George Jessel, to whom the 11-year-old Miss Gumm had appealed for help after being billed as Glumm at the theatre where they were both appearing. Her first name came from a Hoagy Carmichael song *Judy*, of which she was fond. French comedian Fernandel was born Fernand Constandin. His wife called him Fernand d'elle (her Fernand). Luis Alonso selected his new name of Gilbert Roland as a tribute to the two stars he most admired, John Gilbert and Ruth Roland. Stepin Fetchit, the startled black manservant of twenties and thirties Hollywood movies, named himself after a racehorse which had obliged him by winning. Marilyn Monroe's Christian name was selected for her by Fox talent scout Ben Lyon because of his admiration for Marilyn Miller—the Monroe was her mother's maiden name. Bette (Ruth) Davis took her screen Christian name from Balzac's *Cousin Bette.* Gary (Frank J.) Cooper was named after his agent's hometown, Gary, Indiana. The actor's own hometown would hardly have been appropriate—he came from Helena, Montana. MGM ran a fan contest in 1925 to find a new name for the extravagantly named Lucille Le Sueur. The winner came up with Joan Arden, but as there was already an actress of that name in Hollywood, Miss Le Sueur adopted the name suggested by the runner-up instead—Joan Crawford. Gretchen Young had her first name changed to Loretta by Colleen Moore, who discovered her as a 14-year-old extra in *Her Wild Oat* (US 26). Loretta, said Miss Moore, was the name of 'the most beautiful doll I ever had'. Bela Lugosi, real name

---

British actor Mark Lindsay was to be signed for the John Lennon role in *John and Yoko: A Love Story* (US 85, TVM), but had to surrender the part to Mark McGann when it became known that his real name was Mark Chapman—same as the name of John Lennon's assassin.

Bela Blasko, took his screen surname from his hometown of Lugos in Hungary. Richard Burton, formerly Richard Jenkins, assumed the name of his old teacher in Port Talbot. Gig Young (Byron Barr) took the name of the character he played in *The Gay Sisters* (US 42) and former child star Dawn O'Day switched to Anne Shirley to play the heroine of that name in *Anne of Green Gables* (US 34). The story put about by her studio (and still believed in some quarters) that Theda Bara's name was an anagram of 'Arab Death' was so much hokum: the name was selected by director Frank Powell on learning that she had a relative called Barranger. Equally unroman-

tic was Carole Lombard's (Jane Peters) decision to call herself after the Carroll, Lombardi Pharmacy on Lexington and 65th in New York. Greta Garbo might easily have become Greta Gabor. Long before meeting young Greta Gustafsson, her mentor Mauritz Stiller had cherished the dream of discovering and moulding a great star. He asked his manuscript assistant, Arthur Norden, to select a name. Norden, an historian, chose Gábor, after the Hungarian king, Gábor Bethlen. Stiller wanted something less East European, however, and amended it to Garbo. Another monarch was rather more personally involved in naming Lili Damita (Lilliane Carré). Holidaying at Biarritz in 1921 when she was 17, she attracted the attention of the King of Spain, who enquired after the *damita del maillo rojo* (*young lady in a red bathing dress*).

Those who retain their own names may also have cogent reasons for doing so. 'Bradford Dillman', said that actor, 'sounded like a distinguished, phoney, theatrical name—so I kept it.'

The most enduring screen team was that of Indian superstars Prem Nazir and Sheela, who had played opposite each other in 130 movies by 1975.

The Hollywood record pales by comparison. Excluding performers billed together solely in 'series' films, the most enduring screen partners were husband-and-wife team Charles Bronson and the late Jill Ireland, who co-starred in 15 films up to and including *Assassination* (US 87). Myrna Loy and William Powell played opposite each other in 13 pictures; Janet Gaynor starred with Charles Farrell and Sophia Loren with Marcello Mastroianni in 12 films; Lila Lee with Thomas Meighan in 11 films; Ginger Rogers with Fred Astaire, Judy Garland with Mickey Rooney, Katharine Hepburn with Spencer Tracy and Paul Newman with his wife Joanne Woodward in 10 films; while three screen teams bring up the rear with 8 films together— Jeanette MacDonald and Nelson Eddy; Greer Garson and Walter Pidgeon; Olivia de Havilland and Errol Flynn.

The most extensive screen tests in the history of motion pictures were held for the role of Scarlett O'Hara in *Gone With the Wind* (US 39). Producer David O Selznick shot 149,000 ft of black-and-white test film and another 13,000 ft of colour with 60 actresses, none of whom got the part. Having discarded 27 hours of test film, Selznick narrowed the choice to three major stars and one unknown— Joan Bennett, Jean Arthur, Paulette Goddard and newcomer Vivien Leigh. The final tests required the four contenders to play the scenes of Scarlett getting into her corset, talking to Ashley in the paddock and drunkenly proposing to Rhett Butler. Miss Leigh's successful test was actually made after shooting of the movie had commenced—perhaps the only instance of a major motion picture going into production before the star role had been cast. Total cost of the 165,000 ft of tests was $105,000—approximately the budget then of an average second feature.

Hollywood's first nude screen tests were held for *Four for Texas* (US 63), which starred Ursula Andress and Anita Ekberg in the *femme* leads. Those actresses who had been unwilling to be tested need not have worried; all nude senes were cut by the censor.

Stars who Failed Screen Tests

Failing a screen test may not be a passport to stardom, but in some cases it has been no barrier. Bette Davis's first screen test was so appalling that she ran from the Goldwyn projection room screaming. Her next, with Universal, was successful enough for her to be given a job—as a stand-in girl for screen tests of male actors. Clark Gable failed a Warner screen test in 1930 because Jack Warner declared (in Gable's hearing) that he was only 'a big ape'. His next was at MGM, where his prominent ears told against him. The fact that he did it in Polynesian costume with a flower in his hair may not have helped—production chief Irving Thalberg reckoned he lacked macho appeal. Although he failed the test, MGM signed him anyway and he stayed with the studio—contributing significantly to its ascendancy—for 23 years. Another star who failed the rigours of a MGM test was Maurice Chevalier; but he was signed by Paramount in 1928 on the strength of the *same* test.

Shirley Temple, probably the greatest box-office attraction of all time, failed a test for the *Our Gang* series. The screen's most prestigious luminary,

François Truffaut was so delighted with 12-year-old Jean-Pierre Léaud's screen test for *The Four Hundred Blows* (Fr 59) that he decided to incorporate it into the film—despite the fact that it consisted of an informal conversation between Léaud and the director. The scene was preserved in the film as an interview between the boy Antoine Doinel and a woman psychiatrist in a reformatory. The psychiatrist was not seen, but a female voice-over substituted for Truffaut's questioning. Fade-outs were used to cover up Léaud's explicit replies to Truffaut's intimate questions about adolescent sex, heightening the effect of disorientation.

Laurence Olivier, was turned down for *Queen Christina* (US 33) after testing opposite Greta Garbo, though it is widely held that Garbo deliberately sabotaged the test in order that the role should go to ex-lover John Gilbert, then in decline.

Paramount gave the thumbs down to young British thespian Archibald Leach on account of his thick neck and bandy legs. A couple of years later Paramount head B. P. Schulberg noticed Leach in the test of an aspiring actress in which he was merely the feed. Notwithstanding his neck and his legs, he was signed at $450 a week and given a brand new name to boot—Cary Grant.

Rock Hudson's screen test for 20th Century Fox was so bad it was preserved and shown to other aspirants as a classic example of how not to perform before the camera.

Occasionally it might be the candidate who said no. The talented Romy Schneider walked out of her 1955 screen test with Walt Disney, furious at being made to pose in a dirndl dress in front of a picture postcard Tyrolean backdrop.

Brigitte Bardot's puppy fat and spots caused her to fail a screen test with Marc Allégret when she was 16. Jane Russell also failed to pass muster. The report on her 1940 test for Fox read 'unphotogenic'. Warner's comments when she tested for them were 'no energy' and 'no spark'. Another star considered physically unsuitable was Robert Taylor. He failed his test for United Artists in 1933 because Sam Goldwyn thought he was too skinny.

Nothing was found wanting in Ava Gardner's physique. After seeing her test for MGM, Louis B. Mayer expostulated: 'She can't talk. She can't act. She's terrific.'

Less enthusiasm was expressed for Fred Astaire in a studio report on his first screen test, even if the words were much the same: 'Can't act. Can't sing. Can dance a little.'

Not even an established star could afford to be overconfident. According to Hollywood legend, at the height of her screen career Gloria Swanson took a test incognito wearing a blonde wig. She was turned down.

The shortest adult performer in movies was 2 ft 7 in tall Tamara de Treaux (1959–90), an actress and singer from San Francisco. Tamara's most celebrated role was E.T., Steven Spielberg's lovable alien from outer space. Although in parts of the film E.T. was an electronic puppet, in others he was played by actors and actresses in costume—beside Tamara, there were 2 ft 10 in Pat Bilson and legless schoolboy Matthew de Merritt, who played the drunk scene walking on his hands inside the E.T. suit. Tamara's main scene was of E.T. shuffling into the spacecraft for his return home. Her weight—she considered she was too heavy at 2 st 12 lb—helped her to perfect what she described as 'a cute Daffy Duck waddle'. Tamara was dwarfed by seven-year-old Drew Barrymore, who towered over her by 17 in.

The shortest actor to play the leading role in a film is Filipino paratrooper and black belt martial arts exponent Weng Weng, who has starred in

Agent 00 (Phi 81) and *For Your Height Only* (Phi 84). Weng Weng measures 2 ft 9 in.

The shortest actor to achieve celebrity in Hollywood and the only dwarf honoured in the Hollywood Walk of Fame is Billy Barty, a 3 ft 9 in veteran of 150 films and founder of The Little People of America Inc.

All-dwarf casts have been used in two films—a western *The Terror of Tiny Town* (US 38) and Werner Herzog's *Even Dwarfs Started Small* (FRG 70). *The Little Cigars* (US 73) had a cast of five midgets and one full-sized actress, described as 'a busty blonde'. The **largest cast of dwarves and midgets** was 116 in *The Wizard of Oz* (US 39), and an equal number in *Under the Rainbow* (US 81), which was the story of what the original Munchkins got up to on and off the set of *The Wizard of Oz* while they were staying at the Culver Hotel in 1938. (What they got up to was miniature mayhem.)

The most enduring dwarf actor is Angelo Rossitte, who debuted in Tod Browning's *Freaks* (US 32) and was recently featured in *From a Whisper to a Scream* (US 87).

The shortest artiste to play major roles, apart from dwarves and midgets, is 4 ft 9 in Linda Hunt, who made her debut in *Popeye* (US 80) as mother of the giant, Oxblood Oxheart, and won the Academy Award for Best Supporting Actress in 1984 for

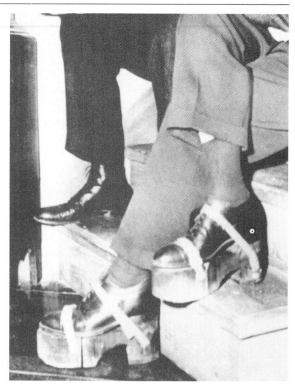

Humphrey Bogart may have been a movie giant, but he needed these platforms to bring his scrawny 5ft 4in body level with Ingrid Bergman's limpid eyes in *Casablanca* (US 42). (*Associated Press*)

Hollywood's most diminutive leading man, five-foot-nothing Danny De Vito strides out to stardom with screen twin Big Arnie in *Twins* (US 88). (*Bruce McBroom*)

her role as Billy Kwan, a male Eurasian cameraman in Indonesia, in *The Year of Living Dangerously* (Aus 82). She has since been in the Merchant–Ivory version of Henry James's *The Bostonians* (GB 84), *Dune* (US 84), *Silverado* (US 85), as Gertrude Stein's lifetime companion Alice B. Toklas in *Waiting for the Moon* (US 87), and *She-Devil* (US 89).

The only leading ladies under 5 ft were silent-screen heroines Florence Turner and Marguerite Clark, each 4 ft 10 in tall, 4 ft 11 in May McAvoy, who starred opposite Al Jolson in *The Jazz Singer* (US 27), and 4 ft 11½ in Gloria Swanson. Janet Gaynor and Mary Pickford were both 5 ft exactly, as was the lesser known Edith Roberts, whose height qualified her to play the title role in *Her Five-Foot Highness* (US 20).

The shortest actor in leading roles is five-foot-nothing Danny De Vito, veteran of a host of cameo roles before achieving stardom opposite Arnold Schwarzenegger in *Twins* (US 88). Most diminutive actor in romantic leads is 'Cuddly' Dudley Moore, who insists that the half is not omitted from his 5 ft 2½ in. Mickey Rooney can look him in the eyebrows at 5 ft 3 in and Michael J. Fox can look down at them both from his 5 ft 4 in elevation—the same height as Humphrey Bogart. Reports that Alan Ladd was only 5 ft tall were quite untrue; he was 5 ft 6 in, which made him an inch taller than Dustin Hoffman and the same height as Al Pacino. Nevertheless, Ladd's lack of inches was proverbial in Hollywood. Sophia Loren has confirmed that he had to stand on a box for his love scenes with her in *Boy on a Dolphin* (US 57) and James Mason, when he was invited to co-star with Ladd in *Botany Bay* (US 54), told the producer that he had no intention of standing in a trench for their scenes together.

The tallest screen artiste was Clifford Thompson, claimed to be 8 ft 6 in and then the tallest man in the world, who played opposite (and above) ZaSu Pitts in Hal Roach's *Seal Skins* (US 32). No other eight-footers are recorded. Artistes of 7 ft or over include Tex Erikson, 7 ft exactly, who was featured in *Jungle Jim in the Forbidden Land* (US 52); 7 ft University of California basketball player Tiny Ron Taylor, seen as Ira in *Seven Hours to Judgement* (US 88); Kevin Peter Hall, at 7 ft 2 in the tallest of six brothers all over 6 ft 5 in, who played the space alien in *Predator* (US 87) and the eponymous ape-man in *Big Foot and the Hendersons* (US 87); Johan Aasen, a 7 ft 2 in character actor who entered Hollywood pictures in 1923; Peter Mayhew, 7 ft 2 in ex-hospital porter, who played a mythical monster in *Sinbad and the Eye of the Tiger* (US 77) and the furry wookie Chewbacca in *Star Wars* (US 77); Richard Kiel, 7 ft 2 in without his size 16 shoes, who played the steel-teethed giant villain in Bond movies *The Spy Who Loved Me* (GB 77) and *Moonraker* (GB/Fr 79) and starred in the title role of *The Humanoid* (It 78); John Bloom, 7 ft 4 in, who was Frankenstein's monster in *Dracula v Frankenstein* (US 71); J. Lockard Martin, the 7 ft 7 in doorman at Grauman's Chinese Theater in Hollywood, who played the robot Gort in *The Day the Earth Stood Still* (US 51) and was so weak he was unable to lift Patricia Neal; and Jack Tarver, 7 ft 10 in, the giant in Fox's feature-length children's picture *Jack and the Beanstalk* (US 17).

The tallest leading men were 6 ft 7 in James Arness, who starred in *Them* (US 54) and *The First Travelling Saleslady* (US 56), and Bruce Spence, 6 ft 7 in, in *Stork* (Aus 71), which was scripted by 6 ft 7 in David Williamson, and *Wo die Grunen Ameisen Trauma* (FRG 84). Christopher Lee is the tallest major star at 6 ft 5 in, an inch taller than Clint Eastwood.

The tallest leading ladies, all at 6 ft, are Margaux Hemingway, Brigitte Nielsen, Sigourney Weaver and Geena Davis (married to 6 ft 4 in Jeff Goldblum, with whom she co-starred in *The Fly* (US 89) and *Earth Girls are Easy* (US 89)).

The heaviest screen artiste was Ethel Greer, who weighed 637 lb when she appeared with Clara Bow in *Hoopla* (US 33). Miss Greer's 140 lb husband, visiting the set, remarked of the slender 118 lb Miss Bow: 'I never could see why some fellows go for these skinny girls'.

The most generously proportioned leading lady of all time was Chesty Morgan, the possessor of a 73-in bust, who starred in *Deadly Weapons* (US 75).

The actor who has played the same role the most times in feature films is the Hong Kong actor Kwan Tak-Hing, who portrayed the great South China martial arts hero Huang Fei-Hong (1847–1924) in 77 films out of a series of 85. His first appearance was in *The True Story of Huang Fei-Hong* (HK 49) and his last in *Magnificent Butcher* (HK 80). During the 1970s, when he played in only one Huang Fei-Hong movie, Kwan Tak-Hing continued the role in a television series.

The Hollywood actor to repeat the same role the most times in feature films was William Boyd (1898–1972), a major star of the twenties whose flagging career was revived in the thirties when Paramount chose him as the gentleman cowboy Hopalong Cassidy. Dressed always in black (usually reserved for villains in 'B' westerns), Boyd rode the range as 'Hoppy' in 66 full-length films, starting with *Hop-a-long Cassidy* aka *Hopalong Cassidy Enters* (US 35) and ending with *Strange Gamble* (US 48). The films were among the first American productions aired on television in the forties and Boyd then embarked on a long-running Hopalong Cassidy TV series, having already played the character in a network radio series.

Typecasting

A number of actors established a reputation for playing particular historical characters: Charles Vanel as Napoleon, Frank McGlynn as Abraham Lincoln and Robert Watson as Hitler. Silent player Roy Travers was cast as the Prince Consort eleven times and as Charles Dickens seven times. The most appearances in one historical role was probably by Mikhail Gelovani, who portrayed Stalin in more than 20 Soviet films. The dictator was so gratified by Gelovani's rather wooden projection of him as the wise, all-seeing, noble proletarian that he was never allowed to give the parts any other dimension.

Other actors have found their niche in occupational roles. Arthur Treacher and Charles Coleman seldom played anything but butlers throughout their screen careers, Irish-American actor Tom Dugan played a slow-witted new York cop in over 100 films following his debut in 1926, while Pat O'Brien was cast as a Roman Catholic priest in at least a dozen of his movies. In 1928 Guy Oliver claimed to have been cast as a sheriff in 150 of the 230 westerns he had made and in 1931 Frank Hagney, invariably seen as a boxer, declared ruefully that he had lost the world's heavyweight title no less than 29 times during his career. A number of performers specialized in courtroom dra-

Mae West fans had to wait 27 years following her performance in *The Heat's On* (US 43) before she made a comeback in *Myra Breckinridge* (US 70). The picture may not have been worth the wait, but Mae still looked a cracker. (*Kobal*)

mas, but none with such dedication as Hollywood character actor Richard Tucker, who is known to have played the prosecuting attorney at least 54 times.

Among performers still active in films, the **record for playing the same occupational** role is claimed by veteran Bombay actor Jagdish Raaj. He has been cast as a uniformed police officer in over 150 films since 1954.

While the greasy, knife-toting Mexican, the shuffling, wide-eyed Negro and the perfidious American Indian have been discarded as offensive stereotypes, there is no such constraint on depicting Arabs as oily and oversexed or shifty-eyed and violent. Nicholas Kaldi is a US-based Iraqi who makes his living playing terrorists, but deplores the racial typecasting. 'There are other kinds of Arabs in the world', he said in a 1990 interview with the *Washington Post*. 'I would like to think that some day there will be an Arab role out there for me that would be an honest portrayal.'

Some were cast against type. German-born Peter van Eyck, who became Hollywood's stock Nazi beast, only came to California because as an active anti-Nazi he was forced to flee Hitler's Germany. Hollywood character actor Mischa Auer was an authentic Russian aristocrat who made his living playing phony Russian aristocrats.

The ability to play a drunk well is a rare one, which enabled Jack Norton and Arthur Housman to specialize in amiable inebriates, seldom playing anything else. Some special talent must also have inspired producers to cast Carmen Nigro as a gorilla in 32 movies, or 33 if his claim to have played the title role in *King Kong* (US 33) can be sustained (it is generally accepted that all the gorilla scenes were acted with models). He last donned his ape suit for *Gorilla at Large* (US 54). 'Cowardly Lion' Bert Lahr was not so lucky. 'After *The Wizard of Oz*', he declared ruefully,

'I was typecast as a lion—and there aren't all that many parts for lions.'

Versatility is harder to quantify. However, it is doubtful whether any performer ever played with a greater variety of accents than Russian-born Hollywood actor Vladimir Sokoloff, who was cast as 35 nationalities during his career ranging from an Italian physicist in *Cloak and Dagger* (US 46) to a blind Chinese beggar in *Macao* (US 52). The only accent Sokoloff never succeeded in mastering was American.

The most delayed comeback: Of the many stars who have retired from films and made a comeback, the one with the longest absence from the screen was George Burns, with a 37-year interval between *Honolulu* (US 39) and *The Sunshine Boys* (US 76). The most delayed comeback by an actress was by Mae West, who retired from the screen after *The Heat's On* (US 43) and returned 27 years later in *Myra Breckinridge* (US 70).

The oldest performer to have played a major role in a movie is French veteran Charles Vanel (1892–1989), who was 95 on the completion of *Les Saisons du Plaisir* (Fr 88) in August 1987. The picture also marked his 75th anniversary as a screen actor. Set during a perfume manufacturers' convention in the south of France, it relates how a centenarian perfumier (Vanel) marries a 90-year-old bride (Denise Grey, who was playing her real age) and plans to name a successor to his dynasty. Vanel's co-star in his previous film, Claude Goretta's *Si le Soleil ne revenait pas* (Fr 87), was Catherine Mouchet, who was somewhat younger than Mme Grey—by 70 years. She had made her debut the previous year in *Thérèse* (Fr 86), 74 years after Vanel had made his debut in *Jim Crow* (Fr 12).

The oldest actress to have played a major role in a movie is Lillian Gish (1893–), who was 93 when she completed principal photography on *The Whales of August* (US 87), in which she co-starred with the comparatively juvenile 78-year-old Bette Davis, in December 1986. Other recent starring roles were in *Hambone and Hillie* (US 84) at the age of 90 and in *Sweet Liberty* (US 86) at the age of 92. Like Charles Vanel (see above), Miss Gish had made her screen debut in 1912. Neither, though, holds the record for the longest screen career (see p. 99), M. Vanel coming second to Curt Bois as the most enduring actor and Miss Gish coming second to Helen Hayes as the most enduring actress. (Note: most reference books cite Miss Gish's year of birth as either 1896 or 1898. In 1984 the American Film Institute was ungallant enough to make public its discovery of her birth certificate, which conclusively proves a birth date of 1893—and secures her place in the record books.)

The greatest age at which anyone has embarked on a regular movie career was 84 in the case of minuscule 4 ft 9 in character actress Lydia Yeamans Titus. She made her screen debut in the Rudolph Valentino film *All Night* (US 18) and played in over 50 features before her death in 1929 aged 95.

Nonagenerian Screen Artistes

Besides Charles Vanel (1892–1989), Lillian Gish (1893–) and Lydia Yeamans Titus (1834–1929) see above, other nonagenerian artistes have been A. E. Matthews (1869–1960) in *Inn for Trouble* (GB 60); Estelle Winwood (1883–1984) in *Murder by Death* (US 76); John Cromwell (1887–1979) in *The Wedding* (US 78); Catherine Nesbitt (1889–1982) in *Never Never Land* (US 80) and *The Second Star to the Right* (GB 81); Sam Jaffe (1891–1984)—who played the 200-year-old High Lama in *Lost Horizon* (US 37)—in *Nothing Lasts Forever* (US 82) and *On the Line* aka *Downstream* (US 84); and George Burns (1896–) in *18 Again* (US 88). Matty, as A. E. Matthews was known, once observed: 'I always wait for *The Times* each morning. I look at the obituary column, and if I'm not in it I go to work.' Estelle Winwood (b. Lee, Kent, 24 January 1883) completed her role as Nurse Withers in *Murder by Death* (US 76) on her 93rd birthday. Miss Winwood was the oldest member of the Screen Actors Guild at the time of her death in California aged 101. She made her professional debut at the Theatre Royal, Manchester, in 1898 and claimed to have been the first woman in America to wear lipstick in public. The oldest screen artiste to appear in a British film was Madoline Thomas (b. Abergavenny, 2 January 1890), who appeared with Emlyn Williams in *Caring* (GB 87 TVM) at the age of 97. She had come to the profession late in life, having been given her first stage role by Emlyn Williams when she was 52 and her first film role, also by her compatriot, in *The Last Days of Dolwyn* (GB 49). She died in 1989 three days short of her 100th birthday.

At least two centenarians were professional extras. William H. 'Dad' Taylor, born Brownsville, Texas, 9 July 1828, appeared in Edwin Carewe's *Evangeline* (US 29) at the age of 101—a unique instance of a person born during the Georgian era playing in a talkie. The other was Walter 'Cap' Field (1874–1976), who joined the Mexican production company Ammex in 1913 and played his last role in *She's Too Hot to Handle* (US 76) when he was 101. He fondly remembered being 'killed or wounded four or five times' in various small roles in *Gone with the Wind* (US 39). The 'sage' in *The Man Who Would Be King* (US 75) was played by a 102-year-old Moroccan.

The oldest performer and the only centenarian to have played a speaking role on screen was 114-year-old Jeanne Louise Calment (b. Arles, 21 February 1875), who appeared as herself in *Vincent and Me* (Can/Fr 90). The film is about a 13-year-old Canadian girl called Jo (Nina Petronzio), passionate about the work of Vincent Van Gogh, who sets out on a European odyssey in pursuit of art forgers and eventually travels through time to 19th-century Arles to encounter the master himself. On her return, having succeeded in her objective of making Vincent smile, she meets the last survivor of those who knew him in person, Mme Jeanne Calment, whose father kept the shop where Van Gogh bought his canvas. She used to serve behind the counter as a girl and remembers vividly how he used to roll the canvas between his fingers to see if it was of good quality. When Jo tells her that Van Gogh was kind to her, Jeanne Calment replies 'Well, good for you, because he was rude to me!'.

The oldest screen performer of all time, Jeanne Louise Calment, who played herself at the age of 114 in *Vincent and Me* (Can/Fr 90). She was the last living person to have known Vincent Van Gogh—and tells the child heroine of the movie what a rude man he was. (*Les Productions La Fête Inc.*)

She also remembers him as 'rough and ugly'. In the year that *Vincent and Me* was released, 1990, Jeanne Calment succeeded Mrs Carrie White of Florida as the oldest person in the world and also became the third oldest centenarian of all time with an authenticated birth date.

One other person is claimed to have appeared in a movie at the age of 114, though not in a speaking role as it was a silent film. She was Mammy Lou, who played an old servant at the Southern mansion depicted in Goldwyn's *The Glorious Adventure* (US 18). The location for the picture was the famous Hermitage estate near Savannah, Ga, where Mammy Lou had been a slave before the Emancipation. If her reported age was genuine, she would have been already over 60 at the time she received her freedom.

The youngest performer in a feature film was Balázs Monori, whose actual birth was shown in *Kilenc Hónap/Nine Months* (Hun 76), the story of a pregnant woman (Lili Monori) torn between two men and striving to improve herself. The director, Márta Meszaros, was reported to be delighted that Balázs's screen debut was so accomplished that no second take was needed.

The youngest performer to receive star billing was Leroy Overacker, known on the screen as Baby Leroy, who was chosen at the age of six months to play the central juvenile role opposite Maurice Chevalier in *Bedtime Story* (US 33). Master Overacker's contract had to be signed by his grandfather, because not only the star but also his 16-year-old mother was under age. The film was about a gay bachelor who becomes encumbered with an abandoned baby whose protruding lower lip matches his own, a circumstance which leads everyone to believe that Chevalier is the father of the motherless child. All is unscrambled when it is found that the distinctive facial feature of the baby is accounted for by nothing more reprehensible than a button lodged under his lip.

After the international success of *Home Alone* (US 90), 10-year-old Macauley Culkin became the highest paid child star in history with a $1 million contract from Columbia.

The youngest performer to win a national award against adult competition was 8-year-old Lee Mete-Kingi, who was honoured as Best Actor at the 1990 New Zealand Film Awards for his performance in *Ruby and Rata* (NZ 90).

The highest paid child performer is Macauley Culkin, who was 10 years old when his success in *Home Alone* (US 90) won him a $1 million contract with Columbia in December 1990 to appear in *My Girl* (US i.p.).

Age and the Leading Lady

As Gloria Swanson said in *Sunset Boulevard*, they 'had faces then' – but most of them were quite a lot younger than the leading ladies of today.

Fewer than 5 per cent of Hollywood leading ladies in the films of 1930 were over 40. In 1990 over 39 per cent had reached these mature years.

In 1920, heyday of silent film output, almost half (46 per cent) the female leads in Hollywood pictures were under 25. In 1980 only a little over 4 per cent

	Under 25	Under 30	Under 35	Under 40
1920	46.3%	73.0%	85.0%	94.6%
1930	33.6%	73.7%	87.5%	95.1%
1940	31.3%	62.6%	81.9%	89.2%
1950	18.6%	61.7%	76.3%	87.4%
1960	18.2%	44.6%	71.8%	86.3%
1970	18.3%	40.9%	62.4%	75.3%
1980	4.3%	19.4%	44.1%	66.7%
1990	9.2%	23.4%	45.1%	60.7%

were as young. Ten years later the figure had risen to 9 per cent, but amongst the leading ladies of 1990 it was the likes of Glenn Close (45), Jessica Lange (41), Anne Archer (42), Cher (44), Susan Sarandon (44), Jane Fonda (53), Karen Black (48), Dyan Cannon (52), Bonnie Bedelia (44), Talia Shire (43), Barbara Hershey (42), Susan Strasberg (52), Diane Keaton (44) and Goldie Hawn (45) who were nearer to the age norm than the sprinkling of young stars like Winona Ryder (18), Annabeth Gish (19),

Uma Thurman (20), Molly Ringwald (22), Nicole Kidman (22), Julia Roberts (22) and Laura Dern (24).

Nearly 70 per cent of leading ladies were in their twenties in 1930 and even in 1950 the figure was over 60 per cent. Thirty years on it had dropped to just over 18 per cent and in 1990 it was 21 per cent.

Why the shift away from youth and towards maturity? There is no clearcut answer, and most likely there is a mixture of reasons. The contract system almost certainly had something to do with it because it was clearly in the interests of the studios to cultivate the careers of their younger talent. The large number of B movies before 1960 gave modestly paid youngsters an opportunity to play leading roles which probably only exists today in independent productions, and mainly the kind of low budget movies in which lissome young ladies lose their clothes. The kind of ingénue role which rocketed 22-year-old Julia Roberts to international stardom in *Pretty Woman* (US 90) is exceptional in major studio productions today. One other important factor is that women under 30 look younger now than they did in previous generations. The heavy make-up, formal clothes and severe hairstyles worn by girls in their late teens or twenties before the youth cult of the 1960s is in marked contrast to the bejeaned and sneakered 'natural look' favoured by most modern women below middle age. It is salutary to remember that when Lauren Bacall played the mature and cooly independent heroine of *To Have and To Have Not* (US 44) she was still a teenager.

The accompanying charts, exclusive to *The Guinness Book of Movie Facts & Feats*, are based on an analysis of the leading ladies of identifiable age in all US productions released in the years indicated.

Insurance

Insurance of stars' more notable physical accoutrements began when silent screen comedian John Bunny (1863–1915) insured his unlovely face for $100,000. Faces were most stars' fortunes and it was an enterprising Los Angeles underwriter, Arthur W. Stebbins, who originated the 'scarred face' policy

	18–19 %	20–24 %	25–29 %	30–34 %	35–39 %	40–44 %	45–49 %	50–54 %	55–59 %	60+ %	Average Age
1920	10.8	35.5	26.7	12.0	9.6	4.0	0.8	0.4	–	0.4	27
1930	4.3	29.3	40.1	13.8	7.6	1.3	2.0	–	–	1.09	28
1940	8.0	23.3	31.3	19.3	7.3	4.7	1.3	3.3	0.3	1.0	29
1950	1.6	17.0	43.1	14.6	11.1	7.1	2.4	0.8	–	2.4	31
1960	–	18.2	26.4	27.2	14.5	5.5	0.9	2.7	2.7	1.8	32
1970	–	18.3	22.6	21.5	12.9	5.4	9.7	2.2	1.1	6.5	35
1980	1.1	3.2	15.1	24.7	22.6	14.0	9.7	3.2	4.3	2.2	37
1990	2.5	6.7	14.2	21.7	15.8	20.8	9.2	4.2	2.5	2.5	36

taken out in the early 1920s by Rudolph Valentino, Douglas Fairbanks and Mary Pickford, the latter for $1 million. Some stars, though, owed their success to individual features, not always facial—Chaplin insured his feet for $150,000. Clara Kimball Young (1891–1960), often described as 'the most beautiful woman in films' at the peak of her career, *c*. 1918, insured her large and luminous eyes for the same amount. Cross-eyed Ben Turpin (1874–1940) insured to the tune of $100,000 against the possibility of his eyes ever becoming normal again—it would undoubtedly have cost him his career. Suave leading man Edmund Lowe (1890–1971) took out a $35,000 policy on his distinguished nose in the mid-1920s and at about the same time Kathleen Key had her lovely neck underwritten at $25,000. A decade later the most famous nose in the business carried a $100,000 risk for Jimmy Durante (1893–1980).

Alberta Vaughn took out a $25,000 policy in 1925 against the possibility of putting on 20 lb weight by 1 June 1927, while Walter Hiers—literally a Hollywood 'heavy'—insured for an equal sum against losing 45 lb. RKO insured Roscoe Ates' (1892–1962) inimitable nervous stutter in the early thirties. A year or two earlier, when sound arrived, First National had insured Corinne Griffith (1898–1979) against loss of voice. Ironically it was her unsuitability for talkies that finished her career. When Anthony Quinn (1915–) had his head shaved for the role of a Greek magician in *The Magus* (GB 68), he insured against the risk of his hair failing to grow back.

The first actress to insure her legs was Hollywood extra Cecille Evans, whose appendages were underwritten for $100,000 in 1921. Miss Evans' speciality was 'doubling' her sensational legs for those of stars less well endowed. The 'Girl with the Million Dollar Legs', Betty Grable (1916–73), actually had them

> Average cost to an insurer when a major motion picture stops production is $500 per minute.

insured for more than that—the sum was $1,250,000. The legs may have been incomparable, but the policy did not stand comparison with the record risk of $5 million accepted on Cyd Charisse's (1921–) long and lovely limbs. No actor has ever been described as 'The Man with the Million Dollar Legs', but Fred Astaire (1899–1987) could have claimed the title— his were insured for just that sum.

It is not only performers who have had parts of their bodies insured. In 1939 the Fleischer Studio took out a $185,000 policy with Lloyd's of London to cover the hands of the 116 animators working on the full-length cartoon feature *Mr Bug Goes to Town* (US 41).

The first artiste whose life was insured for the duration of a picture was Lillian Gish (1893–), covered for the sum of $1 million during the filming of *Way*

Lillian Gish was insured for $1 million for the duration of *Way Down East* (US 20). Had the insurance company known that she was to be exposed on an iceflow in sub-zero temperature every day for three weeks, they might have had second thoughts. (*Kobal*)

Down East (US 20). The insurance company turned down director D. W. Griffith's application for insurance on the other principal players on health grounds. Had they known that Miss Gish was to be exposed on an ice floe in sub-zero temperature wearing only a thin frock every day for three weeks, and that she was to be rescued by the hero just before the floe went over the falls without any trick or stunt work, nor any safety precautions in case the rescue

> Irwin Allen took out a $70 million policy to insure the cast of *The Swarm* (US 78) against bee stings.

failed, doubtless the application on her behalf would have been refused with even greater promptitude.

When seven-year-old Shirley Temple's life (1928–) was insured with Lloyd's, the contract stipulated that no benefit would be paid if the child met death or injury while drunk.

Siobhan McKenna's insurance policy for *Of Human Bondage* (GB 64) forbade her to drive a car while the picture was in production. The first time the Irish actress had taken the wheel she had ended in a ditch, the second time against a wall, the third time up a tree.

FILM MAKING AND FILM MAKERS

The first animal star to appear regularly in films was 'Hepworth Picture Player Rover', an English collie belonging to pioneer producer Cecil Hepworth who made his debut in his master's outstandingly successful low-budget (£7 13s 9d) box-office hit *Rescued by Rover* (GB 05). A simple melodrama about a dog rescuing a baby who has been kidnapped by gypsies, it was in such demand by exhibitors that the negative wore out and the film had to be made twice. Rover, whose real name was Blair, starred in at least seven other films before his death in February 1914. American historian Kenneth Macgowan dryly observed that Rover was the first screen performer who did not overact.

One of the first animals to achieve something akin to 'superstar' status was Strongheart, an ex-Red Cross dog who had served in the trenches in World War I. Strongheart was a consummate screen actor, but had an aversion to being made to howl. According to Lawrence Trimble, who directed Strongheart in most of his films, he would get so depressed that

There are many hundreds of footprints set in the sidewalk outside Grauman's Chinese Theatre in Hollywood—also three sets of hoof-pints. They belong to Tony (Tom Mix), Trigger (Roy Rogers) and Champion (Gene Autry).

his work would be below par for several days afterwards. Once he had graduated to canine stardom, however, there was little choice but to indulge these displays of temperament. A double would be brought in to do the howling for him.

Serving on the other side of the line in World War I was the German Army dog Rin Tin Tin (1916–32), who came to Hollywood in the early twenties and became an animal 'megastar'. He was the only dog in America with a valet, a personal chef, his own limousine and a chauffeur for his exclusive use. He also had a five-room dressing room complex of his own on the studio lot.

The largest cast of living creatures in a film were the 22 million bees employed by Irwin Allen in *The Swarm* (US 78).

The largest number of horses ever assembled for a film was 11,000 in the case of Alexander Ptushko's

The hit moppet picture *Benji* (US 74), about a dog who rescues two children from kidnappers, was shot mainly at a height of 18 in (46 cm) from the ground—the camera was showing the action from Benji's viewpoint. In Samuel Fuller's *White Dog* (US 84), the story of a dog trained to attack black people, all shots through the eyes of the dog were in black and white—dogs are colour blind.

Ilya Muromets/Sword and the Dragon aka *The Epic Hero and the Beast* (USSR 56). The Hollywood record was established the same year when King Vidor used 8000 horses in *War and Peace* (US 56).

The largest assemblage of assorted animals in a movie totalled 8552 in *Around the World in Eighty Days* (US 56), to wit: 3800 sheep, 2448 buffalo, 950 donkeys, 800 horses, 512 monkeys, 17 bulls, 15 elephants, 6 skunks, 4 ostriches.

Just a few of the 22 million bees let loose for *The Swarm* (US 78). Forty years on from *Gone With the Wind* (US 39) Olivia de Havilland was still having a hard time. (*Kobal*)

Animal Casts

There have been four full-length fiction films with all-animal casts. *Bill and Coo* (US 48), produced by comedian Ken Murray, was a comedy feature with a cast of Love Birds in miniature sets. Most of Walt Disney's True Life Fantasies were documentaries about wildlife, but *Perri* (US 57) was based on a novel by Felix Salten about the life of a squirrel. There were no credited human performers in *Jonathan Livingstone Seagull* (US 73), though some fishermen in a boat are seen in the opening sequence. Apart from this, the cast was composed entirely of seagulls. The story, adapted from the novel by Richard Bach (who also wrote the screenplay), is a mystical one of a seagull who acquires grace, is killed doing a noble act, rises from the dead and becomes a bird messiah. Kon Ichikawa's *The Adventures of Chatran* (Jap 87) had a cast of cats, dogs and farm animals with not a human in sight and became Japan's box office hit of the year.

The scrupulous care that film-makers take to ensure that no harm comes to animals appearing in their pictures now extends even to insects. Steven Spielberg's *Arachnophobia* (US 90), about a Californian town invaded by marauding mutant killer spiders, claimed a zero spider mortality rate, despite one scene in which the town exterminator is seen stomping on one which is manifestly the real-life hairy horror. The trick? A cavernous, spider-sized hole crafted in the sole of his boot. The sound of crunched spider was achieved simply but effectively—crushed potato crisps.

*C*AMERA AND CAMERAWORK

The largest number of cameras used for a single scene was 48 for the sea battle in *Ben Hur* (US 25). Another 42 cameras were employed on the chariot-race scene. Concealed in statues, in pits in the ground, and behind soldiers' shields, the 42 operators took 53,000 ft of film—equivalent to seven full-length features—in a single day.

The practice of using more than one camera on a scene was introduced by D. W. Griffith, who used three for the big fight between Dorothy West and Mabel Normand in *The Squaw's Love* (US 14). The three cameramen on this occasion were Billy Bitzer, P. Higginson and Bobby Harron. The use of multiple cameras was not confined to special scenes in Hollywood's silent days. Nearly all feature films were shot with twin cameras, one supplying the master negative from which all release prints for the domestic market were struck, the other the negative for all overseas prints.

The largest number of cameras used on one film was 160 in the case of *One Day of War* (USSR 42). A feature-length documentary, the film was shot in

The shower scene in Alfred Hitchcock's *Psycho* (US 60) involved 70 camera set-ups for 45 seconds of edited footage and took seven days to shoot.

a single day by 160 newsreel cameramen at the Russian Front and behind the lines.

The widest aperture lens ever used in production of a feature film was f0.7 by cameraman John Alcott on *Barry Lyndon* (GB 75). Developed for the US space programme, the lens was fitted to a specially modified camera and employed in filming an interior scene lit only by candlelight.

The first motorized camera (professional) in series production was the all-metal Bell & Howell of 1912, manufactured in the USA with the motor as an optional fitment.

The first feature film made with a motorized camera was *A Sainted Devil* (US 24) with Rudolph Valentino, which was photographed at Famous Players' Long Island studio by Harry Fishbeck with an electrically-driven camera of unidentified make. Generally cameramen continued to crank by hand throughout the silent era, due to the fact that it enabled action to be speeded up or slowed down at will. The coming of sound rendered hand-cranking impractical, since variations in film speed would have caused a corresponding and unnatural variation in the delivery of synchronized speech.

The earliest known multi-shot scene (different camera positions being used within a single scene)

The shower scene in *Psycho* (US 60) involved 70 camera set-ups for just 45 seconds of screen-time. The mouth belonged to the unfortunate Janet Leigh as she succumbed.

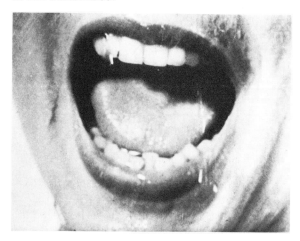

occurs in G. A. Smith's *The Little Doctors* (GB 01), in which there is a cut from a shot of two children administering medicine to a sick kitten to a close-up of the kitten with the spoon in its mouth.

Prior to the rediscovery of this film (see *Sight & Sound*, Summer 1978), the innovation had generally been attributed to D. W. Griffith. In *For the Love of Gold* (US 08), Griffith used a medium shot and a three-quarter shot in a card-game scene where he wanted to register the expressions on the gamblers' faces, and this has been credited as the first use of camera movement within a scene. Another recent discovery of the use of close-up (q.v.) shots within a scene in *The Yale Laundry* (US 07), must cast doubt on whether Griffith was the pioneer of the multi-shot scene even as far as the US industry is concerned.

The first panning shots were used by Max Skladanowski in *Komische Begegnung im Tiergarten zu Stockholm* (Ger 96), a short comedy shot on location in Sweden, and by Lumière representative Eugène Promio in *View of St Mark's Square, Venice* (Fr 96), a panorama of the Square taken from a boat on the Grand Canal.

The first 360° panning shot was made by Edwin S. Porter in *Circular Panorama of the Electric Tower* (US 01), in which the whole of the exhibition grounds of the Pan-American Exposition at Buffalo, NY are seen as the camera slowly revolves. Porter used a geared mounting of his own design for this effect.

The first use of a 360° pan in a full-length dramatic film was by James Whale in *Frankenstein* (US 31), and the following year Rouben Mamoulian employed the technique in *Dr Jekyll and Mr Hyde* (US 32) to give an effect of vertigo during the transformation scene.

Other films with 360° pans are *Rain* (US 32), Herbert Wilcox's *Bitter Sweet* (GB 33) —notable for its double 360° pan (the second much faster than the first) —*La Signora di Tutti* (It 34), *La Strada* (It 54), *Lola Montes* (Fr/FRG 55), *Vertigo* (US 58), *On the Beach* (US 59), *Judgement at Nuremberg* (US 61), *The Manchurian Candidate* (US 62), *Providence* (Fr/Swz 77), *The Swarm* (US 78), *Eagle's Wing* (GB 79), Mai Zetterling's *Scrubbers* (GB 82) and *Highlander II: The Quickening* (US 91). *Laughter in the Dark* (GB 69) was another British film with a double 360° pan, while Brian de Palma's *Obsession* (US 76) is notable for both a 360° and a 540° pan. The latter shot shows all four walls of a room entered by Genevieve Bujold, then pans on past the door to pick her up on the side opposite.

The first slow-motion film was made in 1898 by Berlin cinematographer Oskar Messter, using a specially constructed high-speed 60 mm camera of his own design. Among the earliest sequences filmed with this camera was one that showed a cat

falling off a wall, with a Hipp millisecond watch inset in one corner to indicate the rate of descent. This was shot at 66 frames a second—over four times normal speed—though the camera was capable of filming at speeds of up to 100 frames a second.

The technique has had its widest application in sports and scientific films. The earliest practical application of slow-motion cinematography was for the purpose of gauging the breaking strain of girders, according to Hopwood's *Living Pictures*, published in 1899.

The fastest speed at which a camera has been operated on any feature film (or the slowest slow motion sequence) was 2500 frames per second for the giant explosion scene in *Star Trek: The Wrath of Khan* (US 82). The scene, shot by Industrial Light and Magic at the Cow Palace in San Francisco, took a single second to film but occupied 104 seconds on screen. The normal speed at which a 35mm motion picture camera operates is 24 fps.

The time lapse technique was pioneered by Oskar Messter of Berlin, who filmed the blooming and wilting of a flower in 1897. The lapse factor was 1500 frames per 24 hours.

The earliest known American example is a 1902 American Mutoscope and Biograph subject of the demolition of New York's Star Theater.

The earliest known wipe appears in G. A. Smith's *Mary Jane's Mishap: or, Don't Fool with the Paraffin* (GB 03), in which Mary Jane does and is blown out of the chimney. A line moving across the screen 'wiped' away the scene of her unfortunate demise and replaced it with one of her forlorn grave. Hitherto the introduction of the wipe has generally been attributed to Georges Méliès in *La Royaume des fées* (Fr 03), but Dr Barry Salt of the Slade School has established that this is a misconception. What looks like a wipe between scenes is in fact no more than the lifting of a backdrop.

The only full-length feature film to have been made without a camera was Barcelona artist José Antonio Sistiaga's remarkable 75-minute animated one-man production in Cinemascope *Ere Ereve Baleibu Icik Subua Arvaren/Scope, Colour, Muda* (Sp 70). Completed in 17 months between October 1968 and February 1970, Sistiaga painted each frame of the film separately and single-handed direct on to the film-stock.

The first close-up was a study of a man called Fred Ott sneezing, copyrighted on 7 January 1894 as *Edison Kinetoscopic Record of a Sneeze* (US 94).

Close-ups of inanimate objects or of hands or feet were not unusual in American films of the early years of the century, particularly in the productions of the American Mutoscope and Biograph Co. (AM & B). Examples include the fire alarm box in Edison's *The Life of an American Fireman* (US 03), a girl's pretty foot in Edison's *The Gay Shoe Clerk* (US 03), the contents of a jewel case in AM & B's

The Great Jewel Mystery (US 05), gifts in AM &
B's *The Silver Wedding* (US 06) and a newspaper
article in AM & B's *Trial Marriages* (US 07).
Facial close-ups were rarer, though the opening
scenes of AM & B's *The Widow and the Only Man*
(US 04) introduce the two principal characters
with separate close-ups. The persistent claim of D.
W. Griffith to have been the only begetter of the
close-up—he even went so far as to suggest he
could have patented the technique—has now been
rejected by most film historians, though many still
credit him with having been the first to employ the
interpolated facial close-up as a dramatic device to
register emotion. Even this had been accomplished
a year before Griffith entered the film industry. In
the AM & B production *The Yale Laundry* (US
07), a comedy about students at Yale playing a jape
on their professors, close-ups are used to show surprise on the faces of the victims. It is precisely this
technique of advancing the narrative by means of a
close-up shot that Griffith was later to claim as his
innovation and his alone. There is a certain irony in
the fact that it had been used earlier by an
uncredited director of the very company with
which Griffith was to establish his reputation. The
great director also seems to have overlooked the
fact that he himself was the subject of a close-up
when he played the part of a clown in *At the French
Ball* (US 08), a film made shortly before his
directorial debut at Biograph.

Despite the pioneering efforts of the Edison Co.,
AM & B and 'the Brighton school' (in England),
elsewhere the notion that a film should give its
audience the same view as a theatre audience
received of the stage persisted for many years. As
late as 1911 the leading production company in
Scandinavia, Nordisk Film, was using a 16 ft long
pole attached to the camera as an indication to the
actors that they must come no closer. Albert E.
Smith recalled that about this period at Vitagraph
the actors were always positioned nine yards in
front of the camera. Mary Pickford, who claimed
that she had been the subject of 'the first close-up'
in D. W. Griffith's *Friends* (US 12), said that the
'front office' at Biograph had vigorously protested
at the idea on the grounds that audiences were paying to see the whole of the performer, not only the
top half.

The longest close-up is to be seen in *Daaera* (Ind
53) and lasts 6½ minutes.

The earliest recorded use of the telephoto lens
(invented in 1891) with a cinematograph camera
was by W. K. L. Dickson, the Biograph cameraman
covering the Boer War in 1900. Dickson recorded in
The Biograph in Battle (London 1901) how he had
sought to film the Boer positions with a telephoto,
an attempt frustrated by poor visibility caused by
haze.

The first feature film to end with a freeze frame
was Abel Gance's epic melodrama *La Roue* (Fr 23),
in which the device was used to intensify the
moment of the old railwayman Sisif's death. The
earliest Hollywood feature to culminate in a freeze
frame was *Poor Little Rich Girl* (US 36), with the
three principals, Shirley Temple, Jack Haley and
Alice Faye, arrested in motion.

The first camera dolly was used by British pioneer
cinematographer R. W. Paul at the studio he built at
New Southgate in 1899. In a lecture he gave before
the British Kinematographers' Society in 1936, Paul
recalled: 'A trolley mounted on rails carried the
camera, which could thus be set at any required distance from the stage, to suit the subject. Sometimes
the trolley was run to and from the stage while the
picture was being taken, thus giving a gradual
enlargement or reduction of the image of the film.' It
is not known whether Paul's dolly dates from the
opening of the New Southgate studios, but a photograph taken in 1902 shows it in use.

**The first known use of a camera dolly in a fea-
ture film** was for a tracking shot in the first reel of
Evgenii Bauer's *The Twilight of a Woman's Soul*
(Rus 13), executed by cameraman Nikolai
Kozlovski of the Franco-Russian Star Film Factory.
This was the innovative Bauer's first film as director. It was unlikely that he was aware that the Spanish cameraman Segundo de Chomon had developed
a camera dolly while working for Pathé in Paris and
that it had been patented in Italy in 1912. It was this
dolly that de Chomon used for his pioneering work
on Giovanni Pastrone's *Cabiria* (It 14).

The dolly arrived in America comparatively late,
no examples of its use being known before 1915.
Tracking shots were used in two feature films that
year, by Allan Dwan on *David Harum* (US 15) to
follow the hero as he walks down the street of his
small hometown, and by William Bowman in *The
Second-in-Command* (US 15). On this film, cameraman William F. Alder employed two dollies, one
for forward and backward tracking and the other for
sideways movement. This was a notable innovation
which did not come to its full fruition until Chi-
nese-born James Wong Howe introduced the 'crab
dolly'—a dolly that moves in any direction, including sideways and diagonally—on *The Rough Riders*
(US 27).

Britain, having pioneered the dolly, then completely forgot about it until the end of the silent era.
The first use of 'mobile camera' in a feature film was
by Graham Cutts on Gainsborough-Piccadilly's
The Triumph of the Rat (GB 26), with Ivor Novello.

Camera mobility could be achieved without the
use of a dolly. F. W. Murnau overcame the problem
of how to depict Emil Jannings' drunken view of the
wedding feast in *The Last Laugh* (Ger 25) by
mounting his cameraman on roller skates. When
Sidney Franklin decided to use a hand-held Bell &
Howell Eyemo camera on *Quality Street* (US 27),

he emulated Murnau's example, but here the scene was not a drunken one and the camera had to be kept steady. The solution was to have an assistant pushing the roller-skated cameraman from behind. James Wong Howe also found roller-skates the answer for the prize fight scene in *Body and Soul* (US 47), but on *He Ran All the Way* (US 51) he needed higher camera angles. A squatting camera operator could not roller-skate, so Howe found another expedient—the cameraman was pushed in a wheelchair.

The earliest known use of a hidden camera was in 1916 when director George Terwilliger used this device in the making of the Van Dyke Film Corporation's *The Lash of Destiny* (US 16), starring Gertrude McCoy and Duncan McRae. Scenes which included diners and dancers at the restaurant of the Ansonia Hotel in New York were shot without the unpaid 'extras' being aware of their participation. There is no other record of the technique before 1924. In that year, concealed cameras were used by Russia's master of the newsreel, Dziga Vertov, in making his feature-length documentary about everyday life in the early Soviet state, *Kino-Eye* (USSR 24). Vertov's brother, the cameraman Mikhail Kaufman, filmed open air scenes at Pioneer camps, in markets, at stations, etc., as well as interiors of low life in bars, cafes and thieves kitchens, without his subjects ever being aware of the camera. In America a hidden camera was used by Erich von Stroheim for the scene in *Greed* (US 24) in which Trina rushes out of the junk shop after finding a murdered body. The film was made entirely on location and it was a real street into which ZaSu Pitts dashes distractedly, grabbing the arms of real passers-by as she shrieks her awful news. The reaction of those unwittingly involved was, as von Stroheim hoped, totally believable, as they registered horror and alarm before rushing for help.

These pioneer efforts were followed by a number of other noted uses of hidden camerawork during the twenties. George Webber filmed exterior scenes for *Night Life of New York* (US 25) from a van parked in the streets of the city. Most of *Berlin, Symphony of a Great City* (Ger 27) was filmed in this way by Karl Freund, but where a van was impracticable he concealed the camera in a suitcase, using a special film-stock that he had hypersensitized himself in order to shoot in poor lighting conditions. King Vidor shot most of the New York exteriors for *The Crowd* (US 28) with a hidden camera.

The first double exposure was accomplished by Georges Méliès in *La Caverne maudite/The Cave of the Demons* (Fr 98), employing the technique of 'spirit photography'. The evil inhabitants of the cave were first filmed against a black backdrop, so that the background was not exposed, then the film was wound back and the cave setting filmed. The effect was of 'ghost' characters superimposed against a solid background.

The more normal use of double exposure was to achieve the effect of two characters played by the same performer appearing on screen simultaneously. This was done by 'duplex cinematography', also pioneered by Georges Méliès and at about the same time as the film above. Méliès adapted a technque already well known to still photographers, by which a small frame enclosing two swing doors was mounted in front of the camera lens. When one door was opened, half the scene was exposed on film. The film was then wound back, one door shut and the other opened, and the rest of the scene shot. If the same performer was filmed each time, he or she would appear to be two characters interacting. Méliès' first attempt at this technique was in *Un Homme de tête/The Four Troublesome Heads* (Fr 98), which shows a magician removing his head three times over and in which he used a combination of both spirit photography and duplex photography.

The first physical contact between two characters played by the same person was accomplished in *Little Lord Fauntleroy* (US 21) when Mary Pickford played both the boy and his mother 'Dearest'. Cameraman Charles Rosher used a camera loaded with 2000 lb of weights to achieve absolute steadiness between one take and the next, but the exact details of his extraordinarily advanced technique are still not known. The preparations for each double exposure were amongst the most meticulous and precise in the history of camerawork. It took 15 hours to shoot the scene in which the boy kisses 'Dearest' on the cheek, a take which lasts three seconds on the screen. In another scene they embrace and, in the most spectacular of all, the Little Lord runs and jumps into his mother's arms. The complexity of the operation was enhanced by the fact that Mary Pickford the mother had to be nine inches taller than Mary Pickford the boy. For her adult role in the double exposure scenes she was given platform heels and stood on a concealed ramp, a hazardous operation since she fell off on a number of occasions.

The attempted suicide of Alex (Malcolm McDowell) in *A Clockwork Orange* (GB 71) was achieved by throwing a Newman Sinclair camera off the top of a building. On the sixth take the camera landed downward as intended. The lens was smashed, but the camera was found to be still in perfect working order.

Double exposure was temporarily abandoned when sound came in, because of the difficulty of post-synching. **The first double exposure with dialogue** was a scene in Fox Movietone's *Masquerade* (US 29) in which Alan Burmingham carried on a conversation with another character also played by Alan Burmingham.

The first triple exposure was achieved by cameraman Al Siegler in Universal's *The Twins' Double* (US 14), in which Grace Cunard played the twin heroines and the villainess, their double—all three characters appearing on the screen at the same time.

Nowadays multiple exposures tend to be used for naturalistic special effects rather than the trick of showing the same person simultaneously performing more than one role. A **septuple exposure** was used in *Star Trek* (US 79) for the elaborate sequence in which the starship *Enterprise* first approaches the alien invaders. The different exposures, which included shots of the spacecraft, fog, yellow lights, a star-field and cloud effects, were combined in a scene which occupied only 30 seconds of screen time but 48 hours of filming.

The first film shot at night out-of-doors was Edwin S. Porter's *Panorama of the Esplanade at Night* (US 01), taken at the Pan-American Exposition at Buffalo, NY, on 5 September 1901. Each frame required a ten-second exposure and it took Porter several hours to expose 27 ft of film.

The first feature film containing outdoor scenes shot at night was the Balboa Feature Film Co.'s *An Eye for an Eye* (US 15), a melodrama about bigamy starring and directed by William Desmond Taylor, which was released in January 1915. A number of other examples date from the same year. The Paramount western *Buckshot John* (US 15), starring and directed by Herbert Bosworth, had a scene shot by moonlight, believed to have been shot at Banning, Ca. *The Patriot and the Spy* (US 15), released in June, had night battle scenes, while the detective mystery *The Game of Three* (US 15), released in September, took to the streets of New York for scenes shot at midnight. Another midnight scene, the meeting of the vigilantes in *A Gentleman from Indiana* (US 15), was filmed by the light of fifty radium flares and ten Windfield Koerner lamps.

Feature films which played entirely at night include *Crossfire* (US 47), *The City that Never Sleeps* (US 50), and *La Notte* (It 61). Most Philippine silent moves of the 20s were made entirely at night, as the ill-paid part-time actors had to take day jobs to support themselves.

Back projection was first employed successfully by special effects maestro Willis O'Brien for a single scene in *The Lost World* (US 25). It is a technique by which outdoor scenes can be shot in the studio by placing the actors against a back projected filmed background. The following year back projection was used in the making of *Metropolis* (Ger 26), but it was slow to catch on because of the technical difficulties involved. The breakthrough came with the development of the Teague Back Projector, which was employed for the first time on the Fox production *Just Imagine* (US 30), a science-fiction film set in 1980. Back projection was used to depict a city of the future, with stars Maureen O'Sullivan and John Garrick coasting along in their private aircraft in the foreground.

Back projection in colour was first used by William Wellman on *Nothing Sacred* (US 37).

The first camera crane was used by cameraman William F. Alder for obtaining elevated shots in Metro's *The Second in Command* (US 15), with Francis X. Bushman. At about the same time Allan Dwan devised a more sophisticated elevator on tracks for use in the Babylonian sequence of D. W. Griffith's *Intolerance* (US 16). The 115 ft high structure enabled Griffith to secure a parabolic shot, commencing at the ramparts of the Palace and descending forwards over a sea of extras to ground level and a close shot of the leading players. These early uses of the crane were exceptional. It was not until F. W. Murnau introduced his 20-ton, 200-hp 'Go-Devil' on *The Four Devils* (US 29), and the appearance of an even larger 28-ton apparatus with a 60 ft elevation on the set of *Broadway* (US 29), that the crane came to be regarded as standard studio equipment.

The first woman camerman was Rosina Cianelli, who made her camera debut with Paolo Benedetti's *Uma transformista original* (Bra 09), a Méliès-style trick film made at Barbacena, Brazil, with the Lazzari brothers as stars.

The first American camerawoman was Grace Davison, who joined the Astor Film Corp. at its Long Island studios as an actress in 1915 but was taught to handle a camera by veteran Harry Fishbeck. Miss Davison photographed *The Honeymooners* (US 15), *Spring Onions* (US 15) and other one-reel comedies.

The first camerawoman to shoot a feature film was Tamara Lobova, who worked on *Suvorov* (USSR 41) together with her husband Anatolij Golovnja. First with a solo camera credit was Galina Pyshkova for *Songs of Abay* (USSR 46).

COSTUME

The largest number of costumes in any one film was 32,000 for *Quo Vadis* (US 51). *Waterloo* (It/USSR 70) used 29,000 costumes and *Cleopatra* (US 63) 26,000 costumes.

The largest number of costume changes by one performer was 201 by poet-musician-film-maker Lee Groban of Chicago in his 85-hour duration *The Cure for Insomnia* (US 87). The most in a commercially-made theatrical feature were by Elizabeth Taylor in *Cleopatra* (US 63). Her 65 costumes, designed by Irene Sharaff, cost $130,000. Another

Producer/director Michael Winner does not believe in designer costumes for lowly mortals like movie stars. Jeremy Irons recalled that he was taken by Winner in his Rolls Royce to buy shoes for his lead role in *A Chorus of Disapproval* (GB 89) at a chain store in London's decaying Notting Hill district which was having a sale. The millionaire movie maker picked out three pairs of shoes which had been marked down to £9.99 ($16) each, then introduced Irons to the store manager as a great British star and asked for a special deal. Only when the reluctant manager agreed to throw in a free tin of polish and a duster did he depart satisfied.

40 costumes and head-dresses designed by Oliver Messel at a cost of $64,800 did not appear in the movie as released. Joan Collins wore 87 different costumes in the television movie *Sins* (US 88, TVM), including 30 by top couturier Valentino.

The most expensive costume ever worn in a movie was the barzucine sable coat that enfolded Constance Bennett in *Madame X* (US 65). It was valued at $50,000.

The most expensive costume designed and made specially for a film was Edith Head's mink and sequins dance costume for Ginger Rogers in *Lady in the Dark* (US 44), which cost Paramount $35,000. By comparison, Elizabeth Taylor's dress of cloth-of-24-carat-gold in which she made her entry into Rome in *Cleopatra* (US 63) cost a modest $6500. However, the total cost of Miss Taylor's wardrobe, which amounted to $194,800, was **the highest sum ever expended on costumes for a single performer in any one film.**

At the other end of the scale, costumes could cost next to nothing even in Hollywood's most extravagant days; except for the studios' insistence that nothing was worthwhile unless it was expensive. When a rough, workaday costume was needed for Ingrid Bergman in *For Whom the Bell Tolls* (US 43), designer Edith Head selected an old pair of men's trousers and a shirt from the extra's wardrobe. Producer Sam Wood was incensed and demanded that Miss Head should design a new costume. She did so, copying the old garments exactly, then bleaching them and dying them to look as worn as the originals.

The record spent on costumes in relation to budget was the $1 million plus for wardrobe in the $7 million production *Chanel Solitaire* (US 81), a biopic of the legendary French fashion designer Coco Chanel.

The largest costume collection in the world is owned by Western Costume Co. and housed in a six-storey building at 5335 Melrose Avenue, Hollywood, California. The collection consists of two and a half million costumes.

Western Costume was established in Los Angeles in 1912. In a curious way its fortune could be said to have been founded on dietary deficiency. Business was slow until a major break came with D. W. Griffith's order for all the Civil War costumes for *The Birth of a Nation* (US 15). Griffith, preoccupied with authenticity, had hoped to use genuine uniforms of the period, but found that progress in nutrition over the intervening 50 years had made the average actor of 1914 too large to fit the average soldier's uniform of the 1860s.

Later Western Costume was to supply Clark Gable's clothes for *Gone With the Wind* (US 39), Errol Flynn's for *The Charge of the Light Brigade* (US 36) and Chaplin's Führer uniform for *The Great Dictator* (US 40). In more recent times they provided all the suits for *Dick Tracy* (US 90), matched to the stark monotone colours of the original comic strip (hence the sickly yellow of Beatty's overcoat). Most unusual request, per floor manager Roger Faustino, came from Woody Allen, who wanted sperm costumes for *Everything You Always Wanted to Know about Sex* (US 72).

The highest price paid at auction for an article of costume was $165,000 by an anonymous bidder at Christie's New York on 2 June 1988 for a pair of the ruby slippers worn by Judy Garland in *The Wizard of Oz* (US 39). Hopefully, the new owner was already aware that Miss Garland wore three other identical pairs during the making of the picture.

Chaplin's Tramp Costume

The costume was devised in response to Mack Sennett's request that he 'get into a comedy make-up' for *Kid Auto Races at Venice* (US 14). Chaplin created the costume in a dressing room where Fatty Arbuckle and Chester Conklin were playing pinochle. The moustache was a scrap of crêpe hair

The truth is now out about the most celebrated bra in history, the cantilevered job designed by Howard Hughes to give Jane Russell support where he felt she needed it most. According to Jane's autobiography, the fabled garment did really exist, but she only wore it once and that was in the privacy of her own dressing room. Hughes had used engineering principles to design the ideal brassière for the well-endowed woman. It simply did not work. Jane found it 'uncomfortable and ridiculous' and changed back into her own custom-made bra. She went on set and everyone assumed she was wearing her mentor's creation. She never let on until years after Howard Hughes's death, but there is little doubt that the legend of the cantilevered bra will long outlive Jane Russell herself.

borrowed from Mack Swain; the trousers were Fatty Arbuckle's—hence the bagginess—and the Derby came from Minta Durfee's father, Fatty's father-in-law; the cut-away coat belonged to Chester Conklin (or Charlie Avery, according to one account); the size 14 shoes were Ford Sterling's and Chaplin had to wear them on the wrong feet to keep them on. Only the whangee cane belonged to Charlie himself.

Chaplin gave the original costume to his assistant Harry Crocker in 1928 as a central exhibit in the newly-opened Crocker Museum of props and costumes on Sunset Boulevard. Nearly 60 years later, in 1987, Chaplin's bowler and cane came up for sale at Christie's in London, where they were bought by Danish shopping mall entrepreneur Jörgen Strecker for $150,000.

Fashion and the Movies

Movie costumes began to influence fashion as early as 1912, when it was reported that the natives of Tahiti had become so addicted to westerns that they had taken to wearing stetsons. A rather more far-reaching fashion was initiated by D. W. Griffith when he invented the first pair of false eyelashes in order to give Seena Owen's eyes an abnormally large and lustrous appearance for her role as Princess Beloved in *Intolerance* (US 16). They were made by a wigmaker who wove human hair through the warp of a 24-inch strip of thin gauze. Each day two small pieces were cut from the end of the strip and gummed to Miss Owen's eyelids. The use of mascara and other eye make-up was directly inspired by the example of screen vamps Theda Bara and Pola Negri, who darkened their eyelids to give themselves an air of brooding mystery. Plucked eyebrows became the rage about 1930 after Jean Harlow had hers trimmed into a slender arch. Beauty editors advised her imitators to dab ether on their brows to ease the pain of plucking out the hairs.

Bessie Barriscale caused a sensation with the backless evening gown she wore in *Josselyn's Wife* (US 19) and soon the middle classes were aping a fashion formerly displayed only by their betters. All classes followed the trend to bobbed hair, which became the style of the twenties after Colleen Moore had created the archetypal flapper role in *Flaming Youth* (US 23). Pola Negri was not only the first to go barelegged and sandalled in summer, but was also the first to paint her toenails. She recalled that when she first did this in about 1923, using a bright red polish, a woman glanced down at her feet and shrieked 'She's bleeding'. Nevertheless, within a few weeks, Miss Negri claimed, women everywhere were lacquering their toenails. Joan Crawford was the first to go barelegged with evening clothes in 1926. She stated that she never wore stockings between then and 1930, when long dresses returned to fashion. Bare legs for ordinary 'streetwear' were pioneered by

blonde starlet Rita Carewe in 1927. To preserve the proprieties, however, Miss Carewe had her legs *polished* to give the impression that she was wearing silk stockings.

Bejeaned teenagers might have made an earlier appearance but for the obduracy of D. W. Griffith. About 1914, 16-year-old Dorothy Gish became the first screen star and one of the first women in America to adopt jeans. She never wore them in films, however, and only once to the studio; a stern message to her mother from Griffith prevented such a solecism from ever being repeated. Another ten years were to pass before a woman wearing trousers as an article of feminine apparel (as opposed to male impersonation costume) appeared on screen in the person of Myrna Loy in *What Price Beauty* (US 24). This seems to have had little impact upon fashion at the time and it was not until Louise Brooks took to wearing silk trousers (indoors only) in 1927 that the practice became accepted amongst the more sophisticated followers of filmdom's fashion decrees. The real breakthrough for emancipated womanhood, though, had to await the release of von Sternberg's *Morocco* (US 30), in which Marlene Dietrich concealed her celebrated legs in slacks. Von Sternberg's purpose was to emphasize the lesbian characterization of the role, but the innovation was imitated by the women of America to an extent that suggests its implication was wholly lost on them.

Probably the single most influential trendsetter, and the star who made least effort to be one, was Garbo. The enormous fur collars of the twenties owed their genesis to the broad collar designed by Max Ree to conceal her long neck in *The Torrent* (US 26). Garbo's berets, which she wore off-screen, became a universal fashion of the thirties and made a comeback in the sixties after Faye Dunaway had worn one as the thirties woman gangster in *Bonnie and Clyde* (US 67). The diagonally placed Eugénie hat, dipping over one eye, worn by Garbo in *Romance* (US 30), hastened the end of the cloche and introduced the basic configuration that was to dominate hat styles throughout the thirties. Although most fashion design of the period reflected a conscious rejection of the past, Adrian's Eugénie hat was created for a film that was set in the 1850s.

The other major trendsetter of the period was Joan Crawford, whom women fans watched spellbound as she suffered in mink. While her taste in furs was beyond the reach of the majority, the padded-shoulder costume Adrian designed for her to wear in *Today We Live* (US 33) started the vogue for tailored suits that sloped upwards from the neck. Crawford herself was so enamoured with the style that she went on wearing padded shoulders long after they had gone out of general fashion.

By this time the big studios were co-operating with the garment trade—most of the moguls had come from that industry themselves—so that the costumes designed for the new genre of 'women's pictures' could be in the shops by the time the film was released. It was another Adrian creation for Joan Crawford that began this mass marketing of star costumes, the celebrated *Letty Lynton* dress which she

> The battered hat worn by Henry Fonda in *On Golden Pond* (US 81) was Spencer Tracy's. Katherine Hepburn, who surprisingly had never met Fonda in the 50 years they had each spent in Hollywood, presented it to him the first day on set.

wore in the film of the same name (US 32). Over half a million copies were sold by Macy's of New York alone. The success of the venture encouraged its development. In 1933 a leading department store in Columbus, Ohio called Morehouse Martens 'completed an arrangement by which copies of movie stars' clothes are on sale at the store prior to or coincident with the opening of their pictures'. The initial offerings were a Joan Blondell double-duty dress, a Jean Arthur frock and Claire Dodd pyjamas. The same year Bamberger's of Newark, NJ opened a 'Cinema Shop' devoted exclusively to copies of the clothes worn by stars, and their lead was followed by other major stores from coast to coast, including such noted names as the Hecht Co. of Washington, Goldsmith's of Chicago, Joseph Horne of Pittsburgh ('The Hollywood Shop') and the May Co. of Los Angeles. The desire to look like the stars was no less fervent in Britain, where a magazine devoted to the subject with the title *Film Fashionland* was started in 1934.

Generally, the adoption of a movie fashion brought fortunes either to the designer or to the entrepreneur who succeeded in adapting it to a mass market. The star who launched the style seldom derived any direct benefit, with the notable exception of Shirley Temple. The astute business sense of Mrs Temple ensured that when Fox sold the manufacturing rights to Shirley's party dresses from *Baby Takes a Bow* (US 35), it was Shirley who garnered the lion's share of the profits.

What stars did not wear could sometimes have as much impact on fashion trends as what they did wear. When Clark Gable opened his shirt to reveal a bare and matted torso in *It Happened One Night* (US 34), men's undershirt sales took a 40 per cent dive. Mae West also enjoyed a quite unlooked for effect on fashion, if the Kansas Restaurant Association is to be believed. In 1934 the Association publicly thanked Miss West for stemming the dieting craze stimulated by the sylph-like figures of Dietrich, Crawford and Harlow and for restoring well-rounded curves to healthy US women.

Hollywood also played its part in bringing an exotic touch to American fashion. When Dorothy Lamour wore the first of her celebrated series of sarongs in *Jungle Princess* (US 36), it generated a demand for tropical fabrics that lasted for the next ten years. The Latin-American look that swept the USA in the early forties was instigated by Edith Head's costumes for Barbara Stanwyck in *The Lady Eve* (US 41), and Charles LeMaire's designs for Jennifer Jones in *Love is a Many Splendoured Thing* (US 55) began a trend towards oriental fashion.

After World War II, Hollywood's main fashion influence was in the direction of casual wear, though even as early as 1922 American males had been persuaded to abandon their stiff collars after heart-throb Wallace Reid had played a romantic lead wearing a soft collar. By the 1950s it was mainly teenagers who took their fashion lead from movie idols. What we now regard as standard leather-biker costume only became so after Marlon Brando had appeared looking butch and menacing in zip-up jacket in *The Wild One* (US 54). It also inspired the leather look among gays. James Dean's windcheater in *Rebel Without a Cause* (US 55) and Elvis Presley's tight trousers in *Jailhouse Rock* (US 57) set the teenage-style of the late 1950s and early 1960s.

Footwear is less often influenced by the movies, but girls with slim ankles took to wearing slip-ons without socks or stockings after Bardot had sloughed off the conventions of the formal fifties in *And God Created Woman* (Fr 57). The sex kitten also made going barefoot acceptable—she seldom wore shoes off-screen—provided you were young and pretty. Ten years later Jane Fonda's knee-length white vinyl boots in *Barbarella* (Fr/It 67) became part of the uniform of the mini-skirt generation.

Hairstyles are often prone to the dictates of Hollywood, with Jean Seberg and Mia Farrow demonstrating that cropped hair went well with an elfin face. Blonde streaks in brunette hair was a fashion inspired by Audrey Hepburn in *Breakfast at Tiffany's* (US 61). Whatever it may or may not have done for the butter industry, *Last Tango in Paris* (Fr/It/US 72) gave the world frizzy hair, as exemplified by sultry Maria Schneider, and revived the neglected art of permanent waving.

Another kind of casual look, for highbrows rather than hoydens, involved wearing the kind of baggy, rumpled clothes sported by Diane Keaton with neurotic chic in *Annie Hall* (US 77). Youth and good looks were not really sufficient if you wanted to get away with this; a certain fey and anxious charm was also imperative.

The decline of the cinema as a cultural force has reduced its fashion impact in the west, but in the Orient, where cinema-going continues to increase, it appears to be breaking down traditional prejudices against western dress. Significant of the trend are reports that jeans are now being worn by Indian women since superstar Zeenat Aman began wearing them in public.

CREWS

The largest production crew on a movie consisted of the 556 craftsmen and technicians employed by producer Sukertaru Taguchi on Kon Ichikawa's *Tokyo Olympiad* (US 65). The largest number on a dramatic feature was 532 for the British World War I flying story *Sky Bandits* (GB 86).

The smallest crew on a major motion picture was two for the final scenes of *Bullseye!* (US 90), shot in Barbados with Michael Caine, Jenny Seagrove and John Cleese in January 1990. The unit consisted of director Michael Winner, who operated the camera, and cameraman David Wynn Jones who held the reflector. John Cleese moonlighted as soundman, but as he was performing at the same time (the sound recorder was concealed in a book he carried), he did not count as crew.

DIRECTORS

The first director—The functions of director and producer were first separated for America's earliest 'spectacle' film *The Passion Play* (US 98). Rich G. Hollaman, the producer, engaged a distinguished stage director, L. J. Vincent of Niblo's Garden Theatre in New York, to direct the picture. Unfortunately, America's first movie director had never seen a movie and nothing could persuade him that the camera was capable of reproducing live action. Convinced that he had been engaged to direct a succession of lanternslide tableaux, he would rush out on to the set whenever the performance of a scene was progressing favourably and scream 'Hold it!' The film was eventually made by subterfuge. Each afternoon cameraman William Paley would declare that the light was no longer strong enough to continue and as soon as Vincent had departed the actors would reassemble and shoot as much as possible before dark. The tworeel drama was a sensation when it was premièred at the Eden Musée on 30 January 1898, but it is difficult to know whether it would be more accurately described as the first film made by a professional director or the first dramatic film made with no director at all.

The first woman director was Alice Guy (1873–1968), originally secretary to Léon Gaumont, who was given an opportunity to direct after she had complained at the lack of variety in Gaumont productions. She made her debut with *La Fée aux choux*, about a young couple walking in the countryside who encounter a fairy in a cabbage patch and are presented with a child. The film is usually said to date from 1896, but since it is listed No. 370 in the Gaumont catalogue it seems more likely that it was made *c.* 1900. Mlle Guy was Gaumont's sole director of dramatic films until Zecca joined the

The world's first woman director, Alice Guy, on the set of her first movie *La Fée aux choux* (Fr *c.* 00)

studios at La Villette in 1905. In 1907 she emigrated to the USA, and founded the Solax Co. on Long Island three years later. Between 1919 and 1922 she directed for Pathé and Metro, then returned to France. Despite her long experience, she was unable to find work as a director in her own country and made a living writing stories based on film scenarios for pulp magazines.

The first feature film directed by a woman was the Rex production of *The Merchant of Venice* (US 14), which had Lois Weber as director. Miss Weber was also **the first American woman director**, starting with Gaumont Talking Pictures in New York in 1907, then working for Reliance in 1908, for Rex 1909–13, for the Bosworth Co. 1914–15 and for Universal 1915–19, after which she went independent. Her best known picture was Universal's highly successful *Where Are My Children?* (US 16), a treatise on birth control. As her films became increasingly controversial, she had difficulty in obtaining distribution, and her last picture, *White Heat* (US 34), about miscegenation, was not released.

Sharon Smith, in *Women Who Make Movies* (New York 75), has listed 36 women directors who were active in the United States during the silent era and believes there were others who directed anonymously. The only one to make the transition to sound was Dorothy Arzner, whose *Manhattan Cocktail* (US 28) was **the first talkie directed by a woman**. At the height of her career in the thirties she was listed as one of Hollywood's top ten directors.

The first woman to direct a British production was Jakidawdra Melford, who made her directorial debut with a highwayman picture called *The Inn on the Heath* (GB 14). The first feature by a woman was Dinah Shurey's *Carry On!* (GB 27), a naval war drama, and the first talkie was Elinor Glyn's *Knowing Men* (GB 30).

Of the 7332 feature films distributed by the major Hollywood studios during the thirty years 1949 to 1979, only 14 were directed by women—less than one-fifth of one per cent.

The first director to direct himself in a full-length feature film was Harold Heath, who played the lead in Anchor Films' detective thriller £1000 *Reward* (GB 13).

The first black American director to direct a film aimed at multi-racial audiences was Melvin van Peebles, former San Francisco cable-car gripman, who made his directorial debut with *La Permission/The Story of a Three Day Pass* (Fr 67). Based on van Peebles' own novel, *The Pass*, it related the story of a black GI on a three-day furlough who has a brief affair with a Parisian shop girl. His first American movie was *The Watermelon Man* (US 70), in which Godfrey Cambridge portrays the white insurance salesman who wakes up one morning to find he has turned black.

The first black American to direct an American film at a major studio was former *Life* photographer Gordon Parks, who directed *The Learning Tree* (US 69) for Warner Bros.

The first black African director was Paulin Soumanou Vieyra, born in Dahomey in 1925, who made his directorial debut with *Afrique sur Seine* (Sen 55).

The first Maori to direct a feature film was Barry Barclay, whose *Ngati* (NZ 87) was selected for Critics' Week at the 1987 Cannes Film Festival and won the award for Best Film at the 1987 Taormina Film Festival.

The first director to make a film on percentage was D. W. Griffith, who made *The Birth of a Nation* (US 15) while earning his regular $300 a week with Majestic and was offered 37½ per cent of net profits after the film had been completed.

The first director to earn a million dollars for a single picture was Mike Nichols for *The Graduate* (US 67).

The longest directorial career lasted for 66 years in the case of King Vidor (1894–1982), beginning

The name Allen Smithee as a director's credit cloaks the identity of those who are so dissatisfied with the studio's handling of their work that they refuse to be publicly associated with the picture. The custom originated with *Death of a Gunfighter* (US 69), though in this case it was the high-handed behaviour of the star, Richard Widmark, who had creative control, that caused first Don Siegel and then his replacement Bob Totten to disclaim a personal credit. They persuaded the Directors Guild to allow a pseudonym, and as it was decided that 'Smith' would be too obvious, 'Smithee' was adopted instead. Still the only name allowed when a director has disavowed a picture, its latest manifestation is for *Catchfire* (US 91). In this case it conceals the identity of Dennis Hopper, who as well as directing the picture starred in it as a professional hit-man developing an obsessive passion for his intended victim, played by Jodie Foster. The production company, Vestron, decreed that Hopper's two-hour film was far too long and trimmed it to 90 minutes—making it difficult to understand why Foster's character suddenly switches from being terrorised by the hit-man to becoming his willing accomplice. An infuriated Hopper responded by removing his name from the credits in favour of Allen Smithee.

with a two-reel comedy about auto-racing called *The Tow* (US 14), filmed at Galveston, Texas, where he grew up, and culminating in another short, a documentary about painting called *The Metaphor* (US 80). Vidor's feature-film career had begun with a Christian Science melodrama titled *The Turn of the Road* (US 18), which oddly enough had been financed to the tune of $9000 by a consortium of ten doctors. Between this and his last feature, *Solomon and Sheba* (US 59), came such notable milestones in movie history as *The Big Parade* (US 25) —the most profitable silent film ever made (see p. 24, 30) —his greatest artistic success *The Crowd* (US 28), the first major all-black movie *Hallelujah* (US 29) —see p. 54—a classic tear-jerker *The Champ* (US 31), and a beautifully crafted adaptation of A. J. Cronin's novel *The Citadel* (GB 38) with Robert Donat. Vidor was a romantic, both on and off screen. Looking for a female lead for his first rather primitive comedy *The Tow*, he saw a beautiful girl passing in the back of a car. When he tracked her down, her father refused to let her debase herself in motion pictures. Vidor was determined to secure her services as an actress, but he had also fallen in love with her. They married and she became a major star of the silent screen as Florence Vidor.

Directors with a career spanning half a century:

KING VIDOR (1894–1982) 66 years from *The Tow* (US 14) to *The Metaphor* (US 80).

ABEL GANCE (1889–1982) 60 years from *La Digue* (Fr 11) to *Bonaparte et la Révolution* (Fr 71).

JORIS IVENS (1898–1989) 60 years from *De Brug* (Neth 28) to *Le Vent* (Fr 88).

GRIGORI ALEXANDRANOV (1903–83) 59 years from *The Battleship Potemkin* (USSR 25), co-directed with Sergei Eisenstein, to *Lubov Orlova* (USSR 84).

MANOEL DE OLIVEIRA (1908–) 59 years from *Douru, Faina Fluvial* (Por 31) to *No, or the Vain Glory of Command* (Por/Fr 90).

YULI RAIZMAN (1908?–) 57 years from *A Circle* (USSR 27) to *A Time for Wishes* (USSR 84).

ALEXANDER MEDVEDKIN (1900–89) 55 years from shorts for military film organization Gosvoyenkino 1925 to *Madness* (USSR 80).

JOHN FORD (1895–1973) 54 years from *Lucille Love—The Girl of Mystery* (US 14) to *Vietnam, Vietnam* (US 68).

ALFRED HITCHCOCK (1899–1980) 53 years from *Always Tell Your Wife* (GB 23) to *Family Plot* (US 76).

GEORGE MARSHALL (1896–1975) 53 years from *The Devil's Own* (US 16) to *Hook, Line and Sinker* (US 69).

RAOUL WALSH (1887–1980) 52 years from *The Life of Villa* (US 12) to *A Distant Trumpet* (US 64).

FORD BEEBE (1888–?) 52 years from *The Honor of the Range* (US 20) to *Challenge to be Free* (US 72).

SIR CHARLES CHAPLIN (1889–1977) 52 years from *Caught in a Cabaret* (US 14) to *A Countess from Hong Kong* (GB 67).

RUDALL HAYWARD (189?–1974) 51 years from *The Bloke from Freeman's Bay* (NZ 20) to *To Love a Maori* (NZ 71).

GEORGE CUKOR (1899–1983) 51 years from *Grumpy* (US 30) to *Rich and Famous* (US 81).

MARK DONSKOI (1901–1981) 51 years from *Life* (USSR 27) to *The Orlovs* (USSR 78).

MICHAEL CURTIZ (1888–1962) 50 years from *Ma Es Holnap* (Hun 12) to *The Comancheros* (US 62).

WILLIAM BEAUDINE (1892–1970) 50 years from *Almost a King* (US 15) to *Jesse James Meets Frankenstein's Daughter* (US 65).

Hollywood's most prolific director was William Beaudine (1892–1970), who directed 182 full-length features from *Watch Your Step* (US 22) to *Jesse James Meets Frankenstein's Daughter* (US 65), of which 32 were silents and 144 were talkies. In addition he directed over 120 shorts from 1916. Runners up are as follows:

RICHARD THORPE (1896–) 179 features from *Burn 'em Up Barnes* (US 21) to *The Scorpio Letters* (US 67), of which 63 were silents and 116 were talkies.

MICHAEL CURTIZ (1888–1962) 164 features from *Ma Es Holnap* (Hun 12) to *The Comancheros* (US 62), of which 61 were made in Europe before 1926 and the remainder in Hollywood.

SAM NEWFIELD (1900–64) 140 talkies.

ALLAN DWAN (1885–1981) 132 features from *Richelieu* (US 14) to *The Most Dangerous Man Alive* (US 61), plus over 200 shorts from *Brandishing a Bad Man* (US 11). Dwan claimed to have been involved in the making of 1400 films since 1910 as writer, producer or director.

JOHN FORD (1895–1973) 132 features from *The Tornado* (US 17) to *Vietnam, Vietnam* (US 68).

Note: It has been claimed that George Marshall (1896–1975) directed 425 features during his career, but only 88 full-length pictures crediting him as director can be traced for the period 1917–69. Ford Beebe (1888–) is said to have directed over 200 westerns, 'B' pictures and serials from 1916, but only 72 known films give him director credit.

The most prolific British director was Darlington-born Maurice Elvey (1887–1967), who directed 149 full-length features from *Her Luck in London* (GB 14) to *Second Fiddle* (GB 57). In addition he directed 41 shorts (mainly two-reelers) from *The Fallen Idol* (GB 13).

The most prolific director still alive is Spanish sex-and-gore film-maker Jesus Franco, who has directed over 200 low budget features since the late 1950s. Nearly 100 of his works are available on video.

The director to make the most films in a single year was Sam Newfield (1900–64), who directed 17 'B' westerns for eight different 'Poverty Row' studios during 1938.

The most co-directors on a single film was 16 in the case of *I misteri di Roma* (It 63), an anti-establishment view of 'one day in the life of the city' directed by Gianni Bisiach, Libero Bozzari, Mario Carbone, Angelo D'Alessandro, Nino del Fra, Luigi di Gianni, Giuseppe Ferrara, Ansano Giannarelli, Guilo Macchi, Lori Mazzetti, Massimo Mida, Enzo Mutti, Piero Nelli, Paolo Nuzzi, Dino Partesano and Giovanni Vento.

Deutschland im Herbst (FRG 78), *Love for Everyone* (Chn 42) and *Paramount on Parade* (US 30) each had eleven directors; *Dreams of Thirteen* (FRG/Neth 74) and *Aria* (US/GB 87) had ten; *If I Had a Million* (US 32) and *Forever and a Day* (US 43) had seven. All the foregoing were either non-fiction or episodic fiction films. The most directors on a straight fiction film was seven for *Casino Royale* (GB 67), a Bond movie directed by John Huston, Ken Hughes, Val Guest, Robert Parrish, Joe McGrath, Richard Talmadge and Anthony Squire; and the same number for *Dungeonmaster* aka *Ragewar* (US 85), which was the collective work of Rose-Marie Turko, John Buechler, Charles Band, David Allen, Steve Ford, Peter Manoogian and Ted Nicolaou.

The youngest director of a professionally-made feature film was Lev Kuleshov (1899–1970), who was 17½ when he embarked on his four-reel *Proyekt inzhenera Praita/Engineer Prite's Project* (USSR 18) at the Khanzhonkov Studios in Moscow. Other teenage directors have been Japan's Masahiro Makino, who made his directorial debut in 1927 at the age of 18; George Palmer, 17½, of Melbourne, Vic., who directed the railroad drama *Northbound Ltd* (Aus 26); Yuli Raizman, director of *A Circle* (USSR 27) at the age of 19; Philippe Garrel, whose feature debut *Anemone* (Fr 66), made when he was 19, starred his father Maurice Garrel; Sam Raimi, a 19-year-old who hustled the money for *The Evil Dead* (US 82) on the strength of a 30-min pilot shot on 8 mm; and 18-year-old Laurent Boutonnat, *enfant terrible* responsible for *La Ballade de la Feconductrice* (Fr 80). Boutannat was just old enough to be allowed to see his own film—it won an adults-only rating for its depiction of castration, child slaughter and bestiality. The only teenage female director was 19-year-old French helmer Christine Ehm, who made her debut with *Simone* (Fr 87).

Latest to join the ranks of these juvenile prodigies is 19-year-old Matty Rich. He not only directed but also wrote, produced and performed in *Straight Out of Brooklyn* (US 91), a film about the struggles of a black working class family which he based on true stories of people he has known. It was released internationally by the Samuel Goldwyn Co. after winning a special jury award at the 1991 Sundance Film Festival.

The oldest director was Dutch-born Joris Ivens (1898–1989), who made the Franco–Italian co-production *Le Vent* (Fr/It 88) at the age of 89. This was 60 years after he had made his directorial debut with *De Brug* (Neth 28).

The most versatile film-maker in terms of the most credits for a single film is Polish director Andrzej Kondratiuk, whose *The Four Seasons* (Pol 85) credited him as producer, director, scriptwriter, cameraman, art director, composer, soundman, props buyer, lighting-man and star. The only technical credit to someone else went to editor Maryla Orlowska. Exceptionally for a professionally made film produced in a Communist country, *Four Seasons* was privately financed—by Andrzej Kondratiuk.

Most credits for a major motion picture went to Charles Chaplin for producing, directing, scripting, composing, editing, choreographing, costume-designing and starring in *Limelight* (US 52). Most versatile femme film-maker is Sweden's Ann Zacharias, director, producer, scriptwriter, production designer and star of *The Test* (Swe 87).

The first woman to take writer–director–star credit on a major feature was Elaine May for *A New Leaf* (US 70). **First with producer–director–star credits** was Barbra Streisand for the Jewish musical *Yentl* (GB 83).

The first and only feature-length film directed by a Roman Catholic priest is *Invisible Things* (It 90, TVM), helmed by Fr Serafino Rafaiani of the Capuchin Monks of the Marches. The cast included 100 cloistered nuns of the Clarissa order, whom Fr Rafaiani praised as 'born actresses'.

EDITING

The most edited film in terms of total negative discarded was Howard Hughes' *Hell's Angels* (US 30), which consumed 2,254,750 ft of film during the four years it took to make. If all this footage had been shown unedited, it would have run for 560 hr or 23 days non-stop. The cost of the film stock was $225,475. The final release print was 9045 ft (2 hr 15 min running time), a reduction in the ratio of 249:1. A single scene without actors—a brief close-up of the valves of an aeroplane engine—occupied 20,000 ft of film (the length of four full-length features) before Hughes was satisfied.

In more recent times Michael Cimino shot 220 hours of film for his $57 million epic *Heaven's Gate* (US 81) to produce a release print which one critic described as 5 hours 25 minutes of 'staggering self-indulgence'. When the long version flopped, it was cut to 2½ hours.

Other films with extravagant shooting ratios: Fritz Lang's *Metropolis* (Ger 26) was reduced from 1,960,000 to 13,165 ft, a ratio of 149:1; Charles Chaplin's *City Lights* (US 31) was reduced from 975,000 to 7784 ft, a ratio of 125:1; *Uncle Tom's Cabin* (US 27) was reduced from 900,000 to 13,000 ft, a ratio of 69:1; Charles Chaplin's *The Kid* (US 20) was reduced from 400,000 to 6000 ft, a ratio of 67:1; Leni Riefenstahl's *Olympische Spiele* (Ger 38) was reduced from 1,300,000 to 20,000 ft, a ratio of 65:1; William Wyler's *Ben Hur* (US 59) was reduced from 1,125,000 to 23,838 ft, a ratio of 47:1; Howard Hughes' *The Outlaw* (US 46) was reduced from 470,000 to 10,451 ft, a ratio of 45:1; Erich von Stroheim's *Foolish Wives* (US 21) was reduced from 360,000 to 10,000 ft, a ratio of 36:1; William Wyler's *The Best Years of Our Lives* (US 46) was reduced from 400,000 to 16,000 ft, a ratio of 25:1; Chuck Wein's *Rainbow Bridge* (US 71) was reduced from 252,000 to 10,300 ft, a ratio of 24:1; three with a ratio of 23:1 were D. W. Griffith's *Intolerance* (US 16), reduced from 300,000 to 13,000 ft, Sergei Eisenstein's *October* (USSR 27), also reduced from 300,000 to 13,000 ft, and *Gone With the Wind* (US 39), reduced from 474,538 to 20,300 ft; and *The Longest Day* (US 72), reduced from 360,000 to 17,000 ft, which had a ratio of 21:1, or about twice the average.

The most edited single sequence of a movie was the chariot race scene in *Ben Hur* (US 25), for which editor Lloyd Nosler had to compress 200,000 ft of film into a sparse 750 ft, a ratio of 267:1. Histo-

---

RIGHT–LEFT
In 1928 a Marxist group in Germany called the Popular Association for Film Art presented a compilation film made up entirely of clips from old UFA newsreels, but cut in such a way as to present a revolutionary viewpoint. It brought outraged protests from audiences who had watched the original newsreels without demur and the film was promptly banned. The Marxists claimed that this effectively demonstrated the power of political prejudice; in fact what it most clearly showed was the extraordinary power of a skilled editor to transform a motion picture.

---

rian Kevin Brownlow commented: 'These 750 ft are among the most valuable in motion picture history.'

The least edited films include D. W. Griffith's *Broken Blossoms* (US 19), which was made with no retakes of any scene and had only 200 ft trimmed from its original length of 5500 ft; and William Wellman's *The Public Enemy* (US 31), which was reduced by only 360 ft from its original 8760 ft.

Narrative features which were released unedited include *My Hustler* (US 65); Andy Warhol's *Chelsea Girls* (US 66); and Laura Mulvey and Peter Wollen's *Penthesilea: Queen of the Amazons* (GB 74). The ultimate was achieved by *The Lacy Rituals* (GB 73), which was unedited to the extent of including shots of the clapperboard being clapped and even retained the director's cries of 'cut!' on the soundtrack.

The first woman editor was Viola Lawrence, who graduated from assistant editor to editor at New York's Vitagraph Studios in 1915.

R2 D2, lovable robot hero of *Star Wars* (US 77), was named after a piece of film editors' jargon— it means 'Reel 2, Dialog 2'.

New Films for Old

Skilful editing can create an entirely new film from rearrangement of shots in an earlier one. This was achieved by Fred J. Balshofer, who had made a spy spoof called *An Adventuress* (US 20) in which the then unknown Rudolph Valentino played a bit part, and wanted to cash in on the Latin lover's meteoric rise to stardom. The locale of the new picture, *The Isle of Love* (US 22), was switched from World War I Germany to a desert island by the simple expedient of inserting stock shots of bathing beauties on a palm-fringed beach throughout the film. The problem of expanding Valentino's minor role in the original into the lead for the new picture was overcome in a number of ways. Various shots were repeated several times; long shots were blown up into close-up and intercut with other footage; some scenes were projected on a loop, so that Valentino repeated the same motions several times over; one scene was used as a flashback; and out-takes from the original were inserted into the new film, notably discarded footage of a car ride, which so expanded the scene as to make it seem interminable. Valentino, it is hardly necessary to add, received no recompense for this unauthorized 'star performance'.

Woody Allen successfully cannibalized and transmogrified a Japanese crime melodrama into a madcap comedy. Retitled *What's Up Tiger Lily?* (US 66), the comedic effect was achieved by re-editing, deliberately mismatching the dubbed dialogue, and by Allen's zany narration.

Blake Edwards did what was in effect a reconstruction job with *The Trail of the Pink Panther* (GB 82), the only film ever to have been embarked upon after the death of its star. Peter Sellers (1925–80) was seen once again as the accident-prone Inspector Clouseau in a story knit together from clips and left-over out-takes from five previous Pink Panther films.

Linking shots were made with an uncredited look-alike filmed at a distance or heavily disguised, as in one scene where the Inspector sets off for England swathed in bandages from head to foot. When all the usable Sellers footage had been exhausted, the film resorted to flashbacks of a teenage Clouseau played by Daniel Peacock and an 8-year-old Clouseau in the person of Lucca Mezzofanti. All this ingenuity failed to pay off. The picture flopped and Sellers's widow Lynne Frederick won an award of $1,687,000 from United Artists for violation of her late husband's contractual rights; United Artists were also ordered to pay $214,000 in costs.

FILM STOCK

Transparent roll film of a kind suitable for motion picture use (though designed for still photography) **was first manufactured** by the Eastman Dry Plate and Film Co. of Rochester, NY in August 1889. Although Thomas Edison ordered some about this date for experiments in cinematography, it was found unsatisfactory and the first stock used for taking films for the Edison Kinetoscope was supplied by the Merwin Hulbert firm in 50 ft rolls on 18 March 1891. In the meantime, however, Louis Aimé Augustin Le Prince of Leeds, Yorkshire, had succeeded in making experimental cinematograph films on Eastman Kodak stock that he had ordered in the autumn of 1889.

The first commercially-produced films in Britain were made in 1895 by Robert Paul and Birt Acres using stock supplied by the European Blair Camera Co. Ltd of St Mary Cray, Kent. By the end of 1896, film stock specially cut and prepared for motion picture use was being advertised by the Celluloid Co. of New York, Dr J. H. Smith & Co. of Zurich, Switzerland, the Blair Co. of Cambridge, Mass. and London, England, the Eastman Kodak Co. of Rochester, NY and Fitch & Co. of London.

The first perforated film was used by Louis Aimé Augustin Le Prince (1842–90?) in his motion picture experiments conducted at Leeds, Yorkshire, in 1889. The inventor's assistant Longley recalled that 'we had brass eyelets fixed in the band [ie film] similar to the eyelets of boots'. The projector built by Le Prince in 1889 had a wheel with pins 'for gearing into the band of pictures'. Perforated film was not used by Thomas Edison until at least three years later.

Commercially-produced film stock was originally sold unperforated and it was not until 1904 that Eastman Kodak began offering perforation as an optional extra. Even as late as 1922 Richardson's *Handbook of Projection* states 'perforation is usually done by the producer'. Unperforated nitrate stock continued to be available from Eastman Kodak until September 1949.

Above: It is very rare for a sequel to appear in the same year as the original film, but both these King Kong movies were released in 1933.

Below: The restored interior of the 1911 Electric Cinema in London's Portobello Road – the oldest cinema in Britain to retain most of its original fabric intact; see p. 207. (*British Film Institute*)

PICTURE·PLAY
MAGAZINE   NOV. 1923
20¢

The
Best
Magazine
of the

ELEANOR
BOARDMAN

Face of the twenties: Eleanor Boardman.

Less than 14 years separate these two cover portraits, yet
the contrast in style could hardly be more marked.

Face of the thirties: Garbo.

Above: The Magic Riddle (Aus 91) was the 94th screen version of Cinderella – a record for remakes (see p. 25). In this Australian version the barefoot waif sports a hip-hugging pair of patched blue jeans. (*Yoram Gross Film Studios Pty Limited*)

Left: Peter Elliott in a solo performance as the last ape-man on earth in *The Missing Link* (US 88), amongst the most recent of a surprisingly long list of films with a cast of one. (See p. 97.) (*British Film Institute*)

Below: Stallone's take-home pay for *Rocky V* (US 90) was $27.5 million plus 35 per cent of the gross, arguably the highest amount earned by any star on any one picture. And he did not even need to box in it! (See p. 76.) (*British Film Institute*)

Above: Two-colour Technicolor. Sam Goldwyn's production of *Whoopee!* (US 30) was one of the earliest colour musicals. There were 14 all-colour features produced in the US in 1930 and another 14 part-colour features. Eddie Cantor starred in this one and the Native American is Chief Caupolean. A Red Indian dance number was led by a 14-year-old from St Louis, Mo. called Betty Grable. *Left:* Three-colour Technicolor. *Becky Sharp* (US 35) was the first feature-length film made in this improved Technicolor process which reproduced all of nature's hues – but not always exactly as nature intended. *Liberty* magazine declared that the performers looked like 'boiled salmon dipped in mayonnaise'. (See p. 147 and p. 148)

Yankee Doodle Dandy (US 42), the George M. Cohan showbiz biopic starring James Cagney, was the first black and white feature to be converted to colour electronically. The practice has aroused fierce controversy, film-makers and buffs claiming that it undermines the integrity of films intended to be seen in monochrome. (See p. 149.)

More films have been based on the works of Shakespeare than any other writer – see p. 38. Douglas Fairbanks and Mary Pickford were the King and Queen of Hollywood, but this 1929 talkie was the only film in which they co-starred.

Above: Forbidden Planet (US 56) was the first picture with an all-electronic score. (See p. 164.) *(Kobal)*

Below: The celebrated race around the Great Court of Trinity College, Cambridge, to beat the striking noonday clock in *Chariots of Fire* (GB 81) was actually filmed in the courtyard at Eton. Trinity refused permission. (See p129.) *(British Film Institute)*

Above: No historical character has been portrayed on screen as often as Napoleon. *Conquest* (US 37) was just one of 194 films to feature the Emperor of the French. Jesus Christ comes second with 162 portrayals and Lenin third with a mere 86. (See p. 48.)

Left: Sherlock Holmes exceeds all other fictitious characters in number of screen portrayals. There have been 204 to date and Basil Rathbone, who starred in 14 of them between 1939 and 1945, was one of 72 actors who have donned the deerstalker. (See p. 45.)

Above: And so say the critics and film-makers who voted *Citizen Kane* (US 41) the greatest film of all time in a poll conducted by *Time Out* in 1990 – though when it was first released it flopped at the box office and only won a single Oscar. (See p. 228.)

The highest price paid at auction for an article of costume from a movie was $165,000 for Judy Garland's ruby slippers from *The Wizard of Oz* (US 39). (See p. 117.) (*National Film Archive*)

Above: The Sioux Indians performing in Kevin Costner's Oscar-laden triumph *Dances with Wolves* (US 90) all spoke in the Sioux language Lakota. The problem was that they had to learn their lines phonetically – it is now a dead language. (See p. 158.) (*Kobal*)

Left: Apart from those in uniform, the leading characters in Hollywood movies seldom have blue collar jobs. Driving a truck is one of the few proletarian livelihoods that rates as the stuff of drama – but it still only comes 30th amongst on-screen male occupations. (See p. 65.)

It has been said that Chaplin was more famous in more countries than any other person who has ever lived. He has been the subject of 339 biographies and innumerable portraits. This one was executed by the caricaturist Arévalo in 1931 for the Chilean magazine *Ecran*.

Above: The Count has been the subject of more horror films than any other character – 160 to date. But many fans still consider that Bela Lugosi's was the definitive performance. (See p. 56.)

Below: . . . just as the Boris Karloff's version of *Frankenstein* (US 31) remains the best remembered out of a total of 113.

Above: Sleeper of the year. Nobody expected anything very remarkable from a Cinderella story starring the little known Julia Roberts about an upwardly mobile prostie and her corporate raider Prince Charming. But *Pretty Woman* (US 90) became the World No. 1 at the box office in 1990 and shot the irresistible Miss Roberts to overnight superstardom. (See p. 30.)

Right: Not a colour TV – there weren't many of those around in 1949, the year that this ad appeared in an Argentine magazine. It was a combined radiogram and home movie apparatus – a much more primitive English version of 1931 is shown on p. 155. (*Backnumbers*)

Below: 'Just a huge thundering camel-opera' was the *New York Times*' verdict on *Lawrence of Arabia* (GB 62). For other jaundiced views from the critics, see p. 220. (*British Film Institute*)

Above: Most cinemagoers agreed that the combination of live action and animation in *Who Framed Roger Rabbit* (US 88) was sensational – but so was the cost at a reputed $70 million. (See p. 33.) (*National Film Archive*)

Left: Although Rudolph Valentino was already a major star by the time this film came out in 1922, his name did not appear with Gloria Swanson's because her contract with Paramount stipulated that she would always receive exclusive billing. For other contractual obligations see p. 83.

THE LARGEST CIRCULATION OF ANY SCREEN MAGAZINE IN THE WORLD

New Movie

A TOWER MAGAZINE

SEPTEMBER

10¢

15¢ in Canada

CELLULOID KISSES
—ARE THEY REAL?

•

GRACE MOORE— THEN AND NOW
By *ELSIE JANIS*

MASK OF KATHARINE HEPBURN BY HELEN LIEDLOFF

Above and opposite: Katharine Hepburn is the only performer to have won four Oscars. She triumphed in *Morning Glory* (US 33), *Guess Who's Coming to Dinner* (US 47), *The Lion in Winter* (GB 68) and *On Golden Pond* (US 81). According to Miss Hepburn, the Academy Award she received for her co-starring role with Spencer Tracy in *Guess Who's Coming to Dinner* was 'doubtless meant for both of us'. The worn old fishing hat sported by Henry Fonda in *On Golden Pond* was a gift to him from Miss Hepburn the first day on set – it had belonged to Spencer Tracy. (See p. 224.)

Above: Noble Johnson was the first black actor to make a career in films, though he was often cast as an Indian or Arab – and on one notable occasion as a white man. (See p. 92). In this 1930 version of *Moby Dick* he played Queequeg.

Right: Claudette Colbert was ordered by Cecil B. De Mille to put on an extra 15lb weight for *Cleopatra* (US 34) because Paramount's researchers claimed that the Egyptian queen had a generously rounded figure. (See p. 138.)

The first safety film on an acetate base was introduced by Eastman Kodak of Rochester, NY, in the
autumn of 1908, but its application was limited due
to the fact that it tended to shrink and cockle. The
negative safety stock was withdrawn in 1912,
though positive safety film continued to be available for use with portable projectors in schools.
Little record of production on safety film in the
USA survives from this period and the earliest commercially-made movie known to have been released
on safety stock, a 345 ft drama titled *La Vendetta del
Groom* (It 09), was produced by Cines of Rome.

Sub-standard safety film was produced in 28 mm
gauge by Pathé for use with the KOK home movie
projector in France in 1912 and in 22 mm gauge by
Kodak for use with the Edison Home Kinetoscope
the same year.

Safety film continued to be confined to the sub-
standard gauges until 1950, when Eastman Kodak
reintroduced 35 mm uninflammable stock, using a
triacetate base immune from shrinkage. The revolution in film stock was total and immediate, so that
since 1951 virtually no film has been made on the
highly inflammable nitrate stock previously in use.

The largest frame format of any film stock was the
2.04×2.805 in dimension used in the 70 mm horizontal feed Imax system, developed by Multiscreen
Corp. of Canada. The first film produced in this
5.242 sq in format, which is nine times the size of
the standard 35 mm frame, was *Tiger Child* (Can/
Jap 70), presented at the Fuji Group's pavilion at
Japan's Expo 70.

The first film shot in High Definition Video
System (HDVS) for theatrical release was *Julia
and Julia* (It 87), starring Kathleen Turner, an English-language film made by RAI of Rome. HDVS
was developed by Sony and NHK to enable feature
films to be shot on tape and transferred to film without loss of quality. The video image has 1125 lines,
about twice the definition of a television picture.
The technique is claimed to cut below-the-line production costs by 20 to 30 per cent. The first HDTV
feature produced in America was *Do It Up* (US
88), starring Robby Benson, which was made by
the Rebo High Definition Studio, New York.

GAUGES

The standard gauge of 35 mm was adopted by
Thomas Alva Edison (1847-1931) of West Orange,
NJ, in the spring of 1891 for use with the Kinetoscope peep-show viewing apparatus developed by
his assistant W. K. L. Dickson. Edison's choice of
four perforations, giving a 4×3 format to the image,
was probably dictated by the fact that the film was
designed for showing in a viewing machine, not on
screen. Had he anticipated that projection would
become the normal method of presenting movies, he
would doubtless have opted for a wider format to

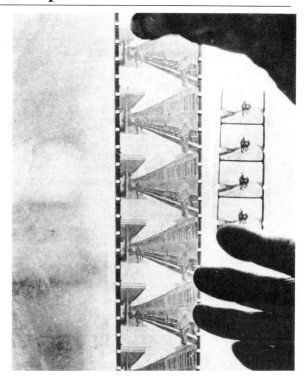

58 mm film stock (*left*) used by Georges Méliès of
Paris in 1896. The narrower gauge was Lumière
film stock of approximately the same date. (*ILN*)

give an aspect ratio approximating more closely to
that of a theatre stage. The Lumière brothers of Lyon,
France, who built the first commercially successful
projectors, decided to conform to the gauge pioneered by Edison and it was undoubtedly their domi-
nance of the nascent film industry in Europe that
established 35 mm as the standard gauge. It was offi-
cially recognized as such by international agreement
in 1907.

The first use of 70 mm film was by Birt Acres
(1854-1918) of Barnet, Herts, for shooting scenes
of Henley Regatta on 7-9 July 1896. He soon abandoned use of wide gauge film because of the high
cost.

A 70 mm projector was produced by Herman Cas-
ter of Canatosta, NY, and introduced into Britain as
The American Biograph on 17 March 1897 at the
Palace Theatre.

The first 70 mm feature film was a special
widescreen version of *Fox Movietone Follies of 1929*,
premièred in the Grandeur process at the Gaiety
Theater, New York, on 17 September 1929.

The first 16 mm feature film to be shot professionally was Lambert Hillyer's *Sundown Riders*
(US 44), a western made in Kodachrome and starring Russell Wade, Jay Kirby and Andy Clyde. The
picture was shot in eight days at a negative cost of
$30,000, less than the cost of a monochrome 'B'
western of the time. Release was through voluntary

bodies and other institutions. The first feature shot on 16 mm and blown up to 35 mm for showing in cinemas—a common practice nowadays for low-budget movies—was Harry Fraser's Kodachrome *The People's Choice* (US 46), with Drew Kennedy as the slowly-turning worm and Louise Arthur as the ever-believing girl. Well-known films containing scenes originally shot on 16 mm include *Doctor Zhivago* (US 65), *Medium Cool* (US 69), *Easy Rider* (US 69) and *Downhill Racer* (US 69).

The smallest gauge ever employed for filming was 3 mm, developed c. 1960 by Eric Berndt and used by NASA in manned space flights in the late 1960s. It had a centre frameline perforation.

The largest gauge ever employed in filming was 75 mm, by the Lumière Co. of Lyons, for special large screen presentations at the Paris Exposition of 1900.

FLASHBACK

The first flashback was used in the Lubin production *A Yiddisher Boy* (US 08) and showed the hero involved in a boyhood street-fight 25 years earlier.

The first sound flashback, in which dialogue and sounds from the past are synchronized with an image of the present in order to conjure up a distant memory, was used by Rouben Mamoulian in *City Streets* (US 31). Dialogue heard earlier in the film was repeated over a huge close-up of Sylvia Sidney's tear-stained face as she recalls the past.

The first flashback within a flashback appeared in Jacques Feyder's *L'Atlantide* (Fr 21); thereafter it was bypassed by film-makers as too confusing until Michael Curtiz challenged the audience's comprehension with a flashback within a flashback within a flashback in *Passage to Marseilles* (US 44). The experiment was repeated in John Brahm's *The Locket* (US 46) and then happily relegated to the limbo of great ideas that do not work.

Unconventional Flashbacks

These include the multiple flashbacks out of sequence employed by William K. Howard in *The Power and the Glory* (US 33) and Orson Welles in *Citizen Kane* (US 41).

Andre Antoine's *La Coupable* (Fr 16) was told entirely in flashbacks, as was *Saragossa Manuscript* (Pol 74), a Decameron-type fantasy of erotic happenings in the 18th century, which went continuously backwards in time. The original version of Sergio Leone's *Once Upon a Time in America* (US 84) jumped backwards and forwards with such confusing irregularity that *Variety*'s correspondent at Cannes actually logged the sequences: 1933—22 min; 1968—14 min; childhood sequence of indeterminate date—54 min; 1920s—25 min; 1968—7 min; 1920s-30s—61 min; 1968—30 min; 1933—7 min.

Bertolucci's first feature *La Commare secca* (It 62),

about the murder of a prostitute in Rome and the subsequent investigation, used the 'against the rules' technique of false flashbacks—deliberately intended to mislead—interspersed with true flashbacks. A charming device was adopted by Keisuke Kinoshita in *Nogiku no gotoku Kimi Nariki/She was like a Wild Chrysanthemum* (Jap 55)—about an old man revisiting his home-town after 60 years and recalling boyhood scenes—when he placed all the flashbacks in an oval-shaped vignette.

LIGHTING

The earliest use of lighting effects for their aesthetic value is generally attributed to D. W. Griffith, who employed artificial lighting to obtain a 'fireside glow' in *The Drunkard's Reformation* (US 09), for the 'sunlight effect' in *Pippa Passes* (US 09) and the 'dim, religious light' in *Threads of Destiny* (US 10). Griffith had to overcome the resistance of his cameramen Harry Marvin and Billy Bitzer, who regarded shadows as 'amateurish'.

The first backlighting by reflectors was introduced by D. W. Griffith's cameraman Billy Bitzer on *Enoch Arden* (US 11), which opens with a superbly backlighted shot of the villagers bidding the sailors goodbye. The technique had been discovered by accident. Normally the camera was never faced directly into the sun, but one day Bitzer

On the set of *California* (US 27) with the most powerful lighting unit in the history of motion pictures.

turned it playfully on to Mary Pickford and Owen Moore as they sat at a shiny-topped table with the sun behind them. Instead of the couple appearing in silhouette, as he expected, Bitzer found that he had obtained a beautifully lit shot with the two artistes' faces bathed in radiance—suitably, since they were in love—the effect of the sun's light reflected in the table top. Bitzer devised a system whereby one mirror would reflect the sun into another, which could then be beamed to the back of a performer's head.

The most powerful lighting used on any film was the 58,000 amps that illuminated the set of *The King and I* (US 56). This is equivalent to the illumination of 258 'brute' arc lights.

The most powerful standard lighting unit currently on sale is the 350-amp Titan Molarc, manufactured by the Mole-Richardson Co. of Hollywood.

The most powerful single arc ever used was a giant 13,940 amp, 325 million candlepower lamp used by Colonel Tim McCoy on the western *California* (US 27). The lamp was 40 times the strength of the most powerful arc available today (see above), 54 times as powerful as the most brilliant lighthouse beam, and said to have a beam that would radiate for 90 miles.

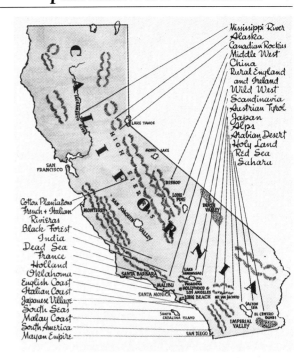

Hollywood could film around the world without anyone having to leave the Sunshine State of California, as this 1935 map betrays.

*L*OCATIONS

Hollywood the World Over

Hollywood has made 4361 feature films set in 125 identifiable foreign countries during the period 1912–90. Comparatively few of these films were shot in the locales they represented, as overseas location shooting was exceptional before the 1950s. The table below, therefore, lists the 25 countries most often depicted in American movies, not necessarily the countries in which the films were actually shot. The most popular overseas locale over the whole period

	1912–19	%	1920–29	%	1930–39	%	1940–49	%	1950–59	%	1960–69	%	1970–79	%	1980–89	%	1990	%	Total	%
Great Britain	256	21.7	166	21.4	160	25.4	134	25.3	53	10.7	24	7.7	11	9.7	22	8.2	4	6.9	831	19.1
France	264	22.4	174	22.5	119	18.9	63	11.9	83	16.8	54	17.3	16	14.2	24	8.9	4	6.9	801	18.4
Canada	196	16.6	99	12.8	45	7.1	25	4.7	20	4.0	4	1.3	4	3.5	9	3.5	3	5.2	405	9.3
Mexico	53	4.5	23	3.0	46	7.3	32	6.0	35	7.0	21	6.7	12	10.6	18	6.7	1	1.7	241	5.5
Italy	43	3.7	20	2.6	18	2.9	13	2.5	30	6.0	38	12.1	7	6.2	13	4.8	2	3.4	183	4.2
Germany	29	2.5	11	1.4	20	3.2	36	6.7	18	3.6	22	7.0	8	7.1	10	3.7	4	6.9	158	3.6
Russia	52	4.4	30	3.9	21	3.3	9	1.7	4	0.8	6	1.9	6	5.3	7	3.5	2	3.4	139	3.2
China	15	1.3	27	3.5	31	4.9	21	3.4	9	1.8	8	2.6	1	0.9	6	3.0	1	1.7	119	2.7
Spain	21	1.8	31	4.0	9	1.4	9	1.7	11	2.2	16	5.1	2	1.8	7	2.6	1	1.7	107	2.5
India	35	3.0	20	2.6	11	1.7	6	1.1	15	3.0	3	1.0	0	–	2	1.0	0	–	92	2.1
Austria	2	0.2	15	1.9	27	4.3	12	2.3	5	1.0	7	2.2	4	3.5	4	1.5	0	–	76	1.7
Japan	23	2.0	4	0.5	0	–	7	1.3	3	0.6	12	3.8	2	1.8	8	3.0	0	–	59	1.4
Egypt	19	1.6	13	1.7	8	1.3	9	1.7	6	1.2	1	0.3	0	–	2	0.7	0	–	58	1.3
Ireland	20	1.7	11	1.4	9	1.4	5	1.0	2	0.4	3	1.0	3	2.7	2	0.7	0	–	55	1.3
Philippines	9	0.8	2	0.3	2	0.3	11	2.1	7	1.4	12	3.8	3	2.7	5	1.9	0	–	51	1.2
South Africa	18	1.5	14	1.8	3	0.5	3	0.6	3	0.6	1	1.0	1	0.9	3	1.1	1	1.7	49	1.1
Vietnam	0	–	2	0.3	2	0.3	2	0.4	6	1.2	2	0.6	4	3.5	27	10.0	3	5.2	48	1.1
Switzerland	8	0.7	6	0.8	9	1.4	6	1.1	5	1.0	3	1.0	1	0.9	4	1.5	1	1.7	45	1.0
Cuba	4	0.3	9	1.2	5	0.8	5	1.0	12	2.4	1	0.3	2	1.8	1	0.4	1	1.7	40	0.9
Korea	0	–	0	–	0	–	0	–	29	5.9	6	1.9	1	0.9	2	0.7	0	–	38	0.9
Morocco	4	0.3	4	0.5	2	0.3	9	1.7	13	2.6	3	1.0	1	0.9	0	–	1	1.7	37	0.8
Algeria	10	0.8	9	1.2	10	1.6	1	0.2	3	0.6	2	0.6	0	–	0	–	1	1.7	36	0.8
Hungary	3	0.3	20	1.3	8	1.3	5	1.0	5	1.0	1	0.3	0	–	4	1.5	0	–	36	0.8
Brazil	1	0.1	5	0.6	3	0.5	9	1.7	6	1.2	3	1.0	1	0.9	4	1.5	2	3.4	34	0.8
Belgium	20	1.7	1	0.1	1	0.2	2	0.4	1	0.2	6	1.9	0	–	1	0.4	0	–	32	0.7
Others	73	6.2	69	8.9	58	9.2	92	17.4	110	22.3	57	18.2	23	20.0	84	31.2	30	51.7	596	13.7
Total	1178		775		631		530		494		313		113		269		58		4361	

Percentage figures represent the proportion of all US productions set, wholly or in part, in overseas locales.

surveyed has been the UK with 831 films (27 of them set in Scotland) or 19.1 per cent of the total, followed closely by France, with 801 films or 18.4 per cent. Hollywood's love affair with Britain, though, has undergone a sharp decline from the 25 per cent of all overseas settings in the 1930s and 1940s to a mere 7.4 per cent (equal with Mexico) in the 1980s. The allure of France has also waned, as America looks beyond Europe, once the epitome of sophistication and romance, to farther flung and more exotic locales.

Where it's at

☆ The scene of the première of Mozart's *Don Giovanni* in *Amadeus* (US 84) was filmed at the Tyl Theatre in Vienna, the actual location of the real première 200 years earlier. It was, however, the only genuine location it was possible to use—for the rest of the movie the unspoiled Old Town of Prague had to stand in for 18th-century Vienna.

☆ Most of the scenes of the eponymous city in Sydney Pollack's *Havana* (US 90) were filmed on a set in the Dominican Republic, as Cuba is strictly off-limits for American film-makers. Interspersed with the reconstructions, though, were shots of the real Havana secured clandestinely by an intrepid second unit.

The Tyl Theatre in Vienna was where Mozart first presented *Don Giovanni*. Two centuries later Milos Forman's *Amadeus* (US 84) replicated the première at the same theatre, still intact with its original interior. Tom Hulce plays Mozart.

☆ Basil Dearden's *The Captive Heart* (GB 46), about a Czech escapee (Michael Redgrave) from a concentration camp who assumes the identity of a dead British PoW, was one of the very few films to have been made on location at a real prisoner of war camp. It was shot at Mariag Milag Nord PoW camp only six weeks after the inmates had been liberated.

☆ The picturesque Pacific coastal town of Canaima, overrun by Venezuelan killer spiders in Steven Spielberg's *Arachnophobia* (US 90), is in reality Cambria, situated in San Luis Obispo County, California. The name Canaima was borrowed from the locale in Venezuela where the jungle scenes of the prologue were shot.

> Starstruck sightseers are the bugbear of most location managers. A sign posted up during a 1988 shoot at New York's Café Luxembourg read: 'The name of this movie is *When Harry Met Sally*. No one famous is in it and you can't be in it either. Thanx. Soon at a theater near you.'

☆ The key scene in *Scandal* (GB 89) in which Christine Keeler's black lover Johnny Edgecombe blasts away at Stephen Ward's front door in Wimpole Mews, Marylebone, was in fact filmed in Bathurst Mews, Bayswater. Although Wimpole Mews was little altered since the scandal involving the War Minister and a Soviet diplomat, it is now surrounded by tall modern buildings. Bathurst Mews still retained its original cobbles and was unusually wide, making it ideal for filming. The changing face of London presented similar problems on *The Krays* (GB 90). As little of traditional Bethnal Green in London's East End survives, the Kray twins' backstreet home was relocated to Victorian back-to-back Caradoc Street in Greenwich.

☆ Not all substitute locations are so close to the real thing. Chicago Town Hall in *Reds* (US 81) was in fact the Zion Institute in Hulme, Manchester. One of the very few location shots in *Who Framed Roger Rabbit* (US 89), set in Los Angeles, was the exterior of the sinister Acme factory. In reality it was the London Transport depot at Shepherd's Bush. 'Metropolis' in *Superman IV* (US 87) was Milton Keynes. In earlier days it was more often England which was recreated Stateside. Sherwood Forest in *The Adventures of Robin Hood* (US 38) was Bidwell Park at Chico, Calif.

☆ The musical *First a Girl* (GB 35), in which Jessie Matthews plays a girl impersonating a boy impersonating a girl, has an extraordinary but justly celebrated finale set in a gigantic bird cage. Reality was less exotic. The 40 ft high cage was built in an open field at Northolt, one of North West London's least picturesque suburbs, and filmed between two and five in the morning with 52 lightly clad and shivering chorus girls perched all over the bars.

☆ Peter Bogdanovich's *The Last Picture Show* (US 71) and his sequel *Texasville* (US 90) were shot in the small town of Archer City, Texas (pop. 1862). The novel on which *The Last Picture Show* was based had been written by Larry McMurty as an evocation of his own experiences as a teenager growing up in Archer City in the 1950s.

☆ The reason that the Los Angeles subway looks so unnaturally clean and tidy in *Predator 2* (US 90) is because San Francisco's BART system was standing in for it.

The City of Florence took such exception to the subject matter of *The Monster of Florence* (It 86), about a series of unsolved maniac murders, that the authorities determined to close down shooting. Their lawyers could not come up with any legal arguments for doing to. Finally they succeeded in ejecting the production by the simple expedient of putting up 'No Parking' signs at all the locations.

☆ The railway station where romance blossomed for Celia Johnson and Trevor Howard in David Lean's *Brief Encounter* (GB 45) was called Milford Junction and was supposed to be in Kent. The actual station was at Carnforth, Lancs and was chosen because it was the only railway junction far enough removed from the flight path of German bombers for blackout restrictions to be lifted for the film-makers. (Although filmed in the last year of the war, *Brief Encounter* was set in the last year of peace.) Today Carnforth is a sorry relic of the last days of steam. Still in use, but unmanned, the only recognisable features from the film are the passageway where the lovers kiss before running to catch their different trains and the station clock which ticked away their stolen hours together. The refreshment room, pivot of the story, has long since vanished. It has been replaced with a foul-smelling room furnished only with a Klix drinks dispenser and a battered dustbin.

☆ First of the Tarzan movies to be shot in a real jungle was *The New Adventures of Tarzan* (US 35), made in Guatemala. Conditions were appalling, with many of the crew laid low by snakes and poisonous insects during the four months it took to complete. The 650 Amerindians hired to play the natives refused to act with Jiggs the chimp and there were further upsets when producer Edgar Rice Burroughs, the creator of Tarzan, ran off with the wife of one of his partners. The story centres on the discovery of a lost city guarded by monster-men and actual Mayan ruins were used to rather greater effect than the flimsy lath-and-plaster studio fabrications constructed for most similar pictures. Star of the film was Herman Brix (later known as Bruce Bennett), who was paid a bit player's $75 a week to brave the real perils of the jungle *and* do all his own stunts.

☆ Harem scenes have been a standby of erotic movies and saucy comedies since the earliest days of movie making. None has been filmed in a real harem, though, until 1989. And perhaps surprisingly the location was the Soviet Union. The international co-production *The Battle of the Three Kings* (Morocco/USSR/Sp/It 90), a 16th century costumer about charismatic Arab leader Abdel-malek, went to Soviet Bachiserai to shoot the scene in an ancient harem which had been preserved by a local Turkish community over the centuries.

☆ *Of Love and Desire* (US 63), the picture in which Merle Oberon attempted a comeback, was literally a home-movie. It was shot at Miss Oberon's 17th-century villa in Mexico City. The Famous Players Lasky version of *Little Women* (US 19) used Louisa May Alcott's family home in Concord, Mass as the home of the March family.

☆ Lindsay Anderson approached the headmaster of his old school, Cheltenham College, for permission to use it as the location for *If* (GB 68), his memorable tale of pupils rebelling against the system which ends with a group of boys machine-gunning the parents and masters on Speech Day. The headmaster enquired what kind of story it was. Similar to *Tom Brown's Schooldays* perhaps?, he suggested helpfully when Anderson hesitated. The director assured him that 'certain features' of the story might be compared with Thomas Hughes' Victorian classic (in which authority is upheld as always right) and permission was willingly granted for a location fee said to have been only £100. Lindsay Anderson has not been invited as a distinguished Old Boy to hand out the prizes at any subsequent Cheltenham Speech Days.

☆ The Merchant-Ivory production *The Ballad of the Sad Cafe* (US/GB 91), set in a small Southern town 'that time had already forgotten by 1925', was shot at Willie Nelson's ranch outside Austin, Texas. Half a million dollars converted 'Willieville', as it is known to everyone except its owner, into a ramshackle main street with a church and cotton mill at one end and the eponymous café, presided over by the formidable fist-fighting Miss Amelia (Vanessa Redgrave), at the other.

☆ The race around the Great Court of Trinity College, Cambridge between Harold Abrahams (Ben Cross) and Lord Lindsey (Nigel Havers) in *Chariots of Fire* (GB 81), in which the Olympic athlete Abrahams becomes the first man to complete the circuit in less time than the 44 seconds it takes the 400-year-old Trinity clock to strike noon, actually took place far from Cambridge. The ultra-conservative Trinity College council, ironically similar to the stuffy dons portrayed in the film, were not prepared to be associated with anything as vulgar as moving pictures, and the scene was filmed in the courtyard of Eton College instead. Lack of an authentic location might have mattered more had the race really taken place, but in fact Abrahams never ran round Trinity Great Court to beat the clock. Nor did Lord Lindsey, because he was a fictitious character, though loosely based on champion athlete Lord Burghley.

> All scenes set on London Underground platforms are filmed at the same tube station— the Aldwych. As one of the few stations only in part-time use, London Transport is prepared to hire it out between 10a.m. and 3p.m. for £2000. The price goes up to £6000 if you want a train.

☆ Forty-five years of communism in Eastern Europe has produced a mixed legacy of some historic locations untouched by development, others blighted by insensitive central planning. The *belle époque* Czechoslovak spa town of Marienbad (Mariánské Lázne in Czech) is one of the latter. It was far too down-at-heel under the communists to serve as the elegant resort depicted in Alain Resnais' *Last Year in Marienbad* (Fr 61). The magnificent formal gardens of Nymphenberg Castle, near Munich, served to depict an idealised Marienbad of the imagination, far removed from the grim socialist reality.

☆ The cornfield which the Iowa farmer played by Kevin Costner turned into a baseball diamond in *Field of Dreams* (US 89) lies just outside Dyersville, Iowa. 'People will come', James Earl Jones as Shoeless Joe Jackson says to Costner in the movie. 'They'll come to Iowa for reasons they can't fathom. They'll arrive at your door, innocent as children, longing for the past.' And come they did, more than 10,000 during the summer following the release of the film, just to see a featureless stretch of grass which had stirred their dreams.

The largest number of different locations used on a motion picture was 168 in the case of Sergei Bondarchuk's four-part *War and Peace* (USSR 1963–67), of which the most prominent were the Battle of Borodino sequence, filmed at Borodino; the 'Moscow on Fire' sequence, filmed at Volokolamsk; and the 'Hunting in Otradnoye' sequence, filmed in the village of Boguslavskiy, near Kashira.

The provincial city most often used for film settings in Britain is Liverpool, which has been featured in 34 films to date: *Her Benny* (GB 20); *Grass Widowers* (GB 21); *Old English* (US 30); *The House of the Spaniard* (GB 36); *Souls at Sea* (GB 37); *Penny Paradise* (GB 38); *Spare a Copper* (GB 40); *Atlantic Ferry* (GB 41); *It Happened One Sunday* (GB 44); *Waterfront* (GB 50); *The Magnet* (GB 50); *These Dangerous Years* (GB 57); *The Key* (GB 58); *Violent Playground* (GB 58); *Sapphire* (GB 59); *In the Wake of a Stranger* (GB 59); *Ferry Across the Mersey* (GB 64); *The Little Ones* (GB 64); *Charlie Bubbles* (GB 67); *The Reckoning* (GB 69); *Letter to Brezhnev* (GB 85); *No Surrender* (GB 86); *Coast to Coast* (GB 86); *Business as Usual* (GB 87); *The Fruit Machine* (GB 88); *The Dressmaker* (GB 88); *Distant Voices, Still Lives* (GB 88); *Appuntamento a Liverpool* (It 88); *Wonderland* (GB 89); *Shirley Valentine* (US 89); *The Man from the Pru* (GB 90, TVM); *Dancin' Thru the Dark* (GB 90); *Blonde Fist* (GB 91); *Film Stars Don't Die in Liverpool* (GB i.p.). Seventeen films have been set in Glasgow, 11 each in Blackpool, Brighton and Edinburgh, and 9 in Oxford. Liverpool evidently does not intend to rest on its laurels. It recently became the first local authority in the UK to appoint a full-time Films Officer responsible for promoting the city to prospective producers and arranging facilities.

MAKE-UP

Little attention was paid to make-up in films before the advent of the close-up (q.v.). **The earliest motion picture in which it is apparent that the actors are wearing make-up** (other than blackface or whiskers) is Edwin S. Porter's *The Whole Dam Family and the Dam Dog* (US 05), in which the

The magnificent formal gardens of Nymphenberg Castle, near Munich, stood in for the down-at-heel Czech spa of Marienbad in *Last Year in Marienbad* (Fr 61). (*British Film Institute*)

cast are made-up to create the illusion of a family resemblance. The pioneer of special make-up techniques for film as opposed to stage performances was D. W. Griffith, who began experiments to achieve a more naturalistic appearance for his performers at Biograph in about 1910. Stage actress Olga Petrova recalled of her film debut in *The Tiger* (US 14): 'I noticed immediately that my co-workers wore a make-up much darker, almost a beige, whereas I wore the usual light Leichner's 1.' There was a good reason for her co-workers' departure from stage practice. The orthochromatic film stock used at this date was insensitive to the red end of the spectrum (scarlet registered as black) and consequently a heavy application of yellow make-up was necessary to create an impression of natural skin tone on screen.

The first make-up specifically for on-screen use was Supreme Greasepaint, introduced by Polish immigrant Max Factor in 1914. The need for special make-up was dictated by the increasing use of artificial lighting for filming from 1912 onwards. Freckles and skin blemishes photographed black, pink cheeks a murky grey, and skin tones a deathly white.

It took 8½ hours daily to transform lovely 37-year-old Francesca Annis into the withered 100-year-old Widow of the Web in *Krull* (GB 82)—and she could not eat until the make-up came off again! (*British Film Institute*)

The first studio make-up department was established at First National in 1924 under British-born Perc Westmore (1904–70). Perc later became head of make-up at Warner's, his brother Bud became head of make-up at Universal, and his other brother Wally spent 38 years in make-up at Paramount.

The largest make-up budget was $1 million for *Planet of the Apes* (US 68), which represented nearly 17 per cent of the total production cost. A team of 78 make-up artists worked under the direction of Fox's make-up specialist John Chambers, who won a special Oscar for his remarkable achievement of creating wholly credible ape faces sufficiently mobile to register the full range of human emotions.

The longest make-up job ever performed on a single artiste was the tattooing applied to Rod Steiger in Warner Bros' *The Illustrated Man* (US 69). It took make-up artist Gordon Bau and his team of eight assistants 10 hours to complete the torso and another full day was spent on the lower body, hands and legs. Bau's longest job previously had been Charles Laughton's make-up for the title role of *The Hunchback of Notre Dame* (US 39), which he finished in a mere 5½ hours.

Other marathon make-up jobs have included the 4 hours daily spent by Wally Westmore on Fredric March's Hyde in *Dr Jekyll and Mr Hyde* (US 32); 4 hours for Boris Karloff's monster in *Frankenstein* (US 31), and a similar time for Jean Marais' make-

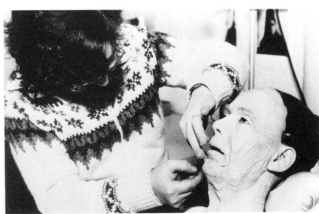

up in *La Belle et la Bête* (Fr 45); 4½ hours on Bull Montana's ape-man in *The Lost World* (US 25) and the same for Lon Chaney in *The Hunchback of Notre Dame* (US 23); 5 hours for the principal apes in *Planet of the Apes* (US 68) and also for the 121-year-old character played by Dustin Hoffman in *Little Big Man* (US 70); Klaus Kinski's Dracula make-up for *Nosferatu* (FRG 79) also took 5 hours daily to apply. Boris Karloff's make-up for *The Bride of Frankenstein* (US 35), an elaboration of Jack Pierce's original monster make-up for the 1931 *Frankenstein*, took 7 hours to complete each day. Shooting of scenes involving Karloff—he was in most—had to be delayed until 1 p.m. In the same film Elsa Lanchester's make-up as the female monster was so rigid she had to be fed lunch through a tube. John Hurt was unable to eat at all after the 7-hour ordeal of having his head monstrously deformed for the title role in *The Elephant Man* (GB 80). It was so exhausting that the full make-up could only be applied every second day. Nick Maley's transformation of 37-year-old Francesca Annis into the 100-year-old Widow of the Web for *Krull* (GB 82) took 8½ hours daily and involved 11 layers of latex compound on her face as well as 12 layers on her hands. The mask extended inside her mouth and prevented eating.

PRODUCERS

The youngest producer to produce a feature-length film for commercial exhibition was 16-year-old George Palmer of Melbourne, Vic., whose thriller *The Mail Robbery* (Aus 25) was released in Victoria and New South Wales. The following year he produced, directed and starred in *Northbound Ltd* (Aus 26), a railroad drama he had written himself. On coming of age Palmer retired from the film business to establish a successful travel agency, but retained an interest in experimental film-making.

America's youngest producer was Matty Rich, who produced and directed his award-winning drama of black working-class life *Straight Out of Brooklyn* (US 91) at the age of 19.

Britain's youngest producer was 22-year-old Norman Hope-Bell, who made his professional debut at Cricklewood Studios with an Ernie Lotinga comedy called *Love Up the Pole* (GB 36).

The first woman producer was Alice Guy (see p. 120), who founded the Solax Co. at Flushing, New York, on 7 September 1910. The first of nearly 300 short films produced by her in the next three years was *A Child's Sacrifice* (US 10), starring 'The Solax Kid' (Magda Foy), which was released on 21 October 1910.

The first feature film produced by a woman was Eros Films' *The Definite Object* (GB 20), a gangster movie set in New York produced by Countess Bubna.

The first talkie produced by a woman was Elinor Glyn's Talkicolor production *Knowing Men* (GB 30), with Carl Brisson and Elissa Landi. She also directed. **The first Hollywood talkie by a woman** was Elsie Janis's *Paramount on Parade* (US 30), which was released in April 1930, two months after Miss Glyn's picture.

The first and only feature film produced by a Roman Catholic priest is *Romero* (US 89), made by Fr Ellwood Kieser for Paulist Pictures, a non-profit making production house operating under the auspices of the Los Angeles Archdiocese. Starring Raul Julia, *Romero* tells the true story of the Archbishop of that name who was assassinated after urging soldiers of the Salvadorean army to refuse to obey orders to attack dissident peasants. Fr Kieser intended to make the story as a TV drama, but decided to go for a full-scale cinema feature after being turned down by the three major TV networks as the subject was too controversial.

The longest career as a producer was by Pierre Braunberger (1905–90), who started producing silent pictures in Paris in 1924 with Jean Renoir's *La Fille de l'eau* (Fr 24) and produced his last film, *Knights of the Round Table* (Fr 89), 65 years later. Amongst his notable productions were Louis Buñuel's controversial debut film *Un Chien Andalou* (Fr 29), Renoir's *Une Partie de campagne* (Fr 36), Truffaut's *Tirez sur le pianiste* (Fr 60) and Godard's *Vivre sa vie* (Fr 62). Many of the French *nouvelle vague* directors began their careers with his Films de la Pléiade production outfit. He was the only producer to have been awarded the prestigious Louis Delluc Prize on three occasions.

> 'You make 5000 to 7000 decisions when you make a film. If you're lucky enough to get 80 per cent of them right you've got a great film. I think so much of life is about percentages.'—David Puttnam on being a producer

The most co-producers credited on a film was seven in the case of abysmal low-budget teen-sex so-called comedy *Summer Job* (US 89). Why it took so many to produce what *Variety* described as 'an amateur night film deficient on all levels' remains one of movies' minor mysteries, but for the record they were: Josi W. Konski, John O'Donnell, Jeffrey Ringler, Ron Gell, David Walker, Ralph Wilson and Kenneth A. Dalton.

The two most successful producer/directors in terms of box office revenue are George Lucas and Steven Spielberg, who between them are responsible for nine out of the twelve films which have garnered more than $100 million in North American rentals. Spielberg has to his credit, as both producer and director, the top earner of all time, *E.T. The Extra-Terrestrial* (US 82), as well as co-producing

Back to the Future (US 85) and directing *Jaws* (US 75), which was the first picture to break the $100 million barrier, and the Indiana Jones blockbusters *Raiders of the Lost Ark* (US 81), *Indiana Jones and the Temple of Doom* (US 84) and *Indiana Jones and the Last Crusade* (US 89). These three were produced by George Lucas, who also directed *Star Wars* (US 77) and produced *The Empire Strikes Back* (US 80) and *Return of the Jedi* (US 83). (For rental figures, see Top 25 Earners chart p. 31.) Lucas also holds the record for the highest earnings from a single film. As producer of *Star Wars* he was entitled to 40 per cent of net profits, worth a sum of nearly $50 million. In addition, Lucas held all the merchandising rights, which Fox had allowed him under the contract because they could see little value in them. His cut of the $2.6 billion revenue from retail sales of *Star Wars* related products is undisclosed.

*P*ROPS

The most valuable assemblage of props ever to be brought together on a single set was the $10 million worth of paintings and sculptures used for the art gallery scenes in Universal's *Legal Eagles* (US 86), starring Robert Redford. They included works by Willem de Korning, Roy Lichtenstein, Alexander Calder and Pablo Picasso.

The most expensive single prop ever used on a movie was the full-scale replica of a Spanish galleon built for Roman Polanski's *Pirates* (US/Tun 86) at a cost of £7 million. Designed by Pierre Guffrey, its construction kept 2000 Maltese shipyard workers in jobs for a whole year.

The most expensive model was Darth Vader's *Star Destroyer* used in *Star Wars* (US 77) and its sequels. Built by Industrial Light and Magic at a cost of $100,000, it had more than 250,000 portholes lit from inside. There are probably numerous tacky 'B' movies which could lay claim to the cheapest model, but points for ingenuity should certainly go to the art director of an engaging Australian sci-fi movie called *As Time Goes By* (Aus 87), about an alien from outer space and his time machine-cum-spaceship. The minuscule budget allowed for nothing more elaborate than a cocktail shaker to represent the latter.

The largest land-based prop ever constructed for a movie was the 60 ft long, 40 ft high Wooden Horse of Troy used in Robert Wise's *Helen of Troy* (US 54). It weighed 80 tons, and 30 full-grown trees and over 1000 lb of nails were needed to build it. A modern air-conditioning system was fitted to save the 25 occupants from heat prostration.

Food facts

When a mock-up aircraft was needed for studio scenes in *Coastal Command* (GB 42), the problem was rivets. Real rivets were too precious to spare in wartime, so the Ministry of Information officer assigned to the film wrote to his opposite number at the Ministry of Food, explaining that for the purpose of simulating rivets 'there is nothing more suitable than large grey Continental lentils which will be glued and painted over. Permission is sought to purchase 7 lb of these'. Lest such a quantity should seem extravagant, he assured the Food Ministry that it was 'unlikely that the whole of the 7 lb would be used, but as the lentils are not of uniform size some selection would be necessary, and any balance would be handed over to the canteen'. An Assistant Divisional Food Officer at the MoF replied a week later: 'I have asked the Food Executive Office, Westminster, to supply you with an authority to purchase, and Gennaros of Old Compton Street to supply.'

The telephone Harpo Marx ate in *The Coconuts* (US 29) was made of chocolate and the bottle of ink he drank was Coke. The boots eaten by Charlie Chaplin in *The Gold Rush* (US 24) were made of licorice.

The raindrops in *Singin' in the Rain* (US 52) had milk added so that they would register better on film.

The blood in the celebrated scene in *Psycho* (US 60) in which Janet Leigh is stabbed in the shower was actually chocolate sauce. The dank green slime that covered Natasha Richardson as she writhed on the muddy floor of a crypt in *Gothic* (GB 86) was chopped boiled spinach.

> The pivotal prop of *Citizen Kane* (US 41), the Rosebud sled which belonged to Charles Foster Kane as a boy, now belongs to Steven Spielberg. He bought it for $60,500.

The green vomit that gushed out of the possessed child Nancy Anglet (Linda Blair) in *The Exorcist* (US 73) was realistic enough to make some spectators throw up themselves. It was in fact only a simple concoction of split pea soup and oatmeal. In the spoof sequel *Repossessed* (US 90) Linda Blair as Nancy grown-up is now a suburban housewife who prepares her family split pea soup for supper.

> A survey conducted during the first six months of 1988 revealed that the percentage of US movies in which alcohol was used was 98 per cent.

*S*CHEDULES

The longest production schedule for a completed feature movie was the 18 years it took to finish Alvaro Henriques Goncalves' *Presente de Natal* (Bra 71). Goncalves, a lawyer by profession, worked on his full-length animated feature single-handed. Two other films are poised to surpass this record on completion. Martin Sharp's idiosyncratic documentary *The Street of Dreams* (Aus i.p.), which combines the seemingly disparate themes of Sydney's defunct Luna Park fairground and the American falsetto songster Tiny Tim, was begun in 1976 and first shown as a work in progress at the 1988 Brighton Festival. The work remains in progress in 1991. Richard Williams' *The Thief and the Cobbler* (GB i.p.) was begun even earlier, in 1967. During the 24 years the animated film has been in production, Williams has spent some $20 million on it. More than half this sum has been put up by the Canadian animator himself, using money earned from his masterpiece *Who Framed Roger Rabbit* (US 89) as well as the proceeds of TV commercials and main-title animation for such features as *What's New, Pussycat?* (US/Fr 65), *Murder on the Orient Express* (GB 74) and the two Pink Panther movies.

The longest production schedule for a dramatic film in terms of start date and completion date was 13 years for Leni Riefenstahl's *Tiefland* (FRG 53) and the same length of time for *Dr Bethune* (Chn 77), Chinese tribute to the Canadian chest surgeon who gave his life while serving as a volunteer with the Red Army in 1939. In the case of *Tiefland*, production of what promised to be the most expensive talkie then made was suspended in 1942 after expenditure of 5 million RMs and the complete breakdown of the director's health. At the end of the war Frl. Riefenstahl was banned from working in the film industry, but following her de-Nazification in 1952 she succeeded in reassembling the original cast and completed the film. It recouped its cost but Frl. Riefenstahl, dissatisfied with her work, then withdrew the picture from distribution and it has not been shown since.

Production of *Dr Bethune* started in 1964 but was halted at the outset of the Cultural Revolution on the personal orders of Mao's wife, Jiang Qing, who asserted that the documentary footage of *Dr Bethune* was sufficient to honour his memory. The cameraman who had taken the documentary footage, Wu Yinxian, was also the cameraman on the biopic. Production was resumed with the collapse of the Cultural Revolution.

The longest production schedule for a British film was the 8 years 20 days (6 May 1956–26 May 1964) it took Kevin Brownlow and Andrew Mollo to complete their fantasy of a Nazi-occupied Britain, *It Happened Here* (GB 66). The picture, which occupied a cumulative shooting schedule of ten weeks, started as an amateur production by a group of enthusiastic teenagers and ended as a professional film with a West End release. (Mr Brownlow has asked the author to point out that in these circumstances he should not be accorded the title of the world's slowest director.)

Other protracted production schedules have included 12 years for Désiré Ecaré's story of women's role in modern African society *Visages de Femmes* (Ivory Coast 85); 11 years (1925–36) for Ladislas Starewitch's animated puppet film *Le Roman de Rénard* (Fr 40); 11 or possibly 12 years for *Pakeezah* (Ind 71), which was so long in the making that the original hero aged too much and had to be recast as the heroine's father; 10 years for Michael and Andy Jones's Newfoundland comedy *The Adventures of Faustus Bidgood* (Can 86), which called on the services of almost every actor and actress in the province; 9 years for the Indian historical epic *Mughal-e-Azam* (Ind 60); 7 years for Harry Hoyt's *The Lost World* (US 25), Fred Zinnermann and Walter Mirisch's *Hawaii* (US 66), Michael Kohler's *The Experiencer* (US) and *Flame Top* aka *Down to Earth* (Fin 81), a biopic of the enigmatic Finnish folklorist Maiju Lassila; 5½ years for Edgar Reitz's *Heimat* (FRG 84), which perhaps is not surprising for a film nearly 16 hours long; 5 years for George Stevens's *The Greatest Story Ever Told* (US 65) and David Lynch's *Eraserhead* (US 77), declared to contain 'one of the most repugnant scenes in film history'; and 4 years for Mel Ferrer's *Vendetta* (US 50), Rudall Hayward's *On the Friendly Road* (NZ 36), which would have been New Zealand's first talkie if he had managed to finish it a year earlier, Francis Ford Coppola's *Apocalypse Now* (US 79), Joseph L. Mankiewicz's *Cleopatra* (US 63) and Terence Young's Korean War epic *Inchon* (Kor/US 81), starring Laurence Olivier as General MacArthur. Sir Richard Attenborough's monumental biopic of *Gandhi* (GB 82) had a schedule of 20 months from the start of pre-production to delivery of prints, with 26 weeks spent on shooting. The gestation of the movie, however, lasted 17 years from the start of the first of 12 draft screenplays to the pre-production date. Attenborough estimated that during this time he gave up some 40 acting parts and a dozen directorial assignments in order to realize what he described as 'my love affair with this project'.

Even this may not represent the ultimate in patience and fortitude. Screenwriter Ted Allan, whose *Bethune: The Making of a Hero* (Can/Chn 90) is based on his own recollections of the Canadian doctor venerated in China for his services on the Long March, first took the project to Darryl F. Zanuck at Fox in 1942. The film went into pre-production with Canadian star Walter Pidgeon signed to play Bethune. When the deal fell through, Allan continued his fight to get the story of his hero on to the screen. Both Columbia and Warner picked up the option and Robert Redford and Paul Newman were amongst those canvassed for the title role. After various independent companies had toyed with the project, Allan finally saw his efforts rewarded when *Bethune* went before the cameras in China in April 1987 as a Canadian/French/Chinese co-production starring Donald Sutherland, some 45 years after he had initiated it. Even then there were further delays. Shooting was suspended after five months and not resumed until November 1988. The picture eventually premièred at the Montreal World Film Festival on 27 August 1990.

The shortest shooting schedule of all time was the one day for Paul Vecchialli's 80-minute feature film *Trou de Mémoire* (Fr 85). Starring Francoise Lebrun and Vecchialli himself, the picture was shot with film stock left over from a documentary he had been commissioned to make.

Other directors who haven't stood around on the job are Rob Nilsson, whose *Heat and Sunlight* (US 87), about a fortyish photographer obsessed with a beautiful dancer, was shot in 60 hours, and Roger Corman, who completed his cult movie *The Little Shop of Horrors* (US 60) in just two days and three nights. Frank Oz's 1986 remake, by contrast, took seven months to shoot.

Also shot in two days (and a couple of hours) was Emile de Antonio's *In the King of Prussia* (US 82), a reconstruction of the attack on the General Electric warhead plant in the mid-west township of King of Prussia by anti-nuclear demonstrators and their subsequent trial. Starring Martin Sheen as himself, and with the defendants, known as the 'Plowshares Eight', as themselves, the film had to be shot in 50 hours to meet the deadline before the defendants had to report for sentencing.

The shortest production schedule for a full-length feature film was 13 days from the start of scripting to the première in the case of *The Fastest Forward* (GB 90), directed by John Gore and produced by Russ Malkin in aid of the Telethon '90 fund-raising event. The 75-minute comedy-thriller was scripted in five days, shot in three and edited in five. It was completed on 27 May 1990, the day of the première at the Dominion, Tottenham Court Road. The volunteer cast included Caroline Bliss, Maurice Denham, Phil Daniels, Fiona Fullerton, Jenny Seagrove, Jerry Hall and veteran character actor Michael Ripper. Fastest time from the inception of a feature film till its general release was achieved by the makers of *Twist Around the Clock* (US 61), which opened 28 days after Chubby Checker reached No. 1 in the charts and gave Sam Katzman the idea of shooting an instant movie to cash in on the new dance craze. Chubby Checker starred.

The shortest time between completion of shooting and the première of a feature film was five hours in the case of Alfred Rolfe's racing drama *The Cup Winner* (Aus 11). The final scenes, consisting of footage of the Melbourne Cup shot by six cameramen, were filmed on 7 November 1911 and the completed drama edited and processed in time for a simultaneous opening at five Melbourne cinemas the same night. It opened in Sydney, 640 miles away, the following day.

The shortest time between the première of a dramatised movie of historical events and the events depicted was nine weeks in the case of telepic *People Vs Jean Harris* (US 81, TVM), aired by NBC in two parts on 7–8 May 1981. It starred Ellen Burstyn as the refined private school headmistress who was convicted of the murder of Dr Herman Tarnower, originator of the celebrated Scarsdale Diet.

SET

The largest film set ever built was the 1312 by 754 ft Roman Forum designed by Veniero Colosanti and John Moore and built on a 55-acre site at Las Matas, outside Madrid, for the last great Hollywod epic of the ancient world, Samuel Bronston's production of *The Fall of the Roman Empire* (US 64). Commencing 10 October 1962, 1100 workmen spent seven months laying the surface of the Forum with 170,000 cement blocks, erecting 22,000 ft of concrete stairways, 601 columns and 350 statues, and constructing 27 full size buildings. The highest point on the set was the Temple of Jupiter, whose bronze equestrian statues surmounting the roof soared 260 ft above the paving of the Forum.

The largest indoor set was the UFO landing site built for the climax of Steven Spielberg's *Close Encounters of the Third Kind* (US 77). With a height of 90 ft, length of 450 ft and 250 ft breadth, the set was constructed inside a 10 million cubic ft dirigible hangar at Mobile, Alabama, which had six times the capacity of the largest sound stage in Hollywood. The structure included 4 miles of scaffolding, 16,900 sq ft of fibreglass, 29,500 sq ft of nylon canopy and 'enough concrete to make a full-scale replica of the Washington monument'.

The largest single structure ever built as a movie set was the vast 450 ft long, 90 ft high medieval castle designed by Wilfred Buckland and erected at Pasadena, California, for Douglas Fairbanks' version of *Robin Hood* (US 22). No

One way of creating the illusion of vast settings on a stage of limited size is to create the set in false perspective. This makes the background look a lot more distant than it really is. One problem, though, in using this technique is the size of the performers at the back of the set. In *Maya* (Fr 49), a set representing a street in a red-light district was built in false perspective. The prostitutes seen at the far end of the street were played by little girls of six to eight years old outfitted in the gaudy raiment of harlotry.

Samuel Bronston's massive set for *The Fall of the Roman Empire* (US 64). It was the largest set ever built.

record survives of its other dimensions, but to be in proportion it must have been at least as big as the *Close Encounters* set (see above), which was exactly the same height and length.

The smallest set used for the entire action of a movie—in terms of confined acting space—was the lifeboat containing the nine protagonists of Alfred Hitchcock's *Lifeboat* (US 44).

It's for real

☆ One of the commonest giveaways in period films and films set in exotic locales is that the clothes of the ordinary people look brand new and probably are. Not so in Bertolucci's *The Sheltering Sky* (GB/It 90), which takes place in North Africa shortly after World War II. Art director James Acheson toured Morocco offering brand new jellabas in exchange for suitably well-worn ones.

☆ Cast as the eponymous pickpocket in *Light-Fingered Sonya* (Rus 15), Nina Gofman played a scene in which she is paying her defence counsel for winning her acquittal for theft and steals his watch at the same time. 'I remember arranging this with the director', she recalled, 'and not wanting to tell anyone of my intention until the scene was over; the actor play-

ing the lawyer suspected nothing. By that time I had acquired a good deal of "experience" and skill in various kinds of theft, which I had been taught by leading specialists in the field. And I managed to extract his watch quite unnoticed. I remember the shot showing my lawyer's bewilderment on finding his watch missing.'

☆ Alan Dwan employed perfumier H. M. K. Smith to prepare an unguent of oil of almonds, honey and cinnamon, impregnated with orange blossoms and henna, for Nita Naldi to rub on her feet in the role of Cleopatra in *Lawful Larceny* (US 30)—also a scent called *Kyaphi* compounded of 28 different aromatics. Both were referred to in ancient Egyptian papyri and although neither the unguent nor the scent could be seen or smelt in the film, Dwan believed their use enhanced the sense of reality for his performers.

☆ Similarly the use of actual historical props may be more for the benefit of the film-makers than the audience, who are often unaware of their authenticity. In *The Crisis* (US 16) Lincoln's despatch box, loaned by the War Department, was used by Samuel Drane in the role of the President. The duelling pistols employed by Carlyle Blackwell as Alexander Hamilton and Arthur Ashley as Aaron Burr in *The Beautiful Mrs Reynolds* (US 18) were the actual ones discharged by the protagonists in the notorious duel which resulted in Hamilton's death. The bugle blown to sound the charge of the Light Brigade was blown again for the charge scene in *Balaclava* (GB 28), while the golden spike which united the Union Pacific and Central Pacific Railroads at Promontory Point, Utah in 1869 was used for the reconstruction of the episode in *Union Pacific* (US 39). More recently the silver candlesticks in the Boston home of Civil War commander Col. Robert Gould Shaw (Matthew Broderick) in *Glory* (US 90) were Col. Shaw's own. Perhaps the most poignant example is of the toys belonging to the Tsarevitch Alexei in *Assassination of the Tsar* (GB/USSR 91), which were the real toys owned by the doomed heir to the Romanov throne. They were lent for the production by the Leningrad Museum.

☆ In his last screen role as *The Brute Man* (US 46), Rondo Hatton played a formerly handsome scientist who turns into a hideously deformed killer after acid is thrown in his face. His distorted features were not attributable to the art of make-up. A formerly handsome actor, he was suffering from the rare disfiguring disease acromegaly. It killed him not long after he completed the distastefully exploitive feature for Universal.

☆ The gaol drama *Riot* (US 68), starring Gene Hackman and Jim Brown, was filmed at the Arizona State Penitentiary with the real Governor, warders and cons playing themselves. The prisoners in

Sylvester Stallone's *Lock Up* (US 90), about a Rambo clone doing time, were also the real thing, inmates of East Jersey State Prison where the picture was shot. Payment for their services was made not in cash but in the form of an outdoor athletics track for their use. On the other side of the wall the Australian picture *Malpractice* (Aus 89), about a medical malpractice suit, had the legal eagles portrayed by real-life lawyers.

☆ The scene in which Lillian Gish is whipped by a viscious hun in *Hearts of the World* (US 18) was enacted with such ferocity that Mrs Gish was horrified to find her daughter's slender back covered in weals when Lillian was bathing that night.

☆ Vanessa Redgrave is another who does not believe in simulating when the screen can show reality. The stinging slap across the face she delivered to 12-year-old Zane Rockenbaugh in *The Ballad of the Sad Cafe* (US/GB 91) was not, like most screen punches, pulled. Unfortunately for young Mr Rockenbaugh the scene requried six takes.

☆ *Attack of the Killer Tomatoes* (US 78) was a science fiction comedy with intentionally crude special effects. One effect, of a helicopter crashing, did look convincing though—it was an unscripted accident.

☆ Forty years after sex had first been simulated on screen in *Extase* (Cz 33), the real thing was to be seen in the love scenes between Julie Christie and Donald Sutherland in *Don't Look Now* (GB 73). Since then Miou Miou and Gerard Depardieu have been seen making out in *Making Out/Les Valseuses*

The cons watching Sly Stallone getting mud on his face in the prison drama *Lock Up* (US 90) were real inmates of Arizona State Penitentiary.

Kenneth Branagh was determined not to glamorise the Battle of Agincourt in his version of *Henry V* (GB 89). He filmed in poor light in a muddy field to capture the historical atmosphere of the conflict—it had rained daily for 11 days when the battle took place in 1415. (*British Film Institute*)

(Fr 74), Jessica Lange and Jack Nicholson in *The Postman Always Rings Twice* (US 81), Maud Adams and Bruce Dern in *Tattoo* (US 81), and Beatrice Dalle and Jean-Hughes Anglade in *Betty Blue* (Fr 86). In most of these cases it was probably the heat of the moment, but the activity shown in the X-rated *Wild Orchid* (US 89) seems to have been deliberate. Speaking of the controversial sex scenes between 37-year-old Mickey Rourke and 19-year-old newcomer Carré Otis, who had fallen in love on set, as 'real and tasteful', producer Mark Damon explained: 'We thought it was a great idea to use this chemistry between them.' The on-screen couplings in the orgy scenes of Bob Guccione's *Caligula* (US 80) turned out to be a less great idea. The female partners were models contracted to Guccione's *Penthouse* magazine, including 1975 Pet of the Year Marjorie Lee Thoreson. In a 1990 suit against Guccione the Supreme Court accepted Miss Thoreson's plea that *Caligula* had done irreparable harm to her acting career and awarded her $4.06 million damages.

☆ Svelte Claudette Colbert was ordered to put on 15 lb for her title role in *Cleopatra* (US 34), because Cecil B. DeMille's team of historical researchers thought there was evidence that the Egyptian queen had a generously rounded figure. No research was needed to establish that middleweight champion Jake La Motta became a bloated slob after his retirement from the ring. For these latter scenes of the La Motta biopic *Raging Bull* (US 80), the trim Robert De Niro force-fed himself until his body had an extra 50 lb of fat and flab.

☆ There are occasions when unreality in historical films cannot be avoided. The Battle of Agincourt in Laurence Olivier's classic *Henry V* (GB 44) was shot in brilliant sunshine because early Technicolor cameras could not be used in poor light. In reality it had rained almost non-stop for 11 days when the great conflict between the French and English armies took place in 1415. But Kenneth Branagh's 1989 remake was true to history—he stopped shooting whenever the sun came out.

☆ There were occasions when the real article was not enough to create the illusion of actuality. D. W. Griffith engaged a genuine evangelist to play upon the emotions of the crowd at the camp-meeting in *True-Heart Suzie* (US 19). The hard-boiled extras composing the crowd remained steadfastly unmoved until Griffith himself took the place of the evangelist on the rostrum. The director preached for an hour until he had brought the crowd to the finest pitch of religious fervour ever caught on screen.

☆ Nor did real events always measure up to what Hollywood could simulate. When one of the last great overland cattle drives of the American West took place in 1924, Paramount sent cameramen to record the episode for a western epic then in production, *North of '36* (US 24). Alas, the real west lacked the gloss of the Hollywood version. The cowboys' clothes were not in keeping with the more colourful variety sported by Hollywood celluloid cowboys, the waggons were drawn by plodding oxen instead of horses, and the horses ridden by the cowboys were less spirited than the trained animals of Hollywood. Only the cattle herd itself looked right. The rest was adapted according to Paramount's vision of the real West, with Hollywood extras replacing the genuine cowboys.

☆ In *The Fabulous Texan* (US 47) there was a scene in which Indians send smoke signals. Wanting to ensure authenticity, director Edward Ludwig recruited some real Indians from a reservation to give technical advice. When the scene had been successfully shot he asked them if the art had been passed down by the elders of the tribe. They shook their heads. 'How did you learn it then?', he asked. 'Easy', said one. 'We've seen it done on the movies.'

☆ Heroin is not difficult to simulate in a film, but in *Traffik* (GB/FRG/Pak 89, TVM) it was the real thing. Benazir Bhutto's new administration in Pakistan bent over backwards to assist the film-makers, including providing large quantities of authentic heroin which had been seized from drug traffickers. It was burned after the shoot.

☆ *Crossing Delancey* (US 89) is based on Susan Sandler's autobiographical play about her relationship with her Jewish grandmother. The granddaughter (Amy Irving) lives on the classy Upper West Side of Manhattan, her grandmother on the Lower East Side. After an exhaustive search for an actress who could play the grandmother with fidelity, the part went to Polish-born Reizl Bozyk. Only after she had been cast in the role was it revealed that Mrs Bozyk lives in the same Lower East Side apartment block that used to be the home of Susan Sandler's grandmother.

☆ Watching the rushes of his Humphrey Bogart gangster movie *Marked Woman* (US 37), producer Hal Wallis objected to the presence of an insignificant and puny looking extra among the gangland tough-guys. He asked director Lloyd Bacon why he had used an actor who looked so unlike a mobster. The mild little man was not an actor, Bacon explained. He was a member of the Lucky Luciano gang who had been cast to add realism.

☆ Reality sometimes goes beyond what the director had intended. When Jean-Paul Belmondo appeared as a boxer for the first of many times on screen, in *L'Aîné des Ferchaux* (Fr 62), he was knocked out— for real—by French champion Anzel.

☆ And it sometimes extends beyond the demands of the script. Although the screenplay for *Vampire's Kiss* (US 90) required only that he swallow a raw egg, wild-man-of-movies Nicholas Cage, known for extravagant behaviour both on and off set, decided that the scene would be more dramatic if he swallowed a live cockroach. 'I wanted there to be a special moment in the film which would really shock', he explained. 'My body was telling me not to do it, but I swallowed a glass of vodka and put the thing straight in my mouth. When I eventually saw *Vampire's Kiss* with an audience and heard their reaction, I knew it had been worth it. That was something they won't forget.'

STUDIOS

The first film studio in the world was Thomas Edison's *Black Maria*, a frame building covered in black roofing-paper, built at the Edison Laboratories in West Orange, NJ, and completed at a cost of $637.67 on 1 February 1893. Here Edison made short vaudeville-act films for use in his Kinetoscope, a peep-show machine designed for amusement arcades. The building was so constructed that it could be revolved to face the direction of the sun.

Reizl Bozyk (left) as an authentic Jewish grandmother in *Crossing Delancey* (US 89). By coincidence she lived in the same building on the Lower East Side as the real-life character she portrayed.

The first studio in Europe and the first in the world in which films were made by artificial light was opened by Oskar Messter at 94a Friedrich Strasse, Berlin in November 1896. For illumination Messter used four Körting & Matthiessen 50-amp arc-lamps on portable stands. His earliest productions by artificial light included *From Tears to Laughter* (Ger 96) and *Lightning Artist Zigg* (Ger 96). The first artificially lit studio in the USA, the Biograph Studio at 11 East 14th Street, New York, was not opened until 1903.

The first film studio in Britain was built at the back of the Tivoli Theatre in the Strand in 1897 by the Mutosope & Biograph Co. Like Edison's *Black Maria*, the studio was mounted on a cup-and-ball fixture that enabled it to be turned in the direction of the sun. It could also be rocked to and fro for 'storm at sea' sequences and similar effects. The glass panels that made up the sides of the studio could be dismantled for 'outdoor' scenes.

The first purpose-built sound stage was Stage Three at Warner Bros Studios, Sunset Boulevard, Hollywood, erected in April 1927. Shooting of *The Jazz Singer* (US 27) commenced on Stage Three the following month.

The largest film studio in the world is Universal City, California, whose 34 sound stages and other buildings cover an area of 420 acres. As many as 6000 staff are employed at times of peak production. Built by Carl Laemmle, the studio was originally opened on a 230-acre lot on 15 March 1915 and had the unique distinction of being a municipality in its own right. Besides the outdoor stages, indoor studio, prop stores, processing labs, zoo and stables, Universal City had its own Town Hall, fire station and police department.

The largest studio stage in the world is the 007 stage at Pinewood Studios, Buckinghamshire, England, which was built in 1976 at a cost of £350,000. It is 336 ft long by 139 ft wide and 41 ft high. Designed by Ken Adam and Michael Brown, the stage was originally built for the James Bond film *The Spy Who Loved Me* (GB 77) and accommodated 1.2 million gallons of water, a full-scale 600,000-ton oil-tanker and three nuclear submarines. The 007 stage is owned by United Artists and Eon Productions and is rented out to other film production companies.

During World War II Pinewood Studios were turned into an outstation of the Royal Mint. According to cynics, this was the only time Pinewood made any money.

STUNTS

The first stuntman was ex-US cavalryman Frank Hanaway, who won himself a part in Edwin S. Porter's *The Great Train Robbery* (US 03) for his ability to fall off a horse without injuring himself.

The first professional stuntwoman was Helen Gibson, who doubled for Helen Holmes in the first 26 episodes of Kalem's serial *The Hazards of Helen* (US 14). Trained as a trick rider and married to cowboy star Hoot Gibson, she was chosen for her ability to do stunts on horseback but proved herself adept at other hair-raising exploits, including jumping a speeding motorcycle on to a fast moving locomotive. Unlike most stunt people, she achieved stardom in her own right, replacing Helen Holmes' successor Elsie McCleod as the lead in the long-running *Hazards of Helen*. Generally at this period,

Jumping through windows could be chancier if they were not made from clear sugar, as in this scene from *Texas Chainsaw Massacre* (US 74). (*British Film Institute*)

In the early days of film-making the Edison Co. used to pay for jump stunts by the foot. Spencer Gordon Bennet recalled jumping off a 62½ ft cliff in 1912 and receiving $62.50 precisely—plus a repeat $62.50 when the director decided he wanted a retake.

actresses were doubled in dangerous scenes by men in drag. Since the introduction of the Sex Equality Act in the USA, it is illegal for stuntmen to double for actresses unless no stuntwoman is willing to take on the assignment.

The Stuntman as Star

The claim made by many stars that they performed all their own stunts seldom amounted to anything more than press agents' ballyhoo. Apart from Helen Gibson (see above), the only star who really did all his own stunting was Richard Talmadge (1896–). The reason was twofold—he was an accomplished stuntman himself; and he never became so valuable a star that the studio feared the consequences if he was put out of action. Perhaps the star most often trumpeted as his own stuntman was Douglas Fairbanks; ironically, it was Talmadge who did most of his stunts, including the celebrated slide down the sail in *The Black Pirate* (US 26). Present-day stars also like to cultivate a macho image by pretending to do stunts performed by professionals. No doubts need to be entertained though about Mel Gibson's claim to have done his own stunts in *Mad Max Beyond Thunderdrome* (Aus 85), since the credits list his name twice: as leading man and as one of the stuntmen.

Stunting at MGM *c.* 1928, from an unlabelled publicity shot. Does anyone know the title of the film or the identity of the flying artiste? And why is he taking a dive over the car? (*Popperfoto*)

The only stuntman who stands in for children is Bobby Porter, who at 4 ft 9 in often substitutes for little girls as well as little boys. Among his more spectacular appearances was the title role of *Annie* (US 82), in which he hung suspended from a 20-storey high drawbridge as stand-in for 9-year-old Aileen Quinn.

The greatest height from which a stuntman has leaped in a free fall was 1170 ft, a stunt performed for *Highpoint* (Can 79) by Los Angeles parachutist Dar Robinson from a ledge at the summit of the CN

> Clint Eastwood's *The Rookie* (US 90) had the rare distinction of featuring more stuntmen than actors—indeed more than twice as many. The men of action outnumbered the ones who just do the talking by 87 to 37.

Tower in Toronto. Robinson opened his 'chute out of shot at a height estimated at 300–350 ft from the ground after six seconds of freefalling, one of reaction time and two for releasing the canopy. The fee, an unconfirmed $150,000, is believed to be a **record payment for a single stunt**.

The highest jump without a parachute by a movie stuntman was 232 ft by A. J. Bakunas, who was doubling for Burt Reynolds in *Hooper* (US 78). He fell on to an air mattress.

The longest leap in a car propelled by its own engine was performed by stunt driver Gary Davis in *Smokey and the Bandit II* (US 81). Davis raced a stripped-down Plymouth up a ramp butted up

against the back of a double-tiered car-carrier at 80 mph and described a trajectory of 163 ft before landing safely on the desert floor.

TAKES AND RETAKES

The longest take in a movie comprises the whole of the second reel of Andy Warhol's *Blue Movie* (US 68) and consists of a 35-minute uninterrupted scene of Viva and Louis Waldon making love.

The longest take in a commercially-made feature movie is a 14-minute uninterrupted monologue by Lionel Barrymore in *A Free Soul* (US 31). Since a reel of camera film only lasts ten minutes, the take was achieved by using more than one camera. Alfred Hitchcock's *Rope* (US 48), the story of two homosexual college men who kill a third for the intellectual thrill of it, was shot in eight ten-minute takes (apart from one cut to the housekeeper in the first reel). The effect was of one continuous shot, since the action of the story occupied the same period of time—80 minutes—as the length of the film.

The greatest number of retakes of a single scene was 342 for the episode in Chaplin's *City Lights* (US 31) in which a blind flower girl (Virginia Cherrill) sells the little tramp a flower under the misapprehension he is a rich man. Chaplin kept reshooting the scene because he was unable to find a satisfactory way of making the blind girl think that the tramp was wealthy. Finally he found a simple yet perfect solution. Chaplin is trying to cross a street jammed with traffic. Unable to reach the sidewalk, he sees a limousine parked by the kerb, gets in at one door and out at the other. The girl hears the door close and assumes it is the owner getting out. She hands him the flower, takes his last quarter, and keeps the change.

  Difficult dialogue is the most common reason for prodigious numbers of retakes. One scene in *Dr Strangelove* (GB 63) was shot 48 times because Sterling Hayden, playing the mad base commander, fluffed his line 47 times. Marilyn Monroe did 59 takes of a scene in *Some Like It Hot* (US 59) in which her only line of dialogue was 'Where's the Bourbon?'. Hollywood rebel Dennis Hopper had an early run-in with veteran director Henry Hathaway when he was made to repeat a scene in *From Hell to Texas* (US 57) no less than 85 times. 'Kid', Hathaway growled at the moody method actor after the 85th take, 'you'll never work in this town again'. It was in fact some ten years before Hopper was offered another worthwhile role. Robert Mitchum claims he stopped taking Hollywood seriously when it took his co-star Greer Garson 125 times to say 'No' in *Desire Me* (US 47). (The picture was such a catastrophe it was released without director credit.)

John Mills declares he was 'drunk as a Lord' after the eighth take of this scene in *Ice Cold in Alex* (GB 58). Never mind, the money from the lager commercials must have made up for it. (*British Film Institute*)

The record number of takes for a dialogue sequence is claimed to be the 127 demanded by Stanley Kubrick of a scene with Shelley Duval in *The Shining* (US 80).

The title of *Ice Cold in Alex* (GB 58) refers to the iced lager dreamed of by the parched members of a long-range desert patrol operating behind the lines in World War II. They survive to reach Alexandria and the cherished libation. John Mills, playing the patrol leader, was required to down the tall glass of lager in one draft. The props man had supplied ginger ale as a substitute, but it did not look right and real Carlsberg was used instead. After eight takes Mills had consumed a gallon of the stuff and was, in his own words, as drunk as a lord. He recalled spending the rest of the day bumping into scenery and props.

One-Shot Directors

At the other end of the scale, there have been those who earned themselves reputations as 'one-shot' directors, notably G. W. Pabst, Cecil B. DeMille, W. S. 'One-Shot Woody' van Dyke, and D. W. Griffith. According to Lillian Gish, Griffith's masterwork *The Birth of a Nation* (US 15) was made with only one retake of one scene. The single repeat shot was necessitated, much to Mr Griffith's displeasure, by the fact that Mae Marsh forgot to drape herself in the Confederate flag for her suicide scene.

*W*OMEN

The first film made with an all-female crew was a comedy titled *Sally Sallies Forth* (GB 28), produced with a women-only cast by the lady members of the Amateur Cinema Association. The 'directress' (as she was called) was Frances Lascott, the camerawoman Mrs A. E. Low and the title role—an inexperienced maidservant who disrupts a pompous tea party—played by Sadie Andrews. It was premièred at the Camera Club on 12 December 1928 and *Film Weekly*'s male critic declared it 'a rattling good effort'.

The first professionally-made feature by women was Savithri Ganesh's *Chinnari Pappalu* (Ind 67), produced and scripted in Telegu by Mrs Sarojini Madhusudana Rao, with music by Mrs P. Leela and art direction by Mrs Mohana. **America's first *femme* production** was *The Waiting Room* (US 73), a psychological drama produced and directed by Karen Sperling (grand-daughter of Harry Warner) and Doro Bachrach. The 32-woman crew was selected from 300 applicants attracted from California, Canada, Europe and New York (where the film was made).

*B*LUNDERS

The most frequent mistakes made in movies are microphone booms visible within the frame, and camera crews reflected in plate-glass windows. Other blunders are legion. Some of the choicest include:

☆ Balthazar Getty as Ralph uses the short-sighted Piggy's glasses to light a fire from the sun in Harry Hook's remake of *Lord of the Flies* (US 90). But glasses to correct short-sightedness do not converge rays of light and in reality the fire would have remained unlit. The error, though, has a literary legitimacy. William Golding made the same mistake in the original novel.

☆ Tom Cruise may have looked every bimbette's idea of a hunk naval pilot in *Top Gun* (US 86), but in fact he was not tall enough for the role. At 5 ft 9 in he is an inch short of the minimum height requirement for officers of the US Navy.

☆ *The Third Man* (GB 49) also features the third cat, though only one cat is in the story. The three separate felines used to portray the puss who 'only liked Harry Lime' each differed in size and colouring.

☆ A British GPO manhole cover is discernible in 1870s Massachusetts in *Heaven's Gate* (US 80).

☆ The bewitching Julia Roberts kicks off her shoes at a polo match in *Pretty Woman* (US 90), revealing the fact—nothing to do with the storyline—that

This fire in *Lord of the Flies* would have remained unlit. Glasses for short-sightedness like Piggy's do not converge the sun's rays.

each of her big toes is encircled by sticking plaster. Arriving back at her hotel she sheds her shoes again and a close-up of her bare feet betrays the absence of the plasters.

☆ In the Reginald Owen version of *A Study in Scarlet* (US 33), Sherlock Holmes resides at 221A (not B) Baker Street.

☆ Despite the gritty realism of *The Krays* (GB 90), the opening scenes contain a curiously elementary error. At the baptism of the twins, they are christened Ronald *Kray* and Reginald *Kray*. Since the sacrament is for the bestowal of Christian names, the surname is never used.

☆ The renegade Southerners engaged in gang rape in *The Scavengers* (US 71), set in the 1860s, have zip flies on their trousers.

☆ In *A Rare Breed* (US 84), an Italian kidnapper demands two million lira in ransom money, which is said to be worth $350,000. In fact at the time the film was made, it was equivalent to about $350.

☆ Trevor Howard and Celia Johnson as the guilt-ridden Home Counties lovers of *Brief Encounter* (GB 45) are revealed to be a long way from Kent when a Yorkshire signpost is momentarily glimpsed in the background.

☆ The teenage boy played by Charlie Shattner in *The Delinquents* (Aus 89) receives a severe whipping from his brutal stepfather. The same evening he strips down to make love to g.f. Kylie Minogue and there is not a mark on his body.

☆ Adventure caper *Jungle Raiders* (It 86) opens with a title reading 'Malaysia, 1938'. There was no such country at that date. The name 'Malaysia' was

Both these felines were supposed to be one and the same cat who 'only liked Harry Lime' in *The Third Man* (GB 49). (*British Film Institute*)

only adopted by the Federated Malay States in 1963.

☆ A character in Basil Dearden's *The Mind Benders* (GB 63) commits suicide by leaping from the right-hand side of a train. The body is then seen lying on the left-hand side of the track.

☆ The forest of Cannon's *Rumpelstiltskin* (US 87), set in the Mittel-Europa of traditional fairy tales, is curiously composed of eucalyptus trees. Location shooting in Israel accounts for the solecism.

☆ In *Ratboy* (US 86), the eponymous alien is seen being driven through Hollywood by black hipster Manny. Shots taken from Ratboy's side of the car show Hollywood Boulevard in the background, while those taken from Manny's side reveal Sunset Boulevard.

☆ Fluffed lines seldom survive on the soundtrack, as it is easy enough to correct them. Notable exception is Cary Grant's spondurgle in Hitchcock's *North by Northwest* (US 59), when he picks up a photograph from a dressing table and says 'Look who's here . . . Our friend who's *assembling* the General Assembly this afternoon'. (The script said *addressing*.)

☆ Yves Montand, playing himself in *Trois places pour le 26* (Fr 88), beds a young actress who is playing her own mother, a former flame of Montand's, in a musical show about the actor's early life. Plot device of the fictional story hinges on the fact that the girl is alleged to be Montand's daughter. As his romance with her mother is shown as having begun and ended some 40 years earlier, and the girl is supposed to be 22, so much for 'is she, isn't she?'.

☆ Philip Marlowe's office window in *Lady in the Lake* (US 46) has his name inscribed on it. Evidently the art director was not familiar with the book. The first name of Raymond Chandler's private eye is spelt on the window as Phillip with two l's.

☆ The gung-ho flagwagger *The Marines Are Here* (US 38) showed a gallant marine scaling a very high wall by climbing on the shoulders of his buddy. The next scene shows him dropping to the ground on the other side—closely followed by his buddy, who has apparently scaled the wall unassisted.

☆ According to locksmith and safe expert Mike Cosnerford, the safecracking scenes in *Breaking In* (US 89) are riddled with inaccuracies. Burt Reynolds says of one safe he robs that it has the highest security rating possible, yet he also refers to it having been installed in 1904 'when the technology was non-existent compared with today'. Using nitroglycerine in the way shown would not have blown open any safe. Instead of dripping a little into the keyhole, the approved safecrackers' technique, the thieves put it on the side of the safe. This, reports Mr Cosnerford, would buckle the safe and jam it absolutely solid.

☆ In Hitchcock's *Family Plot* (US 76), Bruce Dern takes the top off a catsup bottle twice in successive shots.

☆ Michael Caine plays a character whose son is being held hostage in a building from which he can see two windmills in *The Black Windmill* (GB 73). But it transpires that he is imprisoned in the black windmill of the title, so he would only have seen the other. And when Michael Caine effects the daring rescue, it is from the second, white windmill.

☆ In *Annie* (US 82) Daddy Warbucks takes Annie to see *Camille* (US 36) at Radio City Music Hall in 1933.

Spot the spelling mistake. And to give you a clue it isn't CLEWS—that's OK Stateside. (*British Film Institute*)

☆ Twenty minutes into *Kelly's Heroes* (US 70) Clint Eastwood is seen in a jeep surrounded by soldiers. And also by two embarrassed studio technicians wearing striped shirts who creep stealthily out of camera.

☆ In *The Accused* (US 89) Jodie Foster put in an Oscar-winning performance as a spunky working class rape victim. The film starts with a hysterical Foster escaping the bar in which the crime has been committed and concludes with a flashback to her arrival at the bar and the subsequent harrowing events. Tension may be too great for any but the most observant to note that the assaulted Miss Foster flees the scene of the gang rape shod in flat white pumps, but had entered the bar in black high heels.

☆ Moviegoers confronted with any filmic version of Genesis should spare a glance at Adam's midriff. If, as in *The Bible* (US 66), he has a navel—well, he shouldn't, should he?

☆ The eponymous Britisher of Nana Dzhordzhadze's *My English Grandfather* (USSR 86) speaks with a Texas accent strong enough to pass muster in *Dallas*. Apparently the only English-speaker available for post-synching, a young American tourist in Tbilisi, swore to the non-English-speaking Dzhordzhadze that his accent was puckka British. (The UK distributor made it a condition of the contract that the grandfather's role should be redubbed in the Queen's English.)

☆ A newspaper featured in *A Tale of Two Cities* (US 36), set at the time of the French Revolution, shows 'a despatch from Reuter's'. Paul Reuter (1816–99), founder of the worldwide press bureau, was not even born at the time.

☆ All the cars seen in the London street scenes in the Danny Kaye movie *Knock on Wood* (US 54) are left-hand drive. In another Danny Kaye film, *Merry Andrew* (US 58), a London bus is progressing along the right-hand side of the road.

☆ *Indiana Jones and the Last Crusade* (US 89) is cherished by blunder buffs. Set in 1938, the film has Indy crossing the Atlantic by airliner a year before the first transatlantic passenger service began, and starting back by airship a year after transatlantic airship services ceased. In the airport lounge two passengers are reading identical copies of the same German newspaper—fine except that the papers date from 1918, twenty years earlier. But the classic 'how-come-no-one-noticed-that-before-release' humdinger of a howler is an intertitle reading 'The Republic of Hatay', followed immediately by a scene in which the ruler of the 'republic' is addressed as Your Royal Highness.

☆ When Anthony Dowson attempts to throttle Grace Kelly in Hitchcock's *Dial M for Murder* (US 54), she picks up a pair of scissors and stabs him in the back. Even before she strikes, though, a pair of scissors already embedded in his back is momentarily visible to any keen-eyed member of the audience.

☆ Assistant D.A. Timothy Hutton is asked why he chose Brooklyn Law School over St John's in Sidney Lumet's *Q and A* (US 90). He explains that his father did not like the political views of the Jesuits. St John's is a Roman Catholic school, but not Jesuit; it is run by priests of the Vincentian Order.

☆ The action of *The Sound of Music* (US 65) is set in the 1930s, yet in one scene an orange box can be discerned stamped 'Produce of Israel'.

☆ Anachronisms are usually visual or in the dialogue. In *The Draughtsman's Contract* (GB 83) it is a background noise that dispels, at least for ornithologists, the illusion of the film's 17th-century setting. The gentle cooing of a collared dove is not a sound that would have fallen on Jacobean ears. The species was unknown in Britain until 1955.

EIGHT

COLOUR, SOUND AND SCOPE

COLOUR

The first commercially successful natural colour process was two-colour Kinemacolor, developed by George Albert Smith of Brighton for the Urban Trading Co., London. Smith made his first colour film by this process outside his house at Southwick, Brighton, in July 1906. It showed his two children playing on the lawn, the boy dressed in blue and waving a Union Jack, the girl in white with a pink sash.

The first commercially produced film in natural colour was G. A. Smith's *A Visit to the Seaside* (GB 08), an eight-minute short featuring the White Coons pierrot troupe and the Band of the Cameron Highlanders which was trade shown in September 1908. Taken at Brighton, it showed children paddling and eating ice cream, a pretty girl falling out of a boat, and men peeping at the Bathing Belles changing in their bathing machines. The first public presentation of Kinemacolor before a paying audience took place at the Palace Theatre, Shaftesbury Avenue, on 26 February 1909 and consisted of 21 short films, including scenes taken at Aldershot, sailing at Southwick, the Water Carnival at Villefranche and the Children's Battle of Flowers at Nice.

The first dramatic film in natural colour was the Kinemacolor production *Checkmated* (GB 10), directed by Theo Bouwmeester, who has also played the lead role of Napoleon. **The first American dramatic film in natural colour** was Eclair's Kinemacolor production *La Tosca* (US 12), with Lillian Russell. A total of 54 dramatic films were produced in Kinemacolor in Britain from 1910–12. In the USA there were only three dramatic productions in Kinemacolor besides *La Tosca*. These were

Mission Bells (US 13), *The Rivals* (US 13) and *The Scarlet Letter* (US 13), the latter starring D. W. Griffith's wife Linda Arvidson.

The first full-length feature film in colour was a five-reel melodrama, *The World, the Flesh and the Devil* (GB 14), produced by the Union Jack Co. in Kinemacolor from the play by Laurence Cowen. Starring Frank Esmond and Stella St Audrie, it opened at the Holborn Empire on 9 April 1914 billed as 'A £10,000 Picture Play in Actual Colours' in 'four parts and 120 scenes'. Like most of the Kinemacolor dramas, the acting and direction (F. Martin Thornton) were execrable, the colour impressive.

Kinemacolor was an additive process in which both filming and projection were done through red and green filters. The drawbacks were the cost of the special projector used and the wear on the film, which passed through the projector at twice normal speed. Nevertheless, it was installed at some 300 cinemas in Britain and achieved success overseas as well, notably in the United States and Japan. On the production side Kinemacolor was limited in its application because it could not be used for indoor work. There was also a virtue to this, since it encouraged location shooting at a time when black-and-white productions were becoming progressively more studio-bound. One enterprising Kinemacolor venture was **the first colour western**, Theo Bouwmeester's *Fate* (GB 11), set in Texas but filmed in Sussex! Kinemacolor was particularly well suited for films of pageantry, two of the most successful releases being a newsreel of King Edward VII's funeral in May 1910—at which no less than nine kings were present—and a spectacular two-hour presentation of the 1912 Delhi Durbar. Others included the Coronation of King

The first all-colour feature film, 1914.

George V, the Naval Review of June 1911 and the Investiture of the Prince of Wales at Caernarvon. Production came to a halt when Charles Urban, the guiding spirit behind Kinemacolor, left for the US in 1914 to propagate the British war effort through films.

The first colour talkie was Frans Lundberg Films' *Vals ur Solstrålen* (Swe 11), directed by Ernst Dittmer and starring Rosa Grünberg, which was premièred at the Stora Biografteatern in Malmö, Sweden, on 1 May 1911. The 215 ft short was made by the Biophon synchronized disc sound process. The colour process is not recorded, but it was probably stencilled.

The first feature-length sound film in colour was MGM's two-colour Technicolor production *The Viking* (US 28), directed by R. William Neill with Donald Crisp as Leif Ericsson, the legendary discoverer of America, and Pauline Starke as the lovely Helga. It was premièred on 2 November 1928 with synchronized score and sound effects.

The first all-colour talkie feature was Warner Bros' two-colour Technicolor musical *On With the Show* (US 29), directed by Alan Crosland with Betty Compson and Joe E. Brown, which was premièred at the Winter Garden, New York, on 28 May 1929.

The first British talking feature in colour was Talkicolor's *Knowing Men* (GB 30), produced, directed and scripted by Elinor Glyn from her own novel in French and English versions with Danish star Carl Brisson playing opposite Austrian actress Elissa Landi. Although made in colour, the film was released in black-and-white. The first to be released in colour was BIP's *A Romance of Seville* (GB 29), which was originally shown as a silent in 1929 but had sound added in July 1930. Colour process unknown. The first film made as a talkie to be released in colour was BIP's *Harmony Heaven* (GB 30), a musical about a composer (Stuart Hall) who wins fame and the hand of his girl (Polly Ward) despite the attentions of a flirtatious socialite (Trilby Clark).

The first Technicolor film was *The Gulf Between* (US 17), a five-reeler starring Grace Darmond and Niles Welch, produced by the Technicolor Motion Picture Corporation in a two-colour additive process and premièred at the Aeolian Hall, New York, on 21 September 1917. It was **the first full-length**

Kodak's Eastman Color SP print film, the stock used for most colour features from the mid-fifties onwards, had a life of seven to ten years before the colour faded. A new film stock, Eastman Color Print film 5384, introduced as standard for professional colour work in 1982, has a life of 90 to 100 years.

---

colour feature produced in the USA and the third in the world.

The first feature in subtractive Technicolor was Chester Franklin's *The Toll of the Sea* (US 22), starring Anna May Wong, which was premièred at the Rialto Theater, New York, on 26 November 1922. **The first Technicolor interior shots** were taken for a colour sequence in *Cytherea* (US 24).

The colour values of Van Gogh's celebrated painting of a cornfield are not true to nature, according to director Vincente Minnelli. When he made *Lust for Life* (US 56), there was a scene in which Van Gogh is seen painting the picture (the original was used in the film), followed by a dissolve to an actual cornfield. In order to make the real corn match the colours rendered in the painting, Minnelli was obliged to spray the entire field with golden dye.

The Technicolor Motion Picture Corporation had been founded by Dr Herbert Kalmus of the Massachusetts Institute of Technology in 1915. The earliest Technicolor process was not unlike Kinemacolor and depended on the use of filters on both camera and projector. Following his development of a reasonably successful two-colour subtractive process, Dr Kalmus took Technicolor to Hollywood in 1923. The main problem was that the double-coated film was given to cupping and scratched more easily than monochrome. To most producers the cost at 27¢ a foot was prohibitive, compared with 8¢ a foot for monochrome stock, but with the coming of talkies the feverish search for novelty by the major studios encouraged its use and 45 Technicolor features were made in the three years 1929–31.

The first film in three-colour Technicolor was Walt Disney's Silly Symphony cartoon *Flowers and Trees* (US 32), premièred 17 July 1932 at Grauman's Chinese Theater, Hollywood. The first dramatic subject was *La Cucaracha* (US 34), released at the RKO-Hill Street Theater, Los Angeles, on 15 November 1934 and the first three-colour Technicolor sequence in a feature was in MGM's *The Cat and the Fiddle* (US 34).

The first feature made entirely in three-colour Technicolor was Rouben Mamoulian's *Becky Sharp* (US 35) with Cedric Hardwicke and Miriam Hopkins. Not everyone appreciated the innovation. A critic for *Liberty* magazine wrote that the performers looked like 'boiled salmon dipped in mayonnaise'. **The first in Britain** was *Wings of the Morning* (GB 37), a race-track drama starring Henry Fonda and French actress Annabella, which opened at the Capitol, Haymarket, in May 1937.

The first three-colour film stock which could be used in any standard 35 mm camera was Technicolor Monopack, which was used for the first time on the exterior shots of *Lassie Come Home* (US 42). Formerly special cameras had to be rented for colour work.

The most widely used colour process: Technicolor held almost a monopoly of the three-colour field from 1932 until 1952, when *Royal Journey* (Can 52) was released in Kodak's new Eastman Color process. Within three years Technicolor had fallen into second place, with 112 films being produced in Eastman Color in 1955 against 90 in Technicolor. Eastman Color is now used for virtually all colour films produced in the West. Metrocolor, Warnercolor and De Luxe are all processes using Eastman Color stock and films credited 'Color by Technicolor' are generally made with Eastman Color negative but printed by Technicolor laboratories.

The shortest colour sequence consisted of two frames of Alfred Hitchcock's *Spellbound* (US 45). Towards the end of the film, a split-second scene of a gun blast was presented in vivid red Technicolor.

Decline of Black-and-White Films

Not surprisingly the USA was the first country to produce more films in colour than black and white, with 157 out of a total of 237 full-length features being shot in colour in 1954. Rather more surprisingly, monochrome made something of a comeback in

COLOUR AND BLACK-AND-WHITE PRODUCTION IN THE US AND UK, 1920-70

	Full Colour		Part Colour		Black and White			
	US	UK	US	UK	US	%	UK	%
1920	0	0	0	0	797	100	155	100
1921	0	0	2	0	852	99.8	137	100
1922	2	1	0	1	746	99.7	108	98.2
1923	2	1	1	1	573	99.5	66	97.1
1924	1	1	1	0	577	99.7	48	98.0
1925	0	0	1	0	578	99.8	33	100
1926	1	0	8	0	731	98.8	33	100
1927	0	0	1	0	677	99.9	48	100
1928	1	0	2	0	638	99.5	80	100
1929	5	1	5	0	552	98.2	80	98.8
1930	14	1	14	1	481	94.2	73	97.3
1931	5	0	0	0	496	99.0	93	100
1932	1	0	0	0	488	99.8	110	100
1933	1	0	2	0	504	99.4	115	100
1934	0	0	3	0	477	99.4	145	100
1935	2	0	1	0	522	99.4	165	100
1936	4	0	0	0	518	99.2	192	100
1937	8	0	2	0	530	98.1	174	98.9
1938	10	3	0	0	445	97.8	131	97.8
1939	10	3	1	0	472	97.7	81	97.6
1940	16	1	1	0	460	96.4	49	98.0
1941	17	0	1	0	474	96.3	46	100
1942	15	1	0	0	473	96.9	38	97.4
1943	19	1	0	0	378	95.0	46	97.9
1944	26	1	1	0	374	92.3	34	97.1
1945	22	2	0	0	328	93.7	37	94.9
1946	30	6	0	0	348	92.1	35	85.4
1947	40	3	1	0	328	88.9	55	94.8
1948	58	7	0	0	308	84.2	67	90.5
1949	52	6	1	0	303	85.1	95	94.1
1950	61	5	0	0	322	84.1	76	93.8
1951	78	7	1	0	312	79.8	68	90.7
1952	108	14	0	0	216	66.7	87	86.1
1953	144	14	0	0	200	58.1	88	86.3
1954	157	32	0	0	80	33.8	78	70.9
1955	138	33	0	0	98	41.5	62	65.9
1956	134	35	0	0	139	50.9	56	61.5
1957	99	31	1	0	203	67.0	84	73.0
1958	91	23	2	0	164	63.8	88	79.3
1959	80	24	1	0	96	79.3	75	75.8
1960	77	20	0	0	74	49.0	90	81.8
1961	72	32	1	0	78	51.7	77	70.0
1962	67	25	1	0	60	46.9	101	80.2
1963	76	31	0	0	54	41.5	76	63.5
1964	80	34	0	0	58	42.0	41	54.7
1965	88	46	0	0	50	36.2	34	42.5
1966	115	58	0	0	24	17.3	11	15.9
1967	136	84	2	0	7	4.8	6	6.7
1968	170	72	1	0	9	5.0	1	1.4
1969	171	86	2	0	4	2.3	0	0
1970	227	103	3	0	1	0.4	3	2.8

Since 1970 nearly all production in the US and UK has been in colour.

the later 1950s, with nearly 80 per cent of 1959s releases being in black and white, but from 1962 onwards colour remained in the ascendant. The number of monochrome releases fell dramatically from year to year until in 1970 there was but a single black-and-white production. Elsewhere, the changeover took a little longer, delayed perhaps by a feeling that colour was inappropriate to naturalistic, 'social realism' films or to subjects of serious concern. In Britain colour became predominant in 1965, when 46 colour films were produced against only 34 monochrome. Only three years later monochrome production was down to a single picture, with 72 colour releases. 1969 was the first year in which British production was 100 per cent colour. France, long the bastion of grainy monochrome effects, had succumbed by 1967, when only four out of 120 films were shot in black and white. Japan had reached a 50–50 stage by 1965, but within three years the proportion of monochrome features had dropped to 25 per cent. Italy maintained some black-and-white feature productions up to 1968, when seven out of 153 films were shot in monochrome, but very few after that.

In the Far East the changeover was generally slower. Out of the total of 763 films produced in India in 1982, 43 were black and white. All Burmese films were black and white before 1983, the year a colour laboratory was established in Rangoon processing Fuji Colour.

The first feature film shot in black and white to be converted to full colour was *Yankee Doodle Dandy* (US 42), biopic of George M. Cohan starring James Cagney. The special prints with their computer-applied colour were released by MGM on 4 July 1985. 'Colorization', as it is known, has become a controversial issue in the industry, with many directors and stars vehemently opposed to the practice on the grounds that it diminishes the visual quality of films never intended to be in colour. Nevertheless, it appears to be popular with a large section of the public—the colorized version of *Miracle on 34th Street* (US 47) achieved the highest ratings of any film on US television in 1985. Color Systems Technology, the company which developed the system, claims that it goes to great trouble to preserve the integrity of the films given their treatment, even maintaining a research department whose sole function is to ascertain the true colour of props, buildings, vegetation, costumes and such physical attributes as hair and eyes.

SOUND

The first presentation of sound films before a paying audience was made by Oskar Messter at 21 Unter den Linden, Berlin, in September 1896. The sound system employed synchronized Berliner discs, but there is no record of the titles of the films or the performers in them. **The first artistes known to have performed in a sound film** were Giampetro and Fritzi Massary, who appeared in a scene from an operetta filmed by Max Skladanowsky, probably before the end of 1896.

The earliest known talking films were presented by Clément Maurice of the Gaumont Co. at the Phono-Cinéma-Théâtre of the Paris Exposition on 8 June 1900. They included: Sarah Bernhardt and Pierre Magnier in the duel scene from *Hamlet*, playing Hamlet and Laertes respectively; Coquelin in Rostrand's *Cyrano de Bergerac*; Coquelin and Mesdames Esquilar and Kervich in Molière's *Les Précieuses Ridicules*; Felicia Mallet, Mme Reichenberg and Gabrielle Réjane of the Comédie Française in scenes from *Madame Sans-Gêne* and *Ma Cousine*. In addition there were synchronized opera films and ballet films.

The earliest known talking film with original dialogue was *Lolotte* (Fr 00), a comedy written and directed by Henri Joly and premièred at the Théâtre de la Grande Roue at the Paris Exposition. The scene takes place in a hotel bedroom and is played by three characters, a newly-married couple and the patron of the hotel, the latter performed by Joly himself. The dialogue script survives.

The first sound films produced in Britain were a series of song subjects made by Walter Gibbons in the autumn of 1900 under the name of Phono-Bio-Tableaux Films. They included Vesta Tilley singing *The Midnight Son*, *Algy the Piccadilly Johnny* and *Louisiana Lou* and G. H. Chirgwin giving a soulful

Jacques Tati's classic debut film *Jour de fête* (Fr 49) was shot in two different versions—colour and black and white. Much to Tati's chagrin, the Thomsoncolor negative could not be converted into successful positive prints and the film had to be released in monochrome. For years he sought a solution to the problem, even going so far as to stencil-colour certain passages of the film for its reissue in 1963. A visit to the Technicolor Laboratories in London in 1967 proved unfruitful and no progress had been made by the time Tati died in 1982. Recently, however, a breakthrough has been made by the Eurocitel Laboratories at Joinville and his daughter, film editor Sophie Tatischeff, is making an inventory of the 65,000 ft of unedited colour negative in an attempt to reassemble the complete film in the same sequence as the black-and-white version. Clips already processed by Eurocitel were shown on the French television programme *Cinéma, Cinémas* in 1988 as a foretaste of what is hoped will be the realisation of Tati's dream 40 years on.

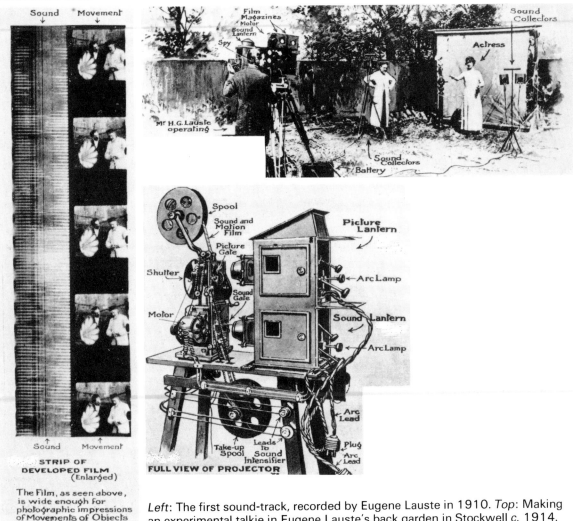

Left: The first sound-track, recorded by Eugene Lauste in 1910. *Top*: Making an experimental talkie in Eugene Lauste's back garden in Stockwell *c.* 1914. (*ILN*). *Above*: World's first talking projector by Eugene Lauste 1913.

rendering of *The Blind Boy*. There was also an actuality with sound effects titled *Turn Out the Fire Brigade*. **The earliest British talking film** was Hepworth's Vivaphone version of *Cinderella* (GB 13) with Gertie Potter.

The first sound-on-film process was patented by French-born Eugene Lauste of Stockwell, London, on 11 August 1906. It was not until 1910, however, that Lauste succeeded in recording and reproducing speech on film, employing an electromagnetic recorder and string galvanometer. He used a French gramophone record, selected at random, for the initial trial, and by coincidence the first words to be heard in the playback were 'J'entends très bien maintenant' ('I hear very well now'). A colleague in the film business, L. G. Egrot, recalled visiting Lauste at his home in Benedict Road about this time: 'He had already started building his camera to take pictures and sound together, the front part of

the camera allowing to test the different systems he was experimenting with for sound recording . . . Very often on a Sunday, a bandmaster friend of his, Mr Norris, would come along with his band and play in the garden of the house where, in 1911, Mr Lauste had had a wooden building erected as an experimenting studio. The machine was taken out, with all leads, some pictures would be made and some sound recorded.'

Lauste completed his sound-on-film projector and reproducing apparatus in 1913, and was about to embark on the commercial exploitation of the process when war broke out. In 1916 he went to the USA with the idea of obtaining financial backing, but the entry of America into the war the following year put an end to his hopes.

The first sound-on-film productions to be presented in public were shown at the Alhambra Kino in Berlin on 17 September 1922 before an invited audience of 1000 people. The films were made by the Tri-Ergon process developed by Joseph Engl, Joseph Massolle and Hans Vogt and included **the first sound-on-film dramatic talkie**. Titled *Der Brandstifter/The Arsonist* (Ger 22), and adapted from Von Heyermann's play of the same name, it had a cast of three with Erwin Baron playing seven of the nine parts. The other films were mainly orchestral with vocal accompaniment. Press reaction was mixed, criticism being made not so much against the level of technical achievement, but at the notion of talking films, which it was said would destroy the essential art of the motion picture—mime—and detract from the cinema's international appeal.

The first American sound-on-film motion picture was *Lincoln's Gettysburg Address* (US 22), a monologue delivered by Ellery Paine, made by Polish-born Prof. Joseph Tykocinski-Tykociner, research professor of electrical engineering at the University of Illinois, and presented in the Physics Building on 9 June 1922. The film was not released commercially.

The first presentation of sound-on-film productions before a paying audience took place at the Rialto Theater, New York, on 15 April 1923, when Lee De Forest showed a number of singing and musical shorts made by the Phonofilm process. The sound films formed a supporting programme to the main (silent) feature, *Bella Donna* (US 23) with Pola Negri. During the following 12 months, 34 cinemas in the eastern United States were wired for Phonofilm sound. The films made at the De Forest Studios between 1923 and 1927 included monologue numbers by Eddie Cantor, George Jessel and Chic Sale; dialogues between Gloria Swanson and Thomas Meighan and between Weber and Fields; Folkina's *Swan Dance*; playlets with Raymond Hitchcock; and orchestral subjects featuring Ben Bernie, Paul Sprecht and Otto Wolf Kahn.

The year 1924 saw three notable sound-on-film 'firsts' from Phonofilm. President Coolidge was filmed delivering a campaign speech on the White House lawn, **the first time that a President of the USA had spoken from the screen; the first Technicolor film with a sound-track** was made, the subject being Balieff's *Chauve Souris* danced in the open air; and **the first dramatic talkie film to be released commercially**, *Love's Old Sweet Song*,

a two-reeler directed by J. Searle Dawley with Mary Mayo and Una Merkel in the leading roles. Although the first to exploit sound-on-film commercially, De Forest failed to establish talking pictures as a major entertainment medium and the Phonofilm patents were eventually taken over by William Fox together with those of the Tri-Ergon system.

One of the effects of the introduction of talkies in the USA was to kill off the theatrical stock companies. In 1929 there were still 200 companies playing stock; by 1939 there were five.

The first public demonstration of sound-on-film in Britain took place at the Finsbury Park Cinema on 14 June 1923, when a programme of

The Talkie Revolution 1928. Did any of Miss Logan's pupils succeed in making it to Hollywood? (*Kobal*)

"From Now On— **VOICE** will be the factor in picking **Movie Stars**"

Jacqueline Logan

"Anyone who thinks at all can see how important a good voice will be in the movies from now on, and what a deciding factor it will be in picking stars for various parts.

I rejoice in the coming of the Talking Movies as an added outlet for the expression of artistic acting and I realize the importance of developing and training the voice to the utmost degree.

With vocal mastery comes poise, confidence and commanding personality. For these things all those who aspire to stardom should labor with all their hearts."

Jacqueline Logan

I Guarantee to Improve Your Voice 100%

Mail coupon below at once—and learn how with my wonderful NEW Silent Method of Voice Culture, I actually *guarantee* to improve your voice at least 100% or refund you every penny. Think what this means—especially now with the great demand the Talking Movie has made for men and women with rich, compelling voices. Movie Directors are now seeking—NOT just pretty faces and nice figures—but FINE VOICES! Practically all the big stars are taking voice culture. See what Jacqueline Logan says in her letter shown above. Here is YOUR one big chance—the chance you've been longing for—to really get into the movies—write me at once and let me show you how you can develop a rich, compelling, commanding voice. But don't delay—mail coupon NOW!

Voice Book—FREE!

Mail coupon now and without any cost or obligation on your part I will immediately send you my wonderful voice book—"Physical Voice Culture" telling all about my *guaranteed* NEW Silent Method of Voice Culture. Take the first step now toward the voice you've longed for—the movie chance you've hoped for—*mail this coupon!*

Prof. E. Feuchtinger, PERFECT VOICE INSTITUTE,
Dept. 12-66 1922 Sunnyside Avenue, Chicago

Prof. E. Feuchtinger, Studio 12-66
1922 Sunnyside Ave., Chicago, Ill.
Please send me, FREE and without any obligation, Prof. tinger's new book, "Physical Voice Culture." I have checked subject in which I am most interested.
☐ Weak Voice   ☐ Singing   ☐ Stammering   ☐ Si
Name
Address
City .... State

When primitive sound-on-disc 'talkies' were introduced during the Edwardian era, volume was sometimes considered rather more important than quality. William Haggar, proprietor of a cinema in Aberdare, Wales, advertised that his films 'can be heard two miles away'.

Phonofilm shorts was trade shown. The *Bioscope* reported: 'Several pictures were projected, including a vocalist rendering a song from *Carmen*, a dancer imitative of Pavlova with dying swan musical effects, and others. The synchronization was as near perfect as possible, but the articulation sounded to me somewhat throaty.'

The first sound-on-film production shown before a paying audience in Britain was the Technicolor dance subject *Chauve Souris* (US 24), which was shown with musical sound-track at the Tivoli in London in the summer of 1925. **The first talking film seen by a paying audience** introduced a programme of Phonofilm singing and orchestral shorts premièred at the Empire, Plumstead on 4 October 1926 and consisted of Sidney L. (now Lord) Bernstein explaining how Phonofilm worked.

The first sound-on-film talkie produced in Britain was De Forest Phonofilms' *The Gentleman* (GB 25), a comedy short directed and scripted by William J. Elliott. The following year four short dramas were produced at the Clapham Studios by the De Forest Phonofilm Co. of Great Britain and in 1927 there were films of Edith Sitwell reading her own poems and Sybil Thorndike in a scene from Shaw's *Saint Joan*.

The first full-length feature film with sound (in part) was D. W. Griffith's *Dream Street* (US 21), a United Artists release. Described by one cinema historian as 'a dreadful hodgepodge of allegory and symbolism', it was a total failure when originally presented as an all-silent picture at the Central Theater, New York, in April 1921. After it had closed, Griffith was persuaded by Wendell McMahill of Kellum Talking Pictures to add a sound sequence. On 27 April the star, Ralph Graves, was brought to the Kellum Studios on West 40th Street to record a love song on synchronized disc, and this was included when the film reopened at the Town Hall Civic Centre on 1 May. A fortnight later a second sound sequence was added, consisting of the shouts and whoops of Porter Strong shooting craps together with other background noises, and this version opened in Brooklyn on 29 May 1921.

The only other feature movie with vocal sound prior to *The Jazz Singer* (see below) was José A. Ferreya's *La Muchacha del Arrabal* (Arg 22), starring Lidia Lis.

The first talking feature film (in part) was Warner Bros' Vitaphone (sound-on-disc) production *The Jazz Singer* (US 27), directed by Alan Crosland and starring Al Jolson, which opened at the Warner Theatre on Broadway on 6 October 1927. The initial, historic talking sequence takes place in Coffee Dan's, where Jack Robin (Al Jolson) has been singing *Dirty Hands, Dirty Face*. Amidst the applause, Jolson holds up his hands and

> When the talkies came to the island of Malta in 1930 with the Valetta première of *Broadway Melody* (US 29), the manager of the Royal Opera House asked all his patrons to wear tennis shoes to lessen the noise of late arrivals. Such precautions were not sufficient to make the innovation the success it had been in other parts of the world. The sound-on-disc system got out of sync, so that the men talked in women's voices and vice versa. Come the half-way interval, the show had to be abandoned because a man was found dead in the stalls.

urges: 'Wait a minute. Wait a minute. You ain't heard nothin' yet! Wait a minute, I tell you. You ain't heard nothin'. You wanna hear *Toot-toot-tootsie*? All right. Hold on.' Turning to the band, Jolson says: 'Now listen: you play *Toot-toot-tootsie*. Three choruses, you understand, and in the third chorus I whistle. Now give it to 'em hard and heavy. Go right ahead . . .'

The second and only other talking sequence was longer and involved a conversation between Jack Robin and his mother (Eugenie Besserer). In view of the many conflicting claims concerning the amount of dialogue in *The Jazz Singer*, it is worth recording that exactly 354 words are spoken in the two talking sequences, 60 in the first and 294 in the second. Jolson speaks 340, Eugenie Besserer 13 and Warner Oland (as the father) one—'Stop!' The dialogue sequences were unscripted, because Warner Bros had only intended to make a film with synchronized music and singing, not a talkie. Jolson, however, ad libbed—the famous line 'You ain't heard nothin' yet' was in fact a catchphrase he used in his stage performances—and studio head Sam Warner liked the snatches of talk enough to keep them in.

The first all-talking feature was Warner Bros' *Lights of New York* (US 28), which was premièred at the Strand Theater, New York, on 6 July 1928. Starring Helene Costello, the picture was so determinedly all-talking that the dialogue continued non-stop from opening credits to end title. Warner's billed it as '100% Talking!'; *Variety* commented '100% Crude'.

The first sound-on-film feature was Fox's *The Air Circus* (US 28), with Louise Dresser and David Rollins, which opened at New York's Gaiety on 1 September 1928. The dialogue sequence lasted 15 minutes. **The first all-talking sound-on-film feature** was Raoul Walsh and Irving Cummins' Fox western *In Old Arizona* (US 28), with Edmund Lowe and Warner Baxter, which was also **the first talkie shot outdoors**. It opened 26 December 1928 at the Criterion, Los Angeles.

The first British talking feature was Marshall

Neilan's *Black Waters* (GB 29), a melodrama about a mad captain posing as a clergyman to murder people aboard a fog-bound ship. Starring John Loder and Mary Brian, the picture was produced in the USA by Herbert Wilcox for British & Dominions Sono Art World Wide.

The first feature-length talkie made in Britain was Alfred Hitchcock's *Blackmail* (GB 29), produced by British Int. Pictures at Elstree with Anny Ondra and John Longden and premièred at the Regal, Marble Arch, on 21 June 1929. The first reel had incidental sound and music only, but the characters began to speak in the second as the plot unfolded. It was billed as '99 per cent talking', a pardonable exaggeration. The posters also carried the slogan 'See and Hear It—Our Mother Tongue As It Should Be Spoken'—a sideswipe at the American-English that had dominated the screen hitherto.

Britain's first all-talking feature was *The Clue of the New Pin* (GB 29) adapted from the Edgar Wallace novel of the same name and produced by British Lion in association with British Photophone. The film was directed by Arthur Maude, starred Donald Calthrop and Benita Hume, and was released on 16 December 1929. An undistinguished production, the film is chiefly memorable

If you thought that was Lauren Bacall singing in *To Have and To Have Not* (US 44), you're wrong. It was none other than Andy Williams!

Lauren Bacall sings in *To Have and Have Not* (US 44), or rather she is seen to sing, because her voice needed to be dubbed. The problem was that she had such a deep speaking voice, no female singer could be found who could match it convincingly. The solution lay in choosing a male singer and the voice heard emanating from Lauren Bacall's lips is actually that of Andy Williams.

for the fact that a rising young stage performer called John Gielgud played a bit part in it.

The first dubbed film was Lee De Forest's Phonofilm production *Love's Old Sweet Song* (US 24). The film contains one exterior scene, in which Una Merkel is strolling down a street when she hears the title song being sung by Mary Mayo from indoors. Since the exterior footage had to be shot silent, the song was dubbed in afterwards.

The first occasion on which another actor's voice was substituted for that of a member of the cast was in *The Patriot* (US 28). The performer concerned, Emil Jannings, threatened legal proceedings if the new sound-track was not erased, and the dubbed voice was removed. The first film released with a substitute voice was *The Wolf of Wall Street* (US 29), in which the heavily accented Hungarian actor Paul Lukas played a partner in a firm of stockbrokers. His dialogue was dubbed by Lawford Davidson. Happily Lukas's accent did not hinder the development of his career—he contin-

In *Singin' in the Rain* (US 52) Jean Hagen plays a spoiled silent screen star whose voice is too *déclassé* for talkies. The producers secretly have her voice dubbed by well-spoken *ingénue* Debbie Reynolds. In reality Miss Reynolds' voice was not considered classy enough and so the voice heard on the soundtrack of the film-within-a-film is not hers at all. It was Jean Hagen's own, speaking in her normal voice.

ued to play major roles in Hollywood pictures for another 40 years.

The first British film to be dubbed was Alfred Hitchcock's *Blackmail* (GB 29). The female lead, Czech actress Anny Ondra, spoke almost no English and her voice was dubbed by Joan Barry (later the mother of heiress Henrietta Tiarks). This was done by the novel method of having Miss Barry read Miss Ondra's lines into a microphone while the latter was performing.

The first use of post-synchronization with the same actors in a feature film was by Ernst Lubitsch for *The Love Parade* (US 29), as a means of freeing the camera from the constraints of the immobile sound-proof booth used in early talkies. By using a silent camera, he was able to counter the static camera positions that marred most of the pioneer sound productions and dub in the dialogue afterwards.

The first film with stereophonic sound was the re-edited version of Abel Gance's *Napoleon Bonaparte* (Fr 27), which was presented with added dialogue and sound effects at the Paramount Cinema, Paris, in 1935. The stereophonic process used had been patented by Gance and André Debrie three years earlier.

Perhaps the most challenging piece of dubbing in recent years was performed by voice-over actor Patrick Floersheim for the French language version of *Dead Poets Society* (US 89). He was required to reproduce not only Robin Williams' bravura vocal performance but also to impersonate his send-ups of John Wayne and Marlon Brando in voices which simulated the way other voice-over artistes had dubbed the Duke and Brando in the French versions of their pictures. While normally a Hollywood picture can be dubbed into French in less than a week, Francophoning *Dead Poets* took two months. The care taken in faithfully matching the tone and timbre of the original voices paid off, with the picture making No. 1 at the French box office in 1990.

The first American productions with stereophonic sound were the Warner Bros' productions *Santa Fe Trail* (US 40) and *Four Wives* (US 40), presented in Vitasound. The first successful system of stereophonic musical accompaniment was Fantasound, developed by Walt Disney Studios in association with RCA and first employed for the sound-track of Disney's feature-length cartoon *Fantasia* (US 41), with music by the Philadelphia Orchestra under the direction of Leopold Stokowski.

The first use of overlapping dialogue—The talking picture borrowed the stage convention, far removed from reality, whereby no more than one character speaks at once. Credit for introducing overlapping dialogue in the interests of naturalism is usually given to Orson Welles for *Citizen Kane* (US 41), but in fact the technique had been used a year earlier in Howard Hawks' wild and witty *His Girl Friday* (US 40), with Cary Grant and Rosalind Russell.

Dolby Sound

Dolby is a noise reduction system designed to eliminate hiss from recorded sound—as its originator has expressed it, 'real high fidelity means reproducing the silence as accurately as the sound'. It was developed by American-born Ray Dolby in an old dressmaking factory in Fulham, where Dolby laboratories were established in May 1965 with four employees and a refusal of credit from the bank. The first practical application was by Decca for disc recording, the units being known as the S/N Stretcher because they were for stretching the signal-to-noise ratio. After Ray Dolby had heard some engineers at Pye referring to his equipment as 'a Dolby', he decided to change the name to his own. **The first film with Dolby sound** was Stanley Kubrick's *A Clockwork Orange* (GB 71). This used Dolby noise reduction on all premixes and masters, though the release prints had a conventional optical sound-track. The first film with a Dolby encoded mono sound-track was *Callan* (GB 74) and the first with a Dolby encoded stereo optical sound-track was Ken Russell's *Lisztomania* (GB 75). At this point Dolby began to take off; less than 10 years later there were 6000 cinemas worldwide equipped to take the new system. The 1000th film with a Dolby stereo sound-track, *Heartbreak Ridge* (US 86), was released in 1986. Since 1977 all the films winning the Oscar for Best Achievement in Sound have been recorded on Dolby.

The first commercial play-off of a movie with digital sound took place at the Plitt Century Plaza Theater in Century City, California over a four-week period during February and March 1985. A specially-recorded version of Disney's 1941 cartoon

Talkies reached the home in 1931. This Synchrophone device consisted of a radiogram which incorporated a synchronised projector. Do any survive? (*Illustrated London News Picture Library*)

feature *Fantasia* (US 41) was used for the presentation, with the sound emanating from a digital audio playback unit synchronized with the projector. The process allows for the exact reproduction of sound. The first feature to be made in digital sound was Disney's *Dick Tracy* (US 90), released on 15 June 1990. Five Los Angeles cinemas, as well as the Embassy I and Loew's 84th Street Sixplex in Manhattan, were fitted with Optical Radiation's Cinema Digital Sound, a playback system providing six-track optical stereo from special 70 mm release prints of the Warren Beatty movie. A specially developed film stock, Eastman Digital Sound Recording Film 2374, had been developed by Kodak to accommodate the newly designed optical sound-track.

The last wholly silent film (ie without a sound-track) **produced in America** for general distribution was George Melford's *The Poor Millionaire* (US 30), with Richard Talmadge (who played both the hero and the villain) and Constance Howard. It was released by Biltmore Pictures on 7 April 1930, just 30 months and a day after the presentation of the first talkie feature. Only four other

silents had been issued in 1930, all of them low budget westerns. The following year there were no silents but four films with synchronized music and sound effects only, including Chaplin's *City Lights* and F. W. Murnau's *Tabu*. Silent production in America, however, was not finished for good. In 1950 Georges Sadoul reported that silent features in colour were being produced in San Francisco for the Chinese population of the United States.

The last British silent feature was Argyle Art Pictures' *Paradise Alley* (GB 31), starring John Argyle and Margaret Delane, the story of a miner who takes the blame when his brother shoots a man during a robbery. It was released in March 1931.

European production had made virtually a complete change-over to sound by the end of 1931. Elsewhere, the last silent feature from Soviet Russia—Alexander Medvekin's *Schastye/Happiness*—was released in 1935 and the last seven Indian silents were issued the same year. Japan took longer to make the change. In 1937, 209 out of 524 movies were without dialogue—50 with sound effects and music, 159 silent. The following year saw the virtual demise of the silent, with 16 'sound effects only' films and 15 wholly silent. As late as 1952 in Burma, where only two of the 22 production companies were equipped to make sound films, production totalled 40 silents and 6 talkies.

The last silent feature films for commercial distribution were produced in Thailand at the end of the 1960s. Although talkies had been produced in the 1930s, World War II totally disrupted both the Thai economy and its film industry and subsequently all films were shot silent on 16 mm stock until 1965. Dialogue was supplied by actors and actresses 'live dubbing' in cinemas from a cubicle next to the projection booth. After 1965 the popularity of Indian-style musicals stimulated producers to shoot sound song-and-dance sequences on 35 mm stock for interpolation with otherwise silent 16 mm footage. According to the Thai Motion Picture Producers' Association 'by 1970 all Thai films were shot on 35 mm with sound'.

Post-Sound Silents

A small number of non-dialogue dramatic films (usually with synchronized music and sound effects) have been produced since the last war. The following list excludes ballet films and similer mime productions and also the Burmese, Thai and Chinese-American silents referred to above.

Russel Rouse's atomic spy thriller *The Thief* (US 52) with Ray Milland; *Los Noces de Sable* (Fr 52) — Jean Cocteau's update of Tristan and Isolde set in the Sahara; *Dementia* (US 55), described by *Variety* as 'the strangest film ever offered for theatrical release', about the dreams of a demented woman; Kaneto Shindo's *The Island* (Jap 60), about a family living on a tiny island, which won the One World Prize at Melbourne in 1962 for 'the feature film which can be most universally understood'; the Bengali production *Ingeet* (Ind 61); Luiz Rosemberg Filho's 2¼-hour *Imagens* (Bra 72), which had no music or sound effects; Yoichi Takabayashi's *Gaki Zoshi* (Jap 72); Andrej Brzozowski's *Obszar Zamknięty/The Closed Area* (Pol 72); *Bez/A Film without Words* (Yug 73); Terry Bourke's spinechilling horror meller *Night of Fear* (Aus 73), about a woman who is terrorized by a crazed hermit after her car crashes on a lonely road; the cast-of-one *Vase de noces* (Bel 73); the cast-of-none *Model* (Gre 74), directed by Kostas Sfikas; Morton Hellig's *Once* (US 74) with Christopher Mitchum; Milos Radivojević's *Testament* (Yug 75); *Robinson Columbus* (Den 75); Jérôme Savetry's *La Fille du garde barrière/The Gatekeeper's Daughter* (Fr 75); James Scott's *Coilin and Platonida* (GB 76); V. Miroshnichenko's *Lone Wolf* (USSR 77), from the Turgenev story about a giant woodsman endeavouring to bring up two motherless children as well as care for the estate; Gérard Myriam Benhamou's *Adom ou le sang d'Abel* (Fr 77), about Cain and Abel; *Pentimento* (Neth 78); Pim de la Parra's *Dirty Picture* (Neth 80); *Le Dernier Combat* (Fr 83), about an apocalypse in which the world has been left with only a handful of men and a single woman survivor; Jos Stelling's *De Illusionist* (Neth 83); *Rebelote* (Fr 84), made by youthful French director Jacques Richard as a tribute to the silent days and with a score by Pierre Jansen for performance by a live orchestra—the picture was billed, less than accurately, as 'The first truly silent film since the advent of sound in 1927' (a claim that ignored the large output of silents between 1927 and 1931, as well as the films listed here); and the only full-length cartoon feature without dialogue, Donyo Donev's *We Called Them Montagues and Capulets* (Bul 84), a social comedy loosely based on *Romeo and Juliet*; *Bolivar* (Ven 82) and *Orinoko-Nuevo* (Ven 84), both by Diego Risquez, the only director to have made two modern silents; *To Sleep so as to Dream* (Jap 86), a detective picture set in the 1920s with all the dialogue presented as inter-titles. Diego Risquez' *Amerika, Terra Incognita* (Ven 88) was a no dialogue re-creation of late 15th-century life at the Spanish court following the discovery of America. Charles Lane's monochrome *Sidewalk Stories* (US 89), about a mute Chaplinesque vagabond, was the most acclaimed picture at the 1989 Munich Film Festival, while Derek Jarman's *The Last of England* (GB 88), about anarchy in a post-apocalyptic Britain, inspired mass walkouts when it was shown at the New York Film Festival. *L'Ange* (Fr 90) had not only no dialogue but, according to *Variety*, 'no plot, no continuity and, to most filmgoers, no sense . . .' Mel Brooks's *Silent Movie* (US 76) nearly qualifies for this list, but there was one word of dialogue.

LANGUAGES

Hollywood's foreign language output was confined principally to the early talkie period, the largest proportion being in Spanish for the Latin American market. Beginning with a dubbed version of RKO's *Rio Rita* (US 29), a total of 96 Spanish language movies were produced in the USA during the ensuing six years, the majority by Fox, and another 17 were made by Paramount at their Joinville studios in France 1930-33. **The first foreign language feature made in America with live dialogue** was *Sombras de Gloria/Blaze of Glory* (US 30). It was a Sono Art-World production.

During the period 1930-35 a total of 63 French language pictures were produced by MGM, First National, Paramount, Warner Bros, RKO, Universal, Fox, Columbia and Twentieth Century. The Paramount productions were made at Joinville, outside Paris, where they also produced in Spanish, German, Italian, Swedish, Portuguese, Romanian, Polish, Czech and Dutch.

The first foreign language talkie to be sub-titled in English was *Two Hearts in Waltz Time* (Ger 29). The titles were written by Herman G. Weinberg (an American), who sub-titled a record number of over 400 films during the ensuing 40 years.

In order to simulate the language of the mutants in *Island of Lost Souls* (US 32), Paramount's director of recording Loren L. Ryder recorded a track consisting of a combination of animal sounds and foreign languages played backwards. He then alternately speeded up the loop and slowed it down, producing cadences that were strange and horrifying. Audience reaction was even more dramatic than had been anticipated; the vibratory effect on the eardrums induced instant nausea.

The first talkie produced in different language versions was British International Pictures' trilingual *Atlantic* (GB 29), which was released with separate English, French and German sound-tracks. Besides its overseas release, the German version was shown at the Alhambra, Leicester Square, to cater for the large German population living in London prior to World War II.

Multilingual films in which foreign characters speak in their own language were comparatively rare before *The Longest Day* (US 62) broke with former Hollywood practice by having the Germans speaking German and the French speaking French. There had been occasional examples, however, from the earliest days of sound, starting with G. W.

Pabst's *Westfront 1918* (Ger 30), with dialogue in French and German. Others included Pabst's *Kameradschaft* (Ger 31), about a mining disaster involving French and German miners; Luis Trenker's *Der verlorene Sohn/The Prodigal Son* (Ger 34), in German and English; Jean Renoir's *La Grande Illusion* (Fr 37), in French, English and German; Nyrki Tapiovaara's *Stolen Death* (Fin 38), a thriller in Finnish, Swedish and Russian; *Carl Peters* (Ger 41), in German and English; *Die Letzte Chance* (Swz 34), in German and French; Guy Hamilton's *The Colditz Story* (GB 54), in English and German; *La Chatte* (Fr 58), in French and German; and Jean-Luc Godard's quadrilingual *Le Mépris/Contempt* (Fr/It 63), in which Michel Piccoli spoke Italian, Brigitte Bardot spoke French, Jack Palance spoke American and Fritz Lang spoke German, the need for sub-titles being effectively reduced by Giogia Moll's role as the interpreter.

Even silent films could be multilingual. Rex Ingram stated in *Motion Picture Directing* (New York 1922) that when making films with foreign settings, he made his principals speak the language of the country. Explaining that 'it helps them materially in keeping to the required atmosphere', he admitted ruefully 'few of them like to go to this trouble . . .'

The most multilingual film producing country is India, which has produced films in the following 47 languages since 1931: Angami Naga, Arabic, Assamese, Avadhi, Badaga, Bengali, Brijbhasha, Burmese, Chhattisgadhi, Coorgi, Dogri, English, French, Garhwali, German, Gorkhali, Gujarati, Haryanavi, Hindi, Kannada, Karbi, Kashmiri, Khasi, Konkani, Magadhi, Maithili, Malay, Malayalam, Manipuri, Marathi, Marwari, Nepalese, Oriya, Persian, Punjabi, Pushtu, Rajasthani, Sambalpuri, Sanskrit, Sindi, Sinhalese, Swahili, Tamil, Telegu, Thai, Tulu, Urdu.

The only film made in Latin was Derek Jarman's *Sebastiane* (GB 76), a homophile interpretation of the legend of St Sebastian. The translator, Jack Welch, used ingenious shifts to put Roman barrackroom language of the third century AD into comprehensible Latin, but in one instance had to resort to a Greek word, rendering the epithet *Motherfucker* as *Oedipus*. *Sebastiane* enjoys the unique distinction of being the only English film ever to have been released in Britain with English sub-titles.

The first talking film made in dialect was *Mieke* (Bel 30), a comedy made in Antwerp by Felix Bell (Gaston Schoukens) in the Anversois patois.

The only feature film made in Esperanto was *Incubus* (US 65), whose star William Shatner is familiar to TV viewers as Capt Kirk of *Star Trek*. The avowed purpose of using Esperanto dialogue was to give the movie an air of the supernatural. It is one of the few American films to have been released with English sub-titles.

The first Hindi film produced in Britain was the Cabana Film Co.'s comedy-thriller *Bhaag Re Bhaag* (GB 78), which had its world première at Leytonstone State Cinema on 4 February 1978. Produced and directed by M. A. Qayyum, it was a cops and robbers caper set in London and Epping Forest, starring Saghir Rahi and an overweight young English lady credited only as Patsy.

A production company called Oscar Films was set up in Newcastle-upon-Tyne in 1990 to make films for the Asian market worldwide. Its inaugural offering was *Princess from Kathmandu* (GB 90), a £3 million production in English and Hindi versions which starred the reigning Miss India, Naveeda Mehdi, in the title role.

The first Cantonese film produced in Britain was *Ping Pong* (GB 86), a comedy thriller starring David Yip and set in London's Chinatown.

The first feature film in Irish was Bob Quinn's *Poitin/Poteen* (Eire 78), with Cyril Cusack as a poteen maker attempting to evade the attentions of the Garda in Connemara.

The first feature film in Welsh was Tom Haydon's documentary reconstruction *The Last Tasmanian* (Aus/GB/Fr 79). The curious circumstance of a film set in Tasmania being filmed in Welsh (there were also English and French language versions) is explained by the fact that Haydon's partner in the enterprise was the Welsh anthropologist Rhys Jones.

The first Welsh language feature to go on general release was *Coming Up Roses* (GB 86), which opened at the Cannon, Cardiff on 6 March 1987 and then crossed the borders of the principality to charm the English (in a sub-titled version) with its engaging story of a fleapit cinema in the valleys which staves off demolition when the projectionist (Dafydd Hywell) and usherette (Iola Gregory) turn it into a mushroom farm.

The first feature film in Gaelic was Barney Platts-Mills' *Hero* (GB 82), a medieval fable about sorcery and magic in a remote corner of the Scottish highlands.

The first feature film in Breton was Gerard Guerin's *Lo Pais* (Fr 73), starring Olivier Bousquet and Nada Stangcar, about a young man trying to make his way to Paris and finally deciding to go home to help his own people. It was premièred at the Cannes Film Festival in 1973.

The only full-length feature film made in pidgin English was *Wokabout Bilong Tonten* (Aus 73), filmed in New Guinea with Anton Sil and Taruk Wabei in the lead roles.

The first feature film in Red Indian was *Windwalker* (US 80), starring Trevor Howard, which was made entirely in the Cheyenne and Crow languages.

The first feature film in Sanskrit (an ancient Indian language) was *Sankaracharya* (Ind 82).

The first feature film in **Frysian**, a language spoken in part of North Holland, was *De Droom* (Neth 85).

The first feature film in **Okinawan**, the language of Okinawa in the Ryuku Is, was *Paradise View* (Jap 85).

The first feature film in **Iban**, the language of Sarawak, was *Bejalai* (Malaysia 87).

The first feature film in **Lapp** was Nils Gaup's *Ofelas* (Nor 87), starring Mikkel Gaup, Ailu Gaup and Sara Marit Gaup. A tale of Lapps resisting Tchude marauders in the Arctic North 800 years ago, it was filmed in temperatures of up to 40 below zero.

The first feature film in **Aymara**, Amerindian language of Bolivia, was Jorge Sanjinés' *Ukamau* (Bol 66).

The first feature film in **Quechua**, Amerindian language of Bolivia, was Jorge Sanjinés' *Yawar mallku/Blood of the Condor* (Bol 69).

The first feature film in **Nahuatl**, the ancient language of the Aztecs no longer spoken, was *In Necuepaliztli in Aztlan* (Mex 90).

The first feature film in **Papiamentu**, the language of Curaçao (Dutch West Indies), was Felix de Rooy's *Ava & Gabriel, Un Historia di Amor* (Curaçao 90), starring Nashaira Desbarida and Cliff San-A-Jong.

The first feature film in **the Gypsy language Romanes** was Emir Kusturica's *Time of the Gypsies* (Yug 90), with Davor Dujmovic as an awkward

The many Indians performing in Kevin Costner's *Dances with Wolves* (US 90) all say their lines in Lakota, the language of the Sioux. In fact, only one member of the cast could speak it in reality. She was Doris Leader Charge, an instructor at a community college on the Rosebud reservation in South Dakota, who plays Pretty Shield, wife of Chief Ten Bears, in the film. It was her task to translate the Indians' dialogue into Lakota and then teach them to deliver the words phonetically.

young man growing up in a squalid Gypsy ghetto outside Skopje and his survival in the criminal underworld of Milan.

The first feature film in **Faroese** was *Atlantic Rhapsody* (Faroes 89).

WIDE SCREEN

The first wide screen process used for a feature film was Panoramico Alberini, devised by Filoteo Alberini in 1914, which was employed by Enrico Guazzoni for a sequence of *Il Sacco di Roma* (It 23).

The first wide screen system to employ the use of an anamorphic lens—a lens that squeezes a wide image on to standard gauge film as in Cinemascope (see below)—was Henri Chrétien's Hypergonar, used by Claude Autant-Lara in making *Construire un feu* (Fr 27).

The first feature film in wide screen throughout was *Happy Days* (US 30), made in the 70 mm Fox Grandeur process.

The first wide screen system to incorporate both wide gauge film and the anamorphic lens was Camera 65, later renamed Ultra-Panavision, which was originally employed on *Raintree Country* (US 57).

Cinemascope

This was developed by the French inventor Henri Chrétien from his original anamorphic Hypergonar system of 1927. Fox bought the patent rights in 1952 and **the first Cinemascope feature film**, *The Robe* (US 53), was premièred at Grauman's Chinese Theater in Hollywood on 24 September 1953. **Britain's first Cinemascope production** was also her first wide screen feature: MGM's *Knights of the Round Table* (GB 54), with Robert Taylor and Ava Gardner.

The peak year for widescreen Hollywood releases was 1957 with 102 or 32 per cent of the total. Of these, 64 were in Cinemascope, 17 in Regalscope, 16 in VistaVision, 4 in Technirama and one in SuperScope. Widescreen achieved its highest proportion of all releases as early as 1955, with

Time of the Gypsies (Yug 90) was the first film to be made in the Gypsy language Romanes. (*Kobal*)

> 'A wide screen just makes a bad film twice as bad'.—Sam Goldwyn

38 per cent. Out of the total of 96 widescreen films, 72 were in Cinemascope.

Cinerama

This was developed by self-taught inventor Frederick Waller of Huntington, New York, who had originated the idea as early as 1939 for an oil exhibit at the New York's Fair. His intention had been to project moving pictures all over the interior surface of the oil exhibit building, but technical difficulties persuaded him to compromise with a half-dome, using eleven 16 mm projectors to cover the vast area of screen. After the war he resumed work on the process, reducing the number of projectors to three and adopting a wide screen ratio of almost 3:1. The first production in the perfected process was *This is Cinerama* (US 52), which opened in New York on 30 September 1952 and ran for 122 weeks. **The first full-length dramatic feature in Cinerama** was MGM's *The Wonderful World of the Brothers Grimm* (US 62).

The widest wide screen system ever was Raoul Grimoin-Sanson's Cinéorama, presented at the Paris Exposition of 1900. Ten synchronized projectors threw a 360° image on to a screen 330 ft in circumference. The audience sat on the roof of the projection booth, which was designed to simulate the basket of a giant balloon. The hand-coloured film took the audience on an aerial voyage of discovery, looking down on the great capitals of Europe. Unfortunately, the show had to be terminated after three performances, since the heat of the ten projectors constituted a fire risk. The concept of 'cinema-in-the-round' was not revived until Walt Disney introduced Circarama at the Brussels World Fair in 1958, though this time on a screen of a more modest circumference.

SMELLIES

The first attempt at combining an appropriate odour with a film was made by S. L. Rothapfel—the celebrated showman 'Roxy'—at the Family Theater, Forest City, Pa., in 1906. Roxy dipped cotton wool in a rose essence and strung it in front of a powerful electric fan during the showing of a news film of the Pasadena Rose Bowl Game. Similar experiments were made in 1929, when Albert E. Fowler, manager of the Fenway Theater, Boston, used a pint of lilac scent tipped into the ventilating system to accompany the credits of *Lilac Time* (US 29). Synthetic orange blossom perfume was sprayed from the ceiling when

Broadway Melody (US 29) opened on Broadway.

The first film made as a 'smellie' was a widescreen travelogue about China, *Behind the Great Wall* (US 59), filmed in Totalscope, DeLuxe Color, stereophonic sound and the new wonder of Aromarama. Premièred at the DeMille Theater, New York, on 2 December 1959, the film was accompanied by a range of 72 smells that included incense, smoke, burning pitch, oranges, spices and a barnyard of geese. The process, devised by Charles Weiss, involved circulating the scents through the ventilating system. Unlike most novelty films, *Behind the Great Wall* had the smell of success even without the gimmicks. It won two awards when it was shown at the Brussels Film Exposition unaccompanied by Aromarama.

The first feature 'smellie' was Michael Todd Jr's *Scent of Mystery* (US 60), a 70 mm Technicolor thriller made in Smell-O-Vision and premièred at the Cinestage, Chicago, on 12 January 1960. The scents used—ocean ozone, pipe tobacco, garlic, oil paint, wine, wood shavings, boot polish, etc.—were piped to each individual cinema seat on cue from the 'smell-track' of the film.

A less sophisticated technique was used to waft the scents of Odorama to spectators of the 'sickie smellie' *Polyester* (US 82), which starred the outsize transvestite Divine playing an all-American housewife whose life stinks. Each member of the audience was given a card numbered from one to ten. When a number was flashed on screen, the spectator scratched the card with a coin, releasing a revolting odour appropriate to whatever disgusting activity was taking place before his eyes.

THREE DIMENSIONAL FILMS

The first presentation of 3-D films before a paying audience took place at the Astor Theater, New York, on 10 June 1915. The programme consisted of three one-reelers, the first of rural scenes in the USA, the second a selection of scenes from Famous Players' *Jim, the Penman* (US 15), with John Mason and Maria Doro, and the third a travelogue of Niagara Falls. The anaglyphic process used, developed by Edwin S. Porter and W. E. Waddell, involved the use of red and green spectacles to create a single image from twin motion picture images photographed 2½ in apart. The experiment was not a success, for much the same reason that 3-D failed 40 years later. Lynde Denig wrote in *Moving Picture World*: 'Images shimmered like reflections on a lake and in its present form the

> Alfred Hitchcock on the shortlived fad for 3-D in the early fifties: 'A nine-days' wonder—and I came in on the ninth day'.

Gig Young throws a punch at the audience in MGM's first 3-D spectacle *Arena* (US 53). Once the novelty of being socked in the face by your favourite star had worn off, the craze for 3-D disappeared overnight. *(Kobal)*

method couldn't be commercial because it detracts from the plot'.

The first 3-D film in colour was *Rêve d'Opium* (Fr 21), produced by the Société Azur in the System César Parolini.

The first 3-D feature film was Nat Deverich's 5-reel melodrama *Power of Love* (US 22), starring Terry O'Neil and Barbara Bedford, premièred at the Ambassador Hotel Theater, Los Angeles, on 27 September 1922. Produced by Perfect Pictures in an anaglyphic process developed by Harry K. Fairall, it related the adventures of a young sea captain in California in the 1840s. The only other American feature in 3-D prior to *Bwana Devil* (US 52) was R. William Neill's *Mars* aka *Radio Mania* (US 22), with Grant Mitchell as an inventor who succeeds in making contact with Mars via television. It was produced in Laurens Hammond's Teleview process.

The first 3-D talkie was a De Forest Phonofilm comedy short titled *Lunacy* (US 24), which opened at the Rivoli and Rialto Theaters in New York as part of the supporting programme on 22 September 1924. The 3-D process was called Plastigram.

The first feature-length talkie in 3-D was Sante Bonaldo's *Nozze vagabonde* (It 36), starring Leda Gloria and Ermes Zacconi, which was produced by the Società Italiana Stéréocinématografica at the Cines-Caesar studios. The 3-D cameraman was Anchise Brizzi.

The first 3-D talkie in colour was an UFA short titled *Zum Greifen Nah/You Can Nearly Touch It* (Ger 37), premièred at the UFA Palast in Berlin on 27 May 1937.

The first feature-length talkie in colour and 3-D was Alexander Andreyevsky's Soyuzdetfilm production *Robinson Crusoe* (USSR 47), starring Pavel Kadochnikov as Crusoe and Y. Lyubimov as Friday. The process used, Stereokino, was the first to successfully dispense with anaglyphic spectacles. Developed by S. P. Ivanov, it employed what were known as 'radial raster stereoscreens'—a corrugated metal screen with 'raster' grooves designed to reflect the twin images separately to the left and right eye. The most difficult technical problem encountered during the production of *Robinson Crusoe* was persuading a wild cat to walk along a thin branch towards the camera. After five nights occupied with this one scene, the cameraman succeeded in getting a satisfactory shot. The effect, according to accounts, was riveting, the animal seeming to walk over the heads of the audience and disappear at the far end of the cinema.

3-D Output

During the 3-D boom that began with the low budget *Bwana Devil* (US 52), over 5000 cinemas in the USA were equipped to show 3-D movies, but the fad was shortlived. 3-D production figures were: 1952—1; 1953—27; 1954—16; 1955—1. In addition there were 3-D movies produced in Japan, Britain, Mexico,

The old adage that the inventor is the last man to make money from his invention may often be true, but Milton L. Gunzburg stole a march on the entrepreneurs ready to reap the richest pickings from his enterprise. Inventor of the Natural Vision 3-D process used for *Bwana Devil* (US 52) etc., he secured the sole distribution rights for the Polaroid glasses necessary for viewing three-dimensional movies. Purchasing the glasses from the Polaroid Land Co. at 6c each, he sold them to theatres at 10c each. For a halcyon six months Gunzburg was distributing six million pairs a week till his contract ran out in July 1953. His $6,240,000 profit represented a better return than the box-office gross on any of the shortlived 3-D movies.

Germany and Hong Kong, but many of these (as well as some of the US productions) were released flat.

Sporadic production resumed in 1960 with the first Cinemascope 3-D movie *September Storm* (US 60), since when there have been 54 further three-dimensional films.

The first 3-D feature with stereophonic sound was Warner Bros' *House of Wax* (US 53). When it was premièred at the Paramount Theater, New York, with 25 speakers, the *Christian Science Monitor* was moved to deplore the 'cacophony of sound hurtling relentlessly at one from all directions'. André de Toth, director of the movie, may have been able to hear the cacophony, but was unable to see the 3-D effect, as he only had one eye.

HOLOGRAPHY

The first successful demonstration of holographic film was given before the Twelfth Congress of the International Union of Technical Association Cinematographers in Moscow in 1977. The system was developed by Prof. Victor Komar of the Cinema and Photo Research Institute and gives an illusion of three-dimensional substance without the use of anaglyphic spectacles. komar's method involved the deployment of laser beams to create a representation of objects in depth based on wave interference. If a spectator moved from one vantage position to another, he would see the object represented from a different angle, as in natural vision. The first film made in holography was a 30-second experimental subject showing a beautiful girl putting jewellery into a glass case. It could be viewed by a maximum of four spectators at a time.

NINE

MUSIC

Cinema music is almost as old as cinema. Felicien Trewey's presentation of films at the Regent Street Polytechnic in February 1896, the first before a paying audience in Britain, had a piano accompaniment described in a contemporary newspaper report as 'a trifle meagre'. It was not long before presenters began to recognize the virtue of appropriate music, though whether the quartet of saxophones engaged by the Cinématographe Lumière when it opened in the Boulevard Saint-Denis, Paris, in March 1897 was able to produce something apposite for every item on the programme is not recorded. In America, Albert E. Smith of Vitagraph recalled that the first of their productions to be shown with musical accompaniment was a news film of the burial of the victims of the sinking of the USN Maine, premièred at a disused opera house on Lexington Avenue, New York, in March 1898 with an orchestra playing a funeral dirge. Similarly, Henry Hopwood recorded in his book Living Pictures (1899) that a news film of the Albion launch disaster, screened only 30 hours after the event, was accompanied by an orchestra playing Rocked in the Cradle of the Deep.

The resident cinema orchestra is recorded as early as 1901, when Britain's first picture house, Mohawk's Hall, in Islington, appointed the 16-piece Fonobian Orchestra under the direction of Mr W. Neale. This remained rare, though, until the advent of the super-cinemas after 1914, which generally employed large orchestras under competent if not distinguished conductors. At the smaller houses, a single pianist would do the job, sometimes far from competent, but occasionally brilliant—Shostakovich supported himself while writing his first symphony in 1924 by playing the piano in an 'old, draughty and smelly' backstreet cinema in Leningrad. (He lost the job a year later because he stopped playing during an American comedy to roar with laughter.) About the same time, less brilliant at the keyboard, but later to achieve celebrity status in another walk of life, was the pianist at the Market Street Cinema in Manchester. She was Violet Carson, the hairnetted Ena Sharples of television's Coronation Street.

Picture houses that could not afford even the meagre wages of a pianist might fall back on the humble phonograph, which was adequate only if there was no intention that the music should relate to the mood of the film being shown. The manager of the first cinema in Leicester, opened in 1906, recalled that he installed a gramophone (later replaced by a mechanical organ) operated by the girl in the pay-box, but that the choice of records bore no relation to

the action on the screen, their only purpose being to drown the noise of the projector.

Inappropriate music could easily destroy the enjoyment of an otherwise meritorious picture, and in the USA the usual practice was for production companies to issue 'cue sheets' of suitable mood music with screen cues, an idea inaugurated by the Edison Co. in 1910 and copied by Vitagraph the following year. The consequence of leaving the choice of music to individual accompanists could be disastrous. Paul McCartney's father Jim McCartney recalls leading a small orchestra providing the music for The Queen of Sheba (US 21) when it was presented in Liverpool. For the chariot race sequence they played Thanks for the Buggy Ride and for the tragic culmination of the picture, the death of the Queen, they chose Horsey Keep Your Tail Up.

The first purpose-built cinema organ (ie a unit organ) was designed by Robert Hope-Jones, a Liverpudlian who joined the Wurtlitzer Co. of North Tonawanda, New York, in 1910 and killed himself four years later after his employers, exasperated at the expense incurred by his constant improvements in design, had locked him out of the factory on full salary. The first Wurlitzer cinema organs were installed in theatres in 1911.

The first cinema organ in Britain was built by Jardine & Co. to the specification of organist George Tootell in 1913 and installed at the Palace Cinema in Accrington, Lancashire.

Britain's first Mighty Wurlitzer was a Model D Unit Orchestra Organ, with six units on two manuals, installed at the Picture House, Walsall, Staffs, in January 1925. Although removed in 1955, the Organ is still in use at the Congregational Church at Beer, South Devon.

The largest cinema organ in the world was the Wurlitzer installed at Radio City Music Hall, New York, in 1932. Still in use, it has 58 ranks of pipes controlled from either or both of the twin four-manual consoles.

The majority of cinema organs which have survived are now in the hands of collectors or preservation societies. Some, though, have been put to practical use. One of the less probable last resting places of a cinema organ is the Chapel of St Francis in Wormwood Scrubs Prison, where the prisoners are uplifted by the strains of the Ealing ABC's Compton.

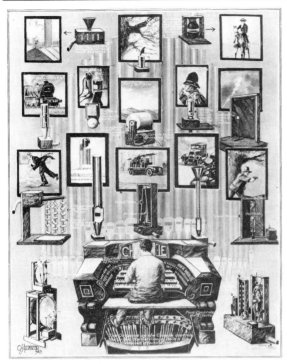

The mammoth 2500 pipe Christie organ at the Regal Theatre, Marble Arch, could create all the effects illustrated. It would also simulate most orchestral instruments as well as a 32-note carillon and a 25-note cathedral chime. But it was too late: the year was 1929 and already movies were being made with all the sound effects recorded on film. (*ILN*)

The largest organ ever installed in a cinema in Britain was a Christie 4/30 (30 units on four manuals), installed at the Regal (now Odeon), Marble Arch and first played by Quentin Maclean in 1928. It incorporated a piano and a carillon, the latter feature being unique.

The first film music to be specially composed for the screen was by Romolo Bacchini for the Cines productions *Malia dell'Oro* (It 06) and *Pierrot Innamorato* (It 06).

Italy was the first country whose major films were regularly supplied with an original score, a practice that did not become widespread elsewhere until the 1920s. Notable early examples were *Lo Schiavo di Cartagine* (It 10), with music by Osvaldo Brunetti, *La Legenda della Passiflora* (It 11), for which Mazzuchi composed the music, and rival scores by Walter Graziani and Colombio Aron for the two simultaneous productions of *The Last Days of Pompeii* (It 13). Pizetti's *Fire Symphony* was written to accompany the sequence in *Cabiria* (It 13) in which the young maidens are sacrificed to the fire god Moloch. Mario Costa wrote a distinctive score for *Storia del Pierrot* (It 13) and Tosti lent prestige to *A marechiare ce sta 'na fenesta* (It 15).

The first composition for a French film was written by Camille Saint-Saëns for Film d'Art's inaugural production *L'Assassinat du Duc de Guise* (Fr 08). This was an arrangement for piano, two violins, viola, cello, bass violin and harmonium. Other pioneer film composers were: Mikhail Ippolitov-Ivanov, who composed scores for *Stenka Razin* (Rus 08), Russia's first dramatic film, and for Vasili Goncharov's *Song About the Merchant Kalashnikov* (Rus 08); R. N. McAnally, whose composition, originally thought to be for the Salvation Army's *Soldiers of the Cross* (Aus 00), is now believed to have been for their similarly titled religious feature *Heroes of the Cross* (Aus 09); the Brazilian Costa Junior, composer of a score for *Paz e Amor* (Bra 10), a two-reel 'talkie' with dialogue spoken by actors behind the screen; and V. Strizhevsky, who wrote the music for *Zaporozhskaya Syetch* (Rus 11).

America and Britain trailed behind the countries mentioned above. **The first original score to accompany an American production** was composed by Victor Herbert for *The Fall of a Nation* (US 16), Thomas Dixon's sequel to *The Birth of a Nation* (US 15). This picture was, however, released five months later (18 September 1916) than *Civilization* (US 16), for which an original score had been composed by Victor Schertzinger.

The first composer to write music for a British film was Sir Edward German, who was paid 50 gns by W. G. Barker for 16 bars of music to accompany the Coronation scene in *Henry VIII* (GB 11). It was reported at the time that Barker 'personally supervised rehearsals of special music which he thinks important in adding to the effectiveness of the subject', which suggests that there may have been a rather more complete score than the single theme by German.

The first film music composed for a sound film was commissioned by Erich Pommer, Gaumont manager for Central and Eastern Europe, for *Les Heures* (Fr 13) aka *Die Stunden*, a 55-minute non-acted 'visual impression' of a day—morning, noon and night. The score was recorded on disc and synchronized with the film. The name of the composer is not known.

The first sound-on-film score was Hugo Riesenfeld's music for Fritz Lang's *Siegfried* (Ger 22), recorded on Phonofilm for its presentation at the Century Theater, New York, in 1925. This was a year earlier than the sound-on-disc Vitaphone accompaniment to Warner Bros' *Don Juan* (US 26), usually claimed as the first synchronized sound feature film.

The first film in which the music was dubbed (ie post-recorded) was *Innocents of Paris* (US 29), a Maurice Chevalier confection whose success was mainly due to the theme song *Louise*.

The first song specially composed for a motion

picture was *Mother I Still Have You*, written by Louis Silvers and sung by Al Jolson in *The Jazz Singer* (US 27).

The first hit-song from a movie was *Sonny Boy*, also an Al Jolson number, from *The Singing Fool* (US 28), composed by Buddy De Sylva, Lew Brown and Ray Henderson. Within nine months of the film's release, the sales of 'Sonny Boy' records had reached 2 million and sheet music 1¼ million.

The first record of a song from a movie was *Mother o' Mine* from *The Jazz Singer* (US 27), sung by Al Jolson and released on the Brunswick label on 6 October 1927 concurrently with the film's première.

The first golden disc awarded for a record selling one million copies was presented to bandleader Glenn Miller on 10 February 1942 for *Chattanooga Choo Choo*, the hit song he and his orchestra had performed in the Fox musical *Sun Valley Serenade* (US 41).

The biggest selling record of a song from a movie is Irving Berlin's *White Christmas*, performed by Bing Crosby in *Holiday Inn* (US 42), which has sold over 30 million copies to date.

The biggest selling soundtrack album is of John Williams's symphony for *Star Wars* (US 77), which has sold over three million copies.

The longest movie song title was *How Could You Believe Me When I Said I Loved You When You Know I've Been a Liar All My Life*, sung by Fred Astaire and Jane Powell in *Royal Wedding/GB: Wedding Bells* (US 51).

The first sound film with a full symphonic score was RKO's *The Bird of Paradise* (US 32), with music by Viennese composer Max Steiner. It was also the **first complete film score to be issued on disc**, released by RCA Victor as an album of 78s. Formerly producers had been unwilling to have music coming from an unidentified source, on the premise that audiences would be confused by hearing music where there was no visible orchestra. Hence, early sound films tended to confine the musical accompaniment to the front and end credits or to passages of the action where it could be clearly seen to emanate from a radio or gramophone. There is no evidence that audiences were confused, for once Steiner had established the symphonic score as integral to certain types of movie the source was never questioned. Steiner scored no less than 290 films during his seven years with RKO and 30 years with Warner Bros, including *King Kong* (US 33), *Gone with the Wind* (US 39), and his three Oscar-winning movies *The Informer* (US 35), *Now Voyager* (US 42) and *Since You Went Away* (US 44). The symphonic score fell into disfavour in the 1960s with the rise of pop and jazz accompaniments, but after a slow climb back in the 1970s reached its apogee with John Williams's Oscar-winning music for *Star Wars* (US 77).

The only time an orchestra composed entirely of strings has been used to record the musical accompaniment to a movie was for *Psycho* (US 60). Hitchcock wanted music that would help to terrify the audience and composer Bernard Herrman responded with what he described as a black-and-white sound to complement a black-and-white film of a black-and-white story. The shrieking violin strings played a significant part in making *Psycho* the film that many people remember as the most frightening they have ever seen.

The first use of electronic music on a soundtrack was for *L'Idée* (Fr 34). The score by Arthur Honegger (1892–1955) was for an orchestra which included an electronic instrument called the Theremin.

The first film with an all-electronic score was MGM's *Forbidden Planet* (US 56), with 'electronic tonalities' by Louis and Bebe Barron.

The first feature-length rock concert film was Lee Robinson's *Rock 'n Roll* (Aus 59), an all-star performance from Sydney Stadium.

The most successful concert film was Paramount's *Eddie Murphy Raw* (US 87), which grossed $50 million at the US box office.

The first woman film composer was Jadan Bai, founder of the Sangeet Film Co. and mother of India's superstar Nargis, who made her musical debut with the score of *Talash-e-Huq* (Ind 35).

The first woman composer to write a complete score for a Hollywood feature was Elizabeth Firestone, daughter of tyre magnate Harvey S. F. Firestone, who scored the Robert Montgomery comedy *Once More, My Darling* (US 47).

The first woman to compose for a British feature was Elizabeth Lutyens, whose score accompanied the Christopher Lee–Diana Dors low-budget thriller *Penny and the Pownall Case* (GB 48).

The most successful film composer of all time—in terms of scoring the music for box-office hits—is Boston Pops resident conductor John T. Williams (1932–) who has composed the scores of eight of the ten highest earning films in history: *E.T.* (US 82), *Star Wars* (US 77), *The Empire Strikes Back* (US 80), *Jaws* (US 75), *Raiders of the Lost Ark* (US 81), *Return of the Jedi* (US 83), *Indiana Jones and the Temple of Doom* (US 84) and *Indiana Jones and the Last Crusade* (US 89). He has won four Oscars for Best Original Score.

Music on Set

Providing music on set to create 'mood' for the performers, a common practice during the production of silent dramas, is usually said to have originated with D. W. Griffith's *Judith of Bethulia* (US 14), though the star of the film, Blanche Sweet, says she has no recollection of it. In fact the idea had originated in

Europe at an earlier date, pioneer woman director Alice Guy playing a gramophone on set to assist the actors in emoting during the production of *La Vie du Christ* (Fr 06).

On occasions the practice got out of hand. Garbo was not satisfied with unadorned orchestral music and insisted on being sung to on set, it was reported in 1927. A soloist would join the studio orchestra and serenade her through a megaphone. Another demanding star caused an even greater onslaught of melody, though not entirely of her own volition. During an epic feud between Pola Negri and Gloria Swanson, whose respective egos were too great to be accommodated together in one studio, Swanson's director Allan Dwan hired a 70-strong brass band to drown the noise being made on Negri's adjacent set and persuade his opposite number to control the temperamental Polish star. In another instance the practice was itself instrumental in inflating a performer's ego to the point of affecting his career. Erich von Stroheim had commanded that whenever Anton Wawerka, who played the Emperor Franz Josef in *The Merry-Go-Round* (US 22) and in *The Wedding March* (US 28) appeared on set, the orchestra should strike up the Austrian national anthem. The custom even prevailed off set, all the Hollywood restaurants honouring Wawerka with the anthem whenever he entered their doors. The actor became so accustomed to this regal treatment that he suffered a breakdown when *The Wedding March* was completed and his imperial privileges withdrawn.

The Star as Composer

Charles Chaplin composed the score for all his films from *City Lights* (US 31) onwards. Noel Coward produced, directed, scripted and starred in *In Which We Serve* (GB 42) as well as composing the music. Less well known instances are: Robert Mitchum's composition of the music for the songs *The Ballad of Thunder Road* and *Whipporwill* in *Thunder Road* (US 58); the use of a portion of Lionel Barrymore's symphony *Tableau Russe* in *Dr Kildare's Wedding Day* (US 41); David McCallum's theme song for *Three Bites of the Apple* (US 67); teenager John Rubinstein's score for *All Together Now* (US 75,

Bob Dylan not only composed the music for Sam Peckinpah's *Pat Garrett and Billy the Kid* (US 73) but had third billing as well. (*British Film Institute*)

TVM) —son of legendary pianist Artur Rubinstein, he also starred; and Brazilian soccer star Pele's score for his auto-biopic *Pele* (Mex 78); Kris Kristofferson's title song for *Trouble in Mind* (US 85), in which he starred as an ex-cop and ex-con. Jeff Bridges composed some of the music for the Dustin Hoffman–Mia Farrow movie *John and Mary* (US 69), but did not appear in it. Phil Collins, who starred as Great Train Robber Buster Edwards in *Buster* (GB 88), wrote three of the songs for the picture (in collaboration with Lamont Dozier), including the hit *Two Hearts* which soared to the No 1 spot in the American Top Ten. The jazz solo performed by Richard Gere on the piano in *Pretty Woman* (US 90), prior to his performance with the irresistible Julia Roberts on top of the instrument itself, was the star's own composition.

TEN

*T*ITLES AND CREDITS

*T*ITLES

The Twelve Longest Film Titles

☆ Lina Wertmüller's *Un Fatto di sangue nel commune di Siciliana fra due uomini per causa di una vedova si sospettano moventi politici. Amore · Morte · Shimmy. Lugano belle. Tarantelle. Tarallucci é vino.* (It 79). The English language title was *Revenge.*

☆ *The Persecution and Assassination of Jean-Paul Marat as Performed by the Inmates of the Asylum of Charenton under the Direction of the Marquis de Sade* (GB 66).

☆ *Les yeux ne veulent pas en tout temps se fermer ou peut-être qu'un jour Rome se permettra de choisir à son tour* (Fr/FRG 70).

☆ *Why Do I Believe You When You Tell Me That You Love Me, When I Known You've Been a Liar All Your Life* (GB 83).

☆ *La' il cielo e la terra si univano, la' le quattro stagioni si ricongiungevano la' il vento é la pioggia si incontravano* (It 72).

☆ *Mais que'es-ce que J'ai fait au Bon Dieu pour avoir une femme qui boit dans les cafés avec les hommes?* (Fr 80).

☆ *Those Magnificent Men in Their Flying Machines: or, How I Flew from London to Paris in 25 Hours and 11 Minutes* (GB 65).

☆ *Film d'amore e d'anarchia, ovvero stamattina alle 10, in via dei Fiori, nella nota casa di tolleranza* (It 72).

☆ *Izrada i otkrivanje spomenika velikom srpskom satiricaru Radoju Domanoviću kao i druge manifestacije povodom 100-godisnjice njegovog rodenja* (Yug 75).

☆ *Caffeteria or How Are You Going to Keep Her Down on the Farm after She's Seen Paris Twice* (US 73). Described as 'the short and sweet story of a girl and her 26 cows', this, the longest titled American fiction film, runs precisely one minute.

☆ *F.F.S.S. Cioé: 'Che mi hai portato a fare sopra a posillipo se non mi vuoi più bene?'* (It 83).

☆ *The Saga of the Viking Women and their Voyage to the Waters of the Great Sea Serpent* (US 57).

> 'It is an axiom of cinema history, one admitting of few exceptions, that the longer the film's title the likelier it is to be an outright dud.'—Gilbert Adair

The Shortest Film Titles

These have all had one letter or digit: (an asterisk signifies a feature movie): *A* (Fr 64); *A* (It 69); *B* (It 69); *C* (It 70); *D* (It 70); *E* (Can 82)*; *F* (US 80); *G* (US 72); *G* (GB/FRG 74)*; *G* (Swe 83)*; *H* (US 60); *H* (Can 90)*; *I* (Rom 66); *I* (Swe 66)*; *K* (US 18)*; *K* (Hun 89)*; *M* (Ger 31)*; *M* (US 51)*; *M* (Cz 64); *O* (GB 32); *O* (Jap 75); *P* (Neth 64); *Q* (Fr/It/Bel 74)*; *Q* (US 83)*; *V* (It 68); *V* (US 83) TVM*; *W* (US 73)*; *W* (Phi 85)*; *X* (Ger 28)*; *X* (Swe 57); *X* (US 62); *X* (S. Kor 82)*; *X* (Nor 86)*; *Y* (Swe 87)*; *Z* (Fr/It 68)*; *$* (US 72)*; *3* (US 56); *3* (US c. 80).

> The average number of letters used in a film title is 17.

Odd Titles

Writing in *Films and Filming*, David McGillivray nominated *Betta, Betta in the Wall, Who's the Fattest Fish of All* (US 69) and *She Ee Clit Soak* (US 71) as 'the most preposterous movie titles ever conceived'. Other unusual titles include *Ojojoj* (Swe 66); *RoGoPaG* (It 63); *I-Ro-Ha-Ni-Ho-He-Yo* (Jap 60); *Ha, Ha, Hee, Hee, Hoo Hoo* (Ind 55); *Sssssss* (US 73); *Phffft* (US 54). Rather more comprehensible curiosities are *Telephone Girl, Typist Girl or Why I Became a Christian* (Ind 25); *After the Balled-Up Ball* (US 17); *In My Time Boys Didn't Use Hair Cream* (Arg 37); *The Film That Rises to the Surface of Clarified Butter* (US 68) and *How to Make Love to a Negro without getting Tired* (Can/Fr 88), but some explanation might be needed for *Egg! Egg?* (Swe 75) and *Cash? Cash!* (Bel 69). *Yes* (Hun 64) was followed by *No* (Hun 65) and the situation remained equally unclear with *Yes No Maybe Maybe Not* (GB 75), though things get less indecisive with *Certain, Very Certain, As a Matter of Fact ... Probable* (It 70). *I Go Oh No* (Tai 84) invites the injunction *Hurry, Hurry* (Sp 81), but then the answer will probably be *I Can't ... I Can't* (Eire 69). The response to *I Know that You Know I Know* (It 82) might be *Okay Okay* (It 83) or perhaps *Augh! Augh!* (It 80), while *I'm Married. Ha Ha* (Mex 62) might elicit something more sympathetic like *Come to My Place, I'm Living at My Girl Friend's* (Fr 81) if the problem is *Feudin', Fussin' and A-Fightin'* (US 48). No answers were vouchsafed to the important questions *Who Created the Yoyo? Who Created the Moon Buggy?* (Phi c. 80), though another, unspoken question, met with the response *No Thanks, Coffee Makes Me Nervous* (It c. 81).

Some odd titles make more sense than first appears. *P'Tang Yang Kipperbang* (GB 83) is a recurring phrase in the film's dialogue, representing part of the codes and rituals of teenagers at school in the 1940s. A sci-fi comedy called *Recharge Grandmothers Exactly!* (Cz 84) was about robot grandmothers who take over the running of households. *Down by Law* (US 86) was released in Italy as *Daunbailò*. No, that isn't an Italian dialect word—that's *Down by Law* spelt phonetically. Similarly, *Nocaut* (Mex 84) is not an unfamiliar word in Spanish, but simply the phonetic spelling of 'Knockout'—the picture is about boxing. Andy Bausch's *A Wopbopaloobop A Lopbambboom* (Lux 89) means about as much in Luxembourgish as it does in any other language, while possibly *Beautiful Lady Without Neck* (S. Kor 66) sounded less odd in Korean.

Wordless titles include Warhol's well-known **** (US 67); . . . (Arg 71)—the English language title was *Dot Dot Dot*; and Michael Snow's ↔ (Can 69). Rather less inventive, but eminently explicit, is *A 100% Brazilian Film* (Bra 87), which is a 100% Brazilian film. Casting about for an apt title for an animated film, Aleksander Skrocynski made an inspired choice with *An Animated Film* (Pol 84), while Netherlands producer Jos Stelling figured that if you are trying to sell a Dutch movie, you might as well call it that, so *Dutch Movie* (Neth 84) it was. *Film Without Title* (FRG 47) was the title of a Rudolph Jugert movie, but it was not apparent whether Vincenzo Ferrari's *Untitled* (It 73) had one or not. The makers of *Don't Worry, We'll Think of a Title* (US 65) evidently had trouble in doing so. Less confidence was displayed by the makers of *Still Lacking a Good Title* (Yug 88).

Home Town

Most of the world's big cities and many of the smaller ones have been used in movie titles. This list is confined to titles which consist only of the names of towns.

Abilene Town (US 46); *Albuquerque* (US 48); *Atlantic City* (US 44) (Can/Fr 81); *Bagdad* (US 49); *Bar-cel-ona* (Sp 87); *Baton-Rouge* (Fr 85); *Bengazi* (US 55); *Benghazi* (It 42); *Berlin* (Ger 27); *Bilbao* (Sp 78); *Birdsville* (Aus 86); *Cairo* (GB 42) (GB 63) (Egypt 91); *Calcutta* (US 47); *Canon City* (US 48); *Caracas* (Austria 89); *Carson City* (US 52); *Casablanca* (US 42); *Casablanca, Casablanca* (It 85); *Chartres* (Swz 90); *Cheyenne* (US 47); *Chicago* (US 27); *Coronado* (US 35); *Dallas* (US 50); *Dimboola* (Aus 79); *Dodge City* (US 39); *El Paso* (US 49); *Fort Worth* (US 51); *Fresno* (US 86, TVM); *Guadalajara* (Mex 43); *Havana* (US 90); *Havre* (Fr 86); *Honolulu* (US 39); *Houston, Texas* (Fr 81); *Istanbul* (US 57) (Bel 84); *Jakarta* (US 88); *Kalamazoo* (Can 87); *Karachi* (Nor 88); *Khartoum* (GB 66); *Lahore* (Ind 53); *L.A.NEWYORK-PARISROMEHELSINKI* (US 91); *Laramie* (US 49); *Lisbon* (US 56); *London* (GB 26); *Madrid* (Sp 87); *Malacca* (Swe 86); *Malaga* (GB 54); *Manaos* (It/Mex/Sp 80); *Mandalay* (US 34); *Maracaibo* (US 58); *Marbella* (It 86); *Matewan* (US 87); *Miami* (US 24); *Monte Carlo* (US 26) (US 30); *Montevideo* (FRG 52) (FRG 64); *Naples and Sorrento* (It 30); *Nashville* (US 75); *New Orleans* (US 29); *New York* (US 16) (US 27); *New York, New York* (US 77); *Palm Beach* (Aus 79); *Palm Springs* (US 36); *Paris* (US 26) (US 29); *Paris, Texas* (FRG 84); *Paris-New York* (Fr 40); *Port Arthur* (Cz 37); *Port Said* (US 48); *Prague* (Cz 85) (GB/Fr 91); *Quebec* (US 51); *Reno* (US 23) (US 30) (US 39); *Rimini, Rimini* (It 87); *Rio* (US 39); *Rome* (It 71); *Saigon* (US 48) (US 88); *San Antonio* (US 45); *San Francisco* (US 36) (Bel 83); *Santiago* (US 56); *Santa Fe* (US 51) (Aut 88); *Shanghai* (US 35); *Shiraz* (Ger/Ind 28); *Sofia* (US 48); *Soweto* (GB/Nigeria 88); *Suddenly* (US 54); *Talpa* (Mex 57); *Tangier* (US 46); *Teheran* (GB 47); *Tel Aviv-Berlin* (Isr 87); *Texas City* (US 52); *Timbuctoo* (GB 33); *Timbuktu* (US 59); *Tobruk* (US 66); *Tombstone* (US 42); *Tucson* (US 49); *Tulsa* (US 49); *Union City* (US 80); *Valencia* (Ger 27); *Valparaiso, Valparaiso!* (Fr 71); *Vegas* (US 78, TVM); *Vera Cruz* (US 54); *Virginia City* (US 40); *Washington* (Iran 83); *Wetherby* (GB 85); *Wichita* (US 55); *Yuma* (US 71, TVM).

When *Men* (US 86) was playing at the Ritz Five in Philadelphia, it was reported that the usherettes had their work cut out redirecting male patrons from the other four auditoria who had mistaken the meaning of the sign over the entrance.

Date Titles

1514 (Hun 62); *1740* (Can 77); *1776* (US 06); *1776* (US 72); *1778* (Fr 78); *1789* (Fr 73); *1793* (Fr 14); *1810* (Arg 60); *1812* (Rus 12); *1812* (Ger 23); *1812* (USSR 44); *1812* (GB 65); *1812* (Hun 73); *1814* (Fr 11); *1848* (Rom 80); *1860* (It 32); *1861*

The longest single word in a movie title, and undoubtedly the most unpronounceable, occurs in *Schwarzhuhnbraunhuhnschwarzhuhnweisshuhnrothuhnweiss oder Put-Putt* (FRG 67).

Battle Shock (Isr 87) starring Alon Abouthoul is not to be confused with *Battle Shock* (Isr 87) also starring Alon Abouthoul. Two entirely different movies, one is directed by Yossi Zomer, the other by Yoel Sharon.

(US 11); *1866* (It 33) —English language title; *1870* (It 72); *1871* (GB 90); *1880* (Fr 63); *1884* (GB 83); *1897* (GB 91); *1900* (US 72); *1900* (It/Fr/FRG 77); *1905* (USSR 52); *1907* (Rom 76); *1913* (Bul 85); *1914* (GB 15); *1914* (Ger 31); *1915* (Aus 82); *1917* (GB 70); *1918* (Fin 55); *1918* (USSR 58) —English language title; *1918* (US 85); *1919* (Sp 83); *1919* (GB 85); *1922* (Gre 79); *1925* (Bul 76); *1929* (Cz 74) —English language title; *1929* (Fin 79); *1931* (GB 32); *1933* (Can/US 67); *1936* (It 81); *1936* (Jap 87); *1939* (Swe 90); *1941* (US 41); *1941* (US 79); *1945* (Ger 45); *1945* (Ger 84); *1948* (Fr 48); *1958* (Nor 80); *1967* (US 67); *1968* (US 68); *1969* (US 88); *1970* (US 70); *1971* (Ven 71); *1972* (FRG 73); *1983* (GB 83); *1984* (GB 56); *1984* (GB 84); *1985* (US c. 70); *1996* (GB 89, TVM); *2010* (US 84); *2084* (Aus 85).

Title Changes

☆ *Livingstone* (GB 25), was reissued in America in 1933 as *Stanley*. (Livingstone was British; Stanley an American citizen.) Numerous British films have needed title changes for the USA—*Carleton Browne of the F.O.*/US: *Man in a Cocked Hat* (GB 59) and *Never Take Sweets from a Stranger*/US: *Never Take Candy from a Stranger* (GB 60) are two obvious examples, but there is only one recorded instance of a simultaneous title change *within* Britain. *This England* (GB 41), a wartime flagwaver with Emlyn Williams and Constance Cummings, was retitled *Our Heritage* for release in Scotland.

☆ In China *Great Expectations* (GB 46) was released as *Bleeding Tears of Lonely Star*, *Nicholas Nickleby* (GB 46) as *Hell on Earth*, and *Oliver Twist* (GB 48) as *Lost Child in Foggy City*. Olivier's *Hamlet* (GB 48) became *The Prince's Revenge*.

☆ *Peyton Place* (US 57) played in Paris as *The Pleasures of Hell*, in Munich as *Glowing Fire Under the Ashes* and in Hong Kong as *The Cold and Warmth in the Human World*. *Guys and Dolls* (US 55) was *Heavy Youths and Light Girls* in Germany. Indonesia changed *I'll Cry Tomorrow* (US 55) to *To Relieve Yourself From the Grief of Your Passions*, while Hong Kong looked for something catchier than *Not as a Stranger* (US 55) and came up with *The Heart of a Lady as Pure as a Full Moon Over the Place of Medical Salvation*. *The Rebel Novice Nun* was the Mexican title of *The Sound of Music* (US 65).

☆ The Tokyo office of United Artists translated *Dr No* (GB 62) as *We Don't Want a Doctor*. The sole-

cism was noticed just in time to stop the posters being printed. No such last minute rescue prevented *Eine Nacht in London* (Ger/GB 34) from being released in Britain as *One Knight in London*.

☆ *Chicago, Chicago* was not the mid-west release title of *New York, New York*, but the Spanish title of Norman Jewison's *Gaily, Gaily* (US 69).

☆ *Dracula 72* (GB 72) did not reach France until a year after its release in Britain. When it did, the title had become *Dracula 73*. Similarly *Airport '79* (US 78) became *Airport '80* on its late arrival in the UK.

☆ The working title of United Artists' *Foxes* (US 80) was *Twentieth Century Foxes* until another film company intervened.

☆ The Spanish word for *Grease* (US 78) is *grasa*, but this translates literally as 'fat'. In Spain the movie was released as *Brillantina/Brilliantine* and in Venezuela as *Vaselina/Vaseline*.

☆ The first movie version of Barrie's play *The Admirable Crichton* had its title changed to *Male and Female* (US 19) after it was discovered some exhibitors were billing it as *The Admiral Crichton*. *Flaming Love* (US 25) was released under that title in New York, but it was considered a bit strong for the hicks in the sticks; for out-of-town dates it became *Frivolous Sal*.

☆ Roland Joffé's *Fat Man Little Boy* (US 89) opened with that title, but the intended audience for this drama about the building of the atom bomb stayed away because they thought the picture was a slapstick comedy. Business picked up under the new title *Shadow Makers*.

In the early days of Hollywood Famous-Players Lasky had the democratic practice of allowing the staff to choose the titles of their movies. The scenario would be circulated round the office and everyone, however junior, was allowed to submit two titles for consideration. In the case of a picture with the working title *Billeted*, the producer chose the title suggested by young Sally Brody of the Sales Department and it was released as *The Misleading Widow* (US 19). Sally was rewarded with an extra $10 in that week's pay packet.

☆ *Whisky Galore* (GB 48) was changed to *Tight Little Island* in the US because the Hays Office would not allow alcohol to be named in a film title.

☆ Before the war it had been the British who were uptight about 'improper' titles. Dorothy Arzner's *Merrily We Go to Hell* (US 32) became *Merrily We Go to ----* for its British release.

☆ The screen version of Christopher Hampton's play *Les Liaisons Dangereuses* was changed to *Dangerous Liaisons* (US 89) after a street poll in the US revealed that only 2 per cent of respondents were prepared to see a film with a foreign title.

☆ Darryl F. Zanuck changed the title of *32 Rue Madeleine* to *13 Rue Madeleine* (US 46) because he reckoned 13 was his lucky number.

☆ *The American Success Co* (US 79) started out under that title without much success, so was recut and re-released in 1983 as *American Success*. American it may have been . . . Three years later the distributors tried again with another cut, this time titled simply *Success*. When that did not bring in the crowds either they just had to accept that for them *Success* meant failure.

☆ Among the odder title changes was the one from the explicit *North Seas Hijack* (GB 80) —which gives a clear idea of what the film is about—to the US release title *ffolkes*, which happens to be the name of the character played by Roger Moore. Equally gratuitous was the retitling of Peter Jackson's adult fantasy

Particular key words tend to recur in film titles, according to the spirit of the age. In the last decade the most dominant of these has been 'dance' (or 'dancing'). Namely: *She Dances Alone* (US/Austria 81); *I'm Dancing As Fast As I Can* (US 82); *Hidden Dances* (Swz 83); *Flashdance* (US 83); *Dance of the Widow* (S. Kor 83); *Breakdance 2* (US 84); *Dance with a Stranger* (GB 85); *Dances Sacred and Profane* (GB 85); *Dancing in the Dark* (Can 85); *The Second Dance* (Ice 85); *That's Dancing* (US 85); *Dancing My Daughter* (S. Kor 86); *Dance of the Puppets* (Br 86); *Dancing Rink* (USSR 86); *Tough Guys Don't Dance* (US 87); *Slam Dance* (US 87); *Square Dance* (US 87); *Dirty Dancing* (US 87); *Dancers* (US 87); *Dance Academy* (It/US 87); *Anita—Dances of Vice* (FRG 87); *One for the Dancer* (Mex 87); *Dance Party* (US 87); *Dancing Through the Summer* (Swe 88); *Dancing in the Forest* (US 88); *Shadow Dancing* (Can 88); *Sweet Hearts Dance* (US 88); *The Dancer* (FRG/Jap 88); *Captives of a Night Dance* (Tur 88); *Afraid to Dance* (Aus 88); *Dances* (US 88); *Salome's Last Dance* (US 88); *The Dancer's Touch* (US 89); *Slash Dance* (US 89); *Dance of Hope* (US 89); *Dance to Win* (US 89); *Bulldance* (US 89); *Dance of the Damned* (US 89); *Macho Dancer* (Phi 89); *Carry On Dancing* (HK 89); *Dance Goddess* (Pak 89); *Dance 'Til Dawn* (US 89, TVM); *Dancin' Thru the Dark* (GB 90); *Dances With Wolves* (US 90); *Dancing Bull* (HK 90); *Deadly Dancer* (US 90); *The Tiger Dancer* (Ind 90); *Dance of the Polar Bears* (Den 90); *Dancing Machine* (Fr 90); *The Forbidden Dance* (US 90); *Shall We Dance* (Aus 90); *She Snake Dances in the Streets* (Ind 91); *Dance With Death* (US 91); *And the Dance Goes On* (Can 91); *War Dancing* (US 91); *Chaindance* (US 91); *Dance on the Dump* (Ger 91); *Dancer* (Ind i.p.); *The Waterdance* (US i.p.).

picture *Meet the Feebles* (NZ 90) as *Just the Feebles* in the US.

☆ The title of *Saturday to Monday* was changed to *Experimental Marriage* (US 19) because exhibitors believed that patrons might be misled into thinking that the picture was only playing over the weekend.

☆ *Down and Out in Beverly Hills* (US 85) was released in Italy as *Up and Down Beverly Hills*— sounds similar, is dissimilar.

☆ Paramount considered 250 alternative titles for the American release of Australian smash-hit *Crocodile Dundee* (Aus 86). After rejecting them all, the distributors decided on one small change for US consumption—the first word was put in quotes, as they felt *'Crocodile' Dundee* would help to avoid the misconception that the film was about crocodiles.

☆ Stanley Kramer's *E.R.N.* (US 91) was to be titled *Eleanor Roosevelt's Niggers*. Kramer had obtained the endorsement of the National Association for the Advancement of Colored People, which was willingly granted as this was the self-selected nickname of the black American tank corps whose World War II heroism was the subject of the film. The production office blanched at the prospect of a title likely to be deplored by white liberals even if it passed muster with blacks and decreed a euphemistic acronymn instead.

Star Titles

When a performer's name was billed above the title, that meant real stardom. But an even greater accolade of fame is for a star's name to appear *in* the title—particularly when the star is not in the movie. (Where the title is marked with an asterisk, the star did

Probably the largest number of alternative titles considered for a film was the 422 possibles devised as a substitute for *The Pinnacle*, the title of the novel by Erich von Stroheim which he himself adapted for the screen. Producer Carl Laemmle reckoned this 'too deep' and invited New York exhibitors to vote from a shortlist of eight. They chose *Blind Husbands* (US 19). Von Stroheim was so incensed that he took a full page advertisement in *Motion Picture News* to protest against 'a name which I would have rejected in disgust had it been submitted to me'. Carl Laemmle responded with another full page the following week, saying of the old title: 'I've even heard it accented pee-nokkle in a joking manner, a thing which would kill your picture deader than a salt mackerel.' The picture triumphed as *Blind Husbands*, but Laemmle failed to outlive a persistent Hollywood legend that he had changed the title because he thought that Pinnacle was the name of a cardgame.

appear.) Omitted from this list are star biopics and also titles containing the names of performers like Abbott and Costello who always played a fictitious version of themselves. The first title listed, therefore, is on account of Karloff rather than the comedy duo. *Abbott and Costello Meet the Killer, Boris Karloff* (US 48)*; *Adolf and Marlene* (FRG 77) —with Margit Carstensen as Marlene Dietrich; *Bacall to Arms* (US 46) —Warner Bros Merrie Melodie; *Bela Lugosi Meets a Brooklyn Gorilla* (US 52)*; *The Black Dragon Revenges the Death of Bruce Lee* (HK 75); *Buster's Bedroom* (Ger/Can/Por 91) —refers to Buster Keaton; *Chaplin! Who Do You Cry* (Jap 32) — porno; *Charlie Chaplin and the Kung Fu Kid in Laughing Times* (HK 81); *Charlie Chaplin Na Vitoscia* (Bul 24); *Come Back to the 5 and Dime, Jimmy Dean, Jimmy Dean* (US 82); *The Curse of Fred Astaire* (US 84); *Dear Brigitte* (US 65)*; *F comme Fairbanks* (Fr 75); *Garbo Talks* (US 86); *Gary Cooper, Who Art in Heaven* (Sp 81); *Ginger and Fred* (It 86); *The Gracie Allen Murder Case* (US 39)*; *Happy Birthday, Marilyn!* (Hun 81) —Yes, it does refer to MM; *In Like Flynn* (US 85); *Ist Eddy Polo Schuldig* (Ger 28)*; *The Kiss of Mary Pickford* (USSR 26)*—shot clandestinely without the star knowing she was in it. *The Little Valentino* (Hun 79); *The Man with Bogart's Face* (US 80); *My Dear Tom Mix* (Mex 91); *Sabu and the Magic Ring* (US 57)*; *The Semester We Loved Kim Novak* (Sp 80); *Shirley Temple se enamora* (Mex 38); *Valentino Returns* (US 86); *The Woman Who Married Clark Gable* (Ire 85); *You Elvis, Me Monroe* (FRG 90).

Meaningless or Misleading Titles

☆ *The Bible* (It 13) was not a biblical epic as its title suggested, but a 6-reel melodrama which included a riot in a theatre, a revolver fight on stage, a car chase, a motorcycle blowing up, and people falling out of trains, fighting to the death in rivers, and kidnapping children. Somewhere amongst all this activity a bible was worked into the plot. Warner's *Tracked by the Police* (US 27) was a Rin Tin Tin vehicle whose title was decided before the script was written. The completed film was certainly about tracking, but the tracker was Rin Tin Tin with never a policeman in sight from first reel to last. Edgar Ulmer's *The Black Cat* (US 34) had nothing to do with the Poe story of the same name (despite a credit to Poe) and nothing to do with a black cat other than the fact that a cat crept in and out of a few scenes, to justify the title.
☆ *The Axe* (US 77) was released in Britain as *California Axe Massacre*, though it was set nowhere near California. *Big Hand for a Little Lady* (US 66) had its title changed in Britain to *Big Deal at Dodge City*. Whoever thought this one up had not seen the picture. It was set in Laredo. *Exiled To Shanghai* (US 37) was not about anyone being exiled and the story did not play in Shanghai, while *Roundup Time in*

In *Haunted Honeymoon* (US 86) Gene Wilder and Gilda Radner play an engaged couple staying with Great Aunt Kate (Dom DeLuise in drag). Haunted they may be, but not on honeymoon. *(Kobal)*

Texas (US 37) was about roundup time on the South African veldt and *Adventures in Iraq* (US 43) was set in Syria. *The Malibu Bikini Shop* (US 86) is about a boardwalk swimsuit store in Venice, California, not in Malibu.
☆ Dore Schary, head of production at MGM and RKO in the forties and fifties, recalled that in his early days in Hollywood at Columbia, it was customary to assign a writer a title and expect him to develop an appropriate story. His first assignment was to devise a plot for the title *Fury and the Jungle* and this was followed by *Fog, The Most Precious Thing in Life* and *Man of Steel*. The titles were deliberately kept general enough to admit of almost any plot line.
☆ *Never Say Never Again* (GB 83), the film in which Sean Connery made his reluctant comeback as James Bond, was so called because the Scottish star had said 'Never Again' after *Diamonds Are Forever* (GB 71).
☆ Gene Wilder's *Haunted Honeymoon* (US 86) is about an engaged couple staying in a spooky old house. Story ends well before the honeymoon.
☆ Rather confusingly *As You Like It* (Bul 85) is based on *Romeo and Juliet*.
☆ Audiences might be forgiven for not knowing that the difficult-to-pronounce *Rocinante* (GB 87), starring John Hurt and set against a background of the 1984 miners' strike in Britain, was actually the name of Don Quixote's horse. Or if they did know it, for failing to see the connection with a recent industrial dispute.

☆ In the early 1930s, piracy of ideas was rife in the Indian film industry and director Dhiren Ganguly was wont to evade questions about the title of his next film with a courteous 'Excuse me, Sir' before hastily switching to another topic. After a while people began asking him when *Excuse Me, Sir* was due to be released, so he decided to call his current project by that title. *Excuse Me, Sir* (Ind 31), released in Hindi and Bengali versions, was one of the most successful pre-war Indian comedies.

☆ Equally meaningless, and for not dissimilar reasons, was the title of a Warner movie starring Errol Flynn. During the thirties there was a Hollywood convention of using the wholly fictitious title of *Another Dawn* for films purportedly showing at any cinema in a film story. When Warner's ran out of ideas for something catchy to title the somewhat slender story for Flynn's next exhibition of sexual bravura, they tagged it *Another Dawn* (US 38).

> MGM's Louis B. Mayer, like many Hollywood moguls, had a deep distrust of literature. Silent star John Gilbert, an erudite man with a strong story sense, had a pet project for making a film based on John Masefield's poem *The Widow in the Bye Street*. Mayer rejected the proposal with derision. With the connivance of director Monta Bell, Gilbert got his way. Bell changed the title to *Man, Woman and Sin* (US 27) and Mayer enthusiastically endorsed the script without realizing it was the same story.

☆ Universal executives admitted that they had no idea what relevance *You Can't Cheat an Honest Man* (US 39) had on the subject matter, nor what writer-star W. C. Fields meant by this scarcely tenable aphorism.

☆ In *Her Twelve Men* (US 54), Greer Garson played a teacher in charge of a class of 13 boy pupils. The original story by Louise Baker, on which the film was based, was called *Miss Baker's Dozen*, which aptly and accurately tallied the 13 young men.

☆ *The Amorous Prawn* (GB 62) was about a general's wife who opens their official home in the Highlands to American paying guests. In America the title was changed to *The Playgirl and the War Minister*, despite the fact that there was no playgirl and no War Minister in the film—the date explains the choice, since 1962 was the height of the Profumo Affair. Similarly *Marilyn and the Senator* (US 75) had nothing to do with Marilyn Monroe and Senator Kennedy, despite its promotors' obvious intention to mislead, and the girl entangled with a senator is not even called Marilyn.

☆ *The Seagull* (Ban 79) was indeed a film based on a classic work of literature. It was not, however, a movie version of Chekhov's celebrated play but of Jack London's famous novel *The Sea Wolf*.

☆ Many people who saw and enjoyed Hitchcock's fast-moving thriller *North by Northwest* (US 59) left the cinema wondering what the title had to do with the story. Those of a literary bent may have devined that it was a reference to the character played by Cary Grant, who feigns madness. The words in the title are slightly misquoted from *Hamlet*: 'I am but mad north-northwest; when the wind is southerly, I know a hawk from a handsaw.'

☆ *Waterloo* (Aus 81) is not a reconstruction of the battle, but an Australian documentary on urban planning. On the other hand *Ran-xerox* (Fr 84), which might be taken to be an industrial film about photocopying, is in fact an erotic feature based on a lascivious French comic strip.

> In November 1988 strong winds in London's predominantly Jewish suburb of Golders Green blew off the final letter of the film being advertised on the canopy of the Cannon Ionic cinema. The title read *Who Framed Roger Rabbi*.

☆ *Special Effects* (US 85) does not have any.

☆ UA's 16th Bond movie *License to Kill* (US 89) was to have been called *Licence Revoked*, a title which would have made a good deal more sense. The storyline has Bond's double-O 'licence to kill' revoked by M as he embarks on a personal vendetta to revenge the slaying of his CIA friend Felix Leiter's wife. It is, therefore, the only Bond movie in which the agent does *not* have a licence to kill. But when UA discovered that less than 20 per cent of the American public knew the meaning of 'revoked', they decided to go for the simpler, even though contradictory, alternative.

☆ *South of Rio* (US 49) took place well north of it and *Krakatoa, East of Java* (US 68) wasn't. Krakatoa was 200 miles *west* of Java.

> The title *Halloween IV The Return of Michael Myers* (US 89) enshrines the name of the bogeyman figure of John Carpenter's *Halloween* series who keeps slicing his way through Middle America. But whence came the name Michael Myers? He is in fact a real person, alive and well and living in London. Far from being a homicidal maniac, though, he is in fact the gently mannered UK distributor who handled Carpenter's early entry into the suspense genre, *Assault on Precinct 13* (US 76). The picture bombed in the US, due mainly to lacklustre promotion, but became a hit in Britain as a result of Michael Myers' enthusiastic and vigorous marketing pitch. As a tribute to the hard working executive, Carpenter conferred on him a measure of screen immortality by namesaking the horrific *Halloween* hatchetman.

Krakatoa wasn't . . . Krakatoa was 200 miles *west* of Java!

INTER-TITLES AND SUBTITLES

The earliest known use of inter-titles was by R. W. Paul in *Our General Servant* (GB 98), at 320 ft the longest story film then produced in Britain. Presented in four scenes, with linking inter-titles, it related how a new maid was compromised by the master of the house. **The earliest known European example** is Georges Méliès' *L'Affair Dreyfus* (Fr 99) and **the earliest American example**, Edwin S. Porter's *Uncle Tom's Cabin* (US 03). **The earliest known use of dialogue in inter-titles** occurs in Edwin S. Porter's *The Ex-Convict* (US 04).

Subtitles superimposed over action—as in foreign language films today—**were first used** in a Lubin serial *Road o' Strife* (US 15) in order to avoid interrupting the fast-paced narrative. The only other silent picture examples known are another serial, *Judex* (Fr 17), the monumental *Ben Hur* (US 25) and *Walking Back* (US 28). The reason it was not done more often appears to be the problem presented with foreign-language versions.

The silent film with the most inter-titles in rela-

tion to its length was *Every Woman's Problem* (US 25), starring Dorothy Davenport. Nat Levine, then sales manager with a Kansas City film exchange, bought the 2300 ft negative, with no titles, for a bargain basement $10,000. By adding 2600 ft of inter-titles he increased it to acceptable feature length and, by choosing an enticing main title, did well enough at the box office to gross four times his investment. Levine used his profit to go into production on his own account, founding the famous

> There are at least two examples of films in which the dialogue was contained in speech bubbles as is the practice with comic strips: the comedy thriller *The Chamber Mystery* (US 20) and the Our Gang three-reeler *Spook Spoofing* (US 28).

Poverty Row studio of Mascot Pictures. *Every Woman's Problem* was probably the only film in which the titles occupied more time than the action.

Silent films with no inter-titles—Murnau's *The Last Laugh* (Ger 25) has often been described as the first feature-length silent movie to rely solely on the action for the development of the narrative, to the exclusion of explanatory titles. Those that preceded it were: Max Reinhardt's *Eine Venzianische*

Nacht (Ger 14); Alexander Tairov's *Le Mort* (Rus 15); *A Page from Life* (It 16); *Remorse* (Den 20); *The Rail* (Ger 21); *The Old Swimming Hole* (US 21); *Warning Shadows* (Ger 22); Karl Grune's *The Street* (Ger 23); Lupu Pick's *Sylvester* (Ger 23); *Lily of the Alley* (GB 23); *The Audacious Mr Squire* (GB 23).

Silent screen audiences were either infinitely more patient than their TV-age counterparts or else much slower readers. The duration of inter-titles for silent films was calculated according to a formula of three seconds for the first word, one second for every subsequent two words. Since substantial dialogue exchanges were often presented in writing, an inter-title could last as much as half a minute, particularly if the producer wanted to pad out insufficient footage to feature length. The maximum acceptable duration for modern subtitles to foreign language pictures is reckoned to be six seconds.

The amount of footage devoted to inter-titles tended to increase as plots became more complex. About 8 per cent of the average one-reeler of 1000 ft was devoted to titles in 1910; by the mid-20s up to 25 per cent of a feature might be titles.

CREDITS

The first screen credits went to André Heuzé for the films he wrote for the French production company Pathé Frères from 1906.

The first person to receive screen credits in the USA was G. M. Anderson, as the leading man of the Broncho Billy westerns in 1908. As producer and author of the films, and part-owner of the Essany studio, Anderson was in a strong position to promote his own name. Generally performers in American films did not receive screen credit until 1911, when the Edison Co. and Vitagraph Co. led the way.

LOCAL GIRL NEARLY MADE GOOD
During the early thirties supporting player Dorothy Jordan was always given the star billing when her films were shown in her home town of Clarksville, Tennessee, however minor the role.

The first British film known to have included screen credits was the Gaumont Co.'s *Lady Letmere's Jewellery* (GB 08), with Maisie Ellis in the title role. The credits were pictorial, each leading character being portrayed next to a card bearing his or her name and role. It is possible that Gaumont had adopted the practice of screen credits earlier the same year when they released a film version of the Lyceum Theatre production of *Romeo and Juliet* (US 08), with Godfrey Tearle and Mary Malone. In this case the cast had been billed in the advertising for the film.

The film-maker with most screen credits was Cedric Gibbons (1893–1960), whose name appeared as art director on over 1500 films between 1917 and 1955. The feat was achieved by Gibbons' insistence on a clause in his 1924 contract with MGM to the effect that every film produced by the studio in the USA would credit him as art director. In practice the art direction for the majority of these films was in the hands of his subordinates.

Demagogic movie mogul Harry Cohn's legendary ruthlessness extended even to the credits on Columbia's releases. Ken Hall's *Smithy* (Aus/US 46), a biopic of the great Australian aviator Sir Charles Kingsford Smith, was made under contract to Columbia by the Australian production company Cinesound with an all-Australian cast and crew. The sole interest of the Hollywood studio was to use up dollar assets frozen in Australia. When Cohn saw the finished product, he ordered fictitious credits substituted for the real ones to disguise its Australian origin. Cohn was nothing if not thorough; even the acknowledgements to the Sydney Symphony Orchestra and the Royal Australian Air Force ended up on the cutting-room floor.

The first pre-credit sequence was in Ben Hecht and Charles MacArthur's *Crime Without Passion* (US 34), which opens with an extreme close-up of the barrel of a gun. The gun fires and blood drips on to the floor. The three Furies of Greek mythology ascend from the puddle of blood in flowing robes and fly over a modern metropolis inciting various crimes of passion. One of the Furies sweeps her arm over the face of a skyscraper, shattering the window glass, which showers down until it forms the words *Crime Without Passion*.

The record for the longest pre-credit sequence is shared by Dennis Hopper's *The Last Movie* (US 71) and Pere Portabella's *Pont De Varsoria* (Sp 90), both movies running for a full half-hour before the credits roll. Portabella's film opens with the award ceremony for a literary prize won by a book with the same title as the movie. The credit sequence begins after 30 minutes of this prologue, which concludes with the book's author deciding to summarise the plot for a guest at the reception. The remainder of the picture, after the credits, consists of scenes from the award winning novel.

The record for the longest credit sequence is shared by Sergio Leone's *Once Upon a Time in the West* (It/US 68) and Richard Donner's *Superman*

(GB 78), each movie running the credits for 12 minutes. Leone disposed of them all at once, Donner in bite-size chunks of five mintues at the start and seven at the end. But Donner's took up more of the movie—9 per cent of the running time against 7 per cent for the longer Leone picture.

The largest number of names credited was 743 for the part-animated *Who Framed Roger Rabbit* (US 89). The majority of these were Richard Williams' skilful team of animators. Highest number on a non-animated movie was 457 for *Superman* (GB 78), which shares the record for the longest credit sequences at 12 minutes (see above). The much greater Roger Rabbit roster sped by in 6½ minutes.

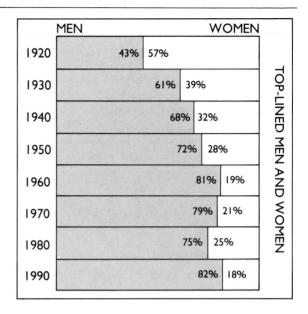

Top-lined

The oft reiterated complaint that there are few good parts for women in modern movies seems to be borne out by the figures for who gets top-lined in the credits—the leading man or the leading lady. Male stars are said to have more pulling power at the box office, but that has to have something to do with the fact that the male role is usually the dominant one—particularly now when one out of eight Hollywood movies feature policemen as the principal characters (see p. 65). It was not always so. In the days of silent pictures, more women were top-lined in American productions than men—as the chart below shows, in 1920 57 per cent of the stars with the main credit were women. By 1930, when talkies had all but ousted the silent film, male stars were in the ascendant, with 61 per cent of the top-line credits. The proportion continued to increase in favour of men at each ten-year point to 1960, when less than a fifth of Hollywood releases gave the major credit to the leading lady. In 1970 and 1980 there was a small decline, but in 1990 there were 256 movies which top-lined the male lead, only 57 the female—a ratio of 82 to 18 per cent. It seems that as opportunities for women have grown greater in the real world, the world depicted by Hollywood has grown inversely more macho. Whatever the reasons, one of the most obvious is the cult of violence. The most prevalent theme in the films of 1920 was dilemma within the family—its resolution, more often than not, lay in the hands of the female protagonist. Few of the films of 1990 were about families—the dominant theme was the resolution of problems by direct action, too often with fists or a gun—and the defender of the American Way was almost inevitably male. This chart, exclusive to *The Guinness Book of Movie Facts & Feats*, records one of the few areas of human activity in the 20th century in which the participation of women has declined dramatically. Figures in brackets are number of films.

Unusual Credits

In *The Terror* (US 28), the novelty of sound inspired Warner's to have the credits spoken by a caped and masked Conrad Nagel. Other films in which the credits have been spoken rather than written include Orson Welles' *The Magnificent Ambersons* (US 42), Truffaut's *Fahrenheit 451* (GB 66), Tony Richardson's *Hamlet* (GB 69) and Robert Altman's *M*A*S*H* (US 70). The last named had a recurring theme of the front line field hospital's nightly film show being announced over the Tannoy. The last film to be so announced is *M*A*S*H* itself, with full credits. A film called *Episode* (Aut 35) was released with conventional credits at home, but with spoken credits in Nazi Germany. In this case the reason was more sinister than a mere desire for novelty. The director of the picture, Walter Reisch, was Jewish. The credits were spoken against a musical background and when Reisch's name was reached, the music swelled to make it inaudible.

One of the few recorded examples of sung credits features in *Por que te engana tu marido/Why Does Your Husband Deceive You* (Sp 69). The vocalists are a priest and his choirboys. The credits were sung also on *Don Juan, My Dear Ghost* (Sp 90).

A mystery credit on *True Blood* (US 89), to the Wyoming Film Commission, remains unexplained. The picture is not set in Wyoming and was not filmed there.

Credits for *Lonely in America* (US 90), about a boy from India coming to New York to work on the family news-stand, has some of the credits as magazine cover-lines, others on a subscription card, a scratch 'n' win lottery ticket and, for the director credit, a trashy tabloid. The *Variety* critic observed: 'This may be the first time a non-industry audience applauded the credits.' *The Gentle Touch* (It 88), a comedy about a proof-reader, has the credits presented as uncorrected proofs, complete with literals, wrong spacing, spelling mistakes etc. As the credits roll, the errors are corrected.

The Bear (Fr 89) has four casting directors credited. Yet the cast consisted of three people, one non-speaking and the others hardly speaking. The credits also included a credit for the credits.

In *Young Toscanini* (It 88), veteran French star Philippe Noiret was billed as making 'a friendly appearance'.

Spike Lee's *Do the Right Thing* (US 89), set in and around a pizzeria in the mainly black Bedford-Stuyvesant district of Brooklyn, has an end credit exhorting audiences to register to vote. The idea was that they should vote against Mayor Ed Koch, whose New York was not to Spike Lee's liking.

If I Ever See You Again (US 78) had several credits to dentists, for no obvious reason other than the fact that leads Joe Brooks and Shelley Hack had teeth of the gleaming perfection seemingly unique to the state of California.

Probably the only film which managed to spell its star's name wrong in the credits was *The Bit Part* (Aus 87), with topliner Chris Haywood billed as 'Heywood'.

In Mike Snow's curiously titled ↔ (Can 69), the credits appear in the middle of the film.

Notorious credits include two for authors. *The Taming of the Shrew* (US 28) bore the attribution 'by William Shakespeare, with additional dialogue by Sam Taylor'; while *The Black Cat* (US 34) was credited to Edgar *Allen* Poe, a misspelling of his middle name. (The fact that the film had absolutely nothing to do with Poe's story did not seem to trouble anyone.)

Fritz Lang's *Hangmen Also Die* (US 43) is probably the only film with credits distinguishing the scriptwriter who wrote the script that was used (Fritz Lang) from the scriptwriter who wrote the script that was not (Bertold Brecht). Incensed that Lang had departed so far from his intended ideas, Brecht won a court decision that allowed him a credit disassociating his script from the shooting script.

Adrian Lyne's *Fatal Attraction* (US 87) boasts one of the odder script credits with 'screenplay, James Dearden, for the screenplay based on his original screenplay'. This last was the screenplay for a 45-minute film called *Diversion* (US 79), rescripted and reshot as a full-length feature under a new title.

Escapade (US 35) ended with William Powell speaking to camera to tell the American public about his co-star, newcomer Luise Rainer, and MGM's high hopes for her Hollywood career. Miss Rainer herself then appeared and was introduced to the audience by Powell.

The role of Crystal Kingsby in *The Lady in the Lake* (US 46) is given as Ellay Mort. In fact the character never appears, because she is dead. Ellay Mort is 'elle est mort'. Story credit for *Lt Robin Crusoe USN* (US 66) went to the somewhat obscure Retlaw Yensid. Reversed it reveals the rather better known Walt Disney.

Marie-Sophie Pochat is billed as Marie-Sophie L. in Claude Lelouch's *Attention Bandits* (Fr 87). The discreet identification masks the fact that the L stands for Lelouch—the director married her immediately after the completion of the picture.

Hollywood feminism is even taking over the credits. The Best Boy on *Slam Dance* (US 87) is credited as 'Electrical Best Person'.

Diangaka (SA 65) had a credit which read 'Original African music composed by . . .' followed by a number of European names.

The sombre Australian melodrama *In Search of Anna* (Aus 78), featuring a pooch called Billy, had a closing credit which informed audiences that 'Billy eats Loyal Dog Food'. Dusan Makavejev's *The Coca Cola Kid* (Aus 85) contained an unusual testimonial in the credits: 'Catering—Kaos (Highly recommended by the whole cast and crew)'. What appears to be an Australian preoccupation with comestibles stimulated another testimonial at the end of *The Marsupials: The Howling III* (Aus 87), which has a credit to the restaurant director Philippe Mora for his Eggs Benedict. Credit for catering on *Cactus* (Aus 86) was to Cecil B. DeMeals.

The Merchant-Ivory production *Mr and Mrs Bridge* (US 90) has an end credit which reads 'Shakespearean tutor to Mr Newman: Sen. Bob Dole'. This refers to the Kansas politician's reading of *Romeo and Juliet* to Paul Newman to assist him in his characterisation of Kansas City lawyer Walter Bridge.

Only a movie as pretentious as *Patti Rocks* (US 89), with its avowed purpose of 'questioning patriarchal language' and 'equalising nudity', could have a credit to the 'Spiritual Adviser'. On a more down-to-earth level there was also a credit for 'Skunk Wrangler'. *The Dark Half* (US 91) has a credit for 'Sparrow Wranglers'. In the finale the villain is attacked by hordes of these vicious little creatures (sparrows, not wranglers).

Making of *The Cotton Club* (US 85) involved so much litigation that the credits even included one for the law firm representing the successful litigants.

Night Patrol (US 84), a knockabout comedy about offbeat Los Angeles cops, had all the credits in French for some inexplicable reason.

Unique credit on a unique version of *Casablanca* (US 43) is 'Copyright Infringements by Joao Luiz Albuquerque'. Brazilian cinéaste Albuquerque recut the classic movie for a private showing at the 1987 Rio Film Festival. In the celebrated airport scene Ingrid Bergman does not get on to the plane leaving Casablanca and comes back into the arms of Bogey. 'Diversions by Irving Schwartz' among the credits

'Tail by Dunlop'. Glynis Johns in *Miranda* (GB 47).
(*British Film Institute*)

for *The Sand Pebbles* (US 66) was, apparently, in tribute to a mysterious, unknown correspondent whose letters proved a morale booster to cast and crew during trying location work in Hong Kong and Taiwan.

Other unusual credits include one for the 'Roach Wrangler' on George Romero's *Creepshow* (US 59) —the film contains a scene involving thousands of cockroaches; for the 'Technical Consultant on Vampire Bats' on *Chosen Survivors* (US 74); for 'Ant Consultant' in *Empire of the Ants* (US 77); for 'Orgy Sequence Adviser' on *Solomon and Sheba* (US 59); for the perfume worn by the leading players in *Marjorie Morningstar* (US 58); for the shoe polish brightening the cast's shoes in *Scent of Mystery* (US 60); for 'Tail by Dunlop' on *Miranda* (GB 47) — Miranda was a mermaid; for the 'Second Second Assistant Director' on *Reform School Girls* (US 86); for the 'Assistant to the Assistant to the Unit Publicist' on *The Greek Tycoon* (US 78); and to Frederico Fellini, who was not on the picture, 'for encouragement at the right time' in *The World's Greatest Lover* (US 77). *The Killing Fields* (GB 84) displayed the enigmatic credit 'Assistant Footsteps Editor', while Gary Graver's low-budget horror pic *Trick or Treats* (US 82) credits Orson Welles as 'Magical Consultant'. 'Fangs by Dr Ludwig von Krankheit' in Polanski's *Dance of the Vampires* (GB 67) should probably be taken with a pinch of garlic salt.

ELEVEN

CENSORSHIP

The first film known to have been suppressed was taken by Lumière cameraman Francis Doublier in Moscow in the summer of 1896 and showed Prince Napoléon dancing with the 'lady of his affections', a professional dancer. The film was seized by the Russian police and destroyed.

Later the same year *Delorita's Passion Dance* (US 96) became **the first film to be banned in the USA** when it was prohibited from exhibition in Atlantic City, NJ, by order of the Mayor.

The world's first regulated film censorship was introduced under a Chicago City Council Ordinance of 4 November 1907 'prohibiting the exhibition of obscene and immoral pictures'. Effective 19 November 1907, the Ordinance required that every film be shown to the Chief of Police before it was exhibited publicly and an exhibition permit obtained. Penalty for violation was a fine of $50–100 (£10–20), each day of exhibition without a permit to be regarded as a separate offence. One of the first films to fall foul of the censorship in Chicago was a Vitagraph production of Shakespeare's *Macbeth* (US 08), banned by a zealous police lieutenant on the grounds that 'Shakespeare is art, but it's not adapted altogether for the five cent style of art'. He explained: 'The stabbing scene in the play is not predominant. But in the picture show it is the feature.'

The first country to establish a State Censorship Board was Sweden. The Statens Biografbyrå was founded on 4 September 1911 and all films released in Sweden after 1 December 1911 were required to be certified by the Board.

Censorship USA

The USA is one of four countries where the film industry has a self-regulatory censorship independent of government (the others are Britain, Germany and Japan). The following is a brief chronology of American censorship as regulated by the Motion Picture Producers of America (MPPA).

1922 The Motion Picture Producers and Distributors of America founded March under the presidency of former Postmaster General Will H. Hays in an attempt to regulate the industry from within and combat growing demands for government intervention. At this date there were already eight State Censorship Boards (Maryland, New York, Florida, Ohio, Pennsylvania, Virginia, Kansas, Massachusetts) plus 90 municipal boards of varying degrees of severity.

Roscoe 'Fatty' Arbuckle, the world's highest paid entertainer, became **the first screen star to be banned**. The announcement was made by Will H. Hays of the MPPDA on 18 April, six days after Arbuckle had been acquitted of the manslaughter of 'good time girl' Virginia Rappe. Shortly afterwards Hays drew up a list of 200 people considered morally dangerous whom it was intended to bar from the industry. Heading the list was Wallace Reid, probably the most popular male star in America prior to Fairbanks' ascendancy, whose drug habit was to finish his career before the MPPDA was able to finish it for him.

1924 The 'Hays Formula' introduced—members agreed to submit scripts in advance for comment and guidance. Few did so unless the script was known to be innocuous.

A scene cut from Mervyn LeRoy's *I Am A Fugitive From A Chain Gang* (US 32). The rule about floggings was that you could show the impact of the whip but not the sound of the blow; or you could have the sound, but not the sight of the whip falling. In the version of the film as released the camera tracked along the faces of the other convicts as they listened to the thud of the heavy belt.

The 'Index' of forbidden books and plays was introduced.

1927 Hays' list of 'Don'ts' and 'Be Carefuls' adopted in June. Eleven 'Don'ts' include 'any licentious or suggestive nudity', 'miscegenation', 'ridicule of the clergy', 'any inference of sex perversion' and 'the illegal traffic of drugs'. 'Be Carefuls' included 'brutality and possible gruesomeness' and 'the sale of women, or of a woman selling her virtue'. Largely ineffective.

1930 First Production Code—known as 'The Hays Code'—drawn up by Martin Quigley, publisher of *Motion Picture Herald*, and Fr Daniel A. Lord of St Louis University. Introduced 31 March. No penalties for evasion.

1931 Prior submission of scripts made binding on members.

1934 Production code Administration Office established in June. 'Resolution for Uniform Interpretation' required producers to abide by Code. Penalties for evasion introduced.

First Seal of Approval granted by Hays Office to Fox's *The World Moves On* 11 July.

1943 Howard Hughes caused the first serious breach of the Code when he exhibited *The Outlaw* (US 43) without a Seal of Approval. Billy the Kid, a criminal and moral transgressor, and his girl Rio, a moral transgressor only, were able to ride off into the sunset without reaping any of the just deserts demanded by the Code. (Or by history—in reality Billy the Kid was shot.)

1954 Code seriously breached when Preminger distributed *The Moon is Blue*, a comedy about virginity, without a Seal of Approval.

1955 *The Man with the Golden Arm* awarded Seal despite explicit treatment of drug addiction.

1956 Revised Code introduced. Nudity, profanity and obscenity remained forbidden in all circumstances. Most other former prohibitions modified.

1961 *The Children's Hour* granted Seal despite theme of sexual deviation—in this case lesbianism.

1964 Sidney Lumet's *The Pawnbroker* was passed uncut with a scene showing a woman naked to the waist. This was the first time nudity had been allowed on screen since the setting up of the Production Code Administration Office 30 years earlier.

1966 The 'blue language' barrier finally crashed by *Who's Afraid of Virginia Woolf*, the Production Code Administration agreeing to give it a Seal (with audiences restricted to over 18s) because it reflected 'the tragic realism of life'.

Code revised again, with no positive prohibitions remaining. Approved films were now divided into 'general audience' and 'mature audience'.

1968 Production Code Administration defied when they refused to approve two British films which contained scenes of oral sex: Michael Winner's *I'll Never Forget Whatshisname* (GB 67) and Albert Finney's *Charlie Bubbles* (GB 68). They were released through subsidiary companies of the intending distributors which were not members of the Association. This device enabled any major distributor to circumvent the Administration and hastened its end.

Code replaced by ratings system under the Motion Picture Association of America Ratings Board, effective 1 November. Four classifications: G = General Audience; M = Mature Audience; R = Restricted (children under 16 to be accompanied by an adult); X = over 16 only.

1970 M was replaced by GP (General Patronage) as 'mature' was being misinterpreted as X+. R was changed to accompanied children under 17 and GP became PG (Parental Guidance).

1981 The last State Censorship Board—Maryland—dissolved after 65 years of activity. During its last full year of operation, the Maryland Censor Board viewed 559 movies and banned eight.

1984 A new PG-13 rating introduced 27 June to designate films which require 'special guidance' from parents for children under 13.

1990 Following increasing dissatisfaction with the X-rating, which impeded the distribution of films of artistic merit but explicit sex content, a new NC-17 rating was introduced by the MPPA to signify no children under 17. At the beginning of October the first film to be released under the new rating, Universal's prestigious *Henry and June* (US 90), was banned unseen in Dedham, Mass. A selectman justified the banning with the statement that an X-rated film by any other rating remains an X film.

Censorship GB

The British Board of Film Censors (BBFC) was inaugurated by the Kinematograph Manufacturers' Association in October 1912 with powers effective from 1 January 1913. The moving spirit behind the venture was the film producer Will Barker, who was concerned at the increase in the number of films being produced 'for the smoking room', which he considered would bring the whole industry into disrepute. Together with Col A. C. Bromhead and Cecil Hepworth, two leading pioneer film-makers, he persuaded the Kinematograph Manufacturers' Association that it was up to the trade to put its own house in order, and with the approval of the Home Secretary the Board was established under the Presidency of G. A. Redford, formerly a playreader for the Lord Chamberlain.

The original classification was into 'U' (Universal) and 'A' (Adult). **The first U Certificate** was granted to the Barker production *Mary of Briarwood Dell* (GB 13) and **the first A Certificate** to the Clarendon picture *A Strong Man's Love* (GB 13), both on 1 January 1913. The A Certificate was originally advisory only. It was not until 1923 that the

London County Council prohibited unaccompanied children under 16 from attending A films. Most other local authorities in England and Wales followed suit by the end of the decade, though in Scotland the A Certificate always remained advisory only.

The BBFC began its life with only two firm prohibitive rules: no film depicting the living figure of Jesus Christ and no film which contained scenes of nudity would be granted a Certificate. During the first year of operation, the Board examined 7510 films (6861 'U'; 627 'A'), of which only 22 were rejected outright. Reasons included 'indelicate or suggestive sexual situations', 'holding up a Minister of Religion to ridicule', 'excessive drunkenness' and the portrayal of 'native customs in British lands abhorrent to British ideas'. In 1917 the new Chairman, T. P. O'Connor, declared that he would not grant a Certificate to any film in which crime was the dominant feature and warned producers that no criminal was to be portrayed as a victim of social deprivation. By 1925 the following were also among the 'Don'ts': 'Women fighting with knives'; 'Animals gnawing men, women and children'; 'Insistence upon the inferiority of coloured races'; and 'Salacious wit'.

An 'H' Certificate (advisory only) was introduced in 1933 to designate horror films, and 'X' for 'Adult Only' in 1951. A revised rating system took effect in 1970 with the A Certificate reverting to advisory status, a new AA classification signifying a minimum admission age of 14, and a raising of the admission age from 16 to 18 for X films. It was found that few people understood the status of A and AA films and by the end of the seventies Britain was one of the only countries still using X for respectable adult films, often of artistic merit; elsewhere it was being used solely as a label for pornography. The current ratings system, introduced in December 1982, retained the U for Universal, but replaced A with PG (Parental Guidance) and AA and X with a simple numerical classification of 15 and 18 respectively to denote the minimum age for admission. It also added an 18R category to classify porno and violent films only for showing in specially licensed cinemas.

The Board's function and powers have remained fundamentally unchanged since its inception, despite modification of its criteria for certification in line with changing social and moral standards. An *aide-mémoire* states: 'The power of censorship is in the hands of Local Authorities. The BBFC exists to act as an intermediary between Local Authorities and the film industry. Its success or failure can be measured simply in terms of the acceptability of its judgements to the majority of Local Authorities in Britain.'

Local Authorities have the power to alter the Certificate issued by the BBFC or to permit the showing of an uncertified film. They also remain the only agency with the power to refuse the right of exhibition.

Censorship was extended to home video movies in Britain in 1985. Unlike cinema films, where the BBFC classification is advisory only, and can be changed on resubmission, the ratings given to video movies are statutory and cannot be altered. The move was generally welcomed, as it meant the end of 'video nasties', but there have been two particularly controversial decisions. The BBFC banned the 20-minute video *Visions of Ecstasy* (GB 89) on grounds of blasphemy, the first occasion any film production had been refused for this reason. The film included scenes of the 16th-century Spanish nun St Theresa of Avila embracing the crucified Christ with more than spiritual devotion and episodes of lesbian fantasy. The Board was legally bound to reject any film which it believed to be in violation of Britain's 17th-century blasphemy law, but its decision was bitterly opposed by libertarians. The following year the Board banned distribution of the video of *International Guerillas* (Pak 90) on the grounds that it might be criminally libellous. The Pakistani film portrayed Salman Rushdie, author of *The Satanic Verses*, as a drunken playboy who tortures and murders Muslims as part of an international plot, before being struck down by Allah with a bolt of lightning. Mr Rushdie himself declared that he was against the ban.

A new '12' certificate (no children under 12 admitted) was introduced by the City of Westminster, which covers London's West End, in 1989. First film to be awarded the new rating was *Madame Sousatska* (GB 89). It was adopted by the BBFC in August of the same year.

The first cut made by censors in a soundtrack was of offensive words sung by Winnie Lightner in a 1927 Vitaphone short produced by Warner Bros.

The first film to receive an X-rating (adults only) under the British Board of Film Censors system of classification was *La Vie commence demain/Life Begins Tomorrow* (Fr 50), which opened in London on 9 January 1951. The reason for the X Certificate was a sequence dealing with artificial insemination. Previously the film would have had to have been either banned or cut. By the end of the permissive 1960s the number of X films had surpassed the number of A and U films combined.

The first film to receive an X-rating under the Motion Picture Association of America system of classification was Brian de Palma's anti-establishment *Greetings* (US 68) with Robert de Niro, which opened in New York on 15 December 1968.

The first film containing a scene of sexual intercourse to be passed fit for juvenile (accompanied) audiences in Britain was *Siddhartha* (US 72), starring Shashi Kapoor and Simi Garewal and based on the Hermann Hesse bestseller.

The largest number of cuts known to have been ordered by a censor to one film is 103 in respect of Faria de Almeida's *Catembe* (Por 64), a critical film by a Mozambique director about the then Portuguese Colony. The most cuts to a Hollywood film was 60 in the case of D. W. Griffith's *Way Down East* (US 20), a heart-rending Victorian melodrama which had been reducing stage audiences to tears for the previous 30 years without apparently undermining their morals. The pivot of the story concerns the waif-like heroine's (Lillian Gish) illegitimate baby and it was this to which the Pennsylvania State Censorship Board took grave exception. Scenes ordered to be cut in their entirety included the mock marriage (the heroine having been deceived), the mock honeymoon, the heroine announcing that she was with child, and all sequences relating to its birth. Indeed the baby made its first, unheralded appearance in the cut version only shortly before it expired, much to the bewilderment of Pennsylvania audiences. (The Board also insisted, for reasons undisclosed, that the title 'I can never be any man's wife' be changed to 'I can never marry any man'.)

The Japanese censor board insisted on more than 450 'blurs' before permitting the release of Bob Guccione's notorious production of *Caligula* (US 79).

'Cinema's Summer of Blood' is how the tabloid press dubbed 1990's season of ultra-violent movies. *Total Recall* (US 90) offered gore fans 110 acts of violence an hour and 35 slayings, 18 of them performed by muscleman Arnold Schwarzenegger in a bad mood—including shooting his on-screen wife through the head with the laconic pronouncement 'Consider this a divorce'. In one of his milder tantrums he rips someone's arms out of their sockets. *Cold Steel* (US 90) had an even higher count of 147 acts of violence an hour and *Die Hard II* (US 90) an all-in total of 200.

The most banned film is open to dispute, but one contender is *Make Them Die Slowly* (US 83), billed as 'The Most Violent Ever'. Publicity for the picture proudly proclaimed that it had been banned in 31 countries.

The country to have imposed the most outright bans is Abu Dhabi with a cumulative total of some 2800. Most of the films affected were declared obscene, anti-Islamic or favourable to Jews.

The first country to abolish censorship of films was Russia under the Kerensky government in March 1917. It was formally reimposed in 1922, though in practice there had been a strong measure of control since the accession of the Bolsheviks to power. In the Stalinist era the Soviet censorship became the most rigorous in the world, to the point of nearly extinguishing the film industry in the 1950s. It remained so until Glasnost.

The brief flowering of liberty in the revolutionary Russia of 1917 had resulted in nothing more stimulating than a spate of anti-Tsarist films, most of them centring on the depraved monk Rasputin as the architect of decay. When Germany abolished censorship in December 1918, the worst fears of its upholders were confirmed by the rash of sex films that followed. Their titles in no way belied their content: *Frauen, die der Abgrund verschlingt/Women Engulfed by the Abyss* (Ger 18), *Verlorene Töchter/Lost Daughters* (Ger 19), *Die Prostitution* (Ger 19), *Hyänen der Lust/Hyenas of Lust* (Ger 19), etc. Homosexuality (q.v.) was also treated on the screen for the first time. It is doubtful whether anything so explicitly sexual was encountered again in films until the 1960s. Censorship was restored by the National Assembly in May 1920.

No other country abolished censorship for adult audiences until 1969, when Denmark took a lead which was to be followed in the 1970s by Austria, Uruguay, Portugal and Upper Volta and in the 1980s by Panama, Argentina, Peru, Brazil, Hungary and, most remarkably of all, the Soviet Union. Belgium is unique in never having exercised any censorship of films for adults.

RIPE FOR CENSORSHIP
The first demand for censorship in Britain came from the cheese industry in 1898, when Charles Urban released one of his scientific films taken through a microscope which revealed the bacterial activity in a piece of Stilton.

The Unkindest Cuts

The vagaries of censorship have taken many forms. Here are some of them.

☆ The State of Illinois demanded excision of the scene in *The Kid* (US 20) in which Jackie Coogan smashes windows. For similar reasons the censorship board of Ohio tried to ban *Treasure Island* (US 20) altogether lest it should encourage children to piracy.

☆ *The Muppet Movie* (US 79) was cut by the New Zealand censor on grounds of gratuitous violence. The offending scene showed Fozzie Bear being menaced by a drunken sailor with a broken bottle. Sweden banned *E.T.* (US 82) for children under 11 because it was claimed the film showed parents being hostile to their offspring.

☆ 20th Century Fox was obliged to cut a shot of a Botticelli nude from its art documentary *Birth of Venus* (US 52) at the insistence of the Hays Office.

☆ The films of Libertad Lamarque, one of Argentina's major stars of the thirties, were banned in

Argentina when Perón came to power in 1945. The reason was that Senorita Lamarque had slapped the face of Perón's mistress Eva Duarte—Evita—on the set of *Circus Cavalcade* (Arg 43) because the aspiring actress had sat in the star's personal chair. When Eva Duarte became the nation's First Lady as Eva Perón, Libertad Lamarque had to flee into exile.

☆ All Grace Kelly's films are prohibited in Monaco, by order of Prince Rainier.

☆ Producer Ismail Merchant was arrested in India for shooting a scene depicting Suttee (the ritual burning alive of widows) for *The Deceivers* (GB 88), as it was held to be 'derogatory to Hindu culture, religion and mythology'—even though it had been Hindu practice.

☆ For local consumption *Manila After Dark* (Ph 81) was retitled *City After Dark* and every mention of Manila on the soundtrack was bleeped out.

☆ *Tarzan of the Apes* (US 31) was banned in Hitler's Germany as contrary to Nazi doctrine on 'hereditary biology'

☆ An unusual ban, which applied only to 12 just men and women, was imposed by Federal Judge Jan E. DuBois when he instructed the jury in a trial about international money laundering not to see *Lethal Weapon 2* (US 89) until after the verdict. The picture is about international money laundering by foreign envoys protected by diplomatic immunity. The judge had been requested to impose the ban by one of the defendants, a foreign envoy but presumably not immune. He successfully contended that plot similarity might influence the jurors.

☆ The eight-reel Josephine Baker picture *Folies Bergère* (US 35—French language version) lost a whole reel to the local censors before it opened at the Odeon in Shanghai, though according to the local society journal *Town and Country* it still held sufficient allure to entice 'many a tired businessman' back for a second or even a third viewing. After two years on release in the interior, it returned to Shanghai again, but considerably shortened. 'Censors all over China had spotted other things that the local censors had missed', reported *Town and Country*, 'and the film had been reduced to a three-reel affair'. Later it went to Manila where further cuts were made. It returned to Shanghai for a third time in 1937, but scarcely a shot of the lightly clad Miss Baker survived intact—the full-length feature had been reduced to a single reel.

☆ South Korea is the only country known to have a censorship provision against movie titles which do not reflect the subject matter of the film. It also has a ban on scenes showing 'school education distordly'.

☆ When a dubbed version of *Becket* (GB 64) was released in Iran, the Shah's censorship authorities required that King Henry should be demoted to a mere Duke, as his portrayal was deemed to be offensive to the institution of monarchy.

☆ Captain Renault (Claude Rains), the devious Police Chief of *Casablanca* (US 42), was conceived by the scriptwriters as a man who sold visas to desperate women seeking escape in exchange for sexual favours. One piece of dialogue found unacceptable by the Hays Office was this, between a subordinate and the Police Chief:

'By the way, another visa problem has come up.'
'Show her up.'

Another was 'The girl will be released in the morning', which had to be changed to 'The girl will be released later'.

☆ Ireland has always been notorious for the vigilance of its censors. Surprisingly, though, Roman Polanski's debut picture *Knife in the Water* (Pol 62), a film with strong homosexual overtones, passed unscathed. It was argued that homosexuality was quite unknown to the Irish and what they did not understand could not harm them. An earlier generation of censors had been less tolerant. The Marx Brothers' *Monkey Business* (US 31) was banned lest it provoke the Irish to anarchy.

☆ The censors objected to a two-second glimpse of Christine Keeler (Joanne Whalley-Kilmer) engaged in some amiable bonking in *Scandal* (GB 89). It was replaced by a two-second out-take of her gazing lustfully at a naked black man.

☆ *Going My Way* (US 44), with Bing Crosby in an Oscar winning role as an easy-going priest, was

---

Going My Way (US 44) was banned in several Latin American countries because RC priest Bing Crosby wore a sweatshirt. (*Kobal*)

banned in several Latin American countries because the cleric wore a sweatshirt and baseball cap.

☆ *Bloody Cry* (Chn 34) was banned by the Kuomintang censors because the villain bore a certain physical resemblance to Chiang Kai-shek. Things did not improve after the revolution. By order of Mao in 1949, no Chinese government leaders were allowed to be portrayed on screen, however favourably.

☆ When the script of *Zaza* (US 39) was returned from the Hays Office, a line in which the heroine screams at the villain 'Pig! Pig! Pig! Pig! Pig!' had noted in the margin against it: 'Delete two pigs'. The Hays Office permitted the saloon queen Frenchie (Marlene Dietrich) to push money down her cleavage in *Destry Rides Again* (US 39), but insisted on the deletion of the accompanying line 'There's gold in them thar hills!'

☆ The Syrian Ministry of Information banned *Kadr* (Syr 81) on grounds that 'it is badly directed and filled with vulgar scenes which are neither edifying nor interesting, that it is cheaply sensational and lacks a coherent plot'.

☆ *La Coquille et la Clergyman* (Fr 28), the surrealist fantasy directed by Germaine Dulac, was banned by the British Board of Film Censors with the comment: 'This film is so cryptic as to be almost meaningless. If there is a meaning, it is doubtless objectionable.'

☆ *Limelight* (US 52) was banned in the USA for 20 years after its release because director–star Charles Chaplin was politically *persona non grata*. When it was eventually shown in America in 1972, it won an Oscar for the best original dramatic score—a uniquely belated Academy Award.

☆ Karate films were banned in Iraq in 1979.

☆ In 1964 the Peking Cinema Institute banned, along with *Hamlet* (GB 48), *Othello* (US/Fr 51) and *The Three Musketeers* (US 48), an educational film titled *Elementary Safety in Swimming in Rivers, Lakes and Seas*. The safety element was considered a bourgeois tendency likely to undermine revolutionary daring.

☆ No films depicting two-piece bathing suits were allowed on Malta's screens before 1964; a similar ban on bikinis applied to Malta's beaches. In that year an English tourist was charged with indecent exposure for having revealed her midriff while sunbathing, but was found not guilty. The court ruling had an immediate effect on film censorship. A large number of banned youth movies, including the whole Elvis Presley repertoire, were given the censor's seal of approval.

☆ *The Wicked Lady* (GB 45), in which Margaret Lockwood played a high-born lady highwayman, had to be almost entirely reshot for the USA due to the depth of Miss Lockwood's *décolletage*.

☆ In New Zealand, two of Shakespeare's works were barred from the University of Wellington's Shakespearian Film Festival in 1985—*The Merchant of Venice* for 'anti-semitism' and *The Taming of the Shrew* for 'sexism'. Doubtless the organizers would have approved of the Act of Parliament passed by the Indian government in 1986 which prohibits the denigration of women in films. Penalty for infringement is up to two years in gaol and a fine equivalent to $200.

☆ Mickey Mouse was banned in Romania in 1935 on the grounds he was frightening to children.

☆ Peter Ustinov's *Memed, My Hawk* (GB 82), from the Turkish novel of the same name, was banned in Turkey lest it 'attract the interest of that portion of the population which is illiterate'.

☆ Joseph Strick's *Ulysses* (GB 67), from the long banned novel by James Joyce, was only passed by the British Board of Film Censors with the deletion of the more outrageously obscene dialogue from the soundtrack. Strick then took the film to the GLC, who as the licensing body for London could ignore the Board's decision. The GLC passed the film without a single cut. It was later revealed that the sound reproduction in the GLC projection room was so faulty that none of the censors had heard a word of the dialogue.

☆ In contrast to the above, Louis Malle's sexually explicit *Les Amants* (Fr 59) passed the British Board of Film Censors only to fall foul of London Transport. The poster, which showed Rodin's beautiful sculpture of a couple in tender embrace, *Le Baiser*, was banned from buses and the Underground.

☆ *The Grapes of Wrath* (US 40) was allowed to be shown in the USSR, because the authorities considered it painted a sufficiently unattractive picture of the life of the American proletariat during the depression. It was later banned when they found that audiences were immensely impressed by the fact that the itinerant family of the story, intended to represent America's dispossessed, owned an automobile.

☆ *The Cow* (Iran 69) was produced under the auspices of the Iranian Ministry of Culture and Arts. On completion it was promptly banned—by the same Ministry of Culture and Arts. Things did not change a lot after the Khomeni revolution. The Ministry of Education financed Abbas Kiarostami's *Homework* (Iran 90), then blocked its release.

☆ The censors demanded that Hitchcock should remove the split-second glimpse of Janet Leigh naked in the celebrated shower scene in *Psycho* (US 60). Unwilling to acknowledge the need to keep it secret that people shower without their clothes on, the master simply returned the sequence to the board, without having cut so much as a frame. Assuming that he had done as they had commanded, they approved it without further ado.

☆ In 1918 the burghers of Villefranche-sur-Rhône banned *Othello* (It 14) from local exhibition because they objected to Desdemona being killed in it.

☆ There was a unique instance in American censorship of a ban on a particular individual being por-

Now you see him, now you don't. Soviet censors have 'unpersoned' Stalin from Mikhail Romm's classic *Lenin in October* (USSR 37).

trayed on the screen. It applied to gangster John Dillinger, whose heroic stature in the mass consciousness had considerably unnerved the American authorities by the time he was gunned down in 1934. For ten years the Hays Office would consider no scripts featuring the gangster, though nine Dillinger movies have been made since 1945.

☆ In 1967 the manager of Center Theater at High Point, NC, was arrested for showing a Julie Andrews picture declared to be obscene. The film, *Hawaii* (US 67), contained scenes of chaste but bare-bosomed native girls. Under a local ordnance, in force since the mid-19th century, any depiction of unclad breasts was an indictable offence.

☆ Probably the most liberal censorship of sexual content during the thirties was that of Nazi Germany. It is doubtful whether such erotic comedies as *Der Ammenkönig* (Ger 35) or Carl Froelich's *Wenn wir alle Engel wären/If We were All Angels* (Ger 36) would have passed any foreign censor. This may well have been because of Josef Goebbels' own sexual predelictions and he was the Chief Censor not only in name but in practice. During the twelve years of the Third Reich he personally viewed every one of the 1363 films produced, as well as all newsreels, cartoons, documentaries and other shorts, before they were passed for public showing. There was one exception to the generally permissive tone. Hitler himself had personally ordered that any woman character in a film who broke up a marriage must die before the end.

☆ *The Adventures of Barrie McKenzie* (Aus 73) — funded by the Australian government—fell foul of the New Zealand censor, who said he could pass it if one cut was made—'from the beginning to the end'.

☆ When *The Sound of Music* (US 65) opened at the

The deletion of 'unpersons' from Soviet encyclopaedias and the retouching of historical photographs to eliminate 'enemies of the state' like Trotsky were familiar practices in the Soviet Union before Glasnost. Evidence has reached the West that a similar revision of history was undertaken with classic films during the Brezhnev era. Writing in *Sight and Sound*, Alexander Sesonske reports how he showed Mikhail Romm's distinguished *Lenin in October* (USSR 37) to a class of film students in 1983. The original film, as Sesonske knew, had attributed to Stalin a leading role in the October Revolution second only to that of Lenin himself; and in nearly every scene depicting Lenin, the tyrant was shown at his right hand, dispensing wise advice and supporting him loyally in committee against Trotsky and other revisionists. The print shown to the students had not a single image of Stalin; he had been eliminated from the film entirely. Some shots had been simply deleted, others cut at the point that Stalin should have appeared. The majority, however, had been skilfully doctored by back projecting the film, then rephotographing the images after placing a large foreground figure, usually a Baltic sailor, to block out Stalin from view. Ironically the revised version of *Lenin in October* is far closer to historical truth than Romm's original.

City Palast in Munich it was with about one third of its running time eliminated. Everything about the Anschluss and the Von Trapp family's daring escape from the Nazis had vanished from the screen. Munich, cradle of the Nazi Party, preferred not to confront that part of the story. The film ended abruptly and bewilderingly immediately after the marriage of Maria to the Baron Von Trapp.

TWELVE

ANIMATION

The first animated film using the stop-motion technique to give the illusion of movement to inanimate objects was Vitagraph's *The Humpty Dumpty Circus* (US 98?). Albert E. Smith, who conceived the idea, borrowed his small daughter's toy circus and succeeded in animating the acrobats and animals by shooting them in barely changed positions one frame at a time—the same principle as that used for animated cartoons.

The earliest known British example of animation is an untitled advertising film made by Arthur Melbourne Cooper of St Albans, Herts, for Messrs Bryant & May. Dating from 1899, it consists of an appeal for funds to supply the troops in South Africa with matches, as it seems this was something the Army authorities had overlooked. The animated 'performers' are match-stick men who climb up a wall and form themselves into the legend: 'Send £1 and enough matches will be sent to supply a regiment of our fighting soldiers'.

Some years later, Melbourne Cooper made two charming films featuring animated toys, *Noah's Ark* (GB 08) and *Dreams of Toyland* (GB 08). Strutting teddy bears were featured in the latter with particularly engaging effect.

Meanwhile, in the United States, J. Stuart Blackton, Albert E. Smith's co-partner at Vitagraph, had produced an unusual novelty with *The Haunted Hotel* (US 07), in which furniture moved about seemingly by its own agency.

The following year Pathé pioneered the animation of paper cut-outs in *Paper Cock-a-Doodle* (Fr 08) —the cut-outs being in the shape of exquisitely wrought birds. The pioneer of animation in Russia was Ladislas Starevitch, who applied the stop-motion technique to bring dead insects 'alive' in *The Grasshopper and the Ant* (Rus 11) and *The Stag Beetles* (Rus 11).

The first cartoon film was J. Stuart Blackton's *Humorous Phases of Funny Faces* (US 06), produced for the Vitagraph Co. of New York. Like nearly all early American film cartoonists, Blackton used the technique of showing an artist drawing a still picture which then magically came alive and moved. Most of the illusions were created by means of cardboard cut-outs, but a few genuinely animated drawings featured at the beginning of the film, showing a man and a woman rolling their eyes and the outline of a gentleman with bowler and umbrella apparently drawing himself.

The first British cartoon film was the Charles Urban production *The Clown and His Donkey* (GB 10), drawn by Charles Armstrong.

The first cartoon film to tell a story was Emile Cohl's *Fantasmagorie* (Fr 08), which was premièred at the Théâtre du Gymnase in Paris on 17 August 1908. Cohl made the film for Léon Gaumont, by whom he was employed as a scenarist. Prior to this, nearly all cartoon films were of the artist-drawing-a-living-picture genre. Robert Desnos has described Cohl as the first to 'cut the umbilical cord which still linked the life of the characters on the screen with the secretions of the fountain pen'. He made about 100 cartoons between 1908 and 1918 and can thus be regarded as **the first professional screen animator.**

The first cartoon series was inaugurated by Emile Cohl with the debut of his character Fantôche, a kind of matchstick man combatting the cruel world, in *Le Cauchemar du Fantôche* (Fr 09). **The first cartoon series in America**, also inaugurated by Cohl, was Eclair's *The Newlyweds*, starting with *When He Wants a Dog, He Wants a Dog* (US 13). Based on the popular cartoon characters originated by George McManus in the *New York World*, the series gave a new descriptive term to the vocabulary of film-making. It was an advertisement for *The*

The first animated cartoon film—J. Stuart Blackton's *Humorous Phases of Funny Faces* (US 06).

Newlyweds, appearing in *Moving Picture World* for 15 February 1913, that contained **the first use of the term 'animated cartoon'.**

The first British cartoon series was *Adventures of Slim and Pim* (GB 18), drawn by Leslie Dawson for Charles Urban's Kineto Co. Slim and Pim were two characters prone to Laurel and Hardy-type misadventures. First to feature animal characters was *The Wonderful Adventures of Pip, Squeek and Wilfred* (GB 21), 26 one-reel episodes based on the popular children's strip in the *Daily Mirror* by A. B. Payne and B. J. Lamb. The series was drawn by Lancelot Speed for Astra Films.

The longest cartoon series was Harry 'Bud' Fisher's *Mutt and Jeff*, which began as a 'Comic Supplement' to *Pathe's Weekly* with the issue of 10 February 1913 and continued as separate weekly reels from 1 April 1916 to 1 December 1926. Allowing for a gap in 1923–4 when no titles have been traced, there were at least 323 *Mutt and Jeff* films. Several have been colorized and synchronized for video release, making them the oldest cartoon films still in regular distribution. A list of all known titles is contained in Denis Gifford's *American Animated Films: The Silent Era, 1897–1929* (McFarland 1990).

The longest series of talkie cartoons for the cinema was Max Fleischer's *Popeye The Sailor Man*, with 233 one-reelers and a single two-reeler (*Popeye the Sailor Meets Sinbad the Sailor* (US 36)) between 1933 and 1957. There were another 220 Popeye cartoons for television produced by King Features in the 1970s. For the first few weeks of the original cinema series Popeye was voiced by William Costello; then for the next 45 years (including the TV cartoons) by Jack Mercer.

The first cartoon film based on a comic strip was Winsor McCay's *Little Nemo* (US 11), a Vitagraph production derived from the artist's *Little Nemo in Slumberland.*

The first animal cartoon character was Old Doc Yak, a tail-coated billy-goat in striped pants, who was brought to the screen by *Chicago Tribune* cartoonist Sidney Smith in a Selig Polyscope series started in July 1913. It was the much-loved animal cartoon characters who eventually gave animated films a distinct appeal of their own as suitable entertainment for children. This development can best be dated from the advent of Pat Sullivan's Felix the Cat in 1919, an animal who 'kept on walking', and who was the first cartoon character to attain the celebrity of a human star. Felix was also **the first animated cartoon character to be merchandised** when Margaret Winkler (who had become the first woman producer and distributor of cartoons in 1922 at the age of 25) issued licences in the US and UK in 1924. Used first as an image on packaging, Felix was also merchandised as a phenomenally successful cuddly toy two years

later. Although his star has waned in the west, in Japan Felix is rated as one of the three most popular cartoon characters (the others are Snoopy and Mickey Mouse). A feature-length movie, *Felix the Cat: The Movie* (US 89), failed to catch on in its home market but was enormously popular with the Japanese.

The earliest known use of cartoon animation in a pornographic movie occurs in *The Virgin with the Hot Pants* (US *c.*24), which opens with a cartoon woman being pursued round a room by a cartoon penis-and-testicles. The pursuer finally catches and penetrates her while she hangs from a chandelier. The next sequence introduces that classic duo of cartoons, the cat and mouse double act, to the world of the dirty movie. In this case the cat is victim, caught and ravished by a mouse with a giant penis.

The first cartoon talkie for theatrical release was Max Fleischer's Song Cartune *Come Take a Trip in my Airship* (US 24), which opens with a 25-second sequence in which the animated figure of a woman in a white dress speaks some patter as the lead-in to the song. The sound-on-film synchronisation was by DeForest Phonofilm.

The first all-talking cartoon was Paul Terry's 'Aesop's Film Fable' *Dinner Time* (US 28), produced by Van Beuren Enterprises in the RCA Photophone sound system and premièred at the

The longest cartoon series—there were at least 323 episodes.

Mark Strand Theater in New York on 1 September 1928. Walt Disney dismissed it as 'a lot of racket and nothing else'. His own initial venture in talkies, *Steamboat Willie* (US 28), presented at New York's Colony Theater on 18 November 1928, was more auspicious; it marked the debut of the most successful cartoon character of all time, Mickey Mouse.

The first British cartoon talkie was *The Jazz Stringer* (GB 28), with 'Orace the 'Armonious 'Ound, made at Wembley Studios by Joe Noble and his brother George ('Orace's voice) for British Sound Productions and premièred at the Tivoli Cinema in the Strand on 15 December 1928. It was claimed as 'the first lip synchronized cartoon in the world'.

The first colour cartoon was *The Debut of Thomas Kat* (US 20), a Paramount release produced by the Bray Pictures Corporation of New York in the Brewster natural-colour process. The drawings were made on transparent celluloid and painted on the reverse, then filmed with a two-colour camera. An unfortunate kitten, Thomas Kat, had been taught by his mother to catch mice, but inadvertently mistook a rat for the smaller breed of rodent.

The first cartoon series in colour was *The Red Head Comedies* (US 23), each a lampoon of an historical event produced by the Lee-Bradford Corporation. Colour process not known.

The first colour cartoon talkie was a three-minute sequence in Universal's *The King of Jazz* (US 30). Made by Walter Lanz in two-colour Technicolor, it depicted a cartoon version of bandleader Paul Whiteman on a big game hunt in Africa. First complete film was Ub Iwerks' two-colour Technicolor

Louis B. Mayer, notwithstanding the advice of MGM studio executives, refused to put aspiring cartoon-maker Walt Disney under contract in 1928 after seeing a preview of the first Mickey Mouse movie because he thought that pregnant women would be frightened of a 10-ft high rodent on the screen.

Fiddlesticks (US 31), featuring Flip the Frog, which was copyrighted on 24 April 1931. Disney's original colour cartoon was not, as often claimed, the world's first, but it was the first in a three-colour process. A Silly Symphony titled *Flowers and Trees* (US 32), the Technicolor short premièred at Grauman's Chinese Theater on 15 July 1932.

Britain's first cartoon talkie in colour was *On the Farm* (GB 33), produced in Raycol Colour and animated by Brian White, Sid Griffiths and Joe Noble from designs by *Punch* cartoonist H. M. Bateman.

The first feature-length cartoon film was Don Frederico Valle's 60-minute *El Apostol* (Arg 17). Based on the book by Alfredo de Lafarrere, the film

was a political satire on Argentina's President Irigoyen. The team of five animators was headed by Diogenes Tabora, a well-known caricaturist, and between them they produced 58,000 drawings for the film over a period of twelve months.

The first full-length cartoon talkie was also surprisingly produced in Argentina. Made by Quirino Cristiani in 1931, *Peludopolis* was another satire on President Irogoyen and used the Vitaphone sound-on-disc system of synchronized sound. Running time was one hour. These two Argentinian cartoon features, and an Italian production *The Adventures of Pinocchio* (It 36), preceded the film which has generally been hailed as the world's first full-length cartoon feature. In fact Walt Disney's *Snow White and the Seven Dwarfs* (US 37) was only the first American cartoon feature, though the world's first to be made in both sound and colour.

Britain's first feature-length cartoon made for commercial release was Halas and Batchelor's *Animal Farm* (GB 54), from George Orwell's savage satire on Soviet repression.

The first 3-D cartoon was Norman McLaren's abstract subject *Around is Around* (Can 51).

The first full-length animated feature in 3-D was the Australian science-fantasy rock musical *Abracadabra* (Aus 82), directed by Alexander Stitt.

The first cartoon films made for television were Alex Anderson and Jay Ward's syndicated series *Crusader Rabbit*, produced in San Francisco as five-minute episodes from 1949 to 1951. For some reason the films were made in colour, despite the fact that there was no colour television.

The most expensive cartoon ever made was Walt Disney's *The Black Cauldron* (US 85), which cost $25 million. One of the least successful of the Disney cartoon features, it returned less than $10 million in North American rentals.

The highest grossing cartoon film of all time is Walt Disney's *Snow White and the Seven Dwarfs* (US 37), with worldwide rentals of $380 million.

The longest cartoon ever made was Osamu Tezuka's erotic feature *A Thousand and One Nights* (Jap 69), which had a running time of 2 hr 30 min in the original Japanese version.

Clarence Nash (1904–85), the immortal voice of Donald Duck, may have been incomprehensible quacking in his native American, but he could be equally hard on the ear in French, Spanish, Portuguese, Japanese, German and Chinese. None of these languages could he understand— Nash had the words written out phonetically and gabbled them in Duckspeak for the delight of audiences from Paris to Peking.

Disney's *Snow White and the Seven Dwarfs* (US 37) is the highest grossing cartoon film of all time. Not a lot of people know that the cartoon dwarfs were modelled on real-life originals, as shown in this 1938 article from Chicago's *Radio Guide*. (*Backnumbers*)

Feature Cartoon Output

Up to the end of 1990, a total of 522 fully animated cartoon features (excluding compilations) had been produced by 34 countries. The most prolific country was Japan, with 169 full-length cartoon features, followed by the USA (92), France (38), Hungary (24), Australia (17), USSR (17), Italy (16), Germany (15), Belgium (14), Spain (13), UK (11), Canada (11), Denmark (11), Czechoslovakia (10), Sweden (9), China (9), S. Korea (6), Romania (5), Cuba (4), Poland (4), Argentina (3), Bulgaria (3), Colombia (3), Finland (3), Brazil (3), Netherlands (2), Iraq (2), Mexico (2), Austria (2), Hong Kong (2), Israel (1), Thailand (1), New Zealand (1), Yugoslavia (1), Taiwan (1), Eire (1) and the United Nations (1).

*C*ARTOON DEBUTS

BETTY BOOP

Max Fleischer's boop-boop-a-doop flapper of the thirties debuted in *Dizzy Dishes* (US 30). Betty started life as a small dog with long ears and only became a human girl in 1932. She was the creation of

'Grim' Natwick, later responsible for animating Snow White in *Snow White and the Seven Dwarfs* (US 37), who died at the age of 100 in 1990. He based her on the singer Helen Kane, whose hit song 'I Wanna Be Loved By You' launched the boop-boo-a-doop catchphrase. The Betty Boop series ran for nine years, her baby-talk voice being dubbed by five different actresses, of whom Little Ann Little (who spoke in boop-boop-a-doop language in real life) and Mae Questel were the best known. Miss Questel reprised the voice when Betty made a welcome return in *Who Framed Roger Rabbit* (US 88). While all the other 'toons' were portrayed in colour, she remained in period—in black and white.

BUGS BUNNY

Started as a hare rather than a 'wabbit' in Ben Hardaway and Cal Dalton's Looney Tune *Porky's Hare Hunt* (US 38). The character only began to assume his real Brooklyn bunny persona in Tex Avery's *Wild Hare* (US 40). Bugs was originally going to be called Happy Rabbit. He was named after his creator Ben Hardaway, whose nickname was 'Bugs', at the suggestion of Mel Blanc, the rabbit's voice and author of the classic line 'Ehh, What's up Doc?' (originally scripted as 'Hey, what's cookin'?'). By 1962 Bugs had appeared in 159 films, including the 3-D *Lumberjack Rabbit* (US 53), and won an Oscar for *Knightly Knight Bugs* (US 58). Following a guest appearance in *Who Framed Roger Rabbit* (US 88), in which he teamed up with Mickey Mouse to play a lowdown trick on a plummeting Bob Hoskins with a snafu parachute, the irrepressible Bugs made a comeback in his own starring vehicle *Box Office Bunny* (US 90). Although long absent from the big screen, the 'wascally wabbit' had been hyperactive on the tube. *Life* magazine asserted: 'For 30 years, Bugs has starred in more programs, on more channels—and has been number one in the ratings more often—than any other artist in the history of television.'

DAFFY DUCK

Tex Avery's Looney Tune *Porky's Duck Hunt* (US 37). After disappearing from cinema screens with his 126th movie in 1964, Daffy made his comeback 33 years later but not a day wiser in WB's *The Duxorcist* (US 87). His voice, originally based on film actor Hugh ('Woo-Woo') Herbert, was later given a raspberry lisp by Mel Blanc. Under the direction of Warner Bros' Chuck Jones, Daffy brought his scatty persona to a range of detective and heroic roles with splendid incongruity.

At the 1989 Santa Barbara Film Festival, Chuck Jones was asked by a grimly earnest cartoon buff a long and rambling question about the nature of Daffy's true being. The veteran animator scratched his head awhile and then drawled, 'I guess I always thought of him as Everyduck'.

DONALD DUCK

Walt Disney's *The Wise Little Hen* (US 34). His

Early Bugs in his pre-Brooklyn bunny persona. The then un-named 'wabbit' made his debut in *Porky's Hare Hunt* (US 38).

opening (and only) words were: 'Who—me? Oh no! I got a bellyache!' Clarence Nash, always Donald's voice, recalled: 'I had an ambition to be a doctor and somehow or other I became the biggest quack in the country.' He was still quacking 49 years later in *Mickey's Christmas Carol* (US 83).

DROOPY DOG

Created by Tex Avery in MGM's *Dumb-Hounded* (US 43). Voice by Bill Thompson.

FELIX THE CAT

Inspired by Kipling's *The Cat that Walked by Himself* in the *Just So Stories* (1902); created for Pat Sullivan by animator Otto Messmer. Prototype Felix, as yet unnamed, debuted in Paramount's *Feline Follies* (US 19). First of the anthropomorphic animal characters to attain the kind of celebrity accorded to human stars; also first to be merchandised. Television debut WXB2S New York 1930.

GOOFY

Walt Disney's *Mickey's Revue* (US 32). Originally called Dippy Dawg and always voiced by Pinto Colvig. Had the honour of starring in the very last of the regular Walt Disney cartoon shorts, *Goofy's Freeway Trouble* (US 65).

MICKEY MOUSE

Born 18 November 1928 with première of *Steamboat Willie*. The artist for the MM cartoons was not Disney but Ub Iwerks, though Walt himself did Mickey's voice. By 1934 the Mouse was receiving more fan mail than any other Hollywood star and the following year Soviet director Sergei Eisenstein declared that he was 'America's one and only contribution to world culture'. There were a total of 119 MM cartoons, of which the majority—87—were made in the thirties. There was a 30-year interval between *The Simple Things* (US 53) and the mouse's triumphant return in *Mickey's Christmas Carol* (US 83). Mickey was voiced in his Dickensian role by Wayne Allwine, who was born the year of the previous Mickey Mouse film.

MR MAGOO

UPA's *Ragtime Bear* (US 49). Created by John Hubley and Millard Kaufman and voiced by Jim Backus, he stumbled his way through 52 shorts and a feature, *1001 Arabian Nights* (US 59).

PLUTO

Walt Disney's *The Chain Gang* (US 30).

POPEYE

Debuted in Max Fleischer's *Popeye the Sailor Man* (US 33); head animator Seymour Kneitel. The voice was that of William Costello, better known as Red Pepper Sam, whose experience as a talking gorilla on a radio show was thought to qualify him for the role. Success went to his head and he was fired as too temperamental, so Jack Mercer, an artist at the Fleischer Studio with a bent for imitations, took over. Popeye's friend Wimpy gave his name to a type of British hamburger.

PORKY PIG

Warner Looney Tune *I Haven't Got a Hat* (US 35). Creator Bob Clampett; voice Mel Blanc.

ROAD RUNNER

Together with the Coyote, created by Chuck Jones and Michael Maltese in *Fast and Furry-ous* (US 48).

SPEEDY GONZALES

The Fastest Mouse in all Mexico debuted in Warner Bros' Oscar-winning *Speedy Gonzales* (US 55). Voice: Mel Blanc.

SYLVESTER

Warner Bros' *Kitty Kornered* (US 45). His constant prey Tweety Pie had preceded him on screen (see below). Voice of both adversaries was Mel Blanc.

TOM AND JERRY

Hanna-Barbera's *Puss Gets the Boot* (US 39). The love-hate relationship of the amiable adversaries was condemned in the '70s for its 'mindless violence'. A full-length feature is scheduled for release in summer 1992 and for the first time in their screen lives the cat and mouse will speak.

TWEETY PIE

Warner Bros' *Birdie and the Beast* (US 44). American essayist S. J. Perelman held Tweety Pie personally responsible for what he regarded as a reprehensible British habit of referring to all felines as 'puddy tats'.

WOODY WOODPECKER

Knock Knock (US 40). The distinctive woodpecker voice was that of Grace Stafford, wife of Woody's creator Walter Lanz, though it was Mel Blanc who recorded the signature tune which went to the top of the hit parade. The series of 192 films lasted until 1972, making Woody the last of the great big-screen 'toon' stars.

THIRTEEN

SHORTS AND DOCUMENTARIES

Two frame enlargements from the earliest surviving advertising film in the world, which dates from 1897. (*Library of Congress*)

ADVERTISING FILMS

The first advertising films were made in France, Britain and the USA in 1897. The single surviving American example of that year was copyrighted by the Edison Co. of West Orange, NJ, on 5 August 1897. The Library of Congress Catalogue records: 'The film shows a large, poster-type backdrop with the words "Admiral Cigarettes". Sitting in front of the backdrop are four people in costume: Uncle Sam, a clergyman, an Indian, and a businessman. To the left of the screen is an ash-can size box that breaks apart and a girl, attired in a striking costume, goes across the stage towards the seated men and hands them cigarettes. Then she unfolds a banner that reads, "We all Smoke".'

Advertising films were also made that year by the International Film Co. of New York, who were the first company to specialize in such productions. Their clients included Haig Whisky, Maillard's Chocolate and Pabst's Milwaukee Beer, and the films advertising these products were interspersed with entertainment films, in the manner of modern TV commercials, in a grand open-air free movie show in the centre of New York. The giant screen was set on top of the Pepper Building at 34th Street and Broadway and the films rear projected with a powerful Kuhn & Webster 'Projectorscope'. The projectionist was Edwin S. Porter, later to achieve fame as director of *The Great Train Robbery* (US 03). On this occasion, however, the only fame he achieved was in the police court, where he was charged with being a public nuisance and causing an obstruction by encouraging people to block the sidewalk.

Three different advertising films are known to date from 1897 in Britain. Walter D. Welford made a film called *The Writing on the Wall* for John Samuel Smith and Co. of Borough High Street, Southwark, manufacturers of bicycle tyres. This was shot in Tottenham and showed a man painting the words 'Ride Smith Tyres' on a brick wall. Rather more ambitious was a production by Arthur Melbourne Cooper of St Albans, which brought to light a contemporary poster for Bird's Custard. An old man is seen walking down stairs bearing a large tray of eggs. He misses his footing, trips, and the eggs cascade on to the floor. Cook has no need to worry, though, because she has a liberal supply of Bird's Custard Powder. The company made an agreement with Melbourne Cooper that he should be paid £1 for every copy of the film distributed. The third example comes from Nestlé and Lever Bros, who joined forces in 1897 to purchase 12 Lumière Cinématographes for a combined promotional exercise. Their initial effort was called *The Sunlight Soap Washing Competition* and was available free to showmen. Besides producing their own advertising films, Lever Bros and Nestlé also sponsored films with no advertising content. On 7 February 1898 they premièred a film of the recent Test Match in Australia at the Alhambra, Leicester Square. This was so successful that it was followed in March by films of the Cambridge crew in training for the Boat Race and later by the Boat Race itself. Mellin's Baby Food also began giving 'advertising

While cinema advertising films have lost some of their appeal to advertisers against the lure of television, product placement in feature films is growing as producers seek to offset spiralling costs. One of the products most often advertised in this way is sunglasses—with luck a star may wear them throughout the picture, even indoors if he is the likes of Jack Nicholson. Manufacturers woke up to the potential after Tom Cruise had sported a pair of Ray-Ban Wayfarers in *Risky Business* (US 84). A 1952 design, the shades were on their way out with sales down to 18,000 a year. Following the release of the movie, sales for the year shot up to 360,000. For *Top Gun* (US 85), Cruise wore Ray-Ban Aviators, with the result that the annual increase in sales rose from 4 per cent a year to 40 per cent. Unique Product Placement, which represents Ray-Ban, now places their glasses in 160 films and TV shows annually. Wayfarers alone sell four million a year and the company had become brand leader in the US.

Not all product placement helps to promote a positive image of the product. Ford executives were worried that the heavies in cops and robbers movies almost invariably drove about in sleek black Lincoln Towncars, one of Ford's models. Most of these were supplied by the Roger & Cowan product placement agency, who maintain a fleet of 550 Fords for rent at a nominal fee to film-makers. The agency had a simple solution when approached by Ford—supply them with the money to buy a stock of Cadillacs, produced by Ford's main rival General Motors. Now the good guys drive Fords, the bad guys drive Cadillacs.

Sales of Ray-Ban Wayfarers increased 20-fold after Tom Cruise gave them star appeal in *Risky Business* (US 84). (*British Film Institute*)

entertainments' with the cinematograph the same year.

The most sophisticated of the pioneer advertising films were made by the great French innovator Georges Méliès, who also made the earliest trick films and the earliest 'blue movies'. Méliès' first advertising film, made at his studio at Montreuil-sous-Bois, was for Bornibus mustard. The scene was a restaurant. Two diners get into an argument which grows so heated that they begin to pelt each other with mustard. The camera then cuts to a black table top on which a jumble of white letters are scattered at random. The letters are seen to form themselves into the slogan *Bornibus, sa moutarde et ses cornichons à la façon de la mère Marianne*—all except the 's' of 'Bornibus', which is unable to find its correct place and keeps bumping into the other letters. Méliès recalled that the erratic 's' was always greeted with gales of laughter.

The earliest known advertising film in colour was *Das Wunder/The Wonder* (Ger 25), an animated cartoon coloured directly on to the prints by means of a stencilling process. Directed by Julius Pinschewer, the two-minute film advertised 'World-renowned Kantorwicz Liqueur' and was notable not only for its colour but also its use of expressionism in the animated designs, some of them wholly abstract, of animator Walter Ruttmann.

The first British all-colour advertising film was *It's An Ill Wind* (GB 29), made for Tintex Dyes of London. The film related the drama of an office boy emptying a bottle of ink over the typist heroine's jumper. However, with the aid of Tintex Colour Remover and Tintex Dye, the jumper is made like new in the latest fashionable colour.

The first talkie advertising film was *Die Chinesische Nachtigall/The Chinese Nightingale* (Ger 28), an animated silhouette version of the Hans Andersen fairy tale made by the Tri-Ergon Co. of Berlin to advertise a new process they had developed for disc recording. Although the use of synchronized discs was common to many early sound film systems, the process Tri-Ergon were promoting had no apparent connection with film-making, their advertising talkie being made by the sound-on-film process they had pioneered six years earlier.

The world's most beautiful woman? Nobody would have said so when this 16-year-old appeared in an advertising short called *How Not to Wear Clothes* (Swe 21), but they did when she conquered Hollywood as Greta Garbo.

Between 1914 and 1942 the standard length for advertising films in Britain was five minutes. Generally they contained some element of narrative and often featured famous stars, such as Jack Hulbert and Cicely Courtneidge in a 1926 comedy made for Rufflette Curtain Tape. Shortage of film stock brought the 'story' advertising film to an end in World War II. In the USA, the use of major stars was rarer, partly due to the contract system but also because most advertising films were made in New York. One notable example, however, was a General Electric advertising film of 1933 which had Dick Powell and Bette Davis cast as a suburban couple extolling the virtues of dishwashers and garden floodlighting. Advertising films could also be an entrée for those who had yet to receive the summons to Hollywood. When the Bergström Department Store of Stockholm allowed a 16-year-old salesgirl to play a small role in *How Not to Wear Clothes* (Swe 21) they were unwittingly launching the screen career of Greta Garbo.

The largest collection of advertising films (including TV commercials) in the world belongs to Jean-Marie Boursicot of Paris, who has amassed 350,000 examples from 42 countries which he stores in an old telephone exchange. He adds to the collection at the rate of 8000 a year, concentrating on the best and worst of the genre—the worst, he claims, come from Canada. He started it in the mid-1960s, when as a boy in Marseilles he used to beg pieces of discarded film from the projectionist of his local cinema. Most were advertising films, predominantly for ice cream. The oldest film in the collection was made by the Lumière Bros in 1904 for Moët et Chandon champagne. Others include a 1917 promotion for holidays in Brittany—while a world war was raging in one corner of France, French Railways were enticing people to vacation in another. Another is a recruitment film for the SS which extols the opportunities offered by that organization for sporting activities and cultivation of the arts. Also in the collection is the shortest advertising film ever made—for Camel cigarettes, it lasts just one second. The Camel logo appears and the beast winks. Boursicot takes choice examples from the collection on tour with a seven-hour non-stop programme entitled 'Nuit des Publivores', or in English 'Night of the Ad-eaters'. The line-up of 450 films changes from year to year except for one perennial. This is a 1975 Perrier advertisement which shows a quarter-litre bottle responding to the caress of a woman's hand until it has enlarged to litre size. Then the cap blows off and the liquid spills over. When it was originally shown, the film had to be withdrawn after five days of mounting protest.

Per a 1990 UK survey, the percentage of people who can recall an advertising film the day after it has been shown in a cinema averages 87 per cent. The equivalent for a TV commercial is 20 per cent.

DOCUMENTARY

The term 'documentary' was first used by Edward Sheriff Curtis, Director of *In the Land of the Head Hunters* (US 14), in a prospectus he issued about 1914 for the Continental Film Co., a Seattle-based venture for the making of films about Amerindian lore and life. It did not pass immediately into the language, only catching on after John Grierson had used it in his February 1926 review of Robert Flaherty's *Moana* (US 26) for the *New York Sun*. Flaherty is generally acknowledged as the first to have brought form and structure to documentary films, commencing with his study of Eskimo life. *Nanook of the North* (US 22); while Grierson himself is regarded as the father of Britain's between the wars 'documentary movement'.

The first documentary film: The majority of pre-1900 films were actualities, but the first of sufficient length to be considered a legitimate documentary record of its subject was *The Cavalry School at Saumur* (Fr 97), which ran for 1330 ft, about 20 min. At around the same time Joseph Perry of the Salvation Army's Limelight Division at Melbourne, Vic., Australia, began shooting some 2000 ft of film illustrating the social work of the Salvation Army. Melbourne had been the first place in the world where the Salvation Army embarked on an organized programme of social work in addition to its traditional evangelism.

The first feature-length documentaries were Paul Rainey's eight-reel *African Hunt* (US 12); a dramatized production in five reels called *One Hundred Years of Mormonism* (US 12); and *Akaky Tsereteli's Journey Along the Racha and Lechkhuma* (Rus 12) by the Georgian director Vasily Amashukeli.

The first sound documentary for theatrical release was Tri-Ergon's *Life in a Village* (Ger 23), premièred at the Alhambra Theatre, Berlin in September 1923.

> Some people are inclined to believe anything if it is shown on a screen. The Nazi-made documentary *Life in the Union of South Africa* (Ger 38) depicted how the starving Europeans were subservient to the prosperous natives.

The most successful documentary film at the box office (excluding concert films) was Allen Funt's X-rated United Artists release *What Do You Say to a Naked Lady?* (US 70), a candid camera survey of people's reactions to nudity in public places. It grossed $10.5 million in the US.

The first news film (other than sporting events,

> In the concert documentary *Woodstock* (US 69), a telephoto lens picks up a young man and a young girl wandering off into the long grass together. Lingering on the reposeful scene, the film records first the grass swaying, then some turbulence, next the abandoned threshing of golden limbs. A vignette of the permissive generation, unlikely to cause offence in the enlightened twilight of the sixties—or so Warner Bros thought until they found themselves served with a writ. The litigant was the young man in the long grass. He was, he deposed, a hairdresser in Montreal. His reputation and livelihood depended on his woman customers assuming him to be gay—the film had revealed his closely guarded secret, that he was really straight!

q.v.) was made by photographer Birt Acres of High Barnet, Herts, on the occasion of the opening of the Kiel Canal by Kaiser Wilhelm II (1859–1941) on 20 June 1895. Besides the arrival of the Kaiser at Holtenau aboard his yacht *Hohenzollern*, Acres took films of the laying of a memorial stone, and of a number of other events held as part of the celebrations, including scenes of the Kaiser reviewing his troops at Hamburg and leading a procession through the streets of Berlin. He also filmed a charge of Uhlan Lancers at the Tempelhof Feld in Berlin, starting a news cameraman's tradition of taking risks in the cause of film reportage by arranging with their commander that the horsemen should charge direct at the camera. Seized with the desire to run for his life as the troop thundered towards him with drawn lances, he nevertheless continued to grind the handle of his camera and was afterwards congratulated by the CO as 'the pluckiest fellow he had ever met'. The first screening took place before the Royal Photographic Society on 14 January 1896.

The first British monarch to be filmed was Queen Victoria (1819–1901) during her autumn holiday at Balmoral in 1896. She recorded the event in her diary for 3 October: 'At twelve went down to below the terrace, near the ballroom, and we were all photographed by Downey by the new cinematograph process—which makes moving pictures by winding off a reel of film. We were walking up and down, and the children jumping about. Then took a turn in the pony chair, and not far from the garden cottage Nicky and Alicky planted a tree.'

Downey was the Royal Photographer. The children who jumped about included the late Duke of Windsor, who must consequently have had one of the longest records of film appearances (including three acting roles) when he died in 1972. 'Nicky and Alicky' were the Emperor Nicholas II (1868–1918) and the Empress Alexandra Feodorovna (1872–1918) of Russia, who had arrived at Balmoral for an informal visit ten days earlier. The film was 'premièred' in the Red Drawing Room at Windsor Castle on 23 November 1896.

The first American President to be filmed was Grover Cleveland (1837–1908), outgoing President on the occasion of President-designate William McKinley's inauguration at Washington DC on 4 March 1897. The inaugural parade, covered by Edison, Biograph and Lumière cameramen, and by one E. H. Amet, included shots of Cleveland, then in the last hour of his Presidency.

NEWSREELS

The first newsreel was *Day by Day*, produced by Will G. Barker and presented at the Empire Theatre, Leicester Square, in 1906. It was issued daily except when fog prevented filming.

The first newsreel produced for general distribution was *Pathé-Faits Divers*, founded in Paris early in 1908 under the direction of Albert Gaveau. The name was soon changed to *Pathé-Journal*. Japan's *Daimai News* is variously claimed to have been founded in 1908 and 1909. This was literally intended as a moving-picture newspaper, having been established by the influential daily *Osaka Mainichi*, *Pathé-Journal* did a reverse operation, founding a weekly illustrated newspaper of the same name in November 1912. The photographic news reportage consisted of stills from the newsreel.

The first regular sound newsreel was *Movietone News*, presented at the Roxy Theater, New York, on 28 October 1928. The subjects covered included Niagara Falls, the Army-Yale football game, 'Romance of the Iron Horse', and Rodeo in New York. Regular weekly issue of *Movietone News* to cinemas throughout the USA commenced 3 December 1928.

The first British sound newsreel was *British Movietone*, commencing with an issue showing the Derby and the Trooping of the Colour which was released on 9 June 1929. It survived as the last remaining newsreel produced in Britain.

The first unscheduled event to be captured by the sound newsreel camera was the assassination attempt on Prince Humbert of Italy on 24 October 1929. Cameraman Jack Connolly of *Movietone* had hidden himself behind the Tomb of the Unknown Warrior in Rome in order to secure forbidden pictures of the Prince and Princess paying tribute to the Italian war dead. He had just been discovered by the police when a shot was fired at the Prince, but fortunately the camera was still running and the sound equipment operating.

The first newsreel footage of an execution was taken by Universal Newsreel's Cuban cameraman Abelardo Domingo, who happened to walk into a prison yard with his camera one day in 1935 just as bandit Jose Costiello y Puentas was about to face the firing squad. Domingo shot the grisly scene unobserved and shipped the film over to New York for inclusion in the newsreel. As soon as it was released in Cuba, Domingo was arrested and condemned to death—also by firing squad. He was released only after Universal's manager in Cuba had paid the appropriate financial sum.

The last newsreel in the United States was *Universal Newsreel*, founded as *Universal Animated Weekly* in 1913, of which the final issue was released on 22 December 1967. At its peak it was showing in 3300 cinema theatres, but with the competition of television declined to 1100.

Cable News Network sponsored a tentative revival of the newsreel format in the summer of 1990 with a three-month trial run of its fortnightly *Reel News* in a dozen New York cinemas. Each 2½-minute film featured four rapid-fire soft news stories, such as the cab driver who had installed a disco in the back of his cab and a demonstration of how mental energy can affect the swing of a pendulum.

The last newsreel in Britain was *Movietone News*, founded as *British Movietone* in 1929 (see above), which suffered a decline from its circulation of over 2000 a week at the peak in World War II to only 200 a week when the final issue was released on 27 May 1979. The sign-off items were the Chelsea Flower Show, 'Our Capital City' (London from the air) and 'Highlights of 50 Years'.

The major remaining producer of newsreels is China, with over 20 studios devoted to their production.

> Early sound newsreels were often shot silent and sound effects added afterwards. According to *Picturegoer* (30 April 1932), 'one firm who owned a specially good crowd track put it on every crowd scene they issued. It was easily recognizable to anyone in the trade because at a certain point a dog barked.'

The most costly newsreel ever made was the *Gaumont British* edition of 24 October 1934, which included scenes of the Centenary Air Race shot at Melbourne, Victoria. The Australian footage was transmitted to Britain frame by frame by beam wireless for 68 hours at a cost of some $4000 a foot or $30,264 for the brief sequence of 160 frames. It was shown in 1500 cinemas within 48 hours of transmission.

The only woman news cameraman was Dorothy Dunn, a member of the *Universal Animated Weekly* crew in America during World War I.

> *Kinematograph Weekly* on newsreels, 25 October 1934: 'Television, of course, will not supplant the celluloid reel for many obvious reasons'. Evidently the reasons were too obvious to be worth stating.

Specialized Newsreels

These have catered to various minorities and sectional interests since the early twenties. The first all-black newsreel was produced by the Monumental Picture Corp. in 1921 and a sound newsreel for blacks called *All-American News* was established in 1942. The last newsreel to be established anywhere in the western world, Heyns Films' *Topical News*, was founded as recently as 1975 to cater to the black population of South Africa. A number of newsreels for women were produced in America, including

Eve's Film Pictorial in the early 1920s, the world's first colour newsreel, *McCall Fashion News* (1925), and Fox's *Fashion Forecast*, which ran from 1938 to 1940.

Children were catered to in America by *The Junior Newsreel* (1934). Other newsreels were made by young people themselves. In England the boys of Mill Hill public school started the *Mill Hill School Animated News* in 1920. On the other side of the Atlantic *Dartmouth College News* (1928) was a regular 16mm newsreel made by the college film club for circulation to alumni, and Culver Military Academy was producing a weekly newsreel in 1929.

In the 1930s the USSR also had its own newsreel for children, geared to teaching them how to be good Soviet citizens. In one edition, which makes distressing viewing today, a proud little girl is being laden with gifts at an official state ceremony as a reward for denouncing her parents as subversives. The commentary says that she has been promised a life of riches where all her needs would be catered for.

A sponsored newsreel, the *Ford Animated Weekly*, was produced by the Ford Motor Co. between 1914 and 1921, succeeded by the *Ford News*, which was for circulation to Detroit theaters only, in 1934. A different type of sponsored newsreel, *Kinograms*, which had commercials interspersing the news items, was introduced on 28 August 1931. The sound was recorded on disc—the only sound newsreel ever to use the synchronized disc system.

Naked capitalism was matched by a socialist newsreel called *The Workers' Newsreel*, of which 16 issues were produced in the USA (1931–32) by the Film & Photo League, an offshoot of the militant Workers' International Relief.

The William J. Ganz Co. of New York began issuing a monthly *Highlights of the News* for home-movie buffs in 1927. A similar enterprise in Britain was Fox Photos' *Film-at-Home News*, inaugurated in September 1933 at an annual subscription of £25 for a 200 ft reel monthly.

Israel produced a *Monthly Newsreel for Immigrants* between 1966 and 1968.

The only all-cartoon newsreel was *Topical Sketch*, founded in Britain in July 1915. Wallace Carlson's *Canimated Nooz Pictorial*, released weekly by Essany from May 1916 to mid-1917, had photographic heads on pen-and-ink bodies. A regular comedy newsreel, titled *Crazy Newsreel*, was issued by 'Gaumont-Skittish News'—otherwise Gaumont-British—from 1937 to 1939.

Even before glasnost Soviet Russia had a satirical newsreel. Called *Fitil/The Fuse*, it dealt chiefly with the shortcomings of the bureaucracy. Established in the days of Khruschev's 'thaw', and allowed to survive as a safety valve against discontent, each ten-minute monthly issue comprised a playlet, a documentary report and a cartoon. The documentary sequence of one *Fitil* showed children walking to

It was not often that the newsreel was billed above the feature. In this case though the slaying of Bonnie and Clyde took precedence over any horse opera.

school in the rain, despite regulations enjoining local authorities to supply transport. When the bureaucracy replied that the situation had now been rectified, another issue of *Fitil* showed the same schoolchildren still walking to school, this time in a snowstorm.

SERIALS

The first serial was the 12-episode Edison production *What Happened to Mary* (US 12), starring Mary Fuller as a foundling seeking her lost inheritance, of which the first episode was released on 26 July 1912. It has been claimed that the film was not a true serial, but a *series* of episodes each complete in itself. Although it is true that the cliffhanger element, an essential element of later serials, was missing from *What Happened to Mary*, in fact the denouement was not revealed until the final episode, and the various adventures were all part of a continuing storyline. *The Adventures of Kathlyn* (US 13) added the missing ingredient, leaving audiences in an agony of suspense at the end of each episode until the final triumph of the heroine.

The first talkie serial was Mascot Pictures' 10-episode jungle yarn *King of the Kongo* (US 29), starring Jacqueline Logan, Walter Miller and Boris Karloff.

The longest serial was *The Hazards of Helen*, directed in 119 one-reel episodes by J. P. McGowan and James Davis for Kalem, and starring Helen Holmes (episodes 1–26), Elsie McLeod (episodes 27–49) and Helen Gibson (episodes 50–119). The first episode was released on 7 November 1914; the last on 24 February 1917. The complete picture had a running time of over 31 hours.

The last Hollywood serial was Columbia Pictures' unremarkable *Blazing the Overland Trail* (US 56), directed by Spencer Bennet.

SERIAL OUTPUT

During the 44-year life of the episode film, American studios put out an estimated 350 silent serials and 231 talkies.

WAR FILM

The first war to be filmed was the Graeco–Turkish War of 1897. Sole cameraman in the field was British war correspondent and pioneer cinematographer Frederick Villiers (1852–1922), who filmed the Battle of Volo in Thessaly, Greece, in April. He wrote in his memoirs: 'Luckily I was well housed during the fighting in front of Volo, for the British consul insisted on my residing at the consulate. To me it was campaigning in luxury. From the balcony of the residence I could always see of a morning when the Turks opened fire up on Valestino Plateau; then I would drive with my camera outfit to the battlefield, taking my bicycle with me in the carriage. After I had secured a few reels of movies, if the Turks pressed too hard on our lines I would throw my camera into the vehicle and send it out of action, and at nightfall, after the fight, I would trundle back down the hill to dinner.' These first historic war films were destined never to be seen by the public. When he finally arrived back in London, Villiers found to his consternation that Star Films of Paris had already flooded the market with dramatized reconstructions of the campaign and there was no demand for the genuine article. He was equally

In the days when newsreel reportage was as important a means of communication as television news today, it was not unknown for battles to be delayed pending the arrival of the cameramen. On 3 January 1914 the Mexican bandit General Pancho Villa signed a contract with the Mutual Film Corporation assigning them the rights to all battle coverage and undertaking that, whenever possible, battles would be fought in daylight hours and at such times as were convenient to the Mutual cameramen. Villa was as good as his word. He postponed his attack on the city of Ojinaga until the camera operator, engaged elsewhere, arrived to record the victory. In a more savage theatre of war, the Nazi destruction of Gdynia in Poland in 1939 was delayed to allow time for cameramen to move forward and film the German forces from in front as they attacked.

unlucky the following year when he filmed the Battle of Omdurman from a gunboat on the Nile. As the gunboat's battery opened up, the camera tripod collapsed and Villiers' camera hit the deck, the magazine fell out and the film was exposed to the light.

The earliest surviving news film taken during a military campaign consists of scenes of the 5th Northumberland Fusiliers at Orange River, South Africa, during the Boer War of 1899–1902. Made by John Bennett Stanford on 12 November 1899, it is preserved in the National Film Archive.

FOURTEEN

PRESS AND PRINT

The first book on cinematography was *The History of the Kinetograph, Kinetoscope and Kineto-Phonograph*, by W. K. L. and Antonia Dickson, New York, 1895. Dickson was Thomas Edison's assistant and the inventor of the Kinetoscope 'peep show' motion picture apparatus and Kinetograph camera patented in his employer's name. The book was published in Britain in October of the same year.

The first poem to mention the cinema was in the British journal *Truth* on 30 July 1896. Titled 'The St Stephens Music Hall', it was about the various attractions to be found at this mythical establishment, including the new-fangled films:

Then, of course, of 'Living Pictures' there are some at which to laugh,
And repeated presentations of 'The Animatographe'.

The first short story about the cinema was 'Our Detective Story' from the *Referee*, a London newspaper, of 24 January 1897. Written by G. R. Sims under the pseudonym 'Dagonet', it centres around a husband whose suspicions are aroused when his wife temporarily disappears in Spain. He has almost forgotten the incident when, some time later, he and she are watching a series of actuality films of Spain at a music hall. Suddenly a lady and gentleman appear on screen arm in arm. It is the wife with the husband's partner: 'The woman was looking up into the man's face . . . His arm stole round her waist—she put up her face—he stooped and kissed her. The audience yelled with laughter.' The husband is outraged and a divorce follows, the films being produced as evidence in court.

Researching the early fiction of the cinema, film historian Stephen Bottomore has identified some 15 short stories published before 1912 which deal with films. Of these, strangely enough, all but two or three deal with a similar theme to 'Dagonet's', i.e. the revelation of some hitherto hidden facts through the showing of a film. The facts in question are usually to do with marital infidelity, but sometimes reveal the perpetrator of a more serious crime.

This constant theme in the fiction of early cinema may have had some basis in reality. As early as January 1897 the well-known British detective Henry Slater was advertising that he would employ the 'Animatographe' for surveillance 'in all cases and . . . produce the pictures in Court in evidence. Consultations free.' In subsequent years there were persistent reports of husbands or wives seeing their spouses two-timing them in newsreel pictures.

The first novel based on a movie was Harold MacGrath's *The Adventures of Kathlyn*, published in Indianapolis with stills from the film in 1914. It was derived from the Selig Polyscope 27-part serial starring Kathlyn Williams, of which the first episode was released on 29 December 1913. Gilson Willets had written the scenario for the film.

The first original work of literature based on a film was Stuart Edward White's *Oil on Troubled Waters*, published in the *Saturday Evening Post* in 1913. Director Allan Dwan had written the film scenario and approached White, a distinguished novelist, with the idea of paying him simply for the use of his name as the supposed author. White was so impressed with the plot, however, that he decided to turn it into a genuine short story for publication. One of the most notable examples of literature derived from a motion picture is Budd Schulberg's novel *On the Waterfront*, adapted from the screenplay of his 1954 film. Novels had been written from screenplays before, but as with cheap paperback adaptations today this was simply a means of publicizing a film at the same time as producing a book with high readership potential. Schulberg's 'book-of-the-film' was probably the first to be conceived as a serious work of literature exploring themes beyond the capacity of the movie camera.

Economically, the book-of-the-film is seldom more than a subsidiary merchandizing operation. In what is believed to be a unique case, however, respecting the Faye Dunaway starrer *The Eyes of Laura Mars* (US 78), the highly-successful paperback is reputed to have made a larger profit than the lacklustre movie.

Another book born of a film was *The Jazz Singer*. In this case a newspaper serial was adapted from the novel (by Arline De Haas), which was based on the film script (by Alfred A. Cohn) of the 1927 talkie, which in turn was a rendering of the Broadway show (by Samson Raphaelson), which had been dramatized from a short story called *The Day of Atonement* (also by Samson Raphaelson).

Similarly, the 1972 TV series *Anna and the King* was a spin-off of the film musical *The King and I* (US 56), an adaptation of the stage musical of the same name, derived from the straight movie version of the story, *Anna and the King of Siam* (US 46), taken from Margaret Landon's fictionalized biography which was based on the autobiography of Anna Leonowens.

Not even Shakespeare is immune. Huddersfield Theatre Royal advertised *Hamlet* in April 1952 as 'The Play of the Famous Film'.

The best-selling book-of-the-film was William Kotzwinkle's *E.T. The Extra-Terrestrial in his adventure on earth*, published in 1982 by MCA Publishing in the US and by Sphere Books in the UK, which has sold over 11 million copies. The Steven Spielberg movie of the same year still holds the all-time box office record (see p. 30).

The first film script to be published in book form was by Carl Mayer for Lupu Pick's *Sylvester* (Ger 23), about a grocer (Eugen Knopfer) who is unable to resolve the jealousy between his wife and his mistress and hangs himself, which was published in Berlin in 1924.

The first dialogue film script to be published in book form was Henri Ette's *The North Pole*, described as 'A 100% Tone and Speaking Picture with Songs, Choruses and Dances', issued by Ette Publications, Faroe Isles, 1931.

The first autobiography of a star was Pearl White's *Just Me*, published by Doran of New York in 1916. It is a lively and wholly unreliable account of her rise as the Queen of the Silent Serials.

The star with the largest number of biographies is Charles Spencer Chaplin (1889–1977), whose life and art have been expounded in 339 book-length works up to and including the first issue of *Charlie Chaplin Journal* (Berlin and New York 1991). This 450-page publication includes a listing of the 338 other works, compiled by Chaplin bibliophile Lennart Eriksson. Among the most recent entries is a biography published in Albania in 1990, believed to be the only life story of a film star available in Europe's last bastion of unreformed Stalinism. The official Albanian press agency explained that Chaplin was *persona grata* as a 'social activist'.

The youngest screen performer to have had a full-length autobiography published is Drew Barrymore (1975–), who shot to instant fame as a seven year old in *E.T. The Extra-Terrestrial* (US 82). Her book *Little Girl Lost*, published in 1990 when she was 15, chronicled misspent years as a tragic Hollywood wild-child. Daughter of alcoholic John Barrymore Jr, she took to drink at age nine and to drugs a year later. At 14 she dried out and returned to film-making.

America's first fan magazine was *Motion Picture Story Magazine*, founded by J. Stuart Blackton of Vitagraph as a monthly in February 1911.

The highest circulation of any film journal was achieved by the Chinese publication *Popular Film*, with a readership peak estimated at 100 million in 1980. Since then it has declined as cinema attendance has slumped, but is probably still read by more people than any other movie magazine in the world.

The first cartoon about the cinema was published in France in the satirical newspaper *Le Charivari* on 19 April 1896. It shows a man giving a cinematograph camera to a couple of newlyweds and advising them cynically: 'In 45 years time you'll be able to see again the only agreeable moment of your marriage.'

The first painting on a cinematic theme is an oil of 1907 by American artist John Sloan (1871–1951) titled *Movies, five cents*. It shows a nickelodeon audience watching a film of a couple kissing and is in a private collection in New York.

The first regular film column in a newspaper began appearing in the *New York Morning Journal* in 1909.

Perhaps the most unusual of the technical books on film is Stephen Ziplow's *Film Maker's Guide to Pornography* (1977), which provides a useful checklist of all the sexual acts capable of being reproduced on screen together with hints on the best ways to shoot them.

Cunnilingus, Ziplow advises, presents particular problems for the cameraman, as the man's head tends to get in the way, whereas orgies are great film fare but beware of the cost. The book also reveals what must be the most specialised job in the movie industry—the 'fluffer'. This is a girl who sits behind the camera on porn movies and whose responsibility it is to have the male performers erect on cue.

FIFTEEN

AUDIENCES AND EXHIBITORS

CINEMAS

The first cinema was the Cinématographe Lumière at the Salon Indien, a former billiard hall in the Grand Café, 14 boulevard des Capucines, Paris, opened under the management of Clément Maurice on 28 December 1895. The proprietors of the show were Auguste and Louis Lumière, the pioneer cinematographers whose films made up the programme. The opening performance included *Le Mur, L'Arrivée d'un train en gare, La sortie des Usines Lumière, Le goûter de Bébé, La pêche des poissons rouges, Soldats au manège, M. Lumière et le jongleur Trewey jouant aux cartes, La rue de la République à Lyon, En mer par gros temps, L'Arroseur arrosé* and *La destruction des mauvaises herbes.* Returns from the box office on the day of opening were disappointingly low, as only 35 people had ventured a franc to see the new form of entertainment. This barely covered the rent of 30 francs a day, and the owner of the Grand Café, M. Borgo, doubtless congratulated himself that he had refused Maurice's offer of 20 per cent of the receipts in lieu of rent. Later he was to come to regret his decision, when the Cinématographe Lumière became the sensation of Paris and box office receipts rose to 2500 francs a day. Most historians have assumed that the Cinématographe Lumière at the Grand Café was simply a temporary show and consequently it has usually been claimed as the first presentation of films before a paying audience (which it was not) instead of the first cinema. Although the exact date of its closure is not known, there is contemporary evidence that it was still functioning as late as 1901. The fact that it operated continuously for at least five years should be sufficient to justify any claim based on permanence.

The first cinema in the United States was Vitascope Hall, opened at the corner of Canal Street and Exchange Place, New Orleans on 26 June 1896. The proprietor of the 400-seat theatre was William T. Rock and his projectionist was William Reed. Most of the programme was made up of short scenic items, including the first British film to be released in America, Robert Paul's *Waves off Dover* (GB 95), but there was sometimes more compelling fare, such as *The Irish Way of Discussing Politics* (US 96) or *The Lynching Scene* (US 96). A major attraction was the movie *May Irwin Kiss* (US 96), which may be said to have introduced sex to the American screen. Admission to Vitascope Hall was 10¢ and for another 10¢ patrons were allowed

USA and UK cinemas from 1945 (total number of screens)

	USA	UK		USA	UK
1945	20,457	4723	1968	13,190	1631
1946	19,019	—	1969	13,480	1581
1947	18,607	—	1970	13,750	1529
1948	18,395	4706	1971	14,070	1482
1949	18,570	4800	1972	14,370	1450
1950	19,016	4584	1973	14,650	1530
1951	18,980	4581	1974	15,384	1535
1952	18,623	4568	1975	15,969	1530
1953	17,965	4542	1976	15,976	1525
1954	19,101	4509	1977	16,554	1547
1955	19,200	4483	1978	16,755	1563
1956	19,003	4391	1979	16,965	1604
1957	19,003	4194	1980	17,372	1590
1958	16,354	3996	1981	18,144	1562
1959	16,103	3414	1982	18,295	1439
1960	16,999	3034	1983	18,772	1327
1961	—	2711	1984	19,589	1226
1962	—	2421	1985	21,145	1226
1963	12,652	2181	1986	22,765	1237
1964	13,750	2057	1987	23,555	1250
1965	14,000	1971	1988	23,234	1284
1966	14,350	1847	1989	23,132	1403
1967	13,000	1736	1990	23,689	1561

to peep through the door of the projection room and see the Edison Vitascope projector. Those possessed of a liberal supply of dimes could also purchase a single frame of discarded film for the same price.

The first cinema in Britain: The earliest attempt at establishing a cinema in Britain was made by Birt Acres, whose Kineopticon opened at 2 Piccadilly Mansions at the junction of Piccadilly Circus and Shaftesbury Avenue on 21 March 1896. The manager was Mr T. C. Hayward. The opening programme (admission 6d) consisted of *Arrest of a Pickpocket, A Carpenter's Shop, A Visit to the Zoo, The Derby, Rough Seas at Dover* (original title of *Waves off Dover* mentioned above), *The Boxing Kangaroo* and *The German Emperor Reviewing his Troops.* After only a few weeks operation, Acres' cinema was gutted by fire.

The first cinema in Britain of any permanence was Mohawks' Hall, Upper Street, Islington, opened by the Royal Animated & Singing Picture Co. on 5

August 1901. The manager was Henry N. Phillips. Principal attractions of the inaugural programme were *The Rajah's Dream or The Enchanted Forest* (Fr 00), billed as 'the finest mysterious picture ever placed before the public', and a number of primitive 'talkies' featuring vocalists Lil Hawthorne, Vesta Tilley and Alec Hurley. There were also war films from South Africa and China, scenes of rush hour at the Angel, a 'graphic representation of the sensational sporting spectacle *Tally Ho* taken at the London Hippodrome', a newsreel of King Edward VII presenting medals to the South African war heroes, and scenes of a motor car explosion, Count Zeppelin's airship and 'a visit to a spiritualist'. The show was nightly at 8 p.m., with matinées on Thursdays and Saturdays, and prices of admission were 6d, 1s, 2s and 3s—considerably more than the average of 3d or 6d that most cinemas charged at the time of World War I. The Mohawk, though, was an ambitious enterprise, for while later cinemas were content to offer a piano accompaniment to the films, the Royal Animated & Singing Picture Co. engaged the 16-piece Fonobian Orchestra under the direction of Mr W. Neale. Within a few days of opening, the Mohawk advertised that it was 'besieged at every performance'. Evidently the cinema-going public was fickle, for within a few months the Mohawk had been forced to close its doors. After a period as a music hall, it was reopened as a cinema in 1908 as the Palace, changed hands ten years later to become the Blue Hall Cinema, and finally became a Gaumont before closing in 1962. The building was demolished in 1985 to make way for the Business Design Centre.

First Cinemas Worldwide

The cinemas listed right were the first to be established permanently (or intended to be permanent) in their respective countries.

ARGENTINA (1901) 467 Calle Maipu, Buenos Aires
AUSTRALIA (Dec 1896) Salon Cinématographe, 237 Pitt Street, Sydney
AUSTRIA (1903) Münstedt-Kino, the Prater, Vienna
BELGIUM (1897) Théâtre de Cinématographie, boulevard du Nord, Brussels
BRAZIL (31 Jul 1897) Salão de Novidades, 141 Rua do Ouvidor, Rio de Janeiro
BULGARIA (1908) The Modern Theatre, Sofia
CANADA (Oct 1907) The Electric Theatre, Vancouver
CHINA (1903) estab. Shanghai by Antonio Ramos
CUBA (c. 1904) Florodora, Palationo, Havana
CZECHOSLOVAKIA (1907) Blue Pike, Prague
DENMARK (7 Sept 1904) Kosmorama, Copenhagen
EGYPT (1904) Pathé Cinema, Cairo
FINLAND (1901) Kinematograph International, Helsinki
FRANCE (28 Dec 1895) Cinématographe Lumière, 14 boulevard des Capucines, Paris
GERMANY (Jul 1896) 21 Unter den Linden, Berlin
GREECE (1907) Constitution Square, Athens
HONG KONG (c. 1909) Bi Zhao Cinema
ICELAND (1906) Biógraftheater, Reykjavik
INDIA (1907) Elphinstone Cinema, Calcutta
IRAN (1905) Avenue Cherâq Gaz, Teheran
IRELAND (EIRE) (1909) Volta Cinema, Dublin (manager: James Joyce)
ITALY (c. 1898) Cinema Silenzioso, 21 Corso Vittorio Emanuele, Milan
JAPAN (Oct 1903) Denkikan, Asakusa
LEBANON (1909) Zahret Sourya, Beirut
MAURITIUS (1912) Luna Park, Port Louis
MEXICO (1901) Salon Pathé, 5 Calle de la Profesa, Mexico City
NEW ZEALAND (1910) King's Theatre, Auckland
NORWAY (1 Nov 1904) Kinematograf-Teatret, 12 Storthingsgd, Oslo
PORTUGAL (1904) Salão Ideal, Lisbon
ROMANIA (May 1909) Volta, Bucharest
SOUTH AFRICA (19 Dec 1908) New Apollo Theatre, 39 Pritchard Street, Johannesburg
SPAIN (c. 1897) Salón Maravillas, Glorieta de Bilbaô, Madrid
SWEDEN (27 Jul 1902) Arkaden Kino, Gothenburg
SWITZERLAND (11 May 1906) Grand Cinématographe Suisse, 17 Croix d'Or, Geneva
SYRIA (1916) Janak Kala'a, Damascus
THAILAND (1907) The Bioscope, Bangkok
TUNISIA (16 Oct 1908) Omnia Pathé, Tunis
TURKEY (1908) Pathé, Istanbul
UNITED KINGDOM (5 Aug 1901) Mohawk's Hall, Upper Street, Islington
UNITED STATES (26 Jun 1896) Vitascope Hall, Canal Street, New Orleans
USSR (RUSSIA) (1903) The Electric Theatre, Moscow
YUGOSLAVIA (CROATIA) (1900) Znasstveno Umjetnicko Kajilste, Zagreb

It is apparent from this list that the oft repeated claim that the first cinema in the world was the Nickelodeon opened by Harry Davis in Pittsburgh, Pa. in June 1905 is wholly without foundation.

CINEMAS WORLDWIDE

AFGHANISTAN
1939-1; 1952-9; 1972-20; 1977-45
ALBANIA
1935-10; 1939-18; 1950-14; 1960-176; 1970-189; 1979-450 (includes mobile); 1985-300
ALGERIA
1935-130; 1939-165; 1950-200; 1962-550; 1979-304; 1990-397
ARGENTINA
1923-800; 1930-1608; 1939-1021; 1950-1855; 1960-1739; 1970-1767; 1979-1794; 1990-527
AUSTRALIA
1919-760; 1925-1216; 1930-1250; 1935-1090; 1939-1371; 1945-1600; 1950-1674; 1960-1800; 1970-1349; 1978-900; 1984-813; 1991-851
AUSTRIA
1921-516; 1925-580; 1930-736; 1935-850; 1949-957; 1956-1210; 1964-1248; 1970-820; 1977-533; 1983-536; 1989-427

BANGLADESH
1976-230; 1984-420; 1988-600
BARBADOS
1981-8; 1991-6
BELGIUM
1920-811; 1930-700; 1939-1100; 1950-1550; 1960-1550; 1972-1081; 1979-545; 1983-652; 1989-427
BELIZE
1991-5
BERMUDA
1989-3
BOLIVIA
1925-16; 1935-23; 1947-60; 1954-60; 1976-41; 1984-160
BRAZIL
1930-1431; 1939-1450; 1947-1514; 1958-3113; 1968-3234; 1978-3200; 1990-1600

BULGARIA
1920-93; 1925-48; 1935-128; 1939-111; 1947-240; 1957-1400; 1967-2957; 1979-3529; 1987-3250; 1991-600
BURMA
1927-58; 1939-131; 1950-150; 1960-380; 1985-435
CAMBODIA
1933-4; 1951-15; 1975-50; 1979-0; 1990-6
CAMEROON
1985-70
CANADA
1922-1087; 1937-1121; 1947-1493; 1955-2085; 1960-1756; 1968-1142; 1977-1392; 1984-2004
CHILE
1930-215; 1939-243; 1947-268; 1960-450; 1972-336; 1988-145

CHINA
1925-120; 1930-185; 1935-276; 1939-275; 1949-596; 1953-770; 1958-1386; 1965-2000; 1982-2670; 1988-3100

COLOMBIA
1930-207; 1939-276; 1947-435; 1972-819; 1980-1000; 1984-700; 1988-536

COSTA RICA
1930-21; 1939-40; 1947-52; 1950-77; 1972-136; 1988-68

CUBA
1939-375; 1947-450; 1950-515; 1972-444; 1976-453; 1985-550; 1991-531

CYPRUS
1985-56

CZECHOSLOVAKIA
1919-490; 1925-680; 1930-1200; 1939-1254; 1945-1656; 1951-1928; 1955-2268; 1966-3584; 1972-3469; 1978-3248; 1984-2847; 1987-2801; 1991-2666

DENMARK
1930-270; 1935-340; 1939-370; 1947-430; 1955-458; 1960-500; 1970-382; 1978-442; 1984-457; 1987-404; 1990-342

DOMINICAN REP.
1984-150; 1988-80

ECUADOR
1930-25; 1935-29; 1939-37; 1950-75; 1960-260; 1977-330; 1983-500

EGYPT
1908-11; 1925-40; 1930-60; 1935-89; 1939-118; 1946-285; 1950-226; 1960-389; 1972-384; 1979-215; 1990-168

EIRE
1945-212; 1950-345; 1955-327; 1960-290; 1970-300; 1975-230; 1980-131; 1988-153

EL SALVADOR
1988-67

ETHIOPIA
1939-33; 1950-11; 1974-31

FINLAND
1911-80; 1922-120; 1927-245; 1932-195; 1937-274; 1942-421; 1947-460; 1952-523; 1957-613; 1962-581; 1970-330; 1979-314; 1983-368; 1987-344; 1990-332

FRANCE
1920-1525; 1925-2947; 1930-3113; 1935-4000; 1939-4600; 1950-5300; 1955-5732; 1960-5821; 1965-5454; 1970-4381; 1975-4328; 1984-5031; 1988-5063; 1990-4440

GERMANY
1912-1500; 1918-2299; 1920-3731; 1925-3878; 1930-5266; 1935-5100; 1940-6900; 1945-11,150. FRG: 1950-5930; 1955-5100; 1960-6950; 1965-5209; 1970-3634; 1975-3094; 1979-3110; 1984-3687; 1987-3242; 1990-3270. GDR: 1960-1550; 1968-1300; 1975-880; 1980-839; 1989-820; 1991-3222

GHANA
1984-80

GREECE
1915-147; 1925-138; 1930-224; 1935-122; 1939-170; 1947-300; 1955-450; 1960-1000; 1970-1034; 1979-1504; 1983-1200; 1987-508

GUAM
1986-19

GUATEMALA
1930-25; 1939-34; 1950-42; 1975-106

HONDURAS
1925-6; 1930-27; 1950-28; 1972-60; 1984-105; 1988-99

HONG KONG
1920-6; 1950-27; 1954-62; 1972-99; 1978-73; 1981-82; 1987-105

HUNGARY
1907-127; 1912-270; 1921-362; 1930-495; 1939-524; 1945-972; 1951-586; 1960-1200; 1972-981; 1979-1045, 1989-925. (NB: Figs refer to 35 mm cinemas only.)

ICELAND
1912-2; 1930-3; 1989-31

INDIA
1910-5; 1920-148; 1924-171; 1930-309; 1936-910; 1941-1136; 1946-1700; 1950-1950; 1960-3200; 1970-4500; 1975-5363; 1979-6232; 1984-7248; 1988-8409. (NB: Excluding mobile cinemas.)

INDONESIA
1930-196; 1939-170; 1950-260; 1960-750; 1972-675; 1982-1581; 1990-2200

IRAN
1925-4; 1930-33; 1939-35; 1945-78; 1950-80; 1960-237; 1972-520; 1976-438; 1984-256; 1989-274

IRAQ
1935-7; 1939-20; 1950-71; 1972-137; 1979-87

ISRAEL
1947-216; 1960-226; 1970-257; 1975-227; 1980-230; 1984-156; 1988-175; 1991-219

ITALY
1907-500; 1922-2019; 1930-2405; 1935-3794; 1939-4049; 1955-9543; 1960-10,500; 1970-9680; 1979-7495; 1991-2450

IVORY COAST
1980-60

JAMAICA
1930-19; 1939-17; 1950-28; 1972-54; 1981-28; 1988-31

JAPAN
1920-600; 1925-1050; 1930-1120; 1935-1600; 1939-1749; 1947-1477; 1950-2157; 1955-7400; 1960-8477; 1963-6164; 1966-4119; 1970-3246; 1973-2974; 1975-2443; 1977-2453; 1979-2392; 1983-2239; 1986-2109; 1990-1836

JORDAN
1950-17; 1972-34; 1988-15

KENYA
1935-8; 1950-44; 1972-28; 1979-35; 1985-50; 1988-44

KOREA
1935-45; 1939-60; 1950-116. South Korea: 1960-273; 1970-658; 1977-752; 1988-710

KUWAIT
1962-4; 1979-10; 1985-11

LAOS
1990-12

LEBANON
1949-48; 1960-82; 1972-170

LIBYA
1951-12; 1962-35; 1972-60; 1977-52

LUXEMBOURG
1933-26; 1939-30; 1950-39; 1955-41; 1972-52; 1975-36; 1979-17; 1988-20

MADAGASCAR
1925-5; 1933-14; 1950-24; 1974-31

MALAWI
1928-5

MALAYSIA
1929-35; 1935-58; 1939-97; 1950-100; 1960-220; 1972-430; 1977-425; 1984-322; 1988-118

MALTA
1915-30; 1950-26; 1960-49; 1972-39; 1979-35; 1982-34; 1988-9

MAURITIUS
1988-40

MEXICO
1930-615; 1935-701; 1939-823; 1946-1369; 1950-1726; 1960-2232; 1972-1850; 1981-3020; 1988-2995; 1991-1765

MONACO
1985-3

MOROCCO
1933-51; 1939-62; 1950-90; 1972-155; 1977-276; 1990-250

NETHERLANDS
1925-264; 1930-236; 1935-308; 1939-333; 1950-461; 1955-573; 1960-565; 1966-490; 1970-435; 1975-387; 1980-507; 1987-436; 1990-426

NEW ZEALAND
1925-350; 1930-443; 1935-366; 1939-576; 1945-568; 1950-570; 1960-581; 1970-260; 1975-228; 1979-200; 1984-154; 1990-106

NICARAGUA
1925-11; 1939-24; 1950-47; 1972-85; 1989-127

NIGER
1983-10

NIGERIA
1939-11; 1950-25; 1973-112; 1979-131

NORWAY
1925-252; 1930-212; 1935-241; 1939-247; 1947-291; 1951-452; 1955-508; 1960-668; 1971-442; 1975-464; 1979-455; 1984-467; 1990-403

OMAN
1988-20

OUTER MONGOLIA
1952-50; 1977-60; 1982-59

PAKISTAN
1947-250; 1957-360; 1960-419; 1970-527; 1975-623; 1979-725; 1984-750; 1990-650

PANAMA
1988-55

PARAGUAY
1930-9; 1939-15; 1950-40; 1972-30; 1988-100

PERU
1925-60; 1930-70; 1935-110; 1939-205; 1950-235; 1960-400; 1972-363; 1977-400; 1985-480; 1988-400

PHILIPPINES
1935-273; 1950-450; 1960-634; 1972-704; 1977-900; 1980-1200; 1984-946; 1988-800

POLAND
1925-383; 1935-728; 1939-769; 1950-574; 1967-3694; 1977-3232; 1984-2112; 1990-1620. (NB: Figs 1967 onwards include 16 mm cinemas.)

PORTUGAL
1925-127; 1939-215; 1950-301; 1967-336; 1975-410; 1984-397; 1991-293

PUERTO RICO
1988-115

ROMANIA
1925-304; 1930-357; 1935-380; 1939-372; 1948-383; 1955-350; 1968-573; 1972-462; 1977-578; 1984-635; 1987-630

SAINT HELENA
1985-1

SENEGAL
1979-75

SEYCHELLES
1988-1

SINGAPORE
1985-57; 1990-48

SOUTH AFRICA
1925-380; 1935-350; 1945-465; 1950-470; 1970-521; 1979-700; 1985-507; 1988-432

SPAIN
1914-900; 1921-570; 1925-1500; 1930-2074; 1935-3252; 1939-3500; 1948-3251; 1955-7325; 1960-6459; 1970-6627; 1974-5178; 1978-4430; 1981-4096; 1984-3663; 1986-2640; 1988-2234; 1991-1306

SRI LANKA
1930-24; 1939-19; 1950-82; 1960-206; 1970-315; 1975-365; 1984-320; 1987-210

SWAZILAND
1988-5

SWEDEN
1920-600; 1930-1182; 1935-843; 1939-1907; 1947-2493; 1955-2494; 1966-1733; 1975-1192; 1979-1210; 1984-1220; 1990-1122

SWITZERLAND
1920-178; 1930-302; 1941-351; 1950-410; 1960-615; 1972-539; 1977-494; 1985-437; 1989-403

SYRIA
1925-14; 1935-26; 1950-50; 1960-70; 1972-90; 1977-70; 1983-70

CINEMAS WORLDWIDE (continued)

TAIWAN
  1960-542; 1972-668; 1991-666
TAHITI
  1988-9
TANZANIA
  1988-35
THAILAND
  1915-3; 1925-42; 1935-68; 1939-80; 1950-118;
  1960-238; 1970-501; 1986-577; 1991-600
TONGA
  1985-10
TRINIDAD
  1988-26
TUNISIA
  1933-61; 1950-50; 1972-65; 1979-76; 1984-85;
  1990-70

TURKEY
  1925-40; 1930-104; 1939-120; 1950-275;
  1960-700; 1970-790; 1990-350
UK
  1914-3170; 1928-3760; 1934-4305; 1939-
  4901. For 1945-1990 see p. 199.
URUGUAY
  1925-101; 1930-122; 1935-137; 1945-175;
  1950-177; 1972-223; 1979-94; 1984-79; 1988-
  85
USA
  1910-9480; 1913-15,700; 1923-15,000; 1929-
  23,344; 1935-15,273; 1940-19,042. For 1945-
  1990 see p. 199.
USSR
  1917-1045; 1987-5257

YEMEN
  1985-20
YUGOSLAVIA
  1921-231; 1930-397; 1939-383; 1950-736;
  1960-1585; 1967-1765; 1977-1385; 1983-
  1278; 1987-1345
VENEZUELA
  1930-121; 1939-147; 1950-350; 1954-575;
  1964-741; 1975-650; 1984-450; 1988-392
VIETNAM
  1912-10; 1925-29; 1930-34; 1939-63; 1950-80;
  1960 (S. Vietnam only) -189; 1970 (S.
  Vietnam only) -102; 1977-199
ZAMBIA
  1988-8

Going to the movies, Connecticut c.1907. (Kobal)

The first purpose-built cinema was the Cinéma Omnia Pathé, on the boulevard Montmartre, Paris, which opened with *Le Pendu* (Fr 06) and supporting programme on 1 December 1906. The world's first luxury cinema, and the first with a raked floor so that everyone could see above the heads in front, it was decorated in classical style with columns and Grecian friezes. The screen, measuring 20 ft by 13 ft, was one of the largest ever installed in a cinema at that time. Admission for the two-hour show ranged from 50c to 3fr—prices at other cinemas were generally in the range of 25c to 2fr.

The first purpose-built cinema in Britain was established by Joshua Duckworth of the Premier Picture Co., a former magic-lantern showman and kinetoscope proprietor, whose Central Hall, Colne, Lancs, was erected at a cost of £2000 and opened on 22 February 1907. At first Duckworth presented both films and variety, but abandoned the latter when he found that pictures alone were a sufficient attraction. In his two-hour programme, he always liked to 'include an educational or travel subject; this I find gives dignity to the show. Good drama and pathetic subjects are always appreciated. The greatest difficulty is experienced in satisfying an audience to which you are playing week after week, with humorous and comic subjects—breaking crockery, tumbling over furniture, or running against the banana cart fails to draw a smile if not positive disapproval.' (*Kinematograph Weekly* 2.7.08). The building continued in operation as a cinema until 1924, then became a spiritualist chapel and later an engineering training workshop. It now houses the Robotics Division of Cleveland-Guest Engineering Ltd, but the exterior remains unchanged from when it was first built.

The large purpose-built cinema followed soon after. First to seat over a thousand people was the 1200 Gem in Great Yarmouth, which opened for business on 4 July 1908 under the management of C. B. Cochran—later to become famous as a West

End impresario. The Gem was an impressively ornate building in the Renaissance style with twin cupolas surmounting towers on either side of the entrance. At night it was lit by 1500 powerful electric bulbs—with that engaging disregard for the literal truth which has always characterized cinema publicity, the management dubbed it 'The Palace of 5000 Lights'. One of the odder characteristics of this pioneer venture in bringing mass entertainment to mass audiences was a condition of the licence granted to Cochran by the local authority. Men and women were not allowed to sit together, presumably for fear of what they might get up to in the dark. The Gem had another curious distinction, being one of the very few purpose-built cinemas ever to have been converted into a theatre. It still operates as the Windmill Theatre, mainly for summer shows and amateur productions. There is even the occasional film show, usually cartoons for the younger holidaymakers.

The first British cinema with a sloping floor was the Picture Palace at St Albans, Hertfordshire, opened by Arthur Melbourne-Cooper of the Alpha Trading Co. in 1908. It was also the first to depart from standard theatre practice by charging more to sit at the back of the stalls than the front. The *Bioscope* reported: 'This arrangement was somewhat resented at first by patrons of the higher-priced seats, but when they found the specially raised floor gave them a better view than could be got from the front, they appreciated the innovation'. The idea was suggested to Melbourne-Cooper by his usherette, whom he later had the good sense to marry.

The first cinema to erect a neon sign was the West End Cinema in Coventry Street, London in 1913. It was also the first building of any kind in Britain to be emblazoned with neon and remained the only one for another ten years.

The first air-conditioned cinema was the Central Park Theater in Chicago, opened in 1917 by former nickelodeon operators Abraham and Barney Balaban and their partner Sam Katz.

The first arts cinema, specializing in minority interest films of artistic merit, was the Cinéma d'Avant Garde, opened in Paris in 1924 by Jean Tadesco.

The first arts cinema in Britain was established by Elsie Cohen when she took over the Palais de Luxe in London's Great Windmill Street in 1929. The following year it was converted into the Windmill, one of the rare instances of a cinema becoming a theatre.

Social Acceptance of the Cinema

Although the cinema was primarily a proletarian form of entertainment in the USA and UK prior to World War I, elsewhere it achieved social acceptance at an earlier date. The first countries in which this was manifest were Russia and Japan, a phenomenon partly accounted for by high admission charges. In Japan seat prices of the earliest cinemas (*c.* 1903) were generally in a range equivalent to 6d (12¢)–3s 9d (90¢), well out of the reach of peasants or artisans. The respectability of the cinema in Russia was attested by the fact that the exclusive Hotel Metropole in Moscow saw fit to open its own cinema in 1906. The interest of the Tsar and Tsarina in films—the court photographer was kept constantly employed filming the Royal Family at leisure—did much to make movies fashionable. An American wrote to a US trade publication in 1913 that the audiences he saw in Russia were of a far better class—and the seats more expensive—than elsewhere in Europe. Cinemas were attended, he said, even by 'very high officials in uniform'.

In France the stage-bound but much admired productions of Film d'Art, with casts drawn from the

USA and UK weekly cinema attendance (millions)

	USA	UK		USA	UK
1922	40	—	1957	45	17.6
1923	43	—	1958	40	14.5
1924	46	—	1959	42	11.2
1925	46	—	1960	40	9.6
1926	50	—	1961	42	8.6
1927	57	—	1962	43	7.6
1928	65	25.2	1963	44	6.9
1929	95	—	1964	—	6.6
1930	90	—	1965	44	6.3
1931	75	—	1966	38	5.6
1932	60	—	1967	17.8	5.1
1933	60	—	1968	18.8	4.6
1934	70	18.3	1969	17.5	4.1
1935	75	—	1970	17.7	3.7
1936	88	—	1971	15.8	3.9
1937	85	—	1972	18	3.0
1938	85	—	1973	16.6	2.6
1939	85	—	1974	19.4	2.7
1940	80	—	1975	19.9	2.2
1941	85	25.2	1976	18.4	2.0
1942	85	28.7	1977	20.2	2.1
1943	85	29.6	1978	21.7	2.4
1944	85	30.3	1979	22.1	2.5
1945	90	30.5	1980	19.8	2.0
1946	90	31.4	1981	20.5	1.6
1947	90	28.1	1982	22.4	1.2
1948	90	29.1	1983	23.0	1.3
1949	87.5	27.5	1984	22.9	1.0
1950	60	26.8	1985	20.3	1.4
1951	54	26.2	1986	21.8	1.4
1952	51	25.2	1987	23.8	1.5
1953	46	24.7	1988	20.9	1.6
1954	49	24.5	1989	21.8	1.8
1955	46	22.7	1990	20.4	1.9
1956	47	21.2			

illustrious Comédie-Française, catered from 1908 for the kind of audiences who looked to film as a silent record of great theatre drama. Around 1910, at a time when even minor American players would only deign to appear in films under the strictest cloak of anonymity, the fact that the leading stars of the Budapest National Theatre were prepared to be seen on screen gave the Hungarian cinema its artistic imprimatur. In Germany *Der Andere* (Ger 12), directed by Max Mack with the distinguished stage actor Albert Basserman in the lead, was the first film to receive serious critical attention in the press and consequent patronage from a new type of cinema audience. The emergence of Denmark's Asta Nielsen as the first star specializing in tragic roles had a profound influence on the cinema in Scandinavia and Central Europe from 1910 onwards, demonstrating the drawing power of original screen drama and 'name' stars to middle-class audiences. As the artistic quality of motion pictures improved, new luxury cinemas opened designed to accommodate the kind of audiences at which these films were aimed Foremost was the giant Gaumont-Palace in Paris (1911), with a seating capacity of 5000; others included Berlin's 2000-seat Alhambra Platz (1911), the Panellinion in

Athens (1911), also with 2000 seats, and Copenhagen's majestic 3000-seat Palads-Teatret (1912).

In America the era of the 'super cinema' began a little later, dating from the opening of the Regent on

---

Between the wars every big cinema had its own restaurant. This one, opened in 1918, was at the Stoll Picture Theatre in Newcastle upon Tyne. During the 1930s, cafés like this served a four-course luncheon with a roll and butter and coffee for as little as 1s 6d (7½d). The last cinema café, at the Odeon in Southampton, closed in May 1982.

The cartoon weekly *Punch* has always been something of a social barometer. When *Punch* publishes a cartoon about a new trend, it is probably here to stay. Note the middle-class audience in this 1912 drawing.

THE CINEMA AS AN EDUCATIVE FORCE.

Tommy (a regular attender at cinematograph shows, during the performance of a society drama). "IS THAT THE TRUSTING HUSBAND OR THE AMOROUS LOVER?"

116th Street and 7th Avenue in February 1913 and the Vitagraph Theater and the Strand on Broadway in 1914. There has been a tendency to oversimplify American film history by suggesting that the cinema remained a primitive entertainment controlled by unlettered immigrants and largely aimed at immigrant audiences until the advent of D. W. Griffith, whereupon, it is said, the movies became an art form. In fact the influence of Griffith in making the cinema socially acceptable is probably less significant than the emergence of the feature-length film in the United States in 1912–13, a development that took place later than it did in Europe. While the simple one-reeler remained standard, the primitive nickelodeon was an appropriate showplace. The rise of the full-length drama, which was contemporary with the creation of the 'star system', broadened the appeal of the movies and stimulated the erection of theatres adequate to their presentation in an atmosphere of 'comfort and refinement'.

In Britain the feature film was also late in supplanting the modest one-reel melodramas and comedies of predominantly backstreet picture houses. Significantly the humour weekly *Punch*, generally alert to social trends, did not publish its first cartoon about cinema-going until 1912. By that date artist Charles Pears was able to show what was clearly intended to represent a sophisticated, middle-class audience. Few of the 4000 cinemas estimated to be operating in Britain by 1912, however, would have aspired to such a level of patronage unless they were of the standard of London's first luxury cinema, Cinema House in Oxford street (1910), with its oak-panelled auditorium, adjoining restaurant, and seats upholstered in a 'delicate shade of Rose du Barri velvet'. Generally speaking, middle-class cinema-going in Britain came in with World War I and was due to a combination of circumstances: the relaxation of chaperonage, the provision of better appointed and more luxurious cinemas, the feverish desire for entertainment by officers home on leave, and not least, the vastly improved standard of film-making after 1914.

The largest cinema ever was the Roxy, built in New York at a cost of $12 million and opened under the management of Samuel Rothapfel (after whom it was named) on 11 March 1927. With an original seating capacity of 6214, the Roxy employed a total of 300 staff, including 16 projectionists and 110 musicians. The Roxy closed on 29 March 1960.

Europe's largest-ever cinema was the Gaumont Palace, opened in Paris with a 6000 seat auditorium in 1931.

The largest cinema auditorium in Britain is the Odeon, Leicester Square, with 1983 seats. The largest number of cinema seats in one building is 3996 at the 12-screen Warner multiplex at Bury, Lancs.

The smallest cinema in the world to operate as a regular commercial venture was the Miramar at Colon, Cuba, which was reported in 1926 to have 25 seats.

The smallest cinema in the USA was the Silver Star Theater in Silver Star, Montana, which had a seating capacity of 26 in 1925. Silver Star, population 75, boasted two cinemas, with a total seating capacity (126) exceeding the number of citizens. Only eleven of the 15,000 cinemas operating in the US at that date had under 100 seats, of which five were in the State of Montana.

The smallest licensed cinema in Britain is the 30-seat CBA Cinema Toftwood in Dereham, Norfolk. Owned by the CBA group (ABC backwards), which arguably can claim to be Britain's smallest cinema chain—it runs one other cinema in Dereham—it has a 6 × 10 ft screen, cherry-red drapes on the walls, and a miniature cinema organ which rises from below the floor to serenade arriving patrons. Four flavours of Aldous ice cream, a Norfolk speciality, are available at 25p a cornet.

The smallest auditorium in a multiple cinema is in the six-screen Biohoellin at Reykjavik, Iceland, which seats 17.

The highest cinema attendance in the world is in China, with 21,000 million admissions in 1986 (about 57.5 million daily). Not all these are paid admissions, however, as cinema shows in public parks and in rural areas are often free. China also has the highest number of attendances per capita, with 21 p.a.

The highest number of admissions for a film per capita of population was achieved by the historical epic *Khan Asparoukh* (Bul 82), of which the first of three parts was seen by 6.5 million of Bulgaria's 8.5 million population, equal to 76.5 per cent. Total admissions for the first run of all three parts (shown separately) were 12 million.

Special Amenities for Cinema Patrons

These were offered by some exhibitors from an early date. A correspondent of the *Kinematograph Weekly* reported in 1907 that it was customary for Italian cinemas to be furnished with a reading-room stocked with the current newspapers and illustrated journals for the benefit of patrons waiting for their friends.

Berlin's first super-cinema, the 2000 seat Alhambra Platz of 1911, served beer during the performance. Each seat had a tip-up tray on the back, similar to those on airliner seats, for the person behind to rest his tankard on. The first air-conditioned cinema was opened in America in 1917, but in hot countries efforts had been made to keep the patrons cool before that date. China Theatres Ltd, which operated a chain of cinemas in the Chinese Treaty Ports, provided cold towels for the audience's comfort. *Moving*

Flint, Michigan—the city with no auto manufacturing and no cinemas. From *Roger and Me* (US 89). (*British Film Institute*)

Michael Moore's *Roger and Me* (US 89), about his quest to interview General Motors chief Roger Smith on the decision to close down the auto factories in GM's and Moore's home town of Flint, Michigan, did spectacular business worldwide and scored the third highest ever gross for a documentary film. One city where it did not get a showing, though, was Flint, Michigan. Despite a population of 150,000, the economically derelict town no longer has a cinema.

Picture World recorded: 'The picture is stopped about every reel for an interval to permit him (the Chinaman) to whizz his towel across to the attendant in the aisle, who immediately wets it in icy water and whizzes it back.'

Many American cinemas have provided a crèche where mothers could leave their babies, the earliest recorded being at the Alhambra, Milwaukee in 1913. The Strand, opened in New York in April 1914, would take telephone calls for patrons, who were asked to notify the Captain of Ushers, in advance, where they were sitting. In the thirties, London's Cameo cinema allowed patrons to telephone out for nothing, besides giving them free cups of tea and free pre-stamped postcards.

A New York cinema which opened in 1925, the Knickerbocker, had a separate 'Carriage Entrance' for the kind of wealthy clientele the movies were begin-

ning to attract. A resident chiropodist ministered to patrons of the Capitol, NY in the 1920s. Club-like amenities existed at New York's Little Carnegie Theater, which opened in 1928 with a ping-pong room, a bridge salon and a dance floor. The Fox, San Francisco, contained an art gallery with paintings personally selected in Europe by Mrs Fox.

Nothing could compare with the 6000-seat Roxy in New York, with its permanent choir of 100 voices, 50-strong ballet troupe, lavishly appointed drawing room, its own broadcasting station and a fully-equipped hospital with separate male and female wards. No less than 12,900 cases were treated in the Roxy's first year (1927–28) and it was claimed that eight lives were saved. There was also the Bilmarjac Seat Indicator System, which consisted of aisle boxes with a row of discs corresponding to the seats. When a seat was vacated, the disc lit up.

After the Roxy, anything offered elsewhere seemed tame by comparison. However, a Paramount representative who visited Australia in the 1940s was particularly impressed with the 'Crying Rooms', in which mothers nursing infants could watch the film from behind a soundproof glass screen. In addition, there would often be a similar room with glass screen for the use of private parties, a facility that the Paramount representative thought highly desirable as Australians visiting the cinema in a group were often drunk.

In 1926 Warner Bros made special provision for the blind at three New York cinemas, the Warner's Theatre, the Capitol and the Colony. Fifty seats in each were fitted with headphones to supply descriptive commentaries on the films shown.

A novel device that failed to catch on elsewhere was the automatic ticket dispenser installed at Loew's 175th Street Theater, New York, about 1960. It would take either coins or notes and give change; if the change was paper money it came in the form of a bill rolled like a cigarette and hygienically wrapped in tissue.

In 1979 the Edmonds Theater, Seattle, made a determined pitch for the teenage market by ripping out 40 seats and installing a dance floor. Live bands played for dancing after each performance, the $3 admission covering both the picture and the rock session.

Open-air cinemas are common in Mediterranean countries, but until recently the Oriente cinema in Barcelona enjoyed the special seasonal amenity of a sliding roof which enabled audiences to sit beneath a star-studded sky in summer—and, less romantically, enabled urchins to lob dead cats over the walls.

The first cinema to present a double bill of feature films was the Glacarium in Melbourne, Australia, on 15 May 1911. The programme for the week was *The Lost Chord* (Aus 11) and *The Fall of Troy* (It 10).

During the 1950s small cinemas in Japanese villages would show up to six features on a single programme. This invariably arose from competition between two rival cinemas, one advertising a triple feature, the other outbidding with a quadruple, and so on.

The longest non-stop show took place at the Variety Arts Center in Hollywood on 29–31 May 1983, when 37 low-budget classics were shown in continuous sequence during a 50-hour 'B Movie Marathon'. Tickets cost $15 for the entire show, patrons bringing their own sleeping bags, food and drink, and what *Variety* described as 'assorted life support systems to get them through the gruelling early morning hours'.

The oldest cinema in the world still remains elusive after four editions of this book. The author invites nominations predating Moscow's Judogestveni Theatre, which opened in 1909.

The oldest cinema in Britain is the Moulin Cinema Complex, Great Windmill Street, London, opened as the Piccadilly Circus Cinematograph Theatre on 5 March 1910. Oldest with the original fabric substantially intact is the Electric Cinema, Portobello Road, also in London, which opened in February 1911. It is now a Grade II Listed Building. Amongst its other distinctions is the fact that mass murderer Reginald Christie (played by Richard Attenborough in *10 Rillington Place* (GB 71)) worked there as a relief projectionist.

The oldest building ever converted to use as a cinema was the Music Hall Cinema, Chester, which was in service as a 'common hall' as early as 1280 and as a place of entertainment by 1616. The building was converted into a legitimate theatre in 1773 and a music hall in 1855. Films were first exhibited there in 1910, but only in 1921 was it reconstructed as a permanent cinema. It closed in 1962 to undergo yet another conversion, this time an ignominious transformation into a supermarket.

The largest cinema chain in the world is the United Artists Theater Circuit of East Meadow, New York, which controls 2506 screens in 34 states, Puerto Rico and Hong Kong.

> General Cinema Theatres, America's third largest cinema chain with 1504 screens, conducts what is literally a straw poll every presidential election. In the months running up to the vote, they issue some two million drinking straws identified with the two major candidates. People buying soft drinks are invited to take the straw of their choice and stock depletion is carefully counted.

The oldest cinema chain is the 108-screen Wehrenberg Corp. of St Louis, Mo., which was established in 1906.

The largest cinema chain in Britain is Metro Goldwyn Cinemas (formerly the Cannon Group), with 406 screens. This represents 26 per cent of Britain's screen total.

The largest UK cinema chain of all time was Rank's Odeon circuit, with 596 cinemas in 1950.

The last silent cinema in Britain was the Electra at Royton, Lancs, run by the Progress Film Co. In contrast to their name the proprietors refused to countenance anything so new-fangled as talkies and only closed down in 1935 when the renters were unable to maintain a supply of silent films.

Elsewhere the silent cinema survived longer. According to US statistics, there were 36 silent picture houses remaining in 1937, though it is possible that some of these were buildings still licensed to show films, but which had ceased to operate. Finland is said to have had some silent houses running during World War II and as late as 1952 only 50 out of the 150 cinemas in Burma were wired for sound. Thailand continued to produce silent films until the mid-1960s (see Silent Film, p. 155).

The longest continuous run of any film at one cinema was 10 years 8 months in the case of *Emmanuelle* (Fr 74), which opened at the Paramount City, Paris on 26 June 1974 and closed on 26 February 1985. In this time it was seen by 3,268,874 patrons.

The longest continuous run at one cinema in Britain was 4 years 9 months for the double bill *Young Frankenstein* (US 74) and *The Rocky Horror Picture Show* (GB 75) at the Times Centa in Baker Street, London from January 1981 until October 1985. *South Pacific* (US 58) ran at the much larger Dominion, Tottenham Court Road, for 4 years 22 weeks ending on 30 September 1962.

The shortest run of any film with a general release was that of *The Super Fight* (US 70), a feature-length movie of a mock championship fight between the then two undefeated heavyweight champions of history, Rocky Marciano and Muhammad Ali, which was released globally on 20 January 1970. In accordance with conditions laid down by the distributor, bonded guards collected all prints after a single showing and took them to be incinerated.

The longest name ever given to a cinema was conferred on a mobile picture show operated by Spanish showman José Fessi Fernandez in the Bordeaux region of France around 1902. It was called the Lentielectroplastiscromomimocoliserpentographe. **The longest name of a cinema currently in operation** is the comparatively terse Cinema-I-Anjuman-I-Khairiya-I-Niswan, a 200-seat picture house in Kabul, Afghanistan. **The longest single word name** is borne by the Kannikaparameswari in Turyvegere, India.

The shortest name ever given to a cinema was borne by the K in Mattoon, Ill. in 1925.

Unusual Cinema Names

These have abounded since the Cabbage opened in Liverpool in 1914 and the Decadence in Harbin, China, the same year. A Bradford clergyman, the Rev. S. Thomas, opened The World's Window about this date and while Brussels offered High Life, Moscow promised Magic Dreams. Brno, Czechoslovakia made an honest declaration with The Illusion, while Estonia's Bi-Ba-Bo may have meant anything at all, even in Estonian. A name which definitely cloaked a secret was the 555 at Brown's Bay, New Zealand, owned by Mrs Olga Brown—it was 'a private family joke, believed to concern cards'. The first cinema in Peking to show talkies was inappropriately called the Peace and Quiet. The Yank Theatre was located far from any indigenous Yanks, in the Grand Duchy of Luxembourg, and it was unnecessary to travel to Milan to attend La Scala when there was one in the Irish village of Letterkenny, Co. Donegal. Greenland Theatre was nowhere near Greenland, but in Palacode, India. The image of suburban gentility conjured up by Bristol's Kosy Korner Kinema was matched by Mon Repos, only the latter was located in the untamed frontier atmosphere of Russia's Baku oilfield in 1916. In India many cinemas are still called 'Talkies', such as Swastika Talkies in Bihar, Tip Top Talkies at Gopichettipalayam, Jolly Talkies in Muttom and Molly Talkies in Nedunganpara, or Baby Talkies, Thiruvarar. English Talkies in Ahmedabad shows movies in Gujarati, not English. The Roxy, now no more than a fading memory to New Yorkers, lives on in Motihari, Champaran, Bohar, and Bombay. The White Elephant and the Black Cat both belonged to World War I Glasgow, as

did a Cinerama long before today's wide-screen spectacle was ever thought of. The Buffalo in Ashington, Northumberland, opened about 1912, was so named because it specialized in westerns.

The oddest names were undoubtedly those found in the United States: Amusu (Lincolntown, Ga.); Hobo (Shawneetown, Ill.); The No Name (Moreauville, La.); Tootles (St Joseph, Mo.); U-No-Us (Rensselaer Falls, NY); Muse-Us (Dayton, Ohio); Tar Heel (Plumtree, NC); Dazzleland (Philadelphia); Glory B (Miami, Okla.); C-It (Ashtabula Harbor, Ohio); The Vamp (Barnwell, SC); Fo To Sho (Ballinger, Texas); Ha Ha (Minneapolis); Hoo Hoo (Doucette, Texas); The Herring (Winton, NC); Cinderella (Detroit); OK (Simpson, Ill.); My (Indianapolis); Your (Detroit); Our (Sparta, Mich.); Why Not (Greenfield, Ind.); It (Huntingdon, W. Va.); Try-It (Buffalo, NY); Hi-Art (Lockport, NY); Good Luck (Seattle, Wash.); Sour Wine (Brazil, Ind.); Oh Gee (Edwardsville, Ill.); Happy Jack (Abilene, Texas); Uses Pictures (Butlerville, Ind.); No Home (Dalton City, Ill.); Pa and Ma's (Cobsden, Ill.); Red Apple (Omak, Wash.); Fattie's (Winchester, Texas); Silent Prayers (Sprigg, W. Va.); Za Za (Plainfield, Ind.); Zim Zim (Cumberland, W. Va.). The Norka in Akron and the Idol in Lodi were simply the town name spelt backwards. In Thibodaux, La., there were two cinemas before the war. The larger was the Grand. Its smaller rival was the Baby Grand.

The largest number of cinemas in one city was 986 in New York in 1913.

The post-war record was held by Tokyo, which had over 600 cinemas in 1958, two and a half times as many as New York.

The largest number of cinemas showing the same film in the same city at the same time was 246 in New York when the sensational sex film *Traffic in Souls* (US 13) was first released.

The first multiple cinema was the Regal Twins, Manchester, opened in 1930. The present nationwide movement into multiples began with the twinning of the Odeon, Nottingham in July 1965. First in the USA was the Alhambra Twin at Alhambra, Calif. in 1939.

A choice of films at the same cinema was not unknown even before the advent of the multiple. In 1926 the Spanish correspondent of the German film journal *Lichtbildbühne* reported that he had visited a cinema in Cairo with twin screens in one auditorium showing two different films at the same time.

The first triplex was the Burnaby Theater in Burnaby, British Columbia, opened by Taylor Twentieth Century Theaters in 1965. Britain's first triplex was the ABC Lothian Road in Edinburgh, opened on 29 November 1969.

The first quadriplex was the Metro Plaza in Kansas City, Mo., opened by the Durwood family (forerunners of the present American Multi-Cinema chain) in 1966. This was followed by a six-plex in 1969.

The largest multiplex in the world is the 7600 seat Kinepolis in Brussels, Belgium, opened in September 1988 and containing 24 auditoria. Proprietor Albert Bert declared that he could have accommodated 8500 patrons, but preferred to trade extra seating for extra comfort. The distance from the back of one seat to the back of another is four feet, obviating a need to skew the knees sideways to admit the passage of other patrons. The front row in each auditorium is the same distance from the screen as the height of the screen; in the case of the auditorium showing IMAX films on a giant screen this means 60 ft of unoccupied space.

The largest multiplex in Britain is the 14 screen Showcase opened by National Amusements at Manchester in October 1989.

The last purpose-built single auditorium cinema to be erected in Britain was the Natraj in Leicester in 1980, one of the Liberty chain of Asian cinemas. All newly built cinemas since then have been multiplexes.

The northernmost cinema in the world is the 329-seat North Cape Municipal Kino at Honningsvåg (pop. 5000), Norway, which lies on latitude 71° 1′, 300 miles north of the Arctic Circle.

The southernmost cinema in the world is the Cine San Martín in Ushuaia (pop. 2200), Tierra del Fuego, Argentina, just north of latitude 55°.

Unusual Cinemas

Cinemas have been located in odd places ever since someone thought of putting one on top of Mt Portofino, Genoa, in 1907. Motion pictures entered the Arabian harem the same year when one Mehdi Russi Khan persuaded Shah Mohammed Ali to allow him to relieve the boredom of the many royal wives with a 'ladies only' cinema showing Pathé films imported from France. Meanwhile in the less exotic atmosphere of one of London's ancient churches, St Mary Axe, the Rev. Wilson Carlisle was relieving the ennui of his parishioners by introducing elevating and instructive movies into his Sunday services. Some years later, in the early 1920s, the Crawford Memorial Methodist church at 218th Street, New York, began doubling as a cinema. The Rev. Lincoln Caswell was worried about dwindling congregations and started up Saturday night cinema performances with full-length features plus a supporting programme of comedies and a newsreel, borrowing the films for nothing from an obliging neighbouring theatre. The following night he would preach on the moral pointed by the 'big picture'. As a further

Entertaining the troops, 1917. (*British Film Institute*)

inducement the stars themselves were invited along, one notable patron being Lillian Gish.

There have been occasional misguided attempts to establish open-air cinemas in Britain, among them the Garden Cinema at Hull, which opened for business on a balmy summer's night in July 1912. Patrons sat on deck chairs in an open-sided marquee. Not surprisingly the cinema was forced to close with the onset of winter and never reopened again. Another attempt was made in 1915, when a roof-top cinema seating 150 was established by Pathé Frères on a building in Wardour Street, London. Two years later an open-air cinema was inaugurated in the middle of Trafalgar Square for the benefit of soldiers and sailors on leave.

In 1913 Secretary of State William Jennings Bryan established a cinema inside the State Department,

Washington, for the leisure-time entertainment of the staff.

There is no record of cinemas in prisoner of war camps, but Allied civilians interned at Ruhleben Internment Camp during World War I enjoyed the benefit of a well-appointed picture house.

One Nazi concentration camp is known to have had a cinema. In November 1944 a barracks at Dora, a concentration camp adjacent to Buchenwald, was converted into a cinema as a special privilege for the slave labourers engaged on the assembly of Hitler's V1 and V2 rockets.

In England during World War II, Chislehurst Caves were converted into shelters at the height of the blitz, special trains being run nightly from London. Some people even moved in with their own furniture and a cave cinema was operated to keep the temporary refugees amused during the long winter evenings.

A number of cinemas have been devoted to the films of a single star. The Crystal Hall on 14th Street, New York, showed only Chaplin movies for nine years, 1914–23, with the exception of one week when they decided to vary the programme. Business was so bad they reverted to Chaplin. In Moscow in 1925 there was a cinema devoted entirely to old Clara Kimball Young movies, despite the fact that Miss Young's career was already over by this date. (She had refused to diet when the fashion for slim figures overtook America. In Russia the rotund look never went out.) There are two cinemas which show only Bond movies—the Camera cinema in Berlin and the Kolosseum Kino in Vienna. The 007 pictures are shown strictly in rotation, each one for a week three–four times a year. In Madras there is a cinema which shows only Sivaji Ganesan movies.

In May 1931 the Grand Cinema in Auckland, New Zealand, changed its name to the London and initiated a policy of showing only British films 'for the first time in the whole Empire'. It was also the last time. Modern-day Helsinki has a Soviet government-owned cinema, The Cosmos, which shows exclusively Soviet films. It runs at a prodigious loss—total box-office take in 1981 was only $83,000.

Cinemas catering to minorities have included one for lepers opened in Trinidad in 1921 and Britain's first and only cinema for negroes, established in Cardiff in 1935. A cinema for children called Smile is run by the pupils of a boarding school at Almetievsk in the Tatar Republic of the USSR. The Harmonic cinema in Frankfurt has women-only performances once a fortnight—the films shown are either made by women or specifically about women. Another cinema with a female bias is the Kineca Omori in Tokyo, which is run by and located in a supermarket. It specializes in European films and silent classics: the people most attracted by such fare in Japan are female and over 25, so supermarket shoppers are prime target audience.

The first cinema in a train was established on the Trans-Siberian Railway by a French company in 1913. Admission was 50 kopeks (12½¢ or 1s). In Britain cinema coaches on trains were introduced by the LNER on the *Flying Scotsman* between Kings Cross and York in March 1924. The premier presentation was *Ashes of Vengeance* (US 23) with Norma Talmadge. 'Talkie Trains' were inaugurated by the LNER in May 1935 and continued in service till outbreak of war.

A floating cinema was instituted in the USA on the Erie Canal between Troy and Newark, NY in 1907. Called the *Star Floating Palace*, it was a converted canal boat with a 'wainscoted inside' which plied the canal towns giving shows at each. The idea was later borrowed by Soviet Russia. When the 'agit-steamboat' *Red Star* was dispatched on a propaganda tour down the Kama and Volga Rivers in 1919, Molotov and Lenin's wife Krupskya, who were in charge, arranged for the construction of a 800-seat cinema on a barge, which was towed behind the *Red Star*.

A cinema called the Fly-In was opened at Asbury Park, NJ, in 1948 with space for 500 cars and 50 aeroplanes.

The only cinema in the world which has never had a change of programme is Screen 6 of Atlanta's CNN Centre 6, which shows *Gone With the Wind* (US 39) twice a day every day of the year.

There is nothing unusual about watching movies in the air, but cinemas are curiously rare at airports. The only one in Europe is at Prague, where it is greatly appreciated by those subjected to the haphazard scheduling of East European airlines. There was another cinema in Prague never visited by foreign travellers. Located in the Praha Hotel, its existence was only revealed with the ending of 40 years of communist dictatorship in 1989. Open exclusively to top party officials, it shows only western made films prohibited for exhibition to the people of Czechoslovakia.

The American Classic Indoor Drive-In Movie is a hard-top simulated drive-in of the 50s at Dezerland on Manhattan's West Side. Patrons sit in classic cars of the period under a sky forever starry while viewing B movies and newsreels of the period.

The first children's Saturday matinees were inaugurated by Sidney Bernstein (now Lord Bernstein) of the Bernstein Group of Theatres (later Granada Theatres) with a performance at the Empire, Willesden, on 23 March 1928. Two thousand children paid 3d each to attend a programme which included *Robinson Crusoe* (GB 27), a *Topical Budget* and two shorts.

The first Mickey Mouse Club was founded in 1930 by Harry Woodin at the Fox Dome Theater in Ocean Beach, Calif. By 1932 over one million

Eager youngsters from the East End slums queueing for the children's matinée at Plaistow, January 1937. Unusually, this one was on a Thursday rather than a Saturday. (*British Film Institute*)

American children belonged to Mickey Mouse Clubs. The earliest known branch in Britain was established at the Arcade Cinema, Darlington, in 1933. There were 200 Mickey Mouse Clubs by May 1937. Gaumont–British cinema clubs were in being by 1936 and the Granadiers, organized by the Granada circuit, were founded in 1937.

> The Globe Cinema, a 300-seat picture house in Norwich, was built in 1934 by 14-year-old Alfred Warminger on a £1500 loan from his father. Alfred himself was manager and projectionist, while his two sisters acted as usherettes, with a boy to sell chocolates. There were two shows a night, the cost of admission to the 5 o'clock performance being a penny and to the 7 o'clock performance twopence.

The first gaol to institute film shows for prisoners was Goulburn Gaol, Sydney, New South Wales, commencing on 3 January 1911 with a programme presented by the Methodist chaplain, the Rev. J. H. Lewin. The *Melbourne Argus* reported: 'Some of the long-sentence prisoners had never previously seen moving pictures and they more especially enjoyed the entertainment. The pictures were of course of an elevating character, including *Water-*

ways of Holland, Dogs of Various Countries, and *The Visit of the American Fleet.*'

In Britain the first regular film shows for gaol inmates were instituted on a weekly basis at Maidstone Prison in November 1937. The inaugural programme was rather dauntingly described as 'three hours of educational and cultural films, specially selected for reformative treatment of prisoners'. The shows were held in the 100-seat prison chapel, admission according to a three-weekly rota (Maidstone held 350 prisoners) being permitted to inmates who had earned a certain number of good conduct marks. The projector was operated by 'lifers'.

The first drive-in cinema was the Camden Automobile Theater, opened by Richard Hollingshead on a 10-acre site off Wilson Boulevard, Camden, NJ, on 6 June 1933 with a presentation of *Wife Beware* (US 33), with Adolphe Menjou. The screen measured 40×30 ft and there was accommodation for 400 cars. The sound came from high-volume screen speakers provided by RCA–Victor.

The expansion of drive-ins began very slowly; twelve years after the opening of the Camden there were still only 60 in the whole of the United States. The growth years were the same as for television, for no clear reason. In 1949 there were 1000 drive-ins and the peak was reached in 1958 with 4063 against 12,291 hard-tops. There are now less than a thousand.

The first in-flight movie was First National's production of Conan Doyle's *The Lost World* (US 25), shown during a scheduled Imperial Airways flight from London to the Continent in April 1925.

America's first in-flight presentation was a more modest affair consisting of a *Universal Newsreel* and a couple of cartoon shorts shown aboard a transcontinental Air Transport Inc. Ford transport aircraft on 8 October 1929.

The first airline to introduce regular in-flight movies was TWA, commencing with the presentation of *By Love Possessed* (US 61), with Lana Turner and Efrem Zimbalist Jr, in the first-class section during a scheduled New York–Los Angeles flight on 19 July 1961.

The world's airlines are estimated to spend about $50 to $60 million per annum on acquiring rights to films. A major airline like Australia's QANTAS pays in the region of $35,000 per picture, with a minimum of about 350 showings. The average age of the in-flight audience is about 20 years older than theatrical audiences, hence films that do well at the box office do not necessarily meet the same response a mile up in the air. Conversely a film like *Raise the Titanic* (US 80), which bombed at the box office, won plaudits from air passengers. According to specialist distribu-

Birth of the in-flight movie—Imperial Airways, April 1926. (*Backnumbers*)

tor Entertainment in Motion, a blockbuster picture can earn an extra $1 million on the wing.

The first cinema aboard a liner was a feature of the 16,000-ton Italian vessel *Patra*, which left Naples for her maiden voyage across the Atlantic in the spring of 1914.

Cinema Cinema

A prodigious number of movies have been made about the business of movie making, from *Merton of the Movies* to *A Star is Born* and beyond. Not many movies have the showing of films as a central theme. Here are the few which do.

☆ *Sherlock Junior* (US 24) Buster Keaton gave one of his best performances as the cinema projectionist who dreams of becoming a detective.

☆ *Paybox Adventure* (GB 36) Enid Stamp Taylor as heiress who works as ticket seller in cinema.

☆ *Contraband* (GB 40) Michael Powell–Emeric Pressburger, spies using cinema as a front.

☆ *The Smallest Show on Earth* (GB 57) Bill Travers and Virginia McKenna as young couple who think they have inherited a luxury picture palace, but find that it is in fact a run-down little flea-pit. Charming story recounts how they make it pay (e.g. turning the heat up during desert movies and then selling iced drinks).

☆ *Targets* (US 68) Peter Bogdanovich's second movie, in which a crazed sniper terrorizes the audience of a drive-in. Notable for Boris Karloff's last major performance.

☆ *The Projectionist* (US 70) A projectionist fantasizes he is Captain Flash under the baleful eye of tyrant cinema manager.

☆ *The Last Picture Show* (US 71) Peter Bogdanovich's evocation of small town life in Texas c. 1950, with the single cinema as the main centre of entertainment and social intercourse.

☆ *The Picture Show Man* (Aus 77) Rivalry between two travelling picture shows in 20s backblocks Australia.

☆ *The Enchanted Sail* (It 82) Two brothers take a travelling cinema wagon round rural Italy in 1920s.

☆ *Variety* (US 83) Set in a sex cinema called Variety, in which the box office girl finds herself being drawn to events on screen and becomes entangled with one of the patrons.

☆ *Mr Love* (GB 85) Barry Jackson as cinema projectionist in Southport who plays Bogey live on stage to the usherette's Bergman when the projector breaks down during *Casablanca*.

☆ *American Drive-In* (US 85) Rare example of a film in which the whole of the action takes place in a cinema—in this case a hick town drive-in during the showing of a double bill of *Hard Rock Zombies 1* and *2*. Mainly a study of audience types, including a biker gang, a hooker, two little old ladies who turn out to be dope dealers, and an intellectual couple who earnestly analyse the hokum on screen.

☆ *The Purple Rose of Cairo* (US 85) Woody Allen's ultimate movie fantasy, in which the fictional hero of a topper and tails thirties society movie walks out of the screen to romance unhappily married working girl and besotted movie fan Mia Farrow.

☆ *Wandering Lives* (Mex 85) José Carlos Ruiz and Ignacio Guadaloupe play itinerant showmen who tour the villages of Durango with a travelling cinema.

☆ *Demons* (It 85) Horror movie set in cinema showing horror movie.

☆ *Dead-End Drive-In* (Aus 86) Relates the story of a group of unemployed in 1990 imprisoned in a sinister drive-in.

☆ *Prunelle Blues* (Fr 86) French Algerian owner of cinema in Barbes quarter of Paris who discovers it is centre of a drugs ring.

☆ *Midnight Movie Massacre* (US 88) 1956: monster-on-the-loose in tacky cinema showing ham sci-fi serial called *Space Patrol*. Latter was shot especially as the film within the film.

☆ *The Man from Bulvara Kapushinov* (USSR 88) Perhaps the most offbeat film about a cinema (and a refreshing change from schlock horror in the back of the stalls), Soviet *femme* helmer Alla Surikova's wacky borsch western relates how a mild mannered pioneer film presenter arrives in a decadent Wild West town with a supply of silent one-reelers and a volume titled *The History of World Cinema*. He proceeds to bring the benefits of cinema's civilizing influence to the rowdy cowpokes, lusty chorus girls and pesky Injuns. All are converted to decorous habits (the town bully joining the church choir) until Our Hero leaves town and the saloon proprietor and the not-so-holy preacher connive to undermine the

Movies showing at cinemas depicted in movies are usually either ones for which the director has a particular regard or spoof titles. In *Gremlins 2 The New Batch* (US 90) there are scenes centred on two movie houses. One is a Times Square cinema with a spoof movie advertised outside, *The Howling XI*; the other is showing a real film for which director Joe Dante had a particular regard—*Gremlins 2 The New Batch*.

new morality with 'smoking parlor' pictures extolling the pleasures of vice . . .

☆ *Splendor* (It/Fr 88) Ageing owner (Marcello Mastroianni) of the ageing and waning Splendor cinema recalls past glories and packed houses as he faces the prospect of having to sell out to a furniture store. Eventually the indifferent townsfolk are rallied to occupy the cinema and prevent its sale.

☆ *The Lady from the Shanghai Cinema* (Br 88) Hero meets heroine in Rio picture house and becomes involved in the action on screen, a gangster picture whose *femme* lead is the girl's lookalike.

☆ *Matinée* (Can 88) Set in a Vancouver cinema where the Horror Film Festival leads to murder most foul.

☆ *Cinema Paradiso* (It 89) The life of a Sicilian cinéaste as a boy, a youth and a man, from childhood visits to the cinema of the title, through adolescent years of friendship with the projectionist (Philippe Noiret), who is blinded in a nitrate fire and whom he succeeds, to his return home from the mainland where he has become a successful film director.

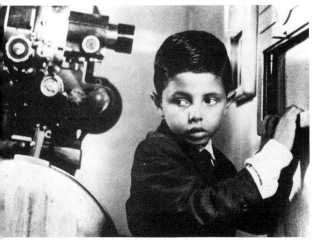

A small boy in a small town falls in love with cinema . . . *Cinema Paradiso* (It 89) captured hearts with its heady nostalgia for the days when the silver screen was a window on the outside world. (*British Film Institute*)

☆ *Bert Rigby, You're a Fool* (US 89) Comic adventures in Hollywood of a screen-struck and striking miner (Robert Lindsay) from the North of England determined to make enough quick bucks to reopen the derelict cinema in his small home town.

☆ *My Cinemas* (Tur 90) About a young woman (Hiilya Avsar) who escapes from her harsh family life through the magic of the cinema, eventually turning to prostitution to buy the clothes worn by the actresses she admires.

Asian cinemas in Britain peaked in the mid-70s, when there were some 120—about 8 per cent of the total—and the UK had become the Indian film industry's biggest export market. The phenomenon had started in 1959 with the opening of the first full-time Indian cinema in Britain, Western Talkies in Manchester Road, Bradford—surprisingly the initiative of an English exhibitor, Eric Douglas. As the Asian population burgeoned in the 1960s, the cinema became the focal point of the immigrants' restricted social lives in a cold and alien land. But almost as rapidly as it had begun, the Asian cinema circuit disappeared again. According to Indian film specialist Edward Hotspur Johnson, by 1980, only three years after the first Japanese VCRs arrived in Britain, Asians in the UK had become the world's first mass video audience, with more than 50 per cent of households owning or renting a video recorder. In 1984, a quarter of a century after the first Indian cinema in Britain, the last two—the Naz in London's Brick Lane and the Aspara in Leicester—succumbed to the competition of video.

*T*ICKETS

The highest seat price (excluding charity performances) was for Kevin Brownlow's reconstruction of Abel Gance's silent classic *Napoleon* (Fr 27) when it was shown in Tokyo in October 1981. Top price was 12,000 yen or $44. Both showings were a sell-out. The same picture carried a price tag of £17 top when it was shown at the Empire Leicester Square the previous March.

The lowest seat price recorded was a farthing by a cinema in London's Whitechapel Road in 1909, though the concessionary admission applied only to four children purchasing tickets together. The regular price for children at the Star Kinema in Newcastle upon Tyne about the time of World War I was ½d, but admission could be obtained by presenting a clean glass jam jar instead. In 1925, during a temporary slump in moviegoing, a desperate cinema manager in Covington, La., admitted patrons in exchange for empty beer bottles. He took $23 and 1812 empties. The cheapest seats noted in the Report of the Indian Cinematograph Committee (1928) were priced at one anna—slightly over one penny. These were 'seats' in a figurative sense, since the lowly price meant only a lowly place on the ground. In the late 1930s some cinemas in Karachi were wont to give free shows, consisting of shorts and long trailers, when their rivals were showing a blockbuster. A cinema opened in Cardiff in 1935 for 'coloured people' only charged a flat rate admission of 1d. Even cheaper was a picture house on Sixth Avenue, New York, which advertised *c.* 1912 a movie of a negro lynching for 1c. On at least one occasion any price for a seat has been accepted. In Victoria, BC, a cinema manager running *The Luck of Ginger Coffey* (Can 64) allowed patrons to pay whatever they thought the film was worth.

> In December 1940 the Globe Theatre on Broadway in New York accepted firearms in lieu of cash for admission to Michael Powell's *Contraband*: US *Blackout* (GB 40). The weapons were shipped to Britain for use by the Home Guard.

Currently the lowest admission charges are in China, where tickets range from the equivalent of 6c to 10c in the cities and are reported to be even cheaper in the country areas.

> France has an annual Fête du Cinéma for one day each summer, the price of a single ticket allowing unlimited admissions to any cinema during the 24 hours. In 1990 there were 2.2 million attendances, about six times the daily average. Ardent young Parisian filmgoers have been known to take in as many as eight movies for the price of one.

*A*UDIENCES

The largest audience ever to view a film simultaneously in the same locale was 110,000 on the occasion of the screening of D. W. Griffith's *Boots* (US 19) at the Methodist Centenary celebration held at the Oval Amphitheater, Columbus, Ohio, on 4 July 1919. Fifty thousand of the audience were accommodated in the stands, the remainder in the arena. The film was projected on a giant screen, with a picture size of 100×75 ft.

The highest number of times a patron has seen the same film is 940 by Mrs Myra Franklin of

Cardiff, Wales, whose favourite picture can only be *The Sound of Music* (US 65).

The film seen by the most cinemagoers. There are no reliable figures to authenticate the most popular film of all time in terms of the highest number of paying patrons. However, *Mother India* (Ind 57), which has been on almost continuous release in various parts of India since 1957, is claimed by some authorities on Indian cinema to have been seen by more cinemagoers than *Gone With the Wind* (US 39). This in turn is challenged by the Chinese. Official government statistics give the cumulative audience for *Taking Tiger Mountain by Strategy* (China 70) as 7.3 billion up to the end of 1974. This seemingly impossible figure—it represents over seven admissions per head of population, including babies—could just be true. In the rural areas, where most of the population of China lives, there were an average of ten film shows per year in each village in the early 1970s. As only eight new films were released in China during the Cultural Revolution 1966–73, and nearly all others were banned, the same films had to be shown over and over again. Non-attendance at film shows was regarded as a mark of political deviation.

The film seen by the least cinemagoers. Of films which have actually secured a release, the lowest reported audience was for Luis Vera's *Accomplished Facts* (Chile 86) with 1880 spectators.

> After seeing 6500 films as a paying customer, fan *extraordinaire* Sloan C. Short of Seattle bought his own cinema in Bellingham, Wash. in 1975. It was cheaper, he reckoned, than buying tickets.

Fan Mail

Mail began to be sent to the uncredited performers of the early silents even before the advent of named stars. Mary Pickford recalled an occasion at the Biograph Studios in about 1912 when she enquired about a letter she was expecting, and was told that it had probably been thrown away together with the hundreds of other letters addressed simply to 'the Girl with the Curls' or 'the Biograph Girl'. She was amazed to learn that people she had never met should feel impelled to write to someone who had no more substance for them than a mute shadow on a silver screen. Biograph's high-handed method of disposing of unsolicited correspondence did not long survive the onslaught of the fan magazines, which soon took to publishing the stars' studio addresses in response to eager enquiries from the fans. Producers came to realize that a mail count was one method of assessing a rising star's popularity and consequently his or her box office potential, while the stars themselves knew that it was in their own interest to maintain a devoted fan following, even at the cost of the $250 a week it was estimated in the twenties that a major star would need to spend on photographs and postage.

The largest fan mail of the immediate post World War I period was received by 'America's Sweetheart' Mary Pickford, with an average of 18,000 letters a month. It was maintained that Miss Pickford employed a fleet of 18 secretaries to answer them.

Mary Pickford's popularity began to decline in the 'flapper era' and in 1927 it was reported that Colleen Moore was leading the fan mail league table with 15,000 letters a month. Miss Moore was obliged to dispatch an average of 12,000 photographs of herself monthly at a cost of 12c each, including postage. A year later she had been overtaken by Clara Bow, whose count for the month of April 1928 was no less than 33,727 items of mail. The cost of replying was $2550 including $450 for three full-time secretaries. The most popular male star at that time was, some-what surprisingly, Charles 'Buddy' Rogers, with 19,618 letters. Douglas Fairbanks, generally thought of as the most consistently popular male star of the twenties, rated only 8000 letters, which gave him equal place in the league table with a dog, Rin Tin Tin. Chaplin, who had once created a fan mail record with 73,000 letters in the first three days of his return home to London in 1921, could muster no more than 5000.

> Donald O'Connor made six films with Francis the Talking Mule but surrendered his leading role to Mickey Rooney when he discovered the mule was getting more fan mail than he was.

The coming of sound virtually ended the screen careers of Colleen Moore and Clara Bow, but ushered in a host of new stars, one of whom was to create a fan mail record which has never been broken. Mickey Mouse, reported Walt Disney at the end of 1933, had received 800,000 letters that year, an average of 66,000 a month. He stressed that all these communications had been addressed to Mickey personally, and not to his creator.

In that heady period of Hollywood history known as 'the era of the Great Stars', neither Gable nor Garbo could compete with a mouse, a child and a singing cowboy. By 1936 seven-year-old Shirley Temple was receiving just over 60,000 letters a month, an all-time record for a mere human being. As age crept up on the golden-curled moppet, the fickleness of film fans once again asserted itself. By the time she had reached the mature age of ten, Miss Temple was no longer at the top. Her place had been taken by the guitar-strumming cowboy Gene Autry, though it may have been some consolation that his peak of 40,000 letters a month came nowhere near her best.

World War II brought a new element into star

> 'I stopped believing in Santa Claus at an early age. Mother took me to see him in a Hollywood department store and he asked me for my autograph.'—Shirley Temple Black

appeal with the advent of the pin-up picture, and it is probable that a high proportion of the dogfaces who wrote from far-away places to the new record holder, the fighting forces' own Betty Grable, had never seen any of her films. The attraction of her million dollar legs, however, was attested by the average of 30,000 letters a month they inspired.

A number of factors contributed to the decline of fan mail after World War II, chief amongst them the parallel decline in the star system, the rise of other cult heroes such as pop singers and sportsmen, and dwindling audiences in the wake of television. Even in recent years, however, it has been possible for stars held high in public esteem to inspire prodigious quantities of mail at times when they are the focus of news attention, as evidenced by the 150,000 letters received by John Wayne from loyal fans during the two months following his heart operation in June 1978.

> For three years after his death, Warner Bros received more fan mail addressed to James Dean than to any of its living stars.

The nature of the fan letter writer has seldom been examined, but in April 1927 *Variety* published the results of a survey in which they reported that 10 per cent of all fan mail sent from within the USA came from Poles (or people with Polish names), while 8 per cent of the 32,250,000 letters received annually from fans worldwide by Hollywood studios originated from South American countries. The greater proportion of requests for photographs, said *Variety*, came from people who never went to the movies—'they are of the poor kind who cannot afford it and simply pick up coupons or read names on billboards of the various stars . . .'. An analysis made the following year at Paramount, the studio which received the most fan mail, revealed that 75 per cent of the correspondents were women, despite the fact that female stars received more letters than men.

Fan mail being traditionally associated with film stars, it is worthy of note that no actor or actress has received in the course of a career the number of letters delivered to Charles Lindbergh following his transatlantic flight—a total of 3,500,000.

Space precludes more than the briefest selection of the last 60 years of fan mail:

☆ To Kathlyn Williams 1916: 'Dear Miss Williams, You are my favourite moving picture actress. I would appreciate it so much if you would give me one of your old automobiles, any one, I wouldn't care how small.'

☆ To Enid Bennett 1920: 'I am making a collection of pictures of the most notorious actresses. Please send me yours.'

☆ To Emil Jannings (whose looks were certainly subordinate to his artistry) 1928: 'Dear Miss Jannings, You are my favourite actress. I go to see all your pictures because I like the way you wear your clothes. To me you are the best-dressed actress on the screen, as well as the most beautiful. I try to imitate your clothes and your stylish way of wearing your hair.'

☆ To Una Merkel (following a request for a signed photo) 1933: 'Do not send picture. Am moving and decided I don't want it.' Miss Merkel to fan: 'Picture is sent. You'll take it and like it.'

☆ To Glenn Ford 1946: 'I am 22, pretty, but I never saved my money. You did. That is the real reason I would like to marry you. Please let me know soon, as I have also written to Dick Powell and Larry Parks.'

☆ To Virginia Mayo from Arab Sheik 1948: 'You are the surest proof to me of the existence of God.'

☆ To Frank Sinatra, from girl fan proposing marriage 1956: 'We've never met, but I'm a singer and I feel I can do so much for your career.'

Film Fans, Famous and Infamous

Royalty have been among the most fervent supporters of the cinema since its earliest days. At a time when 'animated pictures' had scarcely moved out of the fairground, Queen Victoria was enjoying frequent film shows at Windsor Castle. An ardent film fan, the Queen had a special predilection for movies about children and her favourite was said to be a Riley Bros production called *The Pillow Fight* (GB 98), in which four mischievous schoolgirls bombarded each other with pillows in their bedroom.

The first royalty with private cinema theatres in their palaces were the Crown Prince of Siam and Tsar Nicolas II, both in about 1913. When war broke out and the Tsar took command of his forces in the field, he missed his cinema at the Tsarkoye Selo palace so much that he had another one installed at the Stavka, headquarters of the Russian Army. The Tsar's favourite film was *The Exploits of Elaine* (US 14), a cliff-hanger type serial which he watched weekly at Stavka throughout the second half of 1916. The deposed Emperor of China, Henry P'u Yi, had a cinema built at the Palace of Established Happiness about 1920, where a steady flow of Charlie Chaplin and Fatty Arbuckle films were maintained, until the emergence of Harold Lloyd, who displaced them as Imperial Favourite. The Emperor's owlish horn-rimmed glasses were said to have been acquired in tribute to the American comedian.

Queen Alexandra's favourite film was *True Heart Susie* (US 19), in which Lillian Gish played the kind

Under a local decree of 1984 in the Maharashtra town of Nandurbar, Muslim women are forbidden to visit the cinema. The penalty for violation is the equivalent of $10. Any man reporting a woman in the audience receives a reward of $5.

of simple, joyful country girl the Queen sometimes wished she could have been. A private print of the film was kept at Buckingham Palace. Queen Mary's taste, on the other hand, ran to rather more robust fare, her favourite star being the romantic and extremely athletic hero of Hollywood adventure movies Eddie Polo. (Reputedly Queen Mary was the only member of the Royal Family who was not a Charlie Chaplin fan—the reason, according to one fan magazine writer, being the fact that she was not endowed with a very developed sense of humour.) The Queen was said to be the Royal Family's most enthusiastic filmgoer and during World War II, when living at Badminton, she gave a weekly film show for servicemen. However, her youngest son, the Duke of Kent, seems to have rivalled her in his passion for the pictures. When he married Princess Marina in 1934, the Earl of Dudley had a squash court converted into a cinema at his seat, Himley Hall, where the Royal Couple were to spend their honeymoon. During the twelve days of their stay, the Duke and Duchess watched 18 feature films, nine comedies, an unspecified number of documentaries, five newsreels and a specially made life-story of His Royal Highness. Every night of the honeymoon was spent at the movies reported an ecstatic Gaumont–British, who had supplied the 202 reels of film shown.

Both the Duke's brothers shared his delight in the cinema. The Duke of York, later King George VI, was reported in America to have a particular weakness for the films of Nancy Carroll. A greater sensation, though, was the revelation in *Photoplay* in 1931 that the Prince of Wales (later Edward VIII) was in the habit of making incognito visits to one of London's less exclusive suburban cinemas, the Grand in Edgware Road, at least once or twice a week. The Prince always attended with the same girl, it was alleged, she taking her seat at 8.45 p.m. and he slipping into his at precisely 9 p.m., after the house lights had gone down.

No recent information is available about HM The Queen's taste in films, the Palace being prepared to say only that 'she most often asks to see those of which she has read favourable reviews'. According to

George Bernard Shaw named Sir Cedric Hardwicke as his fifth favourite actor. The distinguished thespian was preceded in Shaw's regard by the Marx Brothers.

a newspaper report of the late 1950s, however, her favourite stars were then Gary Cooper, Laurence Olivier and Dirk Bogarde. Curiously Her Majesty does not have a private cinema. At Sandringham the shows are held in the Ballroom, at Balmoral in the Large Drawing Room and at Windsor Castle in the Waterloo Room. Films are not shown at Buckingham Palace. Royal film shows are the responsibility of the Equerry in Waiting, who selects the films unless the Queen has made a particular request.

The Princess of Wales frequents the Odeon in Kensington High Street, the cinema nearest to her home at Kensington Palace. She usually attends with girl friends—the so called 'Throne Rangers'—and joins the queue for tickets with humbler patrons, often paying herself. She always sits in the back row of the stalls for privacy. Princess Diana's favourite film is reported to be *Rain Man* (US 88), in which Dustin Hoffman plays an autistic. The condition is one of the Princess's special concerns.

World leaders have also been in the forefront of the world's film fans. Both Stalin and Churchill named *Lady Hamilton* (GB 42) as their favourite film, the British Prime Minister seeing it four times. Churchill's passion for films was not shared by all his wartime colleagues, a number of whom have testified to their displeasure at the PM's habit of breaking off the evening's work to watch the ritual movie and then expecting them to match his alertness and vigour as top-level discussions continued until three in the morning. At Kremlin film shows, according to Khruschev, Stalin 'used to select the movies himself. The films were usually what you might call captured trophies: we got them from the West. Many of them were American pictures. He liked cowboy movies especially. He used to curse them and give them their proper ideological evaluation but then immediately order new ones.'

Hitler's favourite movie at the time he became Chancellor of Germany was *The Blue Angel* (Ger 30), of which he had a private print. Trenker's *The Rebel* (US 33), was said to be his favourite American film. *The Blue Angel* was later displaced in his affections by Willi Forst's *Mazurka* (Ger 35), which he watched as often as two or three times a week in the small hours of the morning when he was suffering from insomnia. Such was the Führer's devotion to the film, a rumour spread that its star, the bewitching Pola Negri, was under his special protection. In fact Miss Negri had never met Hitler, but found that whenever she went to Nazi Germany she was treated with the kind of privileged deference accorded only to intimates of the Reich's Chancellor. (She later won a libel action against the French cinema magazine *Pour Vous*, which alleged she was Hitler's mistress.)

The Führer is said to have indulged in film shows of a less conventional kind. Pauline Kohler, who served on the staff at Berchtesgaden, claimed that Hitler had a special film made of a prominent German star stripping and exhibiting 'various exercises' which 'threw a terrible light on the perversity of Hitler's sexual desires'. This was shown in the Führer's private cinema at Berchtesgaden, where a selected group of staff were invited to view it on Christmas Day 1937.

Arturo Alessandri, President of Chile in the 1930s, was besotted with the infant Shirley Temple. He had each of her films shown at his official residence in Santiago as soon as it was released and prevailed upon the Chilean Navy to adopt her as their official mascot.

President Anwar Sadat of Egypt watched a movie every day. President Tito of Yugoslavia saw an average of 200 a year—one virtually every night he was in Belgrade. His favourite was the Humphrey Bogart–Bette Davis movie *The Petrified Forest* (US 36), about a group of travellers at a way-station in Arizona who are held up by gangsters.

With the passing of Presidents Sadat and Tito, the most devoted film fan among current heads of state is President Bongo of Gabon. He is reported to watch 'several films every night' at the Presidential Palace, mainly karate movies from Hong Kong and Hindu melodramas. He has personally financed the making of three feature films, two of them scripted by his wife Joséphine and the third, *Demain un jour nouveau* (Gab 78), based on his own autobiography.

Pope John Paul II has a penchant for pouting blonde child-woman Patsy Kensit. He asked to meet her after she had starred in *Il Ragazzo delle Crocette* (It 89). Said a breathless Miss Kensit of the encoutner: 'I felt holy for a week afterwards.' Another fan, from the opposite end of the social spectrum, is gangland boss Reggie Kray (played by Martin Kemp in *The Krays* (GB 90)), a long-time friend of her family. His opportunities to see her films are limited, as he is serving a life sentence in a maximum security gaol, but they write to each other regularly.

American Presidents have been enjoying films at the White House since June 1914, when Giovanni Pastrone's epic *Cabiria* (It 14) was screened before President Wilson and his Cabinet. The President's favourite star was the statuesque Katharine Mac-Donald, known as 'The American Beauty'. If FDR had any preferences when it came to the ladies, he was not letting on to his wife. Eleanor Roosevelt confided that 'the President never has an evening of his own planning without at least one Mickey Mouse film'. It is not recorded whether President Truman was obliged to sit through *The Scarlet Pimpernel* (GB 34) the 16 times his daughter Margaret—a devotee of Leslie Howard—had it screened at the White House. Eisenhower's favourite films while President were *Angels in the Outfield* (US 52) —described by Leslie Halliwell as 'unamusing, saccharine whimsy' —*Springfield Rifle* (US 52), *To Catch a Thief* (US 55), and *Rear Window* (US 54). The latter two starred his favourite actress, Grace Kelly. President Kennedy left the selection of films to aide Arthur Schlesinger, who arranged a show every Sunday evening at the White House. A President's predilection for a particular movie could have sinister overtones. Richard Nixon had repeated private screenings of *Patton: Lust for Glory* (US 69) shortly before ordering American bombers into Cambodia. President Carter was too discreet to mention a favourite film, but it did not escape attention on the other side of the Atlantic that he was enrolled as an honorary member of Britain's Errol Flynn Fan Club. It also behoved Hollywood's own incumbent of the White House not to be too forthcoming about his personal preferences, but in answer to the obvious question, the President's Director of Media Relations revealed that Mr Reagan had 'viewed one of his own films at the request of his staff'. Amongs films not starring Ronald Reagan which he admired, one was certainly the Gary Cooper American Civil War drama *Friendly Persuasion* (US 56). It was a copy of this movie which he presented to Mikhail Gorbachev during his visit to Moscow in 1988. President Bush's taste in movies remains an enigma. Per the White House: 'The President and Mrs Bush frequently view movies at the White House and at Camp David because they entertain often. However, they do not have a preference for one particular movie, actor or actress. They view a variety of the currently running films.'

PREMIÈRES

The largest audience to attend a world première were the 23,930 persons who paid $2.50 to $50 each to see Robert Altman's *Brewster McCloud* (US 70), starring Bud Cort and Sally Kellerman, at the Houston Astrodome on 5 December 1970. A special 70 mm print was made exclusively for the première at a cost of $12,000, since a standard gauge film would have given insufficient definition on the 156×60 ft 'astroscreen'. The *Houston Chronicle* reported in inimitable Texan style: 'The reaction was what you might call mixed. The audience was mostly your younger hip crowd, but the low intelligibility and the film's wierdness in general caused things to be a bit subdued. Miss Kellerman runs around nekkid a lot and there are what you might call bad words . . .'.

The largest number of simultaneous openings was for Warner Bros' *Batman* (US 89) at 2850 screens throughout the USA on 23 June 1989.

The first performer to achieve simultaneous premières on stage and screen was Marie Dressler, who opened in *A Mix Up* at the 39th Street Theater on the same night, Monday 30 December 1914, that her feature length comedy *Tillie's Punctured Romance*, in which she starred with Charlie Chaplin and Mabel Normand, had its world première at the New York Theatre.

The only simultaneous opening of a movie and a Broadway show derived from the same source took place in January 1914, with the New York première of Pierce Kingsley's *The House of Bondage* ((US 14), starring Lottie Pickford, and the play based on Reginald Wright Kaufmann's novel of the same name. The story, controversial for its day, was of a working class girl from Pennsylvania who is forced into prostitution in New York, eventually escapes from her pimp, but is rejected by her family for the dishonour she has brought them.

Unusual Premières

Not all premières take place in glittering and star-studded surroundings. *Oliver Twist* (US 22) had its British première at London's historic Foundling Hospital, presumably in tribute to the protagonist's orphan origins; while the world première of MGM's Agatha Christie whodunnit *Murder at the Gallop* (GB 63) took place in a tent at a church garden party in rural Cheshire. The Barbara Stanwyck starrer *My Reputation* (US 46) was premièred in a Nissen hut on an airfield 'somewhere in England'. After this somewhat downbeat launch, it went on to become a major box office success in America.

There was only one place to hold the world première of *Dodge City* (US 40). The last of the real razzmatazz preems before the austerities of war, the celebration began with a special train bringing 150 Warner Bros executives and stars, including the movie's topliners Errol Flynn and Olivia de Havilland, which was escorted into Dodge City by an aerial fleet of 50 private aircraft. Overnight the little Kansan town underwent a temporary population explosion from 10,000 to 150,000.

There was no problem in accommodating everyone who wanted to come to the world première of *King of the Coral Sea* (Aus 54), an adventure story about pearlers in the South Seas. It took place on the tiny Pacific atoll of Thursday Island. With a population of less than a thousand, everyone was invited.

Two films have been premièred off-shore. John Ford's *The Informer* (US 35) was presented for the first time aboard the French transatlantic liner *Normandie*, while *Valley of the Dolls* (US 67) had its inaugural screening aboard the Italian cruise ship *Princess Italia*.

The première of *The Incredible Mr Limpet* (US 64) was held underwater. The oddball story of a man who turned into a fish, the picture was preemed by Warner Bros on the ocean floor with a submerged screen at Weeki Wachi, Fla. The invited audience of 250 sat in a glass tank 20 ft below the surface.

The only world première held in the air was organized by master showman Joseph E. Levine, who held the first showing of Lewis Gilbert's *The Adventurers* (US 70), glitzy filmization of the Harold Robbins novel, in a jet airliner crossing the USA.

Far-flung simultaneous opening are not so rare, but when Stanley Kramer decided to hold the world première of *On the Beach* (US 59) on both sides of the Iron Curtain at the same time there was certainly no precedent. Based on Nevil Shute's novel about the doomed survivors of a nuclear holocaust, the film opened in 17 cities on 17 December 1959, including New York, Moscow and the city in which the story was set, Melbourne.

If Kramer's intent was to stimulate peace among nations, very different sentiments must have actuated the Nazis' decision to première Veit Harlan's epic *Kolberg* (Ger 45) in the besieged fortress of La Rochelle. *Kolberg* was about the fortitude of the inhabitants of the Baltic town of that name during the Napoleonic Wars; the staging of its première in such unpropitious circumstances a symbolic act. Since the print could not be brought through the lines of the besieging army, it was dropped into the town by parachute.

Robert Warwick, star of *Alias Jimmy Valentine* (US 15), promised the inmates of Sing Sing that they would see the picture before anyone else, as they had helped him with the scenes shot in the 'Big Pen' of the notorious gaol. The world première took place before an audience of murderers, gangsters and rapists on 14 February 1915. It was another 60 years before the next prison première, this time at the New York City Correctional Institution for Women, when Lech Kowalski's study of drug addiction *Gringo* (US 85) was shown for the first time.

The première of *The Jeweller's Shop* (Can 88) was held in the rather more grandiose setting of the Vatican's magnificent Paul VI Hall. Reason for such a privilege was to honour the playwright whose work had been adapted for the screen—none other than Pope John Paul II. He had written the drama in 1960 when he was Bishop of Cracow.

The most belated première of a feature film took place at the Cinémathèque Française in Paris in April 1984, when the completed version of André Antoine's 64-year-old *L'Hirondelle et la Mésange* (Bel 20) was presented for the first time. Six hours of unedited rushes had been discovered in the State Film Archive and edited by Henri Colpi as he perceived Antoine had intended. The reason the unedited film had been shelved in 1920 was that distributor Charles Pathé was so disconcerted by the rushes, which revealed a story of canal life shot in

cinéma verité style, that he refused to release it. The audience at the première, by contrast, were captivated by the film's lyrical beauty as well as its understated realism.

Film Criticism

This was born with a brief review of *May Irwin Kiss* (US 96) in the *Chap Book* for 15 June 1896: '. . . absolutely disgusting'.

The first regular film critic was Frank Woods, who began reviewing for the *New York Dramatic Mirror* with the issue of 1 May 1909. Woods used the pen-name 'Spectator'. His salary was $20 a week.

None of the performers were identified in early reviews. *Variety* seems to have been the first to discard this anonymity, the issue for 21 January 1911 referring to Mary Pickford's 'cute ways and girlish manner' in *The Italian Barber* (US 11).

The first newspaper to carry film reviews was *Vilag* (*World*), a Budapest daily, which engaged Sándor Kellner as its critic in August 1912. Kellner's sojourn with the paper was brief, since he was determined to get into the production side of the movie business, which he did with spectacular success as (Sir) Alexander Korda.

The first American newspaper to employ a regular film critic was the *Chicago Tribune* with the appointment of John Lawson in 1914. Lawson was killed in an accident soon after and his place was taken by Miss Audrie Alspaugh, who wrote under the by-line 'Kitty Kelly'. Movie historian Terry Ramsaye recalled: 'Kitty Kelly could make or break a picture in the Middle West . . . Her column was a large success, and she became the best disliked name in the world of the film studios'.

The most enduring film critic is London-based Dilys Powell (1902–), who began reviewing for the *Sunday Times* in 1939 and now does five film reviews a week for the humorous weekly *Punch*. Amongst her earliest reviews were those she wrote on *Only Angels Have Wings* (US 39) and *Stagecoach* (US 39). When *Gone With the Wind* (US 39) was reissued in 1989, Miss Powell was the only critic whose 'reassessment' was in relation to a review written when it was first released. She decided that Clark Gable's performance was really rather better than she had given him credit for half a century earlier. Dilys Powell spends Mondays and Tuesdays at press shows, always sitting in the third row of the viewing theatre and entering precisely two minutes late. Her arrival is the signal for the picture to start.

Stay Away Crits

Verbal annihilation has been the stock in trade of the film critic ever since the very first review. Here are a few intimations that the critic did not think the picture deserved his unqualified approval.

☆ Anthony Slide on Marguerite Duras's *India Song* (Fr 75) 'Without question the most boring, pretentious feature ever foisted on the general public'.

☆ Alan Brien of the *Sunday Times* on Irwin Allen's *The Swarm* (US 78) 'Simply the worst film ever made'.

☆ *Variety* on *The Gong Show Movie* (US 80) 'Bong-g-g-g-g'.

☆ Vincent Canby on the $48 million *Inchon* (US/Kor 82) 'The most expensive B-movie ever made'.

☆ *Variety*: 'Lonesome Cowboy is Andy Warhol's best movie to date, which is like saying a three-year-old has graduated from smearing faeces on the wall to the occasional use of finger paints'.

☆ Anonymous critic on *Cleopatra* (US 63) 'Elizabeth Taylor is the first Cleopatra to sail down the Nile to Las Vegas'.

☆ *New York Daily News* on *Hawk of Powder River* (US 48) 'Eddie Dean's latest is in black and white rather than color but the improvement is hardly noticeable; you can still see him'.

According to Julius Crist of the *New York Times, The Agony and the Ecstasy* (US 65) was 'All agony, no ecstasy'. Here, Rex Harrison as Pope Julius II is piling on the agony for Michelangelo. (*Kobal*)

☆ Judith Crist on *The Agony and the Ecstasy* (US 65) 'All agony, no ecstasy'.

☆ *Variety* on *Way Back Home* (Bel 81) 'So poor that it gives amateurism a bad name'.

☆ Gary Arnold of the *Washington Post* on Ken Russell's biopic of Tchaikovsky *The Music Lovers* (GB 71) 'Awful . . . the worst experience I ever had in a cinema'.

☆ *Variety* on *Les Enfants du Paradis* (Fr 44) —which is probably the most universally admired foreign language film of all time—'Downright dull'.

☆ Colin Bennett of the *Melbourne Age* on Australia's first sexploitation movie *The Set* (Aus 70) 'At last my 18-year search for the worst film ever made has ended'.

☆ Alan Parker on *The Draughtsman's Contract* (GB 83) 'A load of posturing poo poo'.

☆ John Simon on *Camelot* (US 67) 'This film is the Platonic idea of boredom, roughly comparable to reading a three-volume novel in a language of which one knows only the alphabet'.

☆ James Agee on *You Were Meant For Me* (US 48) 'That's what you think'.

☆ *Variety* on *Movie Movie* (US 78) 'Awful Awful'.

☆ David Aasen of *Newsweek* on *A Dream of Passion* (US 78) 'As one endures the spectacle of Mercouri bearing her soul . . . it seems one has wandered into the home movies of a demented culture maven'.

☆ C. A. Lejeune on *No Leave No Love* (US 46) 'No Comment'. (This was the complete review.)

☆ *Variety* on *The American Prisoner* (GB 29) 'Save for direction, story, dialog, acting and being a period picture, this is a good one'.

☆ The *Reporter* magazine on *Guess Who's Coming to Dinner* (US 67) 'Abie's Irish Rose in Blackface'.

☆ 'Cart' of *Variety* on *The Lion with the White Mane* (Cz 87) 'All concerned should run and hide . . .'.

☆ Pauline Kael on *Blue Collar* (US 78) 'Jukebox Marxism'.

☆ *Variety* on Vadim's *And God Created Woman* (Fr 57), which became the most successful foreign film ever released in America, 'Just average for any US possibilities . . . questionable attributes of the new star here, Miss Bardot'.

☆ David Denby of *New York* magazine on Sylvester Stallone's *Cobra* (US 86) 'Senselessly crude, laughably unbelievable . . . unimaginably degraded'.

☆ *Newsweek*: 'The Sentinel is the perfect film for those who like to slow down and look at traffic accidents.'

☆ The *Observer* on the most successful cartoon feature of all time, Disney's *Snow White and the Seven Dwarfs* (US 37) 'Has all the roughness and error of a first try.'

☆ Bril of *Variety* on *Beverly Hills Brats* (US 89) 'Atrocious almost to epic proportions . . .'.

☆ The *New York Times* on *Lawrence of Arabia* (GB 62) 'Just a huge thundering camel-opera . . .'.

☆ Alan Stanbrook of *7 Days* on *Dick Tracy* (US 90)

'. . . a charter for the illiterate.'
☆ Val Lewton on *Gone With the Wind* (US 39) 'Ponderous trash.'
☆ Vincent Canby on *Gandhi* (GB/Ind 82) '. . . a laboriously illustrated textbook.'
☆ Sheila Johnston of *The Independent* on the Soviet Union's first explicit sex picture *Little Vera* (USSR 89) '. . . one of the more dubious achievements of glasnost is the freedom to make bad soap opera.'
☆ Berg of *Variety* on *The Hollywood Knights* (US 80) '. . . seems determined to set the *Guinness Book* record for the most gross-outs ever packed into one picture.'

*T*HE GOOD NOTICE GUIDE

Leading showbusiness trade paper *Variety* publishes weekly lists showing the number of favourable, unfavourable and mixed notices received by films reviewed in five main centres: New York, Los Angeles, Washington DC, Chicago and London. The chart below shows the percentage of each over a 60-week period in 1990–91 and is presented in rank order of cities giving favourable notices. The total number of reviews surveyed was 7656, of which 3005 appeared in New York, 1582 in London, 1209 in Chicago, 931 in Washington and 929 in Los Angeles.

	Favourable %	*Unfavourable* %	*Mixed* %
Los Angeles	38.5	38.9	22.6
London	37.8	34.6	27.6
New York	36.1	42.1	21.8
Washington	33.8	42.3	23.8
Chicago	27.0	48.5	24.5
All	35.0	41.2	23.8

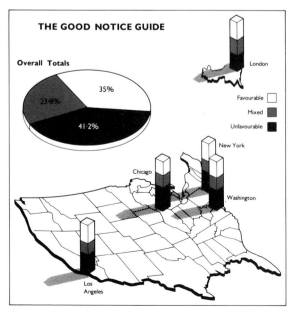

According to the figures, producers wanting a clutch of favourable reviews for starters stand a better chance if they open in Los Angeles.

And anyone expecting New York critics to be the most vituperative may be surprised to see that in fact they come closest to the norm both in the favourable and unfavourable categories. Chicago is where they like to cut film-makers down to size. Birthplace of film criticism in the US (see p. 219), it is out on a limb both for its very low score of favourable reviews (27 per cent) and very high score of unfavourable reviews (48.5 per cent).

Perhaps it is apposite that Los Angeles should be the most evenly balanced between favourable (38.5 per cent) and unfavourable (38.9 per cent) notices. Movie critics may feel that they can only handle having half the town against them at any one time.

London's individuality is belied by its second place in the table. Not only does it have the lowest score (34.6 per cent) for unfavourable notices, but it is the only city of the five where favourable notices outnumber unfavourable ones. And some may feel it is not wholly uncharacteristic of the island race that its critics score the highest rating (27.6 per cent) for ambivalence.

The only film reviewed during the survey period which received no unfavourable notices in any of these five centres was Martin Scorsese's acclaimed Mafia movie *GoodFellas* (US 90). It received 28 favourable reviews in New York (3 mixed), 7 in Los Angeles (1 mixed), 10 in Chicago, 9 in Washington and 11 in London (2 mixed).

*S*CREEN

The largest screen ever used for projecting a motion picture was the 115 × 85 ft installation at the Tsukuba Expo '85 in Japan, on which a 20 minute $2 million production *Skywards* (Can 85) was presented by the Canadian Imax system.

It had taken 'state of the art' technology 87 years to catch up with and surpass the previous record for the largest screen image, set by Louis Lumière in 1898 at the Galérie des Machines on the site of the forthcoming Paris Exposition with a picture measuring 99 ft × 79 ft 2 in. The distance from the projector was 650 ft and the screen was kept wet to increase its reflection of light, a task undertaken by the Paris Fire Brigade, who trained their hoses on the mammoth sheet before the show began.

The largest screen in the world today belongs to the Imax Theatre at the Taman Mini Park in Jakarta, Indonesia and measures 96 ft × 70 ft 6 in. It was manufactured by Harkness Screens of Boreham Wood, Herts, England.

The largest screen in Britain measures 62 × 45 ft and is used with the Imax projection system at the National Museum of Photography, Film and Tele-

The giant screen used by the Lumière brothers, Paris, 1898.

vision at Bradford. The screen is the height of a five-storey building.

> Among the odder surfaces on which movies have been publicly projected was a circular screen of egg shells for a presentation of Marcel Duchamp's *Anemic Cinema* (Fr 26) at the Soviet Union's first independent film festival in a glasnost-happy Riga in 1988.

The widest screen ever used for projecting motion pictures was erected at the Palais d'Electricité et de la Lumière at the Paris Exposition of 1937 for showing Henri Chrétien's *hypergonar* films, the precursor of Cinerama. The concave

> Hamburg's annual 'Low-Budget Film Festival' boasts something unique in film presentation—a floating screen. It is moored on the Alster and anyone who cares to can simply sit on the bank and enjoy the midnight shows for free.

screen had a breadth of 195 ft and was 32 ft 6 in high. By comparison the Cinerama screen size was 90 × 26 ft.

The widest screen in use today was installed at the Mercury Cinema, Paris, in 1981 and measures 133 ft in breadth.

360° screens, with the audience wholly surrounded by the projected image, exist at the China Pavilion of Walt Disney's EPCOT Center in Florida, where the system is called 'Circle Vision'; and at the L'Espace Gaité cinema in Paris, which presents the 'Panrama' system on a 350 square metre screen.

AWARDS AND FESTIVALS

The first film awards were made in respect of a festival which opened in Monte Carlo on New Year's Day 1898. The competition was open to professionals and amateurs alike but subjects had to be taken in Monaco. The first prize was worth £80, and there were two others worth £40 and £20. The following year the competition was expanded. Prize money was increased to a total of £1200 (30,000 francs) plus a number of honourable mentions and this time it was purely for amateurs. It was organized by the Societé des Bains de Mer who stipulated that each competitor must send in three films of any place or subject which should never previously have been exhibited. The jury was to be composed of 'artists and amateurs' and films were judged on 'originality, artistic merit and photographic quality', according to the *British Journal of Photography*. The prizes were awarded in February 1900 by the Prince of Monaco and the winning entries were shown at the Palais des Beaux Arts. The titles of the winning films are not recorded.

The first award-winning film known by name was Giovanni Vitrotti's *Il Cane riconescente* (It 07), an Ambrosio production which won a gold plaque awarded by the Lumière brothers at an international contest held in Italy in 1907.

The first award made to a feature film was also won by Ambrosio. The Grand Prix of 25,000 francs at the International Exhibition at Turin in 1912 went to *After Fifty Years* (It 12), an historical drama set in the Austro–Italian War of 1859.

The first annual awards and the oldest extant were instituted in 1917 by America's National Board of Review of Motion Pictures.

Britain's first film festival was the International Festival of Women's Films, held in London in 1928. The first prize went to Dorothy Arzner's *Fashions For Women* (US 27). The only other pre-war festival on record was a non-competitive event held at Malvern in 1931, notable chiefly for the pre-release presentation of the first Bernard Shaw talkie, *How He Lied to Her Husband* (GB 31) with Edmund Gwenn.

The first regular film festival was held as part of the Venice Biennale and took place at the Hotel Excelsior from 6 to 21 August 1932, the purpose behind it being an attempt to revive the depression-hit tourist trade. A total of 18 pictures were entered by Germany, the USA, France, Italy and the UK, three of them directed by women. No awards were made.

ACADEMY AWARDS

These were instituted by the Academy of Motion Picture Arts and Sciences and first presented on 16 May 1929. The awards that year were to dignify the efforts of film-makers during the 12 months August 1927 to July 1928—and at the same time to dignify, the Academy hoped, the somewhat tarnished reputation the film industry had earned itself in the 'roaring twenties'.

Oscar, the Academy Award trophy, is the figure of a man with a crusader's sword standing on a reel of film. Until 1931 it was known simply as 'The Statuette', but in that year Academy librarian Margaret Herrick chanced to remark 'He looks like my Uncle Oscar' and the name stuck. Plated in 10 carat gold, Oscar has always stood 13½ inches tall, except in war time when the trophy consisted of a gold-plated plaster plaque with the Oscar figure in relief. The value of

Casting the Oscars at the Southern California Trophy Company in 1949. The 'high hats' were knocked off before the figures were dipped in a bath of liquid gold. (*Popperfoto*)

an Oscar is $295. Recipients pledge never to sell their statuette except back to the Academy, who will pay $10 for it. Nevertheless, Oscars have changed hands for rather more than this. In 1988 the 1951 Best Picture Oscar for *An American in Paris* was bought by a Swiss collector of movie memorabilia for $15,760 and at an unspecified earlier date Brando's Oscar for *On the Waterfront* had been sold (not by Brando) for $13,500. Double Oscar winning scriptwriter Frances Marion said that she saw the statuette as 'a perfect symbol of the picture business: a powerful athletic body clutching a gleaming sword, with half of his head, that part which held his brains, completely sliced off'.

The most awards in any category have been won by Walt Disney (1901-66), who was honoured with 26 regular and six special trophies.

The most awards for individual creative achievement are the eleven won by Cedric Gibbon (1893-1960) of MGM for art direction; the most won by a woman are the eight by costume designer Edith Head (1907-81).

The largest number of films qualifying for consideration for an Academy Award was 264 for the 47th Awards in 1974. During the 1980s the figure has fluctuated around the 250 mark, representing a little less than half the films released annually in the USA. To qualify a film has to have played publicly in Los Angeles for at least a week within specified dates.

The most awards won by any one film went to *Ben Hur* (US 59) and numbered eleven: Best Picture; Best Director; Best Actor; Best Supporting Actor; Cinematography; Art Direction; Sound; Music Score; Film Editing; Special Effects; Costume.

The most awards won by a British film went to *Gandhi* (GB 83) and numbered eight: Best Picture; Best Actor; Best Director; Best Original Screenplay; Cinematography; Film Editing; Art Direction; Costume Design.

The most nominations for awards were made in respect of *All About Eve* (US 50) with 14. It won six.

The most nominated films to receive no awards were *The Turning Point* (US 77) and *The Color Purple* (US 86), each with 11 nominations.

The only occasion on which no film won more than one Oscar was the second Academy Awards in March 1930.

Only two films have won 'The Big Five' major awards—Best Picture; Best Director; Best Actor; Best Actress; Best Screenplay. They are: *It Happened One Night* (US 34)—Frank Capra; Clark Gable; Claudette Colbert; Robert Riskin; and *One Flew Over the Cuckoo's Nest* (US 75)—Milos Forman; Jack Nicholson; Louise Fletcher; Lawrence Hauben and Bo Goldman.

The most Best Director awards have been made

Scriptwriter Robert Towne was so dissatisfied with the liberties he reckoned Hugh Hudson had taken with his script for *Greystoke: The Legend of Tarzan, Lord of the Apes* (GB/US 84) that he had his name replaced on the credits with that of his sheepdog, an animal called P. H. Vazak. The dog was nominated for an Oscar.

to John Ford, who won four times: *The Informer* (US 35); *The Grapes of Wrath* (US 40); *How Green was my Valley* (US 41); *The Quiet Man* (US 52).

The only time that all five Best Director nominations went to non-American directors was in 1988: Bernardo Bertolucci (It) for *The Last Emperor*; John Boorman (GB) for *Hope and Glory*; Adrian Lyne (GB) for *Fatal Attraction*; Lasse Hallström (Swe) for *My Life As a Dog*; and Norman Jewison (Can) for *Moonstruck*. The winner was Bernardo Bertolucci.

The most Best Actor awards have been won by five actors, each with two Oscars: Spencer Tracy for *Captains Courageous* (US 37) and *Boys Town* (US 38); Fredric March for *Dr Jekyll and Mr Hyde* (US 32) and *The Best Years of our Lives* (US 46); Gary Cooper for *Sergeant York* (US 41) and *High Noon* (US 52); Marlon Brando for *On the Waterfront* (US 54) and *The Godfather* (US 72); and Dustin Hoffman for *Kramer vs Kramer* (US 79) and *Rain Man* (US 88). Tracy, though, received nine nominations during his career, against seven for Brando, six for Hoffman and five each for March and Cooper. Sir Laurence Olivier equalled Tracy's nominations, but won only a single Best Actor award for *Hamlet* (GB 48). Perhaps Tracy should also take first place by virtue of the fact that Katharine Hepburn is on record as saying that one

The Oscars for Best Picture and Best Director have been won in respect of the same film on 46 occasions out of 63 (to 1991), including a ten-year unbroken run from 1958 to 67. The only directors of the Best Picture who were not even nominated in the directing category were William Wellman when *Wings* won in 1929, Edmund Goulding when *Grand Hotel* won in 1933 and, most notoriously, Australia's Bruce Beresford when the landmark *Driving Miss Daisy* won to enormous popular acclaim in 1990. On accepting the Oscar for Best Picture, producer Richard Zanuck spoke for the whole cast and crew when he said 'We're up here for one very simple reason—the fact that Bruce Beresford is a brilliant director'.

of her Academy Awards was doubtless intended for both of them.

The most Best Actress awards have been won by Katharine Hepburn, whose four Oscars were awarded for *Morning Glory* (US 33), *Guess Who's Coming to dinner* (US 67), *The Lion in Winter* (GB 68) and *On Golden Pond* (US 81). Miss Hepburn also enjoys the distinction of having received the most nominations of any performer (13), and of having the longest award-winning career, spanning 48 years.

The first co-stars to win Best Actor and Best Actress award in the same year were Clark Gable and Claudette Colbert, for *It Happened One Night* (US 34). Miss Colbert was so sceptical of her chances of winning the Oscar that she decided not to postpone a trip to New York on a train scheduled to leave on the evening of the ceremony. She was just stepping into the carriage when officials of the Academy arrived to tell her she had won. A motorcycle escort rushed her to the Biltmore Bowl to receive the award, still dressed in her travelling clothes.

Other co-stars who won in the same year have been: Jack Nicholson and Louise Fletcher: *One Flew Over the Cuckoo's Nest* (US 75); Peter Finch and Faye Dunaway: *Network* (US 76); Jon Voight and Jane Fonda: *Coming Home* (US 78); Henry Fonda and Katharine Hepburn: *On Golden Pond* (US 81).

The only tie for Best Actor was between Wallace Beery in *The Champ* (US 31) and Fredric March in *Dr Jekyll and Mr Hyde* (US 31).

The only tie for Best Actress was between Barbra Streisand in *Funny Girl* (US 68) and Katharine Hepburn in *The Lion in Winter* (GB 68).

The following members of the same family have won Oscars in the same year: brother and sister Douglas and Norma Shearer, he for Sound Recording on *The Big House* (US 30), she as Best Actress in *The Divorcee* (US 30); father and son Walter and John Huston, both for *The Treasure of the Sierra Madre* (US 47), as Best Supporting Actor and Best Director, respectively; brothers Richard M. and Robert B. Sherman for Best Song, 'Chim-Chim Cher-ee' in *Mary Poppins* (US 63); and father and son Carmine and Francis Coppola, both for *The Godfather Part II* (US 74), as composer of Best Original Dramatic Score and Best Director respectively. The Hustons also established the record for **most generations of Oscar winners** when Anjelica, John's daughter, Walter's granddaughter, won Best Supporting Actress for *Prizzi's Honor* (US 85).

The shortest performance to win an Oscar was Anthony Quinn's eight-minute *tour de force* as Gauguin in *Lust for Life* (US 56), which won him the 1956 Best Supporting Actor award.

The first Oscar winning debut performance was by Gale Sondegaard in *Anthony Adverse* (US 36), for which she won the Best Supporting Actress award. First neophyte in the Best Supporting Actor category was Timothy Hutton for *Ordinary People* (US 80).

The first Best Actress award for a debut performance went to Shirley Booth for *Come Back, Little Sheba* (US 52). Others to have won for their first film were Barbra Streisand for *Funny Girl* (US 68) and Marlee Matlin for *Children of a Lesser God* (US 86). There has been no Best Actor award for a debut performance.

The only occasion all ten nominees for Best Actor and Best Actress have been US born was in 1985.

Seats at the Academy Awards ceremony are amongst the highest priced of all 'bootleg' tickets—those in the first 15 rows of the auditorium fetch up to $1,800 each.

The first performer to win an award for a foreign language film was Sophia Loren, whose role in *Two Women* (It 61) secured her the Oscar for Best Actress.

The youngest Oscar winner was Shirley Temple, who won a Special Award at the age of six for 'her outstanding contribution to screen entertainment during the year 1934'.

The youngest person to receive a regular Academy Award was 9-year-old Tatum O'Neal, who won the Oscar for Best Supporting Actress for her role in *Paper Moon* (US 73). The youngest nominee was 8-year-old Justin Henry for *Kramer vs Kramer* (US 79).

The oldest performer to win an Oscar was British-born Jessica Tandy, who was 80 years and 8 months old when she was awarded Best Actress for her standout role in *Driving Miss Daisy* (US 89). She was five months older than George Burns was when he won his Best Supporting Actor award for *The Sunshine Boys* (US 75). Miss Tandy might have won a Best Actress Oscar a lot earlier if she had not been the only member of the New York cast of Tennessee Williams' play *A Streetcar Named Desire* who was not brought to Hollywood to appear in the 1951 film version. Vivien Leigh, who substituted for her in the superlative role of Blanche Dubois, carried off the Academy Award for Best Actress.

The oldest nominee was Eva Le Gallienne, 82, as Best Supporting Actress for *Resurrection* (US 80).

The first black Oscar winner was Hattie McDaniel, who was awarded Best Supporting Actress for her role as Mammy in *Gone with the Wind* (US 39). Twenty-four years elapsed before another black performer won a regular Oscar:

Hattie McDaniel as Mammy—first of a very short roster of Oscar winning black artistes. There have only been four to date. (*National Film Archive*)

Sidney Poitier was awarded Best Actor for *Lilies of the Field* (US 63).

Only two non-professionals have won acting Oscars: Canadian war veteran Harold Russell for his role as the handless ex-soldier (Russell himself had had his hands blown off) in *The Best Years of Our Lives* (US 46); and Cambodian refugee Dr Haing S. Ngor for his moving performance as a victim of Cambodia's Pol Pot regime in *The Killing Fields* (GB 84).

The longest Oscar ceremony was in 1984 and lasted for 3 hr 40 min. Winners took an average of 99 seconds each to thank 7.8 'wunnerful' people.

Some winners' sense of gratitude has bordered on the excessive. Probably the longest roster of people thanked by a gushing Oscar winner was the 27 named by Olivia de Havilland when she won Best Actress for *To Each His Own* (US 46).

The longest speech was made by Greer Garson on receiving the Best Actress award for *Mrs Miniver* (US 42) and lasted for 5½ minutes. (The author extends his apologies to Miss Garson for repeating, in earlier editions of this book, the canard that she rambled on for over an hour.) Acceptance speeches were restricted to 45 seconds for the first time at the 1990 awards ceremony. After 25 seconds a red light flashes a warning. If the recipient is still thanking co-workers, friends and relatives after the alloted three quarters of a minute loud music intervenes.

THE ACADEMY AWARD FOR THE BEST FILM

Dates given are year award was made
(NB: no ceremony in 1933).
1929 *Wings* (US)
1930 **(March)** *Broadway Melody* (US)
1930 **(Nov)** *All Quiet on the Western Front* (US)
1931 *Cimarron* (US)
1932 *Grand Hotel* (US)
1934 *Cavalcade* (US)
1935 *It Happened One Night* (US)
1936 *Mutiny on the Bounty* (US)
1937 *The Great Ziegfeld* (US)
1938 *The Life of Emile Zola* (US)
1939 *You Can't Take It With You* (US)
1940 *Gone with the Wind* (US)
1941 *Rebecca* (US)
1942 *How Green was my Valley* (US)
1943 *Mrs Miniver* (US)
1944 *Casablanca* (US)
1945 *Going my Way* (US)
1946 *The Lost Weekend* (US)·
1947 *The Best Years of Our Lives* (US)
1948 *Gentlemen's Agreement* (US)

1949 *Hamlet* (GB)
1950 *All the King's Men* (US)
1951 *All About Eve* (US)
1952 *An American in Paris* (US)
1953 *The Greatest Show on Earth* (US)
1954 *From Here to Eternity* (US)
1955 *On the Waterfront* (US)
1956 *Marty* (US)
1957 *Around the World in 80 Days* (US)
1958 *The Bridge on the River Kwai* (GB)
1959 *Gigi* (US)
1960 *Ben Hur* (US)
1961 *The Apartment* (US)
1962 *West Side Story* (US)
1963 *Lawrence of Arabia* (GB)
1964 *Tom Jones* (GB)
1965 *My Fair Lady* (US)
1966 *The Sound of Music* (US)
1967 *A Man for All Seasons* (GB)
1968 *In the Heat of the Night* (US)
1969 *Oliver!* (GB)
1970 *Midnight Cowboy* (US)

1971 *Patton* (US)
1972 *The French Connection* (US)
1973 *The Godfather* (US)
1974 *The Sting* (US)
1975 *The Godfather, Part II* (US)
1976 *One Flew Over the Cuckoo's Nest* (US)
1977 *Rocky* (US)
1978 *Annie Hall* (US)
1979 *The Deer Hunter* (US)
1980 *Kramer vs Kramer* (US)
1981 *Ordinary People* (US)
1982 *Chariots of Fire* (GB)
1983 *Gandhi* (GB)
1984 *Terms of Endearment* (US)
1985 *Amadeus* (US)
1986 *Out of Africa* (US)
1987 *Platoon* (US)
1988 *The Last Emperor* (It/GB/Chn)
1989 *Rain Man* (US)
1990 *Driving Miss Daisy* (US)
1991 *Dances with Wolves* (US)

THE BERLIN FILM FESTIVAL AWARD FOR BEST FILM

The Berlin Film Festival was established in 1951. There was no overall Best Film award in the first year and from 1952–55 the films were voted for by the audience. The Golden Bear award for Best Picture was inaugurated 1956.
1952 *She Danced for the Summer* (Swe)

1953 *The Wages of Fear* (Fr)
1954 *Hobson's Choice* (GB)
1955 *The Rats* (FRG)
1956 *Invitation to the Dance* (GB)
1957 *Twelve Angry Men* (US)
1958 *The End of the Day* (Swe)

1959 *The Cousins* (Fr)
1960 *Lazarillo de Tormes* (Sp)
1961 *La Notte* (It)
1962 *A Kind of Loving* (GB)
1963 *Oath of Obedience* (FRG); *The Devil* (It)
1964 *Dry Summer* (Tur)

1965 *Alphaville* (Fr)
1966 *Cul de Sac* (GB)
1967 *Le Depart* (Bel)
1968 *Ole Dole Doff* (Swe)
1969 *Early Years* (Yug)
1970 No award
1971 *The Garden of the Finzi-Continis* (It)
1972 *The Canterbury Tales* (It)
1973 *Distant Thunder* (Ind)
1974 *The Apprenticeship of Duddy Kravitz* (Can)

1975 *Orkobefogadas* (Hun)
1976 *Buffalo Bill and the Indians* (US) —award declined
1977 *The Ascent* (USSR)
1978 *The Trouts* (Sp); *The Words of Max* (Sp)
1979 *David* (FRG)
1980 *Heartland* (US); *Palermo Oder Wolfsburg* (FRG)
1981 *Di Presa Di Presa* (Sp)
1982 *Die Sehnsucht der Veronica Voss* (FRG)
1983 *Ascendancy* (GB); *The Beehive* (Sp)

1984 *Love Streams* (US 84)
1985 *Wetherby* (GB); *Die Frau und der Fremde* (FRG)
1986 *Stammheim* (FRG)
1987 *The Theme* (USSR)
1988 *Red Shorghum* (Chn)
1989 *Rain Man* (US)
1990 *Music Box* (US); *Larks on a String* (Cz)
1991 *House of Smiles* (It)

BRITISH FILM ACADEMY

Best British Film Award (1948-68)
Best Film Award (1969-)
1948 *Odd Man Out*
1949 *The Fallen Idol*
1950 *The Third Man*
1951 *The Blue Lamp*
1952 *The Lavender Hill Mob*
1953 *The Sound Barrier*
1954 *Genevieve*
1955 *Hobson's Choice*
1956 *Richard III*
1957 *Reach for the Sky*
1958 *The Bridge on the River Kwai*
1959 *Room at the Top*
1960 *Sapphire*
1961 *Saturday Night and Sunday Morning*

1962 *A Taste of Honey*
1963 *Lawrence of Arabia*
1964 *Tom Jones*
1965 *Dr Strangelove*
1966 *The Ipcress File*
1967 *The Spy who Came in from the Cold*
1968 *A Man for All Seasons*
1969 *The Graduate* (US)
1970 *Midnight Cowboy* (US)
1971 *Butch Cassidy and the Sundance Kid* (US)
1972 *Sunday Bloody Sunday* (GB)
1973 *Cabaret* (US)
1974 *La Nuite Americaine/Day for Night* (Fr)
1975 *Lacombe, Lucien* (Fr)
1976 *Alice Doesn't Live Here Anymore* (US)
1977 *One Flew Over the Cuckoo's Nest* (US)

1978 *Annie Hall* (US)
1979 *Julia* (US)
1980 *Manhattan* (US)
1981 *The Elephant Man* (GB)
1982 *Chariots of Fire* (GB)
1983 *Gandhi* (GB)
1984 *Educating Rita* (GB)
1985 *The Killing Fields* (GB)
1986 *The Purple Rose of Cairo* (US)
1987 *A Room with a View* (GB)
1988 *Jean de Florette* (Fr)
1989 *The Last Emperor* (It/GB/Chn)
1990 *Dead Poets Society* (US)
1991 *GoodFellas* (US)

CANNES FILM FESTIVAL

Palme d'Or for Best Film
1946 *La Bataille du Rail* (Fr)
1946 *Antoine et Antoinette* (Fr)
1948 No festival
1949 *The Third Man* (GB)
1950 No festival
1951 *Miracle in Milan* (It); *Miss Julie* (Swe)
1952 *Othello* (Mor); *Two Cents Worth of Hope* (It)
1953 *Wages of Fear* (Fr)
1954 *Gate of Hell* (Jap)
1955 *Marty* (US)
1956 *World of Silence* (Fr)
1957 *Friendly Persuasion* (US)
1958 *The Cranes are Flying* (USSR)
1959 *Black Orpheus* (Fr)
1960 *La Dolce Vita* (It)
1961 *Viridiana* (Sp); *Une aussi longue absence* (Fr)

1962 *The Given Word* (Bra)
1963 *The Leopard* (It)
1964 *The Umbrellas of Cherbourg* (Fr)
1965 *The Knack* (GB)
1966 *A Man and a Woman* (Fr); *Signore e Signori* (It)
1967 *Blow-Up* (GB)
1968 Festival disrupted; no awards
1969 *If* (GB)
1970 *M*A*S*H* (US)
1971 *The Go-Between* (GB)
1972 *The Working Class Goes to Paradise* (It); *The Mattei Affair* (It)
1973 *Scarecrow* (US); *The Hireling* (GB)
1974 *The Conversation* (US)
1975 *Chronicle of the Burning Years* (Alg)
1976 *Taxi Driver* (US)
1977 *Padre Padrone* (It)
1978 *L'Albero Degli Zoccoli* (It)

1979 *The Tin Drum* (FRG); *Apocalypse Now* (US)
1980 *All That Jazz* (US); *Kagemusha* (Jap)
1981 *Man of Iron* (Pol)
1982 *Missing* (US); *Yol* (Tur)
1983 *The Ballad of Narayama* (Jap)
1984 *Paris, Texas* (FRG)
1985 *When Father Was Away On Business* (Yug)
1986 *The Mission* (GB)
1987 *Under the Sun of Satan* (Fr)
1988 *Pelle the Conqueror* (Den)
1989 *Sex, Lies and Videotape* (US)
1990 *Wild at Heart* (US)
1991 *Barton Fink* (US)

VENICE FILM FESTIVAL

Best Foreign Film Award (1934-42)
Best Film Award (1946-68)
Golden Lion for Best Film (1980-)
1932 No official award
1933 No festival
1934 *Man of Aran* (GB)
1935 *Anna Karenina* (US)
1936 *Der Kaiser von Kalifornien* (Ger)
1937 *Un Carnet de Bal* (Fr)
1938 *Olympia* (Ger)
1939 No award
1940 *Der Postmeister* (Ger)
1941 *Ohm Kruger* (Ger)
1942 *Der grosse König* (Ger)
1943-45 No festival
1946 *The Southerner* (US)
1947 *Sirena* (Cz)
1948 *Hamlet* (GB)

1949 *Manon* (Fr)
1950 *Justice is Done* (Fr)
1951 *Rashomon* (Jap)
1952 *Forbidden Games* (Fr)
1953 No award
1954 *Romeo and Juliet* (It/GB)
1955 *Ordet* (Den)
1956 No award
1957 *Aparajito* (Ind)
1958 *Muhomatsu no Issho* (Jap)
1959 *Il Generale della Rovere* (It)
1960 *Le Passage du Rhin* (Fr)
1961 *Last Year at Marienbad* (Fr)
1962 *Childhood of Ivan* (USSR)
1963 *Le Mani sulla città* (It)
1964 *Red Desert* (It)
1965 *Of a Thousand Delights* (It)
1966 *Battle of Algiers* (It)

1967 *Belle de Jour* (Fr)
1968 *Die Aristen in der Zirkuskuppel* (FRG)
Jury and award system discontinued 1969-79.
1980 *Gloria* (US); *Atlantic City* (Fr/Can)
1981 *Die Bleierne Zeit* (FRG)
1982 *The State of Things* (FRG)
1983 *Prénom Carmen* (Fr/Swz)
1984 *Year of the Quiet Sun* (Pol)
1985 *Sans toit ni loi aka Vagabonde* (Fr)
1986 *Le Rayon Vert* (Fr)
1987 *Au Revoir les Enfants* (Fr)
1988 *The Legend of the Holy Drinker* (It)
1989 *A City of Sadness* (Taiwan)
1990 *Rosencrantz and Guildenstern Are Dead* (GB)

To celebrate the publication of its first *Film Guide* in 1989, the weekly listings magazine *Time Out* invited 60 film directors and critics to choose their top ten films. The overall top hundred films were determined by giving three points for each contributor's first choice, two to the second and one to each of the following eight. The result was a not unexpected runaway victory for *Citizen Kane* (US 41), the film which has topped virtually every such compilation made in the last 30 years. With four other films in the top 100, Welles' score is only surpassed by Hitchcock with six. *Time Out*

commented on the list: 'The results are cosmopolitan and catholic—even if Spielberg only scraped into the bottom five—with France racking up almost twice as many classics as England; and statistics freaks might like to note that while the '40s, '70s and '80s come out on roughly level pegging (15–18 films), the '60s marked a definite low (12), while the '50s come out as the Golden Age of film (25).' A notable omission from the list is Eisenstein's *Battleship Potemkin* (USSR 25) — perhaps the first time the silent classic has failed to appear in a list of this kind.

1 *Citizen Kane* (US 41)
2 *The Third Man* (GB 49)
3 *The Night of the Hunter* (US 56)
4 *Some Like It Hot* (US 59)
5 *The Godfather* (US 71)
6 *Vertigo* (US 58)
7 *L'Atalante* (Fr 34)
8 *Raging Bull* (US 80)
9 *Les Enfants du Paradis* (Fr 45)
10 *North by Northwest* (US 59)
11 *Once Upon a Time in the West* (It 68)
12=*Touch of Evil* (US 58)
   =*La Règle du Jeu* (Fr 39)
14 *Psycho* (US 60)
15 *The Wizard of Oz* (US 39)
16 *Blue Velvet* (US 86)
17 *Apocalypse Now!* (US 79)
18=*A Matter of Life and Death* (GB 46)
   =*Chinatown* (US 74)
20 *The Searchers* (US 56)
21 *Tokyo Story* (Jap 53)
22 *Brazil* (GB 85)
23 *Kiss Me Deadly* (US 55)
24=*Sweet Smell of Success* (US 57)
   =*Beauty and the Beast* (Fr 46)
26 *Once Upon a Time in America* (US 83)
27 *Don't Look Now* (GB/It 73)
28 *Rear Window* (US 54)
29 *The Life and Death of Colonel Blimp* (GB 43)
30 *The Big Sleep* (US 46)
31 *Notorious* (US 46)
32 *A Streetcar Named Desire* (US 51)
33 *The American Friend* (FRG/Fr 77)
34=*The Tree of Wooden Clogs* (It 78)

   =*The Magnificent Ambersons* (US 42)
36 *Singin' in the Rain* (US 52)
37 *The King of Comedy* (US 82)
38 *Bonnie and Clyde* (US 67)
39=*Jean de Florette* (Fr/It 86)
   =*Kind Hearts and Coronets* (GB 49)
41 *Mean Streets* (US 73)
42=*Seven Samurai* (Jap 54)
   =*Written on the Wind* (US 56)
44 *Gospel According to St Matthew* (It/Fr 64)
45 *Double Indemnity* (US 44)
46 *Ivan the Terrible* (USSR 44/46)
47=*Red Balloon* (Fr 56)
   =*The Passion of Joan of Arc* (Fr 28)
49 *Out of the Past* (US 47)
50 *Earth* (USSR 30)
51 *The Philadelphia Story* (US 40)
52 *Une Partie de Campagne* (Fr 36)
53 *Voyage to Italy* (It 53)
54 *Lawrence of Arabia* (GB 62)
55 *Pickpocket* (Fr 59)
56=*Klute* (US 71)
   =*The Ghost and Mrs Muir* (US 47)
58 *All About Eve* (US 50)
59 *Dr Strangelove* (US 63)
60=*Modern Times* (US 36)
   =*The Exterminating Angel* (Mex 62)
62 *Rue Cases Nègres* (Fr 83)
63=*The Exorcist* (US 73)
   =*The Sacrifice* (Swe/Fr 86)
65=*Stalker* (USSR 79)
   =*Workers Leaving the Factory* (Fr 95)
67 *Dawn of the Dead* (US 79)
68 *Meet Me in St Louis* (US 44)

69 *Strangers on a Train* (US 51)
70 *King of the Children* (China 87)
71 *2001: A Space Odyssey* (GB 68)
72 *Blade Runner* (US 82)
73 *Babette's Feast* (Den 87)
74 *The Bad and the Beautiful* (US 52)
75 *Kitchen* (US 66)
76=*The 39 Steps* (GB 35)
   =*The Story of the Late Chrysanthemums* (Jap 39)
78 *Umberto D* (It 62)
79 *The Scarlet Empress* (US 34)
80 *Gentlemen Prefer Blondes* (US 53)
81 *The Big Easy* (US 86)
82 *The Grapes of Wrath* (US 40)
83=*White Heat* (US 49)
   =*This Is Spinal Tap* (US 83)
85 *Rebel Without a Cause* (US 55)
86 *Withnail and I* (GB 86)
87=*The General* (US 26)
   =*Fear Eats the Soul* (FRG 73)
89=*The Battle of Algiers* (Alg/It 65)
   =*The Discreet Charm of the Bourgeoisie* (Fr 72)
91 *October* (USSR 27)
92 *The Long Goodbye* (US 73)
93 *Chimes at Midnight* (Sp/Swz 66)
94 *The Conversation* (US 74)
95=*Kings of the Road* (FRG 76)
   =*Silent Running* (US 71)
97 *ET The Extra-Terrestrial* (US 82)
98 *The Green Ray* (Fr 86)
99 *Sunset Boulevard* (US 50)
100 *The Jungle Book* (US 67)

INDEX

Page numbers in italics signify an illustration